Praise for
The Network Challenge

"In global businesses today, managing the value net well is both a need for survival and a way to gain competitive advantages. But networks are equally important in studying biological sciences, information systems, political systems, and social networks. Each network can learn from the evolution, theories, and practices from other networks, and that is the power of this book. It is the cross-studies of multiple networks that enable us to have much deeper insights and new perspectives in each of the networks, which cannot be gained from the study of a single respective network."

Lee Hau, Thoma Professor of Operations, Information, and Technology
at the Stanford Graduate School of Business,
and founding Co-Director of the Stanford Global Supply Chain Management Forum

"*The Network Challenge* is an extraordinary work focusing on and capturing a broad range of dynamics that make the various networks in our world so very critical. This book is amazing in its breadth—covering as wide an array of networks and the related economic, communications, and social factors as one can imagine. This book is the seminal text for the role of networks; it looks at networks' all-important role from as many angles as cameras shooting the Super Bowl. And it draws far and wide from different fields to illuminate the role of networks in our world today and our imagination tomorrow. It's a must buy."

David E. Morey, Founder, President, and CEO of DMG, Inc.,
a partner in Core Strategy Group,
and one of the leading strategic communications consultant

"*The Network Challenge* will force every leader to rethink the mental model of what they can manage, what they don't know, and be comfortable with sharing knowledge in order to prosper in this new era of expanded, high-speed networks. This timely book offers in-depth insights from thought leaders on the risks and rewards of embracing networks as the new paradigm for leadership. The potential of networks for marketing and marketing research is particularly exciting reading."

Joe Plummer, Adjunct Professor of Marketing at Columbia University
and Former Chief Knowledge Officer, McCann Worldgroup

"This book offers important new insights and methods for anyone involved in managing innovation, improving the supply/manufacturing/distribution process, creating successful customer relationships, and managing risk. Networks have become central to each of these business processes, offering exciting opportunities for value-creation, as well as important new kinds of complexities requiring firms to reinvent management techniques and skills. The authors illustrate important new trends via a deep base of experience and a commitment to insights that are both reliably sound and eminently practical."

David Schmittlein, Dean,
MIT Sloan School of Management

"We're entering an age of networked intelligence. *The Network Challenge* marshals a cast of savvy thinkers and practitioners to tackle a broad range of the fascinating and important unanswered questions. Completely stimulating."

Don Tapscott, author of 13 books about networks in business and society,
including *Wikinomics*, and most recently, *Grown Up Digital*

"Networks are our future. This book synthesizes valuable insights into the network challenge and provides fantastic strategies for enterprises to enhance their competitiveness. It is a must read by business leaders who wish to succeed in the new age of network challenges."

Victor Fung, Group Chairman of the Li & Fung Group of companies,
which includes major subsidiaries in trading, distribution, and retailing

The Network Challenge

The Network Challenge

Strategy, Profit, and Risk in an
Interlinked World

Paul R. Kleindorfer
Yoram (Jerry) Wind

with
Robert E. Gunther

Vice President, Publisher: Tim Moore
Associate Publisher and Director of Marketing: Amy Neidlinger
Wharton Editor: Steve Kobrin
Editorial Assistant: Pamela Boland
Operations Manager: Gina Kanouse
Digital Marketing Manager: Julie Phifer
Publicity Manager: Laura Czaja
Assistant Marketing Manager: Megan Colvin
Cover Designer: Chuti Prasertsith
Managing Editor: Kristy Hart
Project Editor: Lori Lyons
Copy Editor: Cheri Clark
Proofreader: San Dee Phillips
Indexer: WordWise Publishing Services
Senior Compositor: Gloria Schurick
Manufacturing Buyer: Dan Uhrig

© 2009 by Pearson Education, Inc.
Publishing as Wharton School Publishing
Upper Saddle River, New Jersey 07458

Wharton School Publishing offers excellent discounts on this book when ordered in quantity for bulk purchases or special sales. For more information, please contact U.S. Corporate and Government Sales, 1-800-382-3419, corpsales@pearsontechgroup.com. For sales outside the U.S., please contact International Sales at international@pearson.com.

Printed in the United States of America

First Printing June 2009

ISBN-10: 0-13-701191-1
ISBN-13: 978-0-13-701191-9

Pearson Education LTD.
Pearson Education Australia PTY, Limited.
Pearson Education Singapore, Pte. Ltd.
Pearson Education North Asia, Ltd.
Pearson Education Canada, Ltd.
Pearson Educación de Mexico, S.A. de C.V.
Pearson Education—Japan
Pearson Education Malaysia, Pte. Ltd.

Library of Congress Cataloging-in-Publication Data

Kleindorfer, Paul R.
  The network challenge : strategy, profit, and risk in an interlinked world / Paul R. Kleindorfer, Jerry (Yoram) Wind. — 1st ed.
    p. cm.
  ISBN 978-0-13-701191-9 (hardback : alk. paper)
 1. Business networks. 2. Strategic planning. 3. International cooperation. I. Wind, Yoram. II. Title.
  HD69.S8K54 2009
  658.4'012—dc22
                                       2009004106

To our colleagues across all disciplines, whose research is the foundation of our knowledge of networks; and to the executives and policy makers whose creative solutions to the Network Challenge continue to inspire our research.

Contents

Authors xviii

Foreword by Dean Thomas S. Robertson and
Dean Frank Brown xxv

Preface xxvi

PART I   **THE NETWORK CHALLENGE**

Chapter 1   The Network Imperative: Community or Contagion? 3
Paul Kleindorfer and Yoram (Jerry) Wind
Abstract 3
The Rise of Networks 5
Challenging the Theory of the Firm 8
The Network That Is This Book 13
Meeting the Challenge of Networks 21
References 23

Chapter 2   Creating Experience: Competitive Advantage in the
Age of Networks 25
CK Prahalad
Abstract 25
An Innovation Continuum 29
A Networked Model for Addressing Diabetes 32
Impediments to Networked Innovation 34
New Sources of Competitive Advantage 34
References 36

Chapter 3   Knowledge as a Social Phenomenon: "Horse Holding"
and Learning in Networks 37
Alan M. Kantrow
Abstract 37
"That" Versus "Why" 38
Knowledge as a Social Phenomenon 40

            Forgetting the "Why's" 40
            Dangers of Horse Holding 45
            Letting Go the Horses 46
            References 48

Chapter 4   **Cross-Cultural Leadership in Networked
            Global Enterprises** 49
            Russell E. Palmer
            Abstract 49
            Introduction 50
            Leadership Across Cultures 51
            Culture and Leadership Styles: The Globe Project 55
            Building a Strong Organizational Culture: The Honeywell Way 59
            Conclusions: Building Cross-Cultural Leadership 62
            References 63

PART II   **FOUNDATIONS**

Chapter 5   **Social Networks: You've Lost Control** 67
            Dawn Iacobucci and James M. Salter II
            Abstract 67
            The Discipline of Social Networks: Examining
            Interdependencies 68
            History of Thought in Social Networks 70
            Concepts and Theories in Social Networks 72
            Key Substantive Findings: What Do We Know? 75
            Implications for Marketing Management and Business 77
            Conclusion: Losing Control 80
            References 80

Chapter 6   **Biological Networks: Rainforests, Coral Reefs,
            and the Galapagos Islands** 85
            Sonia Kleindorfer and James G. Mitchell
            Abstract 85
            Biological Networks 88
            Network Structure: What Determines Food Web Stability? 89
            Network Evolution 91
            Conclusions: Biology and Business 96
            References 99

Chapter 7 Information Networks in the History of Life 105
Robert Giegengack and Yvette Bordeaux
Abstract 105
Senses and Network Communication 108
Communication in Colonial Structures 111
Implications for Human Networks 119
Conclusion 122
References 123

Chapter 8 Artificial Intelligence: How Individual Agents
Add Up to a Network 125
Steven O. Kimbrough
Abstract 125
Cellular Automata Models: Localized Decisions
Combine for Unexpected Effects 127
Agent-Based Models 133
Evolutionary Models 137
Conclusion: Lessons Learned and Looking Forward 139
References 141

PART III **INNOVATION AND COORDINATION IN NETWORKS**

Chapter 9 Network-Centric Innovation: Four Strategies
for Tapping the Global Brain 147
Satish Nambisan and Mohanbir Sawhney
Abstract 147
Network-Centric Innovation 149
Models of Network-Centric Innovation 151
Organizational Competencies and Capabilities for
Network-Centric Innovation 158
Implications for Research and Practice 161
Conclusion 162
References 163

Chapter 10 Coordination Networks in Product Development 165
Manuel E. Sosa
Abstract 165
The Development Process as a Web of Design Activities 166

Complex Products as Networks of Components 171
The Informal Communication Network of Design Teams 175
Conclusions and Future Directions 180
References 181

**Chapter 11   Organizational Design: Balancing Search and Stability
in Strategic Decision Making** 185
Jan W. Rivkin and Nicolaj Siggelkow
Abstract 185
A Model of Organizational Search and Organizational Design 189
Schwab: The Benefit of Sequencing Organizational Structures 194
Toyota: Beyond a Modular Approach 198
Conclusion: Organizing to Search for an Effective Strategy 201
References 202

PART IV   STRATEGY AND BUSINESS MODELS

Chapter 12   Complexity Theory: Making Sense of Network Effects . . . 207
Colin Crook
Abstract 207
Key Concepts of Complexity Theory for Business 208
Key Implications for Managers 213
Key Unanswered Questions 220
Becoming Comfortable with Complexity 221
References 222

**Chapter 13   Supply Webs: Managing, Organizing, and Capitalizing
on Global Networks of Suppliers** 225
Serguei Netessine
Abstract 225
Managing Supplier Relationships: The Automotive Industry 228
Leveraging Coordinating Technology: The Aerospace and Defense
Industry 231
Research on Managing Supplier Networks 235
Conclusion 237
References 239

Chapter 14   Leveraging Customer Networks 243
Christophe Van den Bulte and Stefan Wuyts
Abstract 243
Rising Interest in Social Networks 244
Why Marketers (Should) Care About Social Networks 245
Toward a More Rigorous Approach to Word-of-Mouth
Marketing 247
Conclusion 256
References 256

Chapter 15   The Business Model as the Engine of Network-Based
Strategies 259
Christoph Zott and Raphael Amit
Abstract 259
Origin and Focus of Business Model Research 262
Perspectives on Strategy and Value Creation 263
Understanding the Business Model Concept in a
Networked World 266
Product Market Strategies and Business Models 269
Conclusions and Managerial Implications 271
References 272

Chapter 16   Extended Intelligence Networks: Minding and
Mining the Periphery 277
George S. Day, Paul J. H. Schoemaker, and Scott A. Snyder
Abstract 277
Minding and Mining the Periphery 278
Research Literature: Learning, Networks, and Scanning 280
Types of Extended Intelligence Networks 283
Utilizing Existing Networks 284
Improving Your Extended Intelligence Network 288
The Leadership Challenge: Managing It All 292
References 292

PART V   ORGANIZING IN A NETWORKED WORLD

Chapter 17 Network Orchestration: Creating and Managing
               Global Supply Chains Without Owning Them 299
               Yoram (Jerry) Wind, Victor Fung, and William Fung
               Abstract 299
               Unbundling Supply Chains 301
               The Four Flows: Where Atoms Meet Bits 302
               The Need for Orchestration 306
               Implications of Network Orchestration for Strategy
               and Competencies 307
               Three Roles of Network Orchestration 309
               Striking a Balance 312
               The Need for Orchestration 313
               References 314

Chapter 18 Managing the Hyper-Networked "Instant Messaging"
               Generation in the Work Force 317
               Eric K. Clemons, Steve Barnett, JoAnn Magdoff,
               and Julia Clemons
               Abstract 317
               Social Networks 318
               Paradoxes of Modern Networks 321
               Trends Shaping Modern Networks 323
               Implications 327
               References 332

Chapter 19 Missing the Forest for the Trees: Network-Based HR
               Strategies 335
               Valery Yakubovich and Ryan Burg
               Abstract 335
               From an Atomized to a Network Approach to Human Resources .. 337
               Recruitment and Hiring: The Power of Weak Ties 338
               Training and Development 342
               Performance Management: Creativity Versus Implementation 344
               Retention 345
               Conclusions 346
               References 347

Chapter 20 Relating Well: Building Capabilities for Sustaining
Alliance Networks 353

Prashant Kale, Harbir Singh, and John Bell

Abstract 353

The Key Decision-Points in Creating Relational
Capability: The Philips Story 356

Developing Alliance Capabilities: A Constant Work in Progress ... 361

Conclusion and Implications 363

References 363

PART VI **NETWORK-BASED SOURCES OF RISK AND
PROFITABILITY**

Chapter 21 Networks in Finance 367

Franklin Allen and Ana Babus

Abstract 367

Applications to Finance 369

Conclusion 379

References 379

Chapter 22 The Weakest Link: Managing Risk Through
Interdependent Strategies 383

Howard Kunreuther

Abstract 383

IDS Scenarios 385

Characterizing the Problem—Investing in a Chemical Plant 388

Developing Risk Management Strategies: Tipping
and Cascading 390

Future Research 393

Conclusion: Using Networks to Address Risks 396

References 396

Chapter 23 Integration of Financial and Physical Networks
in Global Logistics 399

Paul R. Kleindorfer and Ilias D. Visvikis

Abstract 399

Globalization and Implications for Logistics Infrastructure 401

Structure and Evolution of Air Cargo and Maritime Logistics 403

Financial Risk Management in Shipping 405
Conclusion 413
References 414

Chapter 24   Telecommunications: Network Strategies for Network
Industries? 417
Kevin Werbach
Abstract 417
A Network-Based View of Telecom 418
Network Monists and Dualists: AT&T and Google 421
The Modular Future 427
Conclusion: A Network View of Networks 430
References 430

Chapter 25   Network-Based Strategies and Competencies
for Political and Social Risk Management 433
Witold J. Henisz
Abstract 433
Sources of Information on Political and Social Risks 436
Developing a Strategy to Manage Political and Social Risks 440
Implementing Political and Social Risk-Management Strategies . . . 445
Conclusion: From Information Overload to Actionable Insight 448
References 449

PART VII   **A DOUBLE-EDGED SWORD: CONTAGION
AND CONTAINMENT**

Chapter 26   Terrorism Networks: It Takes a Network To Beat
a Network 453
Dr. Boaz Ganor
Abstract 453
Terrorism and Social Network Analysis 455
Network Structure 458
The Internet and Other Enabling Technologies 462
Countering Terrorist Networks 464
Implications for Management and Business 468
References 469

Chapter 27   Global Diseases: The Role of Networks in the Spread
and Prevention of Infection 471

J. Shin Teh and Harvey Rubin

Abstract 471

Introduction 472

Network-Based Perspective of Infectious Diseases 473

Controlling Global Infectious Diseases 481

Conclusions: The Rising Challenge and Lessons from the Past 487

References 489

Chapter 28   Lessons from Empirical Network Analyses on
Matters of Life and Death in East Africa 495

Jere R. Behrman, Hans-Peter Kohler, and Susan Cotts Watkins

Abstract 495

General Overview of Survey Data and Contexts 499

Social Networks and Life—The Diffusion of Family Planning 500

Social Networks and Mortality and Death—The Diffusion
of Worry About HIV/AIDS 506

Conclusion 508

References 509

About the Authors 513

Index 537

Authors* for *The Network Challenge*

Franklin Allen
Nippon Life Professor of Finance and Professor of Economics
The Wharton School, University of Pennsylvania

Raphael Amit
Robert B. Goergen Professor of Entrepreneurship and Professor of Management
The Wharton School, University of Pennsylvania

Ana Babus
Research Fellow for Centre for Financial Analysis and Policy
University of Cambridge

Steve Barnett
Anthropologist, Co-Founder and Chief Executive Officer
Bardo Consulting

Jere R. Behrman
William R.Kenan, Jr. Professor of Economics and Associate
Population Studies Center, University of Pennsylvania

John Bell
Head of Strategy & Partnerships
Philips Research

*For biographical details on authors, please see page 513.

Yvette Bordeaux

Director of Professional Masters Programs in Earth & Environmental Science

School of Arts and Sciences, University of Pennsylvania

Ryan Burg

PhD Candidate in Sociology and Business Ethics

University of Pennsylvania

Eric Clemons

Professor of Operations and Information Management and Management

The Wharton School, University of Pennsylvania

Julia Clemons

Undergraduate Student

University of Chicago

Colin Crook

Senior Fellow, SEI Center for Advanced Studies in Management

George S. Day

Geoffrey T. Boisi Professor and Professor of Marketing

The Wharton School, University of Pennsylvania

Victor Fung

Group Chairman

Li & Fung Limited

William Fung

Group Managing Director

Li & Fung Limited

Boaz Ganor
Deputy Dean of the Lauder School of Government and Diplomacy
Interdisciplinary Center Herzliya, Israel

Robert Giegengack
Professor Emeritus of Earth & Environmental Science
School of Arts and Sciences, University of Pennsylvania

Witold J. Henisz
Associate Professor of Management
The Wharton School, University of Pennsylvania

Dawn Iacobucci
E. Bronson Ingram Professor of Marketing and Associate Dean of Faculty Development
Owen Graduate School of Management, Vanderbilt University

Prashant Kale
Professor of Strategic Management
Jones School of Management, Rice University

Alan M. Kantrow
Professor of Management and Director, Infrastructure Research Center
Moscow School of Management, Skolkovo

Steven Kimbrough
Professor of Operations and Information Management
The Wharton School, University of Pennsylvania

Paul R. Kleindorfer
Paul Dubrule Professor of Sustainable Development and Distinguished Research Professor
INSEAD, Fontainebleau

Sonia Kleindorfer

Senior Lecturer in Biodiversity and Conservation

School of Biological Sciences, Flinders University, South Australia

Hans-Peter Kohler

Professor of Sociology and Research Associate

Population Studies Center, University of Pennsylvania

Howard Kunreuther

Cecilia Yen Koo Professor of Decision Sciences and Public Policy

The Wharton School, University of Pennsylvania

JoAnn Magdoff

Psychotherapist and Licensed Clinical Social Worker

Marriage and Family Therapist

James G. Mitchell

Head of the School of Biological Sciences

Flinders University, South Australia

Satish Nambisan

Associate Professor of Technology Management and Strategy

The Lally School of Management, Rensselaer Polytechnic Institute

Serguei Netessine

Associate Professor of Operations and Information Management

The Wharton School, University of Pennsylvania

Russell E. Palmer

Chairman and Chief Executive Officer

The Palmer Group

CK Prahalad
Paul and Ruth McCracken Distinguished University Professor
Ross School of Business, University of Michigan

Jan Rivkin
Bruce V. Rauner Professor of Business Administration
Harvard Business School, Harvard University

Harvey Rubin
Professor of Medicine
School of Medicine, University of Pennsylvania

James M. Salter II
Principal
Customer Lifecycle, LLC

Mohanbir Sawhney
McCormick Tribune Professor of E-Commerce and Technology
Kellogg School of Management, Northwestern University

Paul J. H. Schoemaker
Research Director, Mack Center for Technological Innovation
The Wharton School, University of Pennsylvania

Nicolaj Siggelkow
Associate Professor of Management
The Wharton School, University of Pennsylvania

Harbir Singh
William and Phyllis Mack Professor of Management
The Wharton School, University of Pennsylvania

Scott A. Snyder
President and CEO
Decision Strategies International

Manuel Sosa
Associate Professor of Technology and Operations Management
INSEAD

J. Shin Teh
Associate Director
Institute for Strategic Threat Analysis and Response (ISTAR)

Christophe Van den Bulte
Associate Professor of Marketing
The Wharton School, University of Pennsylvania

Ilias Visvikis
Assistant Professor of Finance and Academic Director of the MBA in Shipping Program
ALBA Graduate Business School, Greece

Susan Cotts Watkins
Professor of Sociology and Research Associate
Population Studies Center, University of Pennsylvania

Kevin Werbach
Assistant Professor of Legal Studies and Business Ethics
The Wharton School, University of Pennsylvania

Yoram (Jerry) Wind
The Lauder Professor and Professor of Marketing
The Wharton School, University of Pennsylvania

Stefan Wuyts
Associate Professor of Marketing
Tilburg University

Valery Yakubovich
Associate Professor of Management
The Wharton School, University of Pennsylvania

Christoph Zott
Associate Professor of Entrepreneurship
IESE, INSEAD

Foreword

The Wharton School of the University of Pennsylvania and INSEAD formed the Wharton-INSEAD Alliance in 2001 to promote scholarship and exchange of students and faculty to advance management thought and business practice. From its start, the Alliance focused not only on education but also on developing the knowledge to meet the challenges of a changing global business environment. This book is a major addition to the fruits of our collaboration.

The theme of network-based strategies and competencies has already become a central element of discourse in business schools and boardrooms around the world. Whether in the context of new governance and leadership challenges from Web-based commerce, or in the current financial crisis and its contagion effects, or in the continuing discussions of the costs and risks of unbundling and outsourcing, the subject of network-based business models is full upon us. Garnering the benefits of extended innovation and global sourcing from such business models will surely be a major theme for researchers and educators going forward. This book aims to contribute to setting the research agenda on this important theme.

The contributions to this volume—arising as they do from scholars from a variety of disciplines, as well as practitioners—are very much in the spirit of the Alliance itself. This collaborative work is a demonstration of the productivity and creativity of the network of scholars who form the core of the Wharton-INSEAD Alliance. We are delighted to see this further evidence of the benefits of our Alliance.

Dean Thomas S. Robertson
The Wharton School
University of Pennsylvania
Philadelphia, USA

Dean Frank Brown
INSEAD
Fontainebleau, France

Preface

This volume is the result of a joint project by the Wharton SEI Center for Advanced Studies in Management and the INSEAD Social Innovation Centre. The original motivation for this book stemmed from several meetings of the SEI Center Board that focused on revisiting work of the early 1990s at the SEI Center on the future of the corporation. These discussions suggested interesting tensions between the established theory of the firm and emerging practice. The underlying factors giving rise to these tensions were the emergence of new communication and information technologies, new governance and regulatory institutions, and corresponding new business models, which were web-centric, not firm-centric. These factors led to an environment of global connectedness and interdependency evoked by Thomas Friedman's notion of a "flat world." These same themes were echoed in the INSEAD Social Innovation Centre's focus on governance and the changing demands on business occasioned by the growing importance of corporate stakeholders representing social and environmental interests.

Given our joint interests, we decided to launch a project under the Wharton-INSEAD Alliance to revisit the earlier SEI project on "the future of the corporation" in light of the emerging environment for global business. The motivating belief for the project was that these "new interlinked enterprises" would require extending the traditional approach to strategy and competencies. We needed to reshape our thinking about business to the contours of these emerging network-based organizations. The required re-conceptualization, we thought, would encompass the traditional sources of profit through efficiency and innovation, but it would also be oriented toward sustainability of the networks within which the company operated.

To examine these themes, we convened a Workshop in May of 2007 to explore the relevance and bounds of such a vision. The results were sufficiently encouraging to warrant a major conference in November 2007, held at the Wharton School and entitled "Network-Based Strategies and Competencies." The Conference was a Wharton Impact Conference, supported by Dean Tom Robertson of Wharton and with primary support from the Wharton-INSEAD Alliance and Dean Frank Brown of INSEAD, which we gratefully acknowledge. The Conference brought together scholars from various non-business disciplines—from anthropology and biology to computer science—as well as diverse traditional business disciplines. We explored together the state of knowledge of networks in each of these disciplines and the relevance of this knowledge for the changing landscape of business and the economic institutions that govern and influence business. The emerging financial crisis in 2007, with its underlying contagion effects, served as a sobering reminder of the potential importance of network-based phenomena and the limitations in our knowledge about them.

The resulting volume certainly exceeded even our ambitious expectations for this project. The reader will see in the contributions to the present volume the huge opportunities and challenges for research, across many disciplines, presented by network perspectives. The reader will also note the richness of network perspectives in expanding the boundaries of traditional business models and strategies to encompass new dimensions of risk, opportunity, and innovation.

This volume owes a debt to many individuals. First and foremost, the SEI Center Board of Directors, and its chairman Al West, were the underlying force that gave rise to this project, and we thank Al and the SEI Board for their continuing support. Our special thanks go to SEI Board Members Colin Crook, Dolf Dibiasio, and Len Lindegren, who commented on many drafts of the Conference Proposal and who served as the intellectual architects for the "network imperative" that shaped this project. The support and encouragement of Luk Van Wassenhove of the INSEAD Social Innovation Centre are also noted with appreciation. We are most grateful to our editor at Pearson, Tim Moore, who has been an essential partner in shaping this venture right from the start and whose vision for this book and so much else has been central to our endeavor.

We are deeply indebted to Robert Gunther, who was our collaborating editor for this project and without whose help a great deal of substance, style, and readability would have been lost from these papers. We also thank Katherine Rohan and Chu Hui Cha of the SEI Center, who bore the brunt of organizing the Workshop and Conference and helped to manage a large and complex book project. Most importantly, we thank the participants at the Workshop and Conference that formed the background and framework for this book. Their splendid and open discussion at these events—and the follow-on papers formed by this discussion—have made the editorial work on this volume a pleasant exercise in intellectual discovery and integration. We hope that the reader will have a similarly enjoyable voyage of discovery in reading these papers, and that this work will provide a stimulus for further research on network-based strategies and competencies.

Paul R. Kleindorfer, INSEAD
Yoram (Jerry) Wind, The Wharton School

PART I

THE NETWORK CHALLENGE

Networks change the fundamental mindsets through which we understand business and the world around us. The first section of the book considers the rise of networks and the way network-based thinking challenges our views of organizations. In Chapter 1, editors **Paul Kleindorfer** and **Yoram (Jerry) Wind** discuss the development of networks and their growing implications for business, as well as providing an overview of the book. In Chapter 2, **CK Prahalad** examines the role of networks in creating innovations that move beyond stand-alone products to networks that deliver a customer experience. In Chapter 3, **Alan Kantrow** examines the role of networks in knowledge management, both the ability to harness knowledge in networks and the challenge in forgetting "horse holding" behavior of the past. Finally, in Chapter 4, **Russell Palmer** draws on his experiences as leader of a major global accounting firm to consider complex issues of leadership across diverse international cultures.

Chapter 1   The Network Imperative: Community or Contagion?   3
Paul Kleindorfer and Yoram (Jerry) Wind

Chapter 2   Creating Experience: Competitive Advantage in the
Age of Networks   25
CK Prahalad

Chapter 3   Knowledge as a Social Phenomenon: "Horse Holding" and
Learning in Networks   37
Alan Kantrow

Chapter 4   Cross-Cultural Leadership in Networked Global Enterprises   49
Russell E. Palmer

1

The Network Imperative: Community or Contagion?

Paul Kleindorfer
Yoram (Jerry) Wind

Abstract

The rising importance of networks creates challenges and opportunities for business enterprises. On the one hand, networks lead to contagion and other risks, as can be seen in the rise of global terrorism and the spread of the 2008 global financial crisis. On the other hand, networks present opportunities for building community, as can be seen in the rapid rise of companies such as eBay, Google, Facebook, and other network-based enterprises. In this chapter, the editors of The Network Challenge *point out that network-based models for business challenge the traditional firm-centric view of competencies and strategies that are the focus of most business education and management thinking. The authors challenge managers to consider the implications of networks in addressing issues such as risk management, strategy, marketing, human resources, and value creation. They emphasize the need to take diverse viewpoints on networks, including drawing upon fields such as biology, infectious diseases, and other areas with a long history of studying networks. Finally, the authors offer a summary of the key sections and chapters in* The Network Challenge, *which provide a broad, multidisciplinary view of networks and their implications for business. This chapter makes it clear that the opportunities and threats presented by networks cannot be ignored.*

The network-based nature of our businesses and financial systems was clearly evident in the deep global financial crisis that unfolded across the summer of 2008. The collapse of U.S. subprime mortgage markets led to a ripple of effects across all sectors of the U.S. economy, necessitating the rescue of Bear Stearns, Fannie Mae and Freddie

3

Mac, and insurer AIG. The U.S. government passed a hastily developed $700 billion bailout package designed to help unfreeze the banking industry, and other governments around the world have followed suit. The ultimate outcome of these emergency measures remains to be seen. However, network contagion and the complexity of cause and effect in a networked world are now routinely put forward as the reasons for the continuing crisis in financial markets. In explaining the conflagration of global markets, network dynamics have become the new phlogiston—a mysterious and ultimately fictitious substance used to explain combustion prior to the discovery of oxygen in the 1770s. We clearly need a deeper and more precise understanding of network interactions.

The network challenge can also be seen in the Chinese "toxic-milk scandal." A few years ago, the logic of outsourcing manufacturing to China and other low-cost producers was irresistible. Any manufacturer who wanted to remain competitive needed to be able to meet the so-called "China price." But a series of problems, including tainted pet foods, recalls of toxic toys, and the spreading scandal of tainted milk powder in China, have revealed the hidden risks of unbundling strategies, with their ensuing more complex supply chains and difficulties in governance of global networks. The results of the tainted-milk event will take months or even years to play out, with global recalls of baby formula, candy, and other food products containing powdered milk now underway. The sheer complexity of uncovering and recalling all potentially contaminated products that have been shipped globally is formidable. The economic damage to the reputation of China's food industry will be staggering as the scandal has heightened concerns in the United States and Europe about the quality of Chinese products. One evident lesson from the toxic-milk scandal is that the spread of information and the measures that are needed to reestablish trust in global networks are of a different and far more complex nature than single-channel, controlled marketing and distribution networks of the past.

At the same time, networks have emerged as a tremendous source of value creation. Companies such as eBay, Google, Facebook, YouTube, and Twitter have risen from the primordial swamps of cyberspace to become major players based primarily on the power of their networks. Established corporations such as Procter & Gamble and Toyota are harnessing networks to tap into new sources of innovation around the globe or engage in word-of-mouth marketing for new products. The successful 2008 U.S. presidential campaign of Barack Obama has been attributed to his deft ability to mobilize and manage an unprecedented network of volunteers and contributors. Networks of suppliers are creating and delivering products through supply webs that stretch around the globe and can be reconfigured rapidly. Networks are now a powerful driver of value creation across society, but they follow different rules than command-and-control hierarchies. To tap into the value of networks, managers need a deeper understanding of how they work.

Companies and governments today face a dilemma: They cannot compete without networks to access resources or markets, but these networks present new risks and challenges that must be managed. The threats that face our world today—from financial crises to global competition to terrorist attacks to global diseases—are network-based. Effective solutions, in many cases, are also network-based. In such an interlinked world, we need a deeper understanding of networks to drive growth and manage risks. We need to understand what makes networks tick. This book is an attempt to provide a starting point for understanding the nature of networks and their implications for business. We brought together a broad cross section of researchers from diverse fields within business and outside—from biologists to antiterrorism experts—to help understand the nature of networks more broadly, and the specific knowledge that managers need to work in a networked world.

The Rise of Networks

A network may be defined mathematically as a set of nodes and the arcs that connect specific pairs of these nodes. These interlinked structures serve as conduits for information, human resources and capital, material flows—and associated risks. The origin of interest in networks in business and economics goes back to studies of transportation networks and mathematical programming solutions for various classes of production and transportation problems in the 1950s (e.g., Dorfman, Samuelson, and Solow 1958; Ford and Fulkerson 1962). Network-based theory also developed rapidly in sociology (as in the work of the renowned sociologist Coleman 1990). The early work was typically grounded in the analysis of a prespecified network, but a number of important contributions have now emerged regarding endogenous network formation (the activation of potential links between various nodes) and information exchange in economic and social networks (see, for example, Jackson 2008). Researchers in other fields have also addressed network phenomena, either explicitly or implicitly. This book presents many of these perspectives on networks. We have not tried to reduce all of these perspectives to a single, general definition of network-based effects, but all of these perspectives imply informational and resource links between actors in some given context. These links, whether preexisting or dynamically activated, imply interdependencies between these actors (see sidebar). It is the study of the nature and evolution of these interdependencies that has provided new insights on the changing landscape of global business, and that provides the major backdrop and rationale for this book.

Networks, Interdependencies, and Externalities

In economics, interdependencies are often referred to as *externalities*. Externalities occur (typically in choice contexts involving resource allocation or economic design decisions) either when the payoffs or information of one agent are influenced by actions of other agents (a pecuniary or informational interdependency or externality) or when the set of feasible actions of one agent are influenced by actions of other agents (a technological interdependency or externality). Sometimes several types of interdependency occur in the same resource allocation problem. Social interdependencies (wherein payoffs to certain agents are influenced by their observed compliance with norms or depend on kinship links) are an example of pecuniary interdependencies, but theories regarding such interdependencies obviously have their own special character. Network interdependencies are a specific form of interdependency in which the effects of the interdependency (pecuniary, informational, technological, or social) operate through identifiable agents/nodes and pathways/links. The specific character of networks (and their interdependency effects) derives from the role played by the structure and typology of the nodes and links connecting individual agents in a specific network. Network theory has come to mean many things in the past several decades, including endogenous formation of links and nodes, information transmission in networks of given structure, computational limits when various agents in a network structure can perform certain local calculations only, social contagion effects, and so forth. All these and more are reflected in the chapters in this book, and each area discussed in the book is also evolving. Thus, we are not going to attempt to provide a general and all-encompassing definition of what network effects are. Rather, for the general purposes of understanding the chapters in this book, you should simply think of networks in the common English-language use of the term as interlinked structures that serve as conduits for information, human resources and capital, material flows, and associated risks.

Sharp declines in the cost of communications, information technology, and logistics have led to explosive growth of outsourcing and offshoring, as global work migrates to where it can be completed best at lowest cost. Cross-border trade has skyrocketed. Total manufacturing exports increased 10% annually between 2000 and 2006, growing at twice the rate of world GDP.[1] While global business once moved from developed to developing

---

[1] "International Trade Statistics 2007," World Trade Organization, http://www.wto.org/english/res_e/statis_e/statis_e.htm.

countries, now global competition means "competing with everyone from everywhere for everything," as Boston Consulting Group's Hal Sirkin, Jim Hemerling, and Arindam Bhattacharya write in their book *Globality* (2008). We have seen waves of mega M&A activity that have created new industries (AOL Time Warner) and reshaped existing ones (Chrysler and Daimler-Benz, Sony and Columbia Pictures, JP Morgan and Chase).

Consumers are networked through interactive and empowered relationships, including the rapid rise of social networking sites such as MySpace and Facebook. By 2009, there are expected to be as many as 250,000 social networking sites. On eBay alone, more than 276 million users bought and sold more than $59 billion in products in 2007, almost equal to the $61 billion in sales by Target in the same year.[2] eBay sellers trade more than $2,000 in merchandise *every second*. New multinational regulatory models and business models are emerging to meet the network challenge. Investors also are placing a high value on network-based firms, as shown by Microsoft's $240 million purchase of a stake in social networking firm Facebook in October 2007, based on a $15 billion valuation of the privately held company that was launched less than four years earlier (Greene 2007).

Companies are using networks as sources of innovation and customer service. We are seeing the rise of consumer-generated advertising and consumer-led R & D and design. Dell's IdeaStorm site has received thousands of suggestions from consumers for new products or services, and consumers then vote for those they think are most important (www.ideastorm.com). As Don Tapscott and Anthony D. Williams write in *Wikinomics* (2006, 10), "We are entering a new age where people participate in the economy like never before. This new participation has reached a tipping point where new forms of mass collaboration are changing how goods and services are invented, produced, marketed and distributed on a global basis. This change represents far-reaching opportunities for every company and for every person who gets connected."

The classic network battle in videocassettes, in which Matsushita triumphed over Sony's superior Betamax technology in the 1970s by building a network of content and equipment, has given way to more complex battles. Even as Sony was battling with Toshiba for next-generation DVD standards (Blu-ray versus HD-DVD), companies such as Apple and Netflix were building their own networks for online movie downloads and other new channels for delivering entertainment (Anthony 2008). Standards wars are just part of a broader competition of network against network.

---

[2] eBay Marketplace Fast Facts, http://news.ebay.com/fastfacts_ebay_marketplace.cfm; Target Corp. Press Release, http://news.target.com/phoenix.zhtml?c=196187&p=irol-newsArticle&ID=1105552.

No One Is Exempt

Every organization is affected by the rise of networks. There are very few quiet backwaters where managers can comfortably take a firm-centric view of their work. This applies to all industries, all sizes of firms, and all countries. All branches of the military are moving to more network-centric models in institutions that had once defined "command and control" hierarchical structures. Networks have both direct and indirect impacts on strategy and competencies, as the chapters in this book make plain. Networks are transforming markets and many of the most important modes through which business and government organizations generate value, assume risks, ensure their long-term viability, and interact with their environment.

We are just beginning to recognize the implications of these changes for how we think about companies and how we design and run our businesses. Companies have experimented with a variety of new models to take advantage of these network opportunities, but we are still in the early stages of discovering what new opportunities and risks are presented by this shift from a firm-centric view to a network-centric view. This book considers some of these implications and opportunities.

Challenging the Theory of the Firm

In this world, the traditional view of the firm no longer serves us well. Adam Smith's famous pin factory, Henry Ford's automobile plant, and Peter Drucker's General Motors have defined how we think about management and strategy. The corporation has been at the center of management study and thinking since the birth of modern business research and education. Our management textbooks are built around the firm. Our laws are based on the corporation. And yet the traditional firm is increasingly an anachronism in a world of diverse and fluid connections—a networked world. New technologies and new business models have transformed the corporation.

The focus of the traditional theory of the firm was on "transformational efficiency" and market power, purchasing inputs and transforming them efficiently into products and services that could be marketed profitably to the firm's customers. The firm and the efficiency of its transformational processes, and its ability to command premium margins in the market, were the focal points of strategy. What has happened in the unbundled economy of the twenty-first century is that this "corporation as king" model has given way to a much more complicated array of interorganizational systems for innovation, for production, for marketing, and ultimately for connecting with customers and investors. On the supply side, outsourcing, offshoring, and the Internet have led to new connections to provide a variety of services, from accounting to manufacturing. On the demand side, open architectures and empowered consumers are driving both innovation and customization of existing products and their marketing. In the process, many corporations have come to view their profits and their risks not in terms of what they control internally, but in terms of their relational capabilities to the networks in which they are embedded.

These networks have done more than connect nodes of independent companies. They have led to second-order and third-order effects that are absent from bilateral transactions. Networked enterprises raise issues of group influence, cascading, contagion, and interdependent risks that cannot be controlled through standard mechanisms. As shown by eBay and other new business models, the distinctions between companies and markets have been blurred. Some of the challenges of the networked world cannot even be considered from a firm-level perspective, any more than a complex ecosystem can be understood by studying one of its actors, or a chemical reaction can be understood by studying a single reagent. The rise of networks has fundamental implications for business strategy and competencies.

Strategy and Competencies

Business strategy has been built around the firm. Michael Porter's (1985) famous Five Forces model puts the firm at the center, and other forces outside. Now the firm is part of the network and the five forces are in the network itself. Concepts such as barriers to entry have less meaning, and the idea of rivalry, buyers, and suppliers is transformed by an environment of "co-opetition" (Brandenberger and Nalebuff 1997).

Core competencies also look different from a network view. Since Hamel and Prahalad identified the importance of core competencies, these competencies have been primarily discussed at the firm level. Companies focused on building and protecting competencies that could not be easily imitated by rivals and could be leveraged across different businesses (such as Honda's expertise in small engines used in products from motorcycles to snowblowers). But as the world has become more networked, the competencies that are important are not so much the ones a company owns as the ones it can connect to.

New technologies, as discussed by Thomas Friedman (2005), are flattening the world. A small village in China or a tiny shop on the back streets of Mumbai can tap into global networks to identify current bids for its products or purchase manufacturing inputs, competing on a relatively level playing field. Entrepreneurial startups can compete against large, well-funded incumbents. Consumer products firm Method (www.methodhome.com), for example, worked with a network of global partners to build a $100 million business in just a few years, competing effectively against giant rivals such as Procter & Gamble. An amateur with a video camera can create content that can compete with large entertainment firms. Large companies can partner with these smaller firms, drawing together swarms of bees into a single productive hive. The challenge for large companies is to develop network-centric business models and strategies to harness the power of the broader network and harvest its usufruct (the right to derive benefit from property that belongs to another person as long as the original property is not damaged).

A Time of Revolutions

The rationale for the firm as an economic and legal entity finds its roots in the very beginnings of modern economics. The cornerstone of this view is Adam Smith's great treatise, *The Wealth of Nations,* published in 1776 on the eve of the birth of the American Republic. It was motivated by Smith's view that the changes that were beginning to be visible in the textile and manufacturing sectors of Britain would transform the economic activity of the world. A new theory was required to think about this. His theory saw economic value as being driven by two fundamental economic factors: "specialization" to achieve economies of scale, and "trade" to rebundle into useful products what specialization had unbundled.

We stand again in a time of revolutions. In the Internet age, the unbundling and rebundling foreseen by Smith has been facilitated by new communications and information platforms. Many of the nontechnical barriers to trade are being dismantled by regional innovations such as NAFTA and the European Union, and by supranational organizations like the WTO. China, India, and other emerging economies are growing rapidly in an interconnected world. Dubai and Abu Dhabi are planning their growth based on serving as a hub for countries within an 8-hour flight. In networked enterprises, the clear lines of specialization and trade have become blurred along with the lines between enterprises.

Perhaps the modern equivalent of Smith's pin factory is Li & Fung in Hong Kong. For a company that produces more than $9 billion in clothing, toys, and other products for some of the world's leading brands, a competency in *manufacturing* might be considered to be central. Yet the company does not own manufacturing plants or employ seamstresses. Instead it orchestrates a network of thousands of suppliers around the globe to create supply chains on-the-fly. Its core competency is not in specialized manufacturing process. Instead, its most important competency is in designing and managing the overall network, what company leaders Victor and William Fung call "network orchestration." This is its area of specialization.

Peter Drucker, exploring the depths of what was the twentieth century's quintessential modern corporation, General Motors, led the way into an understanding of modern management principles that still shapes the way managers are educated and practice. Today, General Motors offers a case in point about how the world has changed fundamentally. It has struggled to keep up with rivals, such as Toyota, with more skill in managing networks for innovation and operations. This new networked organization is, to echo the words of GM's infamous advertising campaign of the late 1980s, "not your father's Oldsmobile." The past two decades have seen immense changes in the forces and institutions that govern economic activity. These changes are leading to a new theory of the firm.[3]

Revolutionary times can be quite dangerous. While networks present opportunities, they also raise a number of risks and challenges as exemplified by the discussion of the financial crisis and the tainted-milk problem that opened this chapter. We have seen waves of change in governance, enterprise risks, and social structures. There are concerns about political risks from corruption, nonstandard accounting practices, and discriminatory regulation in international transactions (www.opacityindex.com). Accountability and transparency can be lost in the complex web of networks. We face network threats of terrorism, diseases, and global warming. These risks are the downside of the opportunities reflected by the network revolution. This revolution has provided huge increases in access to resources and markets, enabled by networks. The same revolution has exposed companies and economies to new complexities and risks because of the increased interdependencies implied by networks. Navigating and balancing the trade-offs between these opportunities and risks is the central challenge for management posed by the new age of networks.

Nodes and Networks

Companies were once seen as self-contained nodes connected with other enterprises; they are now increasingly an integral part of networks. New technologies and logistics platforms have allowed for the unbundling of the vertical organization. This is

---

[3] For an excellent summary of the foundations of the theory of the firm, see Roberts (2004). For a contrasting net-centric view, see Crook, Kleindorfer, Lindegren, and Wind (2006), which served as the background paper for the "call for papers" for the workshop and conference underlying this book.

changing relationships of companies with one another, their employees, customers, and other stakeholders. What happens across organizations is often more important than what happens within them. This transformation and its implications for managers and researchers are the subject of this book.

As our attention shifts from companies to the white space and relationships between them—like the famous optical illusion that shifts from two faces to the vase contained between them (see Figure 1-1)—we need a more fundamental rethinking of our view of business. These dramatic shifts mean that we need to challenge our traditional mental models of management (Wind and Crook 2004). Holding to old models that no longer fit the environment can lead to missed opportunities or the failure to see potential threats.

Figure 1-1   Node or network? Two faces or a vase? As our focus shifts from the firm (nodes) to the network, the white space between enterprises has become increasingly important. Is it time for a shift in our view of strategies and competencies?

The node and network exist together. The faces and the vase are both there, so sometimes it makes sense to look at the firm, sometimes the network. The fortunes of companies still rise or fall based on their own earnings and stock performance—not the strength of their networks—although networks are playing an increasing role in their performance. Investors still buy stock in companies, but the extraordinary valuation of a company such as Google depends in large part on the network in which it is embedded. Like the wave or particle theory of light in physics, both the node and the network view have a place in explaining the phenomenon of our current business world. In particular, the success or failure of many modern enterprises cannot be well understood at the firm level. They demand a network view.

The Network That Is This Book

It takes a network to understand a network. In this book, we have assembled scholars from business disciplines and experts from outside to help you understand network-based phenomena and its implications for management. These experts offer a multifaceted view of the emerging implications of our networked world. We have drawn together the broadest possible kaleidoscopic view from diverse disciplines in social sciences; computer, natural, and life sciences; and diverse business disciplines. The contributors came together for a major conference at the Wharton School in November 2007, sponsored by the INSEAD-Wharton Alliance, where they brought their different views together in a common crucible. The result is this book. Let us briefly examine insights that will be explored by these authors in the following sections of the book.

Part I: The Network Challenge

The first section of the book considers the way networks challenge our fundamental views of organizations, leading to a rethinking of innovation, knowledge management, and leadership. Among the challenges presented by networks are these:

- *Challenge of network-based innovation*—In Chapter 2, "Creating Experience: Competitive Advantage in the Age of Networks," **CK Prahalad,** who was a pioneer in framing the discussion on core competencies more than two decades ago, discusses the role of networks in the design of product and service offerings. He considers how the locus of innovation has moved from the firm to the network and presents examples of networked models that have been applied in medical technology, such as cardiac pacemakers, and in an innovative system for diabetes management in India. Instead of merely assembling a supply chain to produce a product, companies can bring networks together to create a customer experience and value.

- *Challenge of knowledge management*—Networks have tremendous power for remembering and sharing knowledge, but **Alan Kantrow** notes in Chapter 3, "Knowledge as a Social Phenomenon: 'Horse Holding' and Learning in Networks," that sometimes networks need the ability to forget and examines the role of networks in knowledge management strategies. Organizational routines often continue in force long after the old practice is obsolete. But memory is rarely lost entirely. It usually lingers, in distributed fragments, in an organization's social networks and can, if needed, be reassembled.

- *Challenge of network-based leadership*—Networked organizations, particularly cross-cultural networks, present challenges for leaders, as **Russ Palmer** discusses in Chapter 4, "Cross-Cultural Leadership in Networked Global Enterprises," where he considers the new leadership that is needed. The kind of leadership style that works in global networks is different from the "do it and do it now" approach that might work in hierarchical organizations. Leaders need to understand that what works in one culture may not work in another.

Part II: Foundations

While business organizations have begun to recognize the need to build and understand networks, business certainly didn't invent networks. The second section of the book turns to rich and varied research on networks, from online dating to food chains to leaf-cutter ants. Among the insights are these:

- *With the rise of social networks, you've lost control*—Beginning with a discussion of a panicked run on Hong Kong cake shops, **Dawn Iacobucci** and **James Salter** consider the implications of the rise of "social networks" in Chapter 5, "Social Networks: You've Lost Control." In a discussion that moves from online dating to marketing, they show that as power shifts from firms to social networks, companies have less control over their own destinies and need to pay more attention to networks.

- *Size and linking improve productivity and survival in biological networks*—Biological networks are as old as life, and in Chapter 6, "Biological Networks: Rainforests, Coral Reefs, and the Galapagos Islands," **Sonia Kleindorfer** and **Jim Mitchell** take us on a journey into rainforests, coral reefs, and Darwin's *Finches on the Galapagos Islands* to understand the structure and evolution of biological networks. They note that biological networks adapt over time, network size is related to productivity, and networks need a balance of strong and weak links to survive.

- *From bees to ants, networks need a system of communication*—The impact of information and communications on network dynamics did not arrive with the rise of computers and cellphones. In Chapter 7, "Information Networks in the History of Life," **Robert Giegengack** and **Yvette Bordeaux** consider lessons from bee dances to the complex agricultural communities of leaf-cutter ants. These biological networks have systems for filtering noise, specialized roles, and mechanisms for signaling, all of which are also important to human networks.

- ***Cooperation and competition lead to different outcomes in networks***—Beyond natural biology, our computer "creations" have their own evolving life in the form of artificial intelligence. In Chapter 8, "Artificial Intelligence: How Individual Agents Add Up to a Network," **Steve Kimbrough,** using agent-based models, shows how outcomes from strategies of cooperation and competition depend on the surrounding environment and on the nature of the interactions embodied in the information and resource networks that connect agents.

Part III: Innovation and Coordination in Networks

Networks are transforming our view of innovation and coordination. After this broad view of networks, in the third section of the book, we turn our attention to specific business implications, beginning with innovation and coordination. Innovation, product design, and new product development are no longer centered in a single firm, so companies need to understand how to get the best ideas and develop products through networks. Among the insights are these:

- ***Different networks are needed for different types of innovation***—In Chapter 9, "Network-Centric Innovation: Four Strategies for Tapping the Global Brain," **Satish Nambisan** and **Mohan Sawhney** show how organizations can tap into the "global brain" for innovation. But they make it clear that not all networks are the same. A jazz band and an orchestra are both networks but operate in very different ways. In particular, the writers identify four models of network-centric innovation—which they call Orchestra, Creative Bazaar, Jam Central, and MOD Station—and outline how companies can select, prepare for, and pursue the approach that best fits their particular business and innovation context.

- ***Design networks need coordination***—Complex products such as airplanes or automobiles are now designed by networks of teams working on different components, often across organizations and countries. The challenge in managing these networks is to decompose the project into manageable pieces but then coordinate the entire network to produce the best overall design. In Chapter 10, "Coordination Networks in Product Development," **Manuel E. Sosa** considers approaches to engineering design based on the information and resource requirements of a given design problem, as captured in tools such as the design structure matrix to drive decisions such as organizational team structure and modularity in design.

- *Networks sometimes need "inefficient" overlaps to ensure broad search and avoid lock-in*—In Chapter 11, "Organizational Design: Balancing Search and Stability in Strategic Decision Making," **Nicolaj Siggelkow** and **Jan Rivkin** examine the intersection between organizing and strategizing. Centralized decision making may be more stable and efficient but can lead to "premature lock-in" rather than a broad search for fresh perspectives. Using a simulation approach motivated by network-based approaches to artificial intelligence, they look at how "inefficient" overlaps across a network can sometimes be desirable in balancing search and stability.

Part IV: Strategy and Business Models

Networks lead to new views of strategy and new business models, as examined in the next section of the book. Among the insights are these:

- *Organizations increasingly must recognize the "network effects" of complexity theory in developing strategy*—Complexity theory addresses the "network effects" that result from interactions between many independent actors. In Chapter 12, "Complexity Theory: Making Sense of Network Effects," **Colin Crook** explores issues such as fads and crowds, reflecting the spread of shared information and technology, and the use of agent-based simulations to understand interaction effects in networks. He considers the implications of complexity theory for business, and how network effects influence key management areas such as making sense of complex environments, strategy formulation, and organization design.

- *Business is moving from supply chains to supply networks*—As manufacturing supply chains have moved from vertically integrated factories to diffused networks, manufacturers need to manage complex, global webs of suppliers. In Chapter 13, "Supply Webs: Managing, Organizing, and Capitalizing on Global Networks of Suppliers," **Serguei Netessine** examines how companies such as Airbus and Boeing have used technology to coordinate and integrate far-flung supply networks.

- *Marketing is increasingly network-based, depending on "social contagion"*—In Chapter 14, "Leveraging Customer Networks," **Christophe Van den Bulte** and **Stefan Wuyts** consider the increasing role of networks in marketing, accelerating the spread of new products, strengthening brand beliefs and preferences, improving corporate status and reputation, coordinating distribution channels, and accessing resources. They consider the key role of social contagion in marketing.

- *Networks create and distribute value in new ways*—In contrast to firm-centric views of value creation such as Porter's value chain, network-based business models build value through different mechanisms. In Chapter 15, "The Business Model as the Engine of Network-Based Strategies," **Christoph Zott** and **Raffi Amit** identify four major interlinked value drivers—efficiency, complementarities, lock-in, and novelty—and discuss their role in new business models that are consistent with network-based strategies.

- *Networks can improve the organization's "peripheral vision" to see opportunities and threats at the edges of the business*—In addition to their direct function, many networks serve as antennae to scan, sense, and adapt to new and important signals from the organization's strategic environment beyond its core focus. In Chapter 16, "Extended Intelligence Networks: Minding and Mining the Periphery," **George S. Day, Paul J. H. Schoemaker**, and **Scott A. Snyder** explore how companies can use existing networks and design new ones to gather intelligence and create "strategic radar" to recognize emerging threats and opportunities sooner.

Part V: Organizing in a Networked World

Networks are changing the design and management of our organizations. The next section of the book explores how networks demand new capabilities in orchestrating networks, managing a new generation of networked employees, finding and hiring staff, and managing alliances. Among the insights are these:

- *Core capabilities may be located outside the organization, drawn together through capabilities in "network orchestration"*—In Chapter 17, "Network Orchestration: Creating and Managing Global Supply Chains Without Owning Them," **Jerry Wind, Victor Fung,** and **William Fung** describe the innovative model of Li & Fung for "competing in a flat world" by orchestrating a far-flung network of suppliers brought together into temporary networks to fulfill a specific customer order. Its connective capabilities in "network orchestration," in contrast to traditional views of core competencies, allowed the company to become one of the top global contract manufacturers without owning a single factory.

- *Companies need to change the way they manage "instant messaging generation" employees*—The IM generation has different views of work, loyalty, decision making, and even reality. In Chapter 18, "Managing the Hyper-Networked 'Instant Messaging' Generation in the Work Force," **Eric K. Clemons**, **Steve Barnett, JoAnn Magdoff**, and **Julia Clemons** consider how organizations need to adapt their training, their managerial styles, and their expectations of employees' motivations.

- *Effective human resources management depends on harnessing networks*—
  While HR management has traditionally focused on the individual, in Chapter 19,
  "Missing the Forest for the Trees: Network-Based HR Strategies," **Valery
  Yakubovich** and **Ryan Burg** point out that core HR processes such as recruitment and hiring, training and development, performance management, and
  retention all depend on networks. Employees come to organizations through networks, "structural holes" within organizations can challenge employees to develop
  new skills, and networks also increase the potential for "lift outs," in which one
  departing employee takes many others. Effective human resources management
  requires seeing this larger forest instead of focusing only on the trees.

- *Relational capabilities are crucial to successful alliances*—In a networked
  world, alliances are central to success, but more than half of alliances fail. In
  Chapter 20, "Relating Well: Building Capabilities for Sustaining Alliance Networks," **Prashant Kale**, **Harbir Singh**, and **John Bell** discuss their research on
  the importance of building relational capabilities to design and manage alliances
  effectively. Using the case of Royal Philips, they explore the role of strategy, structure, systems, people, and culture in alliance success, underlining the central role
  of relational capabilities in an increasingly networked world.

Part VI: Network-Based Sources of Risk and Profitability

Networks transform our view of risks. Risk management is less about fortifying the
walls around a single firm and more concerned with understanding how many links
among network partners lead to greater security or vulnerability. The next section
explores insights on this challenge, including these:

- *Interlinked global financial systems create new risks*—Our financial systems
  are networks, and today these networks have grown increasingly complex and
  interlinked. In Chapter 21, "Networks in Finance," **Franklin Allen** and **Ana
  Babus** examine how a network perspective can help you understand and address
  challenges such as financial contagion and freezes in the interbank market. They
  examine how social networks can improve investment decisions and corporate
  governance, and the role of networks in distributing primary issues of securities.

- *Risks in networks are interdependent, as are solutions*—The effectiveness of
  airline security depends on the level of security of the "weakest link" in the network, as tragically demonstrated when a bomb introduced on a Malta Airlines
  flight made its way onto the trans-Atlantic PanAm Flight 103. In Chapter 22, "The
  Weakest Link: Managing Risk Through Interdependent Strategies," **Howard**

Kunreuther explores how such interdependent security risks often require interdependent solutions, involving all parts of the network and sometimes requiring a combination of public and private strategies.

- *Global logistics networks present new risks and demand new strategies*—As global logistics networks have grown and developed, they also have presented new challenge in managing risk and volatility across these broad, global networks. In Chapter 23, "Integration of Financial and Physical Networks in Global Logistics," **Paul Kleindorfer** and **Ilias Visvikis** discuss changes in logistics and financial instruments such as derivatives that have emerged to value and hedge the cost of capacity and services in these markets. The approaches to address risks in global logistics illustrate the emerging tools and competencies that have been needed to manage new network risks.

- *Networks can lead to battles between those who seek greater control and those who advocate greater freedom*—Although telecom is a "networked" industry, incumbents have often fought against a network view of strategy and business models. In Chapter 24, "Telecommunications: Network Strategies for Network Industries," **Kevin Werbach** contrasts the worldview of "Monists" such as AT&T, who see the infrastructure as inseparable from the network, and "Dualists" such as Google, who see the network and its applications as distinct from the underlying infrastructure. He suggests that a more modular future might bridge the gap between those who seek to own and capitalize on the network and those who seek to expand it through more neutral offerings.

- *Addressing political and social risks requires a deep understanding of networks*—Companies such as an oil company seeking drilling rights face complex risks from interactions among political leaders, media, and social activists. The company's fate often is in the hands of a complex set of actors. In Chapter 25, "Network-Based Strategies and Competencies for Political and Social Risk Management," **Witold Henisz** examines how information about the structure of political and social networks can be integrated into data acquisition and analysis, as well as strategy implementation, to better manage political and social risks.

Part VII: A Double-Edged Sword: Contagion and Containment

Networks have a dark side. They speed the flow of communication and commerce, but diseases, terrorism, computer viruses, and other threats can ride on these same smooth rails. Extended chains with more partners in different countries create channels for contagion. The final section of the book explores the dark side of networks and strategies for addressing challenges, including these:

- *Network-based global terrorism demands a network-based solution*—Al-Qaeda and other global terrorist networks have moved from hierarchy to a resilient, network-based structure and leadership. In Chapter 26, "Terrorism Networks: It Takes a Network to Beat a Network," **Boaz Ganor** examines how the evolving structure of these networks is redefining global terrorism, and how antiterrorist agencies have had to build their own networks to address them. As he notes, "It takes a network to beat a network."

- *Diseases spread through global networks, so countries need to join together to prevent them*—In Chapter 27, "Global Diseases: The Role of Networks in the Spread (and Prevention) of Infection," **J. Shin Teh** and **Harvey Rubin** examine the role of global networks of air travel and connections in the spread of infectious diseases. Networks can help to meet these challenges, such as those that contribute to the development and distribution of drugs and vaccines for infectious diseases. Network-based analyses help to better model the spread of diseases. The authors also argue that effectively addressing the risks of global infection requires a collaborative international solution, or "global compact," that will allow effective diagnosis, prevention, and treatment of infectious diseases.

- *Interpersonal social networks spread diseases but also can help prevent them*—In Chapter 28, "Lessons from Empirical Network Analyses on Matters of Life and Death in East Africa," **Jere R. Behrman**, **Hans-Peter Kohler**, and **Susan Cotts Watkins** explore the impact of informal social networks in preventing HIV infection in Kenya and Malawi, using longitudinal quantitative and qualitative data from more than a decade. They show that both the context (e.g., the degree of market development) and the density of networks matter (possibly interactively), as well the endogeneity of network partners.

These chapters, collectively, represent a multidimensional view of the shifting landscape. They help managers to raise important questions about a networked world and wrestle with the core issues they need to address in meeting the network challenge: How do we need to rethink our approach to innovation? What new coordination mechanisms do we need? What strategies do we need to compete effectively network against network rather than firm against firm? What business models will help us create and appropriate value in a networked world? How do we need to redesign our organization and change our approach to managing our employees? What new risks are created by networks, and how can we address their dark side?

As noted previously, these approaches are not either/or. We are not in a completely networked world. In each area, we need to be able to see the network as well as the individual nodes. Both perspectives are accurate and important. Firm-level strategies and competencies still need to be part of management thinking, but these decisions need to be made in the context of the broader network.

Meeting the Challenge of Networks

Shifting thinking and action is particularly challenging for mature and established companies. In our discussion of these issues with senior executives, they have raised practical questions such as this: How can managers move from the theory of network effects to implementing these concepts with a management team when the next item on the agenda is the quarterly financials? Ground-up new ventures such as eBay, Wikipedia, and Google have brought a radically different worldview, but their lack of a legacy has been an advantage in this process. Established firms face the more daunting challenge of making the leap from the firm-centric world to a networked world, without undermining their existing business and commitments of current stakeholders in it.

In some cases, the changes may appear at first to be incremental. This can lead to the "boiled frog" syndrome, in which managers don't recognize the significance of the change until it is too late. The development of the Internet itself percolated behind the scenes for many years, confined primarily to academic and military circles, before the minor innovation of the web browser made it a transformational force in business. This is what Ron Adner and Dan Levinthal (2000) have called "technology speciation," using a term from evolutionary biology to describe how technologies are transformed by a leap into a new domain. What might initially have looked like a difference of degree becomes a difference in kind. It appears that we may see the same kind of speciation with respect to networks, in which a number of small changes add up to very different models for business and different approaches to developing strategy and competencies.

The speed of network development is one uncertainty, and another is the models for networks that might emerge. Although we sometimes discuss "networks" as if they were a single concept, the models for networks that could emerge—and are emerging—are diverse. We need to understand the differences among these networks. Some, for example, may operate like formal orchestras, whereas others may more closely resemble the improvisational performance of a jazz quartet. Some will need conductors, whereas others will self-organize. What are the different types of networks and which ones work best in a given situation?

Some of the implications of this shift to a network-centric view are already beginning to emerge, as illustrated in Table 1-1.

TABLE 1-1   Network-Centric Thinking

	Firm-Centric Thinking	Network-Centric Thinking
Leadership	Command and control	Self-organizing/empowered
Value creation	Firm-centric products	Network-centric experience
Innovation	Internal R & D	Open innovation
Core competencies	Firm-based core competencies	Network orchestration and learning
Competition	Firm against firm	Network against network
Risks	Local and direct	Systemic and interdependent
Finance	Appropriating rents	Building and sharing value
Marketing	Mass marketing	Mass contagion
Operations Focus	Efficiency	Flexibility
HR	Superstars	Supernetworks

The insights summarized in Table 1-1 are just the beginning. The role of networks and our understanding of them continue to evolve rapidly. This is largely uncharted territory, both for business disciplines and for the social and natural sciences that inform these disciplines. We are all learning what this world means. The challenge of understanding networks is like the old fable of the blind men trying to provide an accurate description of an elephant—except that it is a herd of elephants and they are all in motion, and they have not only observable physical characteristics but also unobserved motivations, knowledge, and attitudes. Any attempt to freeze the action to see what is going on or predict where the herd will go next, though useful, is necessarily limited. The act of concentrating on a specific aspect of networks such as human resources or alliances, or a type of networks such as terrorist networks or biological networks, necessarily leaves out part of the picture. We hope that by gathering individual experts from many disciplines and probing this phenomenon from many angles, we can overcome some of the blind spots that each may bring to the task and help illuminate the true nature of these networks and their significant implications for business.

The implication of networks ranges from the survival and growth of our businesses to the future of the planet, as we address highly networked issues such as international trade, global warming, and terrorism. Understanding networks is critical at every level, from personal decisions to business decisions to the broadest policy issues facing our world. We hope this book will help put the changes that are playing out in the structure of the global economy into a broader context for managers facing the challenges of leadership in the emerging networked world and for our colleagues as we attempt to shed new light on these phenomena through research.

References

Adner, R., and D. Levinthal. 2000. Technology speciation and the path of emerging technologies. In *Wharton on Managing Emerging Technologies,* ed. G. S. Day and P. J. H. Schoemaker. New York: Wiley & Sons.

Anthony, S. 2008. Sony: Winning the DVD battle but losing the innovation war? *Innovation Insights*, February 19, http://discussionleader.hbsp.com/anthony/2008/02/sony_winning_the_wrong_war.html.

Brandenburger, A. M., and B. J. Nalebuff. 1996. *Co-opetition.* New York: Currency Doubleday.

Chandler, A. D. Jr. 1977. *The Visible Hand: The Managerial Revolution in American Business.* Cambridge, MA: Harvard Belknap.

Coleman, J. S. 1990. *Foundations of Social Theory*. Cambridge, MA: Harvard University Press.

Crook, C., P. R. Kleindorfer, L. Lindgren, and J. Wind. 2006. Toward a new theory of the firm, working paper, SEI Center for Advanced Studies in Management. Philadelphia: The Wharton School.

Fine, C. H. 2000. Clockspeed-based strategies for supply chain design. *Production and Operations Management,* 9 (3), 213-221.

Ford, L. R., and D. R. Fulkerson. 1962. *Flows in Networks*. Princeton, NJ: Princeton University Press.

Friedman, T. 2005. *The World Is Flat: A Brief History of the 21st Century.* London: Allen Lane.

Fung, V. F., W. K. Fung, and Y. Wind. 2008. *Competing in a Flat World.* Upper Saddle River, NJ: Wharton School Publishing.

Greene, Jay. 2007. Microsoft and Facebook hook up. *BusinessWeek,* October 25.

Hamel, G., and C. K. Prahalad. 1990. The core competence of the corporation. *Harvard Business Review*, vol. 68, no. 3, May-June, 79-93.

Hamel, G., and C. K. Prahalad. 1994. *Competing for the Future: Breakthrough Strategies for Seizing Control of Your Industry and Creating the Markets of Tomorrow.* Boston: Harvard Business School Press.

Hammer, M. 1990. Re-engineering work: Don't automate, obliterate. *Harvard Business Review,* July-August, 104-112.

Hart, S. L. 2005. *Capitalism at the Crossroads.* Philadelphia: Wharton Publishing.

Hendricks, K. B., and V. R. Singhal. 2005. An empirical analysis of the effect of supply chain disruptions on long-run stock price and equity risk of the firm. *Production and Operations Management,* 14 (1).

Jackson, M. O. 2008. *Social and Economic Networks.* Princeton, NJ: Princeton University Press.

Kleindorfer, P. R., and L. N. Van Wassenhove. 2004. Risk management in global supply chains. In *The Alliance on Globalization,* ed. H. Gatignon and J. Kimberly. Cambridge University Press.

Micklethwait, J., and A. Wooldridge. 2003. *The Company: A Short History of a Revolutionary Idea.* New York: Modern Library.

Porter, Michael. 1985. *Competitive Advantage.* New York: Free Press.

Prahalad, C. K. 2004. *The Fortune at the Bottom of the Pyramid.* Philadelphia: Wharton Publishing.

Roberts, J. 2004. *The Modern Firm.* New York: Oxford University Press.

Sirkin, Harold, James Hemerling, and Arindam Bhattacharya. 2008. *Globality: Competing with Everyone from Everywhere for Everything.* New York: Business Plus.

Smith, A. 1776. The Wealth of Nations (An Inquiry into the Nature and Causes of the Wealth of Nations). Republished in 1991. New York: Prometheus Books.

Stern, J. M., and J. S. Shiely. 2001. The EVA Challenge. New York: John Wiley & Sons.

Tapscott, D., and A. D. Williams. 2006. Wikinomics: How Mass Collaboration Changes Everything. New York: Penguin.

Williamson, O. E. 1996. The Mechanisms of Governance. Oxford: Oxford University Press.

Wind, Y., and V. Mahajan. 2001. Convergence Marketing. New York: Financial Times Prentice Hall.

Wind, Y., and C. Crook. 2004. The Power of Impossible Thinking. Upper Saddle River, NJ: Wharton School Publishing.

Womack, J. P., and D. T. Jones. 2005. Lean consumption. Harvard Business Review, March-April.

2

Creating Experience:
Competitive Advantage in the Age of Networks

CK Prahalad

Abstract

The locus of innovation is shifting from the firm to the network. In contrast to develop-ing stand-alone products, innovators are drawing together networks that deliver a per-sonalized co-created experience to the customer. In this chapter, C. K. Prahalad describes a model in which nodal firms link communities of customers with communities of pre-qualified vendors. Examining cases from cardiac pacemakers to addressing diabetes, he explores the implications of this shift for product and service innovation, value creation, and new sources of competitive advantage.

The process of innovation and value creation is changing. Consider, for example, the new logic of value creation through personalized co-creation of experiences demon-strated by the case of Build-A-Bear Workshop®. Manufacturers of stuffed toys typically tried to anticipate consumer demand, manufacture the right line of products to meet the demand, and place it on the shelves in time for seasonal sales. The results of this approach have been mixed. Some product innovations catch the fancy of consumers; many others languish. This is an expensive proposition for both retailers and manufacturers.

In contrast, the Build-A-Bear Workshop creates a platform for customer innovation, co-creation, and experience. It doesn't try to predict the right product portfolio that will appeal to customers. Instead, it invites children and their families to design their own stuffed animals. The children first buy an empty shell of the bear or other animal. Then, they give it life with a personal identity, adding stuffing, a heart, and chips that generate sounds (even personalized sounds). They give the bear its first shower and get a birth certificate. Most families spend a disproportionate amount of money for this experience. The value in the case of Build-A-Bear Workshop is not in the product; it is a unique, co-created (by the child and the company) experience. This is not company-centric product innovation; it is co-creation.

Then the children create a unique lifestyle for the bear and can create a community, including adding siblings. They sign a "Bear Promise," which shows how the process is centered around the child rather than the product. Pay attention to how often the words "I," "my," and "me" are used:

> My Bear is Special
>
> I brought it to Life
>
> I chose it
>
> I stuffed it
>
> Now I am taking it home
>
> Best Friends are forever
>
> So I promise right now to make
>
> My bear My # 1 Pal.

Although there is a product involved, Build-A-Bear is not merely a product or customer solution, but rather is an engaging customer experience. The customer is a co-creator of this experience. The company does not sell a specific product. Instead, it gives the customer a platform for innovation. Build-A-Bear has found a way to monetize innovation.

Yes, toys are fun. Some of you are more concerned about complex, mission-critical products. So let us start with a very mission-critical product—a cardiac pacemaker. The success of a cardiac pacemaker once depended primarily on the quality of the product itself. The focus of innovation efforts were directed at making the product better, smaller, and cheaper. Consider an alternative. Imagine the pacemaker connected through a network such that the patient can be remotely monitored. The doctors can connect with the patient and provide advice whenever needed. But now, the value of the pacemaker depends increasingly on the peace of mind it provides to the patient at all times. The pacemaker, as a physical product, is still critical, but the real value is in the personalized experience and peace of mind created by connecting it to a network of doctors and hospitals (Prahalad and Venkat Ramaswamy 2004; Prahalad and Krishnan 2008).

With information technology and wireless communication, a pacemaker becomes part of a network that includes the patient, doctor, other experts, hospitals, and family, as illustrated in Figure 2-1. Fully developed, such a system can help a patient, even when he is traveling. If there is an abnormality that is detected, the network of suppliers—the entire ecosystem—can spring into action. The information from the device can be sent to the patient's doctor and family, who can connect the patient with a doctor on location and a local hospital, drawing upon a network of approved providers. A network of other experts can be drawn in for reviews or a conference on the best treatment strategy. In theory, the system could even call a priest or lawyer, if preprogrammed to do so.

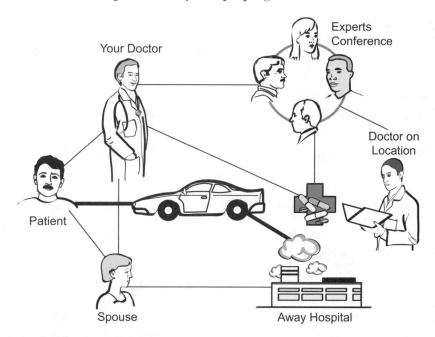

Figure 2-1   Cardiac pacemakers

Where is the value here? Is it in the pacemaker (the physical product) or in the network? In this context, a pacemaker is not just a product. It is the nexus of a network. The network in which the device is embedded represents the capacity to deliver enhanced healthcare and cardiac emergency services. The value of the pacemaker derives from the experience and the ongoing sense of security and peace of mind that it provides the patient. The pacemaker is just one element of this network-based co-created value.

The development of complex ecosystems for co-creating value is becoming common. Consider, for example, the OnStar system at General Motors. OnStar monitors engine performance just as pacemakers do for humans. More important, OnStar can provide additional services such as making reservations in restaurants. OnStar changes the concept of a car. Instead of seeing the car as a stand-alone product, it transforms the car into a node in a seamless network that links drivers to a variety of resources. Value is not just in the car alone but in the networks in which it is embedded as well. It is in the personalized experience of a driver—be it in calling the ambulance in case of an unfortunate accident or in the pleasant prospect of a great meal in a French restaurant—both orchestrated by the OnStar system. Network connectivity due to OnStar has made GM one of the largest reseller of wireless minutes in the world.

Changing Processes of Value Creation and Innovation

The traditional view of value—the firm-centric view—assumes that value is created by the firm and exchanged with the consumer. Value is embedded in products. Given this view, the managerial focus was on the internal efficiencies in the development and the manufacture of products. This *product and firm-centric view of value* worked well for more than a century. With ubiquitous connectivity, digitization, emergence of social networks, and convergence of technology and industry boundaries, we are seeing the emergence of a new model for value creation with a new set of key drivers: personalized experience, co-creation, individuals, thematic communities, experience-based platforms, and delivery network (Prahalad and Krishnan 2008). We can already see this value-creation process in companies such as Google, Li & Fung, Netflix, Starbucks, Amazon, Aviva, Nike, and ICICI-Prudential.

In the old paradigm, the firm was the center of the value chain. It dealt with suppliers and consumers on its terms. Now a nodal firm—such as Medtronic in the pacemaker example, or General Motors for OnStar—organizes many partners who collectively deliver the personalized co-created experience demanded by customers. This shift is critical to recognize. Value creation is about one consumer experience at a time. But in order to do this, we need an ecosystem. The ecosystem is orchestrated by nodal firms such as Medtronics or GM. These nodal firms have specific roles. They provide the intellectual influence, define the network infrastructure, set standards, and manage the customer interface. They do not own the firms in the ecosystem or necessarily have legal control as in joint ventures. They typically have privileged access to the network partners without ownership. These networks have effectively divorced ownership and legal control from access and influence.

Co-creation of value using a network results from a *participatory process*. Innovations are no longer dreamed up in a lab and pushed out to customers. Customers are brought into "the lab" and asked to engage in co-creation, as illustrated by the Build-A-Bear model. Rather than the focus on the laboratory and the traditional market research undertaken before product launch, innovation now has become a continuing process of interaction among a company, its suppliers, and its customers, throughout the life of the product family. Involving customers reduces risks, investment, and time in product development. This is the new logic of innovation.

The innovation process begins with the customer and moves to the company, the reverse of the traditional approach. Consumers and consumer communities participate in setting the agenda, and orchestrate the flow of ideas, products, and services. They draw upon a community of suppliers and talented individuals to create and share value. The nodal firm draws together these two communities (customers and suppliers). Orchestrating both networks drives innovation.

An Innovation Continuum

The networked paradigm has shifted the locus of competence. Before the 1990s, most managers assumed that competence resided primarily in the business unit, with specific units developing highly refined competencies. In the 1990s, companies began to see their organizations as a portfolio of competencies that they could apply to different types of businesses. The ideas of "core competencies" (Prahalad and Hamel 1990), transcending business units, as a new avenue for innovation was born. By 1995, some competencies began to migrate through outsourcing and offshoring to the extended supply network. Beginning in about 2001, however, the locus of competencies has been extended to include an enhanced network of suppliers, partners, and consumers. The network-based approach to competencies focuses on the network, not the individual nodes, as the centerpiece for survival and profitability. Of course, individual firms, as nodes in such networks, must also possess the requisite competencies to provide added value to their networks and thereby to remain preferred pathways for product origination and order fulfillment. In a word, core competencies in this new environment are as important as ever, but defining these properly requires a network-based perspective rather than the firm-focused perspective.

The consequences of this shift have been most significant in the area of innovation. Before 1995, innovation largely referred to product innovations. Then, the focus of innovation shifted to customer-specific solutions. Finally, around 2001, with the emergence of new information and communications technologies, as well as changes in the role of consumers, innovation has begun to focus more on customer experiences and co-creation. In the world of after-sales support for technical products, for example, the focus shifted from failure time of key components to the uptime and value-added of the customer in the use of the product. Aircraft-engine manufacturers now sell their aircraft engines not as products to be maintained but rather in terms of the useful hours of service such engines provide for customers before they need maintenance. The emphasis for innovation has shifted very clearly to the value-added as experienced by the airline customer.

These twin shifts in the locus of competence and the focus of innovation define an innovation continuum, as illustrated in Figure 2-2. This continuum stretches from innovation around products to solutions to experiences.

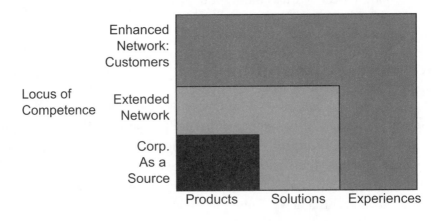

Figure 2-2   We can identify an innovation continuum.

This shift is the result of the changing focus of markets and the changing capabilities for accessing global resources. A significant part of the research and practice of innovation management continues to be firm- and product-focused. As we can see in the innovation continuum, the opportunities for extending the resource base (locus of competence) exists. This requires managers to access resources from across the network. Simultaneously, they have to think of value not in products but in co-created experiences—one consumer at a time.

This perspective of innovation anchored by access to resources in the network and one consumer experience at a time is a significant departure from the legacy of the industrial system that has served us well for more than 100 years. Consider, for example, Ford Motor Company and its Model T. Ford offered the standardized Model T to an undifferentiated mass market. Ford was also a vertically integrated firm. The model was this: All resources are within the firm; we create the product and sell it to an undifferentiated consumer base. This was the starting point. Needless to say, we have moved away from this perspective. The migration has been from an undifferentiated consumer to specific segments of customers, such as adolescents or seniors. Companies such as Dell then offered mass customization, making products more individualized. The natural progression of this movement is to a model of personalized co-creation. Companies now deliver one personalized experience at a time, drawing resources from multiple locations to satisfy a single customer (N=1), as illustrated in Figure 2-3a.

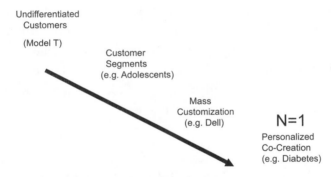

Figure 2-3a   The centrality of personalized experience

At the same time, there has been a parallel shift in accessing resources. From a totally vertically integrated factory such as Ford Motors' River Rouge plant, companies are rapidly moving to a system of distributed resources of a flexible supply base, and global supply chains. Resources are increasingly accessed through a multi-institutional, multivendor ecosystem. We can label this shift R=G as illustrated in Figure 2-3b. The result has been the emergence of nodal firms that are not part of any fixed supply chain but rather are at the center of a web of prequalified vendors ready and able to respond to customer demands as they materialize anywhere on the Web.

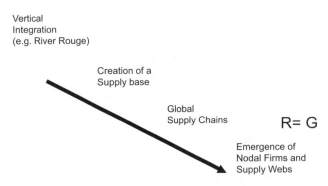

Figure 2-3b The need for accessing distributed resources

An important part of this supply web is access to global networks of talent. Using collaborative and integrative capabilities, companies can access talent of workers, customers, or partners on a global scale. Companies are not exporting jobs; they are importing competitiveness. InnoCentive, for example, links networks of inventors with companies that need their ideas and expertise. By involving hundreds of thousands of customers in its software beta testing, Microsoft gains a commitment to its development worth billions of dollars. Professors who see their students as co-creators of knowledge in the classroom can engage them in developing new knowledge. (Of course, the professors also cannot predict where the class will end up.)

A Networked Model for Addressing Diabetes

The potential of networked approaches to innovation can be seen in a new strategy for addressing Type 2 diabetes that is being pioneered by ICICI-Prudential. As a lifestyle disease, diabetes requires not only effective testing and treatment but also effective, ongoing management by individuals. Compliance with a prescribed personalized routine is key. As with the Build-A-Bear example, the solution, therefore, has to be highly personalized (N=1).

Economic incentives are a source of feedback to individuals, and can improve compliance. By offering patients variable pricing for insurance, we can provide the incentive for individuals to change their behavior. Patients who demonstrate strong compliance are offered lower premiums; those with poor compliance, and thus increased risks, must pay higher premiums. The critical value-creation element of this process is network-based. All parts of the network contribute some essential elements, from decreased risk, to scientific monitoring and feedback, to treatment, to actuarial assessments for improved insurance rates. This is a virtuous cycle induced by a cooperating network of service providers.

No single firm can provide the resources required; it needs an ecosystem for ensuring patient compliance. Success depends on a multivendor ecosystem with a nodal firm. This ecosystem around the individual requires access to doctors and hospital networks. The network also includes companies such as Metropolis and Well Spring that can provide diagnostic testing, and companies such as Johnson & Johnson and Nicholas Piramal that offer systems for ongoing monitoring. Pharmaceutical companies such as Wockhart and Biocon also need to be included. Finally, gyms and health clubs can help to ensure that patients engage in fitness programs and other activities that support wellness. At the center of this network is an insurer such as ICICI-Prudential that can offer variable pricing based on behavior, as shown in Figure 2-4. In this case, ICICI-Prudential serves as the nodal firm in this network, drawing together other parts of the ecosystem. It takes a network to support such a model.

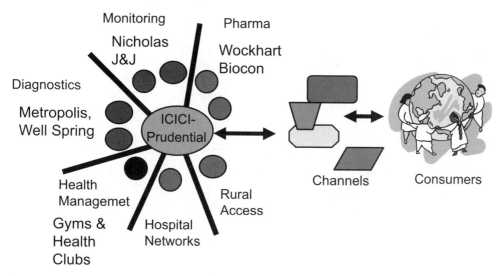

Figure 2-4   The diabetics management ecosystem

Impediments to Networked Innovation

Two primary impediments prevent the development of networked capabilities for innovation. First, the *social infrastructure* of the firm is a serious hurdle. This includes the legacy mindset, dominant logic, skills, attitudes and behaviors, decision processes, and incentives. The impact of this legacy mindset can be seen in the way the previous diabetes model challenges the traditional mindset of the insurance industry in many ways. As summarized in Table 2-1, the shift to a networked approach requires not only creating new systems, but also giving up past traditions and beliefs about "how to compete and create value." The most significant of these beliefs, perhaps, is the centrality of the firm rather than the network in innovation and value creation.

TABLE 2-1   A Networked Mindset

Traditional Insurance Perspective	Health Perspective
A class of customers and actuarial data	One customer at a time (N=1)
	Real-time behavioral data
Pricing based on segment	Pricing based on compliance of an individual
	Economic incentive to stay healthy
Protect from catastrophic illness, death	Help customers improve their lifestyle, contain diseases, protect from catastrophic illness and death
Customers are on their own	Customers get help, feedback, and certified periodic testing

The second hurdle is the technology infrastructure of the firm. Its existing databases, information and communications technology (ICT) architecture, and applications may make it difficult to adopt new approaches. Even if the organization can adopt a networked mindset, it might not have the right infrastructure to follow through.

New Sources of Competitive Advantage

Networked models lead to new sources of competitive advantage. Traditional sources of advantage such as access to capital, raw materials, and technology are increasingly becoming "table stakes." They are important to have but do not give the firm a unique advantage. Competitive advantage derives from linking strategy and operations, through resilient business processes, and focused analytics. For example, in the case of diabetes, the success of the model depends in part on analytics that can isolate one patient who needs specialized attention and knowing how to change prices for one patient based on her compliance.

The N=1, R=G competitive environment forces us to think of new sources of competitive advantage and innovation in new ways. For example, it forces us to develop capabilities such as these:

- Efficiency and innovation
- Co-creation
- Rapid reconfiguration of resources
- Real-time action
- Improved risk management and financing
- Intelligent products
- Cycle-time reduction
- Global scale
- Flexible logistics and fulfillment architecture

These various advantages are explored in other papers in this book. Let me note the key issue here: Ecosystems of diverse businesses can help to build advantage and, as a network, be more responsive to global sources of comparative advantage. New entrants to the global stage may be moving rapidly in the direction of N=1 and R=G—be it Google, Amazon, or Netflix—so are firms from capital-starved countries such as India. For example, consider the global reach of IT outsourcing in India. India's lack of capital and legacy systems enabled it to take new approaches to contracting, funding, and project management in multiple cultures. India created industries with a global focus, such as IT. This approach has now spread to other industries as well, such as pharmaceuticals. Indian companies also have addressed local challenges linked to global opportunities, in industries such as automobiles (Tata) or finance (ICICI). The creation of an ecosystem of diverse businesses in India—from IT to microfinance—presents new opportunities for Indian and global firms to leverage their resource and innovation base.

Industries will continue to be transformed through new business models. These models will focus attention on building an ecosystem that demands collaborative capacity, common shared standards and platforms, and resilient and adaptive systems. These forces come together to redefine and drive innovation. In addition, transformation requires imagination, passion, courage, humanity, humility, intellect, and a healthy measure of luck.

As this discussion highlights, networks create a new platform for innovation and value creation. Competencies necessary for survival and growth are now as rooted in network architectures and ecosystems as they are in the fiber of individual companies. Strategies are no longer the limited purview of a company-focused view of value and control over its resources. Rather they stretch as far as the boundaries of the global networks within which companies must find their place. Innovation and marketing are also increasingly networked, and expand considerably the boundaries of the firm to encompass organizing networks of consumers and networks of suppliers around a nodal firm. The nodal firm and its competencies and capital structure will, of course, remain critical elements of strategy and management. However, these can be properly understood and designed only against the background of the networks connecting the nodal firm to the communities of consumers and potential suppliers. These represent the sandbox for innovation and competitive advantage for the firm.

References

Prahalad, C. K., and Gary Hamel. 1990. The core competence of the corporation. *Harvard Business Review*, May-June, 79-91.

Prahalad, C. K. 2004. *The Fortune at the Bottom of the Pyramid.* Upper Saddle River, NJ: Wharton School Publishing.

Prahalad, C. K., and M. S. Krishnan. 2008. *The New Age of Innovation.* McGraw-Hill.

Prahalad, C. K., and Venkat Ramaswamy. 2004. *The Future of Competition.* Cambridge, MA: Harvard Business Press.

3

Knowledge as a Social Phenomenon: "Horse Holding" and Learning in Networks

Alan M. Kantrow

Abstract

Human knowledge and traditions can persist long after their relevance disappears, particularly in an environment of abundant information and rapid change. Organizational routines often continue in force long after memory of their purpose has been lost. But memory is rarely lost entirely. It usually lingers, in distributed fragments, in an organization's social networks and can, when needed, be reassembled. In this chapter, Alan Kantrow examines the role of such networks in the process of memory loss and recovery.

According to Elting Morison, noted technology historian (1966), at the outset of World War II:

> *When armaments were in short supply, the British...made use of venerable field pieces that had come down to them from previous generations. The honorable past of this light artillery stretched back, in fact, to the Boer War. In the days of uncertainty after the fall of France, these guns, hitched to trucks, served as useful mobile units in the coast defense. But it was felt that the rapidity of fire could be increased. A time-motion expert was, therefore, called in to suggest ways to simplify firing procedures. He watched the gun crews of five men at practice in the field for some time. Puzzled by certain aspects of the procedures, he took some slow-motion pictures of the soldiers performing the loading, aiming, and firing routines.*

When he ran these pictures over once or twice, he noticed something that appeared odd to him. A moment before the firing, two members of the gun crew ceased all activity and came to attention for a three-second interval extending throughout the discharge of the gun. He summoned an old colonel of artillery, showed him the pictures, and pointed out this strange behavior. What, he asked the colonel, did it mean. The colonel, too, was puzzled. He asked to see the pictures again. "Ah," he said when the performance was over, "I have it. They are holding the horses." (1966, 17-18).

Long after horses had left the battlefield, soldiers, even in the heat of battle, were still following routines from the long-forgotten days of cavalry. Like them, we face ever greater demands for ever higher levels of performance. And like them, we suffer from a kind of amnesia—a failure of organizational memory that derives in large measure from the gradual, imperceptible erosion of the recollection, even the awareness, of specific, idiosyncratic, granular detail. Until recently, there was no realistic way to repair this loss. Now—through networks—there is.

"That" Versus "Why"

There is a simple reason for horse holding. It results from how knowledge is stored in an organization. What people remember is "that" something is the case; what they forget is "why." Over time, detailed recollection of the nuanced context that gave rise to specific decisions, attitudes, approaches, and assumptions erodes. It decays, silently, at a remorseless, steady rate. It leaches away. What it leaves behind is the dry, dehydrated husk of the structure or belief or procedure or attitude that it once filled with life and vitality. The husk lingers on long after the life-giving fluid that animated it has disappeared. But few, if any, notice. Indeed, most continue to treat that husk as if it were still live and vital. They remain blindly loyal to the "that" it once implied, even though the "why" has long since gone. And that's when they wind up holding horses.

Early in the twentieth century, for example, according to company old-timers, the old kettle house at Procter & Gamble had pipes that ran from everywhere to everywhere, generations of pipes that had built up much the way a coral reef does. No one really knew which ones did—or carried—what. All they knew was that, en masse, the piping worked. On the wall was a large valve, which only the most senior operators were allowed to touch and which they turned, only so far, at a critical point in the process.

Years later, when the old plant was finally torn down, it became clear that the wheel did not connect to anything—and had not for some time. The murmurs of surprise almost, but not entirely, drowned out the background noise of some four-legged beasts being held somewhere off in the distance.

Louis Gerstner, former CEO of IBM, recalls that IBM's famous dress code—dark suits and white shirts—had grown up at a time when the executives served by IBM dressed in much the same way. Thomas Watson, Sr.'s initial framing of the rule was, as Gerstner notes, "eminently sensible….Respect your customer, and dress accordingly." Over time, as customers started to dress differently, what was remembered and obeyed by rote and custom was the strict rule of formal dress. What was forgotten was the sensible connection of any such rule to the customer.

Much the same decay of careful original thought into the reflex of unthinking custom affected IBM's core set of Basic Beliefs. According to Gerstner (2003, 185),

> There is no arguing with [such Basic Beliefs]. They should be the standard tenets of any company in any industry, in any country, at any period in history. But what the Beliefs had come to mean—or, at least, the way they were being used—was very different in 1993 than in 1962, when Tom Watson had introduced them.

> Consider "superior customer service." The supplier-customer power relationship had become so one-sided during IBM's hegemony that "customer service" came to mean, essentially, "servicing our machines on the customers' premises," instead of paying real attention to their changing businesses—and, where appropriate, challenging customers to expand their thinking [as IBM had famously done during the launch of the System/360]. We basically acted as if what customers needed had been settled long ago, and our job was to ship them our next system, whenever it came out. Customer service became largely administrative—like going through the motions in a marriage that has long since lost its passion.

Horse holding at work represents just the kind of half-hearted "going through the motions" that Gerstner describes. It is an unthinking, nearly absent-minded deference to the outward manifestations of accustomed routine and to the underlying judgments that everyone knows to be true. Equally important, it is the persistence of deference long past the point when such judgments remain accurate and such routines make sense.

Knowledge as a Social Phenomenon

As these examples illustrate, organizational knowledge loses vitality, even meaning, when separated from the social contexts of its creation and application. It is the product of social networks, which shape it as much as it shapes them. Indeed, it is—as much first-rate scholarship has told us over the years—a social phenomenon.

Ever since the formative work of Thomas Allen, for example, the field of R & D management has paid close attention to how information flows within organizations—that is, to who communicates with whom about what. Closer to the present, the work of Robert Cross and others on social networks has extended this attention to all aspects of organizational life. In the specific area of knowledge management, Dorothy Leonard, David Garvin, Larry Prusak, Tom Davenport, and Leigh Weiss have all explored the social dimension of knowledge creation, capture, transmission, and use within both formal and informal professional communities. No surprise here. The modern conceptual ground for this view of things has been solidly in place ever since Berger and Luckmann's formative work on the "social construction" of reality.

Forgetting the "Why's"

Although "that's" may be captured by—even fossilized in—current routines, oft-forgotten "why's" are inextricably woven into the fabric of history. Without the historical record, they cannot be reconstructed through logic or speculation. Facts, after all, are unrelieved singularities. They cannot be inferred; they have to be known—that is, remembered. And their effects linger. Like black holes, they shape the universe around them and continue to shape it long after they have themselves disappeared from view. Recovering them is hard.

Uneven Records: The Problem of Missing Information

As late as the mid-1940s, the standard product of the American recording industry was the 78 rpm shellac disk. To a generation raised on the wonders of modern consumer electronics, the distorted sound quality and short playing time of these records are nearly intolerable. At the time, however, they were the state of the art. Toward the end of 1945, Peter Goldmark, later the president of CBS Laboratories, got corporate support to work on a systemic fix to these problems. Everything was fair game: amplifiers, the material (shellac) of the record, the shape of the recording grooves, the cartridge and stylus used, the method of recording, the turntable drive—in fact, everything but the microphone, which everyone knew to be nearly perfect as it was. With near inevitability, Goldmark found that the microphone technology in use was causing phase distortion and had to be replaced. That helped, but problems with sound quality still remained.

As the contents of old 78 rpm disks were transferred onto disks of the new format, careful electronic timing filtered out much of the jerkiness caused by the original splicing. By itself, however, better timing could not remove regular, but unexplained, changes in orchestra pitch. What technical shortcomings were responsible for them? None, as it turned out. The reason for the shift in tone could not be found in the recording itself.

A bit of clever historical research uncovered the interesting fact that, when the original disks were made, the orchestra would record in a series of separate four-minute sessions that were, as a practical matter, spread out over a period of several days. That was why the pitch of the orchestra would vary from segment to segment. There was no way for Goldmark to guess this, no way to derive it from some convenient rule of thumb. The only way to get to the answer was to know—or painstakingly reconstruct—a set of unique, particular historical facts. "Why's" are forgotten because they cannot be inferred from general principles or deduced from first causes. They are unique and unpredictable. They have to be known.

The Problem of Bias and Distortion

Even when the historical record is intact, getting an accurate read on the "why's" is hard. In the 1790s a yellow fever epidemic struck Philadelphia, and medical opinion about its causes broke down pretty much along lines defined by the emergent political parties. Physicians of Federalist affiliation thought the disease must be the result of some foreign, imported contagion. Republican doctors thought it the result of some local corruption of the soil. The best available science had not much to offer by way of support to either opinion. There is no way to make sense out of this odd difference in diagnosis without knowing that there was another great ideological "fever" disturbing the world of these doctors at the same time, the French Revolution. Men of a Federalist turn of mind were deeply distrustful of the political infection that such a European upheaval might carry to their own shores; Republicans were perfectly willing to believe that things were already rotten enough at home without looking abroad for sources of infection. Absent close knowledge of the source of these views and the political differences of the doctors—which might not seem relevant at all to the discussion of disease—the competing diagnoses make no sense. With them, they do.

The Problem of Path Dependence: Artifacts and Artifice

The outcomes of history are also shaped by the distinctive path of evolution of a product, idea, or procedure. The Science Center at Harvard University, a major building designed by Jose Luis Sert, has far more architectural detail on one side than the other. A carefully rendered intention? Not at all. As someone who worked in Sert's office at the time recalls,

> *A huge cardboard model of the proposed Science Center stood in Sert's drafting room, oriented in such a way that the Littauer end [the one more richly developed] faced the door. Sert would enter the room and immediately begin working on that model at the nearest point. The side of the model hardest to reach was the long side facing north, and in the finished building this shows the least elaboration.*

Guessing or intuition cannot help here. The only thing that works is knowledge of the actual, day-to-day process by which the building was designed—precisely the kind of knowledge that leaches away over time.

Path dependence shapes the design not only of buildings but also of much more central artifacts of history such as calendars and clocks. In China of the Sung Dynasty, the calendar was not a set of neutral facts put together according to the best astronomic and scientific knowledge. It was not an objective reality available to all, a set of universal reference points. Nothing of the sort. In China, as David Landes (1983) remarks in his history of clockmaking,

> *The calendar was a perquisite of sovereignty, like the right to mint coins. Knowledge of the right time and season was power, for it was this knowledge that governed both the acts of everyday life and the decisions of state. Each emperor inaugurated his reign with the promulgation of this calendar, often different from the ones that preceded it. His court astronomers were the only persons permitted in principle to use timekeeping and astronomical instruments or to engage in astronomical study. His time was China's time.*

Examined closely, much of the seemingly objective texture of the day-to-day world is an artifice, a thing constructed. Consider, for example, something as basic as the hour as a unit of time. Is its duration "given" in the nature of things? Has the duration always been the same as it is now? The answer to both questions is no. In fact, before the middle decades of the fourteenth century, an hour was not a standardized unit of time. Nor were there necessarily 24 of them in a day. Nor did they all have to be of equal length.

In the very early life of the Church, the day was divided into a series of canonical or devotional hours, but their absolute number depended on local custom. It was not until the sixth century that that number was fixed at seven, and, even then, the precise time and duration for each depended on geographical location and season. By the middle of the fourteenth century, when the lay keeping of time had fixed the length of a day at 24 hours of equal duration, the first hour began not upon the stroke of midnight, but upon the stroke of noon. There was, moreover, a long period before then during which the agreed-on total (24) for the number of hours in a day had been established, but their need to be of equal length had not. The day was split evenly between periods of light and dark, which therefore had a total of 12 hours each. As a result, the duration of any individual hour inevitably reflected the vagaries of location and season.

An hour, then, is not a self-evident matter of fact, but an artifice—the cumulative, archaeological result of custom, practice, and scientific discovery in many cultures and religions over several millennia. But it is the apparently hard fact that gets remembered, not the wild complexities of the underlying archaeological record. Much the same is true of the minute, which did not get applied to a subdivision of the hour until the thirteenth century or so. (Indeed, neither the hour nor the minute began as a unit for the measurement of time; both were initially devised for other reasons, like the measurement of distance.) The system of counting now used for both derives from the Egyptians, who probably measured their day in 24 hours of unequal length because their numerical system was derived, in turn, from that of the Babylonians, which was based on multiples of six. As Daniel Boorstin (1983, 42) concludes in his account of the discovery of time, "when we mark each hour of our 24-hour day, and designate the minutes after the hour, we are living, as a historian of ancient science reminds us, by 'the results of a Hellenic modification of an Egyptian practice combined with Babylonian numerical procedures.'"

Once established, such artifice—whatever the shreds and patches out of which it is initially formed—tends to have immense staying power. Fundamental social and cultural choices have great inertia. Certainly, their contours can and do change over time, but such change tends to some slowly, imperceptibly. The problem, of course, is that the teeming detail they organize and arrange changes much more quickly. The hard shell—the "that"—of categories remains clearly visible in the field of vision long after the complex, organic realities for which it was once a convenient handle have mutated beyond recognition and, in so doing, slipped out of collective memory.

Similarly, language in use today is also a historical record that is stripped down to its skeleton. Many turns of phrase that now roll off the tongue as uncomplicated, literal expressions were once metaphors lively enough to catch the attention up short. There was, for example, a time when such phrases as "tail of a kite" or "river bed" or even "foot of a bed" were sufficiently novel and striking to change the way people saw things. There was a time when speaking of a situation as being "in a shambles" carried all the visceral associations of the slaughterhouse. No longer. "That's" build up the way coral does: As vital fact and detail gradually seep away, living things die and leave their hard skeletons behind. "That's" harden, and then horses get held.

Learning the Right Lessons from History

Even when the historical facts have not been lost, it is not an easy matter to read them correctly. Mark Twain had it right. A cat that once sits down on a hot stove will never sit on a hot stove again. But it will never sit on a cold stove either. Experience is, indeed, a very good teacher, but the question remains whether the lessons it teaches are the right ones.

From the mid-1960s on, RCA's most significant corporate R & D effort had to do with videodisc technology. Justifiably concerned that government dollars for R & D would not keep pace with the costs of staying at the forefront of advances in electronics, the leaders of RCA's corporate research efforts needed a project that would have an indisputable call on the financial support of the company's operating divisions. The videodisc was just such a project. From the outset, however, those leaders framed the project in ways that stressed rigid cost constraints rather than the high-performance goals favored by the business units that would ultimately need to deploy the technology in their products. This, in turn, pushed R & D efforts down a path—the capacitance approach—that was relatively cheap, but that was also not very supportive of the high-end performance characteristics favored by those units. The unsurprising outcome: an internal technology that never really caught on, and a series of decisions by business unit managers to market products based on a competitive technology developed by others.

The RCA Laboratory managers who insisted on the capacitance approach did not do so out of laziness or accident or inattention. They believed—and confidently explained to all who would listen—they had learned an important, albeit painful, lesson from past experience. RCA's earlier technological success in developing color television had not translated into equivalent commercial success because the costs of development had gotten out of hand. They had learned their lesson. Had they ever! Fierce cost control was what really mattered. Performance was, of course, important too, but not if it were colored by a flood of red ink. After their searing experience with color television, no one in a position of responsibility in the Labs wanted to be holding the bag if, once again, runaway costs snatched defeat from the jaws of victory.

In retrospect, it is easy to see how smoothly the bold drama of "that" overshadows the nuanced complexities of "why." For RCA, the lesson learned was inarguably clear: Watch your R & D costs. Much less clear was the fact that that lesson applies to some, but not all, situations. Was the development of the videodisc one of them or not? The challenge, of course, is to know, within reason, which kind of situation one is in. Absent such knowledge, there will likely be a blind adherence to "that," and such adherence provides the energy supply on which horse holding, with all its quiet frustrations, depends. Under the too-simple umbrella of "that," correlation easily masquerades as causation, and universal generalizations readily cascade from sample sizes of one.

Dangers of Horse Holding

This matters. In the practical world of knowledge work, horse holding can have serious consequences, By the late 1920s, for example, Alcoa had some 32 operations underway in countries other than the United States. In 1928, a variety of specific considerations led management to retrench from its aggressive postwar thrust into international activities, which were first transferred to a Canadian subsidiary and then severed from Alcoa entirely when that subsidiary was spun off. Arthur Vining Davis, then the company's chairman, had doubts about the company's capability to run matters well both at home and abroad at the same time. The proliferation of tariff barriers in foreign markets added fuel to his concern about keeping international activities within Alcoa proper. Splitting off the Canadian subsidiary had another benefit: It would allow him to create a suitable top-level job for his brother, who would become president of the newly independent Canadian firm.

Thirty years later, all the company remembered was that it was—and had long been—a U.S.-based and U.S.-focused outfit with a strong domestic orientation. Why this was the case had been forgotten. That it was the case was a simple, self-evident, unremarkable matter of fact, a nugget of corporate truth too obvious to be debated. Looking back on this period of false, but untroubled certainty from the vantage point of the mid-1980s, a later chairman of Alcoa, Charles W. Parry (1985), saw matters differently. According to Parry,

The spin-off of our foreign activities in 1928, for reasons peculiar to that time, interrupted Alcoa's international development. It was an attitude about this event in our history, and not anything inherent in the nature of our abilities, our technology, or our markets, that subsequently kept us isolated in the U.S. market for so many years....It was a mindset that long outlasted the context of its creation.

When "that's" get remembered and "why's" are forgotten, mindsets can easily outlast the context of their creation—and that is when horses get held.

Letting Go the Horses

What do networks have to do with the managerial consequences of horse holding? In a word, they may provide the remedy. True, they cannot prevent the leaching away of "that." It is a natural human process and follows an immutable law of social gravity, a kind of epistemological physics. But they may just provide a way to reverse its effects— perhaps not entirely, but enough to make a significant real-world difference.

The problem is immensely difficult but simple to state. To avoid unintended horse holding, professionals need to "remember"—that is, reconstruct—the rich contexts of fact that gave rise to the structures, beliefs, forms, and procedures they now follow. As a practical matter, however, this is nearly impossible. The details of these various contexts are virtually infinite. Full, exhaustive reconstruction of each lies outside the bounds of doable, let alone affordable, effort. Where, then, to begin?

- *Look for anomalies*—The best place to start is with any features on the landscape of belief, structure, or practice where things do not quite fit with each other or with their ostensible purpose. Loose ends, tatters, and fragments are the most visible evidence that something has outlived the context of its creation. As the evolutionary biologist Stephen Jay Gould (1992, 29) nicely put it, "Remnants of the past that don't make sense in present terms—the useless, the peculiar, the incongruous—are the signs of history. They supply proof that the world was not made in its present form. When history perfects, it covers its tracks."

  Star Trek fans will remember that Klingon warships, those great Birds of Prey, must intentionally uncloak before firing their weapons. When context erodes, the uncloaking is unintentional, but the effect is the same: Careful observers can see the mechanisms that had previously been hidden—and can, as a result, make judgments about whether they pose a threat that needs to be addressed. Loose ends, then, are a useful clue.

- ***Identify performance declines***—A breakdown in the effectiveness of current mental models and routines can also be a sign of forgotten context. When the epicycles of Ptolemaic astronomy could no longer keep the dates of the annual vernal equinox from wandering randomly through the calendar, even the die-hard defenders of the old system—that is, of what Thomas Kuhn (1962) calls the established "normal science" of the established paradigm—grudgingly opened themselves to the consideration of alternatives.

- ***Recognize patterns***—There is an ample body of work, increasingly being tapped by the management community, on the gathering and interpretation of intelligence. Here, the core challenge has long been not just the mechanics of gathering information but, perhaps even more important, the disciplined ability to sift the material thus gathered through lenses that correct for biases, distortions, and tacit assumptions, whether intentional or not.

In a large organization or sphere of activity, however, no one individual has the scope of vision to discover and synthesize the evidence of such loose ends and performance problems. The relevant patterns are usually not visible from an individual's eye level. But they are visible to a network. Noting, describing, and collating the tatters and fragments of evidence of imperfect, awkward fit are tasks that well suit the way that networks operate. When that many eyes look independently from that many angles, the odds go up that meaningful patterns will emerge.

To up the odds, it helps greatly to design networks and their operating protocols from the outset in ways that flexibly "tag" chunks of content ("that") with the rich contextual information ("why"), which might otherwise slowly get forgotten. The happy news is that the new technologies that support knowledge management systems have precisely this capability. Management thinkers like Chris Meyer have long focused on the modes of context-sensitive collaborative work made possible by these technologies, as have practitioners such as Xerox PARC's long-time head, John Seely Brown. Of late, the activities of a variety of knowledge-intensive professions have similarly come in for close attention of this sort. Just think, for instance, of Beth Noveck's research into the use of wikipedias and other mechanics for addressing the legal complexities of democratic participation and patent review processes in developing and developed economies. Or, for that matter, of Steve Weber's examination of open-source behaviors and protocols in bio-pharma and high-technology industries.

A wiki, for example, can retain knowledge and context with a richness that a database with narrowly defined fields might lack. Advances in digital storage mean that we may soon have the capacity to make a video record of our entire lives, and networks mean that we will be able to link to the records of others. Advances in search technologies may make it possible to make use of this avalanche of data to answer questions about the present and the past. In this world, we might be able to pinpoint the first time a horse was held and perhaps gain insights into why. We can only do this, however, if we feel that information about context is valuable. This is the kind of knowledge that many organizations discard, however, in a push for efficiency.

Even with advances in data gathering and analysis, however, the process of recognizing and changing horse-holding behaviors still requires creative managers. As Elting Morison himself observed, "The Executive exists to make sensible exceptions to every rule." Properly managed, networks have an unmatched capability to register and aggregate point observations of loose ends, filter them for bias and distortion, and then review them to determine whether the belief or process or structure or protocol in question still makes compelling sense and, thus, still merits adherence. If not, it will be far easier to convince professionals to let go the reins and set free at least some of the horses they have been, without knowing it, holding.

References

Boorstin, Daniel. 1983. *The Discoverers: A History of Man's Search to Know His World and Himself*. New York: Random House.

Gerstner, Louis. 2003. *Who Says Elephants Can't Dance? Leading a Great Enterprise Through Dramatic Change*. New York: Collins Business.

Gould, Stephen Jay. 1992. *The Panda's Thumb: More Reflections in Natural History*. New York: WW Norton & Company.

Kantrow, A. 1987. *The Constraints of Corporate Tradition*. New York: Harper & Row.

Kuhn, Thomas. 1962. *The Structure of Scientific Revolutions*. Chicago: University of Chicago Press.

Landes, David. 1983. *Revolution in Time: Clocks and the Making of the Modern World*. Cambridge, MA: Belknap Press.

Morison, Elting E. 1966. *Men, Machines and Modern Times*. MIT Press.

Parry, Charles W. 1985. "Alcoa: A Retrospection." Newcomen Society of the United States.

4

Cross-Cultural Leadership in Networked Global Enterprises

Russell E. Palmer

Abstract

Global networks of firms are rapidly replacing top-down, hierarchical organizations. Such networks, thanks to information technology and global communications systems, can respond to changes in international demand faster and more flexibly than rigid corporate organizations of the past could. But by drawing together diverse cultures and individuals, these networks present new challenges to leaders. Traditional styles of leadership are not enough for this emerging environment. The kind of leadership style that leads to efficient execution in these global networks is different from the "do it and do it now" approach that might work in hierarchical organizations.

This chapter, based on the author's experience in leading global accounting firm Touche Ross, serving as dean of the Wharton School, and heading his own corporate investment firm, discusses leadership in a networked, global environment. The chapter, drawing on principles described in Chapter 9 of his book, Ultimate Leadership, *shows that a leader's ability to execute is deeply influenced by the culture and society in which the organization itself operates. What followers expect of their leaders and the traits that make leaders effective vary across different societies and cultures. Although basic principles of leadership may be universal, leaders cannot afford to take a one-size-fits-all approach toward society and culture.*

Introduction

Even in a world of instant global communications and broad networks, leadership still depends on personal relationships. To build these relationships in a world of more diverse global cultures and networked organizations, leaders need to understand cultural differences and manage across cultures. This chapter examines some of the differences and commonalities that leaders need to balance in heading global networks and firms.

For example, when I served as CEO of Touche Ross, we had a good working relationship with Tohmatsu Awoki & Co in Japan. It was the Japanese accounting firm with which everyone wanted to do business. We had talked to the head of the firm on several occasions about becoming a member of our firm and working on an exclusive basis. I had developed a pretty good personal relationship with the managing partner, Iwao Tomita. In 1975, we invited him to Williamsburg for our big international meeting. This was where the heads of Touche Ross firms from 80 countries came, mostly with their spouses. We had a good meeting and then it was time for the final night's dinner. During the dinner I went to Tomita-san and asked if we could meet privately. We went to an adjacent room and I said, "Do you know something that would be totally spectacular if we did it here tonight?" When he asked what I had in mind, I said, "It would be great if we announced that Tohmatsu Awoki has joined Touche Ross International. We could go out right now and tell everybody here and it would be a tremendous surprise and you would be a hero."

We talked over a few issues, and then he said, "Okay." Just like that. We went back to the dining room to announce it. We stopped the band, got up on the stage, and said, "We want to tell you something terrific and we know you are going to be as thrilled about it as we are. Tonight, Tohmatsu Awoki has joined Touche Ross." As we had expected, cheers and loud applause followed. Eventually, the firm's international name was changed to what it still is today—Deloitte Touche Tohmatsu. Tohmatsu Awoki is now the largest accounting firm in Japan. It never would have happened without a history of careful cultivation of our personal relationship with Iwao Tomita that convinced him of our integrity and to seal the deal at the right moment.

To be sure, our partner firms joined us out of self-interest as well. But even when we could not offer the best business deal, they did ultimately get what they wanted from the association. But the most important reason was that they valued the relationship we had with them and they believed in our integrity. That is what made it work.

Leadership Across Cultures

It is fashionable these days to speak of the global business world as being "flat." It is true that top-down, hierarchical organizations are rapidly being replaced by global networks of firms. The reason for the change is that such networks, thanks to information technology and global communications systems, can respond to changes in international demand faster and more flexibly than rigid corporate organizations of the past.

What leadership skills do such international networks demand? Can the kind of leadership that leads to efficient execution be exercised in these global networks in the same way that it could in hierarchical organizations? The answer is obviously not.

This chapter, drawn from my book *Ultimate Leadership* (Palmer 2008), shows that a leader's ability to execute is deeply influenced by the culture and society in which the organization itself operates. In addition to leading Touche Ross (now Deloitte & Touche), which is a network of professional services firms and partners spanning several countries, I also served as Dean of the Wharton School of the University of Pennsylvania, a network of faculty, alumni, and student networks. I now head the Palmer Group, an investment firm that created a network of professional colleges.

Today's firms are increasingly operating in a global system of interrelated businesses. Many have expanded their businesses by buying and selling their products and services internationally; an increasing number of others now operate full businesses in many— sometimes more than 100—countries. In this chapter, I discuss the differences in leadership across cultures. The world is simply too diverse to take the same approach in every context. To succeed, leaders will have to understand and adapt their leadership to the national cultures in which they are doing business. Leaders cannot afford to take a "one-size-fits-all" approach toward society and culture.

I begin by describing experiences I had working with companies that operate in very different cultures from our own. This raises the question of whether there are global principles of leadership that apply to all cultures, and I discuss those that I believe are, indeed, universal. Then I combine my own experience with other research, illustrated with insights from some of the major national cultures you are likely to encounter in today's "flat world." I consider some of the pitfalls for managers who are unprepared to understand national difference. Finally, I point to the example of Honeywell, which has done a tremendous job in setting up a program that can help its executives manage across national borders.

Universal Principles, Different Practices

Unlike our competitors, who staffed their overseas offices mainly with Americans, Touche Ross International took the opposite approach. The bedrock of our international firm was local leaders, not U.S. expatriates whom we sent overseas. We took this approach because we had to do it; we really had no other choice because we were the youngest firm and coming into the global game late. We did not want to change local leaders' business culture or impose our ideas upon them; we wanted them to come up and actively work with us in building our global enterprise, making it truly an international firm, not a U.S. firm. We would help them with training and with finding clients, but trusted them to be our equals in every respect. That was what made Touche Ross International's approach different from that of other firms, and it turned out to be our greatest global strategic advantage.

This experience illustrates how important it is to tailor your approach to working with people in different cultures. It does not mean that what we did will work in every culture. For instance, an egalitarian, consensus-building approach may be seen as a positive leadership trait in some cultures, but in others it could well be viewed as failure to "manage" and provide direction, and thus be interpreted by followers as a sign of weakness. This leads me to address the question of whether any leadership principles are universal.

The truth is, most of the principles of leadership are universal, but they are practiced differently in different parts of the world. Consider, for example, personal integrity, which is the foundation of leadership. I believe that integrity and leadership go together all over the world; I cannot imagine people in different parts of the world accepting a person without integrity as a leader over a long period. Idi Amin, Adolph Hitler, Benito Mussolini, Saddam Hussein—all these people played leadership roles, but eventually they came to a bad end. You might go astray from the principles of leadership, but in time it catches up with you. The *basic principles* of leadership are universal. Global leaders need to recognize differences, understand the power of self-interest and relationships, respect other cultures, maintain integrity, and hire local leaders.

Recognize Differences

The point to remember is that cultural differences run deep. You not only have to accept them, but you also have to acknowledge them. As opposed to these underlying principles, the style of leadership has to be different in various cultures. Japanese society, for example, has a great reverence for age. Young people may come along, and while they may be very bright and talented, Japanese society generally regards them as potential leaders who may reach leadership roles in the future but are not there yet. That is not the case in the United States. Most Americans believe that the young bucks of Silicon Valley or relatively young executives like Bill Gates have the leadership ability to change the world. We'll examine research on these specific cultural differences later in the chapter.

Understand the Power of Self-Interest and Relationships

Taking a broader look at national differences, I argue that leadership and business are not very different from what we read in the newspapers every day. The United States can almost always count on the UK, for example. Why? To some extent the reasons are cultural, but it also often serves the interests of the UK to support the United States. In the same way, the United States can almost always count on France to say the Americans are doing something wrong. Again, to some extent it's cultural—the cards are stacked against the United States because many people in France regard Americans as boorish cowboys who don't understand the world or how it works. What makes a difference when we go from the world's political structures down to business? Just this: self-interest and personal relationships. When it is in the self-interest of other countries to support what the United States is doing, they do so. When it's not in their self-interest, they go their own way. And so it is in business.

The lessons about self-interest and the importance of personal relationships were brought home to me many times while I was CEO of Touche Ross. These two factors helped us maintain business relationships between the U.S. firm and our partner firms in other countries. We could cater to the self-interest of foreign firms by providing them with business that they could not generate for themselves, and they could provide us with opportunities that we could not tap on our own. Also, we could provide new products and educational opportunities. We also built strong personal relationships with international firms that resulted in relationships of trust.

However, if you think about it, this is a pretty rickety structure because these relationships could change. One of our competitors could come along to one of our international partner firms and say, "You've got X amount of referral business from the United States, but we'll give you double that." Or they could schmooze with the leaders of our partner firms, take them out to dinner, offer them positions on international committees or boards, and do things that generally undermine our personal relationship. That did happen to us, and we did lose some partner firms that way. Only a few; we kept most of them.

Respect Other Cultures

You have to treat people so they know that you do not in any way believe you are superior to them. If anything, you almost need to treat them as if they are superior to you. You have to make them think that their country is great—because it really is—and that the meeting their firm has organized is a most spectacular one. You have to tell them how important they are, send them notes, dance with their wives at firm dinners, and do what you need to do to maintain your relationship. If they don't think they can trust you on a personal level, you are in big trouble. Americans should not be tempted to impose our business practices and customs in different parts of the world any more than we can expect to press our form of democracy on Iraq, Iran, or Afghanistan. These customs and cultures have developed in many cases over more than a thousand years. How can we believe that we can—or even should—change all this overnight? We should first clean up some of the practices in City Hall or in Congress, and, for that matter, in parts of the business world, before we feel we are the shining example for others to emulate.

Maintain Integrity

Touche Ross had an affiliate firm in the Philippines. I was warned that this firm had been bribing tax authorities on behalf of their clients. This was illegal, so I said we ought to find another affiliate. But that was a problem. When we asked around, we were told that this was a common practice among most of the independent accounting firms in the Philippines. One exception was the SGV Group headed by Wash SyCip, but they already served several firms in the Big Eight. Eventually we ended up starting our own firm. But this experience helped us understand that this is how business was being done in that part of the world. After we had our own firm, we were able to serve our U.S. clients or German clients in that country, but obviously we did not get a whole lot of local business from clients that expected us to follow the local practices. Even if you are operating in an environment of questionable practices, it's essential that you maintain the integrity issue between yourself and your associates. Fundamentally, if you act with integrity, they will believe that they can trust you.

Culture and Leadership Styles: The Globe Project

Given the importance of understanding leadership in different countries, we now turn to academic research that addresses this challenge. There are real differences in how people in different cultures view and approach leadership. In 1993, Wharton Management Professor Robert House launched The Global Leadership and Organizational Behavior Effectiveness Research Program (GLOBE), one of the largest and most far-reaching studies of global leadership (House et al. 2004). Over time, GLOBE involved 170 investigators from more than 60 cultures representing all major regions of the world. The study examined the interrelationships among societal culture, organizational culture and practices, and organizational leadership by asking middle managers whether certain characteristics and behaviors would help or hinder a person in becoming an outstanding leader. This approach was designed to ensure a systematic and reliable understanding of the differences in leadership styles in diverse national cultures.

House and his colleagues found that "there are universally endorsed leader attributes," as reported in *Knowledge@Wharton*, the online research and business analysis journal of the Wharton School (*Knowledge@Wharton* 1999). "In addition," the report continued, "the study also found that there are attributes that are universally seen as impediments to outstanding leadership. The most important finding, however, is that there are culturally contingent attributes that can help or hinder leadership. What is seen as a strength in one culture may be a considerable impediment in another culture."

House and his colleagues noted that to "see how cultures might come into play, we can easily imagine a situation in which a British executive who was trained at an American business school is asked to run the Argentine manufacturing facility of a Japanese firm. What leadership attributes should this executive work to develop: Japanese? Argentine? American? British? This executive needs to understand the culture within which he works and how his employees perceive leadership" and develop "leadership attributes, tailored to the unique culture within which he or she works."

The GLOBE project showed that "different cultural groups may vary in their conceptions of the most important characteristics of charismatic/transformational leadership. In some cultures one might need to take strong, decisive action in order to be seen as a leader, whereas in other cultures consultation and a democratic approach may be the preferred approach to exercising effective leadership." In studying management practices, the researchers found that "many attributes associated with charisma are seen as contributing to outstanding leadership, but the term 'charisma' invokes ambivalence in several countries. There is concern in some cultures that people tend to lose their balance and perspective as a result of an excessive focus on achievement created by charismatic leaders. Certainly the most notorious example of a charismatic leader is Hitler."

The researchers also found that seemingly universal leadership qualities such as vision and risk-taking carry considerable cultural baggage. "Leaders are expected to have vision, but how this is displayed differs from culture to culture," the report says. "In China, the influence of Confucian values makes people wary of leaders who talk without engaging in specific action. Indian managers, on the other hand, care less about visionaries, preferring bold assertive styles of leadership. Leaders are often thought to be risk-takers, but GLOBE found that risk-taking is not universally valued as contributing to outstanding leadership."

Communication skills are extremely important for leaders, but what "constitutes a good communicator is likely to vary greatly across cultures," the report pointed out. "American managers are more likely to provide directions to subordinates on a face-to-face basis while Japanese managers are likely to use written memos. In the U.S. subordinates are usually provided negative feedback directly from their supervisors, while in Japan such feedback is usually channeled through a peer of the subordinates. These differences reflect the U.S. individualistic norm of 'brute honesty' and the Japanese collectivistic norm of 'face-saving.'"

Characteristics of Some Major National Cultures

To illustrate differences in culture, I spoke with Tom Presby, who worked with me at Touche Ross and has spent a good part of his life doing business globally. Some of his observations are summarized in Table 4-1. Although they may sound like cultural stereotypes, they are based on his personal experience working in these countries.

Table 4-1 Illustrative Cultural Differences

Latin-Based Europe (France, Spain, Italy, French Belgium, French Switzerland)	Germanic Europe (Germany, Austria, Flemish Belgium)	Japan	Russia
Elegance is important in business arrangements, which can lead to convoluted transactions. Honor and pride trump pragmatic solutions. Unlike many other cultures where a calm exterior is important, people get angry all the time, but it's generally just a transaction and not necessarily a fracture in a relationship. Social standing counts. This can stem from either family or successful completion of education at an elite university. People tend to be very loyal to personal friendships. Tax minimization schemes (sometimes illegal ones) are often employed.	Very conservative about change and particularly attached to doing all things "the German way," which is thought to be superior in every aspect. Hierarchical approach to business based on position and university diploma. Makes collaboration and teamwork difficult. Formal approach to doing business, business relationships, contracts, regulations, etc. Not as scrupulous as their formal approach might suggest.	"Face" counts most. Never suggest in public or in private that a Japanese person is wrong or has made a mistake. Trust is the key to relationships. Trust must be earned by persistence and by showing respect for Japanese institutions. Generally loyal, once trust has been established. Good partners, and generally deliver on commitments. Often incapable of taking public, negative action against other Japanese people or institutions.	Corruption is commonplace. It does not stem from a person's decision to transgress from proper and honest behavior; it is simply the way normal business gets done. Most people hold the belief that business is a zero-sum game. Younger managers have a Putin mindset, whereas managers from pre-1990 have a different mindset. The country is full of young, attractive, well-educated, multilingual Russians. If they were educated in Russia, outsiders should be careful about trusting them with information and/or responsibility. There is little loyalty to a company or an enterprise, whether foreign or Russian owned. Negotiations never stop until (and sometimes after) documents are signed. Don't rely on the classic "handshake agreement" or the Russian courts (or even Russian lawyers). Management style is hierarchical rather than collaborative. East-West joint ventures generally fail. Be sure to include a buyout provision.

It is impossible to describe all the national cultures you can encounter in the global marketplace. The references at the end of the chapter provide a guide to further reading that can help you adapt to a wide range of specific national cultures.

The Potential Pitfalls of Leading in Diverse National Cultures

Understanding these cultural differences is vital to effective leadership across different cultures. Failure to recognize cross-cultural differences can result in problems for leaders. In the book *The Transplanted Executive: Why You Need to Understand How Workers in Other Countries See the World Differently,* Professors P. Christopher Earley and Miriam Erez (1997) cite the instance of CTX, a high-tech printing equipment maker headquartered in Israel, which ran into great difficulties because of the failure of Israeli executives to communicate effectively with their overseas subsidiaries. The company made its equipment in Israel, and the subsidiaries were expected to provide service and maintenance in their respective countries. The subsidiaries were required to provide daily reports about service and maintenance issues, which they often failed to do. In frustration, the general manager in Israel invited the managers of all subsidiaries to attend a communications workshop at headquarters. The Israeli general manager began by lashing out at executives from the subsidiaries for not filing their reports, and added that he would give them two minutes to explain their failure to do so. The European managers were both offended and outraged at this treatment, and the communication problem worsened instead of improving, as the Israeli leaders had hoped.

The reason that the cure was worse, in a sense, than the disease had to do with the cultural nuances that underlay these communications. In Israel, many managers develop a forceful, authoritarian style as a result of that country's compulsory military service and other factors—and Israeli workers, who are used to this culture, not only do not feel offended by such behavior but also generally see it as a sign of strength and decisiveness. In contrast, the European managers interpreted the Israelis' behavior as being domineering and offensive—and they responded by refusing to submit their reports. As the authors observe, the European "cultural values were similar to but not identical to the Israelis'." According to the authors, companies need to use an integrated approach to managing cultural values if they want to overcome such challenges.

Building a Strong Organizational Culture: The Honeywell Way

In contrast, Honeywell, a manufacturer with revenues of $31 billion, shows how companies can build a strong and consistent organizational culture despite differences in national cultures. The company's operations span the globe, and it recruits and develops executives to manage across different national cultures. It has been doing business in the Asia Pacific region for more than 70 years, licensing manufacturing products in Japan since the 1930s. Its Asian operations are headquartered in Singapore, from where the company oversees operations in 13 Asian countries including Australia, India, China, Korea, and Taiwan, among others. More than 13,000 employees work for Honeywell in the Asia Pacific region. In addition, the company has a strong manufacturing base in Europe, the Middle East, and Africa. These operations are managed from regional headquarters in Brussels, and they involve 25,000 employees who work for Honeywell establishments in 49 European, African, or Middle Eastern countries. Moreover, Honeywell has affiliates in 10 Latin American countries including Argentina, Brazil, Chile, Colombia, and Ecuador, among others. The company has more than 7,000 employees in Latin America.

Given its global footprint, how does Honeywell train its executives to be successful leaders in different parts of the world? The company employs a program called the "12 behaviors," according to David M. Cote, the company's present Chairman and Chief Executive. "We created it about five years ago to lay out what we expect of all Honeywell employees and particularly from Honeywell leadership. During the annual appraisal process, everyone gets measured on those 12 behaviors." Cote explains that the reason the 12 behaviors program is significant is that when Honeywell recruits people in different parts of the world, it employs those who will fit the 12 behaviors best. "In other words, we don't hire them first and then train them in those behaviors; we hire them based on their ability to work in conjunction with these behaviors," he says.

For example, one of the behaviors is teamwork. "It is an overused word. After all, who would not be in favor of teamwork?" Cote asks. "But it is not always well understood, because teamwork sometimes implies that everyone must agree." Honeywell, however, defines teamwork in a specific way: The company sets out the requirements of a team member and how these differ from those of a team leader. If an issue is being discussed, it is incumbent upon team members to speak up and express their opinion and to make sure that their point of view is heard. Cote explains that it is also incumbent upon the team leader to make a decision. He or she cannot just sit there and wait for consensus. If, after you've been heard, the decision goes against you, it is up to you to support the decision.

This is precisely an area where differences in cultural or social context could lead to different behaviors. Whereas in countries like the United States people might be willing to speak up openly, in many Asian cultures dissent within a team might be regarded as being disrespectful of the leader or even as being insubordinate. How does Honeywell train its team leaders to manage teams in such contexts? Cote's answer is that this is why they hire people who fit the 12 behaviors. "If I am told that people in India or China will not speak up to disagree at team meetings, my response is that no people in any country are all the same. They are not. You only need to find 2,000 or 3,000 people out of more than a billion people in India who are predisposed to thinking this way." Cote adds that sometimes "more issues are made of cultural differences than are really there. I firmly believe that all people want to be treated with basic respect and courtesy and recognition that they and their country are of value. That is not hard to do."

Cote recognizes, of course, that in some cultures authoritarian leaders are treated with respect rather than being resented. "If you try to hire people in South Korea, you tend to find people who are autocratic leaders, and employees who expect an autocratic leader. However, we have also learned that when you put someone there who is more team-based, instead of laying down the law about how they expect things to work, most people seem to get there. That is why it is not right to stereotype a country. All the people are not like that."

As the leader of a company with operations in more than 70 countries, Cote regularly conducts town hall meetings around the world for audiences ranging from 100 to 2,000 people. He has conducted at least 40 meetings outside the United States, and in almost every country he has visited, he has been told not to be surprised if no one asks questions at the end of his presentation. Local experts say, "Our culture is just not like that." And yet, Cote says, "In not one case has there been a problem with people asking questions. What it comes down to is, what kind of an environment do you set up upfront, and how do you make people feel comfortable asking questions? You find that the experts—the communications people—are wrong."

Cote offers another example of the problem that stereotypes can create. "In the UK we had to move a plant from one location to another, and we had decided to offer packages to people who agreed to move." Cote was warned not to expect a high response because "nobody moves in the UK." Cote asked the local Honeywell executives, "How do you know if you don't offer the packages? Why don't you make the offer and see what happens?" When the offer was made, Honeywell's British executives were astonished to see that large numbers of people accepted the packages and agreed to move. Cote says, "They said they liked what they did, and they agreed to move for the job. People get too hung up on their stereotypes."

Using Humor to Bridge Cultures

A sense of humor can go a long way toward bridging cultural gaps. "No matter what culture you go to, people have a sense of humor," Cote says. "If you can find some way to tap into that sense of humor, so that it's not just completely serious, you can make progress. It's one of those universal truths about people."

One time, Cote was involved with negotiations in Japan with people whom he had not dealt with before. In the beginning of the conversation, he began to joke about cultural differences involving food. "I talked about how I preferred a cheeseburger to a traditional Japanese bento box, and then I started teasing them about why we couldn't have a cheeseburger bento box. Everyone laughed, and as we did that, we started to develop a rapport. Then the negotiations began, and we ended up in a tough spot. Both sides knew it was a tough issue, and finally the Japanese executives said yes. Then I said, 'We were talking about this before. There are cultural differences—so, is this a Japanese yes or an American yes? I'm wondering which one this is.' Again, everyone smiled and laughed, and then we went on to discuss the issue even further until it was resolved. The point is that there are cultural differences, and you have to recognize them; but as long as you have basic respect for people—and you use a sense of humor—that can get you through a lot of situations."

Even as Cote recognizes that cultural and social contexts differ around the world, he acknowledges that there are some universal principles that people need in order to become successful leaders anywhere: "You need integrity. No matter what culture you belong to, people need to be able to trust you."

A Tool for Success: The 80-20 Rule

How should companies prepare leaders who have been successful in one part of the world become effective leaders in a different region and culture? Cote says he has found that moving from one part of the world to another is "analogous to moving from one business to another in the same country. When you look at cultural differences, they exist between different countries but also within different companies and sometimes even within different businesses in the same company."

Cote suggests that the way to deal with such change is to use what he calls his "80-20 rule: 80 percent of what you deal with in the new situation is exactly the same as what you have dealt with in the past, and you have to deal with it the same way; 20 percent is different. The people I have seen fail—when they change companies or businesses or countries—are those who go in saying that since they did things a certain way in the past, they will do it the same way again, or those who think they are in a totally new situation and nothing of what they have learned in the past is applicable. Both of those are failure modes. The person who is in success mode walks in saying, 'I know it's 80-20. My trick is to figure out what's in the 80 (and I should do it exactly the way I did before) and what's in the 20 (and I need to modify my way of working to comply with the new company, or country).'"

Conclusions: Building Cross-Cultural Leadership

These principles—and practical advice—from the Honeywell chairman can go a long way in helping leaders of all organizations manage more effectively across different national and social contexts. As organizations become more networked globally, managing across the interfaces of different corporate and national cultures becomes more important. Leaders need to recognize cultural differences and build the personal relationships that are crucial to the success of networked enterprises.

To summarize some of the key insights from research and practice:

- Just as success in execution depends on the leader's ability to understand and navigate through an organizational context, it also depends on understanding national cultures and social context in which organizational networks operate. Leaders cannot hope to be effective if they use a one-size-fits-all model of leadership everywhere.

- The principles of leadership are mainly universal, but the way in which they are applied depends on the cultural context. Leaders need to recognize the 80 percent of a situation that is the same, and the 20 percent that is different. In particular, relationships and integrity are important in any culture. They also need to recognize that they can hire employees in any country who are aligned with the corporate culture, even if they do not fit the local norms.

- Cultural differences run deep. You not only have to accept them, but also have to acknowledge them in the way that you treat people. They must come to know that you do not in any way believe you are superior to them. If anything, you almost need to treat them as if they are superior to you. Humor can play a powerful role in bridging cultural gaps.

As global networks, formal and informal, become more important, cross-cultural challenges will become an increasingly significant leadership challenge. Even in a more borderless world, navigating the borders and interfaces between cultures is essential to effective network building and leadership.

References

Earley, P. Christopher, and Miriam Erez. 1997. *The Transplanted Executive: Why You Need to Understand How Workers in Other Countries See the World Differently.* New York: Oxford University Press, 5-7. (The authors provide an interesting table of Cultural Profiles with Example[s of] Management Practice, listing many countries, p. 27.)

House, Robert J., Paul J. Hanges, Mansour Javidan, Peter W. Dorfman, Vipin Gupta. 2004. *Culture, Leadership, and Organizations: The GLOBE Study of 62 Societies.* Sage Publications.

Knowledge@Wharton. 1999. "How cultural factors affect leadership," July 23. http://knowledge.wharton.upenn.edu/article.cfm?articleid=38.

Palmer, Russell E. (2008). *Ultimate Leadership: Winning Execution Strategies for Your Situation,* Upper Saddle River, NJ: Wharton School Publishing.

PART II

FOUNDATIONS

Although business organizations have begun to recognize the need to build and understand networks, business certainly didn't invent networks. The second section of the book offers foundational insights into the nature of networks, based on perspectives from diverse fields. In Chapter 5, **Dawn Iacobucci** and **James Salter** examine insights from sociology and marketing, demonstrating the rising importance of networks and their impact on social relationships and organizations. In Chapter 6, **Sonia Kleindorfer** and **James G. Mitchell** examine the rich variety of biological networks, including food chains from coral reefs to rainforests, and consider the evolution of networks such as communities of finches on the Galapagos Islands. In Chapter 7, **Robert Giegengack** and **Yvette Bordeaux** examine information exchange in biological networks, including termite colonies and bees, and how these networks mediate communication across their nodes. Finally, in Chapter 8, **Steven Kimbrough** considers recent advances in artificial intelligence and agent-based simulations that have been used to explore the impact of network relationships on the evolution, efficiency, and survival in a variety of social and biological systems.

Chapter 5   Social Networks: You've Lost Control   67
             Dawn Iacobucci and James Salter

Chapter 6   Biological Networks: Rainforests, Coral Reefs, and the
             Galapagos Islands   85
             Sonia Kleindorfer and James G. Mitchell

Chapter 7   Information Networks in the History of Life   105
             Robert Giegengack and Yvette Bordeaux

Chapter 8   Artificial Intelligence: How Individual Agents Add Up
             to a Network   125
             Steven O. Kimbrough

5

Social Networks: You've Lost Control

Dawn Iacobucci
James M. Salter II

Abstract

This chapter provides an overview of social networks—the basic discipline from which ideas and terminology are drawn when characterizing popular phenomena such as "social networking" Internet sites like Facebook and MySpace. The authors offer the reader a flavor of the theoretical and empirical research conducted by social network scholars since the 1930s. They explore how researchers have used social networks to generate and test economic, sociological, and organizational theories. The authors examine broad insights from this research, as well as management implications in areas such as advertising, brands, loyalty, authenticity, and segmentation. The overriding message is that as power shifts from firms to social networks, companies have less control over their own destinies and need to pay more attention to networks.

In the 1990s, a chain of cake shops in Hong Kong experienced firsthand the power of social networks in commercial contagion. A Japanese firm, which owned a department store chain and a cake-shop chain, both of which had retail presence in Hong Kong, closed the Hong Kong department stores. Consumers holding gift certificates to be redeemed at the stores were left with worthless pieces of paper. Around the same time, the Japanese company spun off the cake stores, so the cake-store chain was financially independent. But consumers still saw the department stores and cake shops as connected. On November 24, 1997, some Hong Kong cake-store employees received pink slips, and a rumor began that the cake-store chain would close. Consumers were afraid that their cake voucher coupons would be worthless, as had happened with the department store gift certificates. Within hours, thousands of people rushed all the chain stores to redeem their cake voucher coupons. *Quelle tragédie!*

A study of the run on Hong Kong cake shops by Lai and Wong (2002) documented the contagion of a commercial rumor. The researchers conducted phone interviews in the week that followed, asking whether and how the respondent had heard of the rumor. They found that family ties spread the word faster than nonfamily ties or commercial media, but the strength of the tie didn't affect the speed of the information diffusion. On average, 22% of the respondents told three other people.

As this example illustrates, the power of social networks means that companies no longer have control over many aspects of their businesses. The company's business can sometimes be driven more by word-of-mouth rumors among its customers than the company's own messaging. In this chapter, we explore the diverse research on social networks in many areas, some key findings, and implications for managers. While traditional research has focused on key actors (the nodes), social network research has focused on the relationships between the players (links). The overriding implication of networks for managers, as the Hong Kong cake-shop chain discovered, is that you ignore the power of the network at your peril.

The Discipline of Social Networks: Examining Interdependencies

What is a social network? Many standard statistical techniques focus on independent actors. Tools such as ordinary least squares and general linear modeling investigate relationships among variables, and assume the observations on which those variables were taken to be independent. Although these approaches are remarkably robust to violations of most underlying assumptions, their Achilles' heel is that assumption of independence among the observations. In some settings, researchers seek statistical corrections for this inconvenience. In social network settings, researchers examine the interdependencies among the observations as the very phenomenon of interest. That is, the lack of independence is not a statistical nuisance; it is the very thing to study.

Networks, then, are collections of nodes and links. The links connect dyads (pairs) of nodes. The links may be simply binary or they may convey the strength of ties. Links may be mutual or asymmetric. They may not exist, and then a tie is said to be null, or two nodes may be linked in several ways, and then the tie is said to be multiplex. The network may be defined as the collection of nodes and their inherent dyadic links, or it may be defined on the links that thereby determine which nodes are included in the network set. A sociogram depicting a network is shown in Figure 5-1.

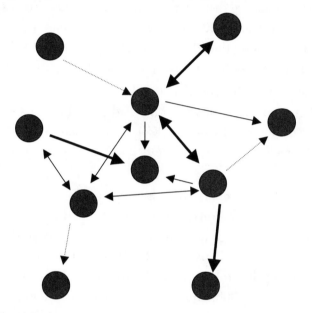

Figure 5-1   A social network

A social network is a network in which the links between the nodes capture some element of social interaction. This term is used very broadly, in part reflecting a philosophy that just about every interaction one observes is social in nature—whether it is a network of children playing, employees e-mailing about a project, firms coordinating to establish an industry policy, countries collaborating on peace efforts (or countries fighting), dolphins determining the seas in which to frolic for the morning, and so on.

In social networks, the entities of "nodes" and "links" are more frequently referred to as "actors" and "relational ties." The actors can be people or collections of people, and the ties can reflect liking, frequency, trust, communication, flows of money or information, and so forth. The diversity of both is captured in the examples that follow.

History of Thought in Social Networks

Social network publications date back to the 1930s, but the focal journal, *Social Networks,* was launched in 1978. In addition to studying cases of commercial contagion, researchers have looked at the impact of social networks in diverse areas. In fact, once one becomes aware of the paradigm, social networks may be seen everywhere. Networkers have examined epidemiology and disease transmission, for example, among children (Del Valle et al. 2007) or among drug sharers and sex partners (Adams and Moody 2007; Bell, Belli-McQueen, and Haider 2007). Social network researchers study social support networks, such as those among the Flemish Belgians (Agneessens, Waege, and Lievens 2006) or among men and women in Tehran (Bastani 2007).

Criminology has found the social networks perspective to be useful, given the propensity for bad guys to hang out with other bad guys. Recent social network studies have included gangs in Boston (Tutzauer 2007), white-collar crime (Baker and Faulkner 2004), terrorism (Morselli, Giguère and Petit 2007), and juvenile crime in Stockholm (Frank 2001).

Some social network researchers study interpersonal politics in organizations, such as knowledge sharing in corporations (Cross, Borgatti, and Parker 2001) or patterns of cooperation in a law firm (Lazega and Pattison 1999). Others study real politics, from historical dealings of Brezhnev (Faust et al. 2002) or Spain's effect on the development of the Caribbean (Bonacich, Holdren, and Johnston 2004), to modern politics in the House and Senate (Fowler 2006), Supreme Court (Brazill and Grofman 2002), and Mexico (Sinclair 2007).

In addition

- Diffusion of innovation is of perennial interest, such as documenting the spatial-temporal implementation of organic farming in Finland (Nyblom et al. 2003).
- Social network researchers also study the intersection of sociology and economics, for example, in studying what kinds of structures are optimal for economic development of a community (Crowe 2007) and the social mobility of parent and child occupations (Roberts 2002).
- And, of course, there's romance. Social networkers study structures of double-dating (Yamaguchi 2000) and online Swedish dating communities (Holme, Edling, and Liljeros 2004).

This diverse assortment of scholarship is all considered networking, because the studies characterize interdependent elements. These studies are also all considered social, because they involve humans or aggregations of humans.

As a final indicator of the diffusion of networks, consider these professional markers. There is the annual Sunbelt Social Networks Conference sponsored by the International Network for Social Network Analysis (www.insna.org), founded in 1978, which also sponsors a journal, *Social Networks*, devoted to the topic. There are numerous courses (many syllabuses are posted on the insna.org site) and several universities in which social networks are a stronghold (for example, University of California at Irvine, Carnegie Mellon, and the sociology department at UCLA). There is a newsletter titled *Connections*, as well as English and Spanish listservs. There is dedicated software (UCINET) and algorithms posted for standard software. The standard comprehensive text is that by Wasserman and Faust (1994); good primers include Knoke and Kuklinski (1982) and Scott (2000), and book on networks in marketing include Iacobucci (1996) and Van den Bulte and Wuyts (2007).

The articles in *Social Networks* have included theoretical papers, case studies, and longitudinal studies, as well as discussions of data collection and modeling issues. Since the journal's inception, theoretical and modeling papers have dominated, as shown in a plot of journal articles in Figure 5-2. All other topics appear less frequently, primarily because of our category definitions. For example, centrality is but one means of analyzing network data, but it is important enough that even its small numbers are noticeable. Longitudinal studies are infrequent, presumably mostly due to the onerous data requirements. Case studies are also effortful data collections. Both categories are represented as fairly infrequent, and fairly steady-state, with exceptional blips attributable to special issues of the journal.

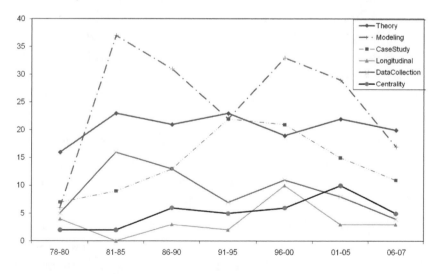

Figure 5-2 Content analysis of *Social Networks* articles

In the sections that follow, we describe several studies of each sort, to give the reader a feel for the kind of scholarly inquiries reported in this journal. Following the report on *Social Networks*, we turn to the contemplation of what it all might mean for marketing and business.

Concepts and Theories in Social Networks

Conceptual and theoretical papers in social networks are of two sorts: theory development and theory testing (usually economics, sociology, and organizational science). We will offer examples of all of these.

Theory Development

In addition to the study of the run on Hong Kong cake shops noted previously, other researchers have explored many other practical examples that have informed theory. For example, Grossetti (2007) examined the impact of mass urbanization on traditional community ties, by comparing a current community network in Toulouse, France, with one documented in the United States in the mid-1970s. He found many structural similarities, from the average size of actors' networks, the network densities, the numbers of friends mentioned who live within a five-minute drive, and so on.

An unfortunately quite topical case study is Morselli, Giguère, and Petit (2007), who mapped two different kinds of networks—those of terrorists and those of criminals. Perhaps on the surface these both seem to be communities of bad guys, but their study unfolded differences. For example, terrorist networks tend to be driven by ideology, whereas nonterrorist criminals tend to be driven by commercial enterprise. Furthermore, the latter were typically functional for shorter durations, so the networks required greater efficiencies.

On a more upbeat note, Holme, Edling, and Liljeros (2004) measured online interactions on pussokram.com, a Swedish online dating site (the term apparently translates roughly to "kiss'n'hug"). They found support for homophily; that is, it is more "birds of a feather flock together" than "opposites attract."

In terms of theorizing, all of these lines of scholarship are thriving—theory development and theory testing, and iterations between the two. Within theory testing, economic and social theories are the primary contenders, but social network theories usually care more about the social networks and connectedness than the source discipline of a possibly interesting and relevant theory, so the journal is informed by more disciplines than just these two.

Theory Testing

Other researchers are using approaches from economics, sociology, and organizational science to test theories. Economics approaches, such as the application of game theory, have been used to test whether traditional economic views hold in social networks. For example, Braun and Gautschi (2006) examined the effect of network structure on power in bargaining games. Other researchers extend traditional economic views to include new twists coming from social networks. For example, Sozański (2006) studied cooperative game solutions to demonstrate that central network actors are key. That observation builds on economics, which had nothing to say on the matter.

Baker and Faulkner (2004) pitted competing economic and sociological theories against each other in an investments arena. They measured the likelihood of an investor losing capital, and found that result was reduced either by the investors engaging in due diligence (research into the investment vehicles) or by the investors having social ties to the machinery of the investment, and the likelihood of loss was further reduced by the presence of both due diligence and a social connection.

Crowe (2007) found that the economic self-development of communities flourished with networks whose parties were cohesive (tightly interconnected). Industrial recruitment, a different sort of economic development, instead was aided by networks that resembled bridges (those with boundary spanners reaching out to other networks).

Sociology, social psychology, and organizational science contribute different theories that are frequently put to the test in social network studies. For example, Plickert, Côté and Wellman (2007) note that reciprocity (or the golden rule) seems to be a universal norm, and they proceed to find strong empirical support. Cross, Borgatti, and Parker (2001) used an organizational science approach, asking employees whom they sought out when they needed information of various types (helping to solve problems, helping to reformulate the problem, knowledge about where to find answers, validation of proposed answers, and name-lending legitimation). They found a hierarchical, nearly Guttman scale in that for most respondents, some people were sought out for everything, whereas other people were sought out only for simple requests. When these researchers dug deeper, they found that this ranking didn't reflect talent or status among individuals in the organization. Rather, most people have a couple of trusted sources from whom they seek everything.

Longitudinal Studies

Longitudinal studies examine the impact and evolution of networks over time (Doreian 2006). Sometimes scientists expect change, as in a study by several teams of researchers documenting the evolution of social support networks as young people leave school and enter the workplace (Bidart and Lavenu 2005; Degenne and Lebeaux 2005). Perhaps not surprisingly, these studies found that network size shrinks with the onset of job responsibilities. They also found that as people "sort out" their networks, they tend to retain those most similar to themselves.

Other researchers study the durability of networks. For example, Adams, Madhavan, and Simon (2006) studied two ethnic groups in rural West Africa. The Bamanan people, who compose 35% of Mali, tend to support themselves by farming and, hence, live in extended families. In contrast, the Fulbe people, who are 10% of Mali, raise cattle and live and move in smaller nuclear families. Networks were sampled and resampled and found to be largely stable.

Social Network Methodologies: Data Collection and Modeling

Researchers use a variety of tools to understand networks, including (1) data collection and network sampling and (2) data representation and network modeling. The first approach examines the quality of data. For example, Adams and Moody (2007) interviewed both members of a sample of dyads, several times each, and found remarkably high reporting reliability over the duration of the study. In addition to such studies of reliability, researchers study other data issues such as comparing self-reports of network ties and observations of actual interactions (Killworth et al. 2006); clearly defined, recent behaviors tend to be reported with less error. Some researchers are concerned with sampling issues—for example, finding that if an actor is not included in the sample, the cohesiveness of the network is underestimated (Kossinets 2006). Other researchers have simulated missing data scenarios and (thankfully) found that most measures of centrality are not completely debilitated, but slowly denigrate monotonically with the amount of missing data (Borgatti, Carley, and Krackhardt 2006; Costenbader and Valente 2003; also see Iacobucci, Neelamegham, and Hopkins 1999).

Researchers also looked at the impact of study and survey design. Kogovsek and Ferligoj (2005) found better measurement quality when a survey question focuses on one friend, and cycles through sociometric questions (such as, "Tell me about this friend as a source of different kinds of support") than when focusing on one kind of support and cycling through friends. They also found that behaviors were easier to report reliably than emotional questions. Bailey and Marsden (1999) studied the rather famous "General Social Survey Name Generator" and found that the names elicited when respondents were asked, "Who would you go to, to discuss important matters?" can be affected by context; for example, when the preceding survey questions asked about health (or politics), the matters deemed important leaned more toward health (or politics), and naturally affected the names generated. Fu (2005) found that a classic survey finding holds for networks, too. Specifically, single survey items were quick and inexpensive, but diary data provided more depth of information.

A second major stream of research focuses on data representation and modeling. Researchers use many approaches to model network data. For example, researchers are trying to hone topological methods for identifying which actors in a network should be deemed those in the core set versus those who are more peripheral characters (Boyd, Fitzgerald, and Beck 2006; Salomé and Ramos 2006). Researchers are trying to model triads (McDonald, Smith, and Forster 2007) and blend individual level data with aggregate level data (Mizruchi and Marquis 2006). Other researchers are refining a newer line of inferential models to examine network effects such as transitivity (Goodreau 2007; Robins et al. 2007). Modeling centrality indices is its own cottage industry in social networks. Borgatti and Everett (2006) created a useful conceptual framework for centrality indices. Butts (2006) offered ideas about how to normalize centrality indices for easier comparison. For readers interested in more information about social networks, there are several good primers, including Knoke and Kuklinski (1982) and Scott (2000).

Key Substantive Findings: What Do We Know?

Based on several decades of research on social network literature, what do we know? In addition to specific knowledge, there are several broader lessons:

- In a myriad of settings, people and firms are interconnected. Information about how they are interconnected is not redundant with information about who they are. A network view of a person's (or firm's) interconnections should not replace, but is complementary information to, a traditional view of the person's (or firm's) attributes.

- Networks and patterns of connectivity show some stability (like traits) and some variability (like particular behavioral predictions).

- Network analysts can proceed pragmatically; if the data have something to say, it will be found. So don't worry (unduly) about sampling or representation.

- Although it is not surprising that an in-depth study (such as a case study on a firm) reveals deep insights, what is perhaps more surprising is that typically many generalizations are possible. We can learn from each other and across contexts.

On the other hand, there are many things we do not know about networks. For example, rare are the models that integrate actor characteristics with network characteristics. As a result, we know little about possible differences between networks among children versus teens versus adults versus seniors, for example. We can hypothesize richly but find few empirical investigations about how network structures differ for men versus women, or Western versus Eastern cultures. As network models mature, certainly these classic survey questions should be folded into network perspectives.

Similarly astonishing to people outside of social networks is that while the term "social networks" has come to popularly connote various online connector services, the technological embeddedness of social networks is as yet understudied. There are some exceptions (for example, Licoppe and Smoreda 2005; Mok and Wellman 2007), but to date, this area is more potential than realization.

Marketing and business applications will be somewhat stunted by the fact that many social network analytical models are very well suited to rather small, bounded networks. This is changing, certainly primarily due to the pressures presented by the availability of large-scale datasets, but as yet, the software for large networks is not as "plug and play" as that for small networks.

Finally, many social network studies still have a fairly scientifically immature ring about them, being more descriptive ("Isn't this network cool?") than theoretical or prescriptive. In business, too, many a network study has been launched, many a lesson learned, many a cool graph plotted. But when the dust settles, networks have to prove their worth with some sort of marketing or managerial insight. We now turn our attention to some of these specific managerial insights that we can derive from research on social networks.

Implications for Marketing Management and Business

Networks have many implications for business. We explore five key implications for marketing management and business: implications for advertising, brands, loyalty, authenticity, and segmentation.

Advertising and Targeted Messaging

Marketers may have been mistaken in their initial perception that the growth of online networks represented the emergence of a highly effective marketing medium. Although top networks continue to show dramatic growth (for example, MySpace has more than 100 million global visitors and 200 million accounts; comScore 2007), such mass and diversity, though good for reach and awareness, don't necessarily ensure effective marketing and messaging results.

Furthermore, as social networks developed, many marketers thought that the wealth of user detail they provided would make it possible to target and control messages more effectively. As technology continues to improve, being able to target advertising to individual profile and behavior information is easier, but fraught with privacy problems, both legal and social (Weber 2007).

In addition, the interactive characteristics of social networks take control out of the hands of the marketer and put it into the hands of the users, who communicate with each other, praising and criticizing, raving and ridiculing. Today's information highway is more about connecting and collaborating than command and control. Although many companies have policies on how to engage with traditional media and even on blogging, few have any in-house rules covering the kind of instant response required by bloggers and social networks.

Managing Brands

Brands are nodes in networks, and consumer network users consistently expressed their desire for brands and organizations to treat them less like customers and more like friends (Fox Interactive Media 2007). In response, some 48% of brand marketers plan to use social marketing tactics in next year's plans, in part because social networkers trust the opinions of their peers more than ads when making a major purchase decision (Jupiter Research 2007). Marketers using social network advertising need to use effective network analysis to identify brand advocates and influentials to provide credibility and acceptance of the brand promise (Schatsky 2007).

The mass and immediacy of social networks are capable of modifying—enhancing or detracting from—attitudes and behaviors toward brands in the off-line world. For example, the size and complexity of networks such as MySpace and Facebook may weaken the normal relationship between weak links and strong links in affecting brand preference, while networks may accelerate belief updating and normative pressure for negative as well as positive consideration of product and service features, benefits, and purchase. There have been both successes (such as, BMW's "The Hire," Chevy Tahoe's apprenticechevy.com) and failures among the wide range of brand promotions on social networks.

Loyalty

Marketers haven't yet considered the effect of networks on loyalty. The nature of social networks is to provide a place where people with common friends and interests can congregate and connect. If their friends start to move to a new, hot site, the socializers will follow their friends (such as the migration from the pioneer Friendster to Facebook, which users perceived as "more interesting"). Success can be transient in the world of social networking, particularly for the notoriously fickle youth who dominate membership on these sites. Thus these spaces are unusually vulnerable to the next "new" thing; just as quickly as users flock to one site, they can move on to another with no warning. The financial benefits of attracting and retaining customers through building customer loyalty are well documented in the marketing literature. However, loyalty via social networks adds new challenges that are not well understood.

Authenticity: Don't Tamper and Don't Try to Fool the Network

Given the size and potential for anonymity on social networks, it is tempting for a marketer to think that a little misinformation here and there could be used effectively to enhance a brand or product via the network. However, such attempts can easily backfire. For example, the 2006 blog by "Jim and Laura" was ostensibly authored by a couple traveling across the United States, parking overnight in Wal-Mart store parking lots and interviewing Wal-Mart employees, who uniformly gave glowing testimonials about the benefits of working at the company. It quickly turned out that it was a fake blog and expenses for the trip were paid for by Working Families for Wal-Mart. The "flogging" (fake blogging) was widely criticized, and a public apology was subsequently issued by the firm's public relations agency (Gogoi 2006).

Marketers have also tried to use fake social network user profiles to promote products, also with backlash because it undermines the credibility of network membership (Leggatt 2007; MacManus 2006). More legitimately, marketers are beginning to include blogs in their mix of communications tools. A new service called PayPerPost.com offers to match companies with bloggers who will blog about them in return for cash (Quinton 2006).

As a result of the uncertainties and misuses, there have already emerged some basic social marketing principles for successful social media marketing (Livingston 2007), including, at least these:

- Do not try to control the message.
- Honesty, ethics, and transparencies are musts.
- Build value for the community with real, exciting information, not corporate propaganda.

Segmentation and Value Propositions

Early market segmentation research created segments primarily on *a priori* bases such as geography, purchase volume, products purchased, income, and similar macrodemographics. Research on customer loyalty makes it possible to develop targeted value propositions and marketing initiatives around drivers of loyalty and retention for particular segments, and marketers are now beginning to develop microtargeting for social networks.

For example, MySpace recently launched the second phase of Hyper-targeting, its new advertising platform technology, to enable online marketers to tap into self-expressed user information in real time and create microtarget campaigns for users in hundreds of subcategories (MySpace 2007). Facebook is similarly developing a behavioral microtargeting application to segment users on favorite activities and preferred music, extracted from the user-provided information and the user's links (Vara and Delaney 2007).

The implications of segments within segments and real-time updating of segment user profiles, like everything else about the "new" media versus the "old," are significant for today's marketers. Social networks can be integrated with the proven history of traditional media to develop a marketing mix that will produce the best returns from both.

Conclusion: Losing Control

Nearly eight decades of formal research on social networks has offered many insights into how they function. This work has begun to hint at the implications of networks for business. As noted, there is still much that we don't know about the impact of social networks on business—and the rising popularly and reach of social networks in consumers' lives means that these effects can be expected to deepen.

One serious implication is that power and control in business is shifting increasingly from the company itself to the social networks that surround it. Given this shift, companies need to pay more attention to these networks. As control shifts from the company to the network, companies need to understand network dynamics and how to influence them or work with networks. Otherwise, companies truly will lose control.

Instead of just looking at the characteristics of customers and segments, managers need to look more closely at the relationships between these customers. In their new position as network nodes, companies may never have the kind of control they had previously. But by better understanding the relationships that surround them, firms can gain greater knowledge and more control over the social networks that will define their future.

References

Business Press References

comScore. 2007. Social networking goes global. Reston, VA. Retrieved November 22, 2007, from http://www.comscore.com/press/release.asp?press=1555.

Fox Interactive Media. 2007. Never ending friending, white paper.

Gogoi, Pallavi. 2006. Wal-Mart's Jim and Laura: "The real story," BusinessWeek.com, October 9, 2006.

Jupiter Research. Social networking sites: Defining advertising opportunities in a competitive landscape, April 2007.

Leggatt, Helen. 2007. "Social networkers fake profile information," BixReport.com, September 19, 2007.

Livingston, Geoff. 2007. "Think liquid," *The Buzz Bin*, July 16, 2007.

MacManus. 2006. "Sex and social networking sells: Fake user profiles in marketing campaigns," Read/WriteWeb, November 26, 2006.

MySpace. 2007. Corporate press release, November 5, 2007.

Quinton, Brian. 2006. Poisoning the well, Directmag.com, November 1, 2006.

Schatsky, David. Jupiter Research, Op. Cit.

Vara, Vauhini, and Kevin J. Delaney. 2007. Facebook gets personal with ad targeting plan. *The Wall Street Journal*, August 21, 2007.

Weber, Jonathan. "Are social networking sites a bad investment?" Times Online, September 25, 2007.

Social Network Books

Iacobucci, Dawn. 1996. *Networks in Marketing*. Thousand Oaks, CA: Sage.

Knoke, David, and James H. Kuklinski. 1982. *Network Analysis*. Thousand Oaks, CA: Sage.

Scott, John P. 2000. *Social Network Analysis*, 2nd ed. Thousand Oaks, CA: Sage.

Van den Bulte, Christophe, and Stefan Wuyts. 2007. *Social Networks and Marketing*. Cambridge, MA: Marketing Science Institute.

Wasserman, Stanley, and Katherine Faust. 1994. *Social Network Analysis: Methods and Applications*. Cambridge University Press.

Social Network Journal References[1]

Adams, Alayne M., Sangeetha Madhavan, and Dominique Simon. 2006. Measuring social networks cross-culturally. *Social Networks*, 28 (4), 363-376.

Adams, Jimi, and James Moody. 2007. To tell the truth: Measuring concordance in multiply reported network data. *Social Networks*, 29 (1), 44-58.

Agneessens, Filip, Hans Waege, and John Lievens. 2006. Diversity in social support by role relations: A typology. *Social Networks*, 28 (4), 427-441.

Bailey, Stefanie, and Peter V. Marsden. 1999. Interpretation and interview context: Examining the general social survey name generator using cognitive methods. *Social Networks*, 21 (3), 287-309.

Baker, Wayne E., and Robert R. Faulkner. 2004. Social networks and loss of capital. *Social Networks*, 26 (2), 91-111.

Bastani, Susan. 2007. Family comes first: Men's and women's personal networks in Tehran. *Social Networks*, 29 (3), 357-374.

---

[1] Contact first author for annotated bibliography of *Social Network* articles since 1999.

Bell, David C., Benedetta Belli-McQueen, and Ali Haider. 2007. Partner naming and forgetting: Recall of network members. *Social Networks,* 29 (2), 279-299.

Bidart, Claire, and Daniel Lavenu. 2005. Evolutions of personal networks and life events. *Social Networks,* 27 (4), 359-376.

Bonacich, Phillip, Annie Cody Holdren, and Michael Johnston. 2004. Hyper-edges and multidimensional centrality. *Social Networks,* 26 (3), 189-203.

Borgatti, Stephen P., Kathleen M. Carley, and David Krackhardt. 2006. On the robustness of centrality measures under conditions of imperfect data. *Social Networks,* 28 (2), 124-136.

Borgatti, Stephen P., and Martin G. Everett. 2006. A graph-theoretic perspective on centrality. *Social Networks,* 28 (4), 466-484.

Boyd, John P., William J. Fitzgerald, and Robert J. Beck. 2006. Computing core/periphery structures and permutation tests for social relations data. *Social Networks,* 28 (2), 165-178.

Braun, Norman, and Thomas Gautschi. 2006. A Nash bargaining model for simple exchange networks. *Social Networks,* 28 (1), 1-23.

Brazill, Timothy J., and Bernard Grofman. 2002. Factor analysis versus multidimensional scaling: Binary choice roll-call voting and the U.S. Supreme Court. *Social Networks,* 24 (3), 201-29.

Butts, Carter T. 2006. Exact bounds for degree centralization. *Social Networks,* 28 (4), 283-296.

Costenbader, Elizabeth, and Thomas W. Valente. 2003. The stability of centrality measures when networks are sampled. *Social Networks,* 25 (4), 283-307.

Cross, Rob, Stephen P. Borgatti, and Andrew Parker. 2001. Beyond answers: Dimensions of the advice network. *Social Networks,* 23 (3), 215-35.

Crowe, Jessica A. 2007. In search of a happy medium: How the structure of interorganizational networks influence community economic development strategies. *Social Networks,* 29 (4), 469-488.

Degenne, Alain, and Marie-Odile Lebeaux. 2005. The dynamics of personal networks at the time of entry into adult life. *Social Networks,* 27 (4), 337-358.

Del Valle, S. Y., J. M. Hyman, H. W. Hethcote, and S. G. Eubank. 2007. Mixing patterns between age groups in social networks. *Social Networks,* 29 (4), 539-554.

Doreian, Patrick. 2006. Actor network utilities and network evolution. *Social Networks,* 28 (2), 137-164.

Faust, Katherine, Karin E. Willert, David D. Rowlee, and John Skvoretz. 2002. Scaling and statistical models for affiliation networks: Patterns of participation among soviet politicians during the Brezhnev era. *Social Networks*, 24 (3), 231-59.

Fowler, James H. 2006. Legislative cosponsorship networks in the U.S. House and Senate. *Social Networks*, 28 (4), 454-465.

Frank, Ove. 2001. Statistical estimation of co-offending youth networks. *Social Networks*, 23 (3), 203-14.

Fu, Yang-chih. 2005. Measuring personal networks with daily contacts: A single-item survey question and the contact diary. *Social Networks*, 27 (3), 169-86.

Goodreau, Steven M. 2007. Advances in exponential random graph (p*) models applied to a large social network. *Social Networks*, 29 (2), 231-248.

Grossetti, Michel. 2007. Are French networks different? *Social Networks*, 29 (3), 391-404.

Holme, Petter, Christofer R. Edling, and Fredrik Liljeros. 2004. Structure and time evolution of an Internet dating community. *Social Networks*, 26 (2), 155-74.

Iacobucci, Dawn, R. Neelamegham, and Nigel Hopkins. 1999. Measurement quality issues in dyadic models of relationships. *Social Networks*, 21 (3), 211-37.

Killworth, Peter D., Christopher McCarty, H. Russell Bernard, and Mark House. 2006. The accuracy of small world chains in social networks. *Social Networks*, 28 (1), 85-96.

Kogovsek, Tina, and Anuska Ferligoj. 2005. Effects on reliability and validity of egocentered network measurements. *Social Networks*, 27 (3), 205-29.

Kossinets, Gueorgi. 2006. Effects of missing data in social networks. *Social Networks*, 28 (3), 247-268.

Lai, Gina, and Odalia Wong. 2002. The tie effect on information dissemination: The spread of a commercial rumor in Hong Kong. *Social Networks*, 24 (1), 49-75.

Lazega, Emmanuel, and Philippa E. Pattison. 1999. Multiplexity, generalized exchange and cooperation in organizations: A case study. *Social Networks*, 21 (1), 67-90.

Licoppe, Christian, and Zbigniew Smoreda. 2005. Are social networks technologically embedded?: How networks are changing today with changes in communication technology. *Social Networks*, 27 (4), 317-335.

McDonald, John W., Peter W. F. Smith, and Jonathan J. Forster. 2007. Markov chain Monte Carlo exact inference for social networks. *Social Networks*, 29 (1), 127-136.

Mizruchi, Mark S., and Christopher Marquis. 2006. Egocentric, sociocentric, or dyadic?: Identifying the appropriate level of analysis in the study of organizational networks. *Social Networks,* 28 (3), 187-208.

Mok, Diana, and Barry Wellman. 2007. Did distance matter before the Internet?: Interpersonal contact and support in the 1970s. *Social Networks,* 29 (3), 430-461.

Morselli, Carlo, Cynthia Giguère, and Katia Petit. 2007. The efficiency/security trade-off in criminal networks. *Social Networks,* 29 (1), 143-153.

Nyblom, Jukka, Steve Borgatti, Juha Roslakka, and Mikko A. Salo. 2003. Statistical analysis of network data—an application to diffusion of innovation. *Social Networks,* 25 (2), 175-95.

Plickert, Gabriele, Rochelle R. Côté, and Barry Wellman. 2007. It's not who you know, it's how you know them: Who exchanges what with whom? *Social Networks,* 29 (3), 405-429.

Roberts, Jr., John M. 2002. Connections between A. K. Romney's analyses of endogamy and other developments in log-linear models and network analysis. *Social Networks,* 24 (3), 185-99.

Robins, Garry, Tom Snijders, Peng Wang, Mark Handcock, and Philippa Pattison. 2007. Recent developments in exponential random graph (p*) models for social networks. *Social Networks,* 29 (2), 192-215.

Salomé García Muñiz, Ana and Carmen Ramos Carvajal. 2006. Core/periphery structure models: An alternative methodological proposal. *Social Networks,* 28 (4), 442-448.

Sinclair, Philip A. 2007. A representation for the Mexican political networks. *Social Networks,* 29 (1), 81-92.

Sozański, Tadeusz. 2006. On the core of characteristic function games associated with exchange networks. *Social Networks,* 28 (4), 397-426.

Tutzauer, Frank. 2007. Entropy as a measure of centrality in networks characterized by path-transfer flow. *Social Networks,* 29 (2), 249-265.

Yamaguchi, Kazuo. 2000. Power in mixed exchange networks: A rational choice model. *Social Networks,* 22 (2), 93-121.

6

Biological Networks: Rainforests, Coral Reefs, and the Galapagos Islands

Sonia Kleindorfer
James G. Mitchell

Abstract

This chapter reviews and illustrates the scope and nature of network phenomena in biology. Biology remains the most extensive and complex information network on the planet. In this chapter, Kleindorfer and Mitchell examine the nature of biological networks, including their inherent stability and risks to their resilience. After a general introduction exploring networks and biological systems, this chapter reviews (1) the evolution of biological networks; (2) principles that govern biological networks; and (3) measures of stability, productivity, and efficiency in biological networks. The authors use examples from food (energy) transfer in rainforests and coral reefs, as well as the creation of a biological network through colonization in Darwin's Finches of the Galapagos Islands. Research shows that while large biological networks are inherently unstable, some are more stable than others.

Over the past few decades, rainforests and coral reefs have been a major focus of biological research, including research on biological networks (see Figure 6-1 and 6-2). Both systems are iconic, beautiful, highly productive, liable for impact and loss, and among the most rich and diverse ecosystems on Earth, and, finally, both are seen as microcosms for the fragility, robustness, and complexity of the entire biosphere. A growing portion of this research assesses the impact of human activity on these ecosystems and takes the viewpoint of biological network function.

Figures 6-1 and 6-2   Coral reef and rainforest: Both systems are among the most biodiverse on the planet, but their different underlying network structures make them susceptible to different risks of species extinction and collapse. Copyright (c) 2007 Gitanjali Katrak for the coral reef image taken off Kadmat Island in the Lakshadweep Islands, India (40m depth). Copyright (c) 2007 Bruce Farnsworth for the rainforest image taken near Tena, Ecuador.

Although rainforests and reefs are indeed similar in their high diversity and productivity, they behave differently due to a structural difference in their respective networks. There are sharp differences in the structure of their respective "trophic levels." Trophic levels refer to the chain of "who eats whom," with primary producers at the bottom of the chain, consumed by herbivores, omnivores, and predators, as well as detritus feeders that feed on the remains. Almost all the food production at the base of the coral reef food web is contributed by just three groups: (1) symbiotic microalgae inside the coral, (2) encrusting macroalgae in some parts of the coral reef lagoon and on dead coral, and (3) cyanobacterial microbes that grow on, over, and in all dead and some living surfaces. On the actively growing portion of the reef, almost all the production is due to the coral symbionts. The result is that the diversity as well as the productivity in coral reef ecosystems depends almost entirely on a single species, the symbiotic microalgae, which links with diversity found at the higher trophic levels (see Figure 6-3). In contrast, tropical rainforests have many primary producers at the bottom of the food chain, as shown by the broad base of the food web illustrated in Figure 6-4, and in some cases maximum diversity may be found at the level of primary producers.

 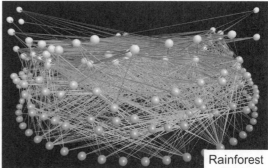

Figures 6-3 and 6-4   Caribbean Coral Reef Network (left image) and El Verde Rainforest Network (right image). Note the few primary producers (red dots) that sustain the entire coral reef network, compared with the many primary producers that sustain the rainforest network. The implication is that loss of a single primary producer will have a large effect on the network in a coral reef, but a small effect in a rainforest. Image produced with FoodWeb3D, written by R. J. Williams, and provided by the Pacific Ecoinformatics and Computational Ecology Lab (www.foodwebs.org, Yoon et al. 2004).

The rainforest ecosystem is more resilient in response to disruption than the coral reef. Loss of a single primary producer species from the bottom of the food web in a rainforest due to disease, competition, or subtle change in the physical environment has little effect on rainforest productivity and diversity. For coral reefs, the impact of such a loss is much greater. The loss of the symbiont species due to rising seawater temperature or attack by bacteria or the crown-of-thorns seastar is catastrophic, because both productivity and diversity are lost. In this case, the network decreases in size and stability, and may disappear completely. To date, such a reef network collapse has occurred only locally, but researchers are concerned that the collapses are increasing in size and frequency. Of course, these processes are more nuanced than presented here. For example, Halaj and Wise (2001) showed that the effects of productivity on food chain length are stronger in aquatic food webs than for terrestrial food webs, making a more complicated analysis of comparisons necessary.

At a basic level, coral reefs and rainforests both are tropical, and the vast majority of the ecosystem nutrients are stored in the organisms. In contrast, in temperate ecosystems the majority of nutrients are stored in the soil or dissolved in the water. This has a profound impact on the way the networks function and, in particular, how industrializing humans have approached the tropical networks. Because temperate nutrients are stored in soil and water, replacement of removed organisms can be achieved through reproduction of remaining organisms that draw nutrients from the environment. Thousands of years ago, this possibility led to agriculture and the idea of cropping. Since nutrients are stored in the organisms in tropical ecosystems, replacing removed organisms is slow or impossible. The general conclusion from these comparisons is that temperate systems have an extensive nutrient bank to draw on, whereas the nutrient savings in the tropics is nearly zero, despite the extensive diversity.

Biological Networks

Biological networks are the most pervasive and largest networks on the planet. Biology presents the most extensive and complex information network known, with at least 10^{31} individual genetic entities, some with as many as 10^{14} cells. Within each cell, there are 10^6 to 10^{10} bits of unique information. The processes of exchange, storage, and retrieval are organized into multiscale, nested, and clustered networks that range across spatial (molecular to planetary) and temporal (nanoseconds to millennia) scales (Newman et al. 2006; Buonomano 2007). Although many clusters of biological networks have no apparent link, they share the same information storage currency of DNA molecules. For this reason, disparate members of the network are capable of sharing information and are believed to have a common origin.

Biological networks form subsets of biological systems. Networks refer to pathways of energy and information transfer, while biological systems generally fulfill a specific function (for example, protein synthesis, reproduction, survival). Specifically, systems biology uses a quantitative approach to measure how its various components functionally interact across time (Aderem 2005). Networks denote associations between individual components within a system that have relationships or carry information (Milo et al. 2002; Newman et al. 2006). To illustrate the relationship between networks and systems, consider the example of neurons. Neurons interconnect to form a network that is part of and interacts with systems that carry out—for example—digestion, reproduction, respiration, and cognition (He, Chen, and Evans 2007; Kastner and McMains 2007; Roudi and Latham 2007).

Networks have attracted rising interest among biology researchers in the past decade. Citations for "Biology Systems" (in the ISI database) rose 400% between 1995 and 2005, from under 300 to more than 1,200; articles on "Biological Networks" rose 350% in the same period, from under 200 to more than 700.

There are many types of biological networks. Weitz, Benfey, and Wingreen (2007) provide a summary, which we briefly outline here. In addition to food webs, or "syntrophic" networks, types of biological networks include regulatory, sensory, and social.

All biological networks exchange information via pathways. In the case of food webs, the information exchange occurs via energy transfer, and is measured using mass (stored energy).

In this chapter, we consider the insights from food webs on network structure and stability, as well as insights on network evolution illustrated by range expansion of Darwin's finches (see Segel and Cohen 2001 and Mitchell 2006 for a further discussion of these ideas and examples). We conclude with a review of underlying principles that underpin these different networks and a brief consideration of potential implications for business.

Network Structure: What Determines Food Web Stability?

Food webs offer perspectives on one of the great and pervading puzzles in ecology: Why is species diversity and complexity so ubiquitous in nature (Gardner and Ashby 1970; May 1972; Pimm and Lawton 1977, Pimm 1984; Cohen, Briand, and Newman 1990; Neutel et al. 2007)? This question arises because of a surprising insight in the 1970s: Large networks are inherently unstable (Gardner and Ashby 1970; May 1972). Subsequently, biologists began to look at food webs in great detail and research focused on determining the stability of food webs (Dunne 2006). The significance of this work is clear 40 years later, as we strive to understand how food webs can be stabilized against damage and erosion of ecosystems.

As shown by rainforest and coral reef food webs, species interaction patterns are crucial for food web stability (Hairsto, Smith, and Slobodkin 1960; de Ruiter, Neutel, and Moore 1995; Martinez, Williams, and Dunne 2006). Research in the past decade has shown that trophic chains with long loops contain many weak links (McCann, Hastings, and Huxel 1998; Neutel et al. 2007). This enhances stability. McCann, Hastings, and Huxel (1998) showed the importance of weak links in dampening oscillations between consumers and resources. The weakness of the links creates stability by preventing a large change in one part of the network to propagate with the same effect throughout the network (Neutel, Heesterbeek, and Ruiter 2002). Having a diversity of predators in a food web also dampens trophic cascades and increases stability (Finke and Denno 2004).

Productivity is the rate at which resource is turned into a consumer (although the definition may vary slightly among biologists). Networks must be very productive to support many-leveled food chains, which are single consumer-consumed pathways from the bottom to the top of the food web (Moore, de Ruiter, and Hunt 1993). This is consistent with the biological principle that at each step in a food chain there is loss of material to waste and heat. Both theory and experiment have shown that it takes many plants to support a herbivore, many herbivores to support a carnivore, and so on (Kaunzinger and Morin 1998).

Food chain length also increases with ecosystem size, but not with productivity (Post, Pace, and Hairston 2000). Although the debate as to whether productivity or ecosystem size controls food chain length remains contentious, ecosystem size and productivity are linked variables, so they are just proxies from different viewpoints for resources. As ecosystem size increases, the total available production increases (Post, Pace, and Hairston 2000; Kaunzinger and Morin 1998). Feedback loops in food webs also influence productivity (Neutel et al. 2007).

The type of links also affects stability. Removing top predators is an effective means of destabilizing food webs (Rooney et al. 2006). An important factor in coupling-driven stability is that the channels of energy flow are strongly asymmetrical. This is consistent with most predator behavior, in which there is a primary food source supplemented by various secondary food sources.

Weak interactions are the stabilizers and strong interactions the destabilizers of food webs. In some circles in the late twentieth century, small may have been considered "beautiful," but in the early twenty-first century, we can say that small is "important." A species or interaction that appears insignificant today might be crucial tonight or next year.

There also appears to be a trade-off between efficiency and robustness in network structure (Pascual and Dunne 2006). In biological systems, individual organisms are not necessarily efficient per se; some are "sloppy eaters." Scavenging takes place all the way down to the molecular scale, where microbes break down the smallest particles. In some sense, there is no natural ecological waste because every organic molecule has utility. In general, in the face of random failures of nodes or links in a network, scale-free networks are far more robust than random networks because they retain their structural characteristics (Mitchell 2006). Network biologists attempt to identify systems that are particularly vulnerable to failure—that is, networks that show low robustness. It is not immediately clear, however, whether high robustness in biological networks is associated with low efficiency.

Network Evolution

Among the attributes of biological networks are their longevity, pervasiveness, impact, and that they evolve. As Dobzhansky (1973) famously stated: "Nothing in biology makes sense except in the light of evolution." Although researchers at least as far back as Darwin have shown that species evolve, the question that network biologists must now ask is this: Do networks of species evolve? And if so, how?

Evolution can be precisely defined as the change in the frequency of alleles across generations (Futuyma 2005). Adaptive evolution refers to a change in population gene frequency via natural or sexual selection; nonadaptive evolution is neutral. (The change in allele frequency is caused by mutation, recombination, or genetic drift.) In biology, the systems are responsive and adaptive with a general trend to increasing complexity over time (for example, single-celled to multicelled organisms; number of trophic levels). Is the same true for biological networks? Observations to date suggest that networks also increase in complexity, from prokaryotes to multicellular eukaryotes. But there is little evidence that this increase in network complexity is driven by adaptive processes. In the most comprehensive review of the issues to date, Lynch (2007) concludes that transcriptional genetic pathways do evolve—however, their evolution is neutral and not adaptive. As Lynch concludes: "Contrary to widespread belief, there is no compelling empirical or theoretical evidence that complexity, modularity, redundancy, or other features of genetic pathways are promoted by natural selection" (p. 810). Genetic variation is generally considered a key feature of resilience in biological populations. Network variation appears to be achieved—at least in part—by random processes of mutation, recombination, and genetic drift. The resultant pathways then set the stage for novel solutions for information transfer.

Biologists frequently refer to the evolution of networks (Weitz, Benfey, and Wingreen 2007). In biology, evolution is measured as a change in the frequency of genotypes in a population (genotype = all alleles), but selection occurs at the level of the phenotype (alleles that are expressed in an individual). So, what are biologists measuring when they study the evolution of networks? Weitz, Benfey, and Wingreen (2007) offer two answers: (1) biological fitness that is network-dependent, whereby selection acts to optimize across a landscape of networks, and (2) density-dependent selection for particular network (pheno-) types. Optimization or game-theoretical models will no doubt provide useful insights into changes in network phenotype—but how do we measure network genotype?

One framework to address the multitude of "correct" answers to a single question in biology is offered by the Nobel Prize winner in ethology Niko Tinbergen. Tinbergen (1963) proposed the "four categories of explanation" for animal behavior. Accordingly, we can examine (1) function or survival value; (2) causation (for example, cue or mechanism), (3) ontogeny (development), and (4) evolutionary history or phylogeny (such as, shared ancestry). Both function and phylogeny are "ultimate" explanations, whereas both mechanism and ontogeny are "proximate" explanations. We can conclude from this framework that systems biologists work at the ultimate/functional level, and network biologists at the proximate level (signals, cues, ontogeny). The distinction between levels of analysis, so widely applied in studies of behavioral ecology, may be useful in the study of biological networks.

Innovation Versus Imitation

Both innovation and imitation contribute to evolution. Innovation of genotypes can be viewed as a two-step process: (1) increasing genetic variation, and (2) selection for particular "solutions" (phenotypes). The sources of genetic variation are—to a large extent—random, and occur through mutation, genetic recombination (sexual reproduction), and genetic drift. Note, however, that mate choice (sexual selection) leads to non-random mating, but the process of genetic reshuffling during reproduction is random. Selection, as outlined previously, is either adaptive or nonadaptive. The key point here is that biological systems are not goal-oriented, and that success (survival) is dependent on the combination of random and nonrandom processes.

Imitation is important because it can potentially decrease genetic variation, for example, through nonrandom mating (and hence increase the speed of evolution), but also increase genetic variation through copying errors. Examples of imitation in biology include mate copying, habitat copying, and the spread of culture (for example, food preparation in macaque monkeys; use of tools by chimpanzees). Bird song is a good example to highlight how imitation may decrease or increase genetic variation. Many songbirds learn their song from a tutor (usually the father). In most birds, the males sing and females use song in mate choice. Through imprinting on the father's song, sons will sing a paternal song, and daughters will prefer a mate that sings a song resembling her paternal song (but will avoid an identical song). Such a process promotes species recognition and reproductive isolation, and hence reduces genetic variation. However, if the father dies during the nesting period, both son and daughter can misimprint on the song of a neighbor who may be a different species. Such misimprinting often leads to hybridization for both the son and the daughter after fledging (reviewed in Grant 1999), and hence increases genetic variation. This new source of genetic variation then sets the stage for selection to act on the novel combinations of genes.

Darwin's Finches: How Can Island Systems Inform Network Biology?

Darwin's Finches are a textbook example of adaptive radiation (Grant and Grant 2008), and a model organism to examine the role of islands in speciation processes. Island systems have not yet been examined in relation to biological networks. Do network structures that operate in island versus mainland systems differ? Island studies in ecology have played a key role in the advancement of speciation and extinction models. Perhaps they will also play an important role in understanding the role of network invasion and compatibility to examine survival or extinction of network types.

In addition to different conditions for island speciation that are largely shaped by nonrandom colonization and exploitation of vacant niches, island systems are particularly vulnerable to risk of extinction (Bennett and Owens 2002). This is well supported by the literature. There has been a shift in island versus mainland extinction outcomes over the past centuries: Until the nineteenth century, 88% of extinctions were reported for islands (driven by introduced predators and disease), whereas now, 46% of extinctions are reported for island systems. Mainland extinction is largely driven by habitat loss (Bennett and Owens 2002). The expansion of human systems across the globe could be usefully examined using a network paradigm that highlights compatible and incompatible human social and economic networks in relation to conservation outcomes and sustainable resource management frameworks (reviewed in Berkes 2002).

Recent Observation: A Darwin Finch Species "Fills a Niche"

Oscillating evolutionary dynamics are a hallmark of Darwin's Finches (Boag and Grant 1981; Price and Grant 1984; Gibbs and Grant 1987; Grant and Grant 1989, 2002). The well-described oscillating dynamics are driven primarily by climatic patterns and the correlated effects of rainfall on seed abundance and seed hardness. Prize-winning research carried out by Peter and Rosemary Grant and colleagues across 35+ years has shown that changes in rainfall and interaction effects with seed dormancy determine seed size, hardness, and abundance, which in turn select for beak size (reviewed in Grant and Grant 2008). Beak size is highly heritable and is strongly correlated with survival under particular ecological conditions. These seminal studies on variation in beak shape and nonrandom survival in Ground Finches were conducted on low and flat islands. In 2000, Kleindorfer et al. (2006) launched a study of clinal variation in beak length in Darwin's Small Ground Finch, *Geospiza fuliginosa,* on an elevated island. (Clinal variation is a gradual change of a character or phenotype in a species over a geographical area.) The period from 2000 onward was characterized by significant and prolonged drought. Our research showed strong selection for beak shape and—notably—population invasion across clines within an elevated island (Kleindorfer et al. 2006; Sulloway and Kleindorferforthcoming). In essence, we have shown evolution by a combined process of adaptation and character displacement using the following series of observations on Santa Cruz Island: First, a niche opened up on this island following the extinction of a highland ground finch species, the Sharp Beaked Ground Finch (*G. difficilis*) by about 1930 (Harris 1973; Sulloway 1982)—this bird had a long beak and long foot span. In the wake of this extinction, *G. fuliginosa* expanded its range into the highlands sometime after the 1960s. Prior to then, breeding was reported only for the lowlands (Lack 1947; Bowman 1961; Curio 1969). By 2000, the highland form of *G. fuliginosa* had evolved a long beak and a small foot span, in contrast to the lowland form, which retained the previous morphology. Following the drought that began in 2001, lowland birds with long toes began to invade the highlands in search of food and water. By 2005, highland birds had evolved an even longer beak as well as a longer foot span more similar to that of *G. difficilis*, the extinct form that disappeared around 1930. In short, it took about 75 years for an existing species of Darwin's Finches to evolve in such a way as to "fill the empty niche" created by the extinction of the Sharp Beaked Ground Finch, a process that included adaptive radiation into a vacant niche as well as "character displacement" set in motion by competition between two different clinal variants of the same species that ultimately filled this niche (see Figure 6-5).

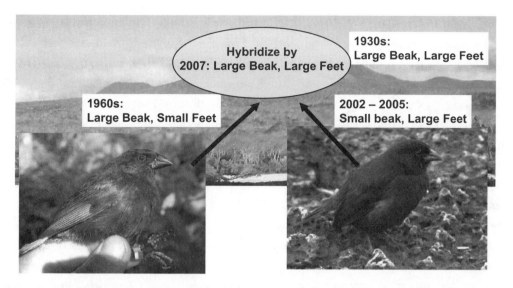

Figure 6-5 Highland (left) and Lowland (right) Small Ground Finches on Santa Cruz Island, Galapagos Archipelago. Arrows indicate possible patterns of range expansion by Small Ground Finches over the past decades following extinction of the highland Sharp Beaked Ground Finch in the 1930s. Sharp Beaked Ground Finches occurred in the highlands and had long beaks and long toes. By 2007, the Small Ground Finches in the highlands also had long beaks and long toes. (Note: The image shows Cerra Pajas volcano on Floreana Island for the purpose of illustration of an elevated island landscape).

Species Invasions: Short-Term Impacts Can Be Huge

Currently, the Galapagos Islands harbor a human population of about 30,000 and are visited by more than 150,000 tourists per year. Only two islands (San Cristobal and Floreana) have a freshwater source. Mostly due to difficult conditions for human habitation (including the lack of fresh water or industry), cargo boats arrive almost daily to the central Santa Cruz Island laden with fruits, vegetables, and supplies. Given this high level of human and cargo mobility from the mainland, Santa Cruz Island may be the source for most introduced organisms to the Galapagos Archipelago (discussed in Wiedenfeld et al. 2007)—despite the efforts of a quarantine system (see also Wikelski et al. 2004; Causton et al. 2006). Currently, 45% of plants (Mauchamp 1997), 23% of insects (Causton et al. 2006), and 14% of birds (Wiedenfeld 2006) are introduced to the Galapagos Islands.

Darwin's Finches are both directly and indirectly affected by introduced organisms. Blood-sucking larvae of the introduced fly *Philornis downsi* are the biggest current threat to Darwin's Finches and cause 19% to 100% total brood mortality across years (Fessl and Tebbich 2002; Dudaniec and Kleindorfer 2006; Fessl et al. 2006a,b). The introduced fly is also implicated in the local extinction of Darwin's Warbler Finch by 2004 (Grant et al. 2005). Introduced predators, like rats, cats, and dogs, also destroy many bird nests (Kleindorfer 2007a). Indirect effects from introduced organisms include the massive destruction of *Opuntia* cacti by rats, feral goats, and donkeys (Curry 1986; Hicks and Mauchamp 1995; Carrion et al. 2007), which are the preferred nesting substrate of the Ground Finches (Grant 1999; Fessl et al. 2006a; Kleindorfer 2007b). On Floreana Island, where most *Opuntia* cacti have been destroyed by introduced donkeys and rats, nest predation was fivefold higher than on Santa Cruz Island, where 97% of birds nested in cacti protected by spines (Kleindorfer 2007b).

As Grant and Grant (2008) conclude, "Food supply, habitat requirements, and competition have guided the development of the whole terrestrial avian community" on the Galapagos Islands (p. 135). Presently, habitat loss and introduced pathogens are the main changes affecting the Galapagos ecosystem and avian community in particular. Both influences are occurring at a large scale over a short period. Natural selection will no doubt lead to evolution in response to such massive impacts—and ultimately to speciation and extinction. For the present, the most appropriate network approach for the Galapagos Islands is that of integrated conservation management across different levels of complexity, both ecological and social (Berkes and Folke 1998; Berkes 2002).

Conclusions: Biology and Business

While biological networks are distinct from business networks, a few insights from the study of biology can raise important questions in considering business networks.

- *Consider adaptation*—Biological networks can be created through nonadaptive processes including mutation, recombination, and genetic drift. It is a mistake to assume that all networks arose through adaptive processes of natural or sexual selection. Similarly, business networks may also result from a combination of systematic adaptation and random mutation and drift. This can lead to the emergence of standards (such as the QWERTY keyboard) that define subsequent evolution of products and companies. Managers need to consider the role of systematic evolution and these chance mutations. Consumer use of cellphone pads to send text messages (not a primary function designed into early phones designed for voice) or using the Internet can change the future direction of industries. Interestingly, Ron Adner and Daniel Levinthal (2000) use the biological term "speciation" to describe dramatic shifts in the evolution of technologies and markets. For example, they note that the Internet existed for many years as a tool for the military and academic researchers. But the relatively minor technological innovation of the Web browser changed the nature of the Internet—creating a new "species" of business tool. Managers need to recognize that networks evolve, be aware of the process of evolution, and understand how they can affect it or respond to it.

- *Understand network behavior*—The four-question framework proposed by Niko Tinbergen may be usefully applied to studies of behavior in biological networks, as well as social networks in business:

    Function or survival value—How is the behavior of consumers and other players in the network based on function or survival? For example, Maslow's hierarchy (ranging from basic needs to higher-level desires and aspirations) is a foundation of work in marketing. How does function or survival shape behavior within networks in business?

    Causation (cue or mechanism)—What are the cues or mechanisms that lead to behavior? In business, these cues have been studied extensively in areas such as marketing or negotiations. How can companies influence the behavior of members of the network?

    Development (ontogeny)—How does the developmental stage of the network or individuals within the network affect their behavior? Networks in business behave differently at different stages, from the more ad hoc networks seen in early-stage ventures to the more structured networks of mature organizations. Social networks also go through stages, from the early and unstable formative networks (such as the many dot-com companies that tried and failed to gain traction) to those more highly developed networks (such as eBay) that are more stable and persistent.

    Evolutionary history or phylogeny (shared ancestry)—Every company and network in business is a product of history and relationships. For example, the shared ancestry of Microsoft and Intel in computers (dominating operating systems and chip design) helped to ensure the phenomenal success of both companies. By studying evolutionary history of their industries, managers may gain insight into opportunities to build on shared ancestry or to overcome problems resulting from their evolutionary history.

- **Be aware of randomness**—In decentralized autonomous networks, randomness and probabilities are essential (exploration, risk, sampling) with a continuous interplay of bottom-up and top-down processes. Managers need to understand this interplay, and work from both the bottom up and top down to influence the evolution of their own networks. They can recognize positive variations that percolate up from the bottom, and drive changes from the top.

- **Size is related to productivity**—By increasing ecosystem size, researchers have experimentally increased available productivity. In general, ecosystem size is a proxy for productivity. Similarly, managers need to consider the impact of the size of a business network on productivity. When do networks reach a critical mass? Given the importance of size, should the company put more resources into building the network in its early stages? For example, companies may sacrifice profit to build market share, with the goal of creating a larger and more productive network.

- **Balance strong and weak links**—The persistence of species diversity and complexity appears to be maintained by having many "weak links" and few "strong links." Managers need to consider the optimal mix of strong links and weak. This may have serious implications for resource allocations. Where should the company invest in forging strong links? How can the company ensure enough weak links so that the network has requisite diversity?

Key questions for the future (modified from Weitz, Benfey, and Wingreen 2007) include these: How does network structure influence and reflect the process of evolution? How do we measure biological resilience? How do we measure signals and what is the effect of noise? How do organisms with a given type of network invade another system? What systems level properties emerge? Although many questions about networks remain, biology has a long head start over business in examining such challenges. This research may offer insights on the dynamics of networks—or at least help raise the right questions—for managers wrestling with the structure and evolution of their own networks.

Acknowledgments

We thank the Santa Fe Institute for use of the network images, and Jennifer Dunne for insightful comments. SK thanks the Galapagos National Park Service and the Charles Darwin Research Station for the opportunity to work on the Galapagos Islands. Field work was funded by Flinders University, Max Planck Institute for Ornithology, Austrian Academy of Sciences, Conservation International, American Bird Conservancy, and the Galapagos Conservation Fund. TAME airlines provided reduced airfare to the Galapagos. JM thanks the Australian Research Council for financial support.

References

Aderem, A. 2005. Systems biology: its practice and challenges. Cell 121, 511-13.

Adner, R., and D. A. Levinthal. 2000. Technology speciation and the path of emerging technologies. *Wharton on Managing Emerging Technologies*, G. Day and P. J. H. Schoemaker, eds., John Wiley & Sons, 57-75.

Bennett, P. M., and I. P. F. Owens. 2002. *Evolutionary Ecology of Birds: Life Histories, Mating Systems, and Extinction*. Oxford University Press.

Berkes, F. 2002. Cross-scale institutional linkages: Perspectives from the bottom up. In *The Drama of the Commons*, ed. E. Ostrom, T. Dietz, N. Dolsak, P. C. Stern, S. Stonich, and E. U. Weber, 293-321. Washington, DC: National Academy Press.

Berkes, F., and C. Folke, eds. 1998. *Linking Social and Ecological Systems. Management Practices and Social Mechanisms for Building Resilience*. Cambridge University Press.

Boag, P. T., and P. R. Grant. 1981. Intense natural selection in a population of Darwin's finches (Geospizinae) in the Galápagos. Science 214, 82-85.

Bowman, R. I. 1961. Morphological differentiation and adaptation in the Galapagos Finches. University of California Publications in Zoology 58, 1-302.

Buonomano, D. V. 2007. The biology of time across different scales. Nature Chemical Biology 3 (10), 594-7.

Carrion, V., C. Donlan, K. Campbell, C. Lavoie, and F. Cruz. 2007. Feral donkey *(Equus asinus)* eradications in the Galápagos. Biodiversity and Conservation 16, 437?445.

Causton, C. E., S. B. Peck, B. J. Sinclair, L. Roque-Albelo, C. J. Hodgson, and B. Landry. 2006. Alien insects: Threats and implications for conservation of Galápagos Islands. Annual Review of the Entomological Society of America 99, 121-143.

Cohen, J. E., F. Briand, and C. M. Newman. 1990. *Community Food Webs: Data and Theory*. Berlin: Springer.

Curio, E. 1969. Funktionsweise und Stammesgeschichte des Flugfeinderkennens einiger Darwinfinken (Geospizinae). Zeitung für Tierpsychologie 26, 394-487.

Curry, R. L. 1986. Whatever happened to the Floreana Mockingbird? Noticias de Galápagos 43, 13-15.

de Ruiter, P. C., A. M. Neutel, and J. C. Moore. 1995. Energetics, patterns of interaction strengths, and stability in real ecosystems. Science 269, 1257-1260.

Dobzhansky, T. 1973. Nothing in biology makes sense except in the light of evolution. American Biology Teacher 35, 125-129.

Dudaniec, R. Y., and S. Kleindorfer. 2006. The effects of the parasitic flies of the genus *Philornis* (Diptera: Muscidae) on birds. Emu 106, 13-20.

Dunne, J. A. 2006. The network structure of food webs. In Ecological *Networks: Linking Structure to Dynamics in Food Webs,* 27-86. Oxford University Press.

Fessl, B., and S. Tebbich. 2002. *Philornis downsi*—a recently discovered parasite on the Galapagos Archipelago—a threat for Darwin's finches? Ibis 144, 445-451.

Fessl, B., S. Kleindorfer, and S. Tebbich. 2006a. An experimental study on the effects of an introduced parasite in Darwin's finches. Biological Conservation 127, 55-61.

Fessl, B., B. Sinclair, and S. Kleindorfer. 2006b. The life-cycle of *Philornis downsi* (Diptera: Muscidae) parasitizing Darwin's finches and its impacts on nestling survival. Parasitology 133, 739-747.

Finke, D. L., and R. F. Denno. 2004 Predator diversity dampens trophic cascades. Nature 429, 407-410.

Futuyma, D. J., ed. 2005. *Evolution.* Sunderland, MA: Sinauer Associates, Inc.

Gardner, M. R., and W. R. Ashby. 1970. Connectance of large dynamic (cybernetic) systems: critical values for stability. Nature 21, 784.

Gibbs, H. L., and P. R. Grant. 1987. Adult survival in Darwin's ground finch *(Geospiza)* populations in a variable environment. Journal of Animal Ecology 56, 797-813.

Grant, B. R., and P. R. Grant. 1989. *Evolutionary Dynamics of a Natural Population.* University of Chicago Press.

Grant, P. R. 1999. *Ecology and Evolution of Darwin's Finches.* Reprint edition. Princeton University Press.

Grant, P. R., and B. R. Grant. 2002. Unpredictable evolution in a 30-year study of Darwin's finches. Science 296, 707-711.

Grant, P. R., and B. R. Grant. 2008. *How and Why Species Multiply: The Radiation of Darwin's Finches.* Princeton University Press.

Grant, P. R., B. R. Grant, K. Petren, and L. F. Keller. 2005. Extinction behind our backs: the possible fate of one of the Darwin's finch species on Isla Floreana, Galápagos. Biological Conservation 122, 499-503.

Hairston, N. G. Sr., F. E. Smith, and L. B. Slobodkin. 1960. Community structure, population control, and competition. American Naturalist 142, 379-411.

Halaj, J., and D. T. Wise. 2001. Terrestrial trophic cascades: how much do they trickle? American Naturalist 157, 262-281.

Harris, M. P. 1973. The Galapagos avifauna. Condor 75, 265-278.

He, Y., Z. J. Chen, and A. C. Evans. 2007. Small-world anatomical networks in the human brain revealed by cortical thickness from MRI. Cerebral Cortex 17, 2407-2419.

Hicks, D. J., and A. Mauchamp. 1995. Size dependent predation by feral mammal on Galápagos Opuntia. Noticias de Galápagos 55, 15-17.

Kastner, S., and S. A. McMains. 2007. Out of the spotlight: face to face with attention. Nature Neuroscience 10, 1344-1345.

Kaunzinger, C. M. K., and P. J. Morin. 1998. Productivity controls food-chain properties in microbial communities. Nature 395, 495-497.

Kleindorfer, S. 2007a. Nesting success in Darwin's small tree finch (*Camarhynchus parvulus*): Evidence of female preference for older males and more concealed nests. Animal Behaviour 74, 795-804.

Kleindorfer, S. 2007b. The ecology of clutch size variation in Darwin's Small Ground Finch, *Geospiza fuliginosa:* Comparison between low- and highland habitats. Ibis 149, 730-741.

Kleindorfer, S., T. Chapman, H. Winkler, and F. J. Sulloway. 2006. Adaptive divergence in contiguous populations of Darwin's small ground finch (*Geospiza fuliginosa*). Evolutionary Ecology Research 8(2), 357-372.

Lack, D. 1947. *Darwin's Finches.* Cambridge: Cambridge University Press.

Lynch, M. 2007. The evolution of genetic networks by non-adaptive processes. Nature Reviews Genetics 8, 803-813.

Martinez, N. D., R. J. Williams, and J. A. Dunne. 2006. Diversity, complexity, and persistence in large model ecosystems. In Ecological *Networks: Linking Structure to Dynamics in Food Webs*, 163-185. Oxford University Press.

Mauchamp, A. 1997. Threats from alien species in the Galápagos Islands. Conservation Biology 11, 260-263.

May, R. M. 1972. Will a large complex system be stable? Nature 238, 413-414.

McCann, K., A. G. Hastings, and R. Huxel. 1998. Weak trophic interactions and the balance of nature. Nature 395, 794-798.

Milo, R., S. Shen-Orr, S. Itzkovitz, N. Kashtan, D. Chklovskii, and U. Alon. 2002. Network motifs: Simple building blocks of complex networks. Science 25, 824-827.

Mitchell, M. 2006. Complex systems: Network thinking. *Artificial Intelligence* 170(18), 1194-1212.

Moore, J. C., P. C. de Ruiter, and H. W. Hunt. 1993. Influence of productivity on the stability of real and model ecosystems. Science 261, 906-908.

Neutel, A. M., J. A. P. Heesterbekk, J. van de Koppel, G. Hoenderboom, A. Vos, C. Kaldeway, F. Berendse, and P. C. de Ruiter. 2007. Reconciling complexity with stability in naturally assembling food webs. Nature 449, 599-602.

Neutel, A. M., J. A. P. Heesterbeek, and P. C. de Ruiter. 2002. Stability in real food webs: weak links in long loops. Science 296, 1120-1123.

Newman, M. E. J., A. L. Barabasi, and D. J. Watts, eds. 2006. *The Structure and Dynamics of Networks.* Princeton University Press.

Pascual, M. and J. A. Dunne, eds. 2006. *Ecological Networks: Linking Structure to Dynamics in Food Webs.* Oxford University Press.

Pimm, S. L. 1984. The complexity and stability of ecosystems. Nature 307, 321-326.

Pimm, S. L., and J. H. Lawton. 1977. Number of trophic levels in ecological communities. Nature 268, 329-331.

Post, D. M., M. L. Pace, and N. G. Hairston. 2000. Ecosystem size determines food-chain length in lakes. Nature 405, 1047-1049.

Price, T. D., and P.R. Grant. 1984. Life history traits and natural selection for small body size in a population of Darwin's Finches. *Evolution,* 38: 483-494.

Rooney, N., K. McCann, G. Gellner, and J. C. Moore. 2006. Structural asymmetry and the stability of diverse food webs. Nature 442, 265-269.

Roudi, Y., and P. E. Latham. 2007. Balanced memory network. PloS Computational Biology 3, 141.

Segel, L. A., and I. R. Cohen, eds. 2001. *Design Principles for the Immune System and Other Distributed Autonomous Systems.* Oxford University Press.

Sulloway, F. J. 1982. The *Beagle* collections of Darwin's finches (Geospizinae). Bulletin of the British Museum of Natural History (Zoology) 43, 49-94.

Sulloway, F. J., and S. Kleindorfer (forthcoming). Selection along a clinal gradient: Evidence for adaptive divergence in Darwin's Small Ground Finch *(Geospiza fuliginosa).* Philosophical Transactions of the Royal Society B: Biological Sciences.

Tinbergen, N. 1963. On aims and methods in ethology. Zeitschrift für Tierpsychologie 20, 410-433.

Weitz, J. S., P. N. Benfey, and N. S. Wingreen. 2007. Evolution, Interactions, and Biological Networks. PloS Biology.

Wiedenfeld, D. A. 2006. Aves, The Galápagos Islands, Ecuador. Check List 2, 1-27.

Wiedenfeld, D. A., G. A. Jiménez, B. Fessl, S. Kleindorfer, and J. C. Valarezo. 2007. Distribution of the introduced parasitic fly *Philornis downsi* (Diptera, Muscidae) in the Galápagos Islands. Pacific Conservation Biology 13, 14-19.

Wikelski, M., J. Foufopoulos, H. Vargas, and H. Snell. 2004. Galápagos birds and diseases: invasive pathogens as threats for island species. Ecology and Society 9 (1), article 5. www.ecologyandsociety.org/vol9/iss1/art5 (accessed: 24.09.07).

Yoon, I., R. J. Williams, E. Levine, S. Yoon, J. A. Dunne, and N. D. Martinez. 2004. Webs on the Web (WoW): 3D visualization of ecological networks on the WWW for collaborative research and educations. Proceeding of the IS&T/SPIE Symposium on Electronic Imaging, Visualization and Data Analysis 5295:124-132.

7

Information Networks in the History of Life

Robert Giegengack
Yvette Bordeaux

Abstract

What can we learn about networks from ants, honeybees, and other animals with evolved social structures? The impact of information and communications strategies on network dynamics did not arrive with the emergence of computers, cellphones, and the Internet. In this chapter, we describe communication networks selected from among many that have been studied in communities of nonhuman organisms. We explore the extent to which communication linkages have controlled the development of those networks. In some of those networks, developmental histories are manifest as evolved body plans and gender roles not represented in human communities. Many of those networks are founded on efficient exchange of information via pathways of which humans are almost fully oblivious.

Insect colonies and other biological communities demonstrate highly developed networks and communications systems. We know from subterranean nests preserved as fossils that, as early as 50 million years ago, colonies of so-called *leaf-cutter* ants had learned to harvest leaves from specific trees and process those leaves to form a growth substrate on which the ants cultivate fungi that represent their principal source of food. Specialist ants, distinguished by task-specific evolved body types, transport the leaves to extensive underground nest chambers; inoculate the processed growth substrate with fecal droplets containing both viable spores of a specific fungus and a chemical cocktail of inhibitors to the growth of pathogens that would adversely affect the growth of that fungus; and manage those underground fungus gardens. Other specialists within the ant colony maintain the nests, each of which may support millions of individuals, and protect the nests from predators. (An extensive literature treats the behavior and evolution of leaf-cutter ants; for example: Weber, 1972; Speight, Watt, and Hunter, 1999; Hölldobler and Wilson, 2009.)

In some tropical forests, the activity of leaf-cutter ants represents 20% of the carbon that is transferred from the leaf canopy to the soil. Students of these intriguing animals have established that the fungi cultivated by leaf-cutter ants have become so dependent on the mutualism represented by that adaptation that the spores cannot grow on a culture medium that has not been processed by the ants, and that the ants cannot subsist on any other food. Leaf-cutter ants have evolved specific body plans among the ants who maintain the fungus garden: a leaf-cutter ant colony includes a reproductive female, or queen; a male ant who contributes sperm to the egg-laying process for the life of the queen; foraging workers who disperse into the forest to collect the leaves; at least four quite distinct classes ("subcastes")of gardening ants; and a specialized cohort of "soldier ants," large insects with massive mandibles, whose only role is to protect the ant colony from other groups of ants, or other animals, who would disturb the nest or steal its food sources.

Ants "invented" agriculture, and developed social institutions to manage that industry, at least as early as 50 million years before humans learned to grow food crops in close proximity to their "nests." Curiously, the earliest known manifestation of agriculture, the cultivation of parasitic fungi on prepared underground substrata, did not directly use photosynthesis from sunlight.

Other groups of ants have learned to capture and "herd" species of aphids that feed on plant juices and manufacture and excrete a substance known as *honeydew*. Honeydew is harvested by honeybees in time of dearth of their regular supplies of nectar, but the honeydew represents the principal diet of the ants that control herds of aphids and protect those herds from other insect predators. (Some aphid-herding ants also eat whole aphids from time to time, thereby adding much-needed protein to their primarily carbohydrate diet.) The fossil record is not as clear on the practice of aphid herding as it is on the origin of fungus gardening, but it is clear that species of ants invented animal husbandry long before humans domesticated their first dog.

What can we learn from the social insects? Philosophers from Plato and Aristotle to Marx and Lenin have invoked the honeybee colony as the exemplar of an efficient, socially integrated, utopian society that manages available resources for the benefit of the entire community. Organizations have adopted the beehive as an iconic representation of their perceived mission (for example, a beehive is the central symbol on the state flag of Utah, under the word "industry"). Science fiction film writers (for example, the *Aliens* sequence, 1979–1997) have modeled the social structure of extraterrestrial communities after the presumed social hierarchy of social insects, offering the suggestion, not explicitly advanced in the films, that the social structure of insects represents the organizational structure that will govern successful human communities of the future.

Other chapters in this book examine the complex system of internal communication linkages within the global human community. The geometry of this network is complicated and fluid, responsive to the changing needs of its users. While engaging humans as its operators, this network is not a human "invention" in the sense that the computer was invented, or even that individual software packages have been invented. It is a system of hard and soft mechanisms, linkages, media, and idioms that have been put in service spontaneously, in constantly changing configurations, in response to specific opportunities as they arise, and subsequently refined and formally codified as the utility of different combinations became apparent. This communication network is an essential aspect of the human condition, but it is not a recent invention. With the earliest trade among humans, which began locally but became regional early in human prehistory, specialized technologies emerged to keep track of commodities being traded, to assess the value of those commodities, and to advertise the availability of those commodities to those who sought them. The earliest examples of human writing seem to be mundane inventories of goods traded and records of commercial transactions.

But these networks are not restricted to human societies. Those who study communication strategies within groups of animals have learned that even organisms that we choose to characterize as "primitive" benefit from the evolved capacity to exchange both materials and information among individuals. Much of this communication is carried on outside the range of human perception and, in many cases, via communication media for which we have evolved no sensory organ.

In this chapter, we will undertake to show that complex communication networks long predate the emergence of the human species and, indeed, have probably been a feature of life on Earth since its inception around 3.7 billion years ago. Communication networks are so securely established within the biosphere that many of them have found expression, via evolutionary processes, in the body plans of fossil and modern organisms. To that extent, the process whereby this network developed is analogous to the biologic processes we characterize as Darwinian evolution.

Senses and Network Communication

Networks of humans and other creatures communicate information through their senses—often remarkably well developed for their specific needs. Among ants, for example, the practice of both fungus gardening and aphid maintenance requires cohorts of highly specialized individuals who carry out the tasks necessary to maintain those food sources in a constantly changing environment. To sustain the host colony, both fungus gardens and aphid nurseries must be managed, and such management requires the exchange of information among the farmers and the consumers. Among ants, most such information is exchanged via release of pheromone molecules that apparently carry a great deal of information. It has become apparent that aphid-herding ants have developed the ability to communicate directly with the aphids they maintain and protect by laying down pheromone barriers that the aphids choose not to cross. The herding task is thus rendered more efficient, and protection of the aphids from other predators is enhanced. Communication within biological networks draws upon the senses of sight, hearing, smell, and touch. We consider each of these senses.

The Sense of Sight

Humans communicate via organs that receive and interpret electromagnetic radiation within the very narrow range of frequencies that we characterize as the "visible spectrum" (0.4 to 0.7 nanometers). Not coincidentally, this is the range of frequencies of the peak of radiation emitted by our Sun; our eyes evolved to take advantage of the strongest electromagnetic signal. Other groups of animals receive and interpret visual signals at short-wave ultraviolet (UV) frequencies (<0.4 nanometers) that we cannot process, and at the long-wave infrared (IR) frequencies (>0.7 nanometers) at which warm-blooded animals emit radiation (~10 micrometers).

Thus, honeybees respond to patterns on flower petals, invisible to us, but visible to them in the near UV (for example, Menzel and Backhaus, 1990); those patterns guide them to the nectaries of those flowers. The class of snakes known as pit vipers, and some lizards, have developed specialized skin cells on their faces that collect and focus long-wave IR radiation emitted by prey animals; apparently, their "primitive" brains process the neurological signals collected by these sensory cells and construct three-dimensional images of the size, shape, and location of potential prey animals in what we would characterize as total darkness (for example, Sichert, Friedel, and van Hemmen 2006).

CHAPTER 7 • INFORMATION NETWORKS IN THE HISTORY OF LIFE

Certain groups of tropical frogs concentrate in their bodies toxins acquired from the insects they eat; those toxins render the frogs distasteful, or in some cases poisonous, to would-be predators. Many of those frogs have developed bright surface pigmentation, the opposite of camouflage, to "warn" would-be predators to leave them alone. That aversion response must represent an evolutionary adaptation rather than a learned response, because a frog that had been injured before being rejected by a predator, or a frog who had poisoned the predator who ingested it, would not be likely to pass its warning coloration on to another generation. Other frogs, who do not concentrate toxins in their bodies, have also evolved bright colors to benefit from the adaptive aversion acquired by predators.

Ranchers in the American west are able to leave fences open where they cross motor roads by installing, in the roadbed, so-called "cattle guards," arrays of rails or pipes separated by cavities that cattle decline to cross. In parts of California, where cattle are either more intelligent or more gullible, cattle guards are simply painted on paved roads, and are fully effective as visible warnings of imaginary barriers.

The Sense of Hearing

Human hearing is sensitive to pulsed signals that cause membranes in our hearing apparatus to vibrate across a broad range of frequencies: from 15 to 20,000 cycles per second (Hz). But bats send and receive information at much higher frequencies, which they use both to communicate with each other and to sense the size and location of flying prey insects. The twittering we hear from a group of roosting bats is the exchange of information ("good morning…nice to *echolocate* you," or "move over—you're crowding me…") at the lowest frequencies they can utter, just within the upper range of human hearing. Baleen whales, toothed whales, and dolphins communicate over vast distances of the world ocean via the efficient transmission of sonic pulses through water, and use echolocation to locate prey animals.

During the Cold War, the U.S. Navy established a global network of submerged hydrophones (the Sound Surveillance System, or SOSUS), expressly for the purpose of tracking the movements of Soviet submarines, each of which emitted a characteristic sound-print that was recognizable to those who monitored the network. Study of that enormous data pool soon revealed that the efficiency of sound transmission in water is also utilized by marine mammals, among whom information is exchanged by efficient transmission in the layer of ocean water confined between the ocean surface and the thermal discontinuity at the base of the near-surface mixed layer. Thus, the energy represented by those waves is not absorbed or attenuated by the entire 4km depth of the ocean, but is propagated efficiently, confined in that shallow near-surface layer.

Vital information about the movement of individual whales, and groups of whales, has been collected incidental to the espionage function of the hydrophone network, and scientists now realize that marine mammals are accustomed to communicating over long distances of open ocean by this efficient transmission of sound. It was the analysts of those data who first realized that modern technology had finally discovered an information superhighway that had been in use by marine mammals for millions of years.

The Sense of Smell

Humans respond to molecules suspended in the air they breathe via the sense we call smell. We probably continuously take in olfactory information, and respond to it in ways we don't immediately recognize. The perfume industry believes that it is able to exploit this subliminal communication pathway in the composition of the fragrances it manufactures, and experienced wine tasters can identify a vineyard and a vintage with a few sniffs of the molecules that evaporate from a wine being tasted. Examination of the role played in identification of potential human sexual partners by subconscious reception and interpretation of olfactory signals is a science in its infancy, despite the probable great age of that communication channel. Cognitive psychologists tell us that a familiar smell invokes human memory of past events more vividly than either a familiar sight or a familiar sound.

But, acute as is the human sense of smell in narrow applications, that sense is far less acute, and far less utilized, than is the capacity among many groups of animals to identify other individuals and transfer information by smell. We marvel at the capacity of a bloodhound to follow the faint scent trace of a human fugitive across varied terrain many hours after the person has passed, and we wonder what kind of information our pet dog is taking in as he sniffs his way around the neighborhood. Few of us realize the extent to which pheromone molecules, deliberately released into the air upon receipt of specific clues, control many aspects of the behavior of insect colonies. Many animals operate in the absence of visible light by their ability to identify specific molecules among the many billions suspended in air or water.

The Sense of Touch

Humans take in a lot of information through their fingertips by tactilely exploring the surface textures of materials they handle, and many among us deprived of sight use those fingertips to interpret the patterns of raised dots that constitute the Braille alphabet. Many other animals, such as star-nosed moles and insects equipped with sensitive antennae, navigate and seek prey exclusively via the sense of touch provided by such apparatus.

The human species is immersed in a cacophony of signals, carried via many media. Animals interpret and exchange information via sensory apparatus that we lack. Each time a behavioral biologist undertakes a study of communication within a specific group of animals, he or she reveals a complex system of communication that enhances the capacity of that group of animals to reproduce, and, thus, to persist in the ever-changing biosphere. Successful communication is a key aspect of Darwinian adaptation, and must be understood in the context of enhancing the potential longevity of the community that benefits from that communication, rather than primarily conferring a reproductive advantage on an individual animal.

Communication in Colonial Structures

Most studies of nonhuman communication have been undertaken with groups of animals much like us. Thus, we know of experiments with use of language in chimpanzees and gorillas; we realize that vast amounts of information is transferred among marine mammals via complex sonic emissions, some of which lie within our hearing capacity; the enormous complexity of wolf vocalization engages so much energy that it can only represent transfer of information that enhances the survivability of a wolf community; and so on. But we seem less well prepared to accept the reality of efficient communication within groups of animals that look very little like us, organisms that we choose to disparage as "primitive." Yet network communication plays a role in so many diverse groups of animals that we are driven to the conclusion that elaborate communication is the rule, rather than the exception, within nonhuman societies.

Some of these communication systems are very old, perhaps as old as life itself. We can only imagine the kind of information exchanged among individual prephotosynthetic chemautotrophs clustered around sea-floor vents spewing hot nutrient cocktails, or among unicellular photosynthesizing organisms suspended in the earliest ocean, or among individual organisms inhabiting the thin veneer of photosynthesizing slime that we suppose coated the first exposed rock surfaces. But even the earliest organisms that have left evidence of their activity in the morphology of hard parts preserved as fossils show evidence of effective associations among individual organisms that, if those associations enhanced survivability within a group of organisms, must have included the exchange of information, however defined.

The communication networks of many of those groups of organisms found expression, through many generations of evolutionary selection, as specialized body plans in which many individual organisms have been integrated into superorganisms. The most complex of these colonial structures are precursors to human cities, in the complexity of their morphology, the number of individuals incorporated in each structure, the range of services offered within the colony, the allocation of responsibilities among individuals in the superorganism, and the internal social organization whereby operational instructions are disseminated.

Corals

Coral animals are only a few centimeters in size, yet those that live in colonies are responsible for building the largest residential structures on Earth, such as the Great Barrier Reef, or the platform on which lie the Bahama Banks. Both structures are clearly apparent in images taken by orbiting satellites.

Each coral colony has a distinctive configuration: Some are shaped like dinner plates, others assume the shape of mounds, and still others develop branching structures like trees on land. Marine biologists have determined that the shape of a coral colony is optimized for the depth at which it lives and for the dynamics of water movement past the colony; when a colony is moved to a different depth, or when a colony is transferred to a site at which flow of water past the individual feeding organisms is different, the colony shape will change to adjust to the new conditions. Since coral organisms feed on microorganisms suspended in the water that flows past them, the configuration of each coral colony must enable that colonial organism to extract food resources from passing water, and dispose of food wastes into the same passing flow. The optimum overall shape of the colony can be maintained only through a complex communication system among all individuals of the colony, and, if environmental conditions surrounding the organism change, the colony must alter its configuration to respond to those changes, or suffer a reduction in its feeding efficiency, which, if maintained long enough, will lead to reproductive failure.

The ability of coral animals to build such large structures is due in part to an ability to share nutrients among members of the colony, and in part to a symbiotic relationship with a photosynthetic alga, *Zooxanthella*. This alga lives within the tissues of each individual coral animal. The coral animal provides protection to the *Zooxanthellae*, as well as CO_2 from respiration, which the *Zooxanthellae* use in photosynthesis. The *Zooxanthellae* produce their own food through photosynthesis, and release both excess sugars and oxygen into the coral animal's tissues. The coral animal uses the oxygen for respiration and the excess sugars (and Ca^{++} and HCO_3^- dissolved in seawater) to carry on all its metabolic activities, including construction of the massive calcite ($CaCO_3$) skeletal structures that make up the major barrier reefs of Earth.

Bryozoans

Bryozoans, a group of colonial marine organisms, have also achieved great structural complexity, but on a much smaller scale than corals (for example, see McKinney and Jackson, 1989). Individual bryozoan animals are a few millimeters in size and can live only as members of fully integrated colonies. The individuals in each colony specialize to perform the necessary functions of the group, becoming physically integrated as a superorganism. Within a single colony, individuals specialize for reproduction, for cleaning the colony surface, or as structural support. As in coral colonies, the majority of the individuals in a bryozoan colony capture food suspended in the water flowing by, digest it, and transfer some of the nutrients to members of the colony who serve other purposes. (Bryozoans have not developed a symbiotic association with photosynthesizing organisms, as have corals.) Other members of the bryozoan colony receive food resources but are specialized to discharge food waste into the surrounding water. If the communal skeleton of the bryozoan colony is damaged, thereby removing some feeding organisms from the resource flow, those organisms will adopt other functions within the colony. If an excreting member of the colony finds itself exposed to passing food resources as a result of such skeletal damage, the excreting organism may become a feeder. If a feeder finds its access to food suspended in the water blocked by structural damage to the colony skeleton, that feeder may become an excreter. (Analogies with changes in worker roles driven by externally imposed infrastructure changes in human communities are compelling.) Each individual in the bryozoan colony, regardless of its role, must also become part of the larger colony structure. Some colonies form simple mats, but fossil colonies have been described that have formed geometrically complex structures, such as the shape of an Archimedes screw (the genus *Archimedes*), which may have controlled the dynamics of flow of water past the colony, maximizing the feeding potential for the community. The communication necessary to coordinate the building of such a structure must be complex.

Modern bryozoan colonies have become even more complex. Circular colonies about the size of a quarter *(Selenaria maculata)* have developed specialized individuals at key positions on the edge of the colony. Each of these individuals grows an elongated appendage, a *flagellum*, and uses this flagellum as a paddle. Individuals with flagella work in unison to move the colony across the bottom of the ocean to better feeding grounds. This new adaptation has allowed a normally sedentary colony to become mobile to seek out food sources and to escape from predators. We know the difficulties encountered in teaching human members of an eight-oared shell to row in unison, and they have the benefit of a coxswain who both steers the shell and offers explicit instructions to the eight oarsmen he faces; bryozoans, however, coordinate the efforts of many more oars-organisms, and somehow communicate instructions that control the velocity and direction of the colony. Thus, an attached (so-called *sessile*) organism has evolved the capacity to become mobile by efficiently assigning highly specialized roles to selected individuals in the colony.

The Social Insects: Communication Among Honeybees

Among land-dwelling organisms, few social structures are as well developed as those that support and govern the *eusocial* insects: ants, honeybees, and termites. These organisms live in highly structured communities in which specific roles are played by particular individuals at particular times in their (usually short) lives. Many of these communities of cooperative individuals construct elaborate residential structures, finely accommodated to environmental variables, that long predate modern sustainable architecture.

A healthy colony of honeybees, *Apis mellifera*, at the peak of the nectar-collecting season, consists of around 50,000 individual honeybees (for example, see Caron 2004). That colony includes only a single diploid reproducing female, the *"queen"*; roughly 50,000 nonreproducing female *workers*, who carry out the many functions of the colony; and about 200 males *("drones")*. The queen may lay 500,000 eggs in her lifetime. Each egg that she fertilizes with a sperm cell that she carries internally from her maiden flight is born as a diploid female; the queen lays a few unfertilized eggs from time to time that emerge as haploid males, or drones. The drones are helpless future sperm donors; they are unable to feed themselves, and they depend on the services of worker bees for all their needs.

As the queen lays each egg in a geometric framework of wax cells, laid down in a precise hexagonal pattern by worker bees, other worker bees tend the eggs. When each egg hatches, other workers systematically feed each larva honey, flower nectar processed by other worker bees. When a larva reaches the age of entry into *pupation*, another worker bee secretes beeswax to seal the cell containing the larva. A few days later the pupa breaks through the wax seal as an adult, winged insect, and enters the honeybee community as another worker bee, destined to pass, in her short (three-month) lifetime, through a series of assignments that support the complex life of the colonial organism that is the hive itself. The primary task that engages the majority of the worker bees during the season of blooming flowers is to fly from flower to flower, collecting nectar from the specialized cells, called nectaries, that the flower constructs. The flower dedicates energy to grow the nectary and supply it with a sugar solution expressly to attract honeybees to the interior of the flower, where each honeybee will brush pollen (sperm) from the *stamens* (the male sexual organs of the flower), to be transferred to the *pistil* (the female sexual organ), on a flower the bee will visit next. This service of the honeybee, presumed to be wholly inadvertent, ensures the successful fertilization of the plants it visits, the propagation of those plants into the next generation, and the continued production of flower nectar to elicit that essential pollination service from future generations of honeybees, who will, of course, depend on that nectar for their own survival and reproduction.

The nectar and pollen that the worker bees carry back to the hive is collected and stored by yet other worker bees, and then still other worker bees fan their wings at the entrance to the hive to draw outside air into the hive, driving it past the collected nectar to evaporate enough water to convert the nectar into honey. Other worker bees inject the drying honey with enzymes they excrete that effectively inhibit the growth of bacteria in the developing honey, enabling the colony to store the excess honey, without risk of fermentation, to sustain the entire community of bees through the season(s) in which no flowers are available.

Still other worker bees station themselves at the entrance to the hive to protect the colony against predatory animals or from bees from other colonies who might undertake to rob the hive of its supply of stored honey. The guard bees first fly at the head and face of a suspected animal intruder (diplomatic posturing?); if the intruder is not repelled by the threat of an attack, the guard bees proceed to sting the intruder with the organ at the end of the worker abdomen, a modified ovipositor connected to a venom sac (a measured "police action"?). When the bee is brushed off or withdraws her stinger, her abdomen is inverted as she leaves the barbed stinger lodged in the intruder, where it continues to inject venom until the supply is exhausted. Inversion of the bee's abdomen releases a specific defense pheromone that alerts other bees in the colony to the fact that an attack has been mounted, and other worker bees leave their assignments elsewhere in the colony and rush to the defense of the hive (a wholesale defense response). The longer the attack is pressed, the more bees sting the intruder; the more pheromone is released, the more guard bees are recruited to the attack (all-out war). The colony is loath to invest resources in the stinging function, however, since each guard who stings an intruder and inverts her abdomen to release the pheromone is mortally wounded in the process. No activity of the hive so confounds the distinction between the individual bee and the individual colony as does this strategy of dispatching a few bees in a suicide attack to protect the hive. The risk/benefit to the bee who sacrifices her life to repel an intruder is far different from the risk/benefit to the colony that loses a few bees to protect the vital food supply. Human societies make similar risk/benefit judgments in deciding how many members of a society can be sacrificed to protect a resource base.

When a colony of bees realizes that its queen is approaching the end of her reproductive career, or when a successful colony stores so much honey that it outgrows the space it can occupy, the colony decides to produce a replacement queen.

This goal is realized by the hive by building a series of beeswax cells, each ~50% larger than a typical worker cell, inviting the declining queen to lay fertilized eggs in those queen cells, and then feeding those larvae as they hatch a specialized diet of *royal jelly* that enables those larvae to mature into reproducing females. When the first of the new queens emerges as a winged insect, she flies out of the hive, closely followed by her colony's retinue of drones, joined by drones from other neighboring colonies who have somehow learned that a virgin queen has embarked upon her maiden flight. As many as 20 of the drones overtake and fertilize the queen; as each act of copulation is completed, the drone drops from the queen, leaving his intromissive organ behind, and falls to the ground to die, either of the injuries he has sustained in copulation or of starvation, since no worker bees follow him out of the hive to feed him. Those few drones who successfully mate with the newly emerged queen are those who follow her most effectively in her high-speed acrobatic maiden flight. Thus, each new queen is fertilized with the sperm of the fastest and strongest drones. Drones that have been unsuccessful in inseminating a virgin queen are denied access to their home colony when and if they return, and die of starvation in the absence of worker bees to feed them. After each episode of virgin-queen pursuit, each colony that contributed drones to the maiden flight must produce a new crop of drones to preen themselves for the next fertilization opportunity.

The newly fertilized young queen returns to her hive with a lifetime's supply of sperm stored in her *spermatatheca*, a specialized organ that can hold viable sperm for the five-year lifetime of a laying queen. Before she sets about the business of laying eggs, she tracks down and kills the old queen, if she is still in the hive, and any later-emerging virgin queens. The new queen then produces many thousands of bees with the mix of sperm she has acquired from many drones, both from her own colony and from other nearby colonies. Within a few months, the community of honeybees with a new queen assumes the genetic makeup dictated by the outcome of her maiden flight.

If the new queen has been raised in response to overcrowding of the hive, or because the egg-laying efficiency of the old queen is in decline, the older queen flies off with about 15,000 of the colony's bees, each engorged with honey, to establish a new colony elsewhere. The swarm achieves this end by setting up temporary residence on the branch of a tree, or under the eaves of a structure, and sends out scout bees to comb the neighborhood for a site suitable to house a new colony. When a scout bee finds a suitable site, she returns to the swarm and communicates detailed information about the conditions, direction, and distance of the proposed site by a highly ritualized process described as a "waggle dance" (see the discussion that follows) on the surface of the swarm. The rest of the swarm observes this performance, often carried on by several scout bees proposing different competing sites, and eventually flies to one of the selected sites to set up a new colony. By this mechanism, the colony reproduces itself, without introducing new genetic material into the community.

The enormous complexity of honeybee society requires elegant management of resources, both material and personnel, to allow the colony to respond to constantly changing environmental conditions. The community makes many decisions: to replace a queen; to enlarge the beeswax comb in which eggs will be laid; to lay unfertilized eggs (drones); to collect nectar and pollen from a given source; to dispatch more bees to repel an intruder; to assign and reassign individual bees to various tasks in the hive; to choose a new site for the colony during swarming; and so forth. For the purposes of this discussion, it is irrelevant whether hive management represents a series of considered decisions by some subset of the community, or simply a series of programmed hard-wired responses to familiar environmental variables. The end result in the hive is a community response based on received information that is somehow processed and somehow elicits appropriate adaptive strategies expressed as instructions that are directed to individuals throughout the hive.

We know something about how essential information is directed through the hive: Karl von Frisch, Konrad Lorenz, and Nikolaas Tinbergen received the Nobel prize in Physiology in 1973 in part for their discovery that foraging bees who have discovered a nectar source communicate that information to other bees in the hive via a complex *waggle dance*, in which the returning forager indicates the direction, distance, quality, and size of a nectar supply by the geometry and intensity of the dance, performed directly on the honeycomb within the hive. Other bees observe this dance and then fly directly to the indicated source, even detouring around artificial obstacles deliberately placed in the most direct pathway by behavioral scientists studying honeybee communication. A similar communication strategy is used by scout bees who leave a swarm after it has departed from the original host colony: Those bees investigate the neighborhood for appropriate colony sites, and then return to the swarm to indicate the quality, direction, and distance of a candidate site to the rest of the community.

Bees also communicate by the release of chemical pheromones, the most important of which seems to be the *queen substance*, a chemical constantly released by the queen, presumably to reassure the other members of the colony that she remains well and continues to lay eggs. (Successful executives of modern businesses know the value of distributing frequent memoranda to their employees, even if those memoranda communicate only trivial information.) Commercial beekeepers routinely replace queens, either to restore reproductive vigor to a colony with a declining queen, or to alter the behavior of the entire colony by introducing a queen from a more productive or gentler stock than the incumbent queen. The replacement of a queen may effect an immediate change in colony behavior through her different queen substance long before she has replaced enough bees through egg laying to alter the hive's behavior by genetic replacement.

Honeybees exchange essential information within each colony, and must also communicate with bees from other, nearby colonies. When a new virgin queen flies out on her maiden flight, she is pursued not only by drones from her own hive but also by drones from neighboring colonies, who have somehow been alerted to what will be their only chance to pass on their genes to the next generation. Is the queen's availability communicated by release of pheromones into the neighborhood? Does that occur fast enough to marshal the drone resources from nearby colonies? Do forager bees, when they encounter bees from other colonies at the flowers they exploit, somehow pass on the information (via gossip at the supermarket?) that their colony is about to hatch a queen?

It seems likely that every essential function of a complex human society is also represented within a honeybee colony.

Implications for Human Networks

Each time we venture into a tropical rain forest, or lower a hydrophone into a coral reef community, we are overwhelmed by the cacophony of signals we encounter, whether those signals assault our eyes, our ears, or our noses—and we are probably oblivious to all but a very small proportion of the signals that swirl around us in each of those environments. The world we inhabit is awash in signals.

These biological networks raise important questions for human networks, particularly the design of business networks. Many communications challenges are effectively addressed within these biological communities:

- *Signal contamination; filtering noise*—As in most examples of human communication, the message pathways used by animals, once established, become flooded with extraneous information that we characterize as "noise," or "spam." In the animal world, parasites and predators learn very quickly how to occupy communication pathways to exploit the predation opportunities that signal mimicry provides. Female fireflies send signals to potential mates as precisely pulsed flashes of cool light, which they generate via chemical reactions in specialized cells in their abdomens. Male fireflies are attracted by those signals, and compete for the privilege of fertilizing the signaler. Females of the firefly genus *Photuris* have acquired the ability to mimic that light signal precisely, but when the aspiring mates arrive the female *Photuris* flies eat them. *Photuris* females have "learned" to take advantage of prey species at a time in their life cycle when they are likely to be least discriminating (Dawkins and Guilford, 1991; Lloyd, 1975). As young as it is, our human Internet is already so infiltrated by identity-theft entrepreneurs, scam artists, and sexual predators that the security and efficiency of this communication network has become compromised. As in biological networks, human users of these networks must learn to distinguish message from noise if they hope to avoid becoming prey.

- *Specialized roles*—In colonies of honeybees, individuals pursue highly specialized roles, often only temporarily assigned, yet they need to communicate across these roles. Individual organisms, whether animal or human, also need to be able to adapt and change their roles in response to changes in the environment, as bryozoan colonies have done in adapting individual functions (from waste excreter to feeder) or developing new collective capabilities (such as colony mobility). Assessing the effectiveness whereby members of nonhuman networks fulfill these roles, communicate across roles, and adapt roles over time may offer fresh perspectives to those who undertake to design and manage human networks.

- **Signaling**—Insects such as honeybees use different ways of communicating information across the network, from pheromones to waggle dances. Designers of human networks must explore many ways of signaling information across the network, using all the senses or diverse channels, to convey information across the network. Networks might be linked using different senses (text, voice, visual, or perhaps even smell) or different channels (print, Web, and mobile, for example). What are the best channels for conveying different types of information? How can the entire network be made aware of changes in the external environment and be enabled to mobilize a response in the way that bees respond to an attack on the hive?

- **Signal contamination; ripple effects**—Just as information about the flight of a new queen is picked up by drones from neighboring hives, human information channels have broader, and sometimes unpredictable, effects, beyond the audience apparently intended. One feature of the network represented by the modern Internet is the near-universality of access it offers. A consequence of that access is the fact that individuals or communities denied what they perceive to be their fair share of the world's resources are immediately aware of that inequity. In earlier times, before the emergence of modern communication media, much of the world's human population labored in obscurity as subsistence farmers without awareness of how well a small proportion of the human community was able to live by seizing a disproportionate share of the world's resources for itself. A threatening consequence of that new awareness is the growing unrest of large numbers of people in underserved cultures, and the willingness of even a very small percentage of those people to lash out in hopelessness at those who have effectively enslaved them. Thus, one aspect of the success of the information network now available to humans is that it has engaged the global human community, rather than being used to control a valuable resource base for the exclusive use of the community that developed the network. An information network has become global for the first time since whales and dolphins learned to exploit the sonic wave guides in the world ocean. It will be some time before the political, social, and economic consequences of the rapid expansion of the human IT network become apparent.

We reason from the 3.7-billion-year history of life that the behavioral patterns and body plans we observe in animals have been selected by a very long process of trial and error (natural selection) because they work well. The only test of efficient operation of the success of a given adaptation is its capacity to enhance reproductive success, not only of the individual animal that possesses a given trait, but also of the community of animals whose potential for survival is enhanced by the efficiency of the mechanism they have developed (by whatever means) to distribute available resources most efficiently among them. Thus, the role of individual reproductive success is eclipsed by the capacity of the community to which that individual belongs to maximize the reproductive potential of the entire community.

Colonialism in Human Societies

We might profitably ask: "How colonial is human society?" We can survive as fully isolated organisms, but few of us choose to do so for any length of time, and, of course, we can't reproduce as isolated organisms. Like colonial organisms, humans live in large concentrations of individuals, and, even in rural communities, the exchange of information among us is of vital importance to sustain the economic and political functions of our extended colony. Within our colonies, individual roles are highly diversified, although that specialization has not been sustained long enough to lead to emergence of additional specialized genders beyond the two we recognize. We congratulate ourselves that each of us enjoys free will, in comparison to the instinctual responses of so-called lower organisms; we indulge the conceit that actions of human colonies are achieved by a process of information exchange and reasoned decision making (we have university departments of *Decision Processes*); and we congratulate ourselves that we are, thereby, operating at a level "above" the hard-wired response of animals. But closer reflection often reveals the extent to which our supposed cognizant responses to external stimuli are, in fact, biologically driven, and investigators of animal behavior now reveal, with some frequency, discomfiting suggestions of the exercise of reason and free will by animals. Our behavior is probably more hard-wired than we care to acknowledge, and the animals whose intellects we disparage probably engage more in reasoned activity than we comfortably accept.

To a very large extent, we judge our performance as individuals in terms of the contribution we make to the welfare of our colony, and many of us find fulfillment in predominantly altruistic roles. In many cases, we are assured that the personal sacrifices we make today will benefit our colony in the future, in some cases the remote future, and many of us find assurance that making those sacrifices now will guarantee rewards in another dimension. Some of us are driven to acts of heroic sacrifice by the promise of eternal salvation. We can imagine that attack bees are conditioned, via the honeybee equivalent of a revivalist camp meeting, to undertake the ultimate sacrifice, in an expression of religious zeal, for the benefit of the colony.

To the extent that human society succeeds, it does so by suppression of individual appetites, and consequent suppression of competition for limited resources. Society achieves that suppression by developing social strategies to distribute those resources more or less equitably across a human population that must be large enough and diverse enough to propagate itself, and its social conventions, into future generations. Human societies that have failed have done so because they have not used their resources as well as other societies competing for the same resource base. (The 2008 turmoil in the global economy is clearly a consequence of the failure of the regulatory structure to suppress individual appetites.)

The development of colonialism elevates the struggle for existence above the individual, and enhances the probability that the group of animals to which that individual belongs will be represented in the next generation. Colonialism lends long-term stability to the group of animals in which it emerges by distributing the risk of nonsurvival among many individuals. The development of colonial structure confers multigenerational longevity that is analogous to the stability conferred on the insurance industry by the emergence of overarching reinsurance markets.

Conclusion

The networks that humans now use to communicate will change with bewildering rapidity as new technologies emerge almost daily. But ancient networks, those that have persisted for so long that their configurations have become codified in specific body geometries, bear testimony to the importance of the development of communication networks in the history of life, and offer a perspective on our modern networks that we must not ignore. The tasks addressed by our human networks are not more complex than those that have been addressed for many millions of years by other groups of organisms, some of whose adapted networks we have described here. Human networks often fall short of the operation of those older biological networks in the efficiency of exchange of information, and in the extent to which that exchange controls every aspect of the life of the organisms that participate in the network.

Human efforts to develop and maintain communication networks, and to facilitate adaptation of those networks to changing environmental pressures, can benefit from consideration of the structure and function of communication networks that have been proven to be effective in the protracted trial-and-error process that has characterized the history of life.

References

Caron, D. M. 2004. *Honey Bee Biology and Beekeeping.* Cheshire, CT: Wicwas Press.

Dawkins, M. S., and Guilford, T., 1991, The corruption of honest signaling: Animal Behaviour, v. 41, p. 865-873.

Hölldobler, Bert, and Wilson, E. O., 2009, The Superorganism: the beauty, elegance, and strangeness of insect societies: W. W. Norton & Co., New York, 521 p.

Lloyd, J. E., 1975, Aggressive mimicry in *Photuris* fireflies: signal repertoires by *femmes fatales:* Science, v. 197, p. 452-453.

McKinney, F. K, and J. B. C. Jackson. 1989. *Bryozoan Evolution.* Univ. of Chicago Press.

Menzel, R., and W. Backhaus. 1990. Color vision in insects. In Vol. 6 of *Vision and Visual Dysfunction,* ed. P. Gouras. MacMillan Press.

Sichert, Andreas B., Paul Friedel, and J. Leo van Hemmen. 2006. Snake's perspective on heat: Reconstruction of input using an imperfect detection system. *Physical Review Letters.* 97, 068105.

Speight, M. R., Allan D. Watt, and Mark D. Hunter. 1999. *Ecology of Insects.* Blackwell Science Ltd.

Weber, Neal A. 1972. *Gardening Ants: The Attines.* Memoirs of the American Philosophical Society.

8

Artificial Intelligence: How Individual Agents Add Up to a Network

Steven O. Kimbrough

Abstract

Artificial intelligence (AI) offers computational methodologies for modeling systems, which can be valuable in understanding networks. In this chapter, Steve Kimbrough examines several types of applications of these methods in exploring how the behavior of individual agents leads to outcomes across networks. For example, he considers how one system, based on a Prisoner's Dilemma that provides a higher payoff for players who don't cooperate, can result in a surprising outcome in which cooperation dominates after many rounds of play. He also considers agent-based models—including turtles in a pond, showing discrimination effects; and sugar and spice trading, showing interactions through trading. Finally, he explores applications to ant colony optimization and swarming optimization of flocks of birds or schools of fish. He concludes that computational models offer important insights into networks, and the procedures used in modeling have a significant impact. The discussion also demonstrates that "networks matter," affecting outcomes in sometimes unpredictable ways.

Artificial intelligence and networks are closely intertwined. Although space limitations prevent a comprehensive treatment, we begin with some basic concepts of artificial intelligence. The mission of AI is to use computational methods to advance the science of complex systems, especially intelligent systems. The goals of AI are indeed scientific (both pure science and engineering); AI seeks to describe, to explain, to predict, and to support intervention in its domain of interest, complex systems. Regarding *computational methods*, the contrast is with purely mathematical representations. We could (more or less) equally well say *procedural methods* or *algorithmic methods.*

In modeling any system, there is a difference between a top-down model and a bottom-up model. Traditional mathematical models were designed for top-down modeling. System behavioral variables are identified and their interrelationships mapped to mathematical relationships. These methods have often proved unsuitable for bottom-up modeling, in which elemental entities are identified and their behavior is described with simple procedures. The system's macro-behavior is then generated by (constructed from) the micro-behavior of its elements. The system's properties so generated are said to be emergent. Procedural modeling has an honored history. Think of Smith's invisible hand and Darwin's theory of speciation. Each originated as a powerful explanation, couched in a procedure, rather than expressed in mathematics (see Kimbrough 2003 for a more extended discussion).

Of the many contributions of AI to the understanding of networks (and to the use of network representations in other sciences), perhaps the most important has been the production of fruitful families of methods for procedural (or computational) modeling. Many readers will be acquainted with *rule-based expert systems,* one of AI's important successes. Particular rule-based expert systems are built by modelers from a large range of specialties, not just AI specialists. The contribution from AI has been to originate and develop the *computational methodology* of rule-based expert systems, for which construction of particular systems was important to prove out concepts. Once these concepts were sufficiently mature, specialists in other fields could use them for particular modeling tasks. Directly relevant to the subject of networks, *neural networks* are another form of computational modeling, one that predates the coining of the term artificial intelligence. Neural networks have also achieved many important successes, and remain vital in the field.

AI has originated several computational methodologies that are valuable for investigating networks. What follows is an overview and discussion of the most important of these techniques and what we have learned with them.[1]

---

[1] Because neural networks are so well known and because, perhaps surprisingly, they have not been much used to shed light on social networks, I shall not discuss them further in this short paper.

Cellular Automata Models: Localized Decisions Combine for Unexpected Effects

"Cellular automata" are computational systems consisting of simple elements—"cells"—arrayed in a network. Cellular automata models typically employ regular networks, of a lattice or grid form, like a checkerboard (although many other options are possible). Each cell in the grid (or square in the checkerboard) is given certain elementary properties, and rules for updating the cells' properties are specified. The network of cells is initialized, each cell having its state or properties—usually a single property—set. Then time unfolds stepwise, discretely. At each tick of the clock, the system's update rules are applied across the network and cell states (properties) are set with (potentially) new values. We watch to see what happens and we draw lessons accordingly. This remarkably simple regime has, as we shall see, remarkably powerful modeling and representation capabilities. Let us see, then, some examples.

Conway's Game of Life (Berlekamp, Conway, and Guy 1982) is surely the most famous, most implemented, and most explored cellular automaton. Its network structure is the regular two-dimensional lattice, or checkerboard. It was originally conceived as being played on an infinite checkerboard, but in many implementations the lattice is finite, wrapping around upon itself as a torus (although displayed as a rectangle, it functionally has the form of a doughnut or bagel).

The rules of Life are elemental simplicity itself. Each cell is either on or off. In visualizations this is indicated by color; typically (and here) light color means off, dark color means on. At each tick of the clock, every cell examines its own state (on, or "alive"; or off, or "dead"—don't ask how a dead cell examines anything) and the states of its eight immediately surrounding neighbors. These are the update rules:

- If the cell is off ("dead") and exactly three of its immediate neighbors are on, the cell goes on (becomes "alive"); otherwise it stays off.
- If the cell is on ("alive") and either exactly two or exactly three of its immediate neighbors are on, then the cell stays on; otherwise it goes off ("dies").

To illustrate, it is convenient to use an implementation of the Game of Life written in NetLogo (Wilensky 1998b). This implementation has the advantage that it is readily, freely, and essentially permanently accessible on the Internet. Searching the Internet will turn up a number of fascinating implementations of Life as well as discussions of the game. (Among my favorites are www.bitstorm.org/gameoflife/, http://en.wikipedia.org/wiki/Conway's_Game_of_Life, and especially, for its library, www.ibiblio.org/lifepatterns/.)

In Figure 8-1 we see the world of Life initiated with six cells on, in two groups of three. After two ticks, the triad at the top has gone extinct (as shown in Figure 8-1c), while the triad on the bottom has switched from three vertically to three horizontally and back. Unless disturbed, it will "blink" like this forever.

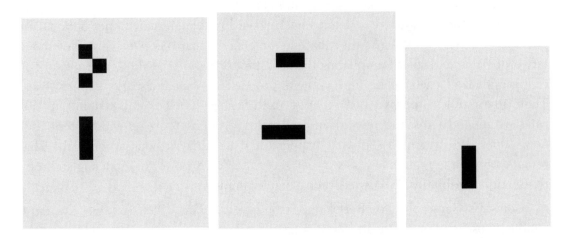

Figure 8-1 The fate of two neighborhoods in the Game of Life. One dies out (on top). The other changes, then changes back to its original configuration (on the bottom). (a) Start: Tick 0; (b) Tick 1; (c) Tick 2.

Figure 8-2 illustrates the evolution of a Life network after a random start with 35% of the cells on. What is not apparent in Figure 8-2b is that although the pattern of cells on has stabilized somewhat, it is far from fixed. Viewed live, the network remains dynamic. It might seem that just about anything could happen on the network of Life. Long experience concurs. Hobbyists have built spaceships that engage in battle, self-replicating machines, and much else. Theory also concurs. In fact, Conway's (1982) original article proves that Life is universal, that is, that it is possible to build a Turing-complete machine in Life. So, under Church's thesis, Life, simple as it is, can make any possible computation. On March 2, 2000, Paul Rendell announced his claim that he had in fact built a Turing machine in Life (see http://rendell-attic.org/gol/tm.htm). This is emergence in the grand. This network game is well-named.

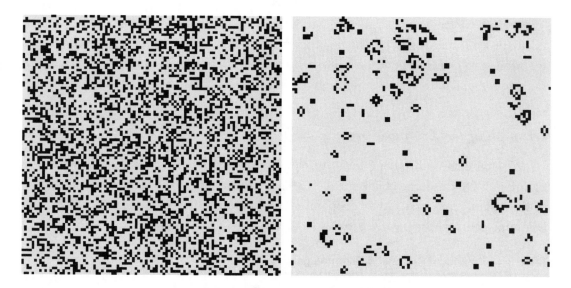

Figure 8-2   Life after a while. After a random start with 35% of the cells on, the network remains dynamic; about 6% of cells are on. (a) Random start, 35% on; (b) later, still dynamic, 6% on.

Life is hardly unique in this sense. Patrick Grim (1994) has defined a two-dimensional cellular automaton on the regular lattice in which the cells play Prisoner's Dilemma with their neighbors and update their strategies as a consequence of the games. This system, too, is universal and can be used to construct a universal computer (Grim 1998). A consequence of this fact, as in the case of Life, is that the general problem of predicting what will happen on the network over time is undecidable. In practice, this means that a single strategy does not dominate to conquest. In the 1930s, Kurt Gödel showed in his "undecidability results" that in certain sufficiently complex formal systems there would always be theorems that could not in principle be proved and nontheorems that could not be refuted.

There is an important practical implication of Grim's results. Given any undecidable system, if we want to understand it better (beyond what can be proved or disproved with the system), we have essentially two approaches available to us. First, it is always possible to study the system empirically. We can ask, for example, which strategies of Prisoner's Dilemma are robust, and which strategies tend to perform well and survive prosperously. From the work of Axelrod (1984, 1987) and others (Nowak and Sigmund 1992, 1993; Nowak, Bonhoeffer, and May,1994), we know that "Tit for Tat" is often the optimal strategy for Iterated Prisoner's Dilemma.

Second, we can explore special conditions for the system in question and hope to be able to prove results regarding the behavior of the system. Whether the special conditions are interesting or not depends, of course, on the larger context. We turn now to an example, one for which the special conditions do arguably teach us something interesting.

Triumph of the Cooperators

We examine a more complex example after a of cellular automaton, illustrated in Figure 8-3. On this large checkerboard, cells are distinguished by their game strategies. In the model, cells may either cooperate (0, black) or defect (1, white) in a Prisoner's Dilemma game whose payoffs are shown in Table 8-1.

Table 8-1   Payoffs of Prisoner's Dilemma game

	S_1 (Cooperate, or 0)	S_2 (Defect, or 1)
S1 (Cooperate, or 0)	A=3, A=3	B=0, C=3.2
S2 (Defect, or 1)	C=3.2, B=0	D=1, D=1

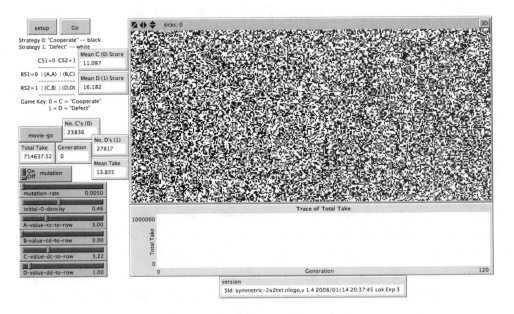

Figure 8-3   Prisoner's Dilemma initialized on the gridscape network.

At initialization, shown Figure 8-3, cells are randomly assigned one of the two strategies, but the payoffs are higher for defection (the probability of the cooperating strategy is 0.46), so the initial outcome is predictable—many cells defect.

After initialization, each cell uses its strategy to play Prisoner's Dilemma with each of its eight immediate neighbors and keeps a running total of the number of points it receives in the plays of the current episode. Having determined its point total, each cell considers the point totals of each of its eight immediate neighbors. If any neighbor has a higher point total, the cell switches its strategy to the strategy of the neighboring cell with the highest point total (ties being broken randomly). This completes the episode and the clock ticks. In Figure 8-4 we see the state of the network after two ticks of the clock. As might be expected, the cooperators have been decimated. Two ticks ago there were 23,836 of them. Now there are only 3,018.

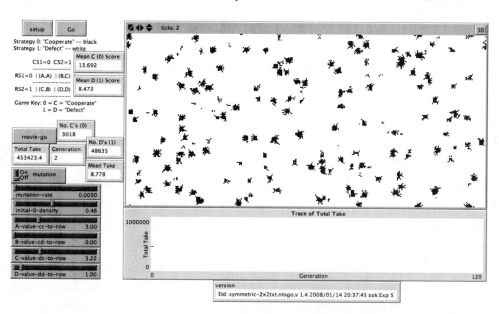

Figure 8-4   Prisoner's Dilemma on the gridscape network, generation 2: cooperators are decimated.

Cooperation appears headed for extinction. This is hardly surprising because whenever a cooperator plays a defector, the defector gets a larger reward. Who would not want to defect under the circumstances? Cooperators do manage to hang on in this particular run, and the system settles after about 45 episodes or ticks of the clock. Figure 8-5 shows the state of the network when this happens.

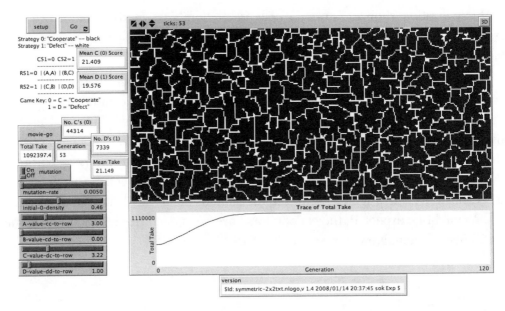

Figure 8-5 **Prisoner's Dilemma on the gridscape network, generation 53: cooperators have conquered.**

What we see, surprisingly, is that the cooperators have recovered and now are permanently ensconced as the majority party. At settlement of this run, there are 44,314 cooperators and 7,339 defectors. I emphasize that the strategies here are completely simple: cooperate or defect. No learning is going on; there is no memory of prior play, as in "Tit for Tat." Cooperators lose every encounter they have with defectors, yet they somehow manage to take over and keep most of the network. How is this possible? Is it inevitable?

The result—conquest by the cooperators—is certainly not inevitable. It depends on the right payoff structure and on the spontaneous appearance of a 3×3 (or larger) rectangle of cooperators. The latter will likely appear in a large network providing the initial probability of cooperation is high enough. If it doesn't, the defectors will eliminate the cooperators. Even assuming the appearance of 3×3 (or larger) rectangles of cooperators, whether cooperators can survive or prosper in the network depends on the game payoffs.

With the right payoffs for Prisoner's Dilemma (or any other game), cooperators, S_1 players, will expand at the expense of defectors, provided there are initial formations of appropriate hypercubes.

Two general observations can be drawn from our simulation model. First, emergence is often non-obvious and may be in defiance of treasured principles. Figures 8-3 through 8-5 embody a kind of emergence or "self-organization" of a system. From a random scattering of cooperators and defectors, a distinctive pattern emerges of areas of cooperation expanding at the expense of defectors, confining them to a very limited existence. That the cooperators—losers in every cooperator-defector encounter—should be doing the pushing must count as surprising, even though it can be predicted from mathematical analysis.

The second observation has to do with the fact that our cellular automaton has modeled in a rudimentary way a society of strategically interacting agents (cells in the network). We see in the simulation and from the analysis a phenomenon we might call the "shadow of society." Cells directly play only their neighbors, but the ultimate outcome on the network—in particular whether a given cell ends up a cooperator or a defector—may well depend on the outcomes of games played neither by the cell itself nor by any of its neighbors. What happens elsewhere in the network may well—and obviously does in our example—have a profound effect on what happens in a particular location.

Agent-Based Models

With examples of cellular automata models clearly before us, we turn to more complex agent-based models (ABMs, also known as "individual-based models," or IBMs) as generalizing cellular automata models. In the cellular automata models we have seen, (1) the agents are fixed in a network and (2) all agents behave according to a single set of global rules. In an ABM, (1) typically at least some agents will be mobile and move about, and (2) there will be different *types* of agents, behaving according to different rules. ABMs, like cellular automata, are (normally) population-oriented: they represent one or more populations of agents and the ensuing interactions among the individuals.

ABMs have received serious applications both in areas of social science (epidemiology and ecology, especially Grimm and Railsback 2005) and in business studies. Several significant recent special issues have been published on agent-based models, including the August 2007 issue of the *Journal of Business Research*, devoted to agent-based modeling, and a special issue of *Proceedings of the National Academy of Sciences of the United States*, as well as issues devoted to economics (Tesfatsion 2001) and sociology (Gilbert and Abbott 2005). Agent-based models have even received discerning treatment in the popular press (Rauch 2002).

Schelling's Segregation Model: Red and Green Turtles

Thomas Schelling's segregation model is one of the first and most famous of agent-based models (see Schelling 1978, Chapter 4, for a nice discussion). Originally developed using "hand simulation" (pencil and paper), the model in one version or another has been widely implemented as an ABM demonstration. We'll conduct our discussion using the one available in the standard release of NetLogo (Wilensky 1997b). It presents the following scenario:

> *This project models the behavior of two types of turtles in a mythical pond. The red turtles and green turtles get along with one another. But each turtle wants to make sure that it lives near some of "its own." That is, each red turtle wants to live near at least some red turtles, and each green turtle wants to live near at least some green turtles. The simulation shows how these individual preferences ripple through the pond, leading to large-scale patterns.*

In Schelling's segregation model as implemented in NetLogo, there are three kinds of agents: the cells of the two-dimensional lattice, which may be vacant or occupied by a single turtle, and two types of turtles (red and green). Each turtle may be either happy or unhappy, with happiness based on the percentage of similarly colored turtles in its immediate neighborhood. Turtles that are happy (more than 30% of its neighbors are similarly colored) stay where they are. Turtles that are unhappy (less than 30% of neighbors like them) move to a randomly selected spot that will make them happy, if one is available. Of course, after they do this, other turtles may become unhappy in consequence.

Figure 8-6a shows an initial random distribution of agents (red and green; black patches are empty). Figure 8-6b shows the end result. In this particular run, everyone ends up happy and on average everyone has 73.8% of its neighbors of the same color. The sad lesson—reinforced by experiments with other threshold levels—is that it takes only modest levels of "prejudice" to effect extensive segregation.

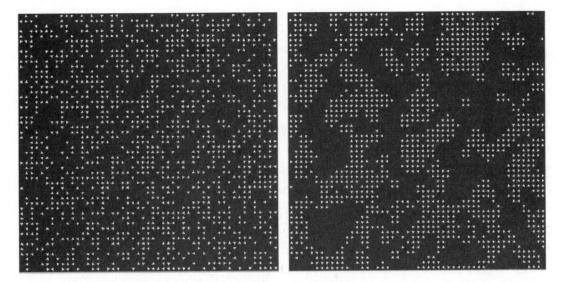

Figure 8-6   Random start and the finish in a run of Schelling's segregation model, using a comfort threshold of 30% (Wilensky 1996). (a) Random start; (b) segregation, stable.

Trade on the Sugarscape

The sugarscape model of Epstein and Axtell (1996) introduced the added dimension of trading between agents. There is the usual regular lattice of patches, and there are agents that move about. Now, however, the patches are heterogeneous. Some patches have sugar growing on them; others have spice. Patches also differ in how vigorous the growth on them is. Some patches are more productive than others. In the sugarscape trading model under discussion here (Epstein and Axtell 1996, Chapter 4), the lattice of patches contains four "hills" of production. There are hills (gradients) of sugar in the northeast and southwest, and hills of spice in the northwest and southeast.

Agents roam about the sugar- (and spice-) scape, harvesting sugar and spice as best they can, metabolizing both at idiosyncratic (heterogeneous) rates. When they find themselves near each other, they consider trading. Some agents have a surplus of sugar, relative to their store of spice, while others have a surplus of spice, relative to their store of sugar. Such pairs of agents encountering each other have a mutual interest in trade. In the sugarscape trading model, trade is effected where it is mutually advantageous. Rules of trade and negotiation are specified exogenously (but reasonably) leading to an *endogenous* discovering of an exchange rate, or price, for sugar and spice.

Challenging Economic Theory

This model offers an interesting contrast to the predictions of economic theory about the behavior of an ideal trading system. Under the Walrasian neoclassical micro-economics theory (or model), agents reveal their situations and preferences to a global "auctioneer" who sets prices so as to clear the market. This theory has a number of interesting properties—real-world fidelity not being among them. How, we might ask as Epstein and Axtell do ask, does the behavior of a more realistic model vary from that of neoclassical theory? The sugarscape trading model is proffered as a start on answering this question. Instead of a centralized, globally knowledgeable authority coordinating the market, Epstein and Axtell offer a different view. What they find is that the realized prices are on average close to the Walrasian price, but the system is far from equilibrium, for the markets at best clear only very locally. Prices vary throughout the sugarscape world. Moreover, social disparity is increased by trade, this disparity resulting primarily from luck rather than superior abilities by certain agents.

We have here an exemplary case in which an agent-based model is used to test and even challenge an established theory. What will be apparent to the reader is how incomplete, or incomprehensive, the two models are. Each is exceedingly simple, perhaps minimally complex for the phenomena being modeled. As a starting point for investigation, this must be judged a virtue. But what comes next? First, features can be added to model explicitly conditions of interest such as wealth effects, mortality, inheritance. Second, we can consider whether social networks spontaneously emerge in these agent-based models. (Typically, yes.) If so, what form(s) do they take and what are their dynamics? Can we experiment with different starting points for existing networks? With different influences on network formation? The agent-based modeling community has delivered an impressive infrastructure of concepts and tools. It awaits full exploitation.

We also can calibrate agent-based models to real-world data. Neither Schelling's segregation model nor Epstein and Axtell's sugarscape trading model has had its parameters set from real-world data or been tested against real-world data. So-called *stylized facts* (data we supposedly don't need to collect because we already know what we will find) rule the day. Uncalibrated models may be useful for purposes other than prediction, such as alerting a decision maker to phenomena of import, without at the same time predicting exactly their timing or magnitude. Even so, in the more mature and established areas of use of agent-based models (epidemiology and ecology, for example), agent-based models often are calibrated and tested with real-world data, successfully so. Given the wealth of social network data potentially available, it would seem that constructing and calibrating agent-based models of social networks is an especially promising venture for the near future.

Evolutionary Models

Darwinian evolution is a process of "blind variation and selective retention" carried out within populations of reproducing individuals. Variation is created blindly, that is to say without foresight with respect to utility or fitness among the reproducing individuals in a population. These individuals compete to reproduce and some are more successful than others, due not only to dumb luck but also to their properties and behavior in the ambient environment. These individuals on balance succeed better than average in reproducing. Although their offspring will typically not be exact copies of themselves—blind variation is introduced during reproduction—offspring will typically resemble their parents to a degree. Properties, good and bad, are inherited to a degree. Carried out in very large scale over very long periods, this process produces the magnificent adaptations we see in living organisms and is "the origin of species."

The notion that the Darwinian evolutionary process might be harnessed in a computational problem-solving context has hardly escaped the attention of artificial intelligence researchers. David Fogel (1998) traces the idea back to the 1940s with proliferating ideas and development since. Genetic algorithms, evolution strategies, evolutionary programming, genetic programming, learning classifier systems, ant-colony optimization, swarm intelligence, artificial immune systems, and coevolution systems are just the main families of related algorithms for implementing computational approaches to Darwinian evolution. Each of these families constitutes a number of specific evolution-based *heuristics* for problem solving. Because of this, a family of such heuristics is said to be a *meta-heuristic*. The grand family, or meta-heuristic, encompassing all of these and more, is now called *evolutionary algorithms* and the area *evolutionary computation* or *evolutionary computing*.

Evolutionary algorithms, or population-based meta-heuristics, have proved highly successful in many areas of search and optimization. The large number of successes and broad uptake of these meta-heuristics precludes, and actually makes unnecessary, rehearsing their application. Instead, I will briefly describe two network-intensive (and network-relevant) varieties of evolutionary algorithms: ant colonies and particle swarming. Each is a group of heuristics falling into the more general category of *swarm intelligence* meta-heuristics. (See http://www.scholarpedia.org/article/Swarm_intelligence for a gentle overview.)

Ant Colony Optimization (ACO)

All the evolutionary algorithms are biologically inspired. The inspiration for ACO is the foraging behavior of ant colonies. Roughly, ant foragers wander about randomly until they find a food site of interest, at which time they pick up some food and head directly back to the colony, depositing pheromone (scent) to mark their path. Other foragers, still wandering at random, may come across a trail with fresh pheromone markings. They will follow the trail away from the colony, find the food source, pick up food, and return on the path to the colony, dropping additional pheromone and, thereby, more heavily marking the path. Other ants will be drawn to the path and the food. Pheromone, however, evaporates so in time the marking on the path deteriorates. If it is not reinforced by new trips back by ants carrying food, it dissipates and eventually the path is ignored. (You can see a nice, albeit elementary, illustration of computational ant foraging in Wilensky 1997a, and more information about ACO in Dorigo, Birattari, and Stutzle 2006; and Dorigo and Thomas Stutzle 2004. ACO research and applications reports are published regularly in the Ants conference, http://iridia.ulb.ac.be/%7Eants/ants2008/; the GECCO conference, www.sigevo.org/gecco-2008/index.html; and PPSN, http://ls11-www.cs.uni-dortmund.de/PPSN/.)

Most of the ACO applications to date involve optimization (usually combinatorial optimization) on networks. In the case of foraging real ants, no network structure need be present. Normally, however, in ACO there is a salient network at hand, and the task is to navigate it in some desirable way (similar to the traveling salesman problem), including simply predicting what individuals will do on a given network. The network forms the space of possible foraging for the artificial ants. Now they wander with random as well as nonrandom components, following and depositing pheromone as with real ants, and using various heuristics to bias their randomized search.

Just as real ants typically are quite effective in scooping up food in the neighborhood, so ACO typically converges to a high-quality solution to the problem posed to it. The possibilities of using ACO to explore and yield insights on complex networks have only begun to be investigated. They hold much promise.

Particle Swarm Optimization (PSO)

PSO is biologically inspired by flocking of birds, schooling of fish, and other such phenomena. (See Wilensky 1998a for a treatment of emergent behavior in NetLogo of flocking phenomena.) Whereas ACO is naturally (but not exclusively) suited to discrete (combinatorial) optimization, PSO is naturally suited to continuous problems.

Each particle (such as a bird or fish) in a PSO model has a position and a velocity in solution space. Each position in solution space has a fitness, or objective function, value that is to be optimized. Each particle considers its "pbest" (personal best position it has encountered so far, "lbest" (local best values encountered so far in its neighborhood), and "gbest" (global best values encountered overall). This information, plus a random component, is used to update its position and velocity. The clock ticks and the process is repeated. As particles compromise among these three types of positions, this typically results in the flock being drawn to a globally high-quality solution.

Networks define systems of neighborhoods that emerge as the particles "fly" about solution space, looking for good solutions and attending to their neighborhoods. This makes PSO a most intriguing way of modeling social learning in social networks. Here, then, we have another very promising model for learning about networks and about learning in networks. (For more information, see Clerc 2006; Kennedy and Eberhart 2001; and Engelbrecht 2006; as well as the journal *Swarm Intelligence,* at www.swarmintelligence.org.

Conclusion: Lessons Learned and Looking Forward

The subject of this essay is AI and the study of networks. There are in this regard four main conclusions that I would emphasize, the first methodological and the others substantive:

1. ***Computational paradigms for investigating networks are available and have proved successful.*** The AI community has originated several powerful computational modeling paradigms that may be used for investigating social networks (broadly understood). These paradigms—particularly cellular automata models, agent-based models, and evolutionary computation—have been largely proved out as successful methodologies. Although much remains to be learned about them, they have delivered many solid successes and offer promise of much more. Their uptake in applications has been substantial and good tools are freely available for using them.

2. ***Procedures matter.*** Classical theories in economics and social science generally, in which agents are assumed to be ideally rational (Rational Choice Theory) are now well known to differ in their predictions from models in which more realistic assumptions are made. Behind Skyrms's (1996) apt but infelicitous phrase—

"evolution does not respect modular rationality"—lies the important finding that computationally plausible models of agent behavior yield outcomes that are often at wide variance with predictions based on Rational Choice Theory.

3. **Networks matter.** With increasing study and understanding, it is fair to say that something we might call Heuristic Choice Theory is emerging. Its mandate is to match heuristic possibilities (the subject of this essay) with heuristic behavior (as in behavioral economics and other empirical disciplines working with living subjects) and real-world data. For the foreseeable future, network models will reside at the nexus of these interests.

Networks are central to this debate, which may well lead to a wholesale revision of the foundations of social science (and perhaps is already doing so).

4. **The "shadow of society" matters.** The study of networks has led to a renewed recognition of the importance of social effects. One is reminded of views developed by 20th-century Pragmatist philosophers, such as John Dewey ("morality is social") and Hilary Putnam ("meanings are not in the head"). Working out a fundamentally social or network view, as distinct to an atomistic view of markets and societies, remains a challenge, albeit an intriguing one, supported by recent findings.

Looking forward, there are methodological challenges and substantive challenges in applying AI to studying networks. On the methodological side is the continuing challenge of validating computational models, and of maximally extracting information from them. The evolutionary computation community is perhaps in the vanguard here, but has only begun to address these issues systematically (Bartz-Beielstein 2006 is a good starting point).

On the substantive side, broadening and deepening the range and scope of network models that are developed and carefully validated remains very much on the agenda. Even without further conceptual developments, there is much to do. And conceptual developments *are* underway. Strategic interaction on nonregular networks—for example, networks other than the regular lattices described previously—is beginning to be investigated in force. Representative theoretical work includes Skyrms and Pemantle (2000) and Galeotti et al (2007). Empirical work has also begun (Kearns, Suri, and Montfort 2006). In fact, the effect of network structure is profound, further supporting the appropriateness of approaching strategic interaction from the perspective of a Heuristic Choice Theory.

Learning by strategically interacting agents in networks is also beginning to be investigated as part of Heuristic Choice Theory. For example, Kimbrough and Murphy (2007) present a simple learning algorithm for adjusting a continuous variable, by which oligopolists can learn to collude tacitly and thereby achieve higher profits. This learning algorithm, however, is subject to so-called number effects: The size and constitution of the collaborating oligopolists matters. Once again our attention is drawn to the network—or neighborhood—structure of industries.

References

Axelrod, Robert. 1984. *The Evolution of Cooperation.* New York, NY: Basic Books, Inc.

Axelrod, Robert. 1987. The Evolution of Strategies in Iterated Prisoner's Dilemma. In Genetic Algorithms and Simulated Annealing, ed. Lawrence Davis, 32-41. Los Altos, CA: Morgan Kaufman.

Bartz-Beielstein, Thomas. 2006. *Experimental Research in Evolutionary Computation: The New Experimentalism.* Natural Computing Series. Berlin, Germany: Springer-Verlag.

Berlekamp, Elwyn R., John H. Conway, and Richard K. Guy. 1982. *Winning Ways for Your Mathematical Plays,* vol. 2: Games in Particular. New York, NY: Academic Press.

Clerc, Maurice. 2006. *Particle Swarm Optimization.* ISTE Publishing Company.

Dorigo, Marco, M. Birattari, and Thomas Stutzle. 2006. Ant colony optimization: Artificial ants as a computation intelligence technique, *IEEE Computational Intelligence Magazine* 1 (4), 28-39.

Dorigo, Marco, and Thomas Stutzle. 2004. *Ant Colony Optimization.* Cambridge, MA: MIT Press.

Epstein, Joshua M., and Robert Axtell. 1996. *Growing Artificial Societies: Social Science from the Bottom Up.* Cambridge, MA: The MIT Press.

Engelbrecht, Andries P. 2006. *Fundamentals of Computational Swarm Intelligence,* Wiley.

Fogel, D. B., ed. 1998. *Evolutionary Computation: The Fossil Record.* Piscataway, NJ: IEEE Press.

Gilbert, Nigel, and Andrew Abbott. 2005. Introduction. *American Journal of Sociology* 110 (4), 859-863.

Galeotti, Andrea, Sanjeev Goyal, Matthew O. Jackson, Fernando Vega-Redondo, and Leeat Yariv. 2007. *Network Games* (September), http://privatewww.essex.ac.uk/~agaleo/wp.htm.

Grim, Patrick, Gary Mar, and Paul St. Denis. 1998. *The Philosophical Computer: Exploratory Essays in Philosophical Computer Modeling.* Cambridge, MA: The MIT Press.

Grim, Patrick. 1994. Undecidability in the spatialized prisoner's dilemma: Some philosophical implications, www.sunysb.edu/philosophy/faculty/pgrim/SPATIALP.HTM, 1994, accessed 2007-3-10.

Grimm, Volker, and Steven F. Railsback. 2005. *Individual-Based Modeling and Ecology,* Princeton Series in Theoretical and Computational Biology. Princeton, NJ: Princeton University Press.

Kennedy, James, and Russell C. Eberhart. 2001. *Swarm Intelligence.* San Francisco, CA: Morgan Kaufmann Publishers.

Kimbrough, Steven O. 2003. Computational modeling and explanation: Opportunities for the information and management sciences. In *Computational Modeling and Problem Solving in the Networked World: Interfaces in Computing and Optimization,* ed. Hemant K. Bhargava and Nong Ye, Operations Research/Computer Science Interfaces Series, 31-57. Boston, MA: Kluwer.

Kimbrough, Steven O., and Frederic H. Murphy. 2009. Learning to collude tacitly on production levels by oligopolistic agents. *Computational Economics* 33(1), 47-78.

Kearns, Michael, Siddharth Suri, and Nick Montfort. 2006. An experimental study of the coloring problem on human subject networks. *Science* 313, 824-7.

Nowak, Martin A., Sebastian Bonhoeffer, and Robert M. May. 1994. Spatial games and the maintenance of cooperation. Proceedings of the National Academy of Science of the United States of America 91, 4877-4881.

Nowak, M., and K. Sigmund. 1992. Tit-for-tat in heterogeneous populations. *Nature* 355, 250-2.

Nowak, M., and K. Sigmund. 1993. A strategy of win-stay lose-shift that outperforms tit-for-tat in the prisoner's dilemma game. *Nature* 364, 56-8.

Rauch, Jonathan. 2002. Seeing around corners. *Atlantic Monthly* 289 (4), 35-48. http://www.theatlantic.com/issues/2002/04/rauch.htm.

Schelling, Thomas C. 1978. *Micromotives and Macrobehavior.* New York, NY: W.W. Norton & Company.

Skyrms, Brian. 1996. *Evolution of the Social Contract.* Cambridge, UK: Cambridge University Press.

Skyrms, Brian, and Robin Pemantle. 2000. A dynamic model of social network formation. Proceedings of the National Academy of Sciences 97 (16, August 1), 9340-9346.

Tesfatsion, Leigh. 2001. Guest editorial: Agent-based modeling of evolutionary economic systems. IEEE Transactions on Evolutionary Computation 5 (5), 437-441.

Wilensky, U. 1997a. NetLogo ants model. NetLogo program at http://ccl.northwestern.edu/netlogo/models/Ants, Center for Connected Learning and Computer-Based Modeling, Northwestern University, Evanston, IL.

Wilensky, U. 1997b. NetLogo segregation model. NetLogo program at http://ccl.northwestern.edu/netlogo/models/Segregation, Center for Connected Learning and Computer-Based Modeling, Northwestern University, Evanston, IL.

Wilensky, U. 1998a. NetLogo Flocking model. NetLogo program at http://ccl.northwestern.edu/netlogo/models/Flocking, Center for Connected Learning and Computer-Based Modeling, Northwestern University, Evanston, IL.

Wilensky, U. 1998b. NetLogo life model. NetLogo program at http://ccl.northwestern.edu/netlogo/models/Life, Center for Connected Learning and Computer-Based Modeling, Northwestern University, Evanston, IL.

PART III

INNOVATION AND COORDINATION IN NETWORKS

Networks create new opportunities for innovation and coordination, and require new approaches. Innovation, product design, and new product development are no longer centered in a single firm, so companies need to understand how to get the best ideas and develop products through networks. In Chapter 9, **Satish Nambisan** and **Mohan Sawhney** present four different models for tapping into the "global brain" for innovation, which they call Orchestra, Creative Bazaar, Jam Central, and MOD Station. In Chapter 10, **Manuel E. Sosa** considers approaches to engineering design based on the information and resource requirements of a given design problem, to drive decisions such as organizational team structure and modularity in design. Finally, in Chapter 11, **Jan Rivkin** and **Nicolaj Siggelkow** examine the intersection between organizing and strategizing, looking at how "inefficient" overlaps across networks can sometimes be desirable in balancing search and stability.

Chapter 9   Network-Centric Innovation: Four Strategies for Tapping the Global Brain   147
Satish Nambisan and Mohan Sawhney

Chapter 10   Coordination Networks in Product Development   165
Manuel E. Sosa

Chapter 11   Organizational Design: Balancing Search and Stability in Strategic Decision Making   185
Jan W. Rivkin and Nicolaj Siggelkow

9

Network-Centric Innovation: Four Strategies for Tapping the Global Brain[1]

Satish Nambisan
Mohanbir Sawhney

Abstract

Most companies realize the need to "look outside" for innovation. However, few have a clear understanding about how they can make such a shift toward network-centric innovation—an innovation strategy that is centered on external networks and communities. Managers need more than anecdotal success stories about externally focused innovation, and they need more specific guidance than the "one size fits all" prescriptions of open innovation. The authors argue that every firm needs to find its own roadmap for tapping the "Global Brain"—the creative potential of the world outside its four walls. There are many different approaches and opportunities for network-centric innovation, based on the nature of the innovation space and the nature of network governance. In this chapter, the authors present a framework for structuring the landscape of network-centric innovation. They describe four models of network-centric innovation—Orchestra, Creative Bazaar, Jam Central, and MOD Station—and outline how companies can select, prepare for, and pursue the approach that best fits their particular business and innovation context.

---

[1] Adapted from *The Global Brain: Your Roadmap for Innovating Faster and Smarter in a Networked World*, by Satish Nambisan and Mohanbir Sawhney, Wharton School Publishing, October 2007.

In recent years, many large companies—for example, Dell, Kraft, Sony, and 3M— have found it difficult to achieve sustained growth in their businesses. The two most favored approaches to achieving growth—cost-cutting strategies, and mergers and acquisitions—seem to have lost their sheen with highly publicized failures such as Time Warner and AOL, or Daimler and Chrysler. This, combined with the increasingly global nature of competition and brutal commoditization of products and services, has led CEOs to the conclusion that innovation is the preferred pathway for sustainable and profitable growth. In a recent CEO survey, more than 86% of respondents indicated that innovation is definitely more important than M&As and cost-cutting strategies for long-term growth (Bain & Co 2005).

Such an innovation-driven growth orientation is also accompanied by a growing real-ization regarding the need to "look outside" for innovative product ideas and technolo-gies—reaching out to customers, suppliers, independent inventors, academic researchers, innovation brokers, and a host of other external entities that constitute the "Global Brain," the vast untapped creative potential that lies beyond company bound-aries. Several companies have set specific goals and targets for such external innovation sourcing—for example, P&G has stated that at least 50% of its innovations in the coming years will be sourced from outside, and both 3M and Henkel have established goals that call for a steady increase in the number of technologies and product concepts acquired from external sources. Moreover, new types of innovation intermediaries and new tech-nological infrastructure (for example, the Internet) have made tapping into such global networks of inventors, scientists, and innovative firms easier than ever before. Thus, the imperative for sourcing external innovation is matched by the rapidly expanding horizon of innovation opportunities.

Making such a shift from innovation initiatives that are centered on internal resources to those that are centered on external networks and communities—that is, a shift from *firm-centric innovation* to *network-centric innovation*—is, however, quite challenging and complex. There are some high-visibility examples of network-centric innovation, such as P&G's Connect+Develop initiative (Huston and Sakkab 2006) and IBM's partnership with open source software communities. However, these are not the only approaches; instead, they indicate the diversity and richness of the network-centric innovation landscape. And it is clear that following the model adopted by P&G or IBM may not be appropriate for your company—in other words, "one size does not fit all." There are different types of entities that companies can reach and many types of rela-tionships and networks that can be developed to harness innovative ideas. There are new types of innovation intermediaries and new innovation infrastructures. The wide range of entities, innovation networks, and approaches indicates the confusing landscape that companies are likely to face when embarking on a network-centered innovation strategy.

Our conversations with managers from almost 30 firms from a wide variety of industries suggest that they have a very limited understanding of the landscape of externally focused innovation, and how exactly their firm should take advantage of the dizzying array of opportunities to partner with external actors. As most CEOs and senior managers admit, harnessing the creative power of the Global Brain is something that is "theoretically easy" but "practically hard to do" (IBM Global CEO Study 2006).

In this chapter, we offer a framework that provides a structure to the landscape of network-centric innovation and informs on how companies can evaluate and identify the opportunities that best meet their particular needs and industry/market context. We start by describing the concept of network-centric innovation.

Network-Centric Innovation

We define network-centric innovation as an *externally focused approach to innovation that relies on harnessing the resources and capabilities of external networks and communities to amplify or enhance innovation reach, innovation speed, and the quality of innovation outcomes.* This definition reflects the essence of network-centricity—the emphasis on the network as the locus of innovation and the associated opportunity to extend, optimize, and/or enhance the value of a stand-alone entity or activity by making it more intelligent, adaptive, and personalized.

At its heart, *network-centric innovation* is an approach to organizing for the production of new ideas. As such, the philosophical roots of network-centric innovation can be traced to the literature on the alternate modes of production. Economists have long maintained that there are two primary modes of producing goods: *markets* and *hierarchies.* Ronald Coase, in his classic work *The Nature of the Firm* (1937), set out the rationale for the existence of the firm (the "hierarchy" mode of production) using the concept of *transaction costs* (that is, costs associated with conducting a market transaction). When the transaction costs increase beyond a certain level, it becomes more profitable to conduct and coordinate the production activities inside a firm than to use a market-based mode of production.

The successful development of Linux and other open source software products in the 1990s implied a third mode of production for new ideas or new products—one that was not just a hybrid of markets and firms. Yochai Benkler called this the *commons-based peer production* model. Using the same transaction cost logic, Benkler (2006) argued that when the "cost of organizing an activity on a peered basis is lower than the cost of using the market, and the cost of peering is lower than the cost of hierarchical organization," the commons-based peer model of production will emerge, as it did in the case of software.

The emerging models in the network-centric innovation landscape, however, reflect not just the internal, market, or commons approach to innovation but instead the mix or the intersections of these three modes of production. To understand the origins of such hybrid modes of production, consider the real-world manifestation of network-centric innovation that can be traced back to two distinct movements that took root in the 1990s: the Open Source movement (social knowledge creation) and the concept of business networks (the "ecosystem" perspective—see Moore 1993).

The boundaries between these two movements—open source communities and business ecosystems—have begun to blur. On the one hand, companies are seeking out open source communities and other communities of creation (for example, customer communities and inventor communities) as partners in innovation. On the other hand, innovations that have emerged from the open source communities are transitioning into the commercial world (for example, commercial open source). So the clear distinction between "purely open" and "purely proprietary" forms of organizing for innovation is giving way to a more complex and nuanced landscape. A wide variety of networks, players, and roles are emerging, including business ecosystems, alliance constellations, open source communities, inventor communities, customer communities, and expert communities. Drawing on the previously identified historical and philosophical roots, we identify four defining principles of network-centric innovation: shared goals and objectives, a shared "worldview," social knowledge creation, and an architecture of participation.

Considerable experimentation is going on in the network-centric innovation landscape, as we will explore next. Given the diverse opportunities, companies embarking on a network-centered innovation strategy need to address three broad sets of challenges:

1. ***Mindset and Cultural Challenges***—Companies need to shift from a "not invented here" view (NIH) and the "we know everything" (WKE) view to a more network-centric view.

2. ***Contextualization Challenges***—Given the different options for network-centric innovation, companies need to systematically evaluate and select from the alternative approaches the one that is most appropriate for its particular industry or market context.

3. ***Execution Challenges***—Once an appropriate network-centric innovation opportunity has been identified, companies need to execute on it, which may require different organizational capabilities and competencies. Companies also need to address issues such as integrating their internal and external innovation processes, managing risks, and protecting intellectual property.

These three sets of challenges—mindset and cultural, contextualization, and execution—represent the range of practical issues that CEOs and senior managers will need to tussle with in order to be successful in promoting and executing external network-centered innovation initiatives. The first step toward addressing them is to acquire a better understanding of the different models of network-centric innovation.

Models of Network-Centric Innovation

The emerging models and trends in the network-centric innovation landscape illustrate two key dimensions of creative endeavor along which we see change happening (see Figure 9-1). The first dimension relates to the nature of the innovation itself—that is, how the innovative idea is defined and how it evolves. The second dimension relates to the nature of network leadership or the structure of the network—that is, how the network partners come together and share in the activities related to development and commercialization of the innovation.

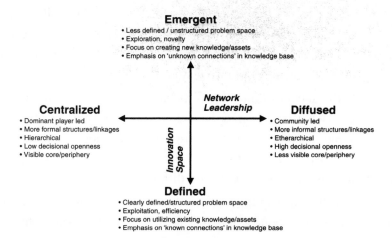

Figure 9-1   Dimensions of network-centric innovation

Consider the first dimension—the *nature of the innovation space.* Different types of projects can be pursued collaboratively in innovation networks. Some of the projects involve making well-defined modifications or enhancements to existing products, services, or technology platforms. In other projects, the innovation space tends to be less well defined, and the outcomes of the innovative effort are not well understood at the outset.

Based on this, we can think about the innovation space as a continuum ranging from "defined" at one end to "emergent" at the other end. On the defined end of the continuum, the definition might occur around a technology platform or a technology standard. Such is the case of AppExchange, the development platform created by Salesforce.com to harness the creative efforts of independent software developers. The innovation space can also be defined by dependencies created by existing products or processes. For example, Ducati, the Italian motorcycle company, engages its customers in innovation primarily to generate product improvement ideas for its existing products. Similarly, 3M's engagement with NineSigma.com was defined in terms of the properties of the adhesive material that the company was seeking. In all these examples, the innovative efforts are defined and limited by existing products, processes, or technology platforms.

At the other end of the continuum, the structure of the innovation space can be less defined and more uncertain. Although the broad contours of the innovative space might be specified or known—for example, the target market for a new product or service or the existing commercialization infrastructure—there might be fewer restrictions on the nature or process of the innovation. For example, when Staples looks around for innovative ideas, it is seeking new product concepts for the office supplies market from an independent inventor network. Similarly, in the open source software arena, many of the projects relate to developing new software applications—whether creating a new development tool or developing a new operating system.

Now, consider the second dimension—the *structure of the network leadership.* An innovation network—whether it is an open source community, an electronic R & D marketplace like NineSigma.com, or an ecosystem of technology firms as in the case of Salesforce.com—consists of a set of independent actors with varying goals and aspirations, diverse resources and capabilities, and different business models.

For all these entities to play together in the innovation initiative, there has to be a mechanism to ensure some coherence among their activities, capabilities, and aspirations. The essence is the need for a mechanism that can provide the vision and direction for the innovation and establish the rhythm for the innovation activities.

Network leadership can be thought of as a continuum of centralization, with the two ends being *centralized* and *diffused*. At the centralized end of the continuum, the network is led by a dominant firm. Leadership may be exercised in different ways—envisioning and establishing the innovation architecture, making the critical decisions that affect or shape the nature and the process of innovation, and defining the nature and membership of the network itself. For example, in its technology ecosystem, Salesforce.com provides the leadership by establishing and promoting the technology platform and by facilitating the activities of its external developers. At the "diffused" end of the continuum, the leadership tends to be loosely distributed among the members of the network. All members of the network share responsibility for leading the network. For example, many open source software projects have a leadership structure wherein the different members of the community share decision-making powers.

Thus, as we move from the left to the right on the continuum of network leadership, we can think about innovation networks that have a clearly defined core with a single dominant firm to networks in which the core and periphery are less well defined, or in which the core consists of all or most of the members.

These two dimensions—innovation space and network leadership—when crossed together, define four archetypical models that help structure the landscape of network-centric innovation: the *Orchestra* model, the *Creative Bazaar* model, the *Jam Central* model, and the *MOD Station* model (see Figure 9-2). In the remainder of this section, we briefly describe each of these four models of network-centric innovation and give some examples.

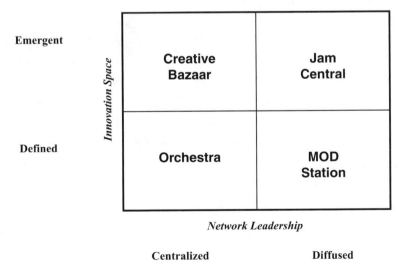

Figure 9-2   The four models of network-centric innovation

The Orchestra Model

The Orchestra model for network-centric innovation closely resembles the organization and the structure of a typical symphony orchestra—a conductor holding sway with his wand, directing a group of musicians—each a specialist in a specific musical instrument. The structure of the innovation space is fairly well defined and network leadership is centralized with a single dominant firm. Innovation architecture provides a clear basis for structuring the activities of the individual actors in the innovation network. And just as the musical instruments in an orchestra need to resonate with each other, the innovative contributions of network members in the Orchestra model also need to complement one another. The leadership provided by the dominant firm is crucial to ensuring that the innovative contributions of individual contributors add up to a valuable whole.

Boeing's development of the Dreamliner 787 offers an example of the Orchestra model of network-centric innovation. Boeing assembled a set of global partners whom it could trust with the process of creating entire sections of the plane, from concept to production. The design and development tasks were not just outsourced to these partners. Instead, partners made financial investments in those tasks. In other words, Boeing made a critical shift from making its partners "Build to Print" to making them "Design and Build to Performance." However, Boeing remained the central decision maker in the network. Although each global partner had significant autonomy with regard to the design of its individual components, there was still a need for a single decision maker on important design and development issues.

The globally dispersed partner companies also needed to converse in real-time using the same vocabulary, interpret the design information gained from others, and integrate that knowledge with the design of their components. Boeing addressed this challenge by creating a sophisticated virtual Global Collaboration Environment for its partners to share information and collaborate on design on a real-time basis. Overall, Boeing's 787 project describes a situation wherein a group of firms come together to exploit a market opportunity based on an explicit innovation architecture that is defined and shaped by a dominant firm. The innovation architecture typically emphasizes efficiency over novelty, so there is a heavy emphasis on modularity.

There are three broad themes that underlie the success of the Orchestra model of network-centric innovation:

1. The firm playing the dominant role in the network has to *provide strong leadership to the innovation activities*—leadership that should be evident in envisioning and clarifying the innovation architecture, facilitating and coordinating the innovation activities of the network partners, and integrating and bringing to market the innovation.

2. The key network partners involved in the design and development should be *sufficiently invested in the project*—in other words, the dominant firm should ensure that the partners share in the risks as well as in the rewards related to the innovation.

3. The lead firm should also *establish an environment* that supports building trust-based relationships and the ability to rapidly share knowledge, thereby ensuring high "situational awareness."

The Creative Bazaar Model

The second model of network-centric innovation—the *Creative Bazaar* model—describes a context wherein a dominant firm shops for innovation in a global bazaar of new ideas, products, and technologies and uses its proprietary commercialization infrastructure to build on the ideas and bring them to the market (Nambisan and Sawhney 2007). The nature of the innovation is, however, emergent—the only constraint is that the innovative idea should fit the company's overall target market and brand portfolio. The term *bazaar* implies a dizzying array of wares on offer, ranging from raw ideas and patents to relatively mature or "market-ready" new product concepts, as well as the presence of different hawkers that companies can deal with, from idea scouts, patent brokers, and electronic innovation marketplaces to incubation agencies and venture capitalists.

Companies that adopt the Creative Bazaar model use these different types of mechanisms to source new ideas and technologies from inventors with implications on innovation risk, reach, speed, and cost (Nambisan and Sawhney 2007). Idea scouts and licensing agents identify promising new product and technology ideas and bring them to large companies for further development and commercialization. For example, idea scouts such as the BIG Idea Group and the Product Development Group (PDG) LLC organize idea contests and Roadshows on behalf of client companies (such as Staples, Gillette, and Sunbeam) to seek out promising ideas from independent inventors. Innovation capitalists not only identity promising innovative ideas but also invest in transforming them into market-ready ideas so that client companies can make better commercialization decisions. For example, Evergreen IP, a Colorado-based innovation capitalist firm, seeks out promising ideas and inventions from individual inventors and makes selective investments to upgrade those inventions via market research, product design, and patent work. It then sells or licenses the resulting innovation and related IP to large consumer product companies such as P&G and Dial. Companies can also shop for more market-ready products (that is, product or technology concepts that have been prototyped and market validated) and acquire them from incubators and venture capital firms.

Regardless of the sourcing approach, the focal company plays the dominant role in the innovation network by offering its infrastructure for developing the innovative idea and by making all the critical decisions regarding commercialization. The commercialization infrastructure might include design capabilities, brands, capital, and access to distribution channels.

In sum, the Creative Bazaar model aims to seek out and bring to fruition innovation opportunities that meet the broad market and innovation agenda of the dominant firm.

Jam Central Model

The third model of network-centric innovation—the *Jam Central* model—involves individual contributors coming together to collaborate in envisioning and developing an innovation. The term *jam* signifies two key themes of this model: It is a group activity and it is improvisational.

The innovation space is typically not well structured and the objectives and direction of the innovation tend to emerge organically from the collaboration. There are no dominant members, and the responsibility for leading and coordinating the activity is diffused among the network members. Even if the leadership is not equally shared by all members, key decisions that shape the innovation processes and outcomes tend to evolve from the interactions of the network members.

Consider the Tropical Disease Initiative (TDI), a typical example of the Jam Central model of network-centric innovation. The TDI is a Web-based, collaborative innovation effort aimed at identifying cures for tropical diseases such as malaria and tuberculosis. The project was launched by a group of scientists and researchers at the University of California at Berkeley, Duke University, and the University of California at San Francisco. The TDI project brings together computational biologists and other volunteer researchers to work collaboratively on specific tropical diseases and then makes the results of such collaborative innovation available in the public domain, where other researchers could use them to guide their clinical research work. The network leadership is diffused among the members. While a core body of founding members provides the broad direction for the community and facilitates collaboration and communication among members, the scientists from all over the world who form the community share in the project-level decision making.

TDI has defined a broad focus on tropical diseases. However, the specific projects are left to individual contributors or community members. Any contributor can propose a new project. As long as the project falls within the broad scope of TDI and there is sufficient interest among the community members, it will be incorporated into the fold. Thus, the specific innovation goals and objectives are emergent.

A critical issue in the TDI network relates to intellectual property rights and production of drugs (Rai 2005). Specifically, who "owns" the output from the TDI projects, and how should such outputs reach the "market"? The TDI community members have at their disposal several intellectual property ownership options. Researchers always have the right to publish their ideas in traditional peer-reviewed scientific journals. In addition, the Science Commons offers public domain licenses (similar to the Creative Commons licensing scheme) that can be used to make available the leads or targets generated through the TDI project to other scientists for follow-up work.

The TDI example illustrates three central tenets of the Jam Central model—an emergent innovation vision and goals, a community-led, diffused leadership structure, and a robust infrastructure to support collaborative knowledge creation and value appropriation.

The MOD Station Model

The fourth and final model of network-centric innovation—the *MOD Station* model—exhibits two key characteristics. First, it largely involves modifying or leveraging an existing (product, process, or service) innovation—that is, activities that occur within the boundaries of a predefined innovation space, and aim to add, enhance, or adapt existing products or services. Second, it occurs in a community context—where the norms and values that govern the innovation activities are established by the community and not by any one dominant firm.

The term *MOD* stands for *modification.* In the computer-gaming industry, games that are modifications of existing games are referred to as "mods." By offering the source of a computer-based game to a community of gamers, a company can enable the creation of variations of the game. These modifications can involve adding new characters, new textures, or new story lines. Depending on the extent of modifications, they can be "partial conversions" or "total conversions." Total conversions typically turn out to be completely new games that happen to use some of the basic content or structure of the original game. Mods are made by the general gaming public or *modders.* Increasingly, the gaming companies have started assisting modders by providing extensive tools and documentation. The mods are then distributed and used over the Internet. The most popular mod is *Counter-Strike,* a game that originated as a modification of another game called *Half-Life* produced by Valve Corporation, a software firm based in Bellevue, Washington.

The individuals who participate in creating the mods, primarily fans of the particular game, play the role of innovators. The online forums associated with such communities provide the platform for the modders to promote and distribute the mods.

The benefits from mods accrue to gamers (for example, more gaming choices, community-based reputational incentives), as well as to the developers of the original games (such as, extended product life cycle, larger customer base) (Rosen 2005). And this has led to many game developers (for example, Epic Games, id Software, Valve Software, and Bethesda Softworks) taking a more proactive approach to promote and support the innovative activities of the gaming community.

The MOD Station model of network-centric innovation is becoming evident in other domains, too. For example, Sun's OpenSPARC initiative involves engaging a community to innovate within the boundaries defined by the SPARC architecture specifications in ways that benefit both the community members and Sun. In sum, the MOD Station model is focused on exploiting existing innovation or knowledge to address market/technological issues by a community of innovators (including innovation users, customers, scientists, and experts).

Organizational Competencies and Capabilities for Network-Centric Innovation

Given these four models, what capabilities do companies need to succeed in network-centric innovation initiatives? Here, we briefly consider two components of a firm's readiness—organizational readiness and operational readiness—as well metrics for measuring success.

Organizational Readiness

Organizational readiness refers to the *people* dimension of the capabilities needed for network-centric innovation. Essentially, it is about creating the right environment within the organization to encourage and support participation in network-centric innovation. This includes creating an "open" mindset, getting leadership onboard, creating the appropriate organization structure, and communicating the innovation strategy internally and externally.

In particular, does the firm need a dedicated unit to lead network-centric innovation? In some firms, existing organizational units (for example, corporate R&D unit or business development unit) can evolve or transform to spearhead the network-centric innovation initiatives. In other cases, new units and new positions need to be established to provide the leadership. Three factors shape such decisions. First, does the company have a history of participating in collaborative R&D ventures? If so, the firm can rely on transforming one or more existing units that already have the experience to take on the new responsibilities related to leading and coordinating the company's network-centric innovation initiatives. Second, is the innovation space the company is mostly focused on for collaboration clearly defined or more diffused in nature? Further, how diverse are the company's innovation partners likely to be? Typically, in a diffused innovation space and with a diverse partner network, the dedicated organizational unit may act less as a process enforcer and more as a clearinghouse for best practices and skills. Third, are the initiatives being considered by the company related to its existing products and services or to new/emerging business areas? If the firm is staying close to existing markets, then it is likely that the company will have to create strong linkages between the organizational unit spearheading network-centric innovation activities and the R&D units within individual business divisions associated with those existing markets/products.

Operational Readiness

Operational readiness refers to the *process* dimension of the capabilities. This includes designing processes for project selection, partner selection, risk management, integrating internal and external processes, and management of intellectual property rights. Operational readiness also involves creating the tools and technologies to support externally focused innovation and metrics to track your progress and assess your success.

Unless the company establishes basic processes to guide and manage its participation in external innovation initiatives, the organization's capability to derive returns from such activities can be seriously hampered. Although the specifics of the different processes and their implementation may depend on the particular organizational context, here we list some of the generic process areas that are needed to support network-centric innovation.

Companies need processes for selecting business areas within the company that would be most appropriate for pursuing network-centric innovation initiatives. Should a company experiment with such external innovation initiatives in its emerging or established businesses? How should the company decide the nature and the level of its involvement in the project? Companies also need processes for selecting external innovation networks and network partners, identifying and managing the risks associated with participating in network-centric innovation projects. In addition, companies need processes for sharing knowledge, coordinating innovation activities, and managing relationships with a diverse set of network partners. The overall objective of the process infrastructure should be to enable the company to use a uniform yardstick to monitor and measure performance in the network-centric innovation activities across the different business units of the organization and to ensure a level of repeatability in such performance.

Over the past few years, a wide range of tools and technologies have emerged that can help companies implement such a network-centric innovation process infrastructure. Some of these tools facilitate communication and knowledge sharing among network members while some other tools enable coordination and management of collaborative innovation processes. Information technology-based tools can be used as process management mechanisms to instill structured product development processes and to bring a level of rigor and stability to the innovation activities. They also facilitate communication and basic project management functions—scheduling, coordinating, and managing resources related to a complex project—whether it is an Orchestra model project such as the Boeing 787 or a Jam Central project such as TDI.

Success Metrics

Another important element of operational readiness is the ability to evaluate the company's performance and returns from network-centric innovation. This ability demands the creation of appropriate "portfolio of innovation" metrics. Some generic network-centric innovation metrics apply to all models, whereas others are specific to the model the company participates in and the role it assumes. Further, whereas some metrics may be defined at the level of the innovation network, others focus on the company and reflect the impact of the company's participation on its internal activities and outcomes. Consider a few examples.

The metrics that are related to the overall network allow a company to evaluate whether it is partnering with the "right" network and also indicate when the company might have to rethink its collaboration strategy. For example, for a company such as Dial, Staples, or P&G that plays the role of an innovation portal in the Creative Bazaar model, a valuable metric would be the reach and geographic scope of its network—the number of inventors and intermediaries. Similarly, for a company playing the role of innovation sponsor in the Jam Central model, a useful measure would relate to the stability of the innovation community—the number of members in the community and the average turnover in membership. Such measures indicate the overall quality of the network and the current and future innovation potential of the network to continuously evaluate whether the company is partnering with the right set of external entities.

Metrics that assess the impact of the collaboration on the company indicate how well the company is fairing or gaining from its participation. Going back to the Creative Bazaar example, the number of external ideas entering a company's product development pipeline or the number of new products that can be traced back to such external sources indicates the clear and most direct impact of the company's participation in the network. Similarly, a company playing the role of innovation catalyst might consider the number of new markets that it has been able to expand as an indication of the impact of its participation in the network.

Some company-specific measures could be more generic and relate to the internal innovation infrastructure or capabilities. For example, an audit of the company's internal innovation processes—process maturity—might indicate its overall preparedness to identify and exploit different types of network-centric innovation opportunities.

Given that each measure provides a unique view or perspective of success in network-centric innovation, it is imperative that a company adopt a portfolio of such measures and employ those best-suited to its desired focus in participating in network-centric innovation.

Implications for Research and Practice

The network-centric innovation framework presented here holds several important implications for both research and practice. First, our discussion emphasizes that companies will need to adopt innovation models that are not just "open" but "network-centric." An explicit acknowledgment of the network brings into focus the characteristics of the network that would shape the company's role in it, as well as the innovation processes and outcomes. From a research perspective, we need to integrate theoretical concepts and constructs from network theory and innovation management to better understand the issues that underlie a company's participation in network-centric innovation.

Second, the framework also highlights the diversity of the opportunities in the network-centric innovation landscape. Companies need to situate their particular organizational and innovation context within this broad landscape to identify the most appropriate innovation model. Here we provided only a brief discussion of the contextual characteristics. There needs to be more rigorous research to develop a deeper understanding of the contextual characteristics that would shape the company's selection of each network-centric innovation model and role in it.

Third, while the focus here has been on the external innovation opportunities, to be successful, companies will need to integrate their internal and external innovation activities. Future studies may focus on identifying the organizational mechanisms that would facilitate such integration, as well as the balance between their internal and external innovation activities.

Finally, most companies with diverse business units or divisions (for example, DuPont, Unilever, 3M) are likely to discover opportunities to pursue more than one innovation role across their diverse innovation contexts. For example, IBM plays the role of a platform leader in some of its traditional business areas including systems and servers, and semiconductors. At the same time, it plays the role of an innovation sponsor in some of the community-led innovation initiatives, most particularly in the Linux open source community. This implies the need to carefully evaluate the potential synergies across these different innovation contexts and to formulate organization-wide network-centric innovation strategies that bring coherence to the different innovation roles within the company.

Conclusion

We started this chapter by emphasizing that tapping into the Global Brain is no longer a matter of choice for most companies. Moving from such an awareness of the promise of network-centric innovation initiatives to their successful execution, however, calls for a better understanding of the types of innovation networks, innovation roles, and organizational capabilities. In this chapter, our primary objective has been to provide a structure to the landscape of network-centric innovation. Companies that invest in processes to systematically identify the "right" network-centric innovation approach and the requisite organizational capabilities are more likely to benefit from such initiatives than those who blindly follow the latest high-visibility example of network-centric innovation.

References

Bain & Company. 2005. Management tools and trends survey.

Coase, R. 1937. The nature of the firm. *Economica* 4 (16), 386-405.

Huston, L., and N. Sakkab. 2006. Connect and develop: P&G's new innovation model. *Harvard Business Review* (March), 84 (3).

IBM Global CEO Study. 2006. Expanding the innovation horizon, www-1.ibm.com/services/uk/bcs/html/bcs_landing_ceostudy.html.

Moore, M. 1993. Predators and prey: A new ecology of competition. *Harvard Business Review.*

Nambisan, S., and M. Sawhney. 2007. A buyer's guide to the innovation bazaar. *Harvard Business Review* (June, 109-118).

Rai, A. 2005. Open and collaborative research: A new model for biomedicine. In *Intellectual Property Rights in Frontier Industries: Biotech and Software.* AEI Brookings Press.

Rosen, Z. 2005. Mod, man, and law: A reexamination of the law of computer game modifications. *Chicago-Kent Journal of Intellectual Property.*

Y. Benkler. 2006. *The Wealth of Networks.* MIT Press.

10

Coordination Networks in Product Development

Manuel E. Sosa

Abstract

Complex products such as airplanes and automobiles are designed by networks of design teams working on different components, often across organizations. The challenge in managing these networks is to decompose the project into manageable pieces but then coordinate the entire network to produce the best overall design. In this chapter, Manuel Sosa offers insights on this challenge. He examines the design structure matrix (DSM) as a project management tool for planning complex development efforts and discusses the engineering and managerial implications of considering complex products as networks of interconnected subsystems and components. In particular, he considers the impact of modularity on interactions among subcomponents. Finally, he examines organizational communications, overlaying product interfaces with communications interfaces of development teams to understand where communication links may be missing or unnecessary. The discussion offers insights on any complex design and coordination challenge, where networks of individuals or teams work together to contribute to a larger whole.

Designing new and complex products requires the interplay of processes, products, and structures across networks of individuals and organizations. From a network perspective, processes are networks of design tasks, products are networks of interconnected components, and organizations are networks of developers or design teams that interact when executing design tasks to develop new products. Because managing interdependences is fundamental to developing new products, taking a network per-spective can advance our understanding of how to coordinate resources in complex development efforts.

Coordination is the result of both system decomposition and system integration. For example, in developing a product such as an airplane, managers decompose the overall project into manageable pieces. Hundreds of specialized cross-functional teams each work on a different component or subsystem of the airplane. Of course, these teams can-not work in isolation; they must integrate and coordinate their efforts to ensure that the system works as a whole. In planning a complex product development process, project managers need to plan and specify just which resources and information different teams will need from each other at particular stages of the project (Sosa, Eppinger, and Rowles 2007b, Sosa 2008).

As we discuss in this chapter, product development managers in large organizations such as Airbus, Ford, or BMW often find themselves lost in their web of design activities and engineering teams, all trying to do the best they can to design their individual piece of the system. Only by taking a network perspective can we navigate the intricate web of activities associated with the design of each of the product components, which is what determines how designers ultimately communicate among themselves during the devel-opment effort.

This chapter is structured in three sections: First, I review the product development literature focused on the use of the design structure matrix (DSM) as a project manage-ment tool that captures development processes as a web of design tasks. Second, I dis-cuss the engineering and managerial implications of considering complex products as networks of interconnected subsystems and components. Finally, I turn to the informal organizational structure to understand how design teams establish and manage their technical communication networks during the design of complex systems.

The Development Process as a Web of Design Activities

In the early 1980s, BMW used to take about six years to complete a new vehicle development. A particularly important milestone in such a long process used to occur 18 months before product launch. That was the date on which the vehicle concept would be frozen so that detailed engineering could be completed, final prototypes built, and production ramp-up started. During the development of the first 7 Series in the mid-1980s, managers at BMW decided to widen the entire vehicle by 40 millimeters just two months before completely freezing the design of the car. This, of course, required redesigning more than one-third of the parts in the vehicle. Yet managers at BMW have agreed that, although costly, carrying out such a major design iteration was strictly necessary to avoid making the car too "cramped." Without such a costly decision, the original 7 Series "would never have succeeded in the market like it has" (Pisano 1996, 6). Although I will not discuss here the specific causes behind this design decision at BMW, this example helps us to illustrate vividly what design iterations are as well as their cost and performance consequences.

Design iterations are the repetition of design tasks due to the arrival of new or more complete information during the development of a new system. Complex products are particularly vulnerable to design iterations because they are complex engineering efforts involving many highly interdependent design activities (Smith and Eppinger 1997b; Mihm, Loch, and Huchzermeier 2003; Sosa, Eppinger, and Rowles 2004). Which design activities are likely to be involved in design iterations? What can managers do to mitigate the negative effects of design iterations? Who is more likely to be involved in design iterations? These are some of the questions that product development managers need to address when planning the development of complex systems such as automobile, airplanes, or jet engines.

Traditional project manager tools such as PERT charts and IDEF diagrams have been typically used during the planning of complex projects. However, because these tools have been devised to plan more sequential engineering efforts such as the ones encountered in the construction industry, they are limited in their capability to explicitly portray design iterations (Eppinger 2001). To address such limitations, Steward (1981) introduced a matrix-based tool called the design structure matrix (DSM), which captures the web of design activities in a product development process. Eppinger et al. (1994) extended the use of DSM-based models to improving complex product development efforts by highlighting the task dependencies that managers can encounter in the process.

A DSM is a square matrix whose rows and columns are identically labeled with the design tasks of a development process (see Figure 10-1). In its simpler form, the nonzero cells of a DSM indicate the existence of an information requirement between two development activities. That is, a mark in cell (i,j) indicates that task i needs information produced by task j in order to be completed. Hence, by examining row i of a DSM, managers can easily identify the other tasks that provide information to task i, and by examining column *j*, managers can easily determine which other tasks are using the information produced by task *j*. As a result, the DSM captures in a compact and visual manner the web of activities that form a development process as determined by the development tasks and their task dependencies. For a review on the various uses of the DSM to improve product development efforts, refer to Eppinger et al. (1994), Eppinger (2001), and Browning (2001).

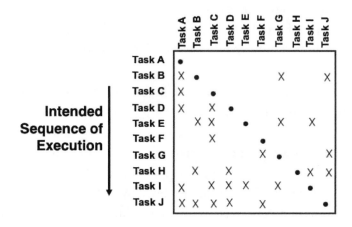

Figure 10-1   A generic design structure matrix

The DSM also captures the order in which activities are sequenced. Typically, the rows (and columns) are ordered in the chronological sequence in which activities are to be executed, from product planning to product launch. Such a chronological arrangement of the rows (and columns) of the DSM allows managers to distinguish between marks below and above the diagonal. Whereas marks below the diagonal are considered feed-forward dependencies because they occur between activities that can be executed in a sequential manner, marks above the diagonal represent feed-back dependencies because they indicate that a design task requires information from another task that will be executed in the future. Therefore, marks above the diagonal represent sources of design iterations because they indicate the arrival of new or updated information that may trigger the rework of a series of design activities. For example, task B in Figure 10-1 would need information from tasks G and J, which are to be executed later in the process. Hence, the arrival of new or updated information to task B may force the team responsible for such a task to revise or rework part of the activities associated with it, which, in turn, can trigger other changes in other design tasks that depend on task B.

Of course, some of these sources of design iterations can be removed by simply resequencing the DSM to minimize marks above the diagonal (Steward 1981; Eppinger et al. 1994), that is, making the development process as sequential as possible (see Figure 10-2). By examining the resequenced (or optimally partitioned) DSM (see Figure 10-3), managers can identify the set of activities that could be executed in a serial fashion (sequential dependency) or those that are independent from each other (parallel dependency). More interesting, managers can also identify the set of design activities that depend on each other in a cyclical manner (coupled dependency). Those are the interdependent (or coupled) development activities that are likely to result in design iterations (Smith and Eppinger 1997a,b).

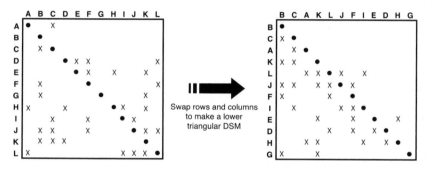

Figure 10-2 Partitioning a DSM into a low triangular DSM

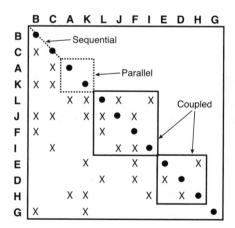

Figure 10-3 Partitioned DSM and types of task dependencies (Eppinger et al. 1994)

An Example from Automobile Design

As an example, Ulrich and Eppinger (2004) examine the task structure used by Fiat to develop the digital mock-up of its engine compartments, as shown in Figure 10-4. The blocks along the diagonal of such a DSM highlight the groups of "activities that are executed together (in parallel, sequentially, and/or iteratively) within each phase." As evident from Figure 10-4, an important contribution of a DSM representation is the simple and explicit representation of complex and iterative processes in which design iterations can be easily highlighted.

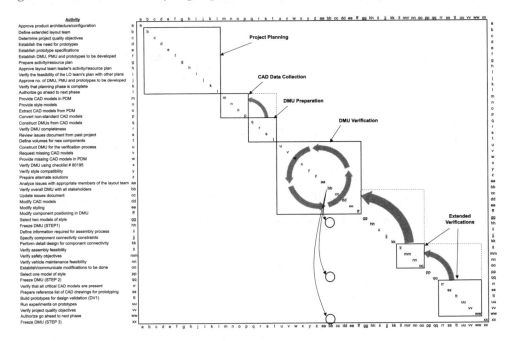

Figure 10-4   Process to develop digital mock-ups at Fiat (courtesy of Steven Eppinger, Ulrich and Eppinger 2004, p. 356; © The McGraw-Hill Companies, Inc.)

Figure 10-5 provides a closer look at the highly iterative set of activities involved in one phase, "DMU verification." It shows which organizational group is responsible for executing each design activity. Note that the group of design activities exhibited in Figure 10-5 forms a highly interdependent network of tasks. As a result, managers must pay particular attention to facilitating the information exchanges between the people responsible for this set of activities. Some information exchanges require more managerial support than others. In particular, managers have to be more actively involved in cross-boundary coordination, when iteration is across people from *different* organizational groups as opposed to people from the *same* organizational group.

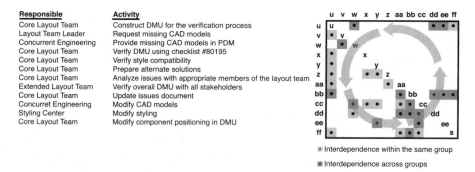

Responsible	Activity
Core Layout Team	Construct DMU for the verification process
Layout Team Leader	Request missing CAD models
Concurrent Engineering	Provide missing CAD models in PDM
Core Layout Team	Verify DMU using checklist #80195
Core Layout Team	Verify style compatibility
Core Layout Team	Prepare alternate solutions
Core Layout Team	Analyze issues with appropriate members of the layout team
Extended Layout Team	Verify overall DMU with all stakeholders
Core Layout Team	Update issues document
Concurret Engineering	Modify CAD models
Styling Center	Modify styling
Core Layout Team	Modify component positioning in DMU

Figure 10-5   Iterative design tasks of FIAT's "DMU verification" phase

In addition to identifying the subset of highly interdependent design activities that are likely to generate design iterations, managers need to understand the specific nature and criticality of the task dependencies of these coupled activities. In the FIAT example, to manage the interdependent design tasks shown in Figure 10-5, managers needed to know which specific engine components and CAD models were involved and how they were connected to one another. In other words, executing the development process shown in Figures 10-4 and 10-5 depends largely on the specific configuration of the product under development, as well as the organization and experience of the people involved. Hence, to effectively manage design iterations in product development, managers have to examine the architecture and organizational structure associated with the development process. This approach illustrates how a network view of product and organizational structures can improve the design and execution of complex product development processes. We now shift our view from the organizational processes to considering the products themselves.

Complex Products as Networks of Components

While complex products result from a network of interlinked design activities, as discussed previously, the products themselves can be seen as networks of interconnected components (Simon 1981). Product decomposition determines the architecture of the product, which is the way components interface with each other, so the product can fulfill its functional requirements (Ulrich 1995, Ulrich and Eppinger 2004). Moreover, the product architecture results in identifiable design interfaces between its various components (Henderson and Clark 1990; Ulrich 1995; Sosa, Eppinger, and Rowles 2007a). These interfaces, in turn, are the main source of technical interdependencies between the design teams responsible for the development of such components, requiring coordination between them (Thompson 1967, Galbraith 1973).

Considering products as networks of components has resulted in two important streams of research in engineering design:

1. **Product decomposition**—Researchers decompose complex products using graphs, trees, and matrices (Michelena and Papalambros 1995; Chen, Ding, and Li 2005), paying particular attention to the identification of *clusters* of similarly dependent components (also called *modules*) to facilitate integration efforts during the design process (Pimmler and Eppinger 1994; Gershenson, Prasad, and Allamneni 1999; Sharman and Yassine 2004).

2. **Design change propagation**—Researchers also have used product-based DSMs to examine how design changes propagate through interconnected components during the design process (Clarkson, Simons, and Eckert 2004; Eckert, Clarkson, and Zanker 2004). Because components are connected with each other to fulfill the functional requirements of the product as a whole, engineering changes in one component are likely to affect other components.

Although the two areas of research previously described have had a great influence in the way complex engineered products are architected and developed, the focus has been on studying the product network as a whole rather than on structural properties of the components as a function of their connectivity with other components. To address this limitation, Sosa, Eppinger, and Rowles 2007a examine "modularity" of a component, defined as its level of independence from the other components. By doing so, we are able not only to quantify component modularity as a function of the lack of *centrality* of the component with respect to other components in the product (Freeman 1979, Wasserman and Faust 1994), but also to relate how the modularity of product components relates to important design decisions such as component redesign.

Two important, and challenging, considerations when modeling complex products as networks of components are (1) defining the level of granularity at the node level; and (2) defining the various types of linkages between any two given components. To illustrate how we have addressed these challenges, consider the architecture of a large commercial aircraft engine developed by Pratt & Whitney (Sosa, Eppinger, and Rowles 2003, 2007a). Figure 10-6 shows both a cross-sectional diagram of the engine studied and its network representation. According to our interviews with systems architects at the research site, the engine was decomposed into eight subsystems, each of which was further decomposed into 5 to 10 components, for a total of 54 components. As a result, there are 54 nodes in the network map shown in Figure 10-6. The nodes are colored to illustrate the eight subsystems that composed the engine: Fan, Low-Pressure Compressor (LPC), High-Pressure Compressor (HPC), Combustion Chamber (CC), High-Pressure Turbine (HPT), Low-Pressure Turbine (LPT), Mechanical Components (MC), and External and Controls (EC). Because this was the third engine derived from the same basic engine design, the product decomposition into subsystems and components was well understood by our informants, and corresponded with the level of granularity used to establish the organizational structure that designed each of the 54 components. Using a higher level of granularity at the subsystem level would have resulted in a network of only eight nodes corresponding to the eight subsystems of the engine, while using a lower level of granularity would have resulted in several hundreds (perhaps thousands) of parts whose individual functionality did not correspond with any important functional requirement of the engine. Using the engine component, also called engineering *chunks* (Ulrich and Eppinger 1994), as the unit of analysis allowed us to represent the engine based on individual elements associated with important functional requirements with dedicated cross-functional teams responsible for their design and development.

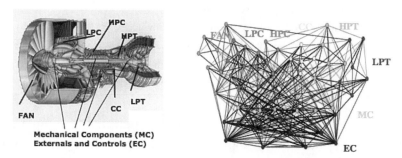

Figure 10-6   Cross-sectional view and network diagram of the PW4098 aircraft engine

After documenting the general decomposition of the product, we identified the network of design dependencies among the 54 components of the engine. We distinguished five types of design dependencies to define the design interfaces (or linkages) of the physical components (see Table 10-1). In addition, we used a five-point scale to capture the level of criticality of each dependency for the overall functionality of the component in question (see Table 10-2), which captures positive or negative design dependencies between components, those that either enable or hinder the component's functionality

(Jarratt, Clarkson, and Eckert 2004). We consider three levels of criticality: indifferent (0), weak (-1,+1), and strong (-2,+2), because we assume that negative component interactions indicate equally important design dependencies to be addressed as positive ones. For additional details on metrics and linkages between product components in complex products, refer to Sosa, Eppinger, and Rowles (2003, 2007a).

TABLE 10-1   Types of Design Dependency

Dependency	Description
Spatial	Functional requirement related to physical adjacency for alignment, orientation, serviceability, assembly, or weight
Structural	Functional requirement related to transferring loads or containment
Material	Functional requirement related to transferring airflow, oil, fuel, or water
Energy	Functional requirement related to transferring heat, vibration, electric, or noise energy
Information	Functional requirement related to transferring signals or controls

TABLE 10-2   Level of Criticality of Design Dependencies

Measure	Description
(+2)	Dependency is necessary for functionality.
(+1)	Dependency is beneficial but not absolutely necessary for functionality.
(0)	Dependency does not affect functionality.
(-1)	Dependency causes negative effects but does not prevent functionality.
(-2)	Dependency must be prevented to achieve functionality.

Those components that are less connected to other engine components are more *modular* because they have more degrees of freedom to fulfill their functional requirements independently of the state of other engine components. Less modular components, which are more integrally connected (via nonstandardized interfaces) to other engine components, are more dependent on other components to fulfill their functional requirements. Interestingly, components in complex products exhibit large variation in terms of their interconnectivity within the product. Figure 10-7 shows two engine components with extreme levels of component modularity.

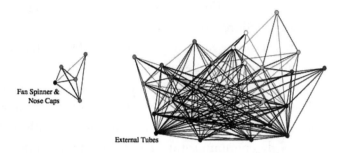

Figure 10-7   Two engine components with the low and high levels of connectivity

Modularity is important because managers should consider the connectivity of components with other components when making important design decisions such as outsourcing or redesigning product components. For example, we found that those components of the engine that were more (directly and indirectly) connected to "transmit forces" (an important engine functional requirement) to other components were the ones that exhibited higher levels of component redesign, whereas those components that were more connected due to spatial consideration (an important design constraint) were the ones that exhibited lower levels of component redesign. Hence, the modularity of a component in a complex product can be associated with both high and low levels of component redesign. Managers can use the knowledge of linkages among components to propagate design decisions or to *avoid* redesigning some components to prevent propagating design constraints that could disrupt certain functional requirements of the product (Baldwin and Clark 2000; Sosa, Eppinger, and Rowles 2007a).

In addition to understanding how process networks and networks of components come together in designing complex products such as an airplane or automobile, managers also have to understand how the *organization* actually coordinates the technical interfaces between the components they design (Allen 1977), as considered in the next section.

The Informal Communication Network of Design Teams

Communication among design teams working on specific product components is crucial to success, as can be illustrated by two cases. In 1999, the Ford Explorer went from being the number one sport utility vehicle (SUV) sold in USA to the least desired one due to quality problems associated with the suspension system of the Ford Explorer and the design of its Bridgestone/Firestone tires. Ford and Bridgestone/Firestone lost billions of dollars after their failure to coordinate the vehicle design of the Ford Explorer with the design of its tires (Pinedo, Sehasdri, and Zemel 2000). Similarly, Airbus's development of the A380 "superjumbo" suffered major delays and cost overruns because of late-emerging incompatibilities in the design of the electrical harnesses of various sections of the plane's fuselage. In this case, the electrical harnesses team in Germany and its counterpart team in France, which were responsible for different sections of the fuselage, were not properly communicating about their design interface specifications (Gumbel 2006). These mistakes likely contributed to the resignation of CEOs and the loss of other senior executives' jobs at both Ford and Airbus.

Although attention to technical interfaces is crucial for successful product development, teams typically ignore (or pay marginal attention to) a number of interfaces during the development process (Sosa, Eppinger, and Rowles 2004). Some level of neglect is perhaps unavoidable given the cognitive and resource limitations of teams (Simon 1947). Although lack of attention to noncritical or standardized interfaces may not be significant (Sosa, Eppinger, and Rowles 2004), the neglect of critical interfaces can have serious negative consequences (Henderson and Clark 1990).

To address this challenge, we need to examine both the architecture of the product and the informal organizational structure. The technical interfaces among product components define the coordination requirements, and technical communication among design teams constitutes one of the primary coordination mechanisms. Figure 10-8 shows a network of technical interfaces between four components and a network of technical communications between six teams, four of which are in charge of designing these components and two others of which are in charge of integration activities (Sosa, Gargiulo, and C. Rowles 2007).

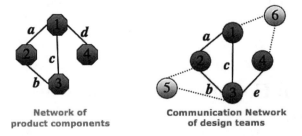

Network of
product components

Communication Network
of design teams

Figure 10-8 Hypothetical networks of components and design teams

By superimposing the maps of product interfaces onto the technical communication structure, we can understand where communications links are missing or may be unnecessary. Managers can identify not only the technical interfaces that are *matched* by technical team interactions (links *a, b,* and *c*) but also the cases of *mismatches* of component interfaces and team interactions. There are two types of mismatches: *unmatched interfaces,* also called unattended interfaces, such as link *d* in Figure 10-8, in which a technical interface is not attended by technical communication between corresponding design teams; and *unmatched interactions* such as link *e* in Figure 10-8, in which teams communicate for technical reasons even though the system architects had not identified technical interfaces between their components. Finally, there are also *external interactions* that occur when teams that are not directly responsible for the design of a component interact with teams designing components. This may be the case with teams that are in charge of overseeing the integration among different aspects of the design but are not responsible for designing any specific component, as is the case with teams 5 and 6 in Figure 10-8.

Most of the complex development projects we have studied in the automobile and aerospace industries exhibit this quasi-direct mapping of product architecture and organizational structure; that is, component X is designed by team X with a few system integration teams in charge of evaluating product-level requirements (for example, the fuel economy of an automobile or the weight requirements of an airplane). In some projects such as software development, however, mapping the architecture and organization is far from one-to-one. (In such cases, we can still adapt the approach described in this chapter; refer to Sosa 2008 for details.)

Although Figure 10-8 shows a simple example, overlaying the actual maps of product and organizational interfaces for a product such as the Pratt & Whitney engine we have studied is a daunting task (see Figure 10-9). As a result, we use a matrix representation to compare complex product and organizational networks, as illustrated in Figure 10-10.

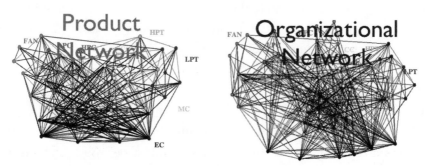

Figure 10-9   Network maps of product and organizational networks of the PW4098 engine

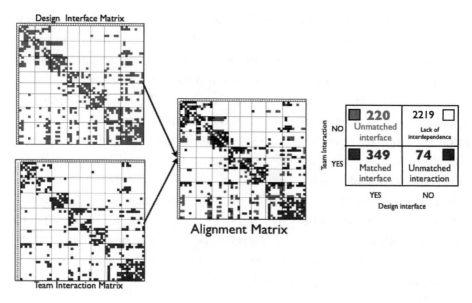

Figure 10-10   A structure approach to map product and organizational structures

In this case, a *design interface matrix* is a 54×54 square with labels corresponding to the 54 engine components while its nonzero cells correspond to the 569 design interfaces among them. In the organizational domain, a similar 54×54 *team interaction matrix* captures how the product component teams represented in the rows request technical information from the teams represented in the columns. Note that both matrices are sequenced in a similar manner so that the component labeling row i (and column i) in the design interface matrix has its corresponding design team labeling row i (and column i) in the team interaction matrix. Finally, to systematically identify matches and mismatches of interfaces and interactions, we overlay the design interface matrix and team interaction matrix to obtain the *alignment matrix*. Because both design interface and team interaction matrices are binary matrices, a cell in the alignment matrix has to be a matched interface, an unmatched interface, an unmatched interaction, or a lack of interdependence. (The original team interaction matrix was of size 60 because it included six integration teams, but we excluded these teams from the comparisons of mismatches. We did, however, take these integration teams into account when analyzing the reasons why mismatches occurred.)

As shown in Figure 10-10, 90% of the cases in the alignment matrix were expected cases (either matched interfaces or lack of interdependences), yet the 10% of mismatched cases are important. Of the 569 design interfaces, 39% of them were unattended by team interactions; of the 423 team interactions, over 17% of them were not associated with design interfaces. Sosa, Eppinger, and Rowles (2004) analyzed the product and organizational factors associated with the systematic occurrence of these mismatches and found that both interface criticality and group boundary matter significantly. Most of the unattended interfaces uncovered in the alignment matrix were low-criticality interfaces. The unmatched interfaces and interactions between team boundaries were at higher risk of being both unattended by team interactions and unidentified by system architects. Sosa, Eppinger, and Rowles (2007b) discuss the managerial implications of this approach in more detail.

By taking a closer look at design interfaces for specific components, we observed that some components had 100% of their design interfaces attended by team interactions while others exhibited less than 40% of their interfaces attended. *Why are some teams better than others at attending the technical interfaces of the components they design? Is it because of attributes of the components they design, or because of the structure of the communication networks with other teams in the organization, or both?* Sosa, Gargiulo, and C. Rowles (2007) found that after controlling for component and team attributes, both the connectivity of product components and the structure of the communication network of design teams matter. Interestingly, these network properties matter in different ways depending on whether the focal team acts as a provider or receiver of technical information.

Components appear to have an impact because teams working on highly *indirectly* connected components have trouble paying attention to technical requests from others because such teams are the ones more likely to suffer excessive and unforeseeable workload due to heavy design iterations. The team's communication network structures also have an effect because, on one hand, teams with sparse communication networks were more likely to search and acquire the technical information about the interfaces of the components they design, and, on the other hand, those teams that were surrounded by a more cohesive communication network structure were the ones that exhibited higher capability to attend the technical requests from other design teams in the network. (This is presumably because such teams enjoyed the benefits of the collaborative environment associated with close and cohesive networks.)

Conclusions and Future Directions

As Simon (1981) suggested, complex systems are difficult to understand because the behavior of the whole depends in nontrivial ways on how its elements interact. This chapter has outlined how a network view of processes, products, and organizations can help us understand how complex product development systems draw together components that form complex systems such as automobiles or aircraft engines. By considering processes not as a sequential set of activities but instead as a web of tasks, some of which can be highly interdependent, we have uncovered the reason design iterations occur. By modeling complex products as networks of interconnected components, we have learned how to cluster components into modules in a more efficient way to make complex systems nearly decomposable systems (Simon 1981). In addition, by taking a network approach to analyzing complex products, we can then consider structural properties of product components that are defined by the patterns of technical interfaces with other components. Finally, by mapping the network of components that form a product with the communication network of teams that design such components, we have been able to evaluate systematically why some interfaces are at higher risk of being unattended than others.

Only by taking a network perspective have we been able to uncover these findings and insights. Yet there is more to learn. Two promising areas in product development that would certainly benefit from a network perspective are product-organizational dynamics and innovation networks. To study the coevolution of product and organizational structures, our current research efforts focus on examining open source software development (Sosa, Browning, and Mihm 2007). One of the advantages of studying the architecture of software products is that their architecture is relatively easy to capture because it is properly codified in their source code (Sangal et al. 2005; MacCormack, Rusnack, and Baldwin 2006). In addition, software products are complex and fast-evolving, which makes them our ideal "fruit flies" to investigate how complex systems evolve over time.

Understanding creativity is imperative for effective innovation management. Creativity is no longer considered an individual attribute but a social activity, yet we are just beginning to understand the role of social networks in the creative process (Fleming, Mingo, and Chen 2007; Sosa 2007). Which attributes of the knowledge exchanged in organizational networks like the ones discussed in this chapter influence creative outcomes? Are more talkative teams more likely to generate more novel and useful ideas than less talkative teams? These are some of the questions innovation managers need to address as they also embark on the challenge of understanding the social networks they are managing.

Finally, as pointed out by Nambisan and Sawhney in Chapter 9, "Network-Centric Innovation: Four Strategies for Tapping the Global Brain," different models for network-centric innovation require different types of coordination and communication. Whether the process is more centralized (such as the Orchestra model) or more decentralized (such as the Global Bazaar model) will determine the type of interfaces that are needed in the network of design teams, the level of creativity that is desired, and the types of communication flows.

As product development increasingly depends on networks of design teams, *network thinking* will be a useful capability for managers in building more successful product development organizations. The frameworks presented in this chapter offer valuable tools for understanding and improving how these networks are structured, communicate, and evolve.

References

Allen, T. J. 1977. *Managing the Flow of Technology.* Cambridge, MA: MIT Press.

Baldwin, C. Y., and K. B. Clark. 2000. *Design Rules: Volume 1: The Power of Modularity.* Cambridge, MA: MIT Press.

Browning, T. R. 2001. Applying the design structure matrix to system decomposition and integration problems: A review and new directions. *IEEE Transactions on Engineering Management* 48 (3), 292-306.

Chen, L., Z. Ding, and S. Li. 2005. A formal two-phase method for decomposition of complex design problems. *ASME J. Mech. Des.* 127, 184-195.

Clarkson, P. J., C. S. Simons, and C. M. Eckert. 2004. Predicting change propagation in complex design. *ASME Journal of Mechanical Design* 126 (5), 765-797.

Eckert, C. M., P. J. Clarkson, and W. Zanker. 2004. Change and customization in complex engineering domains. *Research in Engineering Design* 15 (1), 1-21.

Eppinger, S. D. 2001. Innovation at the speed of information. *Harvard Business Review.*

Eppinger, S. D., D. E. Whitney, R. P. Smith, and D. A. Gebala. 1994. A model-based method for organizing tasks in product development. *Research in Engineering Design* 6 (1), 1-13.

Fleming, L., S. Mingo, and D. Chen. 2007. Brokerage and collaborative creativity. *Administrative Science Quarterly* 52: 443-475

Freeman, L. 1979. Centrality in social networks. Conceptual clarification. *Social Networks* 1, 215-239.

Galbraith, J. R. 1973. *Designing Complex Organizations.* Reading, MA: Addison-Wesley Publishing.

Gershenson, J. K., G. J. Prasad, and S. Allamneni. 1999. Modular product design: A life-cycle view. *Journal of Integrated Design and Process Science* 3 (4), 13-26

Gumbel, P. 2006. Trying to untangle wires. *Time,* October 16 (European edition), 36-37.

Henderson, R., and K. Clark. 1990. Architectural innovation: The reconfiguration of existing product technologies and the failure of established firms. *Administrative Science Quarterly* 35 (1), 9-30.

Jarratt, T., J. Clarkson, and C. Eckert. 2005. Engineering Change. In *Design Process ImprovementA Review of Current Practices,* 266-285.

MacCormack, A., J. Rusnack, and C. Baldwin. 2006. Exploring the structure of complex software designs: An empirical study of open source and proprietary code. *Management Science* 52 (7), 1015-1030.

Michelena, N., and P. Y. Papalambros. 1995. A network reliability approach to optimal decomposition of design problems. *ASME Journal of Mechanical Design* 117 (3), 433-440.

Mihm, J., C. Loch, and A. Huchzermeier. 2003. Problem-solving oscillations in complex engineering projects. *Manag. Sci.* 46 (6), 733-750.

Pimmler, T. U., and S. D. Eppinger. 1994. Integration analysis of product decompositions. *ASME Conference on Design Theory and Methodology,* in Minneapolis, MN, 343-351.

Pinedo, M., S. Sehasdri, and E. Zemel. 2000. The Ford-Firestone case. *Teaching case.* Department of Information, Operations, and Management Sciences, Stern School of Business, NYU.

Pisano, G. 1996. BMW: The seven series project. *HBS case 9-692-083.*

Sangal, N., E. Jordan, V. Sinha, and D. Jackson. 2005. Using dependency models to manage complex software architecture, *Proceedings of the 20th Annual ACM SIG-PLAN Conference on Object Oriented Programming, Systems, Languages, and Applications,* in San Diego, CA.

Sharman, D., and A. Yassine. 2004. Characterizing complex products architectures. *Systems Engineering* 7 (1), 35-60.

Simon, H. A. 1947. *Administrative Behavior: A Study of Decision-making Processes in Administrative Organizations.* Chicago, IL: Macmillan.

Simon, H. A. 1981. *The Science of the Artificial.* 2nd ed. Cambridge, MA: MIT Press.

Smith, R. P., and S. D. Eppinger. 1997a. A predictive model of sequential iteration in engineering design. *Manag. Sci.* 43 (3) 276-293.

Smith, R. P., and S. D. Eppinger. 1997b. Identifying controlling features of engineering design iteration. *Manag. Sci.* 43 (8) 1104-1120.

Sosa, M. E. 2007. Where do creative interactions come from? The role of tie content and social networks. *INSEAD working paper 2007/49/TOM.*

Sosa, M. E. 2008. A structured approach to predicting and managing technical interactions in software development. *Research in Engineering Design* 19(1) 47-70.

Sosa, M. E., T. Browning, and J. Mihm. 2007. Studying the dynamics of the architecture of software products. *Proceedings of the 19th ASME Design Theory and Methodology Conference.*

Sosa, M. E., S. D. Eppinger, and C. M. Rowles. 2003. Identifying modular and integrative systems and their impact on design team interactions. *ASME Journal of Mech. Design* 125 (2), 240-252.

Sosa, M. E., S. D. Eppinger, and C. M. Rowles. 2004. The misalignment of product architecture and organizational structure in complex product development. *Management Science* 50 (12), 1674-1689.

Sosa, M. E., S. D. Eppinger, and C. M. Rowles. 2007a. A network approach to define modularity of components in complex products. *ASME Journal of Mechanical Design* 129 (11), 1118-1129.

Sosa, M. E., S. D. Eppinger, and C. M. Rowles. 2007b. Are your engineers talking to one another when they should? *Harvard Business Review,* November.

Sosa, M. E., M. Gargiulo, and C. Rowles. 2007. Component connectivity, team network structure, and the attention to technical interfaces in complex product development. *INSEAD working paper 68/TOM/OB.*

Steward, D. 1981. The design structure matrix: A method for managing the design of complex systems. *IEEE Transactions on Engineering Management* EM-28 (3), 71-74.

Thompson, J. D. 1967. *Organizations in Action.* New York: McGraw-Hill.

Ulrich, K. T. 1995. The role of product architecture in the manufacturing firm. *Res. Policy.* 24, 419-440.

Ulrich, K. T., and S. D. Eppinger. 2004. *Product Design and Development.* 3rd ed. New York: McGraw Hill.

Wasserman, S., and K. Faust. 1994. *Social Network Analysis.* New York: Cambridge University Press.

11

Organizational Design: Balancing Search and Stability in Strategic Decision Making[1]

Jan W. Rivkin
Nicolaj Siggelkow

Abstract

Managers often must make decisions that depend on decisions in other parts of the organization. These interactions create a network of interdependent choices and make strategizing difficult. In this chapter, the authors explore the intersection between organizing and strategizing. Motivated by real examples that run contrary to conventional wisdom, Rivkin and Siggelkow examine how firms organize themselves to strategize well. In particular, they examine "premature lock-in"—how a firm's strategizing efforts can become stuck in a web of conflicting constraints prematurely, before managers have explored a wide enough range of possibilities. A key role of organizing is to free strategizing efforts and encourage broad search. At the same time, organizing must ensure that strategizing efforts stabilize after the firm discovers an effective set of choices. Balancing search and stability, the authors argue, is a central challenge of organizing. They explore this challenge with an agent-based simulation that shows (1) how a change in organizational structure—for example, a shift from decentralization to integration—may reflect not a reversal of early mistakes but an effective sequence of organizing and (2) why firms

[1] We are grateful to the Mack Center for Technological Innovation and the Division of Research and Faculty Development of Harvard Business School for generous funding. Please note that this chapter is a modified version of "Organizing to Strategize in the Face of Interactions: Preventing Premature Lock-in," a paper that appeared in *Long Range Planning* 39, 2006, pp. 591-614. The reprint of common parts occurs with permission from Elsevier.

may benefit from unnecessary overlap between departments. They conclude that a period of decentralization and unnecessary overlap can be seen as organizational mechanisms to ensure the broad, early search that a firm needs to cope with interactions among strategic decisions.

Despite five decades of research on organizing, real organizations continue to surprise us. Consider two examples:

1. Conventional wisdom holds that when top managers restructure their organization, it is to rectify past mistakes, often large and serious ones. In launching its e-commerce business, for example, discount broker Charles Schwab started with an independent subsidiary, but it soon reintegrated its online and conventional operations—seemingly reversing an earlier organizational error. We will argue, however, that such sequencing from a decentralized to an integrated organizational structure may reflect not a mistake, but an effective way to reach good sets of strategic choices in a novel environment.

2. It is generally held that good organizational structures modularize decisions as much as possible: Integrally related decisions should be grouped under the purview of a single management team, and managerial overlap should be avoided across departments that do not affect one another. Yet in its vehicle development efforts, Toyota intentionally leaves "unnecessary" overlap across departments. As we describe later in the text, the company does not modularize sets of decisions that, in concept, are decomposable, and it seems to benefit as a result.

These examples suggest that conventional wisdom about organizing is sometimes false. Students of organizational design have long recognized that there are few universal truths in their field and, accordingly, have adopted a contingency outlook: Prescriptions for organizing may be valid, but each prescription holds true only for some of the possible environmental conditions (Burns and Stalker 1961; Lawrence and Lorsch 1967). This begs the question, on what environmental conditions is organizational design contingent? And precisely how do environmental conditions lead to different prescriptions for organizing?

To tackle such ambitious questions, we bring two perspectives to bear. First, we focus on one particular role played by organizing: to enable strategizing. A firm's management team faces a set of decisions about how to procure, sell, deliver, service, hire, design, finance, and so forth. *Strategizing* is the search for a combination of choices about such decisions that, together, generate strong performance. *Organizing* is the allocation of rights over decisions as well as the coordination of choices through, for instance, incentives, communication, and hierarchy.[2] Organizing shapes how a firm strategizes—how it searches for a set of choices and what set it eventually adopts. Schwab's early decision to organize e-commerce as a separate subsidiary, for example, affected how it marketed, priced, executed, and serviced online trades.

In Figure 11.1 we provide a simple example of the two main concepts of this paper. A firm is assumed to have to resolve three decisions: "having a sale or not," "increasing its advertising budget or not," and "increasing its product breadth or not." Organizing is the allocation of rights over these decisions and the possible use of coordinating mechanisms and incentive systems. In this case, the firm decided to assign the first two decisions to one department, the third decision to another department, and to coordinate the departments via some type of coordinating mechanism. A different organizing choice could have been to assign all three decisions to one department, or to forgo any coordinating device and to give the departments full autonomy. Strategizing is the search for a high-performing set of choices. Given that each decision can be resolved in different ways, different combinations of choices can arise; for example, "having a sale, increasing the advertising budget, and increasing product breadth," or "not having a sale, increasing the advertising budget, and not increasing the product breadth." Which combinations arise and eventually are chosen is intimately affected by the particular choice of organizing.

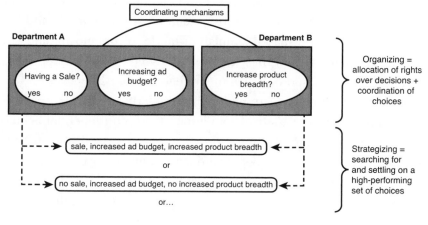

Figure 11-1   Organizing and strategizing

---

[2] Throughout this paper, the term "decision" refers to a variable on which management has multiple alternatives, and "choice" refers to a particular resolution of a decision. Whether or not to train a firm's sales force is a decision, for instance; to train the sales force is a choice.

The second perspective we bring to bear is that *interactions among decisions* make strategizing difficult. Two decisions interact if the resolution of one decision affects the costs and benefits associated with the other. Thus, in this chapter, we consider the challenges that arise when the activities of a firm create a network of interdependent choices. Strategy and organizational scholars have long emphasized that the decisions managers face are highly intertwined (Miller and Friesen 1984; Thompson 1967).[3]

Strategizing—that is, searching for an effective set of choices—is relatively easy when decisions are independent. In this case, organizing is less important because allocation of decisions would not affect their resolution; the firm could assign each decision to autonomous managers with little or no coordination. Strategizing is harder when decisions depend on one another. Trade-offs then arise across decisions, and the danger looms that an incremental approach may produce a solution that is optimal locally, but might be far from the global optimum. To the first question we posed previously—"on what environmental conditions is organizational design contingent?"—we would offer a partial answer: The right way to organize is contingent in part on the nature of interactions among a firm's strategic decisions. This echoes prior contingency literature, which focuses on the complexity of a firm's task environment as a key contingency (Khandwalla 1977).

The second question posed previously—"precisely how do environmental conditions lead to different prescriptions for organizing?"—is harder to address. To tackle it, we first narrow it, focusing on how degrees of interaction affect prescriptions for organizing. We then explore the counterintuitive examples from Schwab and Toyota, discussed earlier, using an agent-based simulation model of organizing and strategizing. The model offers explanations for these examples, related to interactions, which provide insights into how a firm should organize to strategize well. Although the two examples appear quite different, they share an underlying similarity: In both cases, the management team needs to explore a variety of configurations of interdependent choices before locking in on one particular configuration. Sequenced organizational structures at Schwab and "unnecessary" overlap between departments in Toyota may serve this purpose. They might help a management team search more broadly and keep from locking into a poor set of choices prematurely. Firms that organize to strategize well balance

---

[3] In recent years, theoretical work on supermodular systems (Milgrom and Roberts 1990), empirical studies of industries and individual firms (Ichniowski, Shaw, and Prennushi 1997; Pettigrew et al. 2003; Siggelkow 2002; Whittington et al. 1999), prescriptive articles for managers (Porter 1996), and simulation studies of firms as complex adaptive systems (Levinthal 1997; Rivkin and Siggelkow 2003) have reflected a renewed interest in the interactions among decisions.

search and stability; they avoid premature lock-in but have the discipline to cease exploration after they have discovered an effective set of choices.

Our plan of attack is as follows. We first lay out a model of organizing to strategize that is simple, yet is general enough to encompass both examples. We then examine the examples, each with corresponding results from the simulation, and finally draw the examples together and offer further reflections.

A Model of Organizational Search and Organizational Design

Decades of research on organizations have produced a rich variety of valuable perspectives on the role of organizing. Organizational design decisions have been viewed in light of their impact on a firm's ability to process information, their influence on firm incentives to invest in relationship-specific assets, and their effect on the motivation of employees to expend effort, for instance (Galbraith 1973; Grossman and Hart 1986; Jensen and Meckling 1976; Williamson 1975). Classic research on organizations emphasizes the effect of organizing on strategizing and stresses the role of interactions. Consider, for instance, the work of Chandler (1962) on structures that enable strategies involving massive coordination of goods; Lawrence and Lorsch (1967) on organizations that integrate differentiated parts; and Thompson (1967) on organizations that handle pooled, sequential, and reciprocal interdependence among tasks.

To visualize how interactions influence both strategizing and organizing, we can apply techniques from studies of complex adaptive systems. The essential task of a firm's management team, in our conception, is to resolve a host of decisions—such as whether to broaden the firm's product line, increase its advertising budget, or invest more heavily in research and development. We can visualize the management team as operating in a high-dimensional landscape where each horizontal dimension represents one of the decisions and the vertical dimension records the performance that results from each possible configuration of choices (Kauffman 1993; Levinthal 1997). In this context, management's challenge in strategizing is to find a good combination of choices—to discover a high point on the landscape. Because managers are bounded in their ability to reason (Simon 1957), the search process involves exploratory, groping behavior—not simply a consideration of all alternatives followed by a leap to the highest point on the landscape, the global peak. A common response to the cognitive limits of individual managers is to distribute authority and responsibility for discrete decisions across a number of managers. The allocation of interdependent decisions to independent managers, accompanied by coordinating devices such as incentives, communication, and hierarchy, is at the heart of organizing.

When a firm's decisions do not interact with each other, in the sense that each decision's contribution to performance does not depend on others, the performance landscape is smooth and single-peaked. Figure 11-2 shows a highly simplified example of this situation, with just two decisions determining firm performance. The decisions do not interact: The marginal impact of decision 1 on performance does not depend on decision 2, and vice versa. In such a situation, starting from any combination of choices, one can move to the global optimum by a series of performance-improving changes to individual decisions. Incremental improvement will eventually yield the very best combination of choices, so strategizing is relatively simple, and the firm's organizational structure has little bearing on this outcome. Each subset of the firm can safely operate as its own fiefdom. A manager in charge of decision 1 and a manager in charge of decision 2, each maximizing his or her independent contributions, will arrive atop the global peak, even without coordination.

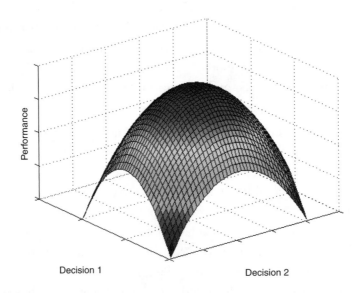

Figure 11-2   Performance landscape with no interactions

When decisions interact, however, the performance landscape becomes rugged. Local peaks, which offer no opportunity for improvement through incremental change, proliferate. Figure 11-3 shows a simple example of such a situation, with each decision maker's impact on performance now dependent on the choice made by the other decision maker. Strategizing becomes challenging: The specter arises that a firm may get stranded on a low local peak, unable to find better options despite poor performance. Also, organizing now affects how well the firm strategizes, since the choice made by one manager may now alter the performance consequences of another manager's decisions.

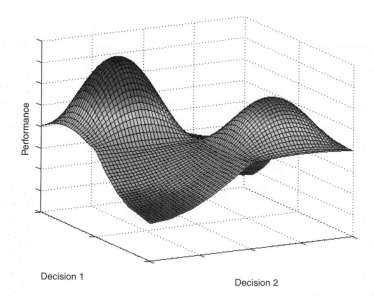

Decision 1

Decision 2

Figure 11-3   Performance landscape with interactions

To examine such complex interactions, we embed the ideas behind this imagery in an agent-based simulation model. Computer simulations have long been used in management science to create "laboratories" in which researchers can conduct rigorous virtual experiments on modeled organizations (Burton and Obel 1984; Cohen, March, and Olsen 1972; Cyert and March 1963). In agent-based simulations, researchers model individual agents—in our case, managers—rather than the system as a whole. (See Chapter 8, "Artificial Intelligence: How Individual Agents Add Up to a Network," for further discussion of agent-based simulations.) We confront these modeled managers with a range of environments, give them heuristics for acting, allow them to interact with one another in a series of periods, and record the resulting behavior over time. By altering the types of environments that managers face and the ways that managers are organized, and by repeating the experiments hundreds of times for each type of environment, we can isolate how well different organizations cope with various types of environments. Let us describe (1) how we model the environment and (2) how we model managers and organizations.

Environments with Interactions

The environment we model requires the management team of each firm to resolve a set of *N* binary (yes or no) decisions, such as increasing the advertising budget or increasing product breadth. In a stochastic but well-controlled manner, the computer generates a payoff for every configuration of choices. The mapping of all possible choice configurations onto payoffs creates the performance landscape on which a firm is operating.

The contribution of a decision to overall performance depends on how the decision itself is resolved (for example, whether the advertising budget was increased) and on how other decisions are resolved that interact with the decision (for example, whether the product line was extended). Formally, an influence matrix tracks the interactions among the decisions, as shown in Figure 11-4. Panel A of the figure illustrates a fully interdependent influence matrix in which each decision affects each other decision, and Panel B shows a modular influence matrix in which decisions 1-4 interact richly, and decisions 5-8 interact richly, but no interactions exist across these two sets of decisions. The payoff associated with a particular set of choices is given by the average across the contributions.[4]

A. Fully interdependent influence matrix

$$\begin{bmatrix} x & x & x & x & x & x & x & x \\ x & x & x & x & x & x & x & x \\ x & x & x & x & x & x & x & x \\ x & x & x & x & x & x & x & x \\ x & x & x & x & x & x & x & x \\ x & x & x & x & x & x & x & x \\ x & x & x & x & x & x & x & x \\ x & x & x & x & x & x & x & x \end{bmatrix}$$

B. Modular influence matrix

$$\begin{bmatrix} x & x & x & x & & & & \\ x & x & x & x & & & & \\ x & x & x & x & & & & \\ x & x & x & x & & & & \\ & & & & x & x & x & x \\ & & & & x & x & x & x \\ & & & & x & x & x & x \\ & & & & x & x & x & x \end{bmatrix}$$

Figure 11-4 Influence matrices

Organizations and Managers

Within these environments, we test how modeled managers in firms with different structures move from the same randomly chosen starting point to find high locations on a performance landscape. In particular, we focus on two organizational features: the task allocation and the presence or absence of a hierarchical structure. The *N* decisions of

4 The particular value of each possible contribution is determined by drawing randomly from a uniform distribution over the unit interval. For further details of the model, see Rivkin and Siggelkow (2006).

the firm can be allocated in various ways to different decision makers. In our model, we focus on firms with either one or two departments and consider how decisions are allocated to these departments. Next, we consider the impact of decentralized or hierarchical structures. A string of a's and b's denotes the allocation of the N decisions to the two departments. For instance, the task allocation aaaaaaaa would denote an integrated firm that has assigned all eight decisions to one department, and aaaabbbb would signify a firm that has assigned the first four decisions to one department and the other four decisions to the other department.

In each period, each department's manager considers one randomly chosen, local alternative to the current status quo choices. (A local alternative is an alternative that differs in one individual choice from the current set of choices.) In a firm with a decentralized structure, each department manager implements the alternative with the highest value for the department or retains the status quo if no alternative yields higher departmental performance. This new choice configuration serves then as the starting point for search in the next period. In a firm with a hierarchical structure, each manager sends his or her most preferred alternatives (which may include the status quo) to a "CEO." The CEO evaluates all possible combinations of alternatives and status quo choices for the two departments and implements the combination that yields highest firm performance. Again, the new choice configuration serves as the starting point for search in the next period. (See Figure 11-5 for a summary of the two organizational structures.) Search continues for up to 200 periods, and we repeat this procedure on 1,000 different performance landscapes.

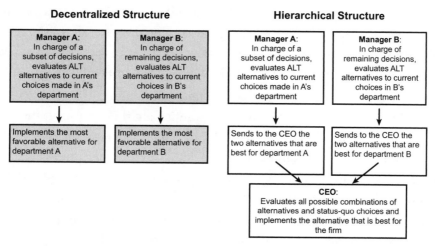

Figure 11-5   Different organizational structures

In the following sections, we will present a number of intriguing results generated with this simulation that shed light on the experiences of Schwab and Toyota discussed previously. (The interested reader will find more detail in the papers cited in the references particularly Rivkin and Siggelkow 2002, 2003, 2006; Siggelkow and Levinthal 2003, 2005; Siggelkow and Rivkin 2005).

Schwab: The Benefit of Sequencing Organizational Structures

In 1995, in its attempt to respond to the successful arrival of Internet-only brokerage firms, Charles Schwab created a free-standing electronic brokerage unit called e.schwab. The unit was given free reign, moved to a separate building, and held responsible for its own profit and losses.[5] Illustrating nicely the effect that organizing has on strategizing, the new unit responded with an array of new practices, including new internal software that allowed for a purely electronic customer relationship, a flat pricing scheme rather than the sliding scale of commissions that Schwab used in its traditional brokerage business, and a limited level of customer services. Although e.schwab was successful, a number of problems arose. In particular, customers were confused and irritated by the different prices and service levels offered under the same Schwab brand name, and the separate computer systems at e.schwab and Schwab made it difficult for customer representatives to gain access to full customer information. In 1998, Charles Schwab decided to reintegrate e.schwab. This included eliminating the separate P&L, renaming e.schwab as Schwab.com, creating flat commissions for all trades, and allowing all customers full access to Schwab's customer services. In sum, the firm became a mix of the e.schwab experiment and the traditional Schwab brokerage.

One reading of this experience is that the initial online organization was a failure. According to this view, Schwab did not correctly anticipate the eventual difficulties that arose from creating a spinoff, and this forced it to reintegrate e.schwab later. Although this might certainly be true, our simulation model indicates that decentralizing and later reintegrating turns out to be a powerful approach for a firm that faces interdependent decisions and needs to reconfigure its set of choices significantly.

To model the effects of different ways of organizing (integration, decentralization, and reintegration), we consider three firms that each face eight decisions ($N = 8$). A fully

---

[5] The description of Charles Schwab and e.schwab draws on Dyer and Hesterly (2000).

integrated firm assigns all eight decisions to "one department" (aaaaaaaa). A decentralized firm assigns decisions to two departments and lets each department implement those alternatives it finds profitable (aaaabbbb). A reintegrating firm operates as a decentralized firm (aaaabbbb) for 50 periods and then adopts the integrated task allocation (aaaaaaaa). (The results are not sensitive to the choice of 50 periods.) For the simulation presented here, we assume that firms operate on fully interdependent performance landscapes, where each decision affects all others. All three firms are placed on the same, randomly chosen starting point, and each firm's performance is recorded over 200 periods. Figure 11-6 charts the average performance trajectories of these three firms over 1,000 landscapes. (Performance is measured relative to the highest performance possible in each landscape.)

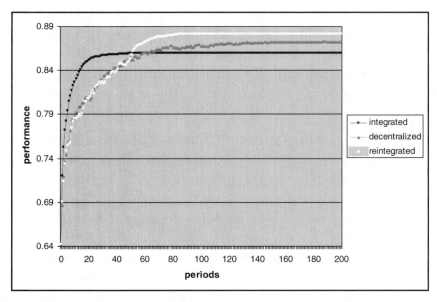

Figure 11-6 The benefits of reintegration in the presence of interactions

As shown in Figure 11-6, in the short run, the integrated firm has a performance advantage over the decentralized firm. Due to the pervasive interactions across the two divisions, each department in a decentralized firm is likely to engage in actions that are beneficial for itself but hurt the firm overall and undermines the improvement efforts of the other department. Such actions slow down the overall performance improvement of the decentralized firm as compared to an integrated firm. In the long run, however, the decentralized firm outperforms the integrated firm. In the presence of many interactions, the typical performance landscape becomes very rugged, with many "local peaks" on which firms can get stuck. As a result, broad search is valuable. The decentralized firm, with each department free to implement changes that benefit it alone, tends to engage in much broader search than does an integrated firm, and this eventually leads to better performance.

What is more striking, however, is that the reintegrating firm outperforms either pure structure. To understand this result—and more broadly to understand the general effect of organizing on strategizing—the concept of an organizational "sticking point" is helpful (Rivkin and Siggelkow 2002). Organizational sticking points are configurations of choices from which a firm will not move. Organizational sticking points are, thus, the eventual outcomes of many periods of strategizing, that is, of searching for high-performing choice configurations. Sticking points have two origins. First, a sticking point can arise when boundedly rational actors have exhausted their knowledge about possible alternatives that they would find more attractive than the status quo. This type of sticking point is very much akin to the notion of a "competency trap" (Levinthal and March 1981; Levitt and March 1988). Second, a sticking point can arise when no alternative can be found that is acceptable to all those in the organization who must consent to its implementation.

Organizational structure has a profound effect on organizational sticking points. For the integrated structure discussed previously, a configuration is a sticking point if no better nearby configuration for overall firm performance can be found. In contrast, for the decentralized structure, a configuration is a sticking point only if *neither* department manager finds a profitable deviation for his or her department. Decentralized firms are less likely to become stuck; they move if either department manager can spot a parochial improvement. For this reason, decentralized firms tend to search rugged landscapes much more broadly than integrated firms. On the other hand, the decentralized firm suffers from two drawbacks. First, it may wander forever, with department managers adopting sequences of changes that undermine each other. Second, the decentralized firm may become stuck at a point where an incremental change that is attractive for the firm as a whole is left unexploited, simply because the change is not parochially appealing to the department that must implement it. The integrated firm, in contrast, never leaves incremental improvements untapped in the long run.

The reintegrating firm couples the broad search of the decentralized firm with the stability and exploitative power of the integrated firm. In its early days, when it resembles a decentralized firm, the reintegrator migrates to a promising area of the landscape. After it changes to become integrated, the reintegrator scales and eventually becomes stuck on a high spot within that area. The early, broad search provided by the decentralized structure puts the firm in a favorable position for further search after the firm reintegrates.

In these results, we see the first instance of a pattern that will recur: Appropriate organizing (or change in organizing) can help a firm by preventing its strategizing efforts from terminating too early—in other words, by shaking it off low-performing sticking points. Similarly, these results also highlight the importance of interaction effects. In the absence of interaction effects—that is, without a network of choices—there would be little need for the broad search that the decentralized structure provides. Figure 11-7 repeats the simulation of Figure 11-6 but with no interactions among choices. The decentralized firm now has a short-term advantage over the integrated firm because its structure benefits from parallel processing of alternatives in each department. In the long run, all three structures end up on the same global peak of the landscape. Thus, in this case, sequencing from a decentralized to an integrated structure does not help the firm at all.

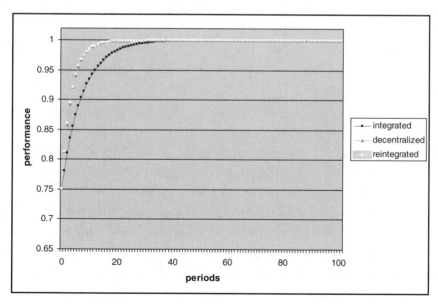

Figure 11-7   Reintegration does not yield a benefit in the absence of interactions.

For managers, our results have two key implications. First, if a firm can afford a period of broad search and needs to reconfigure its choices substantially, it can benefit by first adopting a decentralized structure with parochially minded subdivisions, and then shifting to a structure that reins in subdivisions and makes them accountable for their firm-wide impact. Second, when a firm's performance stagnates—a sign that it may have reached an organizational sticking point—a change in organizing may help the management team dislodge itself from its current set of choices and restart its strategizing efforts, heading toward higher regions of its performance landscape.

Toyota: Beyond a Modular Approach

A central tenet of organizational design theory is to group those tasks that interact with each other in order to attend to all interactions. (See Chapter 10, "Coordination Networks in Product Development," for a nice application of these concepts.) The goal of this modular approach is to decompose a system into subsystems that are entirely independent of each other or that interact with each other in predictable ways via tightly specified interfaces. Decisions made in one subsystem then do not affect other subsystems in unanticipated ways. As a result, no further coordination is necessary and project teams can work on subsystems in parallel. Such modularity has been touted to lead, for instance, to faster product innovation. The search for good sets of choices—the equivalent of strategizing in this context—is enhanced by modular organizing (Baldwin and Clark 2000).

In light of these potential benefits, a number of U.S. car manufacturers embraced the idea of modular product design. Cars were decomposed into various subsystems, and cross-functional teams were assigned to each module. To achieve this structure, firms such as Chrysler disbanded their functional organizations in favor of organizing around products and assigning people to temporary project teams.[6] It is thus somewhat surprising to see that Toyota's vehicle-development process—still the most efficient in the industry—has maintained a functionally based organization, with very limited use of cross-functional teams. At Toyota, coordination is achieved not by a modular design, but rather by high-level chief engineers who provide coordination and integration.

Why might Toyota intentionally organize so that interdependencies are not contained within group boundaries? To shed light on this question, we consider how two different organizations would tackle a decision problem that is perfectly decomposable: the interaction structure shown in Panel B of Figure 11-4. The first organization uses the task allocation aaaabbbb, thereby creating two subsystems that capture all interactions within the two departments and that leave no interactions across departments. The

---

[6] The description of Toyota's product development process draws on Sobek, Liker, and Ward (1998).

second organization uses a task allocation, similar to Toyota's, that does not perfectly decompose the decision problem, but it also employs high-level coordination. This would correspond, for instance, to a task allocation aabbbbaa embedded in a hierarchical structure. In this case, interactions across the two departments (the two functions) still exist, and each department needs to involve the chief engineer (or in our model, the CEO) before implementing choices.

The first two columns in Figure 11-8 show the average performance in period 200 of firms with these two structures. Surprisingly, even though the decision problem is perfectly decomposable, a task allocation that completely decomposes the decision problem (column 1) does not produce the highest performance. The incompletely decomposed task allocation embedded in a hierarchical structure (column 2) does better. To achieve the performance boost, one needs *both* the task allocation aabbbbaa *and* the hierarchical structure. Adding a chief engineer to the decomposed task allocation aaaabbbb creates no benefit, as a comparison of the first and third columns in Figure 11-8 shows: After the decision problem is perfectly decomposed and no cross-departmental interdependencies remain, coordination is unnecessary and the extra hierarchical level does nothing (for example, the first and the third columns show identical performance). Likewise, as the fourth column in Figure 11-8 shows, adopting a task allocation with overlap but leaving the departments decentralized leads to the worst outcome.

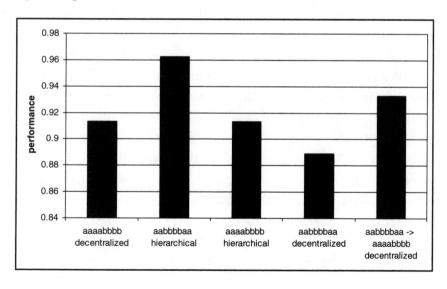

Figure 11-8   The benefits of unnecessary overlap

Why does an incompletely decomposed task allocation with a hierarchy perform better than complete decomposition? Even with complete decomposition, each department faces rich interactions internally; its strategizing problem has many local peaks. Each department tends to lock into a mediocre set of choices prematurely. In the firm with incomplete decomposition, interactions *across* modules create a very different search dynamic: Changes in each department alter conditions in the other, prying departments off of equilibria and requiring each department to continue its search. If this firm did not have a coordinator, such conflict between departments could lead to instability and low performance (as seen in the fourth column of Figure 11-8). A coordinator, however, vetoes parochially beneficial proposals that undermine total firm performance. The combination of extra search generated by "unnecessary" overlap between departments and the stability of the coordinator can produce superior final results.

Sobek, Liker, and Ward (1998) portray exactly this dynamic in their description of Toyota's product development process. For instance, in designing a new model of the Celica sports car, the styling department suggested a design change to the front panel to give the car a more exciting look. This change, however, forced manufacturing to rethink its existing tooling. In response, manufacturing made suggestions, which, in turn, led to changes in design. The chief engineer and the general manager of manufacturing orchestrated this exchange. From this "conflict" emerged an innovative and easily manufactured design—one that likely would not have arisen without interdependencies across these functions.

This example illustrates our general pattern: A good choice of organizing prevents strategizers from locking into sets of choices prematurely, while still allowing the firm to hold on to good solutions. In this case, the "unnecessary" overlap between departments dislodges each department from early solutions and rejuvenates the search process, while the coordinator makes sure that great sets of choices are not lost.

To show that the underlying mechanism in this case and the Schwab example are similar, we conduct one further simulation. Rather than using the hierarchical form to create coordination, we construct a decentralized firm that sequences its task allocation from one with overlap (aabbbbaa) to one that perfectly decomposes the system (aaaabbbb). As the fifth column in Figure 11-8 shows, this sequencing also produces better performance than the perfectly decomposed structure alone can achieve.

Conclusion: Organizing to Search for an Effective Strategy

As the examples in this chapter show, a fragmented, incremental search for optimal solutions may ultimately lead to suboptimal results because of the interactions among choices—in other words, because choices form a network. Due to these interactions, organizations can become stuck or locked in prematurely—saddled with poor performance, yet lacking a clear path for improvement. How the firm is organized affects whether strategizing efforts suffer from premature lock-in. By moving between decentralized and integrated structures, or by leaving overlap between departments in a hierarchy, a firm can break free from low sticking points early yet retain the stability to lock-in later, after it finds an effective strategy. In this light, Schwab's decision to create a separate online business and then to reintegrate it into the broader firm and Toyota's decision to leave "unnecessary" overlap between departments make sense, even if they run counter to conventional wisdom.

We feel that recent research has paid too little attention to the role of organizing in setting the stage for strategizing and, in particular, to the way that interactions affect this role. Good organizational structures help a firm achieve two ends that may seem at odds with each other: to search broadly for a good combination of strategic choices, and to lock in on such a combination after it is discovered. Good structures balance search with stability.

The onus for striking this balance falls on senior management. More broadly, senior managers bear responsibility for dealing with interactions among decisions, particularly interactions that span departmental borders. In a sense, it is such cross-cutting interactions that make senior management necessary. Our perspective is that effective senior managers usually cope with intricate interactions not by "figuring it all out" and enacting the perfect strategy up front, but by crafting an organization that can search effectively for and stabilize around a great strategy. This is consistent with Crook's observation (see Chapter 12, "Complexity Theory: Making Sense of Network Effects") that as the environment becomes more and more complex, predictability decreases. As a result, it becomes crucial for top managers to engage in a shift in mindset from "my job is to design a great strategy" to "my job is to design an organization that can search well for a great strategy."

Interdependencies require specific managerial capabilities—for instance, to spot interactions that span divisional boundaries, to anticipate how decisions in one part of an organization will reverberate elsewhere, and to design incentives that account for cross-divisional interactions. Modularization of activities can help by reducing the need for cross-divisional coordination. Yet as our findings show, modularization may not always be the best organizational response; retaining interdependencies across divisions can create helpful search, as long as it is coupled with a device that creates stability. Finally, this discussion argues for broad strategizing. Initiatives that are narrowly conceived and assessed ("should we have a sale?" or "should we have a broader product line?") can lead to unexpected and unwelcome outcomes if interdependencies are ignored. Managers might fruitfully consider *bundles* of choices such as "having a sale; decreasing the ad budget; and reducing the product line" or "not having a sale; increasing the ad budget; and increasing the product line." If strategizing stays at the level of individual choices, potential interdependencies are likely to be ignored, and firms may not even make it to "local peaks" on their performance landscapes. By considering underlying interaction patterns as they craft a process to search for a strategy, managers can create an organization that is more likely to find its way onto a high performance peak.

References

Baldwin, C. Y., and K. B. Clark. 2000. *Design Rules: The Power of Modularity.* Cambridge, MA: MIT Press.

Burns, T., and G. M. Stalker. 1961. *The Management of Innovation.* London: Tavistock.

Burton, R. M., and B. Obel. 1984. *Designing Efficient Organizations: Modelling and Experimentation.* Amsterdam: North-Holland.

Chandler, A. D., Jr. 1962. *Strategy and Structure: Chapters in the History of Industrial Enterprise.* Cambridge, MA: MIT Press.

Cohen, M. D., J. G. March, and J. P. Olsen. 1972. A garbage can model of organizational choice. *Administrative Science Quarterly* 17, 1-25.

Cyert, R. M., and J. G. March. 1963. *A Behavioral Theory of the Firm.* Englewood Cliffs, NJ: Prentice Hall.

Dyer, J. H., and W. Hesterly. 2000. *Winning the Web Wars: A Blueprint for Advantage in the Online Marketspace.* Brigham Young University and University of Utah.

Galbraith, J. R. 1973. *Designing Complex Organizations.* Reading, MA: Addison-Wesley.

Grossman, S. J., and O. D. Hart. 1986. The costs and benefits of ownership: A theory of vertical and lateral integration. *Journal of Political Economy* 94, 691-719.

Ichniowski, C., K. Shaw, and G. Prennushi. 1997. The effects of human resource management practices on productivity: A study of steel finishing lines. *American Economic Review* 87, 291-313.

Jensen, M. C., and W. H. Meckling. 1976. Theory of the firm: Managerial behavior, agency costs and ownership structure. *Journal of Financial Economics* 3, 305-360.

Kauffman, S. A. 1993. *The Origins of Order: Self-Organization and Selection in Evolution.* New York: Oxford University Press.

Khandwalla, P. N. 1977. *The Design of Organizations.* New York: Harcourt Brace Jovanovich.

Lawrence, P. R., and J. W. Lorsch. 1967. *Organization and Environment.* Boston: Harvard Business School Press.

Levinthal, D. A. 1997. Adaptation on rugged landscapes. *Management Science* 43, 934-950.

Levinthal, D., and J. March. 1981. A model of adaptive organizational search. *Journal of Economic Behavior and Organizations* 2, 307-333.

Levitt, B., and J. G. March. 1988. Organizational learning. *Annual Review of Sociology* 14, 319-340.

Milgrom, P. R., and J. Roberts. 1990. The economics of modern manufacturing: Technology, strategy, and organization. *American Economic Review* 80, 511-528.

Miller, D., and Friesen, P. H. 1984. *Organizations: A Quantum View.* Englewood Cliffs, NJ: Prentice Hall.

Pettigrew, A. M., R. Whittington, L. Melin, C. Sanchez-Runde, F. A. J. Van den Bosch, W. Ruigrok, and T. Numagami, eds. 2003. *Innovative Forms of Organizing.* London: Sage.

Porter, M. E. 1996. What is strategy? *Harvard Business Review* 74 (6), 61-78.

Rivkin, J. W., and N. Siggelkow. 2002. Organizational sticking points on NK-landscapes. *Complexity* 7 (5), 31-43.

Rivkin, J. W., and N. Siggelkow. 2003. Balancing search and stability: Interdependencies among elements of organizational design. *Management Science* 49, 290-311.

Rivkin, J. W., and N. Siggelkow. 2006. Organizing to strategize in the face of interdependencies: Preventing premature lock-in. *Long Range Planning* 39, 591-614.

Siggelkow, N. 2002. Evolution toward fit. *Administrative Science Quarterly* 47, 125-159.

Siggelkow, N., and D. A. Levinthal. 2003. Temporarily divide to conquer: Centralized, decentralized, and reintegrated organizational approaches to exploration and adaptation. *Organization Science* 14, 650-669.

Siggelkow, N., and D. A. Levinthal. 2005. Escaping real (non-benign) competency traps: Linking the dynamics of organizational structure to the dynamics of search. *Strategic Organization* 3, 85-115.

Siggelkow, N., and J. W. Rivkin. 2005. Speed and search: Designing organizations for turbulence and complexity. *Organization Science* 16, 101-122.

Simon, H. A. 1957. *Models of Man: Social and Rational; Mathematical Essays on Rational Human Behavior in a Social Setting.* New York: John Wiley.

Sobek, D. K., J. K. Liker, and A. C. Ward. 1998. Another look at how Toyota integrates product development. *Harvard Business Review* 76 (July-August), 36-49.

Thompson, J. D. 1967. *Organizations in action.* New York: McGraw-Hill.

Whittington, R., A. Pettigrew, S. Peck, E. Fenton, and M. Conyon. 1999. Change and complementarities in the new competitive landscape: A European panel study, 1992-1996. *Organization Science* 10, 583-600.

Williamson, O. E. 1975. *Markets and Hierarchies.* New York: Free Press.

PART IV

STRATEGY AND BUSINESS MODELS

As companies move from firm-centric to network-centric models, they need to rethink their approaches to strategy and the business models they use to generate and capture value. In Chapter 12, **Colin Crook** examines insights from complexity theory in making decisions about issues such as strategy formulation and organizational design. In Chapter 13, **Serguei Netessine** considers how companies such as Airbus and Boeing have used technology to manage complex, global webs of suppliers. In Chapter 14, **Christophe Van den Bulte** and **Stefan Wuyts** consider the increasing role of networks in marketing, accelerating the spread of new products, strengthening brand beliefs and preferences, improving corporate status and reputation, coordinating distribution channels, and accessing resources. In Chapter 15, **Christoph Zott** and **Raphael Amit** identify four major interlinked value drivers—efficiency, complementarities, lock-in, and novelty—and discuss their role in new business models that are consistent with network-based strategies. In Chapter 16, **George S. Day**, **Paul J. H. Schoemaker**, and **Scott A. Snyder** examine the role of networks in sensing information at the periphery and how companies can create "strategic radar" to recognize emerging threats and opportunities sooner.

Chapter 12   Complexity Theory: Making Sense of Network Effects   207
             Colin Crook

Chapter 13   Supply Webs: Managing, Organizing, and Capitalizing on
             Global Networks of Suppliers   225
             Serguei Netessine

Chapter 14   Leveraging Customer Networks   243
             Christophe Van den Bulte and Stefan Wuyts

Chapter 15   The Business Model as the Engine of
             Network-Based Strategies   259
             Christoph Zott and Raphael Amit

Chapter 16   Extended Intelligence Networks: Minding and
             Mining the Periphery   277
             George S. Day, Paul J. H. Schoemaker, and Scott A. Snyder

12

Complexity Theory:
Making Sense of Network Effects

Colin Crook

Abstract

As Colin Crook explores in this chapter, complexity theory offers valuable insights into the interactions of complex systems such as networked enterprises. Complexity theory addresses the "network effects" that result from interactions between many individual actors. This chapter examines the implications of this theory for business, and how these effects influence key management areas such as making sense, strategy, and organization. Crook explores issues such as fads and crowds, using information and technology, and the use of agent-based simulations. Finally, he explores the shifts in management thinking, and business education, needed to utilize complexity theory—a shift in mental models that may be crucial to success in a networked world.

A principal task of senior business managers is to make sense of their business environment. So how do we explain the following report in *The Financial Times* in August 2007?

> *In a rare unplanned investor call, the bank revealed that a flagship global equity fund had lost over 30 percent of its value in a week because of problems with its trading strategies created by computer models. In particular, the computers had failed to foresee recent market movements to such a degree that they labeled them a "25-standard deviation event"—something that only happens once every 100,000 years or more. (Tett and Gangahar 2007)*

We surely understand that markets are inherently uncertain—bubbles are created and inevitably burst. We just do not know beforehand whether it is a bubble and exactly when it will burst. These so-called 25,000- or 100,000-year events may occur *several times* within the career of a financial professional!

Other surprising events are occurring: How could YouTube, Facebook, MySpace, and Flickr appear so quickly and become so successful, with tens of millions of customers? How could China possibly achieve such a dominant position in so short a time, displacing Germany as the world's largest exporter in 2007? Why is eBay so successful with few competitors when its model seemed so easy to imitate? How could Intel and Microsoft achieve market shares on a global scale of over 90%?

It turns out that these "extreme events" (bubbles) are a logical consequence of a phenomenon recognized by complexity theory as "scaling." *The Financial Times* said the bank claimed that "the computers failed to foresee" the problems, yet complexity theory makes it clear that the future in this context is unknowable. The other examples, such as Microsoft's market share and the new Internet companies, can also be explained by complexity theory (Arthur 1994).

Complexity theory works especially well when we are looking at large scale—many molecules, individuals, automobiles, or businesses. Today, we have commercial networks on a scale previously thought inconceivable: tens of millions of businesses, billions of consumers, tens or even hundreds of millions of customers per business, transaction flows of trillions of dollars per day, billions of networked devices, and so on. These businesses have two noteworthy CT characteristics: sheer numbers and extensive interconnectivity.

Given this rising complexity, an understanding of complexity theory can help managers make sense of their environment, and develop the right strategy and organizational design for it (Roberts 2004). But making sense of this environment, in today's networked world, requires managers to understand complexity theory. In this chapter, we examine what complexity theory is and what it means for networked, "flat world" businesses.

Key Concepts of Complexity Theory for Business

While there are some outstanding resources for readers who want a thorough exploration of complexity theory (Kogut 2007; Johnson 2007; Santa Fe institute), we offer here a brief and nonmathematical introduction to core concepts, with a focus on networked businesses. The first challenge in discussing complexity theory is that there are many definitions (Kauffman). Complexity theory embraces such terms as chaos theory, complex adaptive systems, fractals, emergence, power laws, nonlinearity, computational complexity, and self-organization. Complexity theory's reputation has swung between being seen as the answer to many fundamental problems in science and being viewed as a suspect, "new age" theory.

Complexity theory embraces things that are complicated, involve many elements and many interactions, are not deterministic, and are given to unexpected outcomes. Complex systems are nonlinear and can be chaotic. A fundamental aspect of complexity theory is the overall or aggregate behavior of a large number of items, parts, or units that are entangled, connected, or networked together. An amazing aspect of complexity theory is that it applies to many types of "units" (grains of sand in a pile, molecules in a magnet, people driving cars on freeways, and so on). The mathematical laws of complexity theory are essentially indifferent to the nature of the "units." This has naturally held the promise of a universal theory with great utility in explaining many aspects of economics and other systems involving humans. In fact, as scientific understanding of biology reveals the nature of evolution and biological processes, it is argued that biology may be the best metaphor for making sense of business in the twenty-first century (Kauffman 2001).

Complexity theory arose from a recognition of shortcomings of traditional science in explaining certain difficult phenomena. The explanatory power and practical utility of traditional analytical and reductionist science has produced spectacular results. But in the scientific process, issues such as turbulent flow in physics and evolutionary dynamics in biology did not yield to this initial analysis. As such issues became increasingly important, addressing them produced the various strands leading to complexity theory. Other developments leading to complexity theory came from cybernetics and systems thinking, in which the overall behavior of a system was the object of the study. Finally, mathematical computing, in which computers were used to simulate the behavior of cellular automata (elementary cells connected together in a matrix) provided a key stimulus to complexity theory development.

Complexity theory is still a work in progress. The results achieved so far in explaining phenomena in the natural sciences as well as human systems (economics, business, and so on), however, clearly show that it is a powerful method. We need to understand what complexity theory can and cannot do.

In contrast to classical scientific methods that directly link theory and outcome, complexity theory does not typically provide simple cause-and-effect explanations. The links are difficult to understand. This makes this approach much more challenging—particularly in the world of business where managers usually assume that actions and outcomes are directly linked.

Networks and Connectedness

Networks comprise a collection of nodes, clusters, and hubs connected by links. Network analysis usually looks at the nodes and the links, and the overall behavior of the complete network. Networks are rapidly becoming the fundamental structure for the "flat world," so a fundamental understanding of networks and their behavior is crucial to operating a twenty-first-century enterprise. These networks may involve financial, logistic, legal, governmental, and human systems. The network becomes the asset. Networks must be carefully defined as to their value proposition, because it appears that many networks follow a power law—all nodes are not equal. We see the effects of increasing returns (Arthur 1994). If networks are created by the incremental addition of nodes, and if each new node links preferentially to the nodes that are more connected, then scale-free networks occur. Large-scale network effects with more users will be inevitably be more difficult to change.

Networks and networked business are vulnerable to problems (security, robustness, availability, and so on) when connected together. All connected agents worry about issues such as privacy and trustworthiness, and specific attacks on their key nodes. When comparing random networks to scale-free networks, scale-free are more fault tolerant since failures are random and the majority of nodes are poorly connected. Conversely, they are highly vulnerable to a specific attack on the dominant hubs or nodes that will crash the network. We see constant evidence of this occurring.

Networks and connectedness are fundamental to complexity theory, since relationships and not things *per se* are the basis for understanding the world. In fact, many complexity theory processes are called "network effects." As illustrated by other chapters in this book, this approach to networks has revealed such effects for many types of networks, including the brain, society, economy, food webs, the Internet, power grids, cell metabolic pathways, pathways of infection, and social networks. Complexity theory also applies to physical entanglements or connections.

Network Design

Complexity theory helps us understand the impact of network design. Metcalfe's law posits that the value of the network increases with the square of the number of nodes or participants. This reflects the intuitive concept that the value of a phone or fax network increases with the number of machines or people in the network.

In contrast, other network topologies such as the hub-and-spoke model emphasize a simpler connection of many users to a central node(s). Hub-and-spoke networks show little complexity theory behavior (network effects). Radial networks were typical of early computer networks using a centralized resource. Any network that emphasizes this type of structure is unlikely to exhibit the effects of complexity theory since multiple local interactions between units are unlikely. Hub-and-spoke networks confer great power on the hub. Amazon.com, at the center of its retail network, essentially controls the process and agents (businesses or consumers), who cannot communicate directly with each other. The central hub mediates the process.

One early business application of complexity theory concerned an analysis of large-scale telephone networks. Analysis (Erdos and Renyi 1959) had first suggested that these types of networks were random. (Random networks or graphs have any pair of nodes with an equal probability of being connected.) Traffic flows also were assumed to be random and follow a normal distribution. Research in the 1990s (Barabási and Réka 1999) using recent data from the Internet revealed a surprising result. These types of computer networks were not random but *fractal*! Fractals are self-similar over scale, meaning they have properties that are invariant over scale. What this means is any reduction in size of the entity still has the characteristics of the original (Mandelbrot 1983).

Fractals have applications in science, art, mathematics, and other areas. They are present throughout nature. This fractal structure meant that the ratio of "very connected" nodes divided by total nodes remains the same as the network grows. These are known as scale-free networks. Large numbers of nodes have few connections and a few nodes have a very large number of links.

Such "scale-free" networks, which are present throughout nature, exhibit power laws, showing that some nodes are more important than others. An interesting feature of power laws is that they have a tail, which declines far less quickly than a normal or bell curve. These are called fat tails. These scaling laws are found all over nature. Extreme events are a consequence of power laws.

Systems and Holistic Thinking

Systems engineering may be at a crossroads. The discipline has been deeply studied and many theoretical and empirical rules have been established. It is heavily influenced by control theory and cybernetics. Yet big, complex projects—especially involving software—usually run into serious problems. In fact, major software projects are often declared to be beyond the ability of anyone to manage or comprehend. Our current tools are not designed for complexity. This makes it hard to adopt a view based on complexity theory while using tools based on conventional systems engineering.

Understanding systems today increasingly means understanding living systems. Technology has become integrated with people; billions of individuals are now festooned with networked devices. People are an integral part of systems but individuals are also a complex adaptive system. The new approach will have to emphasize people and their interactions with an emphasis on "living the experience" as opposed to the classical command and control methodologies. We can already see advantages here from embodiment and robotics (Brooks 1991) and online gaming (Second Life).

Complexity theory is all about things that are connected, but importantly, it is also about their aggregate behavior. What does all this local interaction of many "agents" produce? People driving on a freeway interact with their adjacent neighbors but, unknown to them, they are producing an aggregate behavior when viewed from afar, in say a traffic control center. Starlings flying and swirling together in a cloud are another oft-quoted example. Complexity theory's great power lies in explaining how such system behaviors arise.

General systems theory tries to discover or create general principles for humans to understand for systems of any nature. Although it is a powerful perspective, it has a mixed reputation. Some researchers have suggested that complexity theory could provide general systems theory with a more scientific foundation. It presents us with a method for mastering complexity—big complicated things or events—and understanding the behavior of many units in the aggregate. It is all about the behavior of the entire system and not just the sum of the individual parts. It provides some rational basis for explaining how complex systems arise.

Self-Organization, Emergence, and Punctuated Equilibrium

One of complexity theory's puzzling features is "emergence." This is the appearance of higher-level structures or behavior brought about by the interactions of relatively simple components. Emergence engenders some controversy because it connotes that "somehow" this higher-level outcome appears. The difficulty lies in explaining and predicting the precise outcome since the characteristics of the total system cannot be traced back to the component parts—there is no master design around which the individual actions are rallied. Emergence and self-organization are connected, and some argue that the process of self-organization is behind many examples of emergence.

This emergence sometimes moves forward in fits and starts, despite the absence of a master plan, creating the phenomenon of "punctuated equilibrium." To try to both understand and explain the process of self-organization and related phenomena, Per Bak and colleagues (1987) examined how a sand pile is built from grains of sand. As the pile grows, there are series of small and then big avalanches. The small events that precede the "big one" are an integral part of the same process and must not be ignored. This led Per Bak to argue for punctuated equilibrium-power laws in which change occurs in a burst. This type of discussion has also influenced thinking about evolution (evolution by natural selection and self-organized criticality). When looking at a system, local interactions can achieve a critical stage where the interactions link up and propagate across the system, thus providing a global shaping force for change.

Key Implications for Managers

Complexity theory affects the three principal tasks of management: (1) making sense of the environment, (2) setting strategy, and (3) organizing the firm.

Complexity theory highlights the challenges of exerting control in a complex environment. The ability to manage in the traditional sense becomes problematic. Managers can decisively shape and influence future outcomes if intervention is applied adaptively, aligned, and coupled to the environment. It means that business can be viewed as an interpretation system, which continuously examines the environment, making sense, learning, and, most important, taking appropriate action to align itself to the new reality. We now consider how managers address the challenges of making sense, setting strategy, and organizing the firm, through the lens of complexity theory.

Making Sense

Most managers have a reasonable desire to find a straightforward explanation for the cause of something; the simpler the better because this is usually followed by an evident course of action. The desire for mono-causality is enormous, even for complicated situations. With complexity theory, we can use multicausality, with relationships as the unit of analysis, to explain (although we cannot specifically predict). To get a grip on something big and complicated, we have to take multiple views, since each viewer has his or her own mental model and resulting perspective. This approach encourages a "making sense" process of engagement with multiple, and ideally divergent, sources. The real skill lies in coherently bringing these views together.

Managers of enterprises must become aware of which fundamental shaping forces are going to influence their environment and how they will shape their business. The global grid will ensure that everyone will be a participant—individuals, businesses, and governments. For example, global warming represents a fundamental shaping force for most businesses. It is huge in its scope, complexity, and impact. Managers need to make sense of the forces that influence the impact of global warming on business (including scientific, regulatory, and consumer actions). These core-shaping forces are the power-law drivers that will shape us all.

Managers need to view business as more of a "living system," enmeshed with its environment, constantly making sense of its situation and always being prepared to take action. We know from complexity theory that we will experience more extreme events that are outside the comfortable normal distribution, but we just do not know when they will occur! We will see more temporal clustering of events—punctuated equilibriums as discussed previously—with bad news or good news coming in waves. We will experience contagion effects as the network effect of relationships of various parties produces shaping waves (good and bad) that travel across the total network. These phenomena must now be regarded as a natural part of making sense. We will, however, have to change how we think of the benefits of "making sense." Rather than inducing a sense of comfort and repose (we "get it" and can relax), it will have to induce a sense of vigilance and reaction, like a soldier in combat who is trained to energetically react to unexpected events.

In the consumer market, the classical view of the consumer has to undergo a revolutionary change. We may well think we have a customer base of individuals, exercising free will and deciding the fate of a business. But we now know better. Complexity theory shows us that each person can be shaped and that the interaction of all these individuals produces surprising outcomes. Are consumers who are participating in a global fad exercising free will or are they being shaped by external forces? These individuals also form clusters around some shared interest. The business can facilitate these clusters but it is not clear that the business can determine them. So increasingly the value of a networked business lies in its customer community. Many businesses have to face the fact that "control" in the traditional business sense is lost.

Sensing and making sense become increasingly important in this complex environment. Businesses must learn to spot fleeting opportunities and be prepared to act very quickly before everyone else sees the same thing. "Total information awareness" means that any insight may be valid for only a short time, and this will place an increased emphasis on the role of arbitrage. It also means that market timing really matters.

Complexity theory can help managers understand how "black swans" and other high-impact events produce many subsequent events (Taleb 2007). The very fact that systems are connected implies that "events" somewhere out there may produce unexpected outcomes far away—the so-called "butterfly effect." Extreme events are an integral part of the networked, flat world, and we must learn to manage accordingly. These events are not predictable. Complexity also presents many "patterns" that turn out to be illusions. People want to see patterns—beware!

In particular, managers need to make sense of how people (or consumers) interact in crowds to generate fads. Managers also need to utilize mountains of data in this process and use technology effectively.

Understanding People, Crowds, and Fads

People are truly complex, adaptive systems. They are intrinsic to business and economics, but both disciplines have treated people as simple entities in their theoretical and practical studies. There is some hope, however, that this is slowly changing; recent Nobel prizes in economics have now acknowledged the role of psychological studies of people in economic theory. People have sensations, perceptions, impulses, emotions, images, and symbols; they categorize and organize information and knowledge and act according to these views.

People like to work in groups to better achieve common goals, but their actions can be shaped to join *fads* with a sense of belonging to a group. In fads and social networks, decision-making agents interact with one another to trigger unpredictable consequences. Across the planet, this network of consumers represents a community of billions, but at the same time, we see the growing importance of the individual within the networked community. People now engage, via the network effect, in swarms, viral marketing, and crowd sourcing.

Understanding Information and Using Technology

The declining cost of mass data storage has now reached a point where companies can contemplate storing all their business data indefinitely. The scale of transactions in networked businesses is generating a torrent of customer data, accelerated by a surge in networked appliances and devices. Companies are now looking at how consumer purchases are influenced, and researchers are developing many techniques to derive meaning from monitoring browsing activity, queries, click-throughs, or other data streams. In a networked flat world, individuals are generating a 24/7 life story of data about themselves and this is available for astute analysis.

In making sense of the environment, managers need to understand how to use these data effectively to extract relevant business meaning. Herein lies a distinct competitive advantage. Who has the algorithms that make sense of these data torrents? Many businesses are trying to extract meaning from massive unstructured data sets, a sign that they believe value to be there.

Harnessing data is not the only technological challenge presented by complexity. Complexity theory has changed the way managers view computer science. In recent years, computer science has been experiencing something of an identity crisis. As Denning and McGettrick (2005) write:

> The old definition of computer science—the study of phenomena surrounding computers—is now obsolete. Computing is the study of natural and artificial information processes.

A fundamental development in complexity theory was the work of Wolfram (2002), who looked at computation as an experimental science involving very simple computer programs (that is, cellular automata) that when interacting produce outcomes of considerable complexity. Wolfram observes: "Mere equations cannot capture complexity, whereas simple computational rules can."

Computer techniques can also be used in such applications as neural networks, fuzzy logic, and probabilistic reasoning. The rising interest in games is no accident, especially when games are seen as models for large, complex, adaptive systems that never terminate. Computing is an infinite game. Computing also plays a central role in simulations, as discussed in the text that follows.

Setting Strategy

In addition to making sense, managers need to set strategy in a complex environment. Strategy involves employing resources to meet the desired objectives of the business over some reasonable length of time. Leaders of networked business need a strategy that can, in an integrated way, make sense of both the big picture and the local situation. Businesses must develop a strategy of both selected node competence, which others will link to, and network orchestration, which enables others to all cooperate and together assemble some desired capability.

In networked environments, businesses must anticipate. They need to redefine their strategy work as understanding better than others the likely future shaping forces, how to align with them, and how to develop a set of capabilities as options to respond as needed. This approach should give businesses enough time to develop the portfolio of capabilities that can be accessed rapidly to handle events. By virtue of its networked morphology, the business can quickly assemble the capability to react to short-term events. Indeed, some of these capabilities may well lie outside the currently defined business, so they are accessed through the network.

In designing capabilities, managers need to make a strategic decision about optimizing a business for maximum performance or retaining more flexibility to handle adaptation for a changing world in the future. The usual complexity theory-based advice would be to avoid optimization unless one is in a relatively benign or dominant niche. However, within a networked world, it may well be a wise and prudent strategy to achieve a portfolio of distinctive node competences provided, of course, that they are highly networked (linked). These links need not be permanent, providing that the company has developed the capability to quickly forge and manage such linkages.

Decision Making

Decision making in a more networked "flat world" uses many of the traditional methods, but it also needs new techniques emphasizing deep knowledge and intuition. This is because timing becomes crucial, especially during an event period when time is compressed. Problem solving is replaced by more of a balancing of issues to maintain flexibility rather than make firm decisions for the next 10 years. The need for an inverted structure for accessing knowledge means there is more of a dialogue and dialectic: top-down concepts and systems thinking and bottom-up, self-organized insights.

Factoring risks into decisions is also more complicated. Risk assessment in decision making must recognize that markets are inherently risky and uncertain and that bubbles occur. The real risks are more than a reassuring bell curve may suggest, and decisions must reflect this. Companies will be at risk more frequently than anticipated.

Adaptation and Simulation

Adaptation is the rule in complex environments. As noted previously, in an unpredictable environment, the ability to align a business to its environment has become a key business goal. Many organizations are experiencing change more rapidly than they can comprehend and control. Maintaining stability and changing at the same time becomes the challenge. Growth progresses by smaller increments, combining needed capabilities and often using other companies—made easier by networking—or by selected acquisitions. Major investments should be made only if a dominant position has been locked in by network effects such as increasing returns. In general, the goal is to pursue no single optimum but to have multiple goals with flexibility, adapting along the way.

Companies that adapt at different rates may find it difficult to cooperate because they are at a different state of adaptation. Both companies and individuals will find it increasingly difficult to be members of communities or groups who have adapted more effectively to their new world. The "edge of chaos" is used to describe the conditions between stability and occasional instability for encouraging innovation and change.

For a strategy of adaptation, simulations can play a critical role in strategy design and evolution. The availability of low-cost, high-powered computing resources, huge data sets, and the fundamental role of computing in complexity theory all combine to make simulation a potentially powerful business tool. Agent simulation has become a very big effort within complexity theory, with wide application from simulation of terrorist networks to consumer behavior. The big challenge with these simulations is deciding on the rules these "intelligent agents" will use with each other. Simulations involving people become more challenging when deciding these rules.

The primary point of simulations is not to forecast an outcome such as a specific future price. All the evidence suggests this would be foolhardy. What simulations can do is to provide a much better feel for the various possible outcomes, risk assessment, and overall system behavior. Simulations, for example, permit the exploration of strategies among interdependent agents, such as the simulation of pricing behavior in electric power markets. They permit the exploration of risk strategies for natural hazards that would otherwise be simply inaccessible to quantification and understanding. (See Chapter 8, "Artificial Intelligence: How Individual Agents Add Up to a Network," for a more detailed discussion of agent-based simulations.)

An exciting development is the role of the massive online multiplayer games and virtual worlds with millions of participants. They can start to represent a parallel virtual world, which can simulate the real one to some extent. Future businesses will no doubt exist within both the real and the virtual worlds. In fact, this has already started to happen (Second Life).

Researchers also use *genetic algorithms* (Holland 1975), a computer-based technique for simulating the characteristics of a set of possible solutions to an optimization problem, which then evolve, seeking a better fit or solution to a particular problem. The simulation involves, say, an initial random set of solutions that then evolve through generations, each generation seeking a solution or fit to the defined task. This may be called the "Darwinian gambit" of seeking effective strategies through random mutation and evolutionary survival of strategies based on local fitness.

Organization

The distributed, networked organization, with the capacity to quickly establish a specific capability, cannot be assembled from a disparate and unrelated group of components or agents. A shared framework of understanding of the current situation and what the future vision is ensures some basis for cooperation and connectivity. Businesses must establish a much simpler set of protocols or methods of working together if rapid, time-dependent capabilities can be assembled. The process for making the various linkages work is crucial for cooperation. Ideally, anyone, anywhere could connect anytime, regardless of systems or processes! This requires considerable information sharing between parties (usually information is power and closely held) and the inherent ability to have sufficient trust in others to quickly connect and disconnect without a bureaucratic or difficult legal process to slow things down. The globalized networked enterprise of the flat world has a problem of identity: Exactly where are the boundaries of the business? Who is an employee? What is a division or group? Exceptional or smart outcomes not previously considered possible will be achieved by combing capabilities in unanticipated ways. This leads to an organization that is fast, agile, and versatile, not optimized for some distinct capability.

Managers need to think beyond their own business units, and often beyond their own organizations, in designing and managing a network to achieve their business goals. Businesses must encourage senior managers to develop the ability to "orchestrate" the working and linking of nodes rather than just managing specific units. Managers have traditionally been trained to manage "chunks" of something such as a manufacturing unit, a marketing department, or HR. Complexity theory, however, places great emphasis on the relationships that govern the chunks or components. This is the crucial role of nodes in a network. Managers will have to give even greater emphasis to understanding the overall purpose of the organization, the relationships between their respective nodes, and the competences of the nodes themselves.

Key Unanswered Questions

There are, unsurprisingly, many unanswered questions related to the networked flat world and complexity theory. The "intelligent" or "smart" business network will be the core of the future business, but we need to more explicitly define the characteristics of these networks and what we mean by "intelligent" or "smart." Networks involve multiple players (including individuals, businesses, NGOs, governments, society, and nonstate actors) and multiple issues (such as security, trust, risk, privacy, reputation, competition, monopoly, and regulation). All of these issues and players will be shaped by complexity theory effects. What is not clear is the process for handling this complex matrix of players and issues. The technology of networks, especially software, now effectively integrates the processes and rules of social systems and business. We need to understand how these networks can facilitate the interaction of disparate agents (customers/businesses) to enable both cooperation and competition.

Among the other key unanswered questions:

- *Modeling global and local interactions*—Agent modeling is based around local interactions and their subsequent production of a complex structure. We are now seeing, in both neuronal structures and the World Wide Web, global interconnections of local clusters. These are system-spanning clusters that somehow imbue the system with special characteristics. We need to better understand the impact of the emergence of global knowledge and global connections on local agent modeling.

- *Driving fads*—We know there are mechanisms for establishing a global consumer fad in short order. We do not know, however, exactly what we have to do to ensure that this process actually happens. This may well be a critical discovery for future business success.

- *Understanding empowered users*—The empowered user (user-centric software, digital social networks, consumer swarms) is interacting in ways not considered previously and beyond what businesses can anticipate. We need to understand how businesses can handle this loss of control to the network.

- *Modeling agents*—The ability to simulate customers as agents in complexity theory depends critically on having a set of authentic rules for their interactions. Will the availability of a huge data set of customer behavior, derived from extensive online data retention and analysis, permit these rules to be derived? Agent-based simulations are only as good as the models used for the individual agents involved.

Becoming Comfortable with Complexity

As noted earlier, many managers find complexity theory a frustrating topic because it can explain but it cannot explicitly predict. In a networked world, managers may experience a feeling of randomness, a loss of control, and subsequent insecurity. They will have to learn to handle this by operating with a different set of criteria for feeling at home in the flat world. They will need to develop the ability to be totally focused on individual things and simultaneously get the big picture. This is the role of the orchestrator. This will require an ability to constantly shift areas of focus—checking context and then working on a focused issue, and then checking context again—always making sense of the overall situation (Wind and Crook 2005).

How can managers do this? It should come as no surprise: Managers will need a broad portfolio of capabilities. Within this portfolio, however, complexity theory can shape and influence the broader education of business managers as they struggle to make sense of an ever-more-complicated and unusual world. Since the flat world is complicated, managers must get used to mutual causality. This means understanding what it means to be "networked" and exploiting network effects.

Managers must become more aware of the power of an "inverted structure" in which ideas and actions flow upward. They will need to focus on detecting and enabling the emergence of desired outcomes from all these interactions. Learning to shape events rather than thinking, mistakenly, that they directly control them will become a key skill. "Stuff happens" in the networked world. Managers must be able to live in a world of events, big and small, driving the agenda, where time is highly nonlinear and events may require multiple actions in a short timeframe.

Human factors will play an ever-increasing role. People, individually and collectively, with have an increasing influence on companies and events, given their integration with networked technology. Managers must pay more attention to people and their behavior—singly and collectively—and understand the irony of the networked world; individuals can seriously shape events, and, paradoxically, individuals, on a global scale, can be shaped and influenced by network effects.

A key need, given the preceding arguments, is how to teach complexity theory and associated views in business school, so it can become more normal and accepted. The "systems approach" needs to be encouraged but in a more concrete way by using complexity theory frameworks. Can we develop a broad set of tools to teach people to think holistically and to handle multiple causalities and actions? Perhaps trying to teach complexity theory as yet another formal scientific method for managers is ill advised since they then expect a direct cause-and-effect paradigm. Complexity theory should be initially taught as a business or management skill or art form with an emphasis on making sense and developing an intuitive approach. This may well be the critical management skill for the networked flat world.

References

Arthur, B. W. 1994. *Increasing Returns and Path Dependence in the Economy.* Ann Arbor: University of Michigan Press.

Bak, P., C. Tang, and K. Wiesenfeld. 1987. Self-organized criticality: an explanation of 1 / f noise. *Physical Review Letters* 59.

Barabási, A., and A. Réka. 1999. Emergence of scaling in random networks. *Science* 286, 509-512.

Brooks, R. A. 1991. New approaches to Robotics. *Science* 13 (253), 1227-1232.

Denning, P. J., and A. McGettrick. 2005. The profession of IT: Recentering computer science. *Communications of the ACM* 48 (11), 15-19.

Erdos, P., and A. Renyi. 1959. On Random Graphs. *Publicationes Mathematicae* 6, 290-297.

Holland, J. H. 1975. *Adaptation in Natural and Artificial Systems.* Ann Arbor: University of Michigan Press.

Johnson, N. 2007. *Two's Company, Three Is Complexity.* Oxford: Oneworld Publications.

Kauffman, S. (2001). http://chronicle.com/colloquylive/2001/05/complexity/.

Kauffman, S. (various publications).

Kogut, B. 2007. *European Management Review* 4 (2).

Mandelbrot, B. B. 1983. *Fractal Geometry of Nature.* San Francisco: W. H. Freeman.

Roberts, J. 2004. *The Modern Firm: Organizational Design for Performance and Growth.* Oxford; New York: Oxford University Press.

Santa Fe Institute. www.santafe.edu/.

Second Life. http://secondlife.com/.

Taleb, N. 2007. *The Black Swan: The Impact of the Highly Improbable*. New York: Random House.

Wolfram, S. 2002. *A New Kind of Science*. Champaign, IL: Wolfram Media.

Wind, Y., and C. Crook. 2005. The Power of Impossible Thinking: Transform the Business of Your Life and the Life of Your Business. Upper Saddle River, NJ: Wharton School Publishing.

13

Supply Webs: Managing, Organizing, and Capitalizing on Global Networks of Suppliers

Serguei Netessine

Abstract

As manufacturing supply chains have moved from vertically integrated factories to diffused networks, manufacturers need to manage complex, global webs of suppliers. In this chapter, Serguei Netessine examines supply networks in two industries in particular: automobiles, and aerospace and defense. He explores how different strategies and technologies have helped companies manage, organize, and capitalize on their networks of suppliers. He discusses how Japanese automakers have used partnerships to outperform their U.S. rivals, who have taken a more adversarial approach to their suppliers. He also considers how companies such as Airbus and Boeing have used technology to coordinate and integrate far-flung networks. While Netessine notes that the formal study of network-based supply chains is just emerging, he offers insights from research and practice on the growing importance of supply networks and strategies for managing them successfully.

Consider…the globe-trotting involved in manufacturing the Intel Pentium processor that powers a Dell computer. The process starts in Japan, where a single crystal is grown into a large ingot of silicon by Toshiba Ceramics. The silicon ingot is then sliced by suppliers, like Toshiba Ceramics or others, into thin wafers that are flown across the Pacific to one of Intel's semiconductor fabs in either Arizona or Oregon. At the fabs, hundreds of integrated circuits are etched and layered on each wafer, forming individual dies on the wafers. Finished wafers are packaged and then flown back across the Pacific to Intel's Assembly and Test Operations in Malaysia. The wafers are treated and cut into dies, and the dies are finished into sealed ceramic "packages." The packages are then placed in substrate trays that are put into Intel's boxes and then packaged again in blank boxes (to conceal that they are Intel products) for shipment back across the Pacific to Intel warehouses in Arizona. Having traveled across the Pacific three times already, the chips are then shipped to Dell factories in Texas, Tennessee, Ireland, Brazil, Malaysia, and China, or one of its contract manufacturers in Taiwan, to be used as components in Dell computers (Sheffi 2007, 11).

As this example illustrates, the past decades have witnessed a radical movement from stand-alone, vertically integrated supply chains toward networked supply chains. At the beginning of the twentieth century, Ford revolutionized the manufacturing industry by mass-producing cars in enormous fabrication facilities. Until the middle of the century, Ford generated electric power, internally procured iron ore and coal, which the company brought to Ford-owned steel mills using Ford-owned railroads and ships, and then made every part required for each automobile (Sheffi 2007, 78). Now, numerous suppliers belonging to several tiers in a network—who sometimes compete and sometimes cooperate—design, manufacture, and assemble products for a few customers. Even a copper wire in a small electric power motor of a GM car starts in the copper mines of Chile, then travels to wire makers in China, then continues on to motor makers in Japan or car-door makers in Canada, and then to final assembly in the United States, before it finishes in the worldwide network of GM's 7,500 distribution dealers (Sheffi 2007, 27).

Flows of information and money through the network are as vital as flows of products themselves. Information conveys demand all the way from customers to manufacturers, and it also helps partners in the supply chain communicate orders, invoices, and payments. The complexity of supply chain networks often results in intricate financial and information flows. For example, the "Big Three" U.S. automakers created the world's largest virtual marketplace, Covisint, which has connected the three virtually through the Internet with thousands of suppliers. Through this business-to-business exchange, all companies have been able to communicate using a common language and make payments without investing in expensive electronic data interchange, or EDI, systems (Koudal et al. 2003). In other industries, such as apparel, a large retailer may want to help its suppliers procure raw materials because it already enjoys economies of scale and more favorable payment terms with raw material suppliers.

This radical transformation from vertically integrated local supply chains to highly decentralized global supply chain networks has been fueled by the emergence of low-cost outsourcing options in Brazil, Russia, India, China (BRIC), and other countries, and by advances in information technology, as well as by the ever-growing complexity of end products. If organized properly, these networks can enable the creation of superior products at the lowest possible cost while ensuring speedy delivery to the consumer.

To realize these benefits, however, a number of new challenges need to be addressed. Among these challenges is the fact that longer supply chains complicate information sharing and demand forecasting and require more inventory; that contractual relationships with suppliers need to be intertwined with other relationships built purely on trust and long-term interactions; that concerns about supply chain disruptions call for preemptive strategies; and so forth. For this reason, Iansiti and Levien (2004) call such networks "business ecosystems" in which every member's fate is tied to the health of the network as a whole. The recent wave of supplier bankruptcies in the automotive industry illustrates the consequences for the manufacturer of financial instability within the supplier network, including parts shortages and production cost overruns (Swinney and Netessine 2007). Thirty-six major automotive suppliers entered bankruptcy since 1999, citing production cost increases, unstable domestic volume, legacy pension plans (resulting in greater overhead expenses), and difficult access to capital.

These events clearly demonstrate the problems arising from a failure to adopt a network perspective. For example, fluctuations in raw material prices affect supplier profitability if contract prices are predetermined and do not include provisions for material price increases. On the other hand, manufacturers' unwillingness to adjust contracts to accommodate raw material price increases often leads to supplier bankruptcy, which, in its turn, hurts the manufacturer that must scramble to keep parts flowing. In 2005, when seat supplier Lear threatened to cease shipping products to Chrysler in an attempt to negotiate higher prices, the automaker promptly took Lear to court to enforce the contract, despite the fact that the supplier posted a net loss of nearly $600 million in the fourth quarter of 2005 alone (Wernle 2006).

Although best-in-class companies manage to achieve superior supply chain performance, other companies fall prey to disruptions, parts shortages, and poor coordination among both customers and suppliers. Supply network disruptions are extremely costly: Empirical evidence indicates (see Figure 13-1) that firms experiencing a supply chain glitch lose approximately 100% in operating income, return on sales, and return on assets relative to control firms that do not experience a disruption. Moreover, during the two-year period after the glitch is announced, operating income, sales, total costs, and inventories do not improve (Hendricks and Singhal 2005). In this study a large portion of supply chain glitches arose due to factors outside of the firm (for example, related to suppliers or customers).

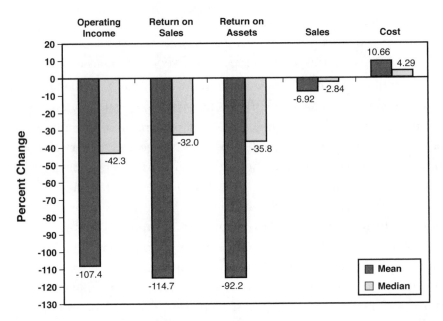

Figure 13-1   Change in control-adjusted operating performance of firms during the year before the announcement of a supply chain glitch. (Reprinted by permission, Hendricks and Singhal, Association between supply chain glitches and operating performance. *Management Science* 51, 695-711, 2005. Copyright, the Institute for Operations Research and the Management Sciences (INFORMS), 7240 Parkway Drive, Suite 300, Hanover, MD 21076 USA)

To summarize, competition between companies has turned into competition between supply chain networks, resulting in a situation whereby one must carefully orchestrate every aspect of moving materials, information, and payments within one's own supply chain network. I will first provide brief case studies illustrating approaches that companies in the automotive and the aerospace and defense industries are using. I will then conclude with a review of emerging academic literature on supply chain networks.

Managing Supplier Relationships: The Automotive Industry

The automotive industry illustrates different approaches to managing relationships with networks of suppliers in an environment of increasing global competition (see Figure 13.2).[1] With increased competition from Japanese, South Korean, and European automakers, the combined market share of the Big Three U.S. manufacturers (GM, Ford, and Chrysler) slipped from 62.2% in 1997 to below 50% in 2007. Since most

---

[1] Much of this section is based on Koudal et al. (2003).

components of vehicle manufacturing are outsourced to suppliers (for both U.S. and foreign companies), success and failure is largely driven by automakers' ability to orchestrate complex supplier networks, representing a case of network-to-network competition in its purest form.

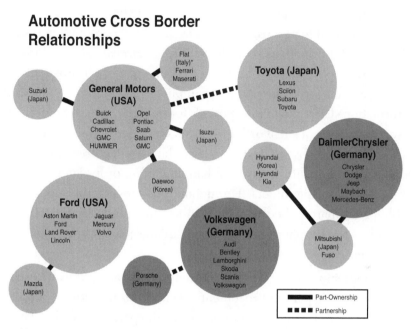

Figure 13-2   Global relationships in the automotive industry (from Trice 2006)

The success of Japanese automotive companies relative to U.S. companies is often attributed to drastically different approaches to managing supplier networks (see Liker and Choi 2004). U.S. companies often keep their relationships with suppliers at arm's length, asking them to bid against each other every year and then selecting on the basis of lowest cost. As a result, the relationships between U.S. automotive manufacturers and their suppliers are often adversarial, built on myriad contingencies written into the contract, and rife with accusations. It is not uncommon, for example, for a manufacturer to demand significant price decreases regardless of suppliers' financial state and business realities. Ford famously demanded an across-the-board 5% price decrease from its suppliers (see Swinney and Netessine 2007). In contrast, Japanese companies operate under the concept of *keiretsu:* a network of closely related vendors that continuously improve, exchange information, and learn together. For a long time, the success of Japanese supplier networks was dismissed as a phenomenon local to Japan and, hence, impossible to emulate outside of Japanese culture. Over the past decade, however, Japanese automotive manufacturers shifted a significant part of their production volume to the United States, with Toyota and Honda locally manufacturing and sourcing 60% and 80% of their U.S. vehicles sales, respectively. Very often these two companies made highly successful partnerships with the same firms that supplied the Big Three U.S. manufacturers, and these suppliers raved about their relationships with Japanese companies while decrying their experiences with U.S. companies.

Although it is as hard to replicate *keiretsu* as the Toyota production system itself, the following fundamental principles seem to underpin *keiretsu* relationships. Toyota tries to learn every part of its suppliers' business and commits to their prosperity. This usually involves placing a manager in the potential supplier's plant and investing in data collection and information sharing for a long period (for example, a year) before committing to using that supplier. Then, a small order is placed, and the supplier's quality and compliance with the schedule is observed. If necessary, the manufacturer shares its own expertise in productivity and quality. Successful handling of an order leads to more orders as well as to more serious assignments. Throughout this process, the supplier is assured of a comfortable profit margin, because the manufacturer understands the supplier's cost structure as well as the supplier does. Toyota maintains joint ventures and stakes in suppliers to share their pains and gains.

Toyota develops suppliers' technical and innovation capabilities by exchanging best practices and conducting joint improvement activities through study groups. Toyota and Honda often do not specify exact requirements for the parts they order. They encourage the supplier to figure out what is needed, stimulating supplier innovation and making the supplier an active participant in the design process rather than a mere provider of "widgets." It is a tradition to have "guest engineers" visiting each other's companies for a year or two at a time, sharing information through well-structured meetings.

Japanese manufacturers are very selective about which parts are designed entirely by suppliers and which parts must be designed on the manufacturer's premises. For example, parts that are independent of the rest of the car can be designed independently by the supplier, but parts that interface with the body of the vehicle must be designed in close collaboration with the manufacturer.

The firm supervises and benchmarks suppliers by providing constant feedback and involving top management in problem solving. Both Honda and Toyota send monthly scorecards to their suppliers that rate each on quality, delivery, performance, incidents, and so on, whereas U.S. manufacturers assess their networks annually, or even biannually.

Finally, Japanese automotive companies tend to multisource by working with two or three suppliers for every subsystem to maintain competition and enable contingency planning. Although existing suppliers are usually assured some part of the business for the entire life of the model, and given preference for new projects, the total volume can fluctuate based on comparative performance with other suppliers. This ensures productive rivalry without placing the supplier at too much risk.

Although the steps outlined previously are intuitively appealing and easy to understand, U.S. automotive manufacturers have struggled to emulate them. Chrysler has made great progress in this direction, but the process stalled after the merger with Daimler. Meanwhile, both Honda and Toyota continue to develop their supplier networks, which grow and improve as the manufacturers themselves advance. Their example seems to indicate that extensive supplier networks can be managed by the manufacturer on a global basis, although new challenges arising in such networks are unique and require novel approaches.

Leveraging Coordinating Technology: The Aerospace and Defense Industry

The aerospace and defense industry illustrates how companies use technology to manage their supply networks. Companies in the industry face ever-increasing product complexity, constant innovation, and uncertainties inherent in multiyear, multibillion-dollar new product development projects. Because a typical product is so expensive to develop and the average life cycle of a product is relatively long (an airplane, for example, might be in active use for 25 years or longer), supply chain costs associated with delivering and maintaining these products are extremely important. Major players in the industry have a truly global presence and provide support to their equipment in most countries throughout the world, either directly or through a network of subcontractors. For example, Airbus Industries[2] has 57,000 employees in 160 offices and 16 production sites worldwide. Its supply chain operates through three customer support centers (in France, the United States, and China), four training centers (in France, Germany, the United States, and China), five spare-parts centers (in France, Germany, the United States, Singapore, and China), and 1,500 suppliers in 30 countries.

Technology is critical to manage such a complex global supply chain. For example, Airbus manages its network of suppliers through several Internet portals. Airbussupply.com provides suppliers with the latest news, projects, and tools, and helps them to manage performance and to exchange product information. Airbussupply.com

---

[2] This material is based on information from Airbus.com.

covers procurement, the supply chain, product development, engineering, aircraft programs, and customer support. Esourcing.airbus.com allows buyers and suppliers to exchange online requirements and proposals during calls for tender and reverse auctions. This paperless process, which covers everything from identifying a potential supplier to developing the final contract, ensures secure information exchanges and fairness among suppliers. Suppliers can inform Airbus buyers about their capabilities through a self-registration process. Airbussupply.com facilitates ordering goods and services from existing suppliers through a harmonized and automated ordering process across all Airbus entities. The system covers the whole supply chain cycle, from initial requests to suppliers all the way to invoicing, including dispatch, transport, receiving, and storage of goods through an integrated, collaborative workplace. Finally, for personnel who work with the end product, there is Airbusworld.com, a portal for Airbus aircraft operators, flight crews, maintenance personnel, and service providers, as well as for airline industry professionals.

Another example of leveraging technology to manage complex products at Airbus is the implementation of RFID (radio-frequency identification) tags. Airbus pioneered the use of RFID technology in aircraft tool management in 1999, enabling identification of each tool with a microchip for radio frequency identification, offering electronic support when tools are lent or used in repairs. The microchips are installed in the tools as well as in the toolboxes and contain data about the history of the tool, as well as shipping, routing, and customs information. In case of product failure, the availability of this groundbreaking technology on aircraft spare parts helps to simplify inventory and repair management. This technology also helps in component repairs, making the repair and flight history of components available electronically and helping identify companies within the supply chain that have the expertise to make a needed repair.

Boeing, Airbus's key U.S.-based competitor, has also implemented new coordination tools and pushed its management of its supply network downstream to sourcing raw materials. The Boeing 787, or Dreamliner, is a family of new, fuel-efficient airplanes that have used advanced carbon-fiber composite materials to achieve an unprecedented 20% improvement in fuel efficiency as well as point-to-point service nearly everywhere in the world. For previous Boeing models, the company designed all major components but outsourced production to suppliers and performed only the final assembly of all parts and pieces. However, such an approach often resulted in schedule disruptions due to missed deadlines by suppliers, capacity shortages, and conflicts among suppliers. Given the unique challenges due to the materials used and its ambitious goals for efficiency and passenger comfort, Boeing took a decidedly different approach to managing the extensive network of suppliers involved in the making of the 787 (see Figure 13-3).

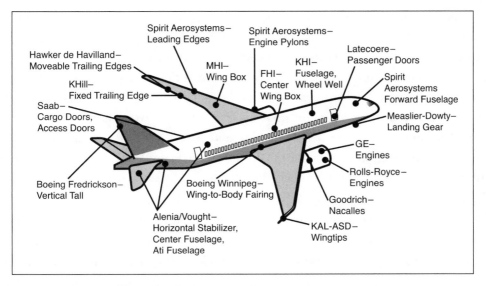

Figure 13-3   Major suppliers for the Boeing 787 (from Georgevitch 2007)

First, the company gave suppliers unprecedented responsibility for designing and delivering major portions of the aircraft, using new tools for coordination. Instead of working out design details, Boeing delegated this task to suppliers who designed, manufactured, and validated parts, then communicated with other suppliers, assembled parts into subassemblies, and delivered them to Boeing's final assembly facility in Everett, Washington. This approach permitted the concurrent rather than serial development of various components of the aircraft, which shortened the development cycle and, therefore, allowed for the latest technologies to be delivered to the market sooner. Forty-three top-tier suppliers helped Boeing to finalize the airplane's configuration in September 2005. Moreover, Boeing previously had to assemble and test even minor pieces of the airplane while obtaining information from scores of suppliers regarding the best way to do so, but now suppliers performed these tasks while directly communicating with one another. This monumental shift also implied that suppliers, who often never communicated with each other before, now had to coordinate delivery schedules and purchase order requirements directly with one another. Such communication and coordination required real-time visibility throughout the entire global supply chain, achieved through Exostar's Supply Chain Management Solution powered by E2open software. Currently, the software virtually links 135 sites across 12 countries located on five continents.[3] However, only 11 major subassemblies will be delivered to Everett, Washington, for final assembly.

[3] Source: http://www.boeing.com.

Second, Boeing implemented advanced sourcing for key raw materials. In the past, the entire manufacturing process could be halted because of raw material shortages. Due to extensive use of new composite materials (50% of the 787's structure is composite, 20% is aluminum, and 15% is titanium), the threat of shortages was even greater. In fact, only a single supplier, Toray, was qualified to supply the key composite material. To avoid raw material shortages, Boeing coordinated capacity development with Toray. This involved tracking closely the aggregate demand across all Toray's suppliers but still allowed individual suppliers to negotiate directly with Toray, because composite materials are usually specific to certain uses or to a single producer (Stundza 2007).

Third, to minimize disruptions in the production process and work-in-process inventory, Boeing streamlined the manufacturing process by reducing variability in parts content. For example, all options and features were standardized, and variations were postponed as late in the production process as possible (for example, to the final assembly stage).

Fourth, the company created a framework for managing the supply network over the product life cycle. For example, early in the production process, when the Dreamliner faces the highest uncertainties in demand and supply, supply chain management processes focus on achieving flexibility to serve fluctuating demand. Later in the product life cycle, when demand matures and achieves high volumes, the supply chain focuses on cost efficiencies. Finally, during the phase-out stage, which is again rife with uncertainties regarding demand, supply chain management is concerned with avoiding excessive inventories through asset flexibility (Georgevitch 2007).

Although Boeing achieved certain successes with its new approach to managing supply chain networks, many problems surfaced in the late stages of the project. In late 2007, the company was struggling to overcome a six-month delay in production due to the "global outsourcing" of development and production to suppliers (see Lunsford 2007), which led to tens of thousands of parts missing at the time of assembly. The reason was that Boeing seems to have overestimated the ability of its suppliers to handle many tasks that Boeing used to handle internally. Furthermore, the company did not commit sufficient resources to overseeing suppliers and, hence, was often ill-informed about progress. (This example illustrates why Toyota pays so much attention to the internal operations of its suppliers.) To address this challenge, Boeing deployed hundreds of its own employees to plants in Italy, Japan, and the United States and set aside about $2 billion in additional money for combating increasing costs due to delays. While there is little doubt among Boeing's leaders that the global sourcing approach is viable (and Airbus has said that it plans to use the same approach to build a competing plane), these added costs probably could have been avoided had Boeing begun with a more network-based perspective on the entire process.

Research on Managing Supplier Networks

The preceding case studies clearly demonstrate the rapid development of global supply chain networks and the strategies and technologies companies are using to manage them. The academic literature on supply chain management, however, has been slow to react to these advances. The main difficulty lies in the methodological challenges of modeling the multifaceted relationships in complex, contemporary supply chains. Although current literature recognizes the need to study contractual relations between buyers and suppliers (see Cachon 2003) and competition/cooperation in supply chains (see Cachon and Netessine 2004), most studies focus on simple supply chains (typically with one upstream and one downstream company) and on monopolistic situations. For example, studies of supplier networks for maintaining and repairing complex equipment such as airplanes or weapons systems have focused on a centrally managed supply chain (see Muckstadt 2005); and more developed models that take into consideration contracting aspects in such supply chains are only beginning to emerge (Kim, Cohen, and Netessine 2007).

Even papers that do study decentralized decision making tend to focus on competition rather than cooperation, while limiting analysis to bilateral rather than multilateral relationships. For example, there is an impressive body of literature on competitive bidding in auctions (see Klemperer 2004), but little is known about when a more cooperative supplier selection process might be preferable. The major exception is the empirical work of Bajari, McMillan, and Tadelis (2006), which shows that there are important limitations to competitive bidding and that contract negotiations might work better when projects are complex, contractual design is incomplete, and there are few potential bidders. Moreover, auctions tend to stifle communication between buyers and sellers, which more or less nullifies the contractor's expertise during the project design stage. This finding is consistent with the examples already given, clearly indicating that successful management of supply chain networks involves significant collaboration and information sharing among network members, with technology playing an important role as mediator.

Because the previous discussion indicates that some of the best supplier networks are managed through cooperation rather than competition, cooperative game theory might offer insights. Brandenburger and Nalebuff (1997) provide a number of fascinating examples indicating that companies often both compete and cooperate to achieve sustainable advantages. Nagarajan and Sosic (2007) provide a comprehensive overview of the recent literature, subdividing this literature into models for negotiation (for example, bargaining models, cooperative bargaining, and negotiation power) and coalition formation/coalition structures (profit allocation rules, structure of the core of the game). Research in this area is very scant, and the focus of this work is on studying ways to share gains from cooperative supply chain management (Anupindi, Bassok, and Zemel 1999; Granot and Sosic 2005; Nagarajan and Sosic 2006) and how the supply chain can be made secure through joint investment by several parties (Bakshi and Kleindorfer 2007).

There is very limited literature on how the entry and exit of firms into various echelons of the supply chain affect the entire network. Corbett and Karmarkar (2001) examine the impact of fixed and variable costs on the structure and competitiveness of supply chains with a serial structure and price-sensitive linear deterministic demand and then characterize the viability and stability of supply chain structures. Majumder and Srinivasan (2006) study multistage serial supply chains, demonstrating the importance of considering the entire sequence of successive contracts when assessing the performance of a supply chain. They also find that sometimes cooperation among nonleader members can increase supply chain efficiency. Majumder and Srinivasan (2005) develop a framework to analyze large supply chain networks involving long sequences of contracts and show that contract leadership and leader position affect the performance of the entire supply chain. They model competition between supply chain networks and show the effect of changes in leader position as well as changes in the cost structure on the equilibrium of the network.

Examples in this article illustrate the important role that the latest technology plays in managing global supply chain networks. For example, Wal-Mart's Retail Link system delivers real-time sales information to its suppliers, which has played a critical role in the company's ability to orchestrate a complex supply chain network. A special issue of *Information Systems Research* on "The Digitally Enabled Extended Enterprise in a Global Economy" (Krishnan, Rai, and Zmud 2007) sheds light on some issues surrounding the use of information technology. For example, Malhotra, Gosain, and El Sawy (2007) investigate the relationship between the use of standard electronic business interfaces (SEBIs) and the adaptive capability of supply chain partnerships, and find empirical support for conceptualizing SEBIs as the mechanism to enable adaptive capability. Bala and Venkatesh (2007) investigate how a firm's role in its supply chain explains differences in the extent to which firms participating in RosettaNet (which allows trading partners of all sizes to connect electronically to process transactions and move information within their extended supply chains) adopted consortium-developed interorganizational business process standards. Wu and Kleindorfer (2005) survey literature on B2B exchanges, while specifically focusing on supply chain contracting in competitive environments arising in capital-intensive industries such as chemicals, electric power, metals, natural gas, plastics, and semiconductors. Steffenson-McElheran (2008) further demonstrates empirically that manufacturing plants that exhibit leading productivity indicators are more likely to adopt e-buying technologies but not necessarily e-selling technologies.

It appears difficult, if not impossible, to reflect in a model many issues that challenge contemporary supply chain networks. For example, Sheffi (2007) illustrates many challenges posed by managing complex supply chain networks due to the possibility of disruptions and security breaches anywhere in the network and emphasizes that public-private collaborations provide one possible solution for securing the network. (See Howard Kunreuther's discussion in Chapter 22, "The Weakest Link: Managing Risk Through Interdependent Strategies," for a further discussion of using public-private collaboration to address interdependent risks.)

Given the challenge of modeling, some researchers have turned to empirical and field studies. Vereecke, Van Dierdonck, and De Meyer (2006) represent one such study in which the authors use network analysis to understand the position of plants in international manufacturing networks. This analysis demonstrates that different types of plants play different strategic roles in a company, each having a different focus and differing in age, autonomy, and level of resources and investments. However, as Nohria (1992, 8) indicates, "If we are to take a network perspective seriously, it means adopting a different intellectual lens and discipline, gathering different kinds of data, learning new analytical and methodological techniques, and seeking explanations that are quite different from conventional ones." This observation is likely to hold true as we learn more about supply chain networks.

One other potentially attractive approach might be the empirical game theoretic analysis through simulations of strategic interactions among multiple agents. See Wellman et al. (2005) and Argoneto et al. (2007) for further discussion. Such an approach helps to overcome the issue of analytical tractability, which otherwise makes analyzing such networks all but impossible. At the same time, it might allow us to obtain insights into supply chain networks with numerous self-interested agents that compete or cooperate.

Conclusion

Although the examples discussed show that supply networks are becoming increasingly important in modern manufacturing, we know very little about what works and what does not in supply network management. Knowledge advances slowly for at least two reasons. First, traditional analytical approaches to modeling supply chains seem to falter when representing complex supply chain networks. Second, data analysis is handicapped by the necessity to collect independent information from multiple companies. Clearly, the challenges are likely to differ greatly between managing a hub-and-spoke network with a central orchestrator such as Toyota, Airbus, or Boeing and managing a much more decentralized network like that of Li & Fung (Wind, Fung, and Fung 2008). The hub-and-spoke network has a relatively stable configuration, whereas the decentralized network has the advantage of being reconfigurable and adaptable to an ever-changing environment. But in either case, technologies such as ERP systems, EDI, and Web-based B2B management tools are likely to play an ever-increasing role in our ability to manage and develop supply chain networks. Furthermore, growing pressure on businesses to focus on environmental issues has led to the emergence of sustainable operations management (Kleindorfer, Singhal, and Van Wassenhove 2005) as a new paradigm. Thus, we can expect to see integration between *forward* networks, or supply chain networks designed to deliver products to customers, and *reverse* networks that maximize product recovery potential over the product life cycle.

Powerful global forces continue to drive the creation of supply chain networks to enable division of labor through outsourcing, to explore cross-country cost differentials, or simply for historical/political reasons. Supply chain management is entering the era of competition among networks rather than at the supply chain level. Old tools inherited from the time when supply chains were much simpler may no longer apply to the new business realities. Although successful supply chain network orchestration is still much more of an art than a science, it is obvious that thinking incorrectly about supply chain management can be very costly (Hendricks and Singhal 2005). Amaral, Billington, and Tsay (2006) describe numerous hazards that can arise in the outsourcing relationship, and they subdivide these hazards into planning, executing, and managing physical, informational, and financial activities.

Finally, sprawling supply chain networks mean that competing companies often work with the same suppliers. Although the relationships may not be exclusive, how companies manage these relationships with the supply network can lead to differential advantages. For example, Sheffi (2007) describes how different responses by Nokia and Ericsson to a supply chain disruption at their common supplier, Philips, led to a 3% market-share shift from Ericsson to Nokia. This illustrates the importance of supply networks, as well as the capabilities and technologies needed for coordinating and managing them.

References

Amaral, J., C. A. Billington, and A.A. Tsay. 2006. Safeguarding the promise of production outsourcing. *Interfaces* 36, 220-233.

Anupindi, R., Y. Bassok, and E. Zemel. 1999. A general framework for the study of decentralized distribution systems. *Manufacturing and Service Operations Management* 3, 349-368.

Argoneto, P., M. Bruccoleri, G. L. Nigro, G. Perrone, and P. Renna. 2007. Production planning, negotiation and coalition: The advanced keys for B2B success. Working paper, University of Palermo, Italy.

Bajari, P., R. McMillan, and S. Tadelis. 2006. Auction versus negotiations in procurement: An empirical analysis. Forthcoming, *Journal of Law, Economics and Organization*.

Bakshi, N., and P. Kleindorfer. 2007. Co-Opetition and investment for resilience in global supply chains. Forthcoming. *Production and Operations Management*.

Bala, H., and V. Venkatesh. 2007. Assimilation of interorganizational business process standards. *Information Systems Research* 18, 340-362.

Brandenburger, A. M., and B. J. Nalebuff. 1997. Co-Opetition: A revolutionary mindset that combines competition and cooperation. New York: Doubleday.

Cachon, G. P. 2003. Supply chain coordination with contracts. In *Handbooks in Operations Research and Management Science: Supply Chain Management,* ed. S. Graves and T. de Kok. New York: North Holland.

Cachon, G., and S. Netessine. 2004. Game theory in supply chain analysis. In *Handbook of Quantitative Supply Chain Analysis: Modeling in the eBusiness Era,* ed. D. Simchi-Levi, S. D. Wu, and Z.-J. Shen. Kluwer.

Corbett, C., and U. Karmarkar. 2001. Competition and structure in serial supply chains with deterministic demand. *Management Science* 47, 966-978.

Georgevitch, S. 2007. 787 Dreamliner: Business model & supply chain overview. Presentation on March 15, 2007, at the Air Force Logistics Transformation Forum. http://www.dla.mil/j-6/AIT/Conferences/AirForce_Log_Trans_Forum/default.aspx.

Granot, D., and G. Sosic. 2005. Formation of alliances in Internet-based supply exchanges. *Management Science* 51, 92-105.

Hendricks, K., and V. Singhal. 2005. Association between supply chain glitches and operating performance. *Management Science* 51, 695-711.

Iansiti, M., and R. Levien. 2004. *The Keystone Advantage.* Harvard Business School Press.

Kim, S.-H., M. Cohen, and S. Netessine. 2007. Performance contracting in after-sales service supply chains. *Management Science* 53, 1843-1858.

Kleindorfer, P. R., K. Singhal, and L. N. Van Wassenhove. 2005. Sustainable operations management. *Production and Operations Management* 14, 482-492.

Klemperer, P. 2004. *Auctions: Theory and Practice.* Princeton University Press.

Koudal, P., H. Lee, B. Peleg, P. Rajwat, and R. Tully. 2003. General Motors: Building a digital loyalty network through demand and supply integration. Stanford Graduate School of Business Case GS-29.

Krishnan, M. S., A. Rai, and R. Zmud. 2007. Editorial overview: the digitally enabled extended enterprise in a global economy. *Information Systems Research* 18, 233-236.

Liker, J. K., and T. Y. Choi. 2004. Building deep supplier relationships. *Harvard Business Review* 82, 104-113.

Lunsford, J. L. 2007. Boeing scrambles to repair problems with new plane. *The Wall Street Journal,* December 7, A1.

Majumder, P., and A. Srinivasan. 2005. Leadership and competition in network supply chains. Forthcoming, *Management Science.*

Majumder, P., and A. Srinivasan. 2006. Leader location, cooperation and coordination in serial supply chains. *Production and Operations Management* 15, 22-39.

Malhotra, A., S. Gosain, and O. A. El Sawy. 2007. Leveraging standard electronic business interfaces to enable adaptive supply chain partnerships. *Information Systems Research* 18, 260-279.

Muckstadt, J. A. 2005. *Analysis and Algorithms for Service Parts Supply Chains.* Springer.

Nagarajan, M., and G. Sosic. 2006. Coalition stability in assembly models. Forthcoming, *Operations Research.*

Nagarajan, M., and G. Sosic. 2008. Game-theoretic analysis of cooperation among supply chain agents: Review and extensions. *European Journal of Operational Research* 187, 719-745.

Nohria, N. 1992. Is a network perspective a useful way of studying organizations? In *Networks and Organizations,* ed. N. Nohria and R. G. Eccles, 1-22. Boston, MA: Harvard Business School Press.

Sheffi, Y. 2007. *The Resilient Enterprise: Overcoming Vulnerability for Competitive Advantage.* The MIT Press.

Steffenson-McElheran, K. 2008. Productivity leadership and strategic investments in innovation: The adoption of e-business capabilities. Working paper, Northwestern University.

Stundza, T. 2007. Composites bring Boeing's buyers, engineers and parts suppliers closer. *Purchasing Magazine Online,* March 1.

Swinney, R., and S. Netessine. 2007. Long-term contracts under the threat of supplier default. Forthcoming in *Manufacturing and Services Operations Management.*

Trice, R. H. 2006. Trade and the defense industrial base. Presentation at the Israel Aerospace Conference.

Vereecke, A., R. Van Dierdonck, and A. De Meyer. 2006. A typology of plants in global manufacturing networks. *Management Science* 52, 1737-1750.

Wellman, M. P., J. J. Estelle, S. Singh, Y. Vorobeychik, C. Kiekintveld, and V. Soni. 2005. Strategic interactions in a supply chain game. *Computational Intelligence* 21, 1-26.

Wernle, B. 2006. Suppliers in "shambles," so why's Ross buying? *Automotive News* April 24, 2006,, 28.

Wind, J., V. Fung, and W. Fung. 2008. Network orchestration: Core competency for a borderless world. Chapter 17 in P. Kleindorfer and J. Wind, *Network-Based Strategies and Competencies.*

Wu, D.J., and P. Kleindorfer. 2005. Competitive options, supply contracting, and electronic markets. *Management Science* 51, 452-466.

14

Leveraging Customer Networks

Christophe Van den Bulte
Stefan Wuyts

Abstract

Social networks and word-of-mouth marketing are increasingly important, yet few current practices are based on a deep understanding of how the structure of networks can affect customer behavior and marketing outcomes. This chapter offers some critical observations on current word-of-mouth marketing practices and identifies four key questions that managers need to ask themselves before engaging in campaigns designed to leverage customer networks: Can we be confident that interpersonal influence or social contagion is really important? Why exactly would social contagion occur? Should we target key influentials? Can we identify and target those influentials? The answers to these questions cannot be taken for granted.

Although marketers are increasingly interested in social networks and word of mouth, there is more to the successful use of social networks than merely recognizing their importance. For example, a large pharmaceutical company commissioned an analysis of the social network of physicians treating a specific medical condition in a metropolitan area. The analysis generated a list of names of physicians who had received the greatest number of nominations as discussion partners from fellow physicians. The people on the top of this list were already well known to the firm sponsoring the study. However, a real eye-opener was the finding that there were two large subgroups in the network, one consisting mostly of physicians with names of European origin and the other mostly of physicians with names of Asian origin. Even more surprising was the finding that only three physicians bridged these two subgroups. One of them—who scored the highest of all physicians in the network on a graph-theoretical metric called "betweenness centrality"—had until then been ignored by the medical education and sales teams of the firm. By understanding the structure of the network and the role of influencers, the company moved beyond a simplistic view of networks. Such a shift in thinking about networks is critical in benefiting from the potential of networks in marketing. This chapter outlines a set of questions that managers need to ask about networks of customers and other stakeholders to fully utilize them in marketing.

Rising Interest in Social Networks

In the past five years or so, marketing practitioners' interest in social networks has surged dramatically. Firms have long recognized that customers constitute a valuable asset. Customer relationship management and customer base valuation are well-established business practices. Firms have also come to recognize the importance of investing in relationships with third parties, especially channel partners. More recently, a growing number of marketers are realizing that not only customers and third parties but also the relations among them can be extremely important to their firm's success. New communication technologies force firms to abandon the long-held assumption that consumers can be treated as if they are isolated from each other. Similarly, channel partners and other third parties are increasingly enmeshed in complex industry networks. As a result of these changes, marketers have come to think about markets not only in terms of firms, customers, and channel partners but also in terms of the ties among all market participants. In other words, marketers have extended their scope of interest to the social networks within which their firms, customers, and other parties are embedded.

As those developments have taken place, social network analysts, economic sociologists, and other researchers have been documenting that some network structures and some positions within networks confer advantages in the form of more information, better reputation, reduced competition, or higher profits. This idea often goes under the label "social capital" (Burt 2005).

Put these two developments together, and the conclusion for marketing is obvious: (1) Markets consist of networks, and (2) networks can convey benefits to (some of) their members, so (3) firms and their marketers should learn how to use networks to their advantage. Of course, the idea that networks matter is hardly novel. Astute entrepreneurs and financiers in Balzac's novels knew so, and so did Benjamin Franklin, Andrew Carnegie, and Thomas Edison. What has changed, though, is that the idea that networks can be leveraged to increase the effectiveness of one's marketing strategies has gone mainstream. Instead of being recognized as something important only to the worlds of high finance or high technology, social networks are increasingly seen as a part, and sometimes an essential part, of marketing practice.

This chapter focuses on the use of customer networks to aid the acceptance of new products and brands, a practice that often goes under the label of word-of-mouth marketing. The key idea of leveraging customer networks through word-of-mouth marketing is to selectively target a few key influential customers who will then—at no additional cost to the firm—propagate the firm's message or product to the rest of the market. In addition to word-of-mouth marketing, networks can also be leveraged to strengthen brand beliefs and preferences, improve corporate status and reputation, coordinate marketing channels, and access resources through alliances. These areas of application cannot be covered within the purview of this chapter, but are discussed in a recent monograph on *Social Networks and Marketing* published by the Marketing Science Institute (Van den Bulte and Wuyts 2007).

Why Marketers (Should) Care About Social Networks

There are several reasons marketers are becoming more interested in social networks:

- ***Eroding effectiveness of traditional marketing***—Marketers have become especially concerned about the declining effectiveness of mass media communication. Media fragmentation caused by an ever-increasing number of magazines, radio stations, television channels, and Web sites may be a boon for firms catering to specialized needs of microsegments but is a bane for firms targeting products of general appeal toward the mass market. Making matters worse, postmodern consumers, particularly teenagers, are increasingly skeptical of advertising and marketing, rendering media communications less persuasive. As traditional marketing communication becomes less effective, marketers are turning to new means of communication, capitalizing on consumers' social networks to propagate their messages. Business-to-business marketers are less affected by changes in the mass media landscape, but they too are concerned about decreasing returns on their marketing efforts. Many feel that managers and other corporate decision makers have less time to listen to sales pitches after years of downsizing, de-layering, and re-engineering. Similarly in healthcare, physicians are now saturated with pharmaceutical sales calls, so some firms are trying to complement or even partially replace their traditional detailing and direct marketing efforts with various forms of word-of-mouth marketing.

- *A focus on brand building*—The potential to use social networks as a platform to connect brands to customers is another reason marketers are taking a closer look at social networks. Marketers are increasingly interested in how consumers use products and brands to build and maintain a social identity. This symbolic use of products and brands does not occur in a social vacuum. Rather, consumers use them as bridges toward or fences against other people (Douglas and Isherwood 1979). Understanding the patterns of positive and negative connections among customers may help marketers in their segmentation, targeting, positioning, and marketing communication, as brands such as Burberry, Diesel Jeans, Red Bull, and Vans illustrate. One specific tactic that has attracted much attention lately is to allow and even facilitate the creation and sharing of consumer-generated (rather than firm-generated) content via the Web. This, the argument goes, may result in stronger and deeper connections between brands and consumers and in more vibrant brand communities. This hope appears to fuel the interest of large fast-moving consumer-goods companies in social networking sites such as MySpace, Facebook, Cyworld, and Bebo, as well as video-sharing sites such as YouTube.

- *Assuring or regaining control*—Managers believe that if they do not take an active role in their customers' networks, they will lose control over the brand discourse. Recommendations in social networks can spread quickly, but so can negative information. Antibrand communities such as ihatestarbucks.com or walmart-blows.com show the risks stemming from the increased interconnectivity among customers. But negative information may also spread, undetected, off-line. A recent study indicates that positive word of mouth is three times more common than negative word of mouth. That may look comforting at first, but it implies that about a quarter of all word of mouth is negative (East, Hammond, and Wright 2007). Moreover, there is some evidence suggesting that dissatisfied customers spreading negative word of mouth are more influential than satisfied customers spreading positive word of mouth if the negative feedback is more vivid than positive feedback, something that seems fair to expect (Herr, Kardes, and Kim 1991). Hence, many marketers have justifiably become concerned about the perils of higher interconnectivity among customers, and have started to systematically monitor the contents of word of mouth and to proactively participate in the discussion.

- ***Challenges in non-Western markets***—As Western firms look to emerging markets to sustain their growth, they often face unfamiliar challenges such as the lack of a strong marketing services industry, the lack of brand heritage, and questions about how to fit products and brands into existing consumption patterns. A social network perspective may help marketers find effective solutions to these problems. For example, both theory and empirical research suggest that engaging in word-of-mouth marketing is especially effective in cultures that are more collectivist, more averse to uncertainty, and more sensitive to status differences than Western cultures typically are (Van den Bulte and Stremersch 2004). Leveraging social networks has also been critical to the success of microlending in developing countries and of credit card companies in Russia. In both cases, astute entrepreneurs have used networks not only to enroll customers but also to screen applicants and to enforce debtor discipline in countries lacking strong credit rating agencies, scoring models based on financial history and debt collection through legal enforcement (Guseva 2008).

- ***Innovation and knowledge management***—As firms become aware that informal and face-to-face interaction is critical to the flow of information and to new product development (Allen 1977), marketers realize that it is important for them to understand the networks within their own organizations to have the voice of the customer heard in the innovation process.

- ***Supply chain management***—Finally, as a consequence of enterprise-level developments described elsewhere in this book, marketers have become increasingly involved in supply chain management issues and in the commercialization of complex systems involving partners such as systems integrators and value-added resellers. Marketers in such situations quickly realize that the firm-customer relationship does not operate in a social vacuum but is enmeshed in a network involving third parties critical to the firm's success (Wuyts et al. 2004).

Toward a More Rigorous Approach to Word-of-Mouth Marketing

Despite the rising interest in word-of-mouth marketing, few current practices appear to be based on any deep understanding of how the structure of networks can affect customer behavior and marketing outcomes. Most egregiously, current uses of "social networking technologies" are mostly old-fashioned marketing communication practices that do not truly seek to leverage network structures. True, a sizable number of advertising dollars have followed consumer eyeballs as they moved from the TV to the Web, but not much else has changed in the nature of campaigns being deployed.

One exception is that marketers are increasingly exploiting opportunities to create more engagement and two-way communication (for example, by involving customers in ad copy development). Another is the use of blogs, discussion groups, and other communities to monitor customer sentiment about one's products, brands, or company, and sometimes even to actively participate in the discourse about them. Neither of those two exceptions really focuses on leveraging the structure of interconnections among customers. But more recent Web 2.0 applications do provide opportunities to observe and act on the actual pattern (rather than simply the presence) of interconnections. One example is how sites such as Epinions, where people state who their trusted advisors are, make it easy for marketers to identify opinion leaders. Another example is how Amazon and other such sites allow users to share shopping lists, purchases, and site visits. However, the tremendous backlash following Facebook's November 2007 attempt to impose this level of transparency on their members rather than to make it optional illustrates that marketers must move carefully in these uncharted waters.

Though it receives less press coverage than Web 2.0 applications, there is a strong renewed interest in old-fashioned word-of-mouth marketing that does not involve the Internet but relies on face-to-face contact. For example, stealth marketing employs (often good-looking) paid enthusiasts to accost you and start a conversation about a new product or have you try it—such as a young couple stopping you on the street and asking you to take a picture of them on their new Sony Ericsson camera phone. But here again, most practices ignore network structure. For instance, buzz marketing through notable stunts, such as the British apparel retailer French Connection UK plastering its windows and shopping bags with the acronym FCUK, does not rely on identifying key opinion leaders. Neither does buzz marketing through paid enthusiasts or volunteers, such as the kind of services provided by BzzAgent. Only a minority of today's word-of-mouth marketing efforts go the extra step and try to really leverage the structure of the network, specifically working through well-connected influentials. Procter & Gamble does so through its network marketing operations Tremor (for teenagers) and Vocalpoint (for housewives). Some pharmaceutical firms do so by collecting data on patient referral, advice, or seeking discussion among physicians, and then targeting those physicians who are best connected in their local community. The example at the start of the chapter illustrates that those local opinion leaders need not be national opinion leaders already known to the firm.

A Checklist for Leveraging Customer Networks

Given the increased attention to social networks among marketing practitioners, researchers, and academics, we will learn a fair deal more over the next few years on how firms can effectively leverage word-of-mouth dynamics in customer networks. In the meantime, decades of research in sociology and communication studies already provide some valuable guidance on how to leverage customer networks through word-of-mouth marketing. These insights can be distilled into four key questions that marketers should ask themselves before engaging in a word-of-mouth campaign in which they try to leverage influential customers:

- Can we be confident that social contagion is really important?
- Why exactly would social contagion occur?
- Should we target key influentials?
- Can we identify and target the influentials?

The next four sections discuss each of those questions and show that the answers cannot be taken for granted.

Can We Be Confident That Contagion Is Really Important?

The basic premise of network-based marketing strategies is that networks actually matter. But can a marketer planning the launch of a new product be confident that word-of-mouth and other contagion dynamics will drive how quickly or slowly the product gains market acceptance? MBA students often say yes, offering as evidence anecdotes such as those found in popular books like *The Tipping Point*. When reminded that such stories, though entertaining, do not qualify as compelling evidence, the better MBA student may recall having learned that new products and technologies often diffuse slowly at first, then quickly, and then slowly again, and add that this bell-shaped pattern is consistent with a process driven by imitation or contagion. Although this pattern is indeed consistent with contagion, it is not compelling evidence either because other processes can lead to the same bell-shaped curve (Van den Bulte and Stremersch 2004). One example is the scenario in which a product's price decreases over time (as it often does) and the maximum price that someone is willing to pay for the new product follows a bell-shaped distribution (as household income does in most countries—there are fewer very poor and very rich households than there are middle-income households). This combination of price declines and customer heterogeneity will result in a bell-shaped adoption curve even without any word of mouth. Failure to control for marketing effort such as sales calls or advertising is another reason that not only practitioners but also seasoned researchers may mistakenly believe that contagion is at work (Van den Bulte and Lilien 2001).

Why Exactly Would Social Contagion Occur?

If we cannot take for granted that bell-shaped adoption curves demonstrate contagion, managers need to look more carefully at why their new product or technology might benefit from contagion dynamics. In general, there are five such reasons, which apply to both consumer and business markets:

1. *Awareness and interest*—Social contact generates awareness and interest as previous adopters, and even nonadopters, discuss the new product with others. Awareness may also spread through observation—seeing houses with satellite dishes or people with iPods are examples. Marketers, however, should not take for granted that adopters become aware through contagion. Word of mouth among peers is not likely to drive awareness for products that are much talked about or advertised in the media. In fact, research shows that, overall, personal channels (including word of mouth) are less important than impersonal channels (including mass media) in creating awareness (Rogers 2003). There are, of course, exceptions such as products that are illegal or otherwise taboo in mainstream media (e.g., Lee 1969).

2. *Belief updating*—People may change their opinions about the costs and benefits of adopting the new product after discussing it with previous adopters or observing the outcomes of adoption (for example, a schoolmate's increased status on the playground). This additional information may lead people to revise their beliefs about how well the product performs on particular attributes or dimensions, or confirm their current beliefs and so reduce their uncertainty about the product. Belief updating through social contagion is particularly important when potential adopters view the product as complex with difficult-to-understand links between features and benefits, when commercial communication channels have little source credibility, or when the product's performance or utility varies across users. In those three situations, input from "people like us" can be critical drivers in the decision to buy. B2B marketers have long capitalized on references from satisfied customers, particularly from companies similar to the target firm.

3. **Normative pressure**—Social influence may also occur through normative pressures. People may experience discomfort when peers whose approval they value have adopted an innovation but they have not. The idea that social influence can operate via both informational and normative routes is quite old and well documented, including in the area of information technology usage (Deutsch and Gerard 1955; Venkatesh and Davis 2000). The importance of normative contagion varies across customers. For example, it is greater in countries with higher levels of collectivism or respect for power and authority (Van den Bulte and Stremersch 2004). There are also differences among consumers from the same country in how sensitive they are to normative pressure (see Van den Bulte and Wuyts 2007). The importance of normative contagion may also depend on the visibility and social acceptability of the product. The use of contraceptives is a classic example of how public norms can impact whether social acceptance by close peers affects one's own adoption.

4. **Competitive concerns**—Social contagion may also be driven by the concern that one's rivals who have adopted the innovation might gain a competitive edge unless one adopts as well. This is likely to be an important driver of contagion among competing firms (Hannan and McDowell 1987). The fierceness with which firms compete against each other, the extent to which they all use the same processes and business models, and the extent to which the new product or technology can contribute to profitability or competitive advantage are likely to affect how much contagion occurs due to competitive pressure (Mansfield 1961). Competitive concerns may also operate among individuals who worry about their status in their community and networks (Burt 1987), at least for products that signal one's social identity or status. The iPod and iPhone most likely benefited from this effect.

5. **Complementary network effect**—This contagion effect occurs when the benefits of use, and hence of adoption, increase with the number of prior adoptions. The effect may be direct, as with point-to-point communication devices such as telephones and fax machines, or it may be indirect, operating through the increased supply of complementary products, as with videocassette recorders and prerecorded tapes, or through the increased supply of supporting infrastructure such as video rental stores. Complementarity issues are typically more pronounced in product categories with competing technological standards. Van den

Bulte and Stremersch (2004) find that product categories with competing standards exhibit patterns of new product diffusion that are more consistent with social contagion than other products do.

Marketers should carefully consider the seemingly simple question of why people would be susceptible to other people's opinions or behavior. The analysis will provide a better sense of how much or how little word of mouth may be at work and offer specific pointers on what elements to emphasize in sales calls, advertisements, and other "standard" marketing communications vehicles to trigger more contagion pressure (for example, word-of-mouth volume) or to increase customers' sensitivity to it.

Should We Target Key Influentials?

Having satisfied oneself that contagion dynamics are likely to be important, the next important question is this: How can marketers exploit the network to speed up the acceptance of new products? The obvious approach is to identify the most influential network members and use them as seeding points in the diffusion process. In short: Target the influentials, convert them, and then free-ride them. Theory and research suggest, however, that the challenge is more complex. The different drivers of contagion discussed previously should lead to different strategies.

First, specific contagion drivers make different types of ties more relevant. Friendship, kin, and perhaps mentoring at work are likely to be the relevant ties for normative issues, whereas asking for technical guidance is likely to be a relevant tie for belief updating. So marketers should first think about the nature of the contagion process, then think about the kind of tie along which the information or influence will propagate, and only then identify the influentials who have many of those ties relevant for the product at hand.

Second, people may be influenced by indirect rather than direct ties. Direct ties will be important for spreading awareness and interest, for belief updating, and for normative pressure. Also, complementarity effects are likely to be stronger if operating across direct ties. People will care about the entire installed base for the PlayStation3, but will be disproportionately affected by friends with whom they can exchange games. For competitive pressure, in contrast, direct ties simply do not matter. What matters is structural equivalence, that is, similarity between actors in terms of commonality of contacts (Burt 1987), so the best "seeding points" for marketing are not necessarily the most connected people but those who are structurally equivalent to the most others.

Third, managers need to consider the overall network structure. If the network is rather dense, meaning that many points in the network are directly connected to many other points, then anything traveling over the network can do so quite rapidly, and strategically selecting special nodes as "seeding points" will hardly affect the speed of diffusion. If the network consists of several dense subgroups that are totally disconnected from one another, then one needs to target at least one person in each group to serve as a seeding point. Exactly which one need not matter much. If the network is a "small world" of dense subgroups that are loosely interconnected, then the people connecting the subgroups are more likely to be key. In the last two scenarios, firms may want to use a decision rule that ensures that each seeding point has many connections but the seeding points have little overlap in their portfolios. Such a rule reduces the number of seeding points needed to "cover" most of the network (Valente et al. 2003).

Can We Identify and Target the Influentials?

Once managers have concluded that it would be beneficial to target influentials, the question arises as to whether this is possible. Ideally, opinion leaders combine four characteristics: (1) being interested in and up-to-date about new products, (2) being early adopters, (3) having a central location in the network, and (4) engaging in many conversations about new products. Before discussing these four characteristics, let us debunk four popular misconceptions about opinion leaders.

The first misconception is that there are "generalized" opinion leaders who influence many kinds of decisions by other people (for example, what brand of skin-care product to buy, what kind of laptop to buy, and what political candidate to vote for). Extensive empirical research shows there are no such generalized opinion leaders in large communities and modern cities (Weimann 1994). A person may be a leader in one category, or even several related categories, but will not have the expertise or source credibility to act as an information leader across the board. Normative leadership may cut across more categories, but people are members of many social groups and have multiple reference groups, and no one has normative opinion leadership in all realms.

The second misconception is that each characteristic or trait of the ideal opinion leader corresponds to a particular type of person. Apart from the obvious early adopters or "innovators," the types sometimes mentioned are "mavens" who are up to date, "connectors" who are well connected, and "salesmen" who convincingly get the word out. However, such typologies are misleading because many people tend to score high or low on more than one such characteristic.

The third misconception is that opinion leaders must combine all four characteristics previously discussed. These are actually far from perfectly correlated (Weimann 1994). Hence, insisting that someone have all four characteristics to qualify as an influential would imply ignoring many people who are actually influencing others, for example, well-connected people who tend to have a negative assessment of new products and do not endorse or adopt them (Becker 1970; Leonard-Barton 1985).

The fourth misconception is that a customer is either an opinion leader (influential) or an opinion seeker (influencee). This idea goes back to the two-step flow hypothesis that "ideas often flow *from* radio and print *to* the opinion leaders and *from* them to the less active sections of the population" (Lazarsfeld, Berelson, and Gaudet 1944, 151; emphasis in original). In fact, word of mouth is typically a two-way process in which people send as well as receive information and opinions. Opinion leading and seeking are only weakly correlated—and positively rather than negatively (Flynn, Goldsmith, and Eastman 1996).

With those misconceptions out of the way, we can now consider in greater detail each of the four characteristics of an ideal opinion leader and why they matter:

1. ***Interested in and up-to-date about new products***—Opinion leaders who are interested in and up-to-date about new products will seek out information and be more convincing to others. There is a strong relationship between opinion leadership and product interest and involvement. From a marketing point of view, this suggests that the cost to contact leaders may be lower than average. However, because opinion leaders tend to have many demands on their time, this advantage may be diminished (in part because it is "competed away" by marketers of other products).

2. ***Adopting early***—Opinion leaders who adopt early have direct experience with the product, which increases their source credibility and ability to influence others. Opinion leaders, however, are not always early adopters. Baumgarten (1975) found that slightly less than half of consumers in the top third in opinion leadership are also in the top third in speed of adoption, indicating that the overlap between opinion leadership and early adoption was small. Other studies have found similar, weakly positive relations between the two constructs. In a very interesting study, Becker (1970) documented an episode in which opinion leaders did not like or endorse an innovation because it conflicted with the source of their power; in this case, people at the periphery of the network were the first to adopt.

Early adoption by peripheral rather than central players has also been observed in business markets. The diffusion of new programming formats and business models among radio stations (Leblebici et al. 1991) and the diffusion of digital technologies in the film business (Grover 2006) are two examples. In such cases, an encirclement strategy of converting peripheral players may prove more effective than the intuitive tendency to target the most central actors. Further, mathematical-theoretical modeling shows that people making up their minds independently (as opinion leaders rather than opinion seekers tend to do) may adopt at any point in time rather than only early on, leading to the somewhat surprising result that the last 30% of adopters may consist not of opinion seekers or followers but of people making up their minds independently (Van den Bulte and Joshi 2007).

3. *Having a central location in the network*—Although centrality is a necessary condition for opinion leadership, operationalizing it is less obvious. Most marketers and market research firms appear to do so in terms of so-called degree centrality, that is, the number of direct ties one has with other members of the network. A refinement might be to think not only about direct contacts, but also about how many network members can be reached in two or three steps (closeness centrality). Yet, further refinements may be required: In network structures with dense subgroups that are loosely interconnected, which is how many human networks are structured, the people linking the subgroups may be of critical importance to how information and products diffuse through the network (betweenness centrality). Moreover, these bridgers are likely to be exposed to more and unique information.

4. *Engaging in many conversations about new products*—Ideal opinion leaders engage in many conversations about new products. However, this characteristic cannot be assumed to be present in all opinion leaders. Some may have a missionary zeal about sharing their opinions, but others—such as the key physician in the example at the beginning of this chapter—may be more reserved and selective. Obviously, the former are more valuable as seeding points, keeping everything else constant. The number of conversations customers engage in is a function not only of their personality or their central location in the network providing the opportunity to influence others, but also of how interesting the message is and, hence, how motivated they are to share it with others. P&G's Vocalpoint word-of-mouth marketing program, for instance, focuses on recruiting homemakers

with large social networks, but also does quite a bit of research to find out what motivates these homemakers to share the information with their friends and acquaintances. Another issue to consider is that opinion leaders may be reluctant to share information with anyone but their closest confidants when the value of information or the cost of sharing it is high (Frenzen and Nakamoto 1993).

Conclusion

Under pressure to increase their marketing ROI through more astute targeting of resources, marketers are rediscovering the importance of social contagion. Targeting well-connected influential prospects who are more in touch with new developments and converting them into customers, many marketers hope, will allow them to benefit from a social multiplier effect on their marketing efforts.

That is sound logic, but we need to take a more rigorous view of using networks in marketing. Before engaging in a word-of-mouth marketing campaign in which one tries to leverage on the existence of especially influential customers, marketers should ask themselves four key questions:

1. Can we be confident that social contagion is really important?
2. Why exactly would social contagion occur?
3. Should we target key influentials?
4. Can we identify and target the influentials?

The answers to these questions are less obvious than many believe. Fortunately, theory and empirical research point to answers. The amount of guidance that is available will increase markedly in the next few years as a growing number of academics and thoughtful market researchers seek to better understand how customer networks operate and how they can be leveraged into better marketing strategies.

References

Allen, Thomas J. 1977. *Managing the Flow of Technology: Technology Transfer and the Dissemination of Technological Information within the R&D Organization.* Cambridge, MA: MIT Press.

Baumgarten, Steven A. 1975. The innovative communicator in the diffusion process. *Journal of Marketing Research* 12 (1), 12-18.

Becker, Marshall H. 1970. Sociometric location and innovativeness: Reformulation and extension of the diffusion model. *American Sociological Review* 35, 267-283.

Burt, Ronald S. 1987. Social contagion and innovation: cohesion versus structural equivalence. *American Journal of Sociology* 92 (6), 1287-1335.

Burt, Ronald S. 2005. *Brokerage and Closure: An Introduction to Social Capital.* Oxford, UK: Oxford University Press.

Deutsch, Morton, and Harold B. Gerard. 1955. A study of normative and information social influences upon individual judgment. *Journal of Abnormal and Social Psychology* 51, 629-636.

Douglas, Mary, and Baron Isherwood. 1979. *The World of Goods.* New York, NY: Basic Books.

East, Robert, Kathy Hammond, and Malcolm Wright. 2007. The relative incidence of positive and negative word of mouth: A multi-category study. *International Journal of Research in Marketing* 24 (2), 175-184.

Flynn, Leisa Reinecke, Ronald E. Goldsmith, and Jacqueline K. Eastman. 1996. Opinion leaders and opinion seekers: Two new measurement scales. *Journal of the Academy of Marketing Science* 24 (2), 137-147.

Frenzen, Jonathan K., and Kent Nakamoto. 1993. Structure, cooperation and the flow of market information. *Journal of Consumer Research* 20 (3), 360-375.

Grover, Roland. 2006. The pornographers vs. the pirates. *Business Week* 3989 (June 19), 68-69.

Guseva, Alya. 2008. *Into the Red: The Birth of the Credit Card Market in Postcommunist Russia.* Stanford, CA: Stanford University Press.

Hannan, Timothy H., and John M. McDowell. 1987. Rival precedence and the dynamics of technology adoption: An empirical analysis. *Economica* 54, 155-171.

Herr, Paul M., Frank R. Kardes, and, John Kim. (1991.) Effects of word-of-mouth and product-attribute information on persuasion: An accessibility-diagnosticity perspective. *Journal of Consumer Research* 17 (4), 454-462.

Lazarsfeld, Paul F., Bernard Berelson, and Hazel Gaudet. 1944. *The People's Choice: How the Voter Makes Up His Mind in a Presidential Campaign.* New York, NY: Duell, Sloan and Pearce.

Leblebici, Huseyin, Gerald R. Salancik, Anne Copay, and Tom King. 1991. Institutional change and the transformation of interorganizational fields: An organizational history of the U.S. radio broadcasting industry. *Administrative Science Quarterly* 36 (3), 333-363.

Lee, Nancy Howell. 1969. *The Search for an Abortionist.* Chicago: University of Chicago Press.

Leonard-Barton, Dorothy. 1985. Experts as negative opinion leaders in the diffusion of a technological innovation. *Journal of Consumer Research* 11 (4), 914-926.

Mansfield, Edwin. 1961. Technical change and the rate of imitation. *Econometrica* 29, 741-766.

Rogers, Everett M. 2003. *Diffusion of Innovations,* 5th ed. New York, NY: Free Press.

Valente, Thomas W., Beth R. Hoffman, Annamara Ritt-Olson, Kara Lichtman, and C. Anderson Johnson. 2003. Effects of a social-network method for group assignment strategies on peer-led tobacco prevention programs in schools. *American Journal of Public Health* 93, 1837-1843.

Van den Bulte, Christophe, and Yogesh V. Joshi. 2007. New product diffusion with influentials and imitators. *Marketing Science* 26 (3), 400-421.

Van den Bulte, Christophe, and Gary L. Lilien. 2001. Medical Innovation revisited: Social contagion versus marketing effort. *American Journal of Sociology* 106 (5), 1409-1435.

Van den Bulte, Christophe, and Stefan Stremersch. 2004. Social contagion and income heterogeneity in new product diffusion: A meta-analytic test. *Marketing Science* 23 (4), 530-544.

Van den Bulte, Christophe, and Stefan Wuyts. 2007. *Social Networks and Marketing.* Cambridge, MA: Marketing Science Institute.

Venkatesh, Viswanath, and Fred D. Davis. 2000. A theoretical extension of the technology acceptance model: Four longitudinal field studies. *Management Science* 46 (2), 186-204.

Weimann, Gabriel. 1994. *The Influentials: People who Influence People.* Albany, NY: State University of New York Press.

Wuyts, Stefan, Stefan Stremersch, Christophe Van den Bulte, and Philip Hans Franses. 2004. Vertical marketing systems for complex products: A triadic perspective. *Journal of Marketing Research* 41 (4), 479-487.

15

The Business Model as the Engine of Network-Based Strategies[1]

Christoph Zott
Raphael Amit

Abstract

In this chapter, Zott and Amit explore the role of business models in creating value through networks. They review earlier, firm-centric views of value creation, including Porter's value chain, the resource-based view, and the transaction costs approach. They point out that business models go well beyond classic views of network theory (for example, topography and structure) and include notions of purpose, acceptance, fairness, coherence, and viability. Based on their earlier framework for e-business models, they explore the role of four major interlinked value drivers: efficiency, complementarities, lock-in, and novelty. They argue that the focal firm's business model acts as both an engine for value-creation and an invaluable construct for understanding the firm's role in relation to other business model participants in the networks in which it is embedded.

Traditional views of value creation—including value chains, the resource-based view, transaction costs models, and even strategic network theory—do not fully explain the value-creation potential of a company such as Priceline.com. This business has established stable interorganizational ties with airline companies, credit card companies,

[1] We gratefully acknowledge the financial support of the Wharton-INSEAD Alliance Center for Global Research & Development. Raffi Amit acknowledges financial support from the Wharton e-Business Initiative (a unit of the Mack Center) and the Robert B. Goergen Chair in Entrepreneurship at the Wharton School. We are grateful to the editors for their constructive and very helpful suggestions.

and the Worldspan Central Reservation System, among others. It is fundamentally anchored in the innovation of its transaction mechanism—namely, the introduction of reverse markets in which customers post desired prices for sellers' acceptance—by which items such as airline tickets are sold. Priceline.com has been granted a business method patent on its innovative transaction method. This method distinguishes the firm from an ordinary, online travel agency. As this example indicates, new business models, based on unprecedented reach, connectivity, and low-cost information processing power, open entirely new possibilities for value creation through the structuring of transactions in novel ways. These new transaction structures are informed, but not fully captured by network theory. Indeed, they go well beyond classic focus of network theory on topography and structure, and include notions of purpose, acceptance, fairness, coherence, and viability. The key issue for a focal firm is to design a value-creating business model that is viable—one that yields a positive net present value for itself and for other business model participants.

The business model can be seen as a structural template that describes the organization of a focal firm's exchanges with all of its external constituents in factor and product markets. It has been brought to the forefront of strategic management thinking through recent rapid advances in information and communication technologies that have facilitated new types of technology-mediated interactions between economic agents. These developments have enabled firms to change fundamentally the ways they "do business"; namely, the ways they organize and conduct exchanges and activities across firm and industry boundaries with customers, vendors, partners, and other stakeholders. In other words, these developments have increased firms' possibilities of *purposeful networking*, that is, of structuring their destiny within the context of the value networks within which they exist. Entrepreneurial managers of focal firms actively design (that is, construct, link, sequence) boundary-spanning exchanges and activities, which are embodied in the business model. As a result, a focal firm is more than just a passive participant in a set of networks. It purposefully structures its destiny in cooperation and interdependence with other firms and players (for example, customers) in its economic network-based ecosystem. This structure is captured by the firm's business model, which could, therefore, be viewed as an "engine" of network-based strategies.

In this chapter, we present a summary of our almost decade-long research program on buisness models (see Amit and Zott 2001, Zott and Amit 2007, 2008). We consider diverse perspectives on value creation, review the theoretical foundations of business models, and point out that a firm's business model is an important locus of innovation and value creation that is enabled by a network-based perspective, that is, one that transcends firm and industry boundatries. In our earlier work (Amit and Zott 2001), we focused on the total value created by the business model. Figure 15-1 depicts the four sources of value creation in business models that emerged from our analysis. The term "value" refers to the total value created in exchanges regardless of whether it is the focal firm, the customer, or any other participant in the transaction who appropriates that value. We identified four major interlinked value drivers: efficiency, complementarities, lock-in, and novelty. We suggested that the presence of these value drivers enhances the value-creation potential of a business model.

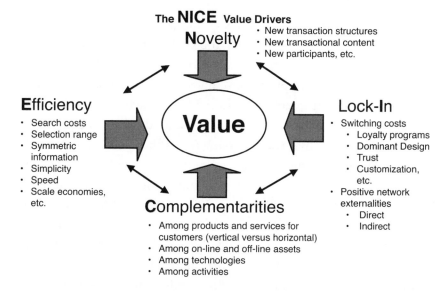

Figure 15-1   Value drivers of business models

In our subsequent work, we shifted attention from value creation to value appropriation by linking some of the value drivers of business models (notably, novelty and efficiency; see Zott and Amit 2007, 2008) to focal firm performance. In our view, the business model is a crucial source for understanding the benefits to each party in the networks in which the focal firm is embedded. Indeed, the notions of value creation and value appropriation need to be simultaneously considered, because entrepreneurial managers who design value-creating business models that do not allow the focal firm to appropriate sufficient value eventually fail, while those who design business models with a strong singular focus on value appropriation may not generate sufficient incentives for other parties to the business model, and therefore fail.

Origin and Focus of Business Model Research

In this chapter we refer to the design of an organization's boundary-spanning transactions as business model design. We formally define the business model as depicting the content, structure, and governance of transactions designed to create value for the focal firm and for other business model stakeholders through the exploitation of business opportunities (Amit and Zott 2001). A business model elucidates how an organization is linked to external stakeholders, and how it engages in economic exchanges with them.

The importance of the business model is grounded in the observation that organizations are increasingly "experimenting with their governance of transactions, that is, adopting new ways of structuring their boundaries" (Foss 2002). A growing body of research has gradually shifted attention from internal organization design toward modes of organizing and managing transactions with the firm's environment (Ilinitch, D'Aveni, and Lewin 1996; Lewin and Volbverda 1999). Recent advances in communication and information technologies, such as the emergence and the swift expansion of the Internet, and the rapid decline in computing and communication costs, have accentuated the possibilities for the design of new boundary-spanning organizational forms (Daft and Lewin 1993; Dunbar and Starbuck 2006; Foss 2002; Ilinitch, D'Aveni, and Lewin 1996). Indeed, these developments have opened new horizons for the design of business models by enabling firms to change fundamentally the way they organize and engage in economic exchanges, both within and across firm and industry boundaries (Mendelson 2000). According to Brynjolfsson and Hitt (2004), this includes the ways in which firms interact with suppliers as well as customers.

One of the central design tasks of entrepreneurs and managers is to delineate the ways in which their new businesses transact with suppliers, customers, and partners. As Ireland et al. (2001, 53) note, entrepreneurs often "try to find fundamentally new ways of doing business that will disrupt an industry's existing competitive rules, leading to the development of new business models." For example, Christensen (2001) highlighted the shift in the locus of profitability in the computer industry as companies like Dell pioneered nonintegrated and flexible business models in which production and distribution were organized in novel ways. And more recently, Nambisan and Sawhney (2008) have pointed to the emerging business imperative for firms to tap into resources and capabilities for innovation of customers, suppliers, and other inventors ("the global brain") that lie outside firm boundaries. Focusing on innovation projects, the authors suggest that firms need to adopt one of several models of network-centric innovation.

Although recent work in organization theory has begun to address the important role of design (Hargadorn and Douglas 2001; Romme 2003), relatively little is known about the specific trade-offs and performance implications of business model design. This is an important gap, however, as Hargadorn and Douglas (2001, 494) suggest, pointing to the failure of Prodigy, an online service in which investors Sears and IBM had sunk $600 million.

While Prodigy's business model was designed and introduced in November 1989, to facilitate selling advertising, merchandise, and online services to casual home users, the end users of the service themselves regarded these offerings as a nuisance, and focused on e-mail and electronic bulletin boards as means of communicating with each other. Prodigy executives, however, were insensitive to the needs and desires of their customers, and refused to adapt their firm's business model. For example, they kept charging customers surcharges on e-mails, and enacted very specific governance rules that made it difficult for customers to interact with each other, or with merchants that were affiliated with the Prodigy business model. Although the business model contained novel and complementary features (it was a very sophisticated early portal), those were not the ones that customers wanted. What is more, Prodigy executives deliberately reduced the efficiency and lock-in of its business model by erecting barriers to customers interacting with each other and with merchants, thereby destroying enormous value. Prodigy failed, despite its highly innovative service offering, largely because of the mismatch between the business model design and customer needs. Hence, business model design is a crucial managerial and entrepreneurial task.

Perspectives on Strategy and Value Creation

There are several firm-centric views of how value is created by firms, which do not fully capture the process of value creation in networks. These views include the following:

- *Value Chains*—Porter's (1985) value chain framework analyzes value creation at the firm level, identifying the activities of the firm and their economic implications. Porter defines value as "the amount buyers are willing to pay for what a firm provides them" (1985, 38). Value can be created by differentiation along every step of the value chain, through activities resulting in products and services that lower buyers' costs or raise buyers' performance. The value chain, however, may be too limited. Value creation opportunities in today's markets may result from new combinations of information, physical products and services, innovative configurations of transactions, and the reconfiguration and integration of resources, capabilities, roles, and relationships among suppliers, partners, and customers.

- ***Resource-Based View*—**A second firm-level perspective, the resource-based view (RBV) of the firm, which views the firm as a bundle of resources and capabilities, also falls short of fully capturing these opportunities. The RBV states that marshaling and uniquely combining a set of complementary and specialized resources and capabilities (which are heterogeneous within an industry, scarce, durable, not easily traded, and difficult to imitate) may lead to value creation (Penrose 1959; Wernerfelt 1984; Barney 1991; Peteraf 1993; Amit and Schoemaker 1993). In a networked economy, however, there is an alternative to ownership or control of resources and capabilities. Accessing resources through partnering and resource sharing agreements is a viable alternative in networked markets, yet the preservation of value, and hence its creation, becomes more challenging, because rivals may have easy access to substitute resources as well.

- ***Transaction Costs*—**Another view of value creation, transaction cost theory, focuses on boundaries between firms, specifically why firms internalize transactions that might otherwise be conducted in markets (Coase 1937). The main theoretical framework was developed by Williamson (1975, 1979, 1983). Transaction efficiency can be a major source of value, with value creation deriving from the attenuation of uncertainty, complexity, information asymmetry, and small-number bargaining conditions (Williamson 1975). Moreover, reputation, trust, and transactional experience can lower the cost of idiosyncratic exchanges between firms (Williamson 1979, 1983). In general, organizations that economize on transaction costs can be expected to extract more value from transactions.

  The theory, however, focuses on cost minimization in bilateral relationships (for example, in intermediate production relationships) and does not specifically address the interdependence between networked exchange parties and the opportunities for joint value maximization that this presents (Zajac and Olsen 1993). In addition, governance modes other than hierarchies and markets (for example, joint ventures) receive relatively little attention, which contrasts with their growing importance of strategic networks. Finally, Williamson (1983) implies that a transaction is a discrete event that is valuable by itself, because it reflects the choice of the most efficient governance form and, hence, can be a source of transactional efficiencies. However, in today's markets, considering any given exchange in isolation from other exchanges that may complement or facilitate that exchange makes it difficult to assess the value created by a specific economic exchange.

Interorganizational Perspective: Strategic Network Theory

The transaction cost approach could be considered a logical precursor to strategic network theory. Strategic networks are "stable interorganizational ties which are strategically important to participating firms," including "strategic alliances, joint-ventures, long-term buyer-supplier partnerships, and other ties" (Gulati, Nohria, and Zaheer 2000, 203). The main questions that strategic network theorists seek to answer are (1) Why and how are strategic networks of firms formed? (2) What is the set of interfirm relationships that allows firms to compete in the marketplace? (3) How is value created in networks (for example, through interfirm asset co-specialization)? and (4) How do firms' differential positions and relationships in networks affect their performance, including both profitability and longer-term survival?

Traditionally, network theorists with a background in sociology or organization theory focused on the implications of certain aspects of network structure for value creation. The configuration of the network in terms of density and centrality (Freeman 1979), for example, has been considered an important determinant of network advantages, such as access, timing, and referral benefits (Burt 1992). Moreover, the size of the network and the heterogeneity of its ties have been conjectured to have a positive effect on the availability of valuable information to the participants within that network (Granovetter 1973).

The appearance of networks of firms in which market and hierarchical governance mechanisms coexist has significantly enhanced the range of possible organizational arrangements for value creation (Doz and Hamel 1998; Gulati 1998). Consequently, strategic management and entrepreneurship scholars have moved beyond structural arguments to explore the importance of governance mechanisms such as trust (Lorenzoni and Lipparini 1999), and the importance of resources and capabilities (Gulati 1999), especially those of suppliers and customers, for value creation. For example, in their study of the Canadian biotechnology industry, Baum, Calabrese, and Silverman (2000) found that biotech startups can improve their performance by configuring alliances into networks that enable them to tap into the capabilities and information of their alliance partners. In addition to enabling access to information, markets, and technologies (Gulati, Nohira, and Zaheer 2000), strategic networks offer the potential to share risk, generate economies of scale and scope (Katz and Shapiro 1985), share knowledge and facilitate learning (Anand and Khanna 2000; Dyer and Singh 1998), and reap the benefits that accrue from interdependent activities such as workflow systems (Blankenburg Holm, Eriksson, and Johansson 1999). Other sources of value in strategic networks include shortened time to market (Kogut 2000), enhanced transaction efficiency, reduced asymmetries of information, and improved coordination between the firms involved in an alliance (Gulati, Nohira, and Zaheer 2000).

The network perspective is very relevant for understanding value creation through business models. However, it may not fully capture the value-creation potential of firms such as Priceline.com, as discussed previously, which enable transactions in new and unique ways.

Understanding the Business Model Concept in a Networked World

The theoretical approaches previously discussed focus on different focal points for value creation. In the value chain framework, it is the firm's activities; in RBV, it is the firm's resources; in transaction cost economics, it is the transaction; and in strategic network theory, it is the network of firms that is both the unit of analysis and the presumed locus of value creation. Using any of these theoretical frameworks in isolation would result in some crucial network-based aspects of value creation either being ignored or not being given due importance. We,therefore, propose the *business model* as an integrative concept for strategy research and practice.

As emphasized earlier, a firm's business model depicts the content (goods and information exchanged), structure (players and how they are linked), and governance of transactions of the firm in relation to the networks in which it is embedded (including control of flows of information, resources, and goods, as well as how value is shared). The business model embodies the strategic intent of the firm concerning value creation and appropriation in its exploitation of business opportunities. While embedded in a network, each business model is centered on a particular focal firm; this is what makes the business model distinct from other network-based concepts (for example, network centrality, egocentric networks) that are less teleological.

Rather than merely construing the focal firm as one of several players in a network, the business model perspective brings the question front and center as to how a particular firm (which we call the focal firm) structures its destiny within the context of the value networks within which it exists. The active construction and design of boundary spanning activities, and their governance, are key tasks for the managers of the focal firm. Without the business model perspective, the focal firm is a mere participant in a sometimes dazzling array of networks, and of passive entanglements. With the business model perspective, the focal firm takes center stage, and purposefully structures its activity system in cooperation and interdependence with other firms and economic agents in its ecosystem. This is why we think of the business model as the "engine," and the embodiment of network-based strategies.

The idea of the business model builds on the main theoretical frameworks of strategic management discussed earlier and entrepreneurship research. The business model focuses on arguments that are central to the value chain framework, particularly the idea that processes and multiple sources of value matter. The resource-based view of the firm took an internal and local perspective on what should constitute resources of interest. Network-based views of the firm expanded the horizon in proper fashion, but they failed to connect to the strategic intent of the focal firm as a source of innovation and an engine of appropriation and purpose. The business model perspective builds on these foundations by recognizing the need for an integrative template that embodies all relevant relations and transactions in the networks in which the focal firm is embedded, exposing the basic design choices for the focal firm as to how it will create and share value with its suppliers, customers, and network partners.

In designing empirical studies of business models, what has come to be known as "configuration theory" provided a useful starting point for developing measures of business model design. This theory is framed in terms of holistic configurations, or gestalts, of design elements (Miles and Snow 1978). Motivated by this approach, and using theoretical and empirical precedents (Miller 1996; Aldrich and Ruef 2006; Zott 2003), we focused in our empirical work (Zott and Amit 2007, 2008) on two independent variables of business model design: design efficiency and design novelty. (Following Figure 15-1, other possible variables that would be consistent with our model would be design lock-in, and design complementarities.) These indicators of efficiency-centered and novelty-centered business model design are listed in Table 15-1. The table illustrates what we considered as design features of a business model.

TABLE 15-1   Indicators for Business Model Value Drivers "Efficiency" and "Novelty"

	Efficiency	Novelty
Business Model Structure	The business model enables fast transactions. Access to large range of products, services and information, and other participants is provided. Transactions are simple from the user's point of view. The business model enables demand aggregation. The business model is scalable (i.e., can handle small as well as large numbers of transactions). The business model enables a low number of errors in the execution of transactions. Certain costs for participants in the business model are reduced through the business model structure (i.e., marketing and sales costs, transaction processing costs, communication costs, etc.). Inventory costs for participants in the business model are reduced through the business model structure.	The business model brings together new participants. The business model links participants to transactions in novel ways. The richness (i.e., quality and depth) of some of the links between participants is novel. The focal firm has been awarded patents for aspects of its business model. The business model (not products) relies on trade secrets and/or copyrights. The focal firm claims to be a pioneer with its business model. The focal firm has continuously introduced innovations in its business model. There are no competing business models with the potential to leapfrog the firm's business model.
Business Model Content	The business model enables participants to make informed decisions. As part of transactions, information is provided to participants to reduce asymmetric degree of knowledge among them regarding the quality and nature of the goods being exchanged. As part of transactions, information is provided to participants about each other. Transactions are transparent: Flows and use of information, services, goods can be verified.	The business model offers new combinations of products, services, and information. The business model gives access to an unprecedented variety and number of participants and/or goods.
Business Model Governance		Incentives offered to participants in transactions are novel (e.g., customers can create content).

Our strongest and most robust finding was that *the more novelty-centered an entrepreneurial firm's business model design, the higher the focal firm's performance* (see Table 3 [Panels A–D] in Zott and Amit 2007). We find that novelty-centered business model design contributes to superior performance during a period of environmental munificence as well as during a period of resource scarcity. The observed effect was thus relatively robust to changes in the environment. Our results suggest that even in times of resource scarcity and uncertainty about the viability of business model designs, innovative business model designs were associated with higher levels of performance. This counterintuitive finding is noteworthy. It attests to the remarkable stability of that relationship, emphasizing the business model as an important and enduring locus of innovation and wealth creation. The results also show that firms can innovate not only by recombining the resources they control, but also by harnessing those of the partners, suppliers, and customers who participate in their business model.

Business model–specific effects may account for some hitherto unexplained variance in the performance of firms. In this sense, they complement, but do not replace, firm-specific and industry-specific effects on firm performance (Rumelt 1991; McGahan and Porter 2002).

Product Market Strategies and Business Models

In Zott and Amit (2008), we show empirically that the business model can be a source of competitive advantage that is distinct from the firm's product market position (Christensen 2001). Product market strategy differs from the business model primarily through its focus on the positioning of the firm vis-à-vis its rivals, whereas the business model is a structural construct that centers on the pattern of the firm's economic exchanges with external parties in its factor and product markets. To illustrate this distinction, consider four firms (all taken from our sample) that have adopted different business model and product market strategy configurations: Priceline, NetBank, Didax, and Multex.

Priceline has chosen a product market strategy of cost leadership, and a business model centered on novelty. In contrast, NetBank, an online bank, has combined its cost leadership strategy with a business model focused more on efficiency than novelty. NetBank clearly aims at achieving cost leadership through cost-effective banking services. It avoids incurring the cost of supporting a branch system, keeps its overhead low, and partners with outside providers of specialized services and technologies that enjoy economies of scale. It enables fast transaction processing, reduces customer search and information costs by providing rate and fee comparisons, and provides lenders with information about account registrations so that they can tailor their offering better to customer preferences. Although the firm had been a pioneer with its online banking business model, the latter had already been copied by competitors such as Wingspan-bank.com, and NetBank had not managed to sustain its innovative edge. So, though Priceline and NetBank both pursue cost leadership strategies, they have emphasized different design themes for their respective business models.

Now consider Didax and Multex, firms that have coupled a product differentiation strategy with different choices of business models. Didax (later acquired by Salem Communications and operating as Crosswalk.com) was an online portal for Christians and Christian-related institutions that offered its clients products and services such as consulting and IT management. The firm aimed at product differentiation by constantly developing and marketing new services and employed a novelty-centered business model based on Christian values and the desire to support charity, which brought together a new range of participants (individuals, businesses, churches, nonprofit organizations).

In contrast to the novelty-centered approach of Didax, Multex combined product differentiation with an efficiency-centered business model. Multex offered and distributed financial information and research via Web platforms to more than 25,000 companies around the world (Reuters acquired the company in 2003). The firm constantly introduced new service features, such as easy-to-read report formats, and developed proprietary technology to enhance its services (for example, software to distribute research reports quickly to specific authorized users). Its business model, however, was that of an efficiency-centered financial information integrator and distributor. The transactions the firm offered to its clients enabled fast access to complex information. The transactions were simple, were mass-customized, and enabled the firm to reach a vast pool of geographically dispersed clients—indicators of an efficiency-centered business model. Our data suggest that a firm's business model and product market strategy are not only distinct concepts, but also complements, not substitutes. Both contribute, independently as well as jointly, to value creation, and positively influence firm performance (Zott and Amit 2008).

Conclusions and Managerial Implications

The business model is a rich and potentially powerful concept. It is a structural template that describes the organization of a focal firm's transactions with all of its external constituents in factor and product markets. It has been brought to the forefront of strategic management thinking through recent rapid advances in information and communication technologies—in particular, Internet and broadband technologies—that have facilitated new types of technology-mediated interactions between economic agents. These developments have enabled an emerging approach to enterprise-level design, as Nadler and Tushman (1997, 120) have asserted. That approach spawns "new designs that extend beyond the corporation's traditional outer walls," and it helps managers recognize the untapped opportunities for competitive advantage that lie outside firm boundaries, for example, the "global brain" (Nambisan and Sawhney 2008). Thus, the focus of organization design seems to have shifted to the structural organization of a firm's exchanges with external stakeholders. Echoing this shift, researchers have observed that the locus of value creation increasingly extends traditional firm boundaries (Dyer and Singh 1998; Gulati, Nohira, and Zaheer 2000), and they have, therefore, called for a broader conceptualization of organizational boundaries beyond the legally relevant demarcation of the firm from its environment (Santos and Eisenhardt 2005). The business model represents this kind of broader concept.

Our research confirms that in a highly interconnected world, entrepreneurs and managers must look beyond the product, process, and firm levels to create and exploit business opportunities. Our analyses show that they can create wealth by paying attention to the holistic design of their business models, notably, by introducing innovative boundary-spanning designs. These give direction and purpose to the networks in which the respective focal firms are embedded, and they are complementary to the firms' internal strategy choices (for example, their product market positioning as differentiators). Our research provides managers and entrepreneurs a coherent design framework that can serve as a compass and a foundation for business model design. Our research further highlights that business model design contributes to the economic performance of the focal firm.

More research is needed into business models. What factors give rise to and shape business model designs? How do regulations, customer preferences, and competition influence the emergence and evolution of these designs? What are the dynamics and costs of business model design change, and how stable are business model designs across time? Organization scholars might be particularly interested in exploring how the firm's architecture of boundary-spanning transactions is linked to its internal organization and how the interaction of the two affects firm performance in a networked world. Strategy scholars could be interested in the ways in which business model design contributes to the competitive advantage of firms and ecosystems (Adner 2006), and how it interacts with other firm strategies and positioning choices.

The study of business models is an important topic for strategic management research because business models affect firms' possibilities for value creation and value capture in an increasingly networked world. The perspective of the business model acknowledges that the locus of value creation has shifted beyond firm boundaries. But at the same time, it asserts that the firm remains an active shaper of its own destiny by purposefully designing the links and activities by which it embeds itself into its multiple networks. These design activities, as well as their outcomes, transcend the firm, but they remain firm-centric, and are intended to help the focal firm not only to create value in concert with its partners, but also to understand and frame its approach to appropriating a fair share of the value created.

References

Adner, R. 2006. Match your innovation strategy to your innovation ecosystem. *Harvard Business Review* 84 (4), 98-107. Business Source Premier. 25 June 2006.

Aldrich, H. E., and M. Ruef. 2006. *Organizations Evolving.* 2nd ed. Thousand Oaks, CA: Sage.

Amit, R. H., and P. J. H. Schoemaker. 1993. Strategic assets and organizational rent. *Strategic Management Journal* 14, 33-46.

Amit, R., and C. Zott. 2001. Value creation in e-business. *Strategic Management Journal* 22, 493-520.

Anand, B., and T. Khanna. 2000. Do firms learn to create value? The case of alliances. *Strategic Management Journal* 21 (3), 295-315.

Barney, J. 1991. Firm resources and sustained competitive advantage. *Journal of Management* 17 (1), 99-120.

Baum, J. A., T. Calabrese, and B. S. Silverman. 2000. Don't go it alone: Alliance network composition and startups' performance in Canadian biotechnology. *Strategic Management Journal* 21, 267-294.

Blankenburg Holm, D., K. Eriksson, and J. Johanson. 1999. Value creation through mutual commitment to business network relationships. *Strategic Management Journal* 20 (5), 467-486.

Brynjolfsson, E., and L. Hitt. 2004. Intangible assets and the economic impact of computers. In *Transforming Enterprise,* ed. W. Dutton, B. Kahin, R. O'Callaghan, and A. Wyckoff, 27-48. Boston, MA: MIT Press.

Burt, R. S. 1992. *Structural Holes: The Social Structure of Competition.* Cambridge: Harvard University Press.

Christensen, C. M. 2001. The past and future of competitive advantage. *MIT Sloan Management Review* 42, 105-109.

Coase, R. 1937. The nature of the firm. In *Economica,* 4 (16), (November) 386-405.

Daft, R. L., and A. Y. Lewin. 1993. Where are the theories for the "new" organizational forms? An editorial essay. *Organization Science. i.* 4, i-vi.

Doz, Y. L., and G. Hamel. 1998. *Alliance advantage: The art of creating value through partnering.* Boston, MA: Harvard Business School Press.

Dunbar, R. L. M., and W. H. Starbuck. 2006. Learning to design organizations, and designing to learn from them. *Organ. Sci.* 17, 171-178.

Dyer, J. H., and Singh H. 1998. The relational view: cooperative strategy and sources of interorganizational competitive advantage. *Academy of Management Review* 23, 660-679.

Foss, N. J. 2002. Introduction: New organizational forms—critical perspectives. *Internat. J. of the Econom. of Bus.* 9, 1-8.

Freeman, L. 1979. Centrality in social networks. Conceptual clarifications. *Social Networks* 1, 215-239.

Granovetter, M. 1973. The strength of weak ties. *American Journal of Sociology* 78 (6), 1360-1380.

Gulati, R. 1998. Alliances and networks. *Strategic Management Journal* 19 (4), 293-317.

Gulati, R. 1999. Network location and learning: The influence of network resources and firm capabilities on alliance formation. *Strategic Management Journal* 20 (5), 397-420.

Gulati R., N. Nohira, and A. Zaheer. 2000. Strategic networks. *Strategic Management Journal* 21, 203-215.

Hargadorn, A. B., and Y. Douglas. 2001. When innovations meet institutions: Edison and the design of the electric light. *Administrative Science Quarterly* 46, 476-501.

Ilinitch, A. Y., R. A. D'Aveni, and A. Y. Lewin. 1996. New organizational forms and strategies for managing in hypercompetitive environments. *Organization Science,* 7, 211-220.

Ireland, R. D., M. A. Hitt, M. Camp, D. L. Sexton. 2001. Integrating entrepreneurship and strategic management actions to create firm wealth. *Academy of Management Executive* 15, 49-63.

Katz, M., C. Shapiro. 1985. Network externalities, competition and compatibility. *American Economic Review* 75 (3), 424-440.

Kogut, B. 2000. The network as knowledge: Generative rules and the emergence of structure. *Strategic Management Journal* 21, 405-425.

Lewin, A. Y., and H. Volbverda. 1999. Prolegomena on coevolution: A framework for research on strategy and new organizational forms. *Organization Science,* 10, 519-534.

Lorenzoni, G., and A. Lipparini. 1999. The leveraging of interfirm relationships as a distinctive organizational capability: A longitudinal study. *Strategic Management Journal* 20, 317-338.

McGahan, A., and M. Porter. 2002. What do we know about variance in accounting profitability? *Management Science,* 48, 834-851.

Mendelson, H. 2000. Organizational architecture and success in the information technology industry. *Management Science,* 46, 513-529.

Miles, R. E., and C. C. Snow. 1978. *Organization Structure, Strategy, and Process.* New York: McGraw-Hill.

Miller, D. 1996. Configurations revisited. *Strategic Management Journal* 17, 505-512.

Nadler, D. A., and M. L. Tushman. 1997. *Competing by Design.* Oxford: Oxford University Press.

Nambisan, S., and M. Sawhney. 2008. Network-centric innovation: A roadmap for tapping the global brain. In *Network-based Strategies,* ed. P. Kleindorfer and J. Wind.

Penrose, E. 1959. *The Theory of the Growth of the Firm.* New York: Oxford University Press.

Peteraf, M. 1993. The cornerstones of competitive advantage: A resource-based view. *Strategic Management Journal* 14, 179-191.

Porter, M. E. 1985. *Competitive Advantage: Creating and Sustaining Superior Performance.* New York: Free Press/MacMillan.

Prahalad, C. K., and V. Ramaswamy. 2000. Co-opting Customer Competence. *Harvard Business Review* 78 (1), 79-87.

Romme, G. 2003. Making a difference: Organization as design. *Organization Science*, 14: 558-573.

Rumelt, R. 1991. How much does industry matter? *Strategic Management Journal* 12, 167-185.

Santos, F.M., and K. M. Eisenhardt. 2005. Organizational boundaries and theories of organization. *Organization Science* 16, 491-508.

Wernerfelt, B. 1984. A resource-based view of the firm. *Strategic Management Journal* 5 (April-June), 171-180.

Williamson, O. E. 1975. *Markets and Hierarchies—Analysis and Antitrust Implications.* New York: The Free Press.

Williamson, O. E. 1979. Transaction cost economics: The governance of transactional elations. *Journal of Law and Economics* 22(2) 233-261.

Williamson, O. E. 1983. Organizational innovation: The transaction cost approach. In *Entrepreneurship*, ed. J. Ronen, 101-133. Lexington, MA: Lexington Books.

Zajac, E. J., and C. P. Olsen. 1993. From transaction cost to transactional value analysis: Implications for the study of interorganizational strategies. *Journal of Management Studies* 30, 131-145.

Zott, C. 2003. Dynamic capabilities and the emergence of intra-industry differential firm performance: Insights from a simulation study. *Strategic Management Journal* 24, 97-125.

Zott, C., and R. Amit. 2007. Business model design and the performance of entrepreneurial firms. *Organization Science* 18, 181-199.

Zott, C., and R. Amit. 2008. The fit between product market strategy and business model: Implications for firm performance. *Strategic Management Journal* 29, 1-26.

16

Extended Intelligence Networks: Minding and Mining the Periphery

George S. Day
Paul J. H. Schoemaker
Scott A. Snyder

Abstract

Although networks in key business areas such as communications, supply chains, R&D, and sales are designed to improve the flow of information, people, or goods, they can also be used to improve the "peripheral vision" of the organization. In this chapter, the authors examine how networks can be used by organizations to scan, sense, and adapt to new and important signals from the organization's strategic environment beyond its core focus. The first part of the chapter emphasizes the importance of peripheral vision in helping organizations not being blindsided by threats while seeing new opportunities sooner. The authors examine some key obstacles to using networks to better mine the periphery for early insight. They then explore how extended networks can help the organization be a responsive open system adapting faster to changes in the environment. They examine to what extent such network constructs as centrality, hierarchy, self-healing, distributed intelligence, multihoming, and latency can be used to improve organizational networks for scanning the periphery. The last section explores some of the leadership challenges associated with using networks to detect weak signals sooner.

Organizations have long used networks to compete more effectively in the marketplace, and are doing so increasingly thanks to major advances in communications and collaboration technologies (Nohria and Eccles 1992; Hannan and Freeman 1989). This enhanced use of external networks presents an important opportunity to improve an organization's peripheral vision, even if these networks were designed for other purposes. We define the periphery as the fuzzy zone at the edge of an organization's vision where early signals of threats and opportunities can first be sensed (Day and Schoemaker 2006). Advances in network design and scanning capabilities can enhance a firm's peripheral vision by extending this zone. But wider scanning also increases the amount of noise received, as well as at times the length of the communications chain. It broadens the gap between the amount of external information received and the capacity of the organization to absorb and interpret such information. In this chapter, we consider various ways to increase the absorptive capacity of organizations by reconfiguring their existing networks and investing in new capabilities.

Minding and Mining the Periphery

A truly vigilant organization is able to *mind* a broad periphery, and *mine* the weak signals for relevance and meaning (Brown, 2004). Whereas "minding" requires divergent attention across many areas of the organization, "mining" requires a strong convergent focus on a few salient parts of the periphery, plus the capacity to act on the insights ahead of rivals. Figure 16-1 portrays this basic challenge using a schematic example.

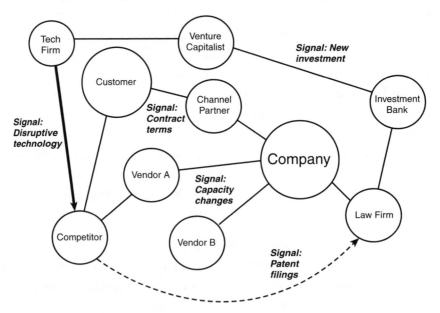

Figure 16-1   Peripheral vision in a network context

Most organizations need to improve their capabilities for learning about the periphery. They are narrowly focused on their immediate environment—a complicated landscape of markets, customers, competitors, regulations, technology, and stakeholders. This unwavering attention benefits short-term performance, but often at the expense of missing subtle signals about changes that could threaten the organization's long-term survival. However, successful peripheral vision—monitoring other industries, remote markets, new research, exotic business models, and tangential data—is much more than sensing incipient change. It is also about knowing where to look more carefully for clues, how to interpret the weak signals, and how to act when the signals are still ambiguous.

Our study of more than 300 global senior executives found that 80% felt that their organizations had less capacity for peripheral vision than they would need (Day and Schoemaker, 2006). It is probably no surprise that two-thirds of corporate strategists in another study (Fuld 2003) said that their organizations had been surprised by as many as *three* high-impact competitive events in the past five years. Moreover, 97% of respondents said their companies lacked an early warning system to prevent such surprises in the future.

Attending to the Periphery Without Being Overwhelmed

Although organizations need to pay more attention to the periphery, one of the most serious challenges is the overload of information that results. Network-centric firms are seeing a geometrically increasing number of weak signals from their expanding periphery, intensified by the Internet, which virtually eliminates signal transmission time and cost. This effect is portrayed in Figure 16-2, as an exponentially growing gap. Unique information per person is growing at over 50% per year while information consumption per person is growing at slightly less than 2% per year (Davenport and Harris 2007). Estimates are that around 70% of the new information is being created by individuals and not necessarily published. It may exist on private intranets, hard drives, or even in email communications, also known as the "deep web."

This flood of information runs up against the barrier of limited ability to process it. Humans are limited by their brain's processing and storage capacities, estimated to be only around 200 megabytes of temporary storage. The human bottleneck can be only partly overcome through technology and collective effort. Most intelligent information consumption and interpretation still requires a "human in the loop." Interpretation is improving only modestly in spite of the aid of technology such as advances in data analysis tools, storage and retrieval technologies, and decision aids, including visualization (Lyman and Varian 2000) and artificial intelligence.

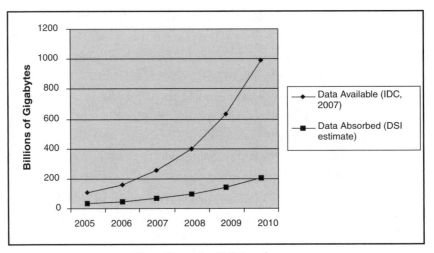

The Gap is Widening...

Figure 16-2   Information explosion and absorption capacity

As Jay Galbraith (1973) highlighted in his cybernetic view of organizational design, companies must match the need to process information (as driven by external change and nonroutine problems or exceptions that may arise) with their limited ability to do so. Various organizational strategies can help bring about this important alignment, ranging from forming self-contained units, to matrix organizations, and formalized communication channels.

The more the organization already knows about an area, the greater its "absorptive capacity" to rapidly and effectively process related new information (Cohen and Levinthal 1990). This concept originally applied to the limit of scientific or technical information a firm could absorb but has been expanded to any new, external information available to the firm (Zahra and George 2002). Weak signals from less familiar areas outside the zone of core competencies are likely to be missed, not assimilated, or misinterpreted.

Research Literature: Learning, Networks, and Scanning

There is little formal literature on the role of external networks in improving an organization's peripheral vision. Various applied papers connect the roles of learning, networks, and the periphery in case studies. For example, Boersma (2003, 2004) describes how the early R&D departments of Philips and General Electric were greatly helped by being deeply embedded in external government, academia, and customer networks. Similarly, the early innovations of Merck and Co. (Dupree 1997) were related to a "series of complex, evolving networks of scientific, governmental, and medical institutions." Nosella and Petroni (2007) examine how an Italian company achieved international success in developing space systems and applications by relying on four strategic networks.

Apart from such case studies, however, little formal literature exists on the topic of this chapter. Nonetheless, several related research streams offer valuable insights, dealing with (1) social networks, (2) innovation clusters, (3) knowledge spillover, and (4) scanning models. Because each of these four research domains is vast, we shall suffice with a brief summary of the main studies and insights relevant to our chapter.

Social Networks

Mark Granovetter (1973, 1985) published several seminal articles on the strength of weak ties and the importance of organizational embeddedness that propelled social networks to a central role in the new field of economic sociology. The ensuing focus on social networks shed new light on such topics as company performance, organizational survival, innovation clusters, R&D productivity, and corporate governance. Ronald Burt (1992; 2004) developed this view further by emphasizing the role of structural holes, that is, areas within the social network where insufficient bridges or brokerage exist such that critical knowledge gaps arise. More applied papers address ways to manage social networks, in terms of how to strategically orient, cultivate, and build them, as well as learn and control them (Cross, Liedtka, and Weiss 2005; Fleming and Marx 2006; Ibarra and Hunter 2007).

Innovation Clusters

Following Michael Porter's (1990) seminal work on regional clusters, there has been extensive research on the role of geographic clusters in R&D (Krugman 1991; Caniels and Romijn 2005). The *Journal of Economic Geography* publishes frequent accounts of the central role that locale plays in innovation. When patent citations, physical locations, membership in professional societies, coauthorship on papers, and so on are examined, a strong picture emerges that social relationship and professional networks play a key role in the sharing of information, including proprietary knowledge and new ideas

(Caniëls and Romijn 2005; Dahl and Pedersen 2004). Although the power of geographic clusters is commonly attributed to resource and knowledge concentration, there are important cross-regional factors as well that explain the appeal of clusters (Rosenkopf and Almeida 2003).

Knowledge Spillover

Knowledge travels across firms through interfirm mobility of employees, including spying and reverse engineering (Tirole 1989, 330). The concept of knowledge spillovers traces back to Alfred Marshall's 1920 book *Principles of Economics* and was further developed in Paul Krugman's 1991 book *Geography and Trade*. In our context, peripheral signals picked up across organizational boundaries, either by accident or on purpose, constitute a form of spillover in the sense that the receiving firm does not pay for the information. An extensive research stream shows that such externalities can create much economic value. One study found that spillovers in the Canadian biotech industry are often highly localized, stemming from microclusters, within 500 meters (Aharonson, Baum, and Feldman 2007); another showed its value for the semiconductor industry (McCann and Arita 2006), and a third in the wine industry (Giuliani 2007).

Scanning Models

Lastly, a separate and burgeoning literature addresses the importance of scanning and various techniques for doing so (Liu 2004; Börjesson, Dahlsten, and Williander 2006). Some studies address the unique management challenges that external scanning activities entail, from information overload to protecting new insights. Academic papers have especially highlighted the links between environmental uncertainty and scanning behavior (Boyd and Fulk 1996; Peteraf and Bergen 2003).

One study of 153 small firms in high-technology manufacturing, for example, found that younger firms responded to increased uncertainty by relying more heavily on personal and external information sources. More established firms, in contrast, used internal networks more, as well as impersonal external sources. Other studies likewise emphasize that the type of scanning leaders engage in depends on the stability of the environment as well as the growth objectives to be pursued (Boyd and Fulk 1996; Ahituv, Zif, and Machlin 1998).

Types of Extended Intelligence Networks

Organizations can use external networks to scan the periphery more widely. There are different ways to create and mine such networks, serving a variety of purposes. Here are some examples:

- *Scanning*—The Global Business Network brings together people from diverse fields to identify events and patterns with implications for their clients. The Mack Center for Technological Innovation at the Wharton School serves as a network for leading companies and academics in scouting emerging technologies and related business models. Newer, Internet-enabled networks, such as FutureMonitor, are designed to capitalize on the wisdom of crowds to surface trends. Insights from these trend spotters are also aggregated and distributed by blogs such as the Business Innovation Factory.

- *Sharing intelligence*—Industry trade associations have long served this role. Participants in narrow industry verticals, or wide agglomerations such as the Business Round Table, the Conference Board, or the Association of National Advertisers, are drawn by shared interests to exchange information or collect new insights. Because these associations function as affinity groups, they tend to reinforce existing beliefs and mental models. In some cases, they become echo-chambers where like-minded managers further confirm their beliefs and biases. To combat this tendency toward conformity, small groups of noncompeting companies often gather in peer networks to exchange information and learn vicariously from the experience of outside peers (Sgourev and Zuckerman 2006).

- *Customized insights*—Sharing information across networks is also critical within large corporations. Customer insights are often widely dispersed or isolated in the research group, making it harder for companies to obtain data at the point where segments, channels, and categories exist, or create a coherent picture of customers. One solution is to create an insights network that integrates internal data and encompasses relationships with expert third parties and key suppliers or customers who can provide data on regional or store-level competitor intelligence (Forsyth, Galante, and Guild 2006).

- *Open innovation*—A variety of networks have emerged to help firms search for ideas and help inventors find markets for their ideas. Networks such as Innocentive and Nine Sigma are designed to find solutions by posing problems to a global community of scientists. Procter & Gamble has similarly extended networks of individuals and institutions that it uses to identify products, ideas, and solutions to technical problems (Chesbrough 2006; Huston and Sakkab 2006; Chesbrough and Appleyard 2007).

Utilizing Existing Networks

Although many of the networks previously mentioned were created specifically for tapping into the knowledge and insights of the periphery, companies should also make use of other kinds of networks. Most ecosystems of firms were designed to execute strategies but can often be leveraged as well to systematically gather intelligence. Many companies naturally live in an ecosystem of tightly integrated partners. Exemplars are Li & Fung, which generates $8 billion per year in garments, toys, and other products without owning a single factory (see Fung, Fung, and Wind 2007, and Chapter 17 in this volume), or Apple, with connections to a million software developers, thousands of accessory makers, and a myriad of content providers, including TV networks and record labels.

Using networks to secure supplies in an efficient and reliable fashion, or reaching customers in a timely manner, for example, can serve a secondary benefit by enhancing the firm's peripheral vision. Unexpected information, beyond the network's main purpose, may arise during the many conversations and information exchanges that must naturally occur for the network to achieve its primary goals. Will such extraneous insight be recognized and transmitted by the early recipients, or remain on the cutting floor because they fall outside the official business purview? For example, will an offhanded comment about a competitor or a weak signal about a shift in customer preferences be magnified or filtered out?

In many cases, managers need to think carefully about the trade-offs between efficiency in pursuing the network's primary purpose and allowing enough slack to scan the periphery effectively. Specifically, organizations will need to consider four critical characteristics of the network: reach, capture, speed, and resilience.

Network Reach—Creating Slack

How diverse is your organization's network in tapping into tangential domains? Does the network function more like an open system, in terms of information detection and transmittal, or is it a closed system, such as a tightly optimized chain that is highly automated with limited slack or even human intervention? And what is the integrity of information accessed by the network? What are the knowledge domains and perspectives covered by the network? Ironically, networks that are run in a very efficient, top-down fashion, for example in a tight supply chain, may be the least capable of detecting weak signals because (1) no one is looking for them, (2) information flows mostly vertically, (3) few outsiders are invited into the network, and (4) the data source is not validated. Just as national intelligence agencies need human spies to pick up unexpected information, by forming personal relationships and deep penetration within key social clusters, employees can connect more deeply with the outside world only if their role in the network allows for some slack. Although slack may be seen as an inefficiency in terms of the network's primary function, it may be a necessary condition to deliver on its secondary function, namely, peripheral scanning. Thus, leaders who architect networks, negotiate terms of agreement with network partners, and design incentive structures may want to assess the intelligence potential of a network before making it too efficient, automated, and task-oriented. Leaders should ask, "How much information did we miss in the past that was resident in a particular network?" This can provide valuable insight into future designs.

Network Capture—Sharing and Interpreting Information

Apart from reach, it is critical that a network can make sense of the information that crosses its nodes. How well does it capture key insights from the disparate information signals that arise at different times and places in the network? A network's effectiveness in capturing key insights will depend on how information is filtered and shared (vertically and horizontally), and how prepared key players are to look for the unexpected. Appropriate filters are necessary to deal with the massive explosion in data, which is expected to grow from 161 billion gigabytes in 2006 to 988 billion gigabytes by 2010, a sixfold increase (IDC 2007). Filters that are too coarse will result in a very high background of noise against which signals may be lost. Conversely, filters that are too tight will exclude potentially significant "weak" signals. An effective signal-to-noise ratio must be set for the network to scan effectively given the resources available.

Trust and open communication are key ingredients in designing networks that generate insights and knowledge beyond their original design or purpose. Information sharing from the network will be blocked if the prevailing organizational mind-set is that information needs to be shared on a "need-to-know basis only." The more a business or an industry relies on serendipity or accidental discovery, the more it needs to share information across networks. For example, it has been estimated that half of the drug discoveries in the pharmaceutical industry—from Fleming's penicillin to Pfizer's Viagra—were accidental in origin (Meyers 2007). Network sociologists use various measures to assess a network's information flow (Burt 1992; Cross, Liedtka, and Weiss 2005). Are all nodes equally connected, or does the network exhibit strong centrality? If a few nodes (for example, people, functions, or departments) see far more of the total picture than others, will these nodes possess the requisite intelligence and wisdom to capture key insights? Whereas hierarchy and centrality in networks may serve efficiency in execution, they can hamper intelligence capture outside the scope of the main task.

Network Speed—Relaying Insights

In addition to reach (how wide is our intelligence gathering net?) and capture (how well do we interpret what we are picking up in distributed form?), it will matter how quickly the network relays the insights to those who can act on them. The movie *Tora! Tora! Tora!*, about the Japanese air attack on Pearl Harbor in 1940, depicts an agonizingly slow conveyer belt transmitting a critical piece of intelligence through the long communication channel from decoders to admirals. Thanks to the information revolution, we can transmit information much faster now. But precisely because of this ease, organizations must filter what is sent to whom. After all, if we use the full power of our IT resources, we would all be inundated by e-mails (and many of us are). So the real issue is not technological but social. What are the norms and procedures that govern the transmission of unexpected, potentially relevant, but ambiguous information along the neural pathways of the organization? Organizational network dynamics resemble the flow of current and resistance in electronic circuits. We can increase the potential of a circuit so that the electrons flow more quickly (within the constraints of Ohm's Law) or slow things down by adding resistance. And we can make the electrons flow sequentially or in parallel (at the price of some dilution of signal strength).

Although various steps can be taken to enhance speed, there are constraints and trade-offs to consider. By analogy, Shannon's Law of Information Theory shows that in addressing signal-to-noise ratio (Shannon and Weaver 1963), we can improve one dimension only at the expense of the other (see Figure 16-3). So, too, with networks, where we cannot simply increase overall network speed (the equivalent of channel capacity) without affecting capture (the equivalent of signal-to-noise ratio), or network reach (the equivalent of network bandwidth).

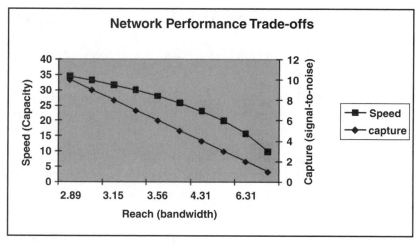

Reference: Shannon's Law of Information Theory

Figure 16-3 Network performance trade-offs

Network Resilience—Capacity to Adapt

Given the importance of peripheral vision in rapidly changing environments, organizations need to be able to adapt their networks in a timely fashion. The Internet was originally created as a scientific intelligence network, known as ARPANET, to easily share information and withstand a large-scale disruption or attack. We can similarly ask how robust or resilient organization networks are when they are damaged, either by accident or on purpose. Such network concepts as multihoming and self-healing speak directly to a network's capability to transmit information along a variety of pathways. Homing refers to a network's capability to reach or transmit a specific piece of information using multiple paths. High-performance content networks, such as, say, Google's search engine, are architected to access and distribute information via several pathways to assure robustness. Self-healing refers to a network's capability to repair itself or extend into areas where it is weak or has gaps. In crisis situations, the network's reliability and speed become especially critical, and ideally the network will function like a good rumor mill, using social connections and low degrees of separation, to spread information fast.

Improving Your Extended Intelligence Network

We have focused on four network characteristics (reach, capture, speed, and resilience) that seem especially relevant to minding and mining the periphery of an organization via its extended networks. Often the very characteristics that make an extended network efficient (such as centrality, hierarchy, focus, and closure) conspire against making it good at picking up weak signals. The latter requires some slack, horizontal communication to help connect the dots, an open systems architecture, and limited centrality to assure a wide-angle view. As leaders design their networks to deliver on both their primary function and peripheral scanning, they should be mindful of these often hidden trade-offs.

How can managers improve the reach, capture, speed, and resilience of their networks? To improve reach, managers can create a visual network map showing all the key nodes, the information content at each node, and the types of information flows between nodes in the network. This map can then be used to identify gateways (entry/exit points), sources, sinks, and broken circuits that can be enhanced with network additions/extensions. To improve capture, scouts or agents can be used to test network performance and integrity at different nodes and along different routes by carrying reference or dummy information through a specific network path. This test is analogous to the childhood game "Whisper Down the Lane" (or "Telephone") in which a message is passed through many people and the final version is compared to the original.

Managers can also improve reach and capture by using active scanning rather than relying on passive scanning. All managers collect intelligence from networks, but they often do so passively. They keep their antennae up and wait to receive outside signals. They are continually exposed to a wealth of data, ranging from the fuzzy impression of rumors gleaned at a trade show, to insights into trends from peer networks and harder data about performance and competitive behavior. Because most of the passive data comes from familiar sources, this mode of scanning tends to reinforce, rather than challenge, prevailing beliefs. There is no room for exploration, and unexpected and unfamiliar weak signals will probably be lost. Active scanning, in contrast, reflects intense curiosity about what is happening in a zone of the periphery and is guided by strategically derived questions. An active scan is often hypothesis-driven and utilizes directed probes by teams of outsiders and insiders that interrogate the network. They use the scientific method of first proposing a hypothesis, and then observing, speculating, and testing actively.

To improve speed, managers should first measure a network's latency for various types of signal information (in real time or via simulation). How long does it take for information to reach those who need it? A tragic example was the tsunami of Dec 2006: The earthquake tremors were registered almost immediately in Hawaii and other scientific stations, and yet it took far too many hours to warn residents in the affected coastal regions of Thailand, Indonesia, and others. In many cases, there were no warnings at all, up to 8 hours after the massive undersea earthquake had been noticed, resulting in more than 200,000 deaths. Wherever high latency exists, parallel paths can be constructed or capacity increased along the primary path (by investing in people resources, knowledge sharing, IT improvements, and such).

Lastly, the resilience of the network can be tested and enhanced. As with the speed dimension, the network can be stress-tested by injecting a specific failure condition (such as taking one node offline), to see how well the network heals itself. Does critical signal information still get to the right destination in the event of a network fault? Such tests are routinely conducted in telecommunication networks or along the electrical power grid. After areas of weakness have been identified, as with brownouts or blackouts in the electricity grid, they can be shored up through early detection of damage, alternative routing capability, and perhaps self-repair. Homeland security is an example in which all four of the key network performance characteristics, including resilience, are a challenge due to rigid organizational boundaries (municipal, state, federal, and international) and the lack of a coordinated focus in all parts of the network to scan and interpret weak signals.

Creating a Strategic Radar

Technological advances enable new, integrated models for collecting, sharing, and encoding information. This includes creating an overarching framework for linking new signals to scenarios and strategies, a "strategic radar." Figure 16-4 diagrams the basic component of such a radar system. We recently applied this approach within a government agency providing military supply chain services, as illustrated in the next section ("Using Networks to Scan the Periphery").

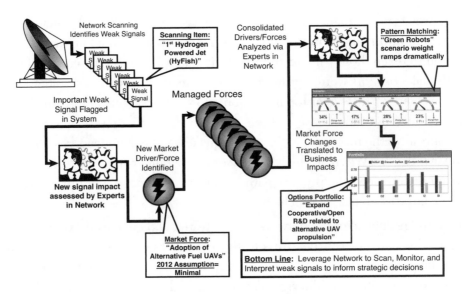

Figure 16-4   Components of a strategic radar (© Strategic Radar)

Using Networks to Scan the Periphery

The Defense Logistics Agency (DLA) supplies the U.S. armed forces with all kinds of critical supplies, from food and medicines to spare parts, tools, fuel, and building materials. After conducting a scenario planning exercise to explore possible future environments relating to logistics and defense operations around the globe, DLA decided to use its extensive networks to monitor for early signals of change. Their networks included vendors, customers, partners, other agencies and employees. Initially, they focused on capturing information on prespecified trends and uncertainties, using various kinds of business analytics. However, they now also scan for new "weak" signals that could result in significant change in the scenarios. For example, the Department of Defense (DoD) and NATO have moved to RFID (radio frequency identification) as the primary technology platform for logistics tracking. DLA is scanning for signals related to this technology that could have significant impact on the DLA. During the monitoring process, signals related to a slowdown in commercial RFID deployments and an increase in new sensor networks were picked up. Increasing energy price coupled with possible requirements for limiting energy consumption for DoD was also identified as a key signal for DLA with potential impacts to the current operating model. In both cases, early identification of these signals helped DLA anticipate future changes and formulate better strategies for the new emerging scenarios.

Importantly, any such new information is interpreted through the lens of multiple future scenarios that the organization may face over the next decade, since this signals are often ambiguous at first. Finally, a DLA uses an interactive dashboard to visualize the forces, scenarios, and a set of suggested strategic responses. A sample Strategic Radar Dashboard for the agency is shown in Figure 16-5.

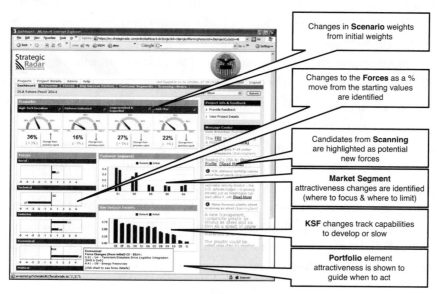

Figure 16-5   Sample radar screen for DLA (© Strategic Radar, Inc.)

In addition to such visualization tools, there are several other technologies that can significantly boost the performance of organizational networks for peripheral vision. Specifically, advances in wireless communication and social networking will increase the ability of employees to self-organize and share signal information with other groups or networks inside and outside the organization. According to a recent survey, executives use less than 50% of the potential of wireless platforms to drive mass collaboration, social networking, and interconnectedness (Snyder 2009). With the advent of new wireless technologies beyond the current 3rd Generation, users will gain more control and can mimic a swarm as they decide to collaborate and organize around specific information needs and objectives. Such social networks are blurring the line between personal and professional domains, presenting both an opportunity and a threat to access employees as consumers and sensors. Privacy and trust will be critical success factors in establishing effective networks that leverage both advanced wireless and social networks.

The Leadership Challenge: Managing It All

As William Gibson once noted, the future is already here but unevenly distributed. Some organizations have learned to harness technological advances to increase their peripheral vision. Others lack the ability to mine their networks, or mind the weak signals without becoming overwhelmed by what appears to be mostly random noise. Each organization must set its own filters to avoid information overload, balancing the error of missing key signals with the cost of paying attention to many signals. However the filters are set, the organization should operate along the efficient frontier concerning these errors. But many are not doing so because they fail to use their extended networks fully.

The difference between those that are ahead and those that are behind is ultimately a matter of leadership. The best organizations are shaped by a leadership team that seeks and values early warnings, and mobilizes the rest of the organization to pay attention to the periphery (Day and Schoemaker 2008). They adopt an inquisitive approach to strategy making that alerts their organization to possible challenges from the periphery, make the necessary investments in knowledge systems and analytical support, and assign clear accountability for detecting, tracking, and sharing weak signals. By creating an environment that promotes vigilance and discovery, they can use their networks to extract better insights from their widened periphery, and do so sooner than rivals.

References

Aharonson, B. S., J. A. C. Baum, and M. P. Feldman. 2007. Desperately seeking spillovers? Increasing returns, industrial organization and the location of new entrants in geographic and technological space. *Industrial and Corporate Change* 16 (1), 89-130.

Ahituv, N., J. Zif, and I. Machlin. 1998. Environmental scanning and information systems in relation to success in introducing new products. *Information & Management* 33 (4), 201-211.

Boersma, F. K. 2003. Structural ways to embed a research laboratory into the company: A comparison between Philips and General Electric 1900-1940. *History and Technology* 19 (2), 109-126.

Boersma, F. K. 2004. The organization of industrial research as a network activity: Agricultural research at Philips in the 1930s. *Business History Review* 78 (2), 255-272.

Börjesson, S., F. Dahlsten, and M. Williander. 2006. Innovative scanning experiences from an idea generation project at Volvo Cars. *Technovation* 26 (7), 775-783.

Boyd, B. K., and J. Fulk. (1996) Executive scanning and perceived uncertainty: A multi-dimensional model. *Journal of Management* 22 (1), 1-21.

Brown, J. S. (2004). Minding and Mining the Periphery, *Long Range Planning*, Volume 37, Issue 2, Pages 143-151.

Burt, R. S (2004). Structural holes and good ideas. *American Journal of Sociology* 110 2, (349-399.

Burt, R. S. (1992) *Structural Holes.* Cambridge, MA: Harvard University Press, 1992.

Caniëls, M. C. J., and H. A. Romijn. 2005. What drives innovativeness in industrial clusters? Transcending the debate. *Cambridge Journal of Economics* 29 (4), 497-515. Chesbrough, H. 2006. *Open Business Models: How to Thrive in the New Innovation Landscape.* Cambridge MA: Harvard Business School Press.

Chesbrough, H. W., and M. Appleyard. 2007. Open Innovation and Strategy. *California Management Review* (Fall), 57-76.

Cohen, W., and D. Levinthal. 1990. Absorptive capacity: A new perspective on learning and innovation. *Administrative Science Quarterly* 35, 128-152.

Cross, R., J. Liedtka, and L. Weiss. 2005. A practical guide to social networks. *Harvard Business Review* 83 (3), 124-+.

Dahl, M. S., and C. O. R. Pedersen. 2004. Knowledge flows through informal contacts in industrial clusters: myth or reality? *Research Policy* 33 (10), 1673-1686.

Davenport, T. H., and J. G. Harris. 2007. *Competing on Analytics: The New Science of Winning.* Cambridge: Harvard Business School Press.

Day, G. S., and P. J. H. Schoemaker. 2006. *Peripheral Vision: Detecting the Weak Signals That Will Make or Break Your Company.* Boston MA: Harvard Business School Press.

Day, G. S., and P. J. H. Schoemaker. 2008. Are You a "Vigilant Leader"? *MIT Sloan Management Review* 49 (3, Spring 2008), 43-51.

Dupree, M. W. 1997. Networks of innovation: Vaccine development at Merck, Sharp & Dohme, and Mulford, 1895-1996. *Business History* 39 (4), 185-187.

Fleming, L., and M. Marx. 2006. Managing innovation in small worlds. *MIT Sloan Management Review* 48 (1), 8-+.

Forsyth, J. E., N. Galante, and T. Guild. 2006. Capitalizing on customer insights. *The McKinsey Quarterly* 3.

Fuld, L. 2003. Be prepared. *Harvard Business Review* (November), 1-2.

Fung, V. K., W. K. Fung, and Y. Wind. 2007. *Competing in a Flat World: Building Enterprises for a Borderless World.* New York: Wharton School Publishing.

Galbraith, J. R. 1973. *Designing Complex Organizations.* Reading, MA: Addison-Wesley.

Granovetter, M. S. 1973. Strength of weak ties. *American Journal of Sociology* 78 (6), 1360-1380.

Granovetter, M. S. 1985. Economic action and social structure: The problem of embeddedness. *American Journal of Sociology* 91 (November), 481-510.

Giuliani, E. 2007. The selective nature of knowledge networks in clusters: Evidence from the wine industry. *Journal of Economic Geography* 7 (2), 139-168.

Hannan, M. T., and M. Freeman. 1989. *Organizational ecology.* Cambridge, MA.: Harvard University Press.

Huston, L., and N. Sakkab. 2006. Connect and develop: Inside Procter & Gamble's new model for innovation. *Harvard Business Review* B4 (March), 58-66.

Ibarra, H., and M. Hunter. 2007. How leaders create and use networks. *Harvard Business Review* 85 (1), 40-+.

IDC. 2007. Expanding the digital universe: A forecast of worldwide information growth through 2010. IDC Whitepaper, March 2007.

Krugman, P. R. 1991. *Geography and trade.* Leuven, Belgium; Cambridge, MA: Leuven University Press; MIT Press.

Liu, R.-L. 2004. Collaborative multiagent adaptation for business environmental scanning through the Internet. *Applied Intelligence* 20 (2), 119-133.

Lyman, P., and H. R. Varian. 2000. How much information? *The Journal of Electronic Publishing* 6 (2, December).

Marshall, A. 1920. *Principles of Economics: An Introductory Volume.* 8th ed. London: Macmillan. (See Book IV, Chapter X: "Industrial organization continued. The concentration of specialized industries in particular localities.")

McCann, P., and T. Arita. 2006. Clusters and regional development: Some cautionary observations from the semiconductor industry. *Information Economics and Policy* 18 (2), 157-180.

Meyers, M. A. 2007. *Happy Accidents: Serendipity in Modern Medical Breakthroughs.* Arcade Publishing.

Nohria, N., and R. G. Eccles. 1992. *Networks and Organizations: Structure, Form, and Action.* Boston, MA: Harvard Business School Press.

Nosella, A., and G. Petroni. 2007. Multiple network leadership as a strategic asset: The Carlo Gavazzi Space case. *Long Range Planning* 40 (2), 178-201.

Peteraf, M. A., and M. E. Bergen. 2003. Scanning dynamic competitive landscapes: A market-based and resource-based framework. *Strategic Management Journal* 24 (10), 1027-1041.

Porter, M. E. 2005. *The Competitive Advantage of Nations.* 1990, New York: Free Press; Marjolein C. J.

Rosenkopf, L., and P. Almeida. 2003. Overcoming local search through alliances and mobility. *Management Science* 49 (6), 751-766.

Sgourev, S. V., and E. W. Zuckerman. 2006. Improving capabilities through industry peer networks. *MIT Sloan Management Review.* (Winter), 33-38.

Shannon, C. E., and W. Weaver. 1963. *A Mathematical Theory of Communication.* Univ. of Illinois Press.

Snyder, S. A. 2009. *Digital Swarms*, Pearson Publishing, 2009.

Tirole, J. 1989. *The Theory of Industrial Organization.* 3rd ed.

Zahra, S. A., and G. George. 2002. Absorptive capacity: A review, re-conceptualization and extensions. *Academy of Management Review* 27, 185-203.

PART V

ORGANIZING IN A NETWORKED WORLD

Networks are changing the design and management of our organizations. In Chapter 17, **Yoram (Jerry) Wind**, **Victor Fung**, and **William Fung** describe the innovative model of Li & Fung for "competing in a flat world" by orchestrating a far-flung network of suppliers brought together into temporary networks to fulfill a specific customer order, and the importance of its connective capabilities or "network orchestration." In Chapter 18, **Eric K. Clemons**, **Steve Barnett**, **JoAnn Magdoff**, and **Julia Clemons** consider how organizations need to adapt their training, their managerial styles, and their expectations to highly networked employees of the "instant messaging generation." In Chapter 19, **Valery Yakubovich** and **Ryan Burg** point out that core HR processes such as recruitment and hiring, training and development, performance management, and retention all depend on networks, yet the typical HR view is to focus on individuals. Finally, in Chapter 20, **Prashant Kale**, **Harbir Singh**, and **John Bell** discuss the importance of relational capabilities in successful alliances, which have become increasingly important in a networked business environment.

Chapter 17   Network Orchestration: Creating and Managing Global
              Supply Chains Without Owning Them   299
              Yoram (Jerry) Wind, Victor Fung, and William Fung

Chapter 18   Managing the Hyper-Networked "Instant Messaging"
              Generation in the Work Force   317
              Eric K. Clemons, Steve Barnett, JoAnn Magdoff, and Julia Clemons

Chapter 19   Missing the Forest for the Trees: Network-Based
              HR Strategies   335
              Valery Yakubovich and Ryan Burg

Chapter 20   Relating Well: Building Capabilities for Sustaining Alliance
              Networks   353
              Prashant Kale, Harbir Singh, and John Bell

17

Network Orchestration: Creating and Managing Global Supply Chains Without Owning Them

Yoram (Jerry) Wind
Victor Fung
William Fung

Abstract

If you accept, in the words of Thomas Friedman, that "the world is flat," how do you need to reshape your organization, management, and thinking for this new terrain? This chapter offers strategies and insights on the capability for "network orchestration" that is essential in designing and managing networks that are centrally controlled. While most management education is focused on competition at the firm level, competition today is increasingly "network against network." This changes the way we approach strategy, supply chains, building competencies, and managing enterprises. The authors examine the strategies used by successful networked companies in diverse industries. Effective network orchestration requires balancing control with empowerment of customers, suppliers, and entrepreneurial managers; and building value more from integration than specialization. While the traditional focus of core competencies has been at the firm level, the rise of networked organizations means that companies need to take a broader view. Success is based less on the competencies that the organization owns than those that it can connect to. The authors point out that this means core competencies in network orchestration and learning may become increasingly important because these meta-competencies allow organizations to assemble and flexibly reconfigure the competencies needed to fulfill a customer-driven value chain.

The emerging "Flat World," as described by Thomas Friedman (2005), presents tremendous opportunities for companies to create networked enterprises. Instead of owning capabilities and assets, companies can connect to these assets fluidly around the globe through connections to other partners. Although organizations have always engaged in partnerships, in this world these partnerships are much broader and more fluid. Companies are using networks to create supply chains that stretch more broadly than ever.

This creates opportunities to build flexible global enterprises that can be reconfigured quickly in a fast-changing world. For example, if Li & Fung Trading receives an order for 100,000 men's dress shirts today, the best place to source the yarn might be Korea, the buttons might come from China, and the weaving might best be done in Taiwan, but in two factories to speed production, while Pakistan might be the best place for the cut, make, and trim (CMT), using three different factories to speed up the process. If the same order came in a month later, it might result in a completely different supply chain. Suppose Pakistan faced political unrest at that point—the entire supply chain could be shifted to another factory in another country. The supply chain is evoked by the customer. Like a message routed through the Internet, the project moves along the best specific path chosen from a broader network. Li & Fung can select the right supply chain from a network of approximately 10,000 suppliers around the globe.

The reason this can be done is that Li & Fung is a networked organization. Although it supplies more than US$14 billion in clothing, toys, and other products for top U.S. brands, it does not own a single factory or employ a single seamstress. It accomplishes all of this through what we call "network orchestration."[1]

This approach shifts the view of the organization and its competencies. Although the focus in the past may have been on building and protecting the core competencies that the firm owns, the focus in such a networked organization is much more on the competencies that the organization can *connect* to. The meta-competency at connecting is "network orchestration." Li & Fung has become a leading supplier without owning competencies in manufacturing. Instead, it has a competency in orchestration that allows the company to draw together many manufacturers and other partners into a flexible and adaptable supply chain. In addition to this capability, companies need the capacity to adapt over time to a rapidly changing environment. This demands capabilities in learning and innovation. With this set of broad capabilities—orchestration, learning, and

---

[1] John Hagel and John Seely Brown first described Li & Fung's approach as "process orchestration" in their book *The Only Sustainable Edge: Why Business Strategy Depends on Productive Friction and Dynamic Specialization*, Boston: Harvard Business School Press, 2005.

innovation—networked organizations can connect to the other specific capabilities they need to create value for customers.

Unbundling Supply Chains

As explored by Serguei Netessine in Chapter 13, "Supply Webs: Managing, Organizing, and Capitalizing on Global Networks of Supplies," traditional supply chains have been transformed into global "supply networks." The supply chain and supply chain management have been an essential part of classic business strategy. Michael Porter recognized that these chains delivered not only products but also value, leading to the concept of the "value chain" (Porter 1985). This allowed managers to consider how value is added at each step along the chain.

Supply chains increasingly are moving from mechanistic and deterministic models to what John Gattorna (2006) calls "living supply chains." As he writes, "Whether we accept it or not, we are already shifting from Newtonian-like thinking to a more organic model." These are supply chains that have the flexibility to respond to the dynamically changing needs of customers and consumers. The way value is created and shared in these "value webs" is also more complex.

In the past, transaction costs represented a limiting factor in making supply chains more flexible and global. The cost of coordinating with different partners and transporting goods and information around the world made it cheaper to keep manufacturing within a single factory, or at least close by. Globalization, improved communications, computing and the Internet, and low-cost shipping reduced transaction costs and contributed to the rise of "borderless manufacturing." As transaction costs have dropped significantly, this has led to the unbundling of the supply chain.

Since Henry Ford set up his famous assembly line near Detroit, the most efficient way to run a factory was to put everything under one roof. Then, companies such as Toyota opened the front doors of the factory and put their suppliers just outside the gates. This created Toyota City. The suppliers were still geographically co-located on the same campus, but they were separate companies outside the factory. Dell and other companies then engaged in global sourcing, purchasing computer chips and other technology from Asia.

As global logistics and coordination have improved, these suppliers can now be virtually anywhere. In fact, "right outside" the factory gates now means anywhere on the planet. Boeing's 777 jet is assembled from three million parts from more than 900 suppliers from 17 countries around the world.[2] Boeing primarily produces the wings and fuselage, as well as assembling the aircraft. Most of the plane's components are outsourced around the globe. For its 787, the company is also outsourcing systems for collision avoidance and landing in zero visibility to Indian engineers at HCL Technologies outside New Delhi. This not only allows the company to find best-in-class providers for each component but also gives each of these nations a vested interest in the success of the aircraft. This, of course, helps in spreading risk and making global sales.

Companies realized that the supply chain could be broken up and spread across the globe. They could do more than source *products or components* from other parts of the world. They could put stages of the supply chain in different parts of the world and coordinate them centrally. This meant breaking up the *processes* of the supply chain, farming them out to different companies in different locations, and then managing these dispersed processes. This is what John Hagel and John Seely Brown (2001) have referred to as "process orchestration." Through orchestration, companies could optimize the overall supply chain to deliver the right product to the right place at the right time at the right price.

Henry Ford's factory was built on the principle of *division* of labor. The new principle was orchestrated *dispersion* of labor. Henry Ford's factory was based on large operations that offered economies of scale, whereas orchestration is based on assembling armies of small and medium business that could act as one.

The Four Flows: Where Atoms Meet Bits

Dispersed manufacturing and network orchestration are made possible because of improvements in four flows required for the manufacturing process: information, financial, physical, and work flows, as shown in Figure 17-1. In traditional supply chains, these four flows were integrated. The shipping information traveled with the physical order, and money changed hands with goods. Physical flows and work flows were essentially the same. Traditional supply chains were difficult to reconfigure, were easily disrupted, and required long lags between placing the order and receiving the finished goods. Even when global supply chains were created, they were fixed. The goal was to keep driving to make them more efficient after they were established, rather than creating the best new design for the chain at any given moment. Flexibility came at a high premium.

[2] "777 Family," www.boeing.com/commercial/777family/pf/pf_facts.html.

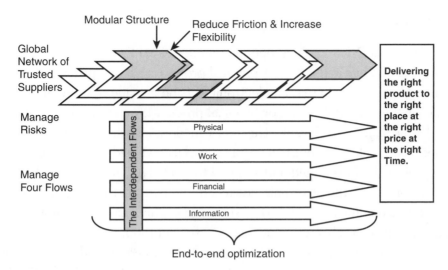

Figure 17-1 Network orchestration

The forces that are flattening the world (see the sidebar "Friedman's Ten Flatteners") have affected these four flows. These forces have accelerated and improved each of the flows. These interrelated forces are flattening the world and transforming management, making logistics more efficient and more global and creating opportunities to rethink the organization. Consider how each of these four flows has been transformed.

Friedman's Ten Flatteners

The ten flatteners identified by Thomas Friedman in *The World Is Flat* (paraphrased slightly):

- End of Cold War and rise of personal computer (IBM PC)
- Internet (Netscape IPO)
- Work flow software (Wild Brain, PayPal)
- Open sourcing (Linux, Apache)
- Outsourcing (Wipro, Infosys)
- Offshoring (Chinese manufacturing)
- Supply chaining (Wal-Mart)
- Insourcing (UPS, FedEx, and Modern Logistics)
- Informing (Google, Yahoo!, and MSN Web Search)
- Digital and wireless (The Steroids)

Information Flows

In *Being Digital,* Nicholas Negroponte, founder of MIT's Media Lab, highlights the distinction between bits and atoms. A physical product such as a printed book or music CD is limited by atoms, whereas an electronic version is made of fluid bits. Transforming an information, entertainment, or financial product from atoms to bits makes geography and time almost irrelevant. The bits can flow anywhere in the world almost instantaneously. Think about music on a CD versus a download through iTunes. The CD has to be packaged and stamped and shipped to a retailer. The customer buys the CD and takes it home. For the electronic download, the customer clicks a button, the payment is made via credit card, and the transfer begins. This transformation from atoms to bits in such products has been the low-hanging fruit of the information revolution. It is not surprising that the services that have been outsourced abroad, such as computer programming or customer service, are those that could be easily digitized. These advances improved and accelerated the information flows.

Information technology has enabled the work and information to become more dispersed. The first separation occurred with the fax machine, whereby paperwork could make its own path separate from the physical products. But with modern information technology, the information flows are now separate from the order and can be accessed from anywhere in the world at any time. An order can clear customs while the shipment is en route because the information travels separately from the physical goods.

Financial Flows

Financial flows also have been digitized and globalized. Through digital technology, hard currency has become liquefied. Global capital can flow more freely, allowing the design and operation of cross-national supply chains and better management of risks. There also has been a shift in the center of economic activity to new countries and regions. As global capital markets have developed, capital flows have been accelerated and separated from physical flows.

Physical Flows

A shirt or a toy cannot be converted into bits. It is a physical product, and at the end of production, it needs to be shipped to its end market by land, sea, or air. Advances in logistics, including global shipping, use of containers, and technology to track shipping, have made moving between remote locations faster and cheaper. A buyer who wanted to change the fabric for a product used to have to get on a plane and fly out to the factory with a sample. Now, the sample can be shipped overnight. FedEx, UPS, DHL, and other carriers have rethought and improved every aspect of shipping and logistics. This is what UPS CEO Mike Eskew has called "synchronized commerce," in which goods, information, and funds "are seamlessly connected to benefit businesses worldwide" (UPS 2003). As costs have declined, every year, more goods are moved by air. For example, 34% of goods from Hong Kong were moved by air in 2006, rising by 1 to 2 percentage points a year, and half of the cargo moves in passenger aircraft, making it less susceptible to spikes in fees from rising fuel costs.

Work Flows

Online retailers such as eBay, Amazon, Netflix, and Audible began addressing the challenge of building interfaces between the bits and atoms to deliver physical products ordered through electronic channels. They began separating financing and information from the product and to take advantage of improvements in shipping to reduce delivery times, accelerating information, capital, and physical flows.

But these improvements only addressed the supply chain after manufacturing was completed. Producing goods such as cotton shorts presents a more complex challenge. Not only does this process require moving atoms from seller to buyer, but also these atoms have to be designed, sewn together, packaged, assembled, and moved around. The challenge here was to improve the *work flows,* to break up and manage processes that are dispersed across diverse geographic locations. Although only part of the modern supply chain could be turned into bits, the improvements in information, capital, and physical flows created opportunities to rethink work flows.

Modularization of manufacturing and other value chains has made it easier to separate parts of the chain to be outsourced. New software to track and manage work processes has helped to keep control in a world of dispersed manufacturing. The first stage in this process was the outsourcing of specific functional areas such as customer service or accounting. The next step is to outsource all but core processes of the chain to the optimal locations in the world.

With a modular structure, the network is the universe of suppliers from which a specific supply chain is precipitated. A specific supply chain is called forth from this universe in response to the demand of the customer. Whereas the old factory ended with the customer, this process begins with the customer.

The Need for Orchestration

Modern management and control systems arose out of the vertically integrated factory. With more fluid value networks, the challenge is to control a supply chain or other value chain through partners that the company does not own. This is a daunting challenge as demonstrated by the many alliances, outsourcing, and offshoring engagements that have run into problems, often due to coordination and control issues. Studies find that half of all strategic alliances fail. Several recent studies have concluded that half the organizations that shifted processes offshore failed to generate the financial returns they had anticipated (Aron and Singh 2005). A study of outsourcing by Deloitte Consulting found that major stumbling blocks include governance, management attention, and change management (Deloitte Consulting 2005). Companies such as Nike, Wal-Mart, and McDonald's have found out the hard way that they are held responsible for what happens in the factories of their outsourced partners—no matter how far removed. This has led to increased scrutiny of working conditions, environmental impact, and other issues throughout the entire network. More recently, we have seen tragic problems with product quality leading to poisonings in products from pet foods to children's toys.

What is missing in many cases is orchestration. It is not enough to set up the network or contract with a partner. Without orchestration, many of the gains of networks and global collaboration can be lost because the resulting supply chains are suboptimized. Orchestration is different from managing a typical internal process. It requires a more fluid approach that empowers partners and employees, while maintaining control at the same time. Network orchestration is the design and management of networks that work together to achieve a common business process. In a networked and flat world, this has become an increasingly important competency.

Although we developed the principles of network orchestration in a manufacturing enterprise, they have broad applications across diverse industries and activities, from research and product development to services. These diverse networks include a business built by Olam International working with small and mid-sized farmers in 40 countries to orchestrate a network for agricultural products and food ingredients. There are research networks such as the Connect & Develop initiative of Procter & Gamble that have linked it with more than 1.5 million independent researchers around the globe, or the external networks that have helped Canadian-based GoldCorp significantly improve the yield of its mining business by orchestrating an eclectic group of experts outside the firm.

Companies have created marketing networks to orchestrate hundreds of thousands of buzz agents to get messages across and promote products. There are networks for innovation such as a system built around Nike and iPod to create an electronic personal trainer. Global sports leagues offer another example of the power of coordinated networks, and even the military is increasingly turning to networked models to meet the complex challenge of fighting modern wars and addressing global terrorist networks.

All these examples have one thing in common: They all are based on networks that come together to create a product or service. And they all require orchestration to keep these networks operating at their peak and prevent them from devolving into chaos. The principles of network orchestration can be applied to these networked enterprises in addition to supply chains and manufacturing.

Although Li & Fung is a large multinational, the opportunities for network orchestration are not limited to large global companies. These opportunities apply equally to companies large and small. In Hong Kong alone, there are at least 50,000 smaller trading companies that manage global (or at least regional) supply chains. They all do some form of network orchestration, although not as extensively as Li & Fung. In fact, the new technologies and other shifts of the flat world lead to a leveling of the playing field that makes it easier for small firms to participate in networks or to engage in network orchestration.

Implications of Network Orchestration for Strategy and Competencies

What the discipline of management was to the old vertically integrated, hierarchical firm, network orchestration is to the company working in the flat world. It is an essential capability for this world. Strategy for network orchestration focuses on competing "network against network," which means that the strategy for the firm is embedded in its strategy for the network. Competencies in this world increasingly are in the network rather than held tightly by the firm (as discussed by CK Prahalad in Chapter 2, "Creating Experience: Competitive Advantage in the Age of Networks"). This means the ability to connect to competencies may be as important as any firm-centric capabilities. This ability to connect and manage competencies in the broader network is a capability for network orchestration, which, along with learning, may be one of the meta-capabilities that is most important for a networked world.

Networks Need Orchestration

In spite of the mythology, not all networked enterprises are grassroots democracies, as they are sometimes portrayed. As Nambisan and Sawhney point out in Chapter 9, "Network-Centric Innovation: Four Strategies for Tapping the Global Brain," some networks have more centralized control whereas others have more diffused leadership. The orchestration involved in a symphony orchestra is obviously different from that for a jazz quartet. But even a group of jazz musicians in a jam session has a leader. Sometimes this orchestration is shared by members of the network, and it may even be largely embodied in a set of rules that guide the relatively autonomous actions of members of the network. Even political democracies are carefully orchestrated through primaries and elections. They sometime need ad hoc orchestration when this system breaks down, as was the case with the 2008 elections in Kenya or the 2000 U.S. election race between George W. Bush and Al Gore, which was referred to the U.S. Supreme Court. Human networks that produce some deliberate product, service, or other outcome often require some type of orchestration.

Wikipedia, for example, while democratic, is not a completely open playing field. A network of some 13,000 writers and editors keep an eye on entries to ensure they are kept current and accurate. Editors weed out nonsense pages, prevent the malicious rewriting of history, and ensure continued development. The architecture of the community, which often is forgotten in celebrating its populist origins, is largely responsible for ensuring that Wikipedia and other open source projects don't disintegrate into chaos. There is active orchestration of this network to ensure that it produces something of value.

A core set of Wikipedia entries has been "protected" so they no longer follow the celebrated "anyone can edit" policy. These are entries such as "Albert Einstein," "George W. Bush," and "Adolph Hitler" that were particularly susceptible to vandalism or "drive-by nonsense," in the words of founder Jimmy Wales. There is also a 14-member arbitration committee that serves as the court of last resort for disputes about entries. Wales ultimately has the last word on difficult issues (Hafner 2006). For open source software collaborations such as Linux, a governing body ensures tight oversight and control of the work of the diffused community of programmers.

The success of a community depends on its design, its governance, and the processes around which it is organized, as well as its motivating power to engage its members and attract new ones. There is no autocratic CEO of Wikipedia, but there is a system for generating and vetting entries that helps to improve the network and ensure that it operates according to a set of core principles. In a supply network, this role of governance and design of processes and motivation is played by the network orchestrator. The orchestrator ensures that the collective "wisdom of the crowd" is tapped, and the network thinks and acts more wisely than any individual member.

Social networks such as MySpace and YouTube, on the other hand, which are less designed to produce a collective product, have less of a need for this governance and orchestration. They are channels and marketplaces, facilitating interactions or transactions. They are valuable in their own right, but because they are focused less on creating a collective deliverable from the network, they have less need for network orchestration. As networks such as YouTube are used to create a collective product, however, they demand more orchestration. For example, when CNN sought to solicit questions by YouTube for a debate among U.S. presidential candidates, the broadcaster stepped in to structure the process and make the selection from the many submissions. Arriving at meaningful questions for the presidential debate required some level of orchestration that goes beyond simply sharing a favorite video with a friend.

Where there is a network coming together to create something, some player or group of players often has to play the role of orchestrator. It could be the company itself, its partners, or a dedicated outside orchestrator. This role of designer and orchestrator of the network is a new role and a new capability, which is often overlooked. But it is perhaps the most important capability for competing in a flat world.

Three Roles of Network Orchestration

What do network orchestrators do? The network orchestrator plays three primary roles related to the focus, management, and value creation of the firm and network, as shown in Figure 17-2. Each of these roles is the expansion of the role of a manager within a more limited fixed factory or traditional firm.

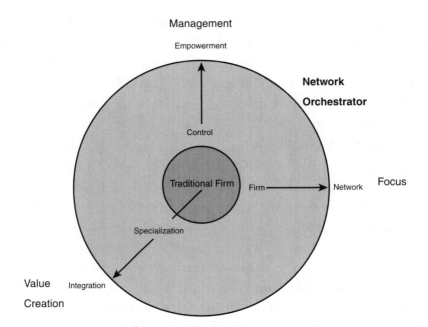

Figure 17-2   Three roles of network orchestration

The movement from a traditional firm toward the network orchestrator requires a shift in focus from the firm to the network, a shift in management from control to empowerment, and a shift in value creation from specialization to integration. Since few companies are "pure" network orchestrators, the world is not completely flat, and companies need to be concerned about their shareholders, employees, and other stakeholders at the center, companies typically need to strike a balance somewhere between the inner circle and the outer one.

Role #1, Design and manage networks—First, the network orchestrator needs to shift focus from viewing the firm as the center of the universe to looking at the network. Companies don't compete against other companies. Networks compete against networks. Two retail stores on opposite corners in New York City may appear to be direct competitors, but this is an illusion. They are not competing against each other in isolation. Each store has a supply chain stretching from its shelves out to the world. The best supply chain will win. Before a customer walks into the store, often the game is over based on the superior supply chain. The best supply chain is drawn from a robust universe of suppliers. It is no longer possible to compete by looking at a company in isolation from the network. The orchestrator creates the broader network and then draws supply chains from it.

Role #2, Control through empowerment—Second, with a dispersed network, the orchestrator needs a different form of leadership and control. In a world in which orchestrators do not own the means of production, what holds this network together? In contrast to rigid control systems used to manage factories, the network orchestrator relies not just on rewards but also on a combination of empowerment and trust, as well as training and certification, to manage a network that it does not own. In addition, the orchestrator empowers its own managers and suppliers to act entrepreneurially. In contrast to command and control systems, the orchestrator works like a guest conductor in an orchestra. The conductor may not have the ability to hire or fire people but coordinates a highly skilled set of independent musicians. Empowered end consumers demand more customization and flexibility, which makes it more challenging to orchestrate networks, but can also create opportunities for companies that have the flexibility to meet these rising demands. Consumers want more transparency from networks and more control over both the end product and the processes used to create it.

This empowerment is created through using "loose-tight" relationships with suppliers that are used to design supply chains around customers. For example, Li & Fung sets a target of having at least 30% of the business of a given supplier but not more than 70% (the 30/70 rule). Li & Fung also establishes units headed by "Little John Waynes" who can act entrepreneurially within a large organization, creating a "big-small" company. Loose relationships and tight controls allow the orchestrator to take responsibility for the whole chain, even though it doesn't own it. Finally, Li & Fung uses a planning process built around three-year stretch goals to balance stability and renewal.

Role #3, Create value through integration—Finally, orchestrators have a different way of creating value. Value in the traditional firm came from specialization, honing skills in specific areas, protecting trade secrets, and keeping out rivals and even partners. Value comes from fighting for a piece of a limited pie and protecting specialized core competencies. Value in the flat world, in contrast, comes from integration, bridging borders as well as leveraging the company's value and intellectual property across the network. This integration means spanning the separate steps of the supply chain to create and capture more value after the product leaves the factory. For a typical $4 stuffed toy, the in-factory costs might be $1 and the ex-factory costs might be $3. In a world in which almost every penny has been squeezed from factory costs, the "soft $3" may be the most attractive target for finding value. In addition, value is created by spanning borders between functions within the company, such as identifying new opportunities for marketing and sales in emerging markets where manufacturing is sourced—to "sell to the source." Orchestrators need to know when to open the doors wide to create value as integrators and when to produce value by focusing on the specialized resources of the firm.

The three roles of orchestrators are interconnected and work together. The more dispersed networks become, the more there is a need for empowerment rather than direct control. The more empowerment if given to suppliers and customers, the more managers need to look across the network rather than focusing on their own firms. The more organizations move toward orchestration, the more they need to be able to build and capture value across the network rather than within the firm. All together, these three roles move companies from the center circle of the figure to the broader outer circle of the networked enterprise.

Striking a Balance

Network orchestration is a multiplier that increases the reach and effectiveness of the organization. It is not a replacement for sound planning and control processes that are currently employed by multinational corporations. These processes are still needed within the organization, and some existing processes can be used with minor modifications. Network orchestration extends standard business processes to a broader network but also requires skills that are distinctive to network orchestration. By doing so, it magnifies the reach and impact of the organization, and increases its flexibility.

The world is not completely flat, and one of the roles of the network orchestrator is to balance the flat and round worlds. For example, in global manufacturing, there are many bilateral trade agreements that create mountains or superhighways for manufacturing supply chains. These bumps in the flat world create a shifting terrain and market imperfections. As with any such imperfections, this presents opportunities for companies with the flexibility to design their businesses around the new realities. The orchestrator needs to come up with the best customer solution given the current landscape and then adjust that solution when the landscape shifts tomorrow, as it will. The orchestrator needs to keep one eye on the possibilities of the flat world and one eye on the very textured realities of the unflat world.

In orchestrating networks, companies also have to balance a focus on the long-term with a short-term interest in maximizing value. For example, it might be advantageous for a network orchestrator to provide financing to a partner in the network. This entails a short-term cost for a loan that might not be something a bank would offer, but it improves the overall functioning of the network. It might allow for the factory to have longer lead times in fulfilling an order, reducing overtime and decreasing shipping costs. This benefits the network overall, and so could justify the investment by the orchestrator. Because the focus is on competing network against network, sometimes the orchestrator will have to sacrifice its own short-term interests to optimize the network—which benefits itself and its partners in the long run. In this case, the orchestrator also knows the risks better than an outside bank, so it can more effectively make such investments.

The Need for Orchestration

With growing concern about environmental impact, working conditions, and product quality, this network orchestration has become more important. Although some see missteps in global outsourcing and offshoring as a sign to pull back and bring more work back home, we need to be careful not to throw out the baby with the bath water. Global networks have created tremendous opportunities and efficiencies that have benefited consumers around the globe. The real lesson in these missteps is the importance of network orchestration. Networks don't run themselves. They are not just designed on paper. Henry Ford didn't just design his factory and then walk away. It required active management to make it work. The same is true for modern networked enterprises. The management required is different from that described by Alfred Sloan and Peter Drucker in the early days of General Motors (which is facing its own challenge in competing against more nimble rivals such as Toyota in a networked world). What is required today is network orchestration.

In the round world, the most important question in developing a supply chain or process chain was to determine *where* it would be handled. As in real estate, the rule was "location, location, location." The costs of moving goods around and tracking information were so high that geography was the first concern. This was an age when toys and garments were made in New York City, close to their market. But as coordination and logistics costs have fallen due to new technology and innovations such as shipping containers, geography has become less important.

There is a new concern, which is not just where but "what do to" and "how to do." After the "what" is determined, companies can find the best place in the world to do it. This is the question at the center of global outsourcing. But the question for network orchestration goes further. It is not just sourcing products but rather designing global processes. What is the best possible way to get this particular job done, the best path through a network of global possibilities? The total quality movement within the factory focused not only on doing things right, but on doing the right thing. Similarly, the network orchestrator looks at more than cost and efficiency. The orchestrator is focused on designing the best possible processes across a global network for delivering the right product to the right place at the right time at the right price.

Many enterprises in diverse settings have begun to recognize the need for network orchestration. This is a meta-competency for a networked world. If your company is part of a network, the questions to ask are, Who is orchestrating? If there is no orchestrator, should you create or play this role? How can the principles of network orchestration—focusing on networks, managing through empowerment, and creating value through integration—be tailored to your own situation? If you don't see your company as part of a network, are you viewing your world too narrowly? Have competitors already created networks that are competing against you? Will you be able to survive in this world?

Competing in a flat world means more than contracting with a company in Bangalore or Shanghai. It requires active orchestration and a different approach to the business. The principles of network orchestration that have been described apply to any organization that is part of a network and needs to seize the opportunities presented by an increasingly flat world. Because networks require orchestration, skills in leading or participating in networks are becoming critical for success.

References

Aron, R., and J. V. Singh. 2005. Getting offshoring right. *Harvard Business Review* (December).

Deloitte Consulting. 2005. Calling a change in the outsourcing market: The realities for the world's largest organizations. April. New York.

Friedman, T. 2005. *The World Is Flat: A Brief History of the Twenty-First Century*. New York: Farrar, Straus and Giroux.

Fung, V. F., W. K. Fung, and Y. Wind. 2008. *Competing in a Flat World*. Upper Saddle River, NJ: Wharton School Publishing.

Gattorna, J. 2006. Supply chains are the business. *Supply Chain Management Review* (September), 42-49.

Hafner, K. 2006. Growing Wikipedia revises its "anyone can edit" policy. *New York Times,* June 17. http://select.nytimes.com/search/restricted/article?res=FB0611F83A550C748DDD AF0894DE404482.

Hagel, J., and J. S. Brown. 2001. *The Only Sustainable Edge: Why Business Strategy Depends on Productive Friction and Dynamic Specialization.* Boston: Harvard Business School Press.

Hamel, G., and C. K. Prahalad. 1990. The core competence of the corporation. *Harvard Business Review* 68 (3, May-June 1990), 79-93.

Porter, M. 1985. *Competitive Advantage: Creating and Sustaining Superior Performance.* New York: Free Press.

UPS. 2003. UPS unveils a new look. March 25, UPS press release. www.underconsideration.com/speakup_v2/ups_media_kit.pdf.

18

Managing the Hyper-Networked "Instant Messaging" Generation in the Work Force

Eric K. Clemons
Steve Barnett
JoAnn Magdoff
Julia Clemons

Abstract

The instant messaging generation, wired and integrated into broad, flat networks almost from birth, will not function as their predecessors did when injected into the social networks that form their professional organizations. IM'ers are creating their own network styles and content, as well as their own informal, back-channel networks, different from those of their more senior coworkers, and more compatible with their personal styles and loyalties. If indeed their adoption of workplace communications norms differs from that of their predecessors, how will these individuals function differently as employees, and how will organizations need to adapt their training, their managerial styles, and their expectations of employees' motivations, performance, and loyalty to incorporate these new employees? After reviewing the literature on social networks, the authors explore a few prominent and visible trends that affect employers and employees: (1) changing communications technologies and their implication for social organization; (2) changing perception of fact, technique, and reality, and implications for authority and decision styles; and (3) outsourcing, downsizing, and the erosion of organizational loyalty. They then offer qualitative impressions, as well as insights from an online survey (of 80 respondents), and explore implications for managers and organizations.

The team responsible for this research is worth a short note:

Eric Clemons is trained as a computer scientist and operations research faculty member; for two decades he directed the Wharton School's research program in information, strategy, and economics, and he has long been at the forefront of the study of the intersection of information, economics, and corporate strategy.

Steve Barnett is an anthropologist who has held academic and business positions. He has taught at Princeton, Brown, MIT, and The Wharton School. He has published widely on consumer culture, business strategy, and modernization. Steve's PhD is from the University of Chicago.

JoAnn Magdoff has a PhD in Cultural Anthropology, augmenting her skills in observation, survey design, and data analysis. Currently, she is a psychotherapist in private practice: a Licensed Clinical Social Worker and a Marriage and Family Therapist.

Julia Clemons is an undergraduate at the University of Chicago with an interest in the social sciences, in particular the relationships between individual motivations and the functioning of groups and societies.

This generation of young employees is the first that has had access to personal computing and personal communications technologies since they began interacting with others. They are the iPod and iMac, e-mail and instant messaging, *blogger* and Second Life and Facebook generation. It is clear that these new workers are bringing a new sense of technology and networking with them, transforming the workplace itself. In this chapter, we explore some of the key trends driving these changes and some of the implications when MySpace meets the workplace.

Social Networks

The Internet has decisively altered the nature and significance of networks. Online networks enable highly visible and yet anonymous interactions. These networks allow experimentation, including the creation of *multiple selves* and rich fantasy lives (Second Life), rendered safe due to the *plausible deniability* that online interactions offer. Online interaction supports the creation of extended networks with an ease and speed not possible in the *"meat space"* world, without the restrictions imposed by geography or the need for face-to-face interaction. Users can create new content that, in turn, generates or reinforces networks (YouTube), and they can redefine ideas of self, other, friend, colleague, or acquaintance (such as MySpace, Facebook, Twitter, LinkedIn, Orkut).

Social network theory was unprepared for these developments. Early social theory from the end of the nineteenth century and the beginning of the twentieth century focused on "sequences," and the approach used by British "armchair" anthropologists tried to fit human societies into evolutionary straitjackets that were soon seen as facile, judgmental, and arbitrary accounts of how we got from there to here, for example, presuming roasting meats as primitive, and boiling meats as civilized. After World War II and into the early 1950s, social scientists began working on "structure," how societies were organized and how they worked day-to-day. Most of these structures were formal—kinship rules and behavior, political and religious systems, and so on. The key insight was that these structures were "functional"—they enabled social continuity. Arranged marriage, for example, facilitated the integration of separate farm lands by linking water supplies for two families, and a religious ritual reinforced social status and thus social stability by allowing high-status groups to participate first (Radcliffe-Brown 1952).

In the late 1950s through mid-1960s, "systems theory" added a more fluid dimension to structural-functionalism (Parsons 1964). This included how people moved through structures and how different subsystems (political, religious, kinship, and so on) fit into an overarching system, with subsystems together forming a whole society. But systems theory remained primarily static, emphasizing continuity and stability. Individuals were secondary; they fit into and moved through antecedent systems.

In the 1970s, the beginnings of a profound change in social theory occurred, shifting the primary focus from the organization to the individual. This allowed an emphasis on individual and organizational transitions and changes, rather than on rules and organizational stability (Barnes 1972). They suggested that systems and structures were secondary, built up from individuals negotiating positions in multiple networks that could and did change, usually more slowly than rapidly. This opened the way for analysis of motivations as well as other rationales for participating in networks—trust, need for information, comfort level, excitement, experimentation, and bonding (Macy and Skvoretz 1998). Mapping interactions and then combining these maps into an overall network became the research method of choice. These maps were then used to understand information flow in networks as well as how networks were organized.

Critical features of networks, elaborated by the shift to the individual and his or her relationships, to a great extent inform current network analysis. These features include the following:

- ***Center and periphery*** (Borgatti and Everett 1999)—Frequencies and types of interactions within a network were mapped, and individuals with the most frequent and most consequential interactions or nodes located at the center of a network; those with the least, at the periphery. This spatial mapping allowed the beginning of evaluating networks as complex and diverse rather than simple and uniform.

- *Significance*—Some interactions were viewed as critical to the ongoing viability of a network whereas others might be valued by the direct parties to the interaction but were not intrinsic to the network—for example, a critical interaction about whether to admit physicians to a mothers' network versus a short discussion about which baby teeth emerge first.

- *Key nodes*—Interactions with some nodes can significantly change, reinforce, or nullify a network's potential for instance, someone telling the boss what is said, presumably in confidence, in a peer network at work.

- *Overlaps*—Different networks can combine and work in tandem; for example, work and leisure networks can overlap with consequences in both arenas. Golf networks can include co-workers, clients (potential and actual), and friends apart from work (Alba and Kadushin 1996).

- *Fragility or stability*—Some networks are limited in time and scope, such as support networks around a specific campaign to raise money for Hurricane Katrina victims, whereas some can persist over long periods, such as networks of high-school and college friends.

- *Contractual or diffuse, enduring solidarity*—Some relationships are well-defined contractual-like interactions in which the parties understand precisely what is expected (such as a pickup game of playground basketball). On the other hand, other relationships are enduring but fuzzy interactions in which the parties realize that the interaction is part of an ongoing dialogue without specific objectives (such as relations within an extended family).

- *Hierarchical/egalitarian*—Who initiates and who sustains a network? Is it a central, dominant figure (or figures) or can it be anyone in the network? Networks can shift from one to the other—for example, a family network dealing with succession in a family business. Generational conflict may morph into resolution when egalitarian children participate as equals after a paternalistic father dies (if it does not devolve into a war of each against all).

Expanding the Idea of Networks

In the past 15 years or so, these network analysis methods have proved fruitful (Wasserman and Galaskiewicz 1994), but recently, real-world developments such as the emergence of Internet networks have required new strategies and concepts:

- ***Emergent networks*** (Strogatz 2003)—Building on complexity theory, networks can be understood as constantly changing entities that emerge in new incarnations from prior interactions, so that interactions do not simply define a network but also continuously create and reposition that network. Small online networks of younger people exchanging music has altered the music industry and created new networks (YouTube, for example) that can create "stars" based on egalitarian networks of listeners telling each other what they like without advertising or promotion and without control by industry professionals.

- ***Virtual networks***—These online networks are not face-to-face and so do not involve the whole "wetware" person. These can be more compelling in some cases than face-to-face networks; people with life-threatening illnesses are often more forthcoming in virtual networks where they don't have to fully identify themselves than they are in face-to-face exchanges.

- ***Multiple selves***—the Internet allows creating distinct selves or personas for use in different networks. These "avatars" can be a different gender, ethnicity, age, or personality from the individual creating the avatars. Using multiple selves across networks blurs the prior centrality of the "true self" in favor of "multiple selves" and opens networks to individual creativity and innovation (Magdoff and Rubin 2003).

We will look at these emerging forms of networks, for implications to network theory and for the ways IM'ers engage each other. In some instances, we can rely on existing theory (Cross and Parker 2004), but in others we will have to develop and expand on existing theory.

Paradoxes of Modern Networks

Our survey and other research on IM-generation networks have revealed several interesting paradoxes. Although the network is important, it is not "selfless." The individuals are not giving up their identities; in fact, they often use their networks to showcase their individual achievements. Second, although the self is important in networks, the definition of the self is more fluid, as people adopt multiple online avatars. This is not "traditional" characterization of self or group; rather, in these immersive networks, the individual can assert primacy in new ways and groups of individuals can link in new ways.

The Paradox of Individualism in Networks

Our survey found that, paradoxically, while networks and network participation is increasingly important, individuals are *not* subsuming their individuality within the group or subordinating their individual aspirations to the goals of the group. Persons in online networks want to claim individual credit for their contributions both within and outside the network and to gain recognition beyond the participants of the network itself. Networks become a means for validating self and for achieving recognition among a group that matters to the person. This is an emerging pattern of relating self to network that resonates with the IM generation. The paradox is clear from our survey: They want to be linked and at the same time they want individual credit. In a sense, Facebook does that by focusing on the minutia of a person's life while providing links to their networked friends.

IM'ers look up to peers who have achieved celebrity, can be emulated, and yet are potential rivals. They are resonating with iconic representations, which we call an "idealized me."

Panopticon Self: The Emergence of Multiple Selves

As noted above, the Internet allows users to create "avatars," distinct selves or personas for use in different networks. In some cases, the avatar may not even have a human referent (it could be an animal, a physical thing, or a totally constructed design). We have seen an "evolution" from self identity exemplified by a single lifestyle to multiple serial self identities expressed in diverse contexts. For example, an individual may be a trader at work, an iMac garage-band software composer at lunch, and a Second Life avatar at night. There is no compulsion to foreground any of these multiple selves. This range of personal expression has morphed into a kind of *panopticon self* wherein the self has a 360-degree view and fluidly adjusts his or her presentation according to the particular environment being faced, thriving on exposure. Network choice opens up a large potential for self-presentation, which can be rejiggered on the fly. The organizational challenge is to pay attention to and encourage both this new individualism and online networks.

This generation may have a different view of what is "real" and what is "self." The sense of self is transformed as people design multiple identities. They may know that muscled hulk is not who they are in everyday life, but it could be anchored in an ironic statement, culturally valued attributes, perception of an idealized self, and even their perception of their essential selves.

Trends Shaping Modern Networks

Three trends are shaping the contours of modern, online networks, and understanding these trends offers insights into how these networks might affect our social organizations.

Trend 1—Rewiring the Organization: Changing Communications Technologies

Changing communications technologies have an influence on social interactions, hierarchies, and behavior. Our online survey, for example, found that 30% of employees learn about company issues via the Internet through exchanges with peers, and not through interactions with their supervisors.

Technology has always influenced the structure of social organizations and of entire societies. In primitive societies, with primitive technologies, social groupings were small (Benkler 2007). As communications got faster, even if only via Roman roads and Incan runners, empires got larger.

The telephone made bilateral coordination easy and changed the effort required for planning; teenagers began to date more extensively in pairs or foursomes. Today, bilateral technologies such as the telephone and e-mail have been augmented, and in some age groups largely superseded, by multilateral network broadcast technologies. With today's new technologies, herding behaviors are once again replacing bilateral dating. Unlike previous herding, which involved *"hanging out"* at a limited collection of congregation points, modern herding is an emergent behavior, as exhibited by the following highly stylized observed sequence of interactions:

1. An instant message is sent out, saying, simply, *"Thursday?"*

2. Numerous responses arrive in no particular order, among which *"mall"* and *"movie/pirates"* predominate.

3. The choice of going to the mall wins, friends congregate at the mall, and they find each other using cellphones.

4. They change their minds and they try to see *Pirates of the Caribbean: At World's End* but can't get tickets.

5. Everyone ends up at Charlie's house.

What will such self-organizing behavior mean for organizations when these young people become the dominant force in the workplace?

The changing capability of available communications technology affects the nature of governance, trust, and of interaction. When the London Stock Exchange introduced screen-based trading in 1986, two centuries of tradition were obliterated (Clemons and Weber 1990). A culture of *dictum meum pactum* (my word is my bond) was replaced with exchanges like *"How could you do that to me?" "That wasn't you, that was your screen!"*

Bilateral technologies like the telephone and e-mail have been augmented, and in some age groups largely superseded, by multilateral network broadcast technologies. In our online survey, 30% of employees learn about company issues via the Internet through exchanges with peers, and not through interactions with their supervisors.

New technologies also change information access and authority. In traditional, bandwidth-constrained organizations, the individuals who were higher up in the hierarchy had superior access to numerous subordinates who provided them with a broad array of information sources. Likewise, individuals positioned higher in the organization were able to communicate orders back down to their numerous subordinates, direct reports, and those subordinate to their direct reports. Both served to underscore the power and authority of leaders.

Not surprisingly, in today's flatter and more universally connected social networks, both the need for explicit and formal hierarchies and the communications-based factors that legitimated them have been eroded. Survey respondents say that the only arena where those senior to them know more about work issues is "overall company problems," not job activities, peer working groups, strategies for respondent's responsibilities, nor areas for employee improvement.

Surely, this will affect workplace behavior, and management's ability to direct and influence employees, as we will explore in the final sections of the chapter.

Trend 2—Challenging Authority: Changing Perception of Reality

Today, online social networks give many people in the organization access to the same data, and this can erode the authority of leaders and affect decision making.

The prominence accorded to "scientific method" has helped determine the zeitgeist and mental paradigms of the times. Galileo, Newton, Gauss, and Descartes left the West with a fascination for logic, reason, observation, data, and analytic styles. Without a doubt it has been the dominant decision paradigm of bureaucrats and executives the world over—so much so that some have charged that we are overreliant on logic (Saul

1992). Today, however, access to data is more widespread and the logic used to determine "reality" is under fire. The authority of leaders based on the unquestioned acceptance of their superior information endowment has been undercut. Our survey indicates that respondents view senior managers as power-based (50%) rather than authority-based, suggesting that they do not have special knowledge or insight that our respondents need to acknowledge. Three developments are emblematic of the shift:

1. ***Younger employees have better access to information.*** The Internet provides ubiquitous access to information and to data. Survey respondents say, almost 4 to 1, that younger employees are more data-driven than older employees. This may be perception, but it reinforces younger employees' sense that they have better access to information, and continues the erosion of the perceived data monopoly previously enjoyed by senior levels of management.

2. ***Younger employees have better access to analytical tools.*** The personal computer in all its forms, spreadsheets, and other analytical tools have made working with data easy and personal. Significantly, 90% of survey respondents say that younger employees use the latest technologies while older employees do not, devaluing the advantage in informed understanding previously attributed to senior management.

3. ***Younger employees have less confidence in information provided by their companies.*** This shift is significant and measurable; 20% of younger employees in our survey say they believe the "company line" and corporate communiqués, versus 45% of older employees.

Preliminary survey analysis indicates provocative areas for further in-depth study. Younger employees identify themselves as more data-driven, wanting to take more personal credit than older employees. They are looking for results, not for process. Technology is a taken-for-granted part of their networking lives, both in and out of the office. Conversely, they assert that older employees are technologically challenged—slow to adapt if not outright Luddites.

Younger individuals also say their immediate superior leads with authority, not personal power. Yet moving up one level up, they reverse their position, saying their bosses' boss rules by personal power primarily, not authority. We think this indicates more about the way younger workers see the larger question of company legitimation than it reflects how senior management actually operates. If they believe authority stops with their direct boss, young workers are freed from the obligation to show fealty to the company. Loyalty thrives on authority, not so much under perceived raw power. This may also be related to the conflict between perception and reality: Although they believe that they enjoy superior access to information and to communications channels, and that this superior access makes them more effective employees than those above them, experience with their direct supervisor contradicts this. Lacking corresponding contact with those further above them, their comfortable and self-aggrandizing perceptions can persist without challenge.

We also note similar changes in the classroom, with diminished authority of the instructor, even if the instructor wrote the case under consideration and consulted with the CEO, the CIO, the CFO, and indeed the entire C-suite. The class will defend its own positions, and will not succumb to *rankism* (Fuller 2006) when reaching its assessment. Even the CEO's own comments during case discussions will not sway them. The class reaches its assessment, not based on deference to the CEO's rank, but based on group interactions as they occur, rather than a formally reasoned or repeatable and logical process. Perhaps the students participate more actively and perhaps they get more out of the discussions; invariably, on some occasions, they will reach incorrect decisions. Certainly it is a slower way to cover any subject.

Consensus is reached through a process of understanding and adopting the beliefs of the majority or of a vocal plurality rather than reason, and the most passionately articulated views will be given more credence. In brief, behavior is emergent rather than planned, the organizational equivalent of herding in a social setting. Action appears based on consensus and consent, rather than on obedience; decisions are followed, not because they are ordered but because they are individually accepted by members of the group.

Surely this will change workplace behavior, speed, performance, and loyalty, and management's ability to direct and influence employees. We explore both changes in behavior and changes in managerial capabilities in the final sections of the paper.

Trend 3—Eroding Loyalty: Group Participation to Advance Individual Goals

American workers no longer expect lifetime employment or lifetime loyalty from their companies, and they no longer offer that loyalty back to their employers. When we started teaching in the 1970s, we were amazed by students who selected an initial employer because of retirement benefits. We are equally surprised by the number of students who view their jobs today—any job, with any firm—as merely a starter job.

The difference is perhaps best characterized by books of two different eras, Whyte's classic *The Organization Man* (1956), and Coupland's humorous novel *Microserfs* (1996). Today, loyalty is not to employer, or even to coworkers merely because they are coworkers. Today, loyalty is to professional affiliations, class affiliations, or *"guild."* Alternatively, loyalty is to friends, and to coworkers because they have become friends. Again, *Microserfs* provides a great example.

We see one additional trend: the transition from group participation to achieve group goals, to group participation to advance individual goals. Work-based friendships and social networks are *instrumental* now, the instrumentality made easier by emerging technologies. The IM generation has goals that are determined by the rewards the organization can allocate. They work together to meet their goals, as long as the company continues to reward them. If rewards are withheld, employees leave. As important, if an individual needs to opt out of the group to advance his or her individual goals, the group understands placing individual goals first. One of our survey respondents described wanting to quit the online game World of Warcraft because it had become worse than a job; it was worse because he felt that he could leave his job, but could not abandon his "guild" in the middle of a quest.

Implications

These apparently diverse trends are connected, creating a portrait of the new worker that is strikingly different from the past. The idea of multiple selves suggests both the primacy of appearance and the relevance of instrumentality. This implies very limited organizational loyalty in the face of network-based loyalties and a flexible rationality that can be shaped to one's instrumental needs and desires. Given this logic, changing communications technologies are enablers of larger cultural shifts for the IM generation.

These changes lead to different cultures and structures. One example of this shift is the emergence of X-teams (Ancona and Bresman 2007), teams that function as creative, emergent networks within organizations and typically go outside the organization to add members with critical skills. X-teams, in this setting, with their focus on outreach beyond company employees, validate an outside-the-company orientation.

IM'ers on Battlefields and Bond Trading Floors

What are the implications of the IM generation on diverse organizations such as a Marine Rifle Company, a GM or Toyota assembly line, a software development team, or a Salomon bond trading desk? For each of these organizations, it is hard to imagine them functioning as well today as they have in the past without recognizing the values and behaviors of IM-generation employees.

The Marine Corps example is particularly striking. Marines have always functioned on the basis of strong loyalty to and close cooperation with fellow Marines. When Marine General Peter Pace was Chairman of the Joint Chiefs, he said that the courage to hang on during a firefight came from the desire to support your buddies to the left and right, rather than solely from any grand principle. He also said that the willingness to remain behind and hold an indefensible position if ordered to do so came from an understanding that your commanding officer would have done the same if ordered to do so and that he would not sacrifice you or your men without a good reason. The preoccupation with appearance is more consistent with Parolles in Shakespeare's *All's Well That Ends Well* than with Dan Daly's leading his fellow Marines at Belleau Woods shouting, *"Do you sons of bitches want to live forever?"* (Battle of Belleau Wood). Historically, Marine riflemen do not opt out for a better offer.

Clearly, small-unit Marine combat teams and Salomon bond traders represent two ends of the spectrum of organizations. Marines fight for their countries, for their units, and above all for their fellow Marines dug into foxholes on either side of them.[1] Respect among junior officers for their more senior officers is deep and pervasive, largely because junior officers know that their seniors have been through similar situations, have acted as they want their juniors to act despite personal risk, and have earned the right to give orders. Their training emphasizes teamwork and cooperation, and rapid action in achieving group goals, with these goals communicated tersely as *commander's intent* (Santamaria, Martino, and Clemons 2003). As long as authority and responsibility are earned, as long as senior officers earn their rank rather than being brought in from outside (clearly an absurdity), and as long as senior officers continue to serve without attempting to trade for better positions at competing military organizations (another absurdity), the IM generation will be incorporated into the Marines without difficulty. The use of the net for private data and private back-channel communications is unlikely to lead to Marines second-guessing their commanders, arranging mutinies, or *fragging* unpopular junior officers.

---

[1] Personal communication with Marine General Peter Pace, Chairman, Joint Chiefs of Staff, while he was addressing classes at the Wharton School.

In contrast, traders' behavior is seldom extremely cooperative. Incentives come largely from bonuses, and bonuses are largely based on individual behavior. Respect and power within the firm comes largely from perception of individual success and relationships with a small number of patrons. The limited importance of loyalty to the firm and to the best interests of the firm while pursuing individual success can be seen in the catastrophic behavior of rogue trader Nick Leeson at Barings and at Société Générale (Clark 2008). We expect that trends toward reliance on individual data and individual social networks, the diminished loyalty to the firm, and the diminished respect for senior officers will all continue, given the reward structure in these firms, the increased individual mobility between firms, and the perception that truly talented individuals can circumvent organizational oversight and control systems. The influx of IM'ers into these firms may proceed smoothly, or it may exacerbate problems with oversight, control, and ethical violations.

Interestingly, we suspect that the impact of video games also will be very different across the two organizations, and different from what is widely expected. Most video games are based on individual combat, requiring total self-reliance, speed of reflexes, and a minimum of thought or analysis. Behaviors have to become instantaneous and instinctive, and there is little time for communication or analysis. Social networking games, like World of Warcraft (www.worldofWarcraft.com) are probably exceptions. This behavior would be a disaster in a rifle company fighting house to house in urban counterinsurgency, where tight coordination, based on constant communication, and leading to rapid, flexible response, is essential. Surprisingly, and at first counterintuitively, individual-reaction shooter video games may represent better training for bond traders than for Marines.

Some Specific Recommendations

The problems that organizations face in integrating, motivating, and leading these new employees will be complex and wrenching. These problems will not occur because IM-generation employees are alienated, disaffected, or disloyal *loners;* they are tightly bound, but not to their employers' organizations. New employees have their own logic, their own reason, their own loyalty and affiliation, their own information sources, and their own decision processes. Their organizations ultimately will have to adapt.

Specifically, we see the following organizational adaptations as required to make the best use of new IM employees:

- *Manage down*—Let networks self-organize and evolve (exploit their emergent aspects), and then have the firm rely on the ones that are most productive. Encourage and sustain them, recognizing the compelling desire of the IM generation to get involved in networks. Learn to manage through Darwinian optimization, letting networks compete for ideas, implementation, and success, and letting success determine which networks will survive.[2]

- *Balance cooperation and competition*—IM-generation folks want to cooperate beyond and across companies and will do so, extending their networks and their loyalties across the boundaries of their firm. It will be interesting to see how this can be accomplished within a capitalist framework and within our current legal protections for trade secrets, patents, and copyrights; this may even suggest an evolution of business practices, laws, and regulation, much as the ubiquitous presence of photocopiers changed fair use rules on distribution of copyright material. Networks are not simply contractual but also affective and diffuse, and this can be valuable to a corporation as well. For example, if IM'ers indicate environmental concern, the organization might open possibilities for learning from relevant environmental actions of other organizations, including competitors, and perhaps becoming involved in joint programs. The networks developed during that process can be kept active for future cooperation.

- *Encourage peer networks* (Tapscott and Williams 2006)—Focusing on the egalitarian emphasis of IM-generation employees, this may perhaps entail allowing immediate supervisor involvement but not higher levels. Among IM'ers, peers trust each other (Stephenson 2006), and deeply distrust senior management. IM peer networking taps into a range of relational experiences, some of which resemble everyday life interactions, but which occur on the Internet rather than in the flesh. Conversations in cyberspace have an implicit dimension: dialogue between and among specific selves, which are one iteration among the several making up an individual's inventory of multiple selves. These interactions blend, experienced as a shared, consensual, group-generating emerging reality.

- *Recognize emergent leaders*—Leadership in a network may come from unexpected individuals, so managers should look at key nodes of interaction, including those that occur at the periphery, rather than making prior judgments about leadership capabilities. To a greater extent than ever before, networks will support self-organizing emergent behavior. The transformation of a potentially gifted employee into a corporate star may be enhanced by employers finding and celebrating those who are already functioning as an *"idealized me,"* functioning for

---

[2] Once again the university environment provides good leading indicators. Although the University of Pennsylvania, like most of its peers, maintained its own social networking Web site for incoming freshman to "meet" each other and to learn about campus from upper classman, it has not survived competition spontaneously arising from user communities on Facebook (Schutz 2007).

themselves and other network members as a desirable model that can be emulated. Network members will see this *"idealized me"* as a leader embodying a set of qualities that they themselves can eventually emulate. Senior management can observe and learn the personal qualities that the network admires and that also improve network output, but they cannot identify or assume these *"idealized me"* qualities in advance. Senior management can focus on qualities these young corporate role models and *"heroes"* demonstrate that can be encouraged and rewarded among the IM staff, rather than expecting the network to follow leaders that managers have picked to be groomed and promoted.

- ***Provide immediate rewards for network success***—IM'ers seem to require faster acknowledgment. The best way to validate useful activity is to reward success during the process. Don't wait until the task is finished.

- ***Encourage diverse voices***—Ensure the availability of alternative ways for loner "geniuses" to provide input, preventing networks from arriving at a banal middle ground. There is a real danger that rapid consensus building online, in the absence of serious analysis, can produce mundane group think as easily as we-are-smarter-than-me breakthroughs.[3] It is important to protect insightful employees who are uncomfortable in networks because these loners may have important insights that can be lost in the increasing reliance on online networks.

- ***Offer the latest technology***—Your network is competing against many alternatives for your employees' attention, and employees usually will migrate to the best technology. Hire the best personnel for tech support functions, respect privacy, and do not "spy" on network processes or spoof or "sock-puppet" to represent the views of senior management anonymously or *"pseudonononymously."* Remember that employees can easily abandon your corporate intranet for open, unprotected, external networks.

- ***Tap into external networks***—Be creative with network possibilities for your employees beyond company-created peer networks. A temporary employee agency and employee placement service is currently operating a "mini-me" company in Second Life, allowing their clients to meet with agency employees and with each other. This changes the placement firm's definition of client—previously the employers who use them to recruit staff, and now the employees themselves.

We are just beginning to see the impact of the IM generation in the workplace. Management will need to develop networks that exist or are potentially emergent in the workplace. Younger workers can then be more readily integrated, not only into their peer's network technology, but into larger company objectives as well.

---

[3] See Libert, Spector, Tapscott (2007) or Tapscott and Williams (2006) for treatment of the power and wisdom of networks in the popular press.

References

Alba, R. D., and C. Kadushin. 1996. The intersection of social circles: A new measure of social proximity. *Sociological Methods and Research* 5, 77-102.

Ancona, D., and H. Bresman. 2007. *X-teams: How to Build Teams That Lead, Innovate and Succeed.* Harvard Business School Press.

Barnes, J. A. 1972. Social networks. Addison-Wesley Module in Anthropology 26, 1-29.

Battle of Belleau Wood. http://en.wikipedia.org/wiki/Battle_for_Belleau_Wood.

Benkler, Y. 2007. *The Wealth of Networks.* Yale University Press.

Borgatti, S. P., and M. Everett. 1999. Models of core/periphery structures. *Social Networks* 21, 375-395.

Clark, N. 2008. French trader in custody. *The New York Times* (January 27). http://www.nytimes.com/2008/01/27/business/worldbusiness/27trader.html?_r=1& partner=rssnyt&emc=rss&oref=slogin.

Clemons, E. K., and B. W. Weber. 1990. London's big bang: A case study of information technology, competitive impact, and organizational change. *Journal of Management Information Systems* 6 (4, Spring).

Coupland, D. 1996. *Microserfs.* Harper Perennial.

Cross, R., and A. Parker. 2004. *The Hidden Power of Social Networks.* Harvard Business School Press.

Fuller, R. W. 2006. *All Rise: Somebodies, Nobodies, and the Politics of Dignity.* Berrett-Koehler Publishers.

Libert, B., J. Spector, and D. Tapscott. 2007. *We Are Smarter Than Me: How to Unleash the Power of Crowds in Your Business.* Wharton School Publishing.

Macy, M. W., and J. Skvoretz. 1998. The evolution of trust and cooperation between strangers. *American Sociological Review* 63, 638-660.

Magdoff, J., and J. Rubin. "Social and Psychological Uses of the Internet," Deciphering.

Parsons, T. 1964. *The Social System.* Free Press.

Radcliffe-Brown, A. R. 1952. *Structure and Function in Primitive Societies.* Free Press.

Santamaria, J., V. Martino, and E. K. Clemons. 2003. *The Marine Corps Way: Using Maneuver Warfare to Lead a Winning Organization.* McGraw-Hill.

Saul, J. R. 1992. *Voltaire's Bastards: The Dictatorship of Reason in the West.* Sinclair-Stevenson Ltd.

Schutz, J. 2007. Diverse freshman class meets on Facebook. *The Daily Pennsylvanian* (August 30). http://media.www.dailypennsylvanian.com/media/storage/paper882/news/2007/08/30/News/Diverse.Freshman.Class.Meets.On.Facebook-2942736.shtml.

Stephenson, K. 2006. *Quantum Theory of Trust: The Secret of Mapping and Managing Human Relationships.* Financial Times.

Strogatz, S. 2003. *Sync: The Emerging Science of Spontaneous Order.* Hyperion Books.

Tapscott, D., and A. D. Williams. 2006. *Wikinomics: How Mass Collaboration Changes Everything.* Portfolio, The Penguin Group.

Wasserman, S., and P. Galaskiewicz. 1994. *Advances in Social Network Analysis.* Sage Publications.

Whyte, W. H. 1956. *The Organization Man.* Simon and Schuster, Inc.

19

Missing the Forest for the Trees: Network-Based HR Strategies

Valery Yakubovich
Ryan Burg

Abstract

Although any manager would recognize the importance of "networking" in finding, developing, and retaining employees, human resource management traditionally has focused on individuals. In this chapter, Yakubovich and Burg point out that core HR processes such as recruitment and hiring, training and development, performance management, and retention all depend on networks. They consider the importance of weak ties in matching employees with jobs and "structural holes" in promoting creativity. They urge managers to make the shift from an atomized view to a network view of human resources—from focusing on the "trees" to understanding the "forest." They show that networks can boost efficiency and productivity by facilitating information sharing, attracting talent, and strengthening employees' commitment to the firm. But networks may also pose risks such as "lift-outs," in which a departing employee takes other workers in his or her network. The authors explore how managers need to understand the impact of networks and how to "manage" them.

In his book, *Seeing Like a State*, James C. Scott (1998) describes the emergence of scientific forestry in late eighteenth-century Prussia and Saxony. Initially, the resource managers were unable to measure the complexity of the old-growth forests they managed. Trees grew around each other, and their timber yield was unpredictable. Moreover, simply counting the trees available on a tract was beyond complex because their shapes were so inconsistent. In time, managers replaced these inconveniently complex forests with homogenous stands of meticulous rows that were easily counted—"legible," as Scott describes them. It was not until two generations later, when the trees became weak, diseased, slow growing, and prone to wind damage, that the forest managers realized their error and revisited the value of the ecology surrounding the trees. They learned to appreciate the complex interactions among the numerous species that help a forest to thrive.

The field of human resource management finds itself in a similar situation. HR managers risk missing the forest for the trees by being broadly individual-centered, treating employees as isolated bundles of talent, skill, and productivity. Even though increasingly common high-performance HR practices emphasize teamwork, the dominant activities of human resource managers, such as hiring, compensation, evaluation, and training, continue to target individuals. Even group-level data, such as peer review evaluations, are used for individual compensation and promotion decisions.

Research in HR reflects this reality. For decades, the field has been dominated by an organizational psychology focused on individuals as carriers of knowledge and skills that organizations can productively engage through appropriate job selection and job design procedures. Accordingly, the research has focused on developing tools that can accurately predict individuals' productivity before they are hired and facilitate the effective training, evaluation, and remuneration of workers once hired. The psychological paradigm in HR research continues to contribute to our understanding of organizations, but this individualist perspective cannot capture the variegated social connectedness experienced by employees. Instead, research tends to strip the interdependencies and ties to the outside world, both of which are critical to the performance of each employee and the performance of the firm as a whole.

In this chapter, we offer a network-based paradigm of human resource management, which translates directly into a firm's long-term performance. As individuals are carriers of *human capital* defined broadly as knowledge, skills, and personality traits, networks are carriers of *social capital* defined by structure and content of the relationships among individuals within and across a firm's boundaries. We argue that long-term performance rests on a firm's capability to expand its financial, human, and social capital through their synergetic interactions in the production process. While the expansion of financial capital, or profit making, is broadly recognized as the source of shareholder value, the need to expand human capital—that is, to develop and train employees—is hotly debated, and the expansion of social capital is barely on the agenda.

From an Atomized to a Network Approach to Human Resources

Business researchers and practitioners widely agree that education, skill, experience, and health are critical human resources, not just to the workers who possess them, but to employers, economies, and whole societies. Numerous studies document the impact of human capital, the umbrella concept for such resources, on workers' compensation and promotion (Becker 1964), companies' bottom line (Becker and Gerhart 1996; Fitz-enz 2000), and societies' GDP (Barro 1991). Yet these studies view human capital as an attribute of an individual and often the single human factor relevant to overall production.

A network approach expands the individualist account and the singular vision of how human capacity turns into economic productivity. As the first step, the network approach asserts that human capital is acquired and actualized through an intrinsically social process. Formal education is acquired in interactions with professors and other students, often supported by family, early childhood nurturing, and cultural predispositions (Coleman 1988). Informal education, in particular on-the-job training, takes place primarily in interactions with supervisors, mentors, and colleagues, who together compose the trainee's intrafirm network (Doeringer and Piore 1971). Human capital becomes productive only if it is invested in entrepreneurial and employment opportunities, which individuals often explore and exploit through their networks (Burt 1992). After all, what is a skill if it is not accessible to the organizational task or productive activity that seeks it out? Formal organizational hierarchies are reasonably effective in assigning and monitoring separable organizational tasks but need the help of informal networks in coordinating complex knowledge-based activities such as simultaneous engineering (Helper, MacDuffie, and Sabel 2000). As a productive asset, networks constitute *social capital* (Bourdieu 1980, Coleman 1988) whose effective acquisition and use require innovative human resource practices.

Managers have long understood that human resources reside in social relationships as much as they do in the hands and brains of individual workers. Managerial practices emerged to capitalize on such relationships, attracting the attention of academic economists and sociologists as early as the 1960s. For example, Rees (1966) noted that employers demonstrated strong preference for using informal networks in hiring, sometimes formalized through bonus packages for employees who referred new hires. It might seem like such recommendations would be narrow and nepotistic, but the reach of interpersonal networks stretches much further than one might casually imagine. In the 1970s, Granovetter ([1974] 1995) theorized how exactly interpersonal networks connect people with jobs.

Together with sociometric studies undertaken by anthropologists and social psychologists, and Milgram's (1967) small-world experiments, Granovetter's argument launched a sustained effort to thoroughly understand HR management implications of social networks, in particular, their role in channeling information and other assets that enhance the effectiveness of individuals and businesses, training, professional development, and strengthening employees' commitment to the firm (Collins and Clark 2003). In this chapter, we offer a general synthesis of these contributions, which provides insights on state-of-the-art practice in human resource management.

Recruitment and Hiring: The Power of Weak Ties

Formal institutions play a fairly minor role in matching workers and employers. Instead, Granovetter ([1974] 1995) found that workers' family, friends, and acquaintances were the primary source of job tips. Most surprisingly, weak ties played the primary role; about 83% of those who got their jobs through contacts used contacts that they saw *infrequently*. Granovetter developed the strength-of-weak-ties argument that suggests that weak ties (based on frequency of interaction, emotional intensity, and reciprocity) are reliable sources of nonredundant information about job opportunities (Granovetter 1973). Weak ties are more likely than strong ones to serve as bridges to new parts of a social universe (Granovetter 1973, [1974] 1995). This statement, widely known as the strength-of-weak-ties hypothesis, gave rise to a vast literature on the role of social networks in labor market processes and outcomes in the United States and other countries (Bian 1997; Boorman 1975; Bridges and Villemez 1986; Lin, Ensel, and Vaughn 1981; Mouw 2003; Wegener 1991; Yakubovich 2005).

Passive Recruitment

While the weak-ties argument was developed from an employee perspective, Manwaring (1984) used ethnographic research to examine the employer's perspective. One can think of a firm's pool of potential job candidates as being organized into three concentric circles, as illustrated in Figure 19-1. The inner circle is the internal labor market (ILM), comprising the firm's current workers who are almost always the first candidates considered for any vacancy (Doeringer and Piore 1971). The outer ring is the external labor market (ELM), which contains the people who have no affiliation with the firm either directly or through social ties. Finally, the area between is the extended internal labor market (EILM), usually defined as the social networks of the firm's current workers (Manwaring 1984).

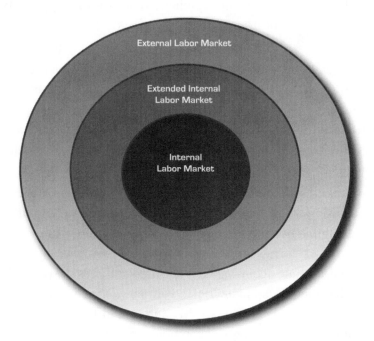

Figure 19-1   The labor market

In the absence of formal hiring policies, the triad ILM–EILM–ELM turns into a surprisingly robust hierarchy whereby positions are filled in the internal labor market first, the vacancies left become available in the EILM, and the external labor market remains the last resort. This hierarchy does not require deliberate strategic action by managers; the social network formed around the firm takes care of it (Granovetter 1995; Marsden and Gorman 2001; Yakubovich 2006). When managers pursue this course of inaction deliberately, this represents a *network strategy of passive recruitment*. It consists, for example, of the delayed broadcasting of new vacancies to give networks of present employees a head start, or avoiding the notification of certain agencies altogether even when the firm is obliged to do so (Manwaring 1984, 163). Sometimes, personnel departments maintain semiformalized waiting lists of the relatives and friends of their workers who are interested in being hired (Windolf 1986; Yakubovich and Kozina 2000).

The limited evidence available suggests that passive recruitment is common. In the 1980 Employer Opportunity Survey, 28% of respondents reported that they did not recruit for the position most recently filled (Barron, Bishop, and Dunkelberg 1985). In Marsden's (1996) study, about 15% to 20% of American employers said that they frequently rely on "direct approaches and unsolicited inquiries by applicants rather than making deliberate efforts to locate prospective workers" (Marsden and Gorman 2001, 472).

Because the search for workers carries high costs of information processing, employers do not strive to maximize the number of applicants but instead identify a few who meet the organization's basic criteria and are worthy of further in-depth investigation (Rees 1966, 561; Barber 1998, 30). The availability of preexisting personal and organizational ties allows employers to do so and therefore makes passive recruitment a prudent cost-saving strategy (Thurow 1975; Waldinger and Lichter 2003).

Passive recruitment is an unintended byproduct of the mere existence of social networks. It is an intrinsic part of social relationships for people to help others in finding jobs, but it brings tangible benefits: Hiring a referral is a "fringe benefit" to the referrer (Manwaring 1984, 168); referrals are at least marginally presocialized into the firm and, therefore, have an easier time acquiring tacit knowledge that is deeply embedded in the social context (Bailey and Waldinger 1991; Castilla 2005; Fernandez, Castilla, and Moore 2000; Manwaring 1984; Reichers 1987, Sutton and Louis 1987); social intermediaries broker information flows between employers and workers and, thereby, can improve matching (Fernandez, Castilla, and Moore 2000; Rees and Shultz 1970; Simon and Warner 1992); and last but not least, employers may benefit from the similarity in characteristics of referrers and referrals, if the former are considered to be good workers (Fernandez, Castilla, and Moore 2000; Rees and Shultz 1970).

With growing awareness of these advantages, employers increasingly adopt referral bonus programs that are supposed to motivate workers to mobilize their contacts for the benefit of the firm, paying a few hundred to thousands of dollars for referred workers who stay for a certain length of time. Dobbin (2007) finds that the number of companies offering referral incentives increased dramatically from single percentage points in 1971 to almost 60% in 2001. Such incentives are particularly effective in bringing in workers who otherwise are less likely to apply. In particular, they appear to help increase the presence of racial minorities in management positions, although referrals may reinforce homogeneity in other positions as workers refer new candidates who are like them.

Are the costs of referral bonus programs justified? Fernandez, Castilla, and Moore (2000) provide the only rigorous analysis in a study of hiring for entry-level positions at a call center of a large financial services institution. The company paid $10 for each referral interviewed and $250 for each referral who was hired and stayed on the job for 30 days. Researchers found that the company spent $416.43 less per hire on referrals than nonreferrals, or a 66% return on the $250 bonus. The savings resulted because a higher percentage of referrals than nonreferrals passed through the stages of the hiring process.

The increasing proliferation of formal referral bonus programs appears to contradict our overall contention that HR is still individually focused. Note, however, that social capital resides in relationships, in this case between a referrer and referral, while the typical referral program rewards one party, the referrer. Neckerman and Fernandez (2003) explain this by employers' interest in motivating referrers to act on their behalf rather than on behalf of referrals. Apparently, employers are not concerned about whether this might create tensions in the referrer's relationship with the referral. Instead of being an investment in employees' social capital, such an approach can deplete it. This suggests a larger point relevant to all the other HR activities we discuss in this chapter: Network-based incentives have to be a part of any network-based HR strategy.

Internet Recruiting

The rapid proliferation of Internet-based venues for matching workers and employers challenges the traditional role of social networks. Firms advertise jobs on their Web sites; workers post their resumes on their personal pages; "virtual" agencies and their "real" predecessors, which expand into cyberspace, do both. Kuhn and Skuterud (2004) find that already between 1998 and 2000 regular Internet job search grew from 6% to 9% in the population at large, from 7% to 11% for employed workers, and from 15% to 26% for unemployed job seekers. In 2004, about 22% of new hires found their jobs online (Stevenson, forthcoming).

Observers of this spurt of activity claim that the Internet opens new channels of communication between workers and firms and thereby reduces the problem of imperfect and asymmetric information pervasive in labor markets (Autor 2001). Do social networks lose prominence with labor markets' expansion into cyberspace? The evidence so far is limited. A 2002 Forrester Research survey, which provides the only longitudinal, albeit retrospective, data, shows that the percentage of jobs found online by the employed workers increased from 6% before October 2000 to 22% between April and September of 2004. At the same time, the percentage of jobs found through personal referrals decreased within the same period from 56% to 44%, while the shares of all the other popular channels, such as headhunters, temp agencies, and newspaper ads, remained the same (reported in Stevenson forthcoming). One can conclude that the Internet is chipping away at networks' share of the labor market.

Nevertheless, there are a few reasons to believe that referral systems are here to stay. First, even the 44% share is still very large and consistent with the findings from decades of research in a variety of economic and sociocultural contexts. Even virtual businesses keep hiring about half of their labor force through the grapevine (Yakubovich and Lup 2006). Second, the sheer numbers of job applications coming over the Internet may force employers to fall back onto personal referrals, unless they can utilize reliable data mining methods and perfect their ability to spot qualified candidates among "passive job seekers." Third, the Internet and networks are not completely independent channels, as some rest on the same social mechanisms that support referral systems. So-called social networking Web sites are hybrids of both. Networks such as Linkedin, which grew to 17 million members between 2002 and 2008, appeal to young professionals whose schooling and transient careers have taken them through several networks. These online networks also open the possibility for employer-initiated employment relationships and for the relatively inexpensive verification of resume claims through the display of peer contacts. Harnessing synergies between social networks and the Internet while preserving the authenticity and trust that characterize face-to-face social ties remains a major challenge for network-based recruitment strategies.

Training and Development

The network perspective points to the effectiveness of the on-the-job training that is a costless byproduct of social interactions in the process of production rather than purposeful investments in human capital (Doeringer and Piore 1971). Because knowledge and skills applicable across firms enhance workers' competitiveness in the external labor market, employers have a strong disincentive to provide them, unless workers share the costs through lower initial wages or make a long-term commitment to the firm. At the same time, employers happily invest in firm-specific human capital that binds workers to the firm. Taken together, these considerations give rise to internal labor markets that guarantee some return on general and firm-specific training to both parties (Becker 1964; Doeringer and Piore 1971).

While traditional in-house training programs have relied on professional coaches and instructors and followed a teacher-student model, companies such as GE and

Southwest Airlines have tapped into their social networks for formal training. They opened their own corporate universities whose teachers were recruited from various levels of the corporate hierarchy. This approach does not just benefit from preexisting ties and affiliations but creates new ones as a byproduct of training experiences shared by employees from disparate parts of an organization. Peer training at Southwest Airlines, for example, acknowledges the experience and expertise of senior employees, while reinforcing the company's distinctive culture and embedding it within a network of relationships. In contrast, formal training programs designed to build firmwide social capital can backfire. For example, Kalev, Dobbin, and Kelly (2007) document that popular diversity training programs are ineffective in promoting minorities to managerial positions. Formal antidiscrimination programs may even cause backlash that increases the prevalence of discriminatory behavior (Dobbin and Kelly 2007).

The choice between the atomistic and network perspectives on training becomes critical as internal markets weaken and the employment relationship becomes increasingly more open to competition (Cappelli 1999). Although the atomistic view of employees might lead companies to invest only in firm-specific training, the network perspective leaves the door open to reciprocity between employers and workers, in which the firm provides general training in exchange for the employee's commitment to the firm.

In addition to training, firms actively use mentoring to increase employees' human and social capital. Despite the long history of research and practice, we know little about the efficacy of mentoring relationships in general, and formal mentoring programs in particular. One vast literature on the topic looks at the effects of mentoring relationships on the advancement opportunities of women and racial minorities, a concern shared by many firms (Burke and McKeen 1990; Ibarra 1995; Thomas 1993). In the most comprehensive study, Dobbin (2007) finds that Asian men and women and Hispanic women are by far the main beneficiaries of formal mentoring programs in terms of the representation in managerial ranks. Burt (1998) finds that women are promoted earlier if they have a few relationships with well-connected high-status people rather than a large but less coherent network, which is more advantageous for men. Podolny and Baron (1997) argue that junior workers are better off establishing close relationships with more senior people with formal authority or informal influence in the same organizational unit.

Executive rotation is another popular tool for developing global executives by rotating promising managers through short or medium-term posts in foreign offices before eventually returning to a leadership position in the home office (Werther, Wachtel, and Veale,1995). A major obstacle to executive rotation, however, is the decay of an expatriate's ties to the headquarters. Proximity is the classic important factor in the establishment and maintenance of social ties (Festinger, Schachter, and Back 1950). Without regular face-to-face interactions with buy-in contacts in the headquarters, young managers stationed abroad may end up forgotten or passed over for promotion. The atomistic approach to executive rotation is blind to this problem. Our network-centered view calls for formal career development plans for expatriates that are assessed and revised on a regular basis jointly by functional and geographic supervisors, and opportunities for face-to-face interactions to keep these managers connected.

Performance Management: Creativity Versus Implementation

The effect of networks on worker performance depends in part on what type of performance is desired. Less dense networks may facilitate idea generation, whereas more dense networks may improve implementation.

Departing from Granovetter's strength-of-weak-ties argument, Burt (1992) argues that the concept of weak ties is a convenient proxy for a more fundamental mechanism, a "structural hole," defined as the absence of a tie between an individual's network contacts. When contacts in an individual's network are disconnected from each other, that person enjoys the benefits of diverse information that passes through him first and increased control over the interactions among disconnected contacts. In turn, the exposure to diverse ideas through sparse networks facilitates learning and creativity (Burt 2004).

Creativity and learning have little value, however, if the ideas generated are not implemented. Implementation tends to be driven by teams that need mutual trust and support, especially if the project outcome is uncertain, and therefore requires densely connected, rather than sparse, networks (Coleman 1988, see also Hansen 1999, Obstfeld 2005). Thus, managers face a trade-off between sparse networks fostering creativity and dense networks engendering trust. Left to their own devices, intraorganizational networks increase in density through ongoing task-driven interactions among employees within the organizational hierarchy and functional units. This does not mean, however, that the hierarchy and functional units have to be demolished, as they are often efficient in distributing information down the chain of command and controlling day-to-day operations (Dodds, Watts, and Sabel 2003). Instead, managers should facilitate interactions across the hierarchy and units on the individual level through job rotations and temporary project teams. On the organizational level, companies can reorganize their space or use company-wide events such as celebrations, retreats, and fairs to bring together people from different functional units and levels of the hierarchy. Managers also build crosscutting ties through the practices of "walk-around" management (Kotter 1982) and 360-degree performance evaluations. The latter reinforces collaboration and reciprocity because the peer who today asks for help may tomorrow be an evaluator. Some firms, for example McKinsey & Company, equip employees with a variety of tools, such as computer databases and yellow pages to facilitate the identification of a colleague outside their unit having the experience in a desired country or industry. McKinsey employees are expected to respond quickly to requests for information, which helps counter the formation of silos and cliques. In the context of globalization, Galbraith (2006) describes Nestlé's dealings with global corporate customers like Wal-Mart, Tesco, and Carrefour. The Nestlé account managers responsible for such customers in individual countries forge relationships and share ideas and experiences at annual sales meetings and maintain regular contact remotely.

Summarizing such experiences, some organization scholars promote "collaborative communities," which formalize collaboration, learning, and knowledge sharing, as a step beyond traditional informal networks (Heckscher and Adler 2006). While undertaking such projects, it is important to keep in mind that managers can nurture collaborative communities but cannot build them. Too forceful formalization may generate networks void of trust and reciprocity, the key ingredients that make networks so effective in the first place.

Retention

New hires with social connections to employees within the firm have increased organizational commitment, an attitude related to job satisfaction (Morrison 2002; Roberts and O'Reilly 1979). Hiring employees who already have a place in the firm's social fabric may make them more likely to stay, contribute, and play the role of good organizational citizens, standard correlates of job satisfaction (Organ and Ryan 1995).

Strong networks are a double-edged sword, however, when it comes to retaining employees. Turnover is a major problem for many organizations, and it is likely to get worse as companies continue "rewriting" their psychological contracts with workers, replacing a promise of long-term employment with an open market-driven relationship

(Cappelli 1999). In searching for solutions, managers increasingly rely on intraorganizational networks. Even if workers are no longer committed to the company, the argument goes, they maintain their commitment to fellow workers and, therefore, stay with the firm (Cappelli 2000).

On the other hand, departing workers often take their contacts with them. Research shows that "network turnover" is a byproduct of hiring through referrals discussed earlier. In the study of the call center at a retail bank introduced previously, Fernandez, Castilla, and Moore (2000) find no significant difference in overall turnover between referrals and nonreferrals in general. They found, however, that referrals whose referrers stay are the least likely to leave the firm, whereas referrals whose referrers leave are undistinguishable from nonreferrals. Practical measures to minimize such turnover, and related replacement costs, include giving preference to referrals from long-term employees, restructuring the payment of the referral bonus, or using strategies to increase frequent referrers' commitment to the firm (Fernandez, Castilla, and Moore 2000).

The damage to a firm is most dramatic when not just individual employees but networks head for the door. Groysberg and Abrahams (2006) analyze so-called "lift-outs," the high-risk, high-reward strategy of luring away a competitor's whole team as a substitute for a merger or an acquisition. The practice runs counter to the common wisdom that effective intraorganizational networks are a sustainable competitive advantage because they are embedded within a firm's culture and, therefore, are relatively immobile (Lengnick-Hall and Lengnick-Hall 2003). If the practice proliferates, firms might become reluctant to encourage self-managed teams or facilitate ties among their employees, particularly when a team's departure threatens the firm's human capital or intellectual property (Almeida and Kogut 1999).

Conclusions

These considerations take us full circle back to the argument that opened this chapter. The field of human resources is focused on individual actors, when networks play a central role. The main implications for strategic HR are clear: Networks vital to a firm's survival do not emerge overnight but take shape in routine interactions over time. As humans maintain fitness when they exercise regularly, firms maintain efficient and robust organizational structures when they create opportunities for meaningful everyday interactions across functional silos.

While barely noticeable under normal circumstances, such structures makes a critical difference in extreme situations, as the terrorist attacks of September 11, 2001, in New York City, illustrate in a tragic but persuasive way. Beunza and Stark (2003) carried out an ethnographic study of the trading room of an investment bank in the World Trade Center in the months preceding the attack. The evening following the attack, the management team developed a plan to resume operations within three weeks to three months, but was surprised when the trading room became fully operational within six days. The researchers found that strong lateral personal ties in the trading room drastically increased the robustness of the organization, which accelerated its adaptation.

Instead of simply looking at the organization as a set of positions to fill, managers might see it as a set of relationships among employees and between the employees and external stakeholders. HR practitioners need to develop and fine-tune network-based strategies to adapt to and benefit from open employment relationships, Internet-based information technologies, and global business environments. As networks are strategically reconstructed and formalized in the process, it is critical that the intrinsic motivation and spontaneity of informal networks be preserved. In so doing, managers will sustain the social structure of their organizations and gain access to important new opportunities.

References

Almeida, P., and B. Kogut. 1999. Localization of knowledge and the mobility of engineers in regional networks. *Management Science* 45, 905-917.

Autor, David. 2001. Wiring the labor market. *Journal of Economic Perspectives* 15 (1), 25-40.

Bailey, Thomas, and Roger Waldinger. 1991. Primary, secondary, and enclave labor markets: A training system approach. *American Sociological Review* 56 (4), 432-445.

Barber, Alison E. 1998. *Recruiting Employees. Individual and Organizational Perspectives*. CA: Sage Publications.

Barro, Robert J. 1991. Economic growth in a cross section of countries. *The Quarterly Journal of Economics* 106, 407-443.

Barron, John M., John Bishop, and William C. Dunkelberg. 1985. Employer search: The interviewing and hiring of new employees. *Review of Economics and Statistics* 67 (1), 43-52.

Becker, Brian, and Barry Gerhart. 1996. The impact of human resource management on organizational performance: Progress and prospects. *The Academy of Management Journal* 39, 779-801.

Becker, Garry S. 1964. *Human Capital: A Theoretical and Empirical Analysis, with Special Reference to Education.* Chicago, IL: University of Chicago Press.

Beunza, Daniel, and David Stark. 2003. The organization of responsiveness: Innovation and recovery in the trading rooms of lower Manhattan. *Socio-Economic Review* 1, 135-164.

Bian, Yanjie. 1997. Indirect ties, network bridges, and job search in China. *American Sociological Review* 62 (3), 366-385.

Boorman, Scott A. 1975. A combinatorial optimization model for transmission of job information through contact networks. *The Bell Journal of Economics* 6 (1), 216-249.

Bourdieu, Pierre. 1980. Le capital social. Notes provisoires. *Actes de la Recherche en Sciences Sociales* 31, 2-3.

Bridges, William P., and Wayne J. Villemez. 1986. Informal hiring and income in the labor market. *American Sociological Review* 51, 574-582.

Burke, Ronald J., and Carol A. McKeen. 1990. Mentoring in organizations: Implications for women. *Journal of Business Ethics* 9 (4-5), 317-332.

Burt, Ronald. 1992. *Structural Holes: The Social Structure of Competition.* Cambridge, MA: Harvard University Press.

Burt, Ronald. 1998. The gender of social capital. *Rationality and Society* 10 (1), 5-46.

Burt, Ronald. 2004. Structural holes and new ideas. *American Journal of Sociology* 110, 349-399.

Cappelli, Peter. 1999. *The New Deal at Work: Managing the Market-Driven Workforce.* Harvard Business School Press.

Cappelli, Peter. 2000. A market-driven approach to retaining talent. *Harvard Business Review* (January-February), 103-111.

Castilla, Emilio J. 2005. Social networks and employee performance in a call center. *American Journal of Sociology* 110 (5), 1243-1283.

Coleman, James S. 1988. Social capital in the creation of human capital. *American Journal of Sociology* 94, S95-S120.

Collins, Christopher J., and Kevin D. Clark. 2003. Strategic human resource practices, top management team social networks, and firm performance: The role of human resource practices in creating organizational competitive advantage. *Academy of Management Journal* 46 (6), 740-751.

Dobbin, Frank. 2007. Best practices or best guesses: Which corporate diversity programs work. Paper presented at the conference "Excellence Empowered by a Diverse Workforce," September 26, in Arlington, VA.

Dobbin, Frank, and Erin L. Kelly. 2007. How to stop harassment: Professional construction of legal compliance in organizations. *American Journal of Sociology* 112, 1203-1243.

Dodds, Peter S., Duncan J. Watts, and Charles F. Sabel. 2003. Information exchange and the robustness of organizational networks. *PNAS* 100 (21), 12516-12521.

Doeringer, Peter B., and Michael J. Piore. 1971. *Internal Labor Markets and Manpower Analysis.* Lexington, MA: Health Lexington Books.

Fernandez, Roberto M., Emilio Castilla, and Paul Moore. 2000. Social capital at work: Networks and employment at a phone center. *American Journal of Sociology* 105 (5), 1288-1356.

Festinger, Leon, Stanley Schachter, and Kurt Back. 1950. *Social pressures in informal groups.* Stanford, CA: Stanford University Press.

Fitz-enz, Jac. 2000. *The ROI of Human Capital: Measuring the Economic Value of Employee Performance.* New York, NY: AMACOM.

Galbraith, Jay R. 2006. Mastering the law of requisite variety with differentiated networks. In *The Firm as a Collaborative Community. Reconstructing Trust in the Knowledge Economy,* ed. C. Heckscher and P. S. Adler, 179-197. Oxford, UK: Oxford University Press.

Granovetter, Mark. 1973. The strength of weak ties. *American Journal of Sociology* 78 (6), 1360-1380.

Granovetter, Mark. 1995. Afterword. *Getting a Job: A Study of Contacts and Careers.* 2nd ed. Cambridge, MA: Harvard University Press.

Granovetter, Mark. [1974] 1995. *Getting a Job: A Study of Contacts and Careers.* 2nd ed. Cambridge, MA: Harvard University Press.

Groysberg, Boris and Robin Abrahams. 2006. "Lift Outs: How to Acquire a High-Functioning Team." *Harvard Business Review* 84(12): 133-140.

Hansen, Morten T. 1999. The search-transfer problem: The role of weak ties in sharing knowledge across organization subunits. *Administrative Science Quarterly* 46, 1-28.

Heckscher, Charles, and Paul S. Adler. 2006. *The Firm as a Collaborative Community.* Oxford, UK: Oxford University Press.

Helper, Susan, John Paul MacDuffie, and Charles Sabel. 2000. Pragmatic collaborations: Advancing knowledge while controlling opportunism. *Industrial and Corporate Change* 9 (3), 443-488.

Ibarra, Herminia. 1995. Race, opportunity, and diversity of social circles in managerial networks. *Academy of Management Journal* 38, 673-701.

Kalev, Alexandra, Frank Dobbin, Erin Kelly. 2006. "Best Practices or Best Guesses? Assessing the Efficacy of Corporate Affirmative Action and Diversity Policies." *American Sociological Review*, 71(4): 589-617.

Kotter, John P. 1982. What effective general managers really do. *Harvard Business Review* 60, 156-167.

Kuhn, Peter, and Mikal Skuterud. 2004. Internet job search and unemployment durations. *American Economic Review* 94 (1), 218-232.

Lengnick-Hall, Mark and Cynthia Lengnick-Hall. 2003. "HR's Role in Building Relationship Networks." *Academy of Management Executive* 17(4): 53-63.

Lin, Nan, Walter M. Ensel, and John C. Vaughn. 1981. Social resources and strength of ties: Structural factors in occupational status attainment. *American Sociological Review* 46, 393-405.

Manwaring, Tony. 1984. The extended internal labour market. *Cambridge Journal of Economics* 8 (2), 161-187.

Marsden, Peter V. 1996. The staffing process. In *Organizations in America: Analyzing Their Structure and Human Resource Practices*, Arne L. Kalleberg, David Knoke, Peter V. Marsden, and Joe L. Spaeth, 133-156. Thousand Oaks, CA: Sage Publications.

Marsden, Peter V., and Elizabeth H. Gorman. 2001. Social networks, job changes, and recruitment. In *Sourcebook of Labor Markets: Evolving Structures and Processes*, ed. Ivar Berg and Arne L. Kalleberg, 467-502. New York: Kluwer Academic/Plenum Publishers.

Milgram, Stanley. 1967. The Small World Problem. *Psychology Today* 2, 60-67.

Morrison, Elizabeth Wolfe. 2002. Newcomers' relationships: The role of social network ties during socialization. *Academy of Management Journal* 45 (6), 1149-1160.

Mouw, Ted. 2003. Social capital and finding a job: Do contacts matter? *American Sociological Review* 68 (6), 868-898.

Neckerman, Kathryn M., and Roberto M. Fernandez. 2003. Keeping a job: Network hiring and turnover in a retail bank. *The Governance of Relations in Markets and Organizations. Research in the Sociology of Organizations* 20, 299-318.

Obstfeld, David. 2005. Social networks, the tertius jungens orientation, and involvement in innovation. *Administrative Science Quarterly* 50, 100-130.

Organ, Dennis W., and Katherine Ryan. 1995. A meta-analytic review of attitudinal and dispositional predictors of organizational citizenship behavior. *Personnel Psychology* 48 (4), 775-802.

Reichers, Arnon E. 1987. "An Interactionist Perspective on Newcomer Socialization Rates." *Academy of Management Review*, 12(2): 278-287.

Sutton, Robert I. and Maryl Reis Louis. 1987. "How Selecting and Socializing Newcomers Influence Insiders." *Human Resources Management*, 26: 347-361.

Podolny, Joel M., and James N. Barron. 1997. Resources and relationships: Social networks and mobility in the workplace. *American Sociological Review* 62 (5), 673-693.

Rees, Albert. 1966. Information networks in labor markets. *American Economic Review* 56 (1/2), 559-566.

Rees, Albert, and George P. Shultz. 1970. *Workers and Wages in an Urban Labor Market*. Chicago, IL: University of Chicago Press.

Roberts, Karlene H., and Charles A. O'Reilly III. 1979. Some correlates of communication roles in organizations. *Academy of Management Journal* 22 (1), 42-57.

Scott, James C. 1998. *Seeing Like a State: How Certain Schemes to Improve the Human Condition Have Failed.* Yale University Press.

Shaw, Jason D., Michelle K. Duffy, Jonathan L. Johnson, and Daniel E. Lockhart. 2005. Turnover, social capital losses, and performance. *Academy of Management Journal* 48 (4), 594-606.

Simon, Curtis J., and John T. Warner. 1992. Matchmaker, matchmaker: The effect of old boy networks on job match quality, earnings, and tenure. *Journal of Labor Economics* 10 (3), 306-329.

Stevenson, Betsey. Forthcoming. "The Internet and Job Search," In David Autor, ed., *Labor Market Intermediation*. University of Chicago Press.

Thomas, David A. 1993. Racial dynamics in cross-race developmental relationships. *Administrative Science Quarterly* 38, 169-194.

Thurow, Lester. 1975. *Generating Inequality.* New York: Basic.

Waldinger, Roger, and Michael I. Lichter. 2003. *How the Other Half Works.* Berkeley, CA: University of California Press.

Wegener, Bernd. 1991. Job mobility and social ties: Social resources, prior job, and status attainment. *American Sociological Review* 56, 60-71.

Werther, William B., Jeffery M. Wachtel, and David J. Veale. 1995. Global deployment of executive talent. *Human Resource Planning* 18.

Windolf, Paul. 1986. Recruitment, selection, and internal labour markets in Britain and Germany. *Organization Studies* 7 (3), 235-254.

Yakubovich, Valery. 2005. Weak ties, information, and influence: How workers find jobs in a local Russian labor market. *American Sociological Review* 70 (3), 408-421.

Yakubovich, Valery. 2006. Passive recruitment in the Russian urban labor market. *Work and Occupations* 33 (3), 307-334.

Yakubovich, Valery, and Irina Kozina. 2000. The changing significance of ties. An exploration of hiring channels in the Russian transitional labor market. *International Sociology* 15 (3), 479-500.

Yakubovich, Valery, and Daniela Lup. 2006. Stages of the recruitment process and the referrer's performance effect. *Organization Science* 17 (6), 710-723.

Relating Well: Building Capabilities for Sustaining Alliance Networks

Prashant Kale
Harbir Singh
John Bell

Abstract

In an environment of rapid and discontinuous change, managers have turned to alliances to access the resources they need. But research on alliances shows that more than half of them fail, demonstrating the difficulty of managing these relationships. In this chapter, the authors explore the relational capabilities needed for building and managing successful alliances, based on their extensive research on alliances. Using the case of Royal Philips, they explore the role of strategy, structure, systems, people, and culture in alliance success. They also discuss the need for ongoing adaptation and renewal of relational capabilities as the business and its environment change.

To meet pressures from globalization and changes in technology and regulation, firms are reaching out to networks to access complementary capabilities. Companies in many industries, such as telecommunications, biotechnology, specialty chemicals, and computer software development, are significantly interconnected among themselves, creating networks of firms with large numbers of direct and indirect ties between them. Each tie between firms can be seen as an alliance. While these ties represent a substantial opportunity to access resources and knowledge of trading partners, research on alliances has shown that the average success rate of such relationships is under 50%. The limited success of such relationships has prompted interest in the factors that may drive higher levels of success in interfirm relationships.

Some of the factors driving poorer performance in alliances include opportunism on the part of a partner, environmental uncertainty surrounding the alliance relationship, and conflict at the interface of the firms involved. Opportunism on the part of one or both partners has led some authors to view alliances as "learning races" in which a higher rate of learning from an alliance can serve as a method of addressing the risk of inadvertent leakage of critically important knowledge to the other partner (beyond what may have been contractually committed). Such arguments have been presented more as an approach to an alliance or network tie rather than the creation of a specific capability to manage the relationship (Hamel 1991; Khanna, Gulati, and Nohria 1998). Other research has pointed to contractual provisions as vehicles to address opportunism in such relationships. More recently, there has been a growing interest in factors leading to higher levels of trust in alliances (Zaheer, McEvily and Perrone 1998). This work makes the distinction between personal trust between representatives of the firms, and trust that can be imputed to the firms involved. There has been subsequent work identifying the conditions under which trust develops in the alliance relationship. Recent work has begun to point to systematic factors driving differences between firms in their success rates of alliances, controlling for factors related to the industry and the firm (Anand and Khanna 2000).

In light of the growing importance of alliances, on the one hand, and the difficulties in managing them, on the other, a capability to manage alliances could become a vital source of competitive advantage. With a well-developed, organization-wide capability to manage alliances, firms could have alliance success rates that are far above the ordinary and derive greater value from them. So, managers realize that having alliance capability is important—they also perhaps recognize that they can "engineer" the development of such a capability in their organization. Yet surprisingly, most firms still have relatively low success rates with alliances, implying that they do not have world-class alliance capabilities.

Firms typically do not invest sufficient time and effort in building their alliance capabilities. First, managers are usually accountable for the short- to medium-term financial performance of their business unit or company, and although alliances have significant impact on the long-term capabilities and competitiveness of their business or company, the direct impact of alliances on near-term financial performance is less discernible. Hence, senior managers may invest less effort in building alliance capability. Second, most firms also simply do not have metrics to assess the performance of their alliances. According to one study, just 30% of firms that create alliances have well-developed measures to evaluate their performance. And what firms do not measure, managers pay less attention to, at least in the near-term. Third, even if managers do invest time and attention in this effort, they simply lack a clear understanding of how to build these capabilities. As a result, they fail to address each of the key decision-points that might be critical to successful development of relational capability.

During the past few years, we have done extensive work to study the development of alliance capabilities in firms. This includes in-depth fieldwork with some Fortune 1000 firms, as well as surveys and archival research with more than 200 firms in which alliances are critical to firms' strategies. Our work shows that alliance capability doesn't merely arise by doing more alliances—in other words, it is not a product of just tacit "learning by doing." Instead it rests on a company's ability to proactively address critical decisions related to strategy, structure, systems, people, and culture. Many firms work on just some of these dimensions but not all, and given that these are tightly integrated with each other, firms end up having alliance capabilities that are far from well developed.

In this chapter, we examine how Royal Philips, one of the leading healthcare and appliance firms in the world, became a more "alliance-capable" organization. This discussion highlights some of the most critical decision-points with respect to the strategy, structure, systems, people, and cultural aspects of building relational capability. By focusing on how one company (Royal Philips) has built up its alliance capabilities, we are able to gain in-depth lessons that can be applied by managers of other firms in designing the strategy, structure, systems, people, and cultural dimensions of relational capability. Wherever relevant, we also supplement our explanation with analysis and information from two other sources: large sample research to examine the relational capability practices in more than 200 firms, and accounts of other firms, such as Eli Lilly and Cisco, that have successfully embarked on a similar journey. Eventually, any company that desires to have relational capability will have to traverse its own idiosyncratic path toward this end. But we feel that even in such a situation, there are some key principles or decision-points that every company must uniformly address (albeit in its own way); and our account of Philips, along with our supplementary analysis of other data, provides a clear insight into what they are and how firms might think about them. At the same time, Philips's own journey in building relational capability should be seen as work in progress, as its own strategy evolves and new structural or process challenges arise in its endeavor. Any company that hopes to have relational capability needs to appreciate that competence is never fully attained; it merely provides a basis for an even higher standard to be achieved in the future.

The Key Decision-Points in Creating Relational Capability: The Philips Story

In 2000, recognizing the growing importance of strategic alliances to its growth and competitive advantage, Philips decided to adopt a more proactive and systematic approach to managing alliances and building alliance capabilities. Some of its actions to build relational capability were deliberate and well thought out; in other cases, things happened by chance and their benefits were incidental or realized in hindsight. The company started with the establishment of a dedicated team to oversee its main corporate partners. Over the years, these actions to build Philips's alliance capability have been discussed, tested, debated, and refined within the company, involving individuals at all levels, including operational-level managers as well as the CEO and the Board of Management. After six years of hard work and trial and error, the company sees itself as being much more competent in forming and managing alliances. Over this period, Philips has established more than 30 alliances with firms from a variety of industries (fast-moving consumer goods, telecommunications, IT, pharmaceuticals, content, and so on). The margins from alliances in one of the divisions have increased from 10% to almost 20% in the past five years. Furthermore, the alliances with firms such as Sara Lee, InBev, Schering, Skype, and Nike have enabled Philips to successfully create new product categories to fuel its growth in the market.

In this section, we highlight some of the key decision-points in the context of Philips's efforts to build alliance capability (as illustrated in Figure 20-1).

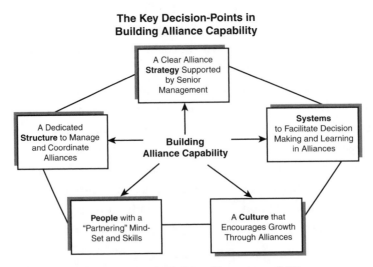

Figure 20-1   The key decision-points in building alliance capability

Strategy—*To build relational capability, senior managers of the company should explicitly "recognize the importance of alliances" to their company and "articulate a clear alliance strategy" to guide their partnering activity.*

In the late 1990s, Philips was struggling to retain its competitive position in various businesses. Recognizing the limitations of its traditional "go it alone" approach in business, the company viewed alliances as an important part of its transformation process. Alliances could help to develop new technologies more rapidly, enhance its cost competitiveness by outsourcing activities, create more innovative products by acquiring consumer insights from firms in completely different industries, establish technology standards in newly emerging industries, and de-risk the ever-shortening product life cycle by consolidating the industry. At the same time, the Philips management also realized that it had multidimensional relationships with certain firms that accounted for a significant part of its business. For instance, firms like Dell, Nokia, and Sony not only bought large numbers of products and services from Philips, but also supplied Philips many of their own products/services, collaborated with Philips in certain technology areas, and even competed with Philips in some product-markets. Traditionally, different units in the company had independently managed the different touch points with these firms. But Philips felt that given the multidimensional nature of these relationships, it might be worthwhile to view them as "partners" and have a more coordinated approach in dealing with them.

Philips' senior management articulated a clear alliance strategy to guide their actions, designating their multidimensional relationships with key players as "corporate alliances" and setting a goal to double their business with these partners in the next five years. Philips's leaders also recognized the need to plan and manage these relationships in a coordinated fashion at the highest levels in the organization, including the CEO and the Board of Management. In addition to these "corporate alliances" across multiple businesses, individual Philips divisions engaged in more narrow "strategic alliances" to meet some of the objectives mentioned earlier (new technology development, manufacturing-outsourcing, and so on). The company also took a more proactive role in forming, managing, and overseeing these alliances. Thus senior management viewed corporate and strategic alliances as a critical part of their strategy going forward, and they visibly exhibited their personal commitment, support, and involvement in developing and articulating the company's alliance strategy.

Structure—*Firms need to create a "dedicated and/or separate management structure" to oversee and support their alliance activity, and adapt the setup and responsibility of this team to meet its evolving partnering needs and priorities.*

Philips set up a separate Corporate Alliance Office to coordinate and oversee its alliance activity. In the beginning, the team's primary role was to manage and coordinate its partnerships with the top 10 corporate partners that accounted for almost 20% of the company's B2B business. The team reported to the company's Head of Strategy, who in turn reported to the CEO. This structure ensured that alliances were seen as being strategically important to the company, and they received close and direct attention of senior management.

Philips changed the structure of the Corporate Alliance Office over time to reflect its changing priorities. After setting up processes and practices to coordinate relationships with corporate alliance partners more effectively, the company realized that "go-to-market alliances" to develop new product categories were critical to the company's divisions going forward. Thus, around this time, managers decided that the Corporate Alliance Office should report to the chief marketing officer, who coordinated marketing and new product development efforts across all divisions and directly reported to the CEO. After this task was accomplished, a Management Board Member who oversaw all the geographical regions and countries became responsible for the Corporate Alliance Office—at this time the Alliance Office was entrusted with coordinating efforts to create alliances and relational capability in Philips businesses spread across different countries. In each case, alliance activity continued to receive the attention and support of the top management in the company.

The role of the Corporate Alliance Office has also evolved over time. In the first two years, the team focused mainly on directly managing its relationships with key corporate partners to leverage synergies across multiple initiatives with those partners. But over time, the office moved from being a center of expertise on alliance management to become a catalyst for developing, spreading, and institutionalizing alliance management skills and processes throughout the organization. As a part of this change, the Corporate Alliance office played a lead role in implementing systematic processes to guide alliance management decisions and actions in the company, and learn and accumulate alliance management know-how to help improve the alliance skills of individual managers involved in doing alliances.

Systems—*Firms with relational capability have excellent "systems and processes" to implement alliances and to develop and institutionalize alliance management competencies.*

Through the Corporate Alliance Office, Philips has established a clear "alliance process" that all divisions and businesses need to follow whenever they form any new alliances. The purpose of the process is to ensure that managers doing an alliance follow best practices in managing each step of the "alliance life cycle": making the alliance business case, selecting the alliance partner, negotiating the alliance, and so forth. It has taken the company several years to gain acceptance for this process, and the support of the senior management and the Management Board was critical.

To ensure success with each phase of the alliance life cycle, the Corporate Alliance Office has created tools that individual managers can use to analyze and make decisions at each step. For this purpose, the company has tools for partner selection, partner due diligence, and doing an alliance health check, and to assist with other phases. These tools ensure that managers engage in systematic analysis and debate in making decisions at any stage of the alliance. The company has also set up systems to capture learning from its prior and ongoing alliance initiatives and experiences, and to internally disseminate that learning to managers. For instance, Philips holds an Alliance Managers Meeting every quarter wherein managers from different alliances get together to share the difficulties and challenges they face in their alliances and offer advice on addressing them. In addition, the Corporate Alliance Office periodically provides formal training programs or coaching to managers who are newly assigned to any important alliance.

People—*Firms with relational capability have people with relevant "partnering skills" and a "partnering mind-set" to coordinate their alliance activity and to manage their individual alliances.*

The capability of any company eventually rests in the skills of its people, and this is also true for relational capability. Our research has found that firms that set up a "dedicated structure to manage their alliances" often struggle in addressing this issue, and the Philips case has some useful lessons in this regard. Although some individuals may incidentally possess partnering skills and mind-sets, firms can take steps to build them in individuals that lack them. Further, firms need to ensure that people with these skills are selected to manage various alliance activities. Perhaps Philips still has a long way to go in systematically addressing the people-related issues in alliances. But it has made some interesting decisions, partly by design and partly by chance, regarding the people in its corporate alliance team.

Broadly speaking, the alliance team in most firms plays (or should play) three different roles: (1) directly managing some of the company's important alliances, (2) leading the company efforts to learn and codify alliance management best practices for the future, and (3) helping individual managers deal with the challenges they might encounter in alliances. Given that it might be difficult to get individuals who simultaneously possess all these skills, the Philips Alliance Team comprises diverse individuals who have one or more of these respective skills and, therefore, can collectively play all the necessary roles. The team has a couple of senior managers who have extensive prior experience in managing either alliances or "key account relationships"—hence they possess the mind-set and experience to directly manage any important alliance for the company. A second set of senior managers has operational experience in doing alliances, but also an academic background (that is, PhD) in this subject. They have the skills and the mind-set to conceptualize the learning and best practices that Philips derives from its alliances, and establish mechanisms to capture and disseminate them in the organization. They are also responsible for developing or implementing the alliance process and the alliance management tools that embed the company's relational capability. Finally, the team has a third set of individuals who do not necessarily have a lot of prior experience in managing alliances themselves, but have a strong background in strategic management consulting. These managers have picked up relevant alliance management skills after joining the alliance team, and they now play a vital role in consulting with managers across Philips with respect to the alliance formation or management issues. Their strong consulting skills, coupled with the alliance management knowledge that they have picked up, is extremely useful in this regard. Over time, these are gradually transferred to other members of the Alliance Team that lack it—and collectively, the Alliance Team can still play all the roles that are necessary to develop and institutionalize the company's overall relational capability.

Culture—*An organizational environment and culture that proactively seeks and supports partnering and alliance activity is vital to developing relational capability.*

Even if the strategy, structure, systems, and people are in place to build strong alliance capabilities, the results will be relatively poor if a company's culture does not stimulate cooperation. Firms that rely on their own skills ("not invented here") or always aim to have majority or full control, will have immense difficulties in developing alliance capabilities. But if they operate in industries where cooperation with other firms is required or beneficial, they will either have to learn to cooperate or opt for more costly and time-consuming alternatives like acquisition or internal development. Firms with a strong partnering culture understand and accept that cooperation requires give-and-take, are less prone to opportunistic behavior, have to be patient to see results, and have to invest into the relationship and sometimes make "one step forward and two steps back." Such firms know that these things are inherent to cooperation and have found a way to feel comfortable about them.

Philips traditionally relied on its own technological competencies to build new products. However, it was also used to cooperating with competitors in technology standardization efforts (for example, with Sony on CD and DVD), as well as with local incumbents (for example, in China) to gain access to certain markets. So, in a way, there was some culture that supported partnering with other firms. What was new for Philips was cooperation with firms from completely different industries, such as sports (Nike), fast-moving consumer goods (Sara Lee, Unilever, P&G), and Internet content (Yahoo). Initially, many internal people were critical about working with firms from such "alien" industries. But what helped open up the culture and internal environment toward partnering was the success of its early industry-spanning alliances (for example, Senseo alliance with Sara Lee, Nike alliance, Coolskin alliance with Beiersdorf). The Corporate Alliance Office actively promoted these quick wins internally. Consequently many businesses were eager to set up new alliances, preferably as carbon copies of Philips's successful Senseo alliance.

The CEO plays a crucial role in driving cultural change. At Philips, the transformation program implemented by CEO Gerard Kleisterlee when he took over in April 2001, emphasized internal and external cooperation. He launched a "One-Philips" program, in which the businesses were challenged and actively stimulated to explore possible synergies and cooperation internally with other Philips businesses. This program was designed to create a "One-Philips" culture, in which depending on others was one of the pillars. The Corporate Alliance Office proactively built on this new culture in its dealings with the corporate alliances. Intensive internal promotion was done by the Corporate Alliance Office to show the benefits of the "One-Philips" approach in alliances with the main partners.

Developing Alliance Capabilities: A Constant Work in Progress

In the past six years, Philips has addressed most of the key decision-points in building its relational capability. Although we have focused on Philips's experience in this chapter, fieldwork with firms such as Eli Lilly, Cisco, and others that have also tried to build this capability highlights the importance of these decision-points, as does our survey of more than 200 U.S.-based firms that have undertaken some effort in this direction. Philips and other firms have derived greater alliance success through their efforts.

We should note, however, that building alliance capabilities will almost always be a work in progress for any company for several reasons: (1) a company's own strategy or alliance priorities might change over time, (2) the company might recognize opportunities to improve its own relational capability practices, or (3) rivals or other firms might have caught up. Accordingly, Philips too needs to reexamine certain dimensions of its strategy, structure, systems, people, and culture in the context of its relational capability needed in the future. For instance, from a strategy standpoint, Philips has recently shed many businesses from its corporate portfolio, making some of its former "corporate partners" less relevant to its overall revenues and business. Does this imply that, going forward, the company needs to revise its overall alliance strategy that has been centered around corporate alliances? From a structure standpoint, the Corporate Alliance Office has embodied Philips's efforts to create a dedicated management structure to lead, coordinate, and support its alliance activity. But if corporate alliance partners are becoming less relevant to Philips, does it need such a structure at the corporate level? Should the company decentralize the responsibility of alliance management to individual divisions, and re-create such a structure within each division? In its attempts to transform itself, Philips has also begun doing acquisitions to develop new capabilities or business. If this is true, and if alliances and acquisitions are alternative modes of achieving the same business goals, should the alliance team be merged with the company's corporate acquisition team?

From a system standpoint, Philips has done an excellent job of creating a well-defined alliance process and a set of tools to facilitate decision making in alliances. Are these processes or tools sufficient or does it require some new ones? For example, one of the challenges facing the company is the turnover of managers who are responsible for individual alliances in the divisions. (Often this turnover happens because managers are assigned new responsibilities.) Whenever this happens, these individuals carry away useful alliance management know-how or learning. In that case, should the company develop some systems or processes to tap into that knowledge and retain it for future use? From the people standpoint, the company has done a nice job of having people with requisite skills in its corporate alliance team—but what are the future growth prospects of these individuals, and where do they go from here? What kind of people should Philips look for to replace them in the future?

As these considerations show, relational capability is not static. Philips and other companies need to consider such issues on an ongoing basis and refine the strategy, structure, systems, people, and cultural dimensions that define their relational capability.

Conclusion and Implications

Networks require managing relationships. As firms become increasingly intercon-nected, their capability to manage relationships with other organizations becomes increasingly important. Considerable research shows that firm-specific capabilities for managing alliances are important in explaining alliance performance (see Anand and Khanna 2000, for example). Firms vary in their capacity to manage alliance relation-ships, but the Philips case illustrates how companies can build alliance capability and embed it in multiple businesses of a diversified firm. It also illustrates the need for con-sistent effort along multiple dimensions—strategy, structure, systems, people, and cul-ture—to create a capability that can help increase their odds of success in each relationship. Building capabilities takes time. For Philips, the process of systematic capability development took over six years to develop and nurture within the firm.

Many of the factors involved in success are considered "soft skills," embedded in strategy, structure, systems, people, and culture. An important element discussed in the story is top-management support. In light of this combination of the softer elements of organizational design, culture, and human assets, firms can rapidly lose relational capa-bility if CEO-level commitment is lost. Since relational capabilities often cross formal lines of organizational structure, there needs to be a high enough priority on creating and managing partnering relationships for firms to remain effective at them. The more durable elements of relational capability, if developed and emphasized long enough, can turn out to reside in the skills of managers and in the firm's culture. In today's environ-ment of frequent restructuring, structure can often shift from facilitating to limiting relational capability within the firm. As we indicated in our discussion of the latter stages of Philips's story of alliance management, the effort to create and nurture relational capability is a continuous exercise in learning and renewal. But given the high failure rate of alliances, and their increasing importance, many companies such as Philips find it well worthwhile to invest in building and renewing these relational capabilities.

References

Anand, B., and T. Khanna. 2000. Do firms learn to create value? *Strategic Management Journal* 21 (3), 291-315.

Dyer, J. H., and H. Singh. 1998. The relational view: Cooperative strategy and interfirm competitive advantage. *Academy of Management Review* 23 (4), 660-679.

Hamel, G. 1991."Competition for competence and interpartner learning within international strategic alliances," *Strategic Management Journal*, Vol 12 Issue S1, 83-103.

Khanna, T., R. Gulati, and N. Nohria. 1998. The dynamics of learning alliances: Competition, cooperation and relative scope. *Strategic Management Journal* 19 (3), 193-210.

Zaheer, A., B. McEvily, and V. Perrone. 1998. Does trust matter? The effects of interorganizational and interpersonal trust on performance. *Organization Science* 9 (2), 141-159.

PART VI

NETWORK-BASED SOURCES OF RISK AND PROFITABILITY

Networks transform our view of risks, from protecting a single firm to dealing with risks from interdependent webs of firms. In Chapter 21, **Franklin Allen** and **Ana Babus** examine how a network perspective can help us understand and address financial contagion and freezes in the interbank market. In Chapter 22, **Howard Kunreuther** explores how interdependent security risks such as airline security—in which the network is only as strong as its weakest link—often require interdependent solutions. In Chapter 23, **Paul Kleindorfer** and **Ilias Visvikis** examine risk and volatility of global logistics networks, and changes in logistics and financial instruments such as derivatives used to address these risks. In Chapter 24, **Kevin Werbach** discusses the battle for the control of networks, contrasting the worldview of "Monists" such as AT&T, who see the infrastructure as inseparable from the network, and "Dualists" such as Google, who see the network and its applications as distinct from the underlying infrastructure. In Chapter 25, **Witold Henisz** examines how information about the structure of political and social networks can be integrated into data acquisition and analysis, as well as strategy implementation, to better manage political and social risks.

Chapter 21 Networks in Finance   367
            Franklin Allen and Ana Babus

Chapter 22 The Weakest Link: Managing Risk Through Interdependent
            Strategies   383
            Howard Kunreuther

Chapter 23 Integration of Financial and Physical Networks in
            Global Logistics   399
            Paul R. Kleindorfer and Ilias D. Visvikis

Chapter 24 Telecommunications: Network Strategies for Network
            Industries?   417
            Kevin Werbach

Chapter 25 Network-Based Strategies and Competencies for Political
            and Social Risk Management   433
            Witold J. Henisz

21

Networks in Finance[1]

Franklin Allen
Ana Babus

Abstract

Modern financial systems exhibit a high degree of interdependence, with connections between financial institutions stemming from both the asset and the liability sides of their balance sheets. Networks—broadly understood as a collection of nodes and links between nodes—can be a useful representation of financial systems. By modeling economic interactions, network analyses can better explain certain economic phenomena. In this chapter, Allen and Babus argue that the use of network theories can enrich our understanding of financial systems. They explore several critical issues. First, they address the issue of systemic risk, by studying two questions: how resilient financial networks are to contagion, and how financial institutions form connections when exposed to the risk of contagion. Second, they consider how network theory can be used to explain freezes in the interbank market. Third, they examine how social networks can improve investment decisions and corporate governance, based on recent empirical results. Fourth, they examine the role of networks in distributing primary issues of securities. Finally, they consider the role of networks as a form of mutual monitoring, as in microfinance.

[1] We are grateful to the editors and to participants at the Wharton INSEAD conference on November 8-9, 2007, where the book's papers were presented for their helpful comments.

The turmoil in financial markets in August 2007, and the following months has revealed, once again, the intertwined nature of financial systems. While the events unfolded, it became clear that the consequences of such an interconnected system are hard to predict. What initially was seen as difficulties in the U.S. subprime mortgage market rapidly escalated and spilled over to debt markets all over the world. As markets plunged, investors' risk appetite was reduced. Banks became less willing to lend money as freely. Interbank lending rates started to rise, and soon the market for short-term lending dried up. The credit crunch ultimately triggered a bank run at the British mortgage lender Northern Rock—something not seen in the UK for over 140 years and in Western Europe for the past 15 years.

Connections in the financial world are varied. The dependencies between financial institutions stem from both the asset and the liability sides of their balance sheets. For instance, direct asset linkages result from exposures between banks acquired through the interbank market. Financial institutions are indirectly connected by holding similar portfolio exposures. When they share the same mass of depositors, banks are connected in a network through the liability side of the balance sheet.

The intricate structure of linkages between financial institutions can be naturally captured by using a network representation of financial systems. The general concept of a network is quite intuitive: A network describes a collection of nodes and the links between them. The notion of nodes is fairly general; they may be individuals or firms or countries, or even collections of such entities. A link between two nodes represents a direct relationship between them; for instance, in a social context, a link could be a friendship tie, and in the context of countries, a link could be a free trade agreement or a mutual defense pact. In the context of financial systems, the nodes of the network represent financial institutions, and the links are created through mutual exposures between banks, acquired on the interbank market by holding similar portfolio exposures or by sharing the same mass of depositors. In this chapter, we argue that network theory may provide a conceptual framework within which the various patterns of connections can be described and analyzed in a meaningful way.

A network approach to financial systems is particularly important for assessing financial stability and can be instrumental in capturing the externalities that the risk associated with a single institution may create for the entire system. A better understanding of network externalities may facilitate the adoption of a macroprudential framework for financial supervision. Regulations that target individual institutions, as well as take into account vulnerabilities that emerge from network interdependencies in the financial system, may prevent a local crisis from becoming global.

More generally, network analysis may help address two types of questions: the effect of the network structure and the process of network formation. Whereas the first type of question captures aspects related to social efficiency, the second type highlights the tension between socially desirable outcomes and the outcomes that arise as a result of the self-interested action of individuals. The first type of question, on network effects, studies processes that take place on fixed networks. For instance, we can study what is the impact of the financial network structure on the way the banking system responds to contagion. We can show not only that network structures respond differently to the propagation of a shock, but also that the fragility of the system depends on the location in the network of the institution that was initially affected. At the same time, financial institutions may gain significant payoff advantages from bridging otherwise disconnected parts of the financial network. Hence, certain network structures may provide additional benefits for those financial institutions that are able to exploit their position as intermediaries between other institutions. Network structure can also play a role in how effective mutual monitoring is for the enforcement of risk-sharing agreements, as in microfinance.

The second type of question, on network formation, studies how financial institutions form connections. We can gain new insights on the issue of systemic risk if we understand how financial institutions form connections when exposed to the risk of contagion. Risk sharing can be an important driving force that explains how financial institutions form connections. Moreover, theories of network formation may help explain freezes in the interbank market of the type we have observed in August 2007, and subsequent months. When the risk associated with lending funds on the interbank market is too high, links become too costly relative to the benefits they bring. In this case, a network formation game would predict an empty network, where no two banks agree to form a link.

This chapter is organized as follows: The following section considers the limited literature in finance that uses network theory and suggests areas for future research where such an approach is likely to be fruitful. The final section contains concluding remarks.

Applications to Finance

Economic research on networks offers insights into how network analyses might be applied to financial systems. Although there would appear to be many applications of network analyses to financial systems, the literature on financial networks is still at an early stage. Most of the existing research using network theory concentrates on issues such as *financial stability and contagion.* Moreover, most of the research done in financial networks studies *network effects* rather than *network formation.* The literature primarily investigates how different financial network structures respond to the breakdown of a single bank to identify which structures are more fragile. In the first subsection that follows, we discuss this literature on contagion. In the second subsection, we consider whether network theory can be used to understand how interbank markets can freeze, as they did in the months after August 2007. The third considers the role of social networks in investment decisions and corporate governance, among other areas. The fourth subsection considers how network theory can be used to analyze investment banking. Finally, we look at how networks can help understand microfinance and other types of network-based relationships.

Contagion

More connections between banks may reduce the risk of contagion. Although the risk of contagion might be expected to be larger in highly interconnected banking system, research indicates that shocks may have complex effects, to the extent that the more complete the set of links between banks is, the lower the risk of contagion in the system.

The literature on contagion takes two approaches: examining direct linkages and examining indirect balance-sheet linkages. In looking for contagious effects via direct linkages, early research by Allen and Gale (2000) studied how the banking system responds to contagion when banks are connected under different network structures. In a setting where consumers have the liquidity preferences introduced by Diamond and Dybvig (1983) and have random liquidity needs, banks perfectly insure against liquidity shocks by exchanging interbank deposits. The connections created by swapping deposits, however, expose the system to contagion. The authors showed that incomplete networks are more prone to contagion than complete structures. Better-connected networks are more resilient because the proportion of the losses in one bank's portfolio is transferred to more banks through interbank agreements. To show this, they take the case of an incomplete network in which the failure of a bank may trigger the failure of the entire banking system. They prove that, for the same set of parameters, if banks are connected in a complete structure, then the system is more resilient in response to contagion effects.

The research that followed, although using stylized models, captured well the network externalities created from individual bank risk. Freixas, Parigi, and Rochet (2000) considered the case of banks that face liquidity shocks due to uncertainty about where consumers will withdraw funds. In their model, the connections between banks are realized through interbank credit lines that enable these institutions to hedge regional liquidity shocks. As in Allen and Gale's study, more interbank connections enhance the resilience of the system to the insolvency of a particular bank. One drawback is that this weakens the incentives to close inefficient banks. Moreover, the authors find that the stability of the banking system depends crucially on whether many depositors choose to consume at the location of a bank that functions as a money center.

Concerned with the optimal financial network, Leitner (2005) constructs a model in which the success of an agent's investment in a project depends on the investments of other agents she is linked to. Because endowments are randomly distributed across agents, an agent may not have enough cash to make the necessary investment. In this case, agents may be willing to bail out other agents to prevent the collapse of the whole network. Leitner examines the design of optimal financial networks that minimize the trade-off between risk sharing and the potential for collapse. Vivier-Lirimont (2004) addresses the issue of optimal networks from a different perspective: He is interested in those network architectures in which transfers between banks improve depositors' utility. He finds that only very dense networks, in which banks are only a few links away from one another, are compatible with a Pareto optimal allocation. Dasgupta (2004) also explores how linkages between banks, represented by cross-holding of deposits, can be a source of contagious breakdowns. The study examined how depositors who receive a private signal about banks' fundamentals may want to withdraw their deposits if they believe that enough other depositors will do the same. To eliminate the multiplicity of equilibria, the author uses the concept of global games. Dasgupta isolated a unique equilibrium, depending on the value of the fundamentals.

Other researchers studied contagion in other industries beyond banking. Cummins, Doherty, and Lo (2002) show how the structure of catastrophe insurance markets can lead to contagion. State guarantee funds, such as the one in Florida, are based explicitly on allocating defaulted policy claims to other solvent insurers, typically in proportion to the net premiums written by these insurers. This network structure limits the capacity of the insurance industry to absorb the effects of a major catastrophic event to well below the total amount of equity capital in the industry.

Parallel to this literature, other researchers applied network techniques developed in mathematics and theoretical physics to study contagion. For instance, Eisenberg and Noe (2001) investigate default by firms that are part of a single clearing mechanism. Similarly, Minguez-Afonso and Shin (2007) use lattice-theoretic methods to study liquidity and systemic risk in high-value payment systems, such as for the settlement of accounts receivable and payable among industrial firms, and interbank payment systems. Gai and Kapadia (2007) develop a model of contagion in financial networks and use similar techniques as the epidemiological literature on spread of disease in networks to assess the fragility of the financial system, depending on the banks' capital buffers, the degree of connectivity, and the liquidity of the market for failed banking assets. As with Allen and Gale, they find that greater connectivity reduces the likelihood of widespread default. However, shocks may have a significantly larger impact on the financial system when they occur.

The impact of indirect linkages on contagion is considered as well in another set of studies. These studies share the same finding with the previous stream of research that financial systems are inherently fragile. Fragility not only arises exogenously, from financial institutions' exposure to common macro risk factors such as economic downturns but also evolves endogenously, through forced sales of assets by some banks that depress the market price, inducing further distress to other institutions.

Lagunoff and Schreft (2001) construct a model in which agents are linked in the sense that the return on an agent's portfolio depends on the portfolio allocations of other agents. In their model, agents that are subject to shocks reallocate their portfolios, thus breaking some linkages. Two related types of financial crisis can occur in response. One occurs gradually as losses spread, breaking more links. The other type occurs instantaneously when forward-looking agents preemptively shift to safer portfolios to avoid future losses from contagion. Similarly, de Vries (2005) shows that there is dependency between banks' portfolios, given the fat tail property of the underlying assets, and this carries the potential for systemic breakdown. Cifuentes, Ferrucci, and Shin (2005) present a model in which financial institutions are connected via portfolio holdings. The network is complete as everyone holds the same asset. Although the authors incorporate in their model direct linkages through mutual credit exposures as well, contagion is driven mainly by changes in asset prices.

The issue of network formation is considered in two studies. Babus (2007) proposes a model in which banks form links with each other as an insurance mechanism to reduce the risk of contagion. At the base of the link formation process lies the same intuition developed in Allen and Gale (2000): Better connected networks are more resilient to contagion. The model predicts a connectivity threshold above which contagion does not occur, and banks form links to reach this threshold. However, an implicit cost associated with being involved in a link prevents banks from forming more connections than are required by the connectivity threshold. Banks manage to form networks in which contagion rarely occurs. Castiglionesi and Navarro (2007) are also interested in decentralizing the network of banks that is optimal from a social planner perspective. In a setting in which banks invest on behalf of depositors and there are positive network externalities on the investment returns, fragility arises when banks that are not sufficiently capitalized gamble with depositors' money. When the probability of bankruptcy is low, the decentralized solution approximates the first best.

Besides the theoretical investigations, *empirical studies* of national banking systems have looked for evidence of contagious failures of financial institutions resulting from the mutual claims they have on one another. Most of these papers use balance sheet information to estimate bilateral credit relationships for different banking systems. Subsequently, the stability of the interbank market is tested by simulating the breakdown of a single bank. Upper and Worms (2004) analyze the banking system in Germany; Sheldon and Maurer (1998), Switzerland; Cocco, Gomes, and Martins (2009), Portugal; Furfine (2003), the United States; Wells (2004), the UK; Boss et al. (2004), Austria; and Degryse and Nguyen (2007), Belgium. These papers find that the banking systems demonstrate high resilience, even to large shocks. Simulations of the worst-case scenarios show that banks representing less than 5% of total balance sheet assets would be affected by contagion on the Belgian interbank market, whereas for the German system, the failure of a single bank could lead to the breakdown of up to 15% of the banking sector based on assets.

These results depend heavily on how the linkages between banks, represented by credit exposures in the interbank market, are estimated (Upper 2006). For most countries, data is extracted from banks' balance sheets, which can provide information on the aggregate exposure of the reporting institution vis-à-vis all other banks. To estimate bank-to-bank exposures, it is generally assumed that banks spread their lending as evenly as possible (that is, the maximum entropy method). In effect, this assumption requires that banks be connected in a complete network. Hence, the assumption might bias the results, in the light of the theoretical findings that better connected networks are more resilient to the propagation of shocks. This is confirmed by Mistrulli (2007), who analyses how contagion propagates within the Italian interbank market using actual bilateral exposures. He also applies the maximum entropy method to the same dataset, and he finds that it tends to generally underrate the extent of contagion.

Other researchers have examined the impact of specific bank failures. Iyer and Peydro-Alcalde (2007) test for financial contagion using data about interbank exposures at the time of the failure of a large Indian bank. They find that banks with higher interbank exposure to the failed bank experience higher deposit withdrawals, and that the impact of exposure on deposit withdrawals is higher for banks with weaker fundamentals.

Freezes in Interbank Markets

Although researchers have devoted a great deal of time to analyzing possible forms of contagion in interbank markets, the actual type of contagion that occurred following August 2007, came as something of a surprise. The interbank markets simply dried up. Even though interest rates were high and in many cases outside the ranges specified by central banks, it was not possible for many institutions to borrow at a range of short-term maturities. An important issue is whether existing contagion theories can be adapted to understand this phenomenon or whether new ones need to be developed.

Freixas, Parigi, and Rochet (2000) do consider the possibility of gridlocks, primarily due to payment systems' breakdowns. The authors analyze different market structures and find that a system of credit lines, while reducing the cost of holding liquidity, makes the banking sector prone to gridlocks, even when all banks are solvent. However, payment systems functioned well during the 2007 crisis and could have smoothly ensured the flow of money. We need an alternative explanation for the freeze in the interbank market.

One way to understand market freezes is through a network formation game, in which the empty network emerges as an equilibrium, using the kind of analysis in Babus (2007). In her model, the endogenous formation of networks worked well and led to efficiency. However, by including frictions it may be possible for exogenous changes in risk that are small to have large effects by causing agents to withdraw from the network. This may help explain what happened in August 2007.

In a study of social networks, Karlan, Mobius, Rosenblat and Szeidl (2009) propose a model of lending and borrowing in which relationships between individuals are used as social collateral. They find that the maximum amount that can be borrowed in a connected network at most equals the lowest value of a link between any two agents. Although the model focuses on trust in social networks, it can be relevant to describe interactions in the interbank market. In interbank markets, links, representing loans between banks, evolve over time. The current network between banks may serve as collateral to form a network in a future period. In this setting, a decrease in the value of the collateral may trigger an adverse effect on how links will be formed in the next period. A small perturbation can, thus, result in a significant drop in lending and borrowing activities across the network.

Social Networks and Investment Decisions

A recent trend of empirical research advances a new important set of questions about the effects of social networks on investment decisions. Cohen, Frazzini, and Malloy (2008) use social networks to identify information transfers in security markets. They use connections between mutual fund managers and corporate board members via shared educational institutions as a proxy for the social network. They find that portfolio managers place larger bets on firms they are connected to through their network, and perform significantly better on these holdings relative to their nonconnected holdings. These results suggest that social networks may be an important mechanism for information flow into asset prices. However, it is less clear whether there are network externalities. In other words, it is less clear how far information travels through the network and whether it affects asset prices across more than two links. Hochberg, Ljungqvist, and Lu (2007) look at venture capital (VC) firms that are connected through a network of syndicated portfolio company investments. They also find that better-networked VC firms experience significantly better fund performance, as measured by the proportion of investments that are successfully exited through an IPO or a sale to another company. This implies that one's network position should be an important strategic consideration for incumbent VCs, while presenting a potential barrier to entry for new VCs.

Another set of studies investigates problems related to corporate governance. Nguyen-Dang (2007) is concerned with the impact of social ties between CEOs and directors within a board of directors on the effectiveness of board monitoring. The paper investigates whether CEOs are less accountable for poor performance depending on their position in the social network. To map the social network, the author uses data on educational background of CEOs from the largest French quoted corporations. Social ties are also formed through interlocking directorships. He finds that when some of the board members and the CEO belong to the same social circles, the CEO is provided with a double protection. She is less likely to be punished for poor performance and more likely to find a new and good job after a forced departure. In later work, Kramarz and Thesmar (2007) ran a similar analysis and found evidence to support that social networks may strongly affect board composition and may be detrimental to corporate governance. Braggion (2008) considers another proxy for social networks between firms' managers: the affiliation with Freemasonry. He finds that social networks help to resolve agency problems between lenders and borrowers in firms that have difficulties in obtaining debt finance. However, in large publicly quoted corporations that were managed by Freemasons, social connections give rise to agency conflicts between managers and shareholders and worsen economic performance.

In related work, Gaspar and Massa (2007) find that personal connections between divisional managers and the CEO within a firm increase the bargaining power of the connected managers and decrease the efficiency of decisions within the organization. Further studies confirm that firms whose directors are better connected and whose connections are with better connected directors exhibit weaker firm governance. In particular, in firms where members of the board are highly connected, CEO pay is higher, CEO pay is less sensitive to firm performance, and poorly performing CEOs are less likely to be fired (Barnea and Guedj 2008). Similarly, in the mutual fund industry, directors tend to hire advisory firms that they have worked with in the past, and, when creating new funds, advisory firms tend to offer board seats to directors they have had business relationships with in the past (Kuhnen 2008).

Pistor (2007) provides a more integrated approach, looking at the financial system from a global perspective. She argues that network-finance is a critical institutional arrangement, allowing the combination of features of different governance systems and leading to innovation when there is great uncertainty about financing choices.

Investment Banking and Networks

Although there is a very large literature that explains the emergence of *commercial* banks, there has been very little work done on why *investment* banks exist. In an important contribution, Morrison and Wilhelm (2007) argue that investment banks exist because they create networks. The researchers suggest that the central role of investment banks is to issue and underwrite securities. This requires that they develop two networks. The first is an information network, which allows them to acquire information about the demand for an issue. This network consists of large-scale investors such as pension funds and insurance companies. When an investment bank is trying to sell an issue, this network provides information on how much investors are willing to pay, helping to set a fair price. In addition to this information network, the bank needs a liquidity network to provide the funds to purchase the securities. This network may overlap to some extent with the information network. These networks are compensated by the average underpricing that has been well documented in the literature. Morrison and Wilhelm argue that the role of trust and reputation is crucial for these networks to function. Contracting technology is insufficient to provide the correct incentives.

Schnabel and Shin (2004) document how in the eighteenth century, networks of merchant banks allowed capital accumulated in one part of Europe to be invested in far distant parts. For example, Amsterdam banks were networked with Hamburg banks that were, in turn, networked with Berlin banks. This allowed savings to flow from Amsterdam to be invested in Berlin and other parts of Prussia. In this case, these networks compensated for asymmetric information due to distance.

Formal network theory has not been used extensively in these studies of investment banks. This is an important and interesting area with many phenomena that are only partially understood, such as long-run underperformance of new issues. Network theory potentially provides a new approach to explain such phenomena and also to provide a basis for normative models to analyze regulation.

Microfinance

Microfinance has emerged as a powerful way for people in the developing world to mitigate risk. Households in developing countries often are faced with unpredictable income streams and expenditures. The uncertainty related to health, weather, crop pests, and job opportunities creates large income variation over time. Medical bills and funeral costs are large expenditures, not always foreseeable (Coudouel, Hentschel, and Wodon 2002). Microfinance may help smoothing fluctuations in consumption that are triggered by shocks in income.

Social interactions play a crucial role in the success of microfinance. For example, in India, Self-Help Groups (SHGs) form the basic constituent unit of microfinance (see, for example, Chakrabarti 2005). An SHG consists of 5 to 20 people, usually poor women from different families. Members pool their savings into a fund that they deposit with the bank. After the bank has observed the accumulation in the fund for a while, it starts to lend to the group, without asking for collateral. Instead, the bank relies on peer pressure and self-monitoring within the group to ensure that loans are repaid.

The success of microfinance in the developing world can be traced to two main factors: (1) a significant decrease in the default rate of loans issued under microfinance terms, and (2) group sanctions that are exercised within the microfinance group to reinforce cooperation. In other words, the social network helps make this financial model work.

Although institutions such as the Grameen bank became widely known, formal microcredit markets are a fairly recent innovation in developing countries. When access to credit is limited, substantial evidence points out that risk sharing occurs through informal bilateral agreements.

While microfinance often depends on local personal networks, such networks have their weaknesses. Group-based models such as microfinance SHGs are often fraught with free-riding and moral hazard problems. These issues and the lack of enforceability of agreements have been identified as the main deterrents for efficient risk sharing (Udry 1994). Inefficiencies arise from the trade-off between the benefits these arrangements provide and the risks involved. Localization is also an issue. Households that live far apart or rely on different occupations are more likely to have different income streams or to be exposed to different sources of risk. Thus, the gains from risk sharing are maximized at large social and geographical distances. However, larger distances make the enforceability of risk-sharing agreements increasingly difficult. For this reason, as has been documented empirically, individuals tend to insure suboptimally, foregoing benefits from risk sharing for better enforceable contracts. For instance, Fafchamps and Gubert (2006) show that the major determinants for the formation of risk-sharing agreements are geographic proximity, as well as age and wealth differences, and not occupation or income correlation. In other words, risk-sharing arrangements are primarily established depending on the enforceability of contracts, proxied by short distances, rather than the diversification of income risk. Understanding the role of networks in this group incentive problem is one potential way of understanding the success of microfinance. We reviewed a few models previously that explore the mechanisms behind cooperation in risk-sharing networks.

Further evidence points out the importance of social networks in emerging economies. Bunkanwanicha, Fan, and Wiwattanakantang (2008) show that marriage might be used to strengthen business alliances. It appears that in Thailand, between 1991 and 2006, more than two-thirds of marriages of big-business owners' offspring were beneficial to the family's firms. This is reflected in the positive reaction the stock market has to the wedding news when the partner is from an economically or politically powerful family.

Most of the work on risk-sharing networks has focused on monitoring and enforceability problems. Other aspects are worth considering as well. For instance, it would be interesting to study the effect that the structure of a preexistent social network has on the formation of a risk-sharing network.

A further question is how introducing a formal institution (that is, a bank) that reduces the need for informal risk-sharing agreements in one region of the network affects the efficiency of risk sharing in the overall network. A closely related issue is to understand the effects of changes in the underlying social network, for example due to migration, on the overall efficiency of the network of risk-sharing agreements.

Conclusion

Our financial systems are networks, and today these networks have grown increasingly complex and interlinked. In this paper, we have argued that network analyses can potentially play a crucial role in understanding many important phenomena in finance. At the moment, this type of approach has mostly been restricted to analyzing contagion in interbank markets. More recent work has focused on the effects of social networks in various contexts, including investment and corporate governance. It seems clear that networks are also crucial in understanding investment banks and microfinance. Another issue to be explored is how some financial institutions exploit their position as intermediaries between other institutions. Financial institutions that bridge otherwise disconnected parts of the network might gain significant payoff advantages. Financial networks will thus be shaped by incentives that drive institutions to acquire the intermediation gains. These are just some of the topics in finance that a network analysis could be useful for, going forward.

Moreover, recent events have made clear that there is a strong need for sound empirical work in this area. Mapping the networks between financial institutions is a first step toward gaining a better understanding of modern financial systems. A network perspective not only would account for the various connections within the financial sector or between the financial sector and other sectors, but also would consider the quality of these links. We need this work to guide the development of new theories that can help us understand events such as the August 2007 crisis, as well as design new regulations that better meet the challenge of an increasingly networked world.

References

Allen, F., and D. Gale. 2000. Financial contagion. *Journal of Political Economy* 108 (1), 1-33.

Babus, A. 2007. The formation of financial networks. Discussion paper 06-093, Tinbergen Institute.

Barnea, A., and I. Guedj. 2008. Director networks and firm governance. Working paper, University of Texas at Austin.

Boss, M., H. Elsinger, S. Thurner, and M. Summer. 2004. Network topology of the interbank market. *Quantitative Finance* 4, 1-8.

Braggion, F. 2008. Managers, firms and (secret) social networks: The economics of Freemasonry. Working paper, University of Tilburg.

Bunkanwanicha, P., J. Fan, and Y. Wiwattanakantang. 2008. Marriage and network formation: A study of family business groups in an emerging market. Working paper, Chinese University of Hong Kong.

Castiglionesi, F., and N. Navarro. 2007. Optimal fragile financial networks. Working paper, Tilburg University.

Chakrabarti, R. 2005. The Indian microfinance experience—Accomplishments and challenges. SSRN: http:/ssrn.com/abstract=649854.

Cifuentes, R., G. Ferrucci, and H. S. Shin. 2005. Liquidity risk and contagion. *Journal of European Economic Association* 3 (2-3), 556-566.

Cocco, J., F. Gomes, and N. Martins. 2009. Lending relationships in the interbank market. *Journal of Financial Intermediation* 18 (1), 24-48.

Cohen, L., A. Frazzini, and C. Malloy. 2008. The small world of investing: Board connections and mutual fund returns. *Journal of Political Economy* 116, 951-979.

Coudouel, A., J. Hentschel, and Q. Wodon. 2002. Poverty measurement and analysis. In *A Sourcebook for Poverty Reduction Strategies*, ed. J. Klugman. Washington, D.C.: The World Bank.

Cummins, J. D., N. Doherty, and A. Lo. 2002. Can insurers pay for the "big one"? Measuring the capacity of the insurance market to catastrophic losses. *Journal of Banking and Finance* 26, 557-583.

Dasgupta, A. 2004. Financial contagion through capital connections: A model of the origin and spread of bank panics. *Journal of European Economic Association* 2 (6), 1049-1084.

De Vries, C. 2005. The simple economics of bank fragility. *Journal of Banking and Finance* 29 (4), 803-825.

Degryse, H. and G. Nguyen. 2007. Interbank exposures: An empirical examination of systemic risk in the Belgian banking system. *International Journal of Central Banking* 3, 951-979.

Diamond, D., and P. Dybvig. 1983. Bank runs, deposit insurance and liquidity. *Journal of Political Economy* 91, 401-419.

Eisenberg, L., and T. Noe. 2001. Systemic risk in financial systems. *Management Science* 47 (2), 236-249.

Fafchamps and Gubert. 2006. "The formation of risk sharing networks," *Journal of Development Economics*, vol. 83(2), 326-350.

Freixas, X., B. Parigi, and J. C. Rochet. 2000. Systemic risk, interbank relations and liquidity provision by the central bank. *Journal of Money, Credit and Banking* 32 (3), 611-638.

Furfine, C. 2003. Interbank exposures: Quantifying the risk of contagion. *Journal of Money, Credit and Banking* 35 (1), 111-128.

Gai, P., and S. Kapadia. 2007. Contagion in financial networks. Working paper, Bank of England.

Gaspar, J. M., and M. Massa. 2007. Power play: Intra-firm corporate connections and firm value. Working paper, INSEAD.

Hochberg, Y., A. Ljungqvist, and Y. Lu. 2007. Whom you know matters: Venture capital networks and investment performance. *Journal of Finance* 62, 251-301.

Iyer, R., and J. L. Peydro-Alcalde. 2007. The Achilles' hell of interbank markets: Financial contagion due to interbank linkages. Working paper, ECB.

Karlan, D., Mobius, M., T. Rosenblat and A. Szeidl. 2009. Trust and social collateral. *Quarterly Journal of Economics* 124 (3).

Kramarz, F., and D. Thesmar. 2007. Social networks in the boardroom. CEPR discussion paper 5496.

Kuhnen, C. 2008. Business networks, corporate governance and contracting in the mutual fund industry. Forthcoming, *Journal of Finance*.

Lagunoff, R., and L. Schreft. 2001. A model of financial fragility. *Journal of Economic Theory* 99, 220-264.

Leitner, Y. 2005. Financial networks: Contagion, commitment, and private sector bailouts. *Journal of Finance* 60 (6), 2925-2953.

Minguez-Afonso, G., and H. Shin. 2007. Systemic risk and liquidity in payment systems. Working paper, London School of Economics.

Mistrulli, P. 2007. Assessing financial contagion in the interbank market: Maximum entropy versus observed interbank lending patterns. Working paper, Bank of Italy.

Morrison, A., and J. W. Wilhelm. 2007. *Investment Banking: Institutions, Politics and Law*. Oxford and New York: Oxford University Press.

Nguyen-Dang, B. 2007. Does the Rolodex matter? Corporate elite's small world and the effectiveness of boards of directors. Working paper, Chinese University of Hong Kong.

Pistor, K. 2007. Network-finance: An institutional innovation for a global market place. Working paper, Columbia University.

Schnabel, I., and H. Shin. 2004. Liquidity and contagion: The crisis of 1763. *Journal of the European Economic Association* 2, 929-968.

Sheldon, G., and M. Maurer. 1998. Interbank lending and systemic risk: An empirical analysis for Switzerland. *Swiss Journal of Economics and Statistics* 134 (4), 685-704.

Udry, C. 1994. Risk and insurance in a rural credit market: An empirical investigation in northern Nigeria. *Review of Economic Studies* 61 (3), 495-526.

Upper, C. 2006. Contagion due to interbank credit exposures: What do we know, why do we know it, and what should we know? Working paper, Bank for International Settlements.

Upper, C., and A. Worms. 2004. Estimating bilateral exposures in the German interbank market: Is there a danger of contagion? *European Economic Review* 48 (4), 827-849.

Vivier-Lirimont, S. 2004. Interbanking networks: Towards a small financial world? Cahiers de la Maison Des Sciences Economiques, Université Pairs Panthéon-Sorbonne.

Wells, S. 2004. U.K. interbank exposures: Systemic risk implications. *Journal of Monetary Economics* 2 (1), 66-77.

22

The Weakest Link: Managing Risk Through Interdependent Strategies

Howard Kunreuther

Abstract

Networks increase interdependencies and this creates challenges for managing risks. This is especially apparent in areas such as security and enterprise risk management, where the actions of a single player in an interconnected network can wreak havoc on everyone in the network. The network, in this case, is only as strong as its weakest link. There are related problems in encouraging investments for prevention and protection, because the expected payoffs from such measures by one player are affected by the actions of other players in the network. In this chapter, Howard Kunreuther examines the challenges of interdependent security (IDS) and strategies for addressing these, including coordination with broader networks such as industry organizations and government.

On December 21, 1988, Pan Am flight 103 exploded near Lockerbie, Scotland. Terrorists had checked a bag containing a bomb in Malta on Malta Airlines, which had minimal security procedures. The bag was transferred in Frankfurt to a Pan Am feeder line, and then loaded onto Pan Am 103 in London's Heathrow Airport. The bomb was designed to explode above 28,000 feet, a height normally first attained on this route over the Atlantic Ocean. Given such interdependencies among different players in a network, this example illustrates that security for the entire network may be only as strong as its weakest link. In this case, the terrorists deliberately exploited the widely varying security procedures across the airlines. This problem is common to other transportation modes, in which there are interconnections between nodes in the network.[1]

Interdependencies create a challenge for airlines in making decisions about investing in security. An airline knows that if it invests in baggage security, it may face a security risk from a dangerous bag loaded onto its plane by another airline. It faces this risk unless it inspects all transferred bags, a policy until recently followed only by El Al Airlines.

In a networked world, the risks faced by any one agent depend not only on that agent's own choices but also on those of others. More specifically, the economic incentive of any agent to invest in protection depends on how she expects others to behave. The strategies can be risk-reducing measures as well as information-gathering and preparedness activities. The fact that such events are typically probabilistic, and that the risk that one agent faces is often determined in part by the behavior of others, gives a unique and complex structure to the incentives that agents face to reduce their exposures to these risks that come under the heading of interdependent security (IDS).

For many IDS problems, if an agent thinks that others will *not* invest in protection, this reduces the incentive for her to do so. On the other hand, should she believe that others will invest in security, it may be best for her to do so also. So it is often the case that there are two equilibria: (1) no one invests in protection, even though all would be better off if they had incurred this cost or (2) everyone invests in protection. In some cases, there may be incentives that can push the system past a tipping point where it shifts from the first equilibrium to the second.

This chapter characterizes the nature of the interdependency problem and suggests risk-management strategies for improving both individual and social outcomes. The first section outlines a series of IDS scenarios to illustrate the range of problems that fall under this rubric. The second section focuses on the problem of a firm with more than one decentralized division, using a simple game theoretic model to illustrate how the expected profits of each division would be improved had all of them invested in risk-reducing measures. The third section introduces risk-management strategies to improve individual and social welfare. We examine how one might induce tipping or cascading by either subsidizing or fining one of the divisions so that it has an economic incentive to invest in protection, leading the others to follow suit. In particular, I focus on coordination measures within a decentralized firm (for example, creating a corporate culture

---

[1] See Heal and Kunreuther (2005a) for more details on this scenario and a formal game theoretic model of the problem.

focused on managing low-probability, high-consequence events) as well as within an industry (for example, private trade associations) to induce cooperative behavior. The public sector can also play an important role through interventions such as taxes, subsidies, insurance, and regulations to deal with the negative externalities caused by interdependent security. The paper concludes with suggestions for future field and experimental research in this area and final comments.

IDS Scenarios

In addition to the airline security case discussed previously, the challenge of interdependent risks can be seen in many areas. In the following scenarios, weak links in the system may lead to suboptimal behavior by everyone. These cases also illustrate possible solutions to address these interdependent risks.

Example 1: Protection of Shared Network Resources[2]

Many workplaces have a complex network of shared resources (such as files, disks, peripheral devices, and bandwidth) along with individual resources (such as desktop machines). The vulnerability of the shared resources to various security risks often depends strongly on the collective actions used to protect individual resources. For example, a shared disk may be erased by a virus entering the local network through the desktop machine of a user who failed to update his or her antivirus software signatures. Individual actions also affect shared resources such as bandwidth. For example, users whose machines are infected with a variety of "malware" can surreptitiously consume huge amounts of bandwidth, at the expense of all other users of the system. Such problems are common among residential commercial cable subscribers to Internet access.

Example 2: Global Supply-Chain Management[3]

Global supply chains face risks from terrorists and other disruptions. One weak link is enough to allow a purposeful agent to penetrate the supply chain and to undermine the risk mitigation actions of all others in the supply chain (Heal et al. 2006). Making these global supply chains less vulnerable depends on the actions of many players.

---

[2] See Heal et al. (2006) and Kearns (2005) for more details on this scenario.

[3] See Heal et al. (2006) for more details on this scenario.

Spurred by the concerns of the U.S. Department of Homeland Security (DHS) for protecting critical infrastructure, major retailers and transportation and logistic specialists came together in 2002 to discuss the responsibilities of the private and public sectors in meeting the new challenges of interdependent security in global supply chains. These early discussions were eventually synthesized in the United States into a voluntary public-private partnership approach to cargo security called the Customs-Trade Partnership Against Terrorism (C-TPAT). The idea of C-TPAT was to develop basic principles, and associated best practices, for all participants in a global supply chain in four areas: site security, personnel (including background checks), material movements, and process control (Kleindorfer and Saad 2005). C-TPAT is designed to integrate the activities of three types of actors: private companies that manufacture and move cargo; port authorities and deconsolidators; and local, regional, and national agencies responsible for homeland security.

Example 3: Meltdown of a Nuclear Reactor[4]

Assume that each country has one nuclear reactor, and that if it invests in a set of safeguards, the chances of an accident from the power plant are reduced to zero. We imagine a group of small adjacent countries (for example, Belgium, Holland, and Luxembourg, or Latvia, Lithuania, and Estonia), where a meltdown in any one will lead to radioactive contamination in all of them. What role could international compacts or trade associations play to ensure that all countries invest in safeguards? A related issue is the ripple effects from an accident that does not result in contamination. For example, in the United States, an accident at any one plant is likely to lead to costly regulatory interventions at all plants.

Example 4: Environmental Treaties[5]

Suppose that countries are asked to sign a treaty to reduce on environmental risk, such as global warming or atmospheric pollution. There is a net cost to any one country for adopting the treaty, but potential benefits to the entire planet if enough countries take this action. What incentive is there for any one country to adopt the treaty if it

[4] See Heal and Kunreuther (2005b) for more details on this scenario.

[5] See Barrett (2003) for more details on this scenario.

knows that a number of other countries will not join? How can one convince countries with leverage to sign the treaty to induce others to follow suit? There are equity-efficiency trade-offs. For example, it might be economically more efficient for only a subset of countries to take preventive actions by being part of a treaty, but more equitable and politically saleable for all countries to sign the treaty.

Example 5: Interdependent Critical Infrastructures[6]

As shown by disasters such as 9/11 and Hurricane Katrina, the failure of infrastructure in one sector can lead to disruptions in other sectors. For example, financial systems and emergency services are highly dependent on telecommunication operations, which are highly dependent on electricity. In a power grid, there is a systematic tendency to underinvest in reliability, individual capacity, or security measures such as trimming vegetation near distribution lines to reduce the chance of a power failure. The costs of failure are passed on to competitors and customers in other parts of the network. When the interdependencies cut across sectors, the natures of the risks are often not well understood so they pose special policy challenges. The private and public sector share an interest in making social and economic systems less vulnerable to disasters. There is growing interest in protecting critical infrastructure to assure the social and economic continuity of the nation (transportation, water distribution, telecommunication, electricity, emergency services, financial services, and so on) in the event of terrorist attacks or severe natural hazard events.

Example 6: Protecting a Firm Against Catastrophic Losses[7]

For large corporations, a failure in one part of the world or one division can lead to disruption or bankruptcy of the entire firm nationwide or even worldwide. For example, a Bhopal-like accident at a chemical plant can lead to losses that are so large that they cause bankruptcy of the entire operation. An ownership group such as Lloyd's, which controls a number of semiautonomous syndicates, can fail if one of the syndicates experiences a severe enough loss. In February 1995, Barings Bank was destroyed by the actions of a single trader in its Singapore unit, and in 2002, Arthur Andersen was sent into bankruptcy by the actions of its Houston branch working with Enron. Similar events

---

[6] See Auerswald et al. (2006) for more details on this scenario.

[7] See Kunreuther and Heal (2005) for more details on this scenario.

have happened to other financial services units in recent years and months, notably the potential collapse of the American International Group (AIG), the world's largest insurer, as a result of a 377-person London unit known as AIG Financial Products that was run with almost complete autonomy from the parent company (Morgenson 2008). Given such an institutional structure, what economic incentive does any division have to incur the costs of protective measures that adversely affect its balance sheet, if other divisions in the organization are not taking similar actions? A culture of risk-taking can spread through the firm, because knowledge that a few groups are taking large risks reduces the incentives that others have to manage their operations carefully.

Characterizing the Problem—Investing in a Chemical Plant

How can these interdependent risks be addressed? As illustrated by some of the examples given, in many cases this is done by looking to the network itself. There may be ways of inducing tipping and cascading so that everyone's welfare is improved. One may thus want to determine the nature of critical coalitions that can tip the entire system. Is there any agent (for example, firm, individual) or group of agents one should focus attention on? More generally, what types of private-sector coordination measures (for example, private trade associations) and public-sector interventions (for example, taxes, subsidies, fines, regulations, and well-enforced standards) are appropriate for dealing with the negative externalities caused by interdependent security?

To illustrate an approach to addressing interdependent risks, consider a simplified case of a single firm with several divisions (as discussed in Example 6). The BeSafe chemical firm has two identical independently operating divisions, each maximizing its own expected returns and having to choose whether to invest in a protective measure. Such an investment would reduce the probability of a catastrophic chemical accident to one of its plants. Suppose Division 1 has invested in protection. There is still an additional risk that BeSafe will go bankrupt if Division 2 has not taken this precautionary measure. In other words, the employees in Division 1 may lose their jobs because of the carelessness of Division 2. In this sense, Division 2 can contaminate other parts of the organization by not protecting its plants against a catastrophic accident. Similarly, Division 1 can contaminate Division 2 if it fails to adopt adequate protection.

From Division 1's perspective, adding a second division creates the possibility of contamination and reduces its incentive to invest in protection. Why? Because in isolation, investment in protection buys the employees in Division 1 freedom from bankruptcy. With the possibility of contamination from others, it does not. Even after investment, there remains a risk of bankruptcy from the other division. Investing in protection buys you less when there is the possibility of contamination from others.

The results for the two-division case carry over to more general settings with some increase in complexity. The incentive for any agent to invest in protection depends on how many other agents there are and on whether they are investing. Other agents who do not invest reduce the expected benefits from each division's own protective actions and hence reduce any single division's incentive to invest.

Suppose there are n divisions in the firm. If n is large and none of the other n-1 divisions have invested in protection, it is highly unlikely that your division will want to invest in protecting itself against a catastrophic accident. Here is the intuition for this somewhat surprising result. One weak link in the organization compromises all the other divisions. In other words, one unprotected division endangers all the other divisions in the firm even if they have all invested in security. The more divisions that have not invested in protection, the greater the chances that the employees of any division will be looking for another job even if its own plants are secure from a catastrophic accident. As more divisions decide *not* to invest in security, the probability of a catastrophic accident becomes greater and there is even less economic incentive for your division to undertake protection. This sets up a negative cycle that leads to declining investments in protection. But the reverse can also be true. If more players invest in protection, there is a greater incentive for others to do so, and, above a certain threshold, this can lead to a positive and reinforcing cycle of investment incentives, as discussed in the text that follows.

Understanding the risks facing individual nodes and the entire network demands rigorous risk assessment and knowledge of varying risk perceptions. As BeSafe collects more accurate information on the risks of chemical accidents at each of its chemical plants, it can develop more effective strategies for planning at its different divisions. Risk perceptions may also vary across the network, and will affect investments in prevention. For example, some managers at BeSafe might invest in preventive actions only if they perceive that the chance of some event rises above a critical probability level.

Developing Risk Management Strategies: Tipping and Cascading[8]

With the right incentives, the network itself can encourage actions by individuals that reduce collective risks. Tipping refers to a situation in which a switch of strategy by a small group of agents will lead all (or most of) the others to follow suit. In the context of the BeSafe chemical plant example, cascading implies that if one division invests in protection, one or more (but not all) other divisions will do the same, inducing others to invest in protection (Dixit 2002). There will be some divisions in an organization that may produce much greater negative externalities by their actions than others. For example, a large division that went bankrupt would be much more likely to have severe impacts on the organization than would a smaller unit. The large division could suffer a catastrophic loss from an accident that would have much more serious repercussions than if the accident occurred at a smaller plant. By providing incentives for the large division to invest in protection, others in the organization might do the same.

If there is a weak link in the network that can cause severe disruptions to others, it may be necessary only to provide economic incentives to this unit to improve its profitability as well as all the others in the system through a tipping or cascading process. It is this weak-link property that characterizes many practical problems in interdependency and can have major impacts on others members of the network. Tipping has been documented in many contexts (Schelling 1978).

Creating Incentives for Tipping

After a point of tipping or cascading is reached, individuals in the network will often begin making their own investments in protection. Coordinating mechanisms and incentives, often through private-public partnerships, can create an appropriate environment for that to occur.

Internal Organizational Rules and Other Coordinating Mechanisms

A large decentralized firm with many divisions will likely need some type of coordinating mechanism from top management to encourage investments if each division's objective is to maximize the expected returns to its own employees. A key question in

---

[8] This section is based on material in Kunreuther and Heal (2005).

this regard is how companies who advertise "Safety is our most important product" actually operationalize this slogan. Larger firms in the chemical industry have formed functional units that play this role across the organization. For example, DuPont has a process safety management group that is responsible for making sure that all the different divisions in the firm follow appropriate procedures.

In the context of the BeSafe example, the company could set up such a cross-cutting unit and institute a specific rule that would require divisions to invest in protective measures when the expected benefits to the firm exceeded the costs of the measure. One way to determine what type of rule to enforce is to consider catastrophic accidents that could cause losses so large that they would threaten the solvency of the firm but where the division itself would not want to incur the costs of investing in protective measures.

Role of the Public Sector

The public sector can play an important role in protection, and has an interest in doing so in areas such as chemical safety in which a company's actions can affect people off-site. A company such as BeSafe may not be held fully liable for the consequences of a chemical accident. For example, the firm causing an accident may not be legally responsible for losses from related decreases in property values of surrounding homes or disruptions in community life.

One way for the government to enforce its regulations is to turn to the private sector for assistance. Specifically, third-party inspections coupled with insurance protection can encourage divisions in firms to reduce their risks from accidents and natural disasters. Such a management-based regulatory strategy shifts the locus of decision making from the regulator to firms, which are now required to do their own planning to meet a set of standards or regulations (Coglianese and Lazer 2003).

The passage of Section 112(r) of the Clean Air Act Amendments (CAAA) of 1990 offers an opportunity to implement such a program. This legislation requires facilities to perform a hazard assessment, estimate consequences from accidents, and submit a summary report to the U.S. Environmental Protection Agency (EPA) called the Risk Management Plan (RMP) (Belke 2001). The challenge currently facing the EPA is how to encourage compliance with these regulations so that firms will improve safety.

There is some urgency for a type of decentralized procedure with appropriate incentives due to the EPA's limited personnel and funds for providing technical guidance and auditing regulated facilities. Chemical firms, particularly smaller ones, have little financial incentive to follow centralized regulatory procedures if they estimate that the likelihood they will be inspected by a regulatory agency is very low and they will face a small fine if caught. In such cases, they may be willing to take their chances and incur the fine should they be caught violating the rule or regulation. This is like putting money into a parking meter. If you know that the chances of a meter being checked are very low and the fine is relatively small, then you might think twice before parting with your quarters.

The combination of two market mechanisms—third-party inspections and private insurance—creates a powerful incentive for firms to implement RMPs to make their plants safer. It also encourages the remaining firms to comply with the regulation to avoid being caught. The intuition behind using third parties and insurance to support regulations can be stated rather simply when the regulatory agency has limited personnel to enforce its own rules: Low-risk divisions, which the EPA has no need to audit, cannot credibly distinguish themselves from the high-risk ones without some type of inspection.[9]

By delegating part of the inspection process to the private sector through insurance companies and third parties, the EPA provides a channel though which the low-risk divisions in firms can speak for themselves. If a division chooses not to be inspected by third parties, it is more likely to be a high-risk one than a low-risk one. If it does get inspected and shows that it is protecting itself and the rest of the organization against catastrophic accidents, it will pay a lower premium than a high-risk division that is not undertaking these actions. In this way, the proposed mechanism not only substantially reduces the number of inspections the EPA has to undertake, but also makes their audits more efficient.

Kunreuther, McNulty, and Kang (2002) show more formally how such a program could be implemented in practice. They provide supporting evidence from pilot studies by the Department of Environmental Protection in Delaware and Pennsylvania, which worked closely with the insurance industry and chemical plants in testing the proposed program. Similar studies for small firms were undertaken by McNulty et al. (1999).

The process safety management unit of a firm should support this program for two reasons. It provides a rationale for the firm to hire third-party inspectors to make sure its

---

[9] The same logic of third-party inspections has been implemented in many domains. Perhaps the best known of these is the ISO 9000 quality standard. Such international standards are intended to reinforce best practices across organizations. These standards are almost always backed by audits as a means of assuring compliance with the standard. Research on ISO 14000 is discussed further in the text. For information on the standards development process at the International Standards Organization (ISO), see www.iso.org/iso/home.htm.

divisions are operating safely. The program also increases the firm's expected profits by reducing the negative externalities that divisions create due to its fear of being contaminated by others.

Future Research[10]

The problem of assessing and managing risks when interdependencies and network effects are present highlights the importance of undertaking research on both the descriptive and the prescriptive aspects of decision making for low-probability, high-consequence events. It also presents new challenges for the foundations of risk and security management in the presence of network interdependencies. Using the BeSafe chemical company example as background, we consider these challenges under the headings of risk assessment, risk perception, and risk management.

Risk Assessment

First, we need to collect more extensive data to estimate the risks and consequences of a catastrophic accident. The Wharton Risk Management and Decision Processes Center has analyzed accident history data from the U.S. chemical industry (Kleindorfer et al. 2007). This accident history data could be linked to financial information so one can analyze the association, if any, between the financial characteristics of the parent company of a facility and the frequency or severity of accidents. Similarly, the property damage estimates, and associated indirect costs from these, can be used to assess the consequences of environmental health and safety incidents on overall company performance and provide valuable insights for insurance underwriting for such accidents. Finally, the same data can be used to assess worst-case scenarios from such incidents, including those that might arise from site security risks associated with terrorism.

The second data collection project is a study of "near misses" in organizations and the systems that have been put into place to report and analyze these data (Phimister et al. 2003). Near misses are defined as incidents that, under different circumstances, could have resulted in major accidents. Linking this data on accident precursors to the accident history database may enable one to identify categories of precursors that give

---

[10] This section draws on Cohen and Kunreuther (2007).

early warnings of the potential for major accidents. Audit tools and other aspects of near-miss management can then focus not just on emergency response but also on the range of prevention and mitigation activities that can help avert major disasters. Even with this data, there will still be considerable uncertainty regarding the estimates of risks associated with these low-probability events (National Academy of Engineering 2004).

Risk Perception

Second, we need more research on how risk interdependencies affect firms' decision processes. The IDS models developed to date assume that individuals or firms make their decisions by comparing expected benefits with and without protection to the costs of investing in security. There is a growing literature in behavioral economics that suggests that individuals and firms make choices in ways that differ from such a rational model of choice (Kahneman and Tversky 2000). For example, there is evidence that people are myopic and do not appropriately take into account the long-term benefits of investing in protective measures, preferring instead to have a return on their investments over a relatively short period. Such short-term horizons may work against protection and prevention measures for low-probability, high-consequence events by the very nature of these events. It would be useful to understand what factors motivate managers' behavior and to consider strategies for making the investment more worthwhile. Some type of accounting arrangement by the firm to convert the upfront payment into a loan arrangement, for example, may enable managers to justify the upfront costs while relieving the division of budget constraints that may deter them from making the investment.

We also need to better understand how managers process information on risk when there is considerable uncertainty on the likelihood or consequences of an accident. We know that individuals have a difficult time dealing with ambiguous risks, particularly those of the low-probability variety (Slovic 2000). One telling example is the way the chemical industry behaved prior to and after the Bhopal disaster. Prior to the accident, there was a tendency to treat an accident such as the one that occurred in the Union Carbide plant in India as one that will not happen to "our firm." Following the disaster, all chemical companies undertook a detailed study of chemicals with catastrophic risk potential and took special measures to deal with them (Bowman and Kunreuther 1988).

Risk Management

Third, with respect to managing risks, we need to understand the impact of certified information, including audits, on behavior and outcomes in risky environments. For the chemical industry, for example, third-party inspection may serve the double purpose of providing information on the level of risk of particular installations as well as providing a signal to insurers and regulators on premiums and inspection levels for firms that invest in protective measures. Incentives implied by improved alignment of insurance premiums with the level of risk of a company can play an important role in inducing investments in risk reduction. Reliable third-party inspections can provide the necessary certification that the chemical firm has an appropriate risk-management plan and is operating in a safe manner. Regulatory agencies and public-interest groups may also find the audits/inspections to be of value, knowing that insurers and auditors are concerned with their own bottom line and would have no incentive to classify a firm as *not risky* if, in fact, it posed a high risk.

Another area that needs to be examined more carefully is the role that certifications, such as ISO 14000, can play in encouraging firms and divisions to operate more safely. In an analysis of ISO data and firm performance, Kang (2005) has shown that facilities that have had serious environmental problems were more likely to arrange to be ISO 14000 certified than lower-risk facilities and that their performance improved over that of the other facilities in the industry after they were certified. There is a tendency for many facilities in a firm to undertake ISO 14000 certification procedures at approximately the same time, suggesting that organizations are using this standard as a way of forcing many of their facilities to undergo an inspection that they might otherwise not consider.

Finally, there may be an important role that trade associations can play in providing guidelines for firms to follow with respect to their operations. The American Chemistry Council (ACC), an association of chemical manufacturers, has undertaken this role through its Responsible Care initiative. Since 1988, members of the ACC have significantly improved their environmental, health, safety, and, in recent years, security performance through the Responsible Care initiative. Participation in Responsible Care is mandatory for ACC member companies, all of which have made CEO-level commitments to uphold requirements that include a management system to drive environmental, health, safety, and security performance, sharing progress and activities with the public and having mandatory certification by independent, accredited auditing firms.[11]

---

[11] For more information on the Responsible Care program of ACC, see www.responsiblecare-us.com/.

Conclusion: Using Networks to Address Risks

Research in these areas can improve our understanding of the nature of interdependent risks and the effectiveness of strategies to address them. These risks arise in the context of networks, so we need to understand network relationships and interactions to understand the true nature of the risks. This requires assessing the risks of individual players and how their actions affect one another. As with the case of airline security discussed in the opening of this chapter, one weak link can erode the security of the entire network and create disincentives for individual investments in protective measures.

Because these risks arise within interdependent networks, effective solutions usually demand looking beyond an individual firm or division. These solutions may involve coordinating efforts across divisions in a firm, across a supply chain, or across the public and private sectors to create a context and supporting information for individual actions that decrease collective risk. These incentives can push the network to a tipping point or cascade that then reinforces behavior that benefits the entire network. The challenge of interdependent risks derives from network interactions. It is, therefore, not surprising that efficient solutions to these problems of interdependency require understanding and harnessing the power of the network.

References

Auerswald, P., L. Branscomb, T. LaPorte, and E. Michel-Kerjan. 2006. *Seeds of Disaster, Roots of Response: How Private Action Can Reduce Public Vulnerability.* New York: Cambridge University Press.

Barrett, S. 2003. Environment and Statecraft: the *Strategy of Environmental Treaty-Making*. Oxford University Press.

Belke, J. 2001. The case for voluntary third party risk management program audits. Paper presented at the 2001 Process Plant Safety Symposium of the American Institute of Chemical Engineers, April 23.

Bowman, E. H., and H. Kunreuther. 1988. Post Bhopal behavior of a chemical company. *Journal of Management Studies* 25, 387-402.

Coglianese, C., and D. Lazer. 2003. Management-based regulation: Prescribing private management to achieve public goals. *Law and Society Review* 37, 691-730.

Cohen, M., and H. Kunreuther. 2007. Operations risk management: Overview of Paul Kleindorfer's contributions. *Production and Operations Management* 18 (5), 525-541.

Dixit, A. K. 2002. Clubs with entrapment. *American Economic Review* 93, 1824-1829.

Heal, G., M. Kearns, P. Kleindorfer, and H. Kunreuther. 2006. Interdependent security in interconnected networks. In *Seeds of Disaster, Roots of Response: How Private Action Can Reduce Public Vulnerability,* ed. P. Auerswald, L. Branscomb, T. LaPorte, and E. Michel-Kerjan. New York: Cambridge University Press.

Heal, G., and H. Kunreuther. 2005a. IDS models of airline security. *Journal of Conflict Resolution* 41, 201-217.

Heal, G., and H. Kunreuther. 2005b. You can only die once. In *The Economic Impacts of Terrorist Attacks,* ed. H. W. Richardson, P. Gordon, and J. E. Moore II. Cheltenham, UK: Edward Elgar.

Kahneman, D., and A. Tversky. 2000. *Choices, Values and Frames.* New York: Cambridge University Press.

Kang, Y. 2005. The impacts of third party inspections on industrial safety and environmental performance. Philadelphia: Wharton School, University of Pennsylvania (mimeo).

Kearns, M. 2005. Economics, computer science, and policy. *Issues in Science and Technology* (Winter) 37-47.

Kleindorfer, P. R., R. Rosenthal, R. A. Lowe, R. Fu, and J. Belke. 2007. Accident epidemiology and the RMP rule: Learning from a decade of accident history from the U.S. chemical industry. Wharton Risk Management and Decision Processes Center Report, December 20, Philadelphia.

Kleindorfer, P. R., and G. H. Saad. 2005. Managing disruption risks in supply chains. *Production and Operations Management* 14 (1), 53-68.

Kunreuther, H., and G. Heal. 2005. Interdependencies in organizations. In *Organizational Encounters with Risk,* ed. B. Hutter and M. Powers. Cambridge: Cambridge University Press.

Kunreuther, H., P. McNulty, and Y. Kang. 2002. Improving environmental safety through third party inspection. *Risk Analysis* 22, 309-318.

McNulty, P., R. A. Barrish, R. C. Antoff, and L. C. Schaller. 1999. Evaluating the use of third parties to measure process safety management in small firms. 1999 Annual Symposium, Mary Kay O'Connor Process Safety Center, October 26, Texas A&M University.

Morgenson, G. 2008. Behind insurer's crisis, blind eye to a web of risk. *New York Times*, September 28, A1.

National Academy of Engineering. 2004. *Accident Precursor Analysis and Management.* Washington, DC: The National Academies Press.

Phimister, J., U. Oktem, P. Kleindorfer, and H. Kunreuther. 2003. Near-miss incident management in the chemical process industry. *Risk Analysis* 23, 445-459.

Schelling, T. 1978. *Micromotives and Macrobehavior.* New York: Norton.

Slovic, P. 2000. *The Perception of Risk.* London, UK: Earthscan.

23

Integration of Financial and Physical Networks in Global Logistics

Paul R. Kleindorfer
Ilias D. Visvikis

Abstract

Logistics is at the center of network-based manufacturing strategies, linking manufacturing sources with intermediate and final markets. As global logistics networks have grown and developed, they also have presented new challenge in managing risk and volatility across these broad, global networks. In this chapter, Kleindorfer and Visvikis discuss changes in logistics and financial instruments such as derivatives that have emerged to value and hedge the cost of capacity and services in these markets. They trace the recent history of maritime logistics and describe the convergence and integration of the physical and financial networks that underlie the valuation and use of logistics services. Global logistics illustrates how network-based strategies have integrated financial and physical networks. It also shows the emerging tools and competencies that have been needed to manage new risks arising from these broader networks.

Keywords: Logistics, Global Supply Chains, Risk Management, Derivatives.

Acknowledgment: The authors would like to thank Colin Crook, Manos Hatzakis, Manolis Kavussanos, Len Lindegren, Andrey Petrichtche, and Jerry Wind for comments on underlying issues related to this paper. Remaining errors and omissions are the responsibility of the authors.

In the past two decades, the forces and institutions that govern global economic activity have undergone immense changes. As shown in Figure 23-1, these include the ongoing development of the European Union, and the changes in liberalization and governance initiated by the World Trade Organization (WTO). Cross-border acquisitions and alliances, together with new markets and new forms of contracting, are supporting outsourcing, unbundling, contract manufacturing, and a variety of other forms of extended-value constellations. On the market side, the Internet has empowered consumers, given rise to peer-to-peer networks, and transformed whole industries. These Internet-related changes include the impact of Skype on the telecommunications industry, search engines such as Google, and the growth of e-retailing with companies such as Amazon and eBay. In tandem, developments in transportation and integrated logistics providers such as FedEx, UPS, and DHL have revolutionized global fulfillment architectures for business-to-business (B2B) and business-to-consumer (B2C) markets.

Continuing Growth in International Trade
Total Exports (M&S) 2001 = $7.6 Trillion
Total Exports (M&S) 2005 = $12.7 Trillion

Globalization
- increasing cross-border trade flows
- increasing demand for cross-border logistic & other services
- BPO&O

Markets, Risk & Volatility
- increasing deregulation and liberalization/WTO
- Markets & Politics/Sustainablility
- Increased Commodity Risks

Technology Drivers
- Decision aids
- Communications
- e-Commerce
- Open Innovation

Customer Empowerment
- Integrated Service Offerings
- Integration with business processes
- e-Empowerment

Growth of Supporting Infrastructure for Logistics and Contracting

Finland Post Corporation, Reprinted with Permission

Figure 23-1   Key trends driving profitability and uncertainty for management (Source: Finland Post Corporation. Reprinted with permission.)

Logistics is a key element of the interdependent megatrends illustrated in Figure 23-1. A mere 20 years ago, logistics (maritime, air, and land-based) was considered a mature industry, operated by "real men," with lots of inefficiencies and empty backhauls, huge cycles of overcapacity and undercapacity, and head-butting competition. The term "logistics" comes from the French *"maréchal de logis,"* the military officer responsible for organizing all camp facilities for troops at war. Reflecting these roots, it has traditionally focused on the physical management of material flows. The communications and information revolution gradually led to improved routing and scheduling, and eventually to improved operating efficiency through regional coordination of capacity. The megatrends shown in Figure 23-1 took logistics to an entirely new level, driven by outsourcing and huge increases in intraregional and international trade. Physical capabilities in international logistics began expanding in the 1990s, and growth has continued unabated, with Hong Kong and Dubai as the most evident examples, but with increases in capacity in nearly every established port. This increase in physical capabilities was accompanied by increased sophistication and intermediation activities of brokers and forwarders, followed by the development of financial overlays and trading instruments for shipping capacity.[1] The logistics industry is an interesting example of how physical markets have dovetailed with financial and information markets in supporting and profiting from globalization and outsourcing (as shown in Figure 23-1). It is also at the heart of the enabling infrastructure that has supported the explosion of international trade in the past decade.

This chapter explores these issues and, in particular, the integration of financial and physical markets as a driving force behind the emergence of global logistics. We first present an overview of the general trends in the global economy, as shown in Figure 23-1, relating the growth in international trade to changes in the accompanying logistics infrastructure. We then examine the evolution of the maritime industry, in particular the growing need for efficient operation of existing capacity and allocation of capital to new capacity. We analyze the evolution of risk-management techniques for hedging the most important sources of risk in the shipping industry, and conclude with a discussion of the managerial implications of the move toward network-enabled strategies and the key role played by financial and physical networks in logistics.

Globalization and Implications for Logistics Infrastructure

Globalization and the unbundling of value chains have been the major factors in the growth of logistics in the past decade. Reflecting the spirit of Adam Smith's *The Wealth of Nations* (1776), the two fundamental factors driving economic growth are specialization (to achieve economies of scale) and trade (to link the most cost-effective sources of product design and manufacturing to end markets). This logic drove international trade

---

[1] Kavussanos and Visvikis (2006, 2007) describe the growth in derivatives trading on shipping capacity. Kaminski (2004) describes related hedging options on aviation fuel and bunker fuel oil.

growth, particularly since the industrial revolution launched mass production of sufficient volume to make international distribution the key to profitability, initially for textiles, spices, and foodstuffs. Adam Smith's logic of specialization and trade became the dominant theme of national economic growth in the 1990s to the present.

In Europe, the fall of the Berlin Wall in 1989 led to the integration of Central and Eastern Europe into the market-based and financial institutions of Western Europe, and to the current 27-country marketplace of the European Union. In Asia, after decades of hesitation and uncertainty, China and India began their ascent to global leadership in low-cost manufacturing and information-based technology support. China's rapidly growing economy has been a major driver of the shipping boom from October 2003 to today. China's high rate of growth and industrialization, together with rapid urbanization, increased its imports of iron ore and oil. Since China entered the World Trade Organization (WTO), its exports also have increased. India's economic growth, which has been more service-sector-oriented, has not attracted as much direct capital investment as China.

Improvements in global logistics are reflected in part in the huge increases in outsourcing and offshoring (see OECD 2007), evident in the past decade as low-cost sources of goods and services and the unbundling of global supply chains. In contrast, U.S. economic growth has slowed (primarily due to the problems in its housing market), where the falling value of the U.S. dollar affected U.S. trade.

While business and entrepreneurship, and rational trade policy, are the natural vehicles for realizing the power of globalization, logistics has become the primary "glue" for integrating multitiered, global networks. The new logistics that has emerged in the past decade reflects a strategic view of the supply chain and greater emphasis on information and financial flows across the network. Starting with Porter's work on the Value Chain, and motivated by the huge success of the supply-chain rationalizations of the 1990s, many of the most successful and innovative companies now formulate their strategies and business models in simple operational terms (Amazon.com; Dell, Li & Fung; Southwest Airlines; Toyota; Zara; among others). They have developed innovative approaches, such as the JIT fulfillment strategies that have been the hallmark of the business model of Dell Computers[2] or the network reconfiguration strategies of Li & Fung (Fung, Fung, and Wind 2008). In this evolution, companies have moved from a narrow focus on costs of logistics to an appreciation of the customer's willingness to pay for reliability and tailored logistics solutions and to a closer scrutiny of the total financial costs of cross-border

---

[2] The saga of the Dell Computer story is described in Gilmore (2008). The original build-to-order supply-chain design has recently been evolving toward a build-to-stock supply chain, driven in part by logistics costs and changes toward retail sales.

relationships. As a result, logistics has become a motive force enabling unbundled value chains and product fulfillment across global networks in nearly every industry. Some details of the logistics evolution in response to these challenges are next.

Structure and Evolution of Air Cargo and Maritime Logistics

The basic structure of international logistics operations, involving many different organizations and economic transactions, is illustrated in Figure 23-2. Logistics operations entail significant investments in capacity, operating systems, and control systems. Some of these are public (terminal and port facilities) and some are private. Integrated logistics operators (UPS, FedEx, Lloyd's) and major shipbrokers/forwarders (Clarkson, SSY, FIS, Panalpina, and Kühne & Nagel) may provide or arrange for end-to-end service for certain classes of goods. Even with the assistance of integrated providers and intermediaries, however, companies that have major logistics operations will be exposed to various elements of risk, from disruptions to congestion to price and availability.[3] How these risks are managed, and how reliable physical availability of various logistics services is coordinated with global trade, is the central focus of this paper.

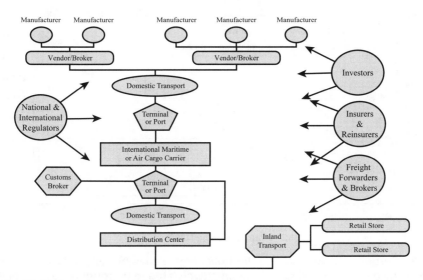

Figure 23-2   Multiple actors in global supply chains

---

[3] Disruption risk management (dealing with disruptions arising from strikes, terrorism, and natural disasters) is a matter of separate concern and has been the focus of heightened interest recently (Kleindorfer and Saad 2005; Bakshi and Kleindorfer 2008), but we will not focus on this issue here.

Logistics has followed the same path as other commodities in recent years.[4] Contracting for logistics services used to focus on physical factors such as domestic trucking and rail, port operations, shipping, or air cargo. The traditional approach was to contract with individual providers for services, usually with the assistance of a freight forwarding company. With the exponential growth of international trade in the past two decades, such piecemeal physical contracting gave way to the growth of integrated service providers and Third-Party Logistics (3PL) providers who would provide brokerage services—one-stop shopping—and arrange all services end-to-end, including warehousing, customers clearance, deconsolidation, and domestic transportation services. Sharp increases in the volume of global trade gave rise to increasingly liquid markets for buying and selling services and underlying capacity. Although initially these markets remained primarily contract markets for physical capacity, eventually financial instruments (as described in later text) began to emerge in international maritime operations. These instruments facilitate price discovery and risk management (hedging) of the primary cost drivers shown in Figure 23-2. During the past decade, we have seen an explosive growth in the use of these instruments to use both existing and new capacity more efficiently.

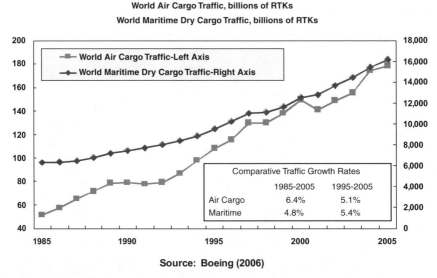

Figure 23-3   Cargo traffic is based on dry-bulk cargo trades (for example, merchandise), excluding crude oil and natural gas shipments (which made up roughly 40% of total international maritime cargo during this period). The results are given in revenue-tonne-kilometers (RTKs).

---

[4] See Kleindorfer and Wu (2003) and Geman (2005) for a discussion of the evolution of other commodity markets in this regard.

Logistics markets are fundamentally driven by the growth of international trade. As shown in Figure 23-3, global air cargo and marine cargo have grown rapidly over the past 20 years.

Less apparent in these figures is the growth in the sophistication of logistics providers over this same period. Four general areas can be noted where information technology, e-markets, and new hedging methods have revolutionized logistics across all sectors of air, maritime, and surface transportation:

1. *Operational control of logistics*, from automated warehousing and container technologies to real-time tracking and control technologies. New technologies include tamper-proof containers and RFID tracking technology, which provides better inventory management and reduces pilferage and theft (Gaukler, Seifert, and Hausman 2007). Moreover, new approaches to security have accompanied these control methods as well (Bakshi and Kleindorfer 2008).

2. *Capacity allocation methods*, to assure efficient utilization of existing capacity in the short and medium run. These include assuring better contracting methods through 3PL providers, and more complete backhaul utilization of freight capacity, as well as better control and routing of containers in cross-docking at ports and deconsolidation centers (Rushton and Walker 2007).

3. *Hedging and risk management*, using financial derivative instruments to mitigate the short- and medium-run financial risks associated with contracting for physical capacity in a world of increasing volatility and uncertainty.

4. *Capacity planning and capacity investment decisions*, for both logistics capacity and investments in logistics infrastructure.

These areas represent the core elements driving the integration of physical and financial networks in maritime logistics. The latter two will be explored in more detail in the next section, following the work of Kavussanos and Visvikis (2006, 2007).

Financial Risk Management in Shipping

Panayides (2006) attributes the convergence and integration of maritime transport and logistics to the "physical integration of modes of transport facilitated by containerization and the evolving demands of end-customers that require the application of logistics concepts and the achievement of logistics goals." Customers of shipping companies have shifted their focus to receiving complete door-to-door service from a single service provider at the least cost and high efficiency. Studies on the integration of maritime transport and logistics have examined specific areas in liner shipping and freight transportation/port integration (Heaver et al. 2000; Robinson 2002), liner shipping logistics services (Lu, Lai, and Cheng 2005), and port and logistics integration (Bichou and Gray 2005). Together with the integration of modes and organizations along the global supply chain, there has also been an integration of physical and financial contracting for maritime capacity.

To reduce risk of an increasingly volatile business environment, financial "paper" (derivatives) markets have grown significantly in the past decade. Although risk-management products based on derivatives, such as futures, forwards, options, and swaps, were originally designed for commodities (Geman 2005), these instruments can now provide risk management and investment (speculative) solutions and contracting in maritime logistics.[5]

Derivatives are important for risk management, as they allow risks to be separated and more precisely controlled. They provide two primary economic and social benefits. First, derivatives are useful in managing risk. Because derivatives are available for risk management, companies can undertake projects that might be impossible without advanced risk-management techniques. Second, derivatives aid in price discovery, generating publicly observable prices that provide information to the market about the true value of certain assets and the future direction of the economy. Thus, companies and individuals can use the pricing information discovered in the derivatives market to improve the quality of their economic decision making.

The benefits of innovations in risk-management strategies arising from the integration of physical and financial markets have been significant. The existence of derivatives products in shipping has made risk management cheaper, more flexible, and available to parties exposed to adverse movements in freight rates, bunker (fuel oil) prices, vessel prices, exchange rates, interest rates, and other variables that affect the cash-flow position of the shipping company and its customers. By using shipping derivatives, market participants in the shipping industry can secure (stabilize) their future income or costs and reduce uncertainty and volatility that arise from the fluctuations in prices and rates. Moreover, shipping derivatives can be used for the construction of speculative and arbitrage strategies. A comprehensive and detailed presentation, with illustrative

---

[5] As noted in Hellermann (2006), similar trends are emerging for air-cargo logistics. However, as shown in Figure 23-3, shipping represents the major mode of transportation of international trade and represents the focal point for value-added logistics services in the global economy.

applications, of the use of derivatives for managing business risks prevalent in the shipping business may be found in Kavussanos and Visvikis (2006).

As an example, the following section describes how alternative financial instruments can be used to hedge the most important source of risk of the maritime capacity: freight rate risk. The dry-bulk and tanker sectors of the shipping industry are covered as these are the most liquid markets and account for roughly two-thirds of seaborne trade movements. Slightly different considerations apply to container trade, where the markets and decisions supported are on a container basis.

Freight Rate Derivatives Products and Markets

Volatility of freight rates represents a major source of business risks for both ship owners and charters in competitive shipping markets. For the charterer wanting to hire in vessels for transportation, increasing freight rates leads to higher costs. In contrast, for the ship owner seeking employment for his vessels, lower freight rates generate less income from hiring out vessels. Freight derivatives contracts can be used to hedge this source of risk in the dry-bulk and tanker sectors of the shipping industry. These derivatives are traded either through exchanges or over-the-counter (OTC).

Compared to more traditional risk-management strategies in shipping, freight derivatives offer significant benefits for both ship owners and charterers. Kavussanos and Visvikis (2006) argue that by using a freight derivatives contract, compared to time-chartering a vessel, ship owners retain operational control of their vessels and at the same time benefit from favorable spot market conditions. On the other hand, derivatives free charterers from the operational risks present in time-charter agreements. The nature of freight derivatives contracts makes it easier to trade in and out of positions, compared to contracts on physical cargo. Freight derivatives do not require physical delivery, as they settle in cash upon conclusion of the contracts, and commissions payable to brokers are lower for freight derivatives than chartering agreements.

The first OTC freight derivatives in the shipping markets since 1992 was the Forward Freight Agreements (FFA) contract. FFAs are principal-to-principal private agreements between a seller and a buyer to settle a freight rate, for a specified quantity of cargo or type of vessel, for usually one, or a combination of the major trade routes of the dry-bulk or tanker sectors of the shipping industry. Because they can be "tailor-made" to suit the needs of their users, they have become very popular with market participants wanting to hedge freight rate fluctuations.

Dry-bulk trading routes, which serve as the underlying assets of the dry-bulk FFA contracts, are based on the Baltic Panamax Index (BPI), the Baltic Capesize Index (BCI), the Baltic Supramax Index (BSI), and the Baltic Handysize Index (BHSI). These indices comprise freight rates designed to reflect the daily movement in rates across dry-bulk spot voyage and time-charter rates. Each route is given an individual weighting to reflect its importance in the worldwide freight market, and routes are regularly reviewed to ensure their relevance to the underlying physical market. The trading routes for tanker trades are the Baltic Dirty Tanker Index (BDTI) and the Baltic Clean Tanker Index (BCTI).[6]

Since their introduction, FFA deals have grown substantially in both value and volume. Figures 23-4 and 23-5 show, respectively, the volume (number of contracts) and market value (in billions of US$) of dry-bulk FFA transactions, from inception until the end of 2006. The volume/value of trading has followed an exponential rise with the volume of 1,500 contracts that traded in 2000 increased to 9,700 by 2006, with a market value of more than US$32 billion (Kavussanos and Visvikis 2007).

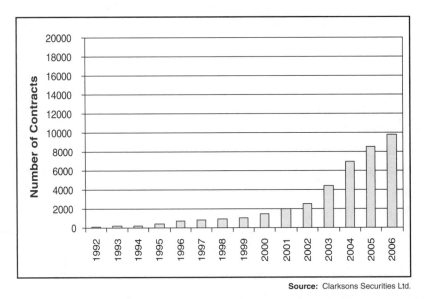

Source: Clarksons Securities Ltd.

Figure 23-4   Yearly volumes of dry-bulk FFA contracts (January 1992–December 2006).

---

[6] For an analytical description of the composition of the Baltic Exchange indices, see Kavussanos and Visvikis (2006, Chapter 3).

The following example illustrates the use of FFAs. Assume that on June 27, 2008, freight rates stand at $87,000/day in the trading route BPI 2a (Skaw-Gibraltar range to Far East—45 days). A charterer, which has to pay the cost of transporting his cargo of grain, believes that in one month freight rates may increase. To protect himself from a potentially more expensive future market, he takes a long (buy) position in an FFA contract to hedge his physical market exposure of $3,915,000 (= $87,000/day × 45 days). On the other hand, say a ship owner, who is the provider of the shipping service by offering his Panamax vessel for hire, believes that freight rates for the same route may fall in one month. The ship owner will then take the opposite position by selling an FFA, which expires in one month, at $87,000/day. These hedges ensure that the charter will pay only this amount, even if rates rise, and the ship owner will receive this amount, even if rates fall.

In the dry-bulk market, voyage-based contracts are settled on the difference between the contracted price and the average spot price of the route selected in the index over the past seven working days of the settlement month. Time-charter-based contracts are settled on the difference between the contracted price and the average price over the calendar settlement month. In the preceding example, say that the settlement price is $79,000/day, which is $8,000 below what the two sides expected ($87,000/day). The charterer, in effect, pays the difference of $360,000 ($8,000 × 45 days) to the shipper.

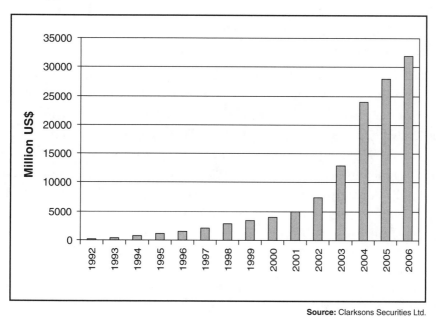

Source: Clarksons Securities Ltd.

Figure 23-5   Yearly market values of dry-bulk FFA contracts (January 1992–December 2006).

Given the increased volatility in energy and shipping rates, the current growth of FFA trades is expected to continue, with FFAs covering increasingly larger proportions of the underlying market. The exponential rise in FFA trading and the increasing liquidity and transparency of the market create increasing benefits to both shippers and direct customers, as well as to 3PL providers and intermediaries, such as forwarders and shipbrokers.

It should also be noted that in OTC derivatives markets, each party accepts credit-risk (or counter-party risk) from the other party. The primary advantage of an OTC market is that the terms and conditions of the contract are tailored to the specific needs of the two parties. This gives investors flexibility by letting them introduce their own contract specifications to cover their specific needs. On the other hand, if someone wants to eliminate the credit risk that emanates from OTC derivatives transactions, he can approach a derivative exchange that offers freight futures contracts. Such instruments can be found in the organized exchanges of the Oslo-based International Maritime Exchange (IMAREX) and the New York Mercantile Exchange (NYMEX), where they are cleared (mark-to-marked) by their associated clearinghouses. Clearinghouses for shipping derivatives are also active in London (LCH.Clearnet) and Singapore (SGX AsiaClear).[7] Clearing offers multilateral netting, removal of credit risk, standardized contracts, daily mark-to-market of positions, and increased trading liquidity, among other benefits. However, it should be noted that in recent years, with the arrival of banks and financial institutions into the FFA market, the credit-risk issue has decreased even further, as banks are ready to take some of the credit risk of FFA transactions.

In addition to futures and forward contracts, options contracts are further derivatives tools available for risk management and investment.[8] This type of financial derivatives contract has been used extensively on a number of underlying instruments, including exchange rates and interest rates. OTC freight options contracts have been available since 1997 on individual routes of the Baltic dry and tanker indices, as well as on baskets of time-charter routes of the indices and on the FFA contracts available on them. The same derivatives brokers that trade FFA contracts offer OTC freight options. The standard freight option contract is either a freight put option (floor) or a freight call option (cap). They settle the difference between the average spot rate over a defined

---

[7] For details on existing exchanges, see the companion electronic version of this paper Kleindorfer and Visvikis (2008), as well as Kavussanos and Visvikis (2006).

[8] See Wu and Kleindorfer (2005) and Geman (2005) for a general discussion of options products for commodities, and Spinler, Huchzermeier, and Kleindorfer (2003) for a discussion of the theoretical developments on options for logistics products.

period and an agreed strike price. A ship owner anticipating falling freight rates will buy a put option, agreeing to sell his freight service in the future at a price agreed today. He will exercise the put option (to sell at the agreed price) if the market freight rate falls below the agreed (exercise) price. Otherwise, he will let the worthless option expire, thus losing only the premium he paid upfront. On the other hand, a charterer can buy a call option, which he will exercise (to buy the freight service at the agreed price) if the market freight rate at expiry is higher than the agreed price. Otherwise, he will let the call option expire and lose only the premium. On June 1, 2005, the first cleared tanker IMAREX Freight Option (IFO) contract was launched, cleared through NOS. The IFOs are now available for trading and clearing to all IMAREX and NOS members, and are structured as monthly call and put Asian style options,[9] with monthly, quarterly, and yearly maturities.

The Impact of Derivatives on Physical Markets

Price discovery, as mentioned previously, refers to the use of one price series (for example, derivatives contract returns) to predict the action of another price series (for example, spot contract returns). The lead-lag relationship between the price movements of derivatives returns and the underlying spot-market returns illustrates how quickly one market reflects new information from another, tied together by arbitrage, and how well the two markets are linked. The informational efficiency of the shipping markets and logistical operations has increased due to the price discovery function of derivatives. Use of this "efficient" information set can lead to more efficient utilization of existing capacity and to the efficient introduction of new capacity.

Kavussanos and Visvikis (2004) investigate this assumption empirically, and more specifically, the lead-lag relationship between freight derivatives (paper) and spot (physical) shipping markets, in both returns and volatility. Results indicate a bidirectional causal relationship between paper and physical markets for all investigated trading routes, implying that derivatives prices can be just as important as sources of information as spot prices are in commodity markets. Further tests suggest that causality from freight derivatives to spot returns runs stronger than the other way around. Also, there is a bidirectional volatility spillover between the freight derivatives and the spot markets.

---

[9] An Asian option is an option that is exercised against an average over a period of time. Asian options are often used in thinly traded, volatile commodity markets to avoid problems with price manipulation of the underlying commodity near or at maturity.

Thus, it seems that freight derivatives prices contain useful information about subsequent spot prices, beyond that already embedded in the current spot price and, therefore, they can be used as price discovery vehicles. This can lead to a better assessment of risk management, ship chartering, budget planning, and logistical decision making.

A second aspect of price discovery refers to the unbiasedness hypothesis, under which derivatives prices must be unbiased (efficient) estimators of spot prices of the underlying asset that will be realized at the expiration date of the contract. Derivatives markets, therefore, can help discover prices, which are likely to prevail in the spot market and, thus, help in eliminating any possible price bubbles and cycles between the short-term cost of providing services and the prices asked. Kavussanos, Visvikis, and Menachof (2004) report that freight derivatives prices one month and two months prior to maturity are unbiased predictors of the realized spot prices in all investigated routes. Thus, market participants can use freight derivatives markets as indicators of the future course of spot markets to guide their physical market decisions and, therefore, minimize or eliminate any potential (abnormal) price discrepancies.

Finally, many derivatives markets have been criticized for increasing (destabilizing) spot market price volatility. This issue has been the subject of considerable empirical research and has received the attention of derivatives users and policymakers. Kavussanos, Visvikis, and Batchelor (2004) investigate the impact of the introduction of freight derivatives on spot market price volatility and on the information asymmetries that existed before in the spot market. The results suggest that the onset of FFA trading (1) has had a stabilizing impact on the spot price volatility of all investigated routes; (2) has had an impact on the asymmetry of volatility (market dynamics); and (3) has substantially improved the quality and speed of information flow. It appears that there has been an improvement in the way that news is transmitted into prices following the onset of freight derivatives trading. The authors conclude (p. 295) that FFA trading has facilitated the incorporation of information into spot prices more quickly "by attracting more, and possibly better informed, participants into the market."

In summary, financial derivatives contracts in shipping markets have helped to better use market information by creating hedging opportunities. Market participants can now better utilize current and new capacity, arrange the transportation transactions and services better and faster (improved transactional efficiency), and minimize the potential extreme (abnormal) values (such as price bubbles) of the underlying traded commodities, leading to improved efficiency in logistic markets.

Conclusion

Logistics is a prime example of how globalization has driven the integration of physical and financial networks to provide primary services and supporting infrastructure. This example also shows the importance of creating new instruments for risk management for buyers, sellers, and investors in these services. Network-based systems may require new ways of thinking about and managing risks across the players in the networks, as with the derivatives that have been created to address logistics risks.

The history of globalization illustrates the tremendous power of specialization and trade as continuing sources of economic growth. It also shows the huge synergies, and inexorable force, driving the integration of financial and physical markets. This integration is necessary to mediate the unbundling of specialization and the rebundling enabled by orchestrated value-added networks that are interconnected by information technology and flexible logistics. Logistics has followed a similar trend to that of nearly every other commodity or near-commodity market, evolving from purely physical and piecemeal contracting to broader, more liquid markets, to the emergence of brokers and intermediaries, to full-fledged derivatives markets for valuation, sourcing, and hedging.

Logistics provides the infrastructure for other networks, deriving its basic value from the more direct value-added activities and products its supports. In this sense, logistics acts as a supernetwork connected to many other physical fulfillment networks (for example, in international retail supply chains, as well as in metals, agriculture, and energy). It enables these networks to function as well as providing financial and risk overlays for the full cost of these subnetworks. The evolution of logistics markets, and their integration with other markets, testifies to the power of markets as integration mechanisms par excellence. Compared to the pre-network age of a decade ago, the network effects of globalization, unbundling, and rebundling encompassed by the new logistics are staggering. What was previously a local and opaque evolution in pricing and the availability of logistics capacity has now become more transparent and more manageable from both a financial and a physical perspective, making it better able to fulfill the central role expected of it as the glue of international trade.

A final area of concern is the risks from the environmental footprint of globalization. If the climate-change mitigation continues as expected, we can expect the integration of carbon markets and footprints with logistics clearinghouses. This could encompass CO_2 emission certificates, just as bunker oil and exchange-rate risks have been integrated with logistics markets and pricing. This adds another layer to the continuing evolution from the prenetwork era of local pricing, piecemeal contract-based trading, and local impact assessment to the increasingly sophisticated postnetwork era of global pricing, market-based trading, and global impact assessment. As such new network challenges move center stage, they will demand new network-based solutions to address them.

References

Bakshi, N., and P. R. Kleindorfer. 2008. Competition and investment for resilience in global supply chains. Forthcoming in *Production and Operations Management*.

Bichou, K., and R. Gray. 2005. A critical review of conventional terminology for classifying seaports. *Transportation Research Part A* 39, 75-92.

Boeing. 2006. World air cargo forecast 2006-2007. Boeing Commercial Airplanes, Seattle (WA).

Fung, V. F., W. K. Fung, and Y. Wind. 2008. *Competing in a Flat World*. Upper Saddle River, NJ: Wharton School Publishing.

Gatignon, H., and J. Kimberly. 2004. *The Alliance on Globalization*. Cambridge University Press.

Gaukler, G. M., R. W. Seifert, and W. H. Hausman. 2007. RFID in the retail supply chain. *Production and Operations Management* 16 (1), 65-76.

Geman, H. 2005. *Commodities and Commodity Derivatives*. Chichester, UK: John Wiley.

Gilmore, Dan. 2008. The new supply chain lessons from Dell. *Supply Chain Digest* (April 10), www.scdigest.com/assets/FirstThoughts/08-04-10.php?cid=1609.

Hammer, M. 1990. Re-engineering work: Don't automate, obliterate. *Harvard Business Review* (July-August), 104-112.

Heaver, T., H. Meersman, F. Moglia, and E. Van de Voorde. 2000. Do mergers and alliances influence European shipping and port competition? *Maritime Policy and Management* 27, 363-373.

Hellermann, R. 2006. *Capacity Options for Revenue Management: Theory and Applications in the Air Cargo Industry*. Verlag, Heidelberg: Springer.

Kaminski, V. 2004. *Managing Energy Price Risk*. London: Risk Books.

Kavussanos, M. G., and I. D. Visvikis. 2004. Market interactions in returns and volatilities between spot and forward shipping markets. *Journal of Banking and Finance* 28 (8), 2015-2049.

Kavussanos, M. G., and I. D. Visvikis. 2006. *Derivatives and Risk Management in Shipping*. 1st ed. London: Witherbys Publishing.

Kavussanos, M. G., and I. D. Visvikis. 2007. Derivatives in freight markets. Special Report Commissioned by Lloyd's Shipping Economist (LSE), A Lloyd's MIU Publication, Informa Business, London, December.

Kavussanos, M. G., I. D. Visvikis, and R. Batchelor. 2004. Over-the-counter forward contracts and spot price volatility in shipping. *Transportation Research—Part E, Logistics and Transportation Review* 40 (4), 273-296.

Kavussanos, M. G., I. D. Visvikis, and D. A. Menachof. 2004. The unbiasedness hypothesis in the freight forward market: Evidence from cointegration tests. *Review of Derivatives Research* 7 (3), 241-266.

Kleindorfer, P. R., and F. H. Saad. 2005. Disruption risk management in supply chains. *Production and Operations Management* 14 (1), 53-68.

Kleindorfer, P. R., K. Singhal, and L. N. Van Wassenhove. 2005. Sustainable operations management. *Production and Operations Management* 14 (4), 482-492.

Kleindorfer, P. R., and D. J. Wu. 2003. Integrating long-term and short-term contracting via business-to-business exchanges for capital-intensive industries. *Management Science* 49 (11), 1597-1615.

Lu, C.-S., K.-H. Lai, and T. C. E. Cheng. 2005. An evaluation of website services in liner shipping in Taiwan. *Transportation* 32, 293-318.

OECD. 2007. Offshoring and employment: Trends and impacts. Organization for Economic Co-operation and Development, Paris.

Panayides, P. 2006. Maritime logistics and global supply chains. *Maritime Economics and Logistics* 8, 3-18.

Porter, M. 1985. *Competitive Advantage.* New York: Free Press.

Robinson, R. 2002. Ports as elements in value-driven chain systems: The new paradigm. *Maritime Policy and Management* 29, 241-255.

Rushton, A., and Walker, S. 2007. *International Logistics Supply Chain Outsourcing.* London: Kogan Page Ltd.

Smith, A. 1776. *The Wealth of Nations (An Inquiry into the Nature and Causes of the Wealth of Nations).* Republished in 1991 (New York: Prometheus Books).

Spinler, S., A. Huchzermeier, and P. R. Kleindorfer, 2003. Risk hedging via options contracts for physical delivery. *OR Spectrum* 25 (3), 379-395.

Wu, D. J., and P. R. Kleindorfer. 2005. Competitive options, supply contracting and electronic markets. *Management Science* 51 (3), 452-466.

24

Telecommunications: Network Strategies for Network Industries?

Kevin Werbach

Abstract

Telecommunications is a networked business, yet it traditionally has resisted a network-based view in its strategies and business models. In this chapter, Kevin Werbach explores this paradox, contrasting the worldview of Monists such as AT&T, who see the infrastructure as inseparable from the network, and Dualists such as Google, who see the network and its applications as distinct from the underlying infrastructure. Not surprisingly, AT&T is a proponent of "tiered access" whereas Google argues for "network neutrality." Finally, Werbach examines how a more modular future might bridge the gap between those who seek to own and capitalize on the network and those who seek to expand it through more neutral offerings.

If there is a sector of the economy that should embrace network-based thinking, it is telecommunications. Surprisingly, the opposite is the case. The leading firms building telecommunications and Internet infrastructure increasingly emphasize consolidation, hierarchy, and exclusive control, rather than collaboration and decentralization. Regulators are dismantling legal frameworks that once promoted openness and interconnection, in favor of misguided efforts to create incentives for proprietary investment. And many scholars, even those challenging the current drift of policy and business models, embrace a static worldview that is a relic of earlier eras. Network-based strategies are thus hard to find today in the so-called "network industries," even as such ideas flourish in adjacent digital information markets. This chapter explores the origins of this paradox, describes its manifestations in the legal and business environment, and traces a more hopeful future.

Telecommunications industry participants and scholars may be divided into two camps: Monists and Dualists. The Monists see physical network infrastructure as the linchpin of the telecommunications and Internet ecosystem. Any activity using that infrastructure must first ensure adequate cost recovery for the massive investments involved in building it. The Dualists, on the other hand, see a division between the network infrastructure, which is an enabling utility, and the activities on top, which are the locus of innovation and value. They urge regulation of the network to free the applications, communication, and content, whereas the Monists believe the network should be permitted to impose greater controls. Both sides recognize that their industries are undergoing dramatic transformation, with the potential to both create and destroy monumental amounts of value. The Monists have been in the ascendancy in recent years, at least in the United States. However, the victories they achieve are pyrrhic. Innovation on top of the network is being stifled, and the forces undermining the Monists' cost-recovery business models are merely being slowed, not stopped.

A Network-Based View of Telecom

Communications systems are nothing more or less than information pathways connecting human and machine nodes.[1] They are, in other words, networks by definition. The telegraph, telephone, radio, television, mobile phones, and online information services are perfectly modeled as network graphs. Engineers use network-based techniques to build and manage telecommunications networks, in areas such as traffic modeling and system architecture. And those in the telecommunications industry invariably describe and represent the infrastructure with the terminology of networks.[2] Nonetheless, truly network-based business strategies are hard to find in today's telecommunications infrastructure sector.

---

[1] This chapter focuses primarily on the networks of telecommunications carriers such as AT&T and Verizon, and to a lesser extent on cable television providers such as Comcast and Time Warner and mobile phone operators such as AT&T and Verizon Wireless. The examples given generally involve the United States, unless otherwise specified.

[2] On the other hand, as noted in Mitchell 2006, at least one U.S. Senator describes the Internet as "a series of tubes."

There is a great deal of network-oriented analyses to draw on. Peter Huber's influential analyses of the modern telephone system as a "geodesic network" more than 20 years ago (Huber 1987) explained in detail how network properties influence cost structures, competition, and innovation. More recently, network scientists have engaged in extensive study of the properties of the Internet and its physical infrastructure (Pastor-Satorras and Vespignani 2004). For example, researchers showed that sites on the World Wide Web (Albert, Jeong, and Barabasi 1999) and Internet routers (Faloutsos, Faloutsos, and Faloutsos 1999) follow a power-law distribution in degree of connectivity. There have also been a few academic efforts to apply network-theoretic techniques to telecommunications policy (Spulber and Yoo 2005; Werbach 2008b). However, such findings have not so far connected with the business models of network operators or those who use their infrastructure.

Most telecommunications infrastructure owners view their assets as nodes—even though those assets are networks. Each network operator's node connects horizontally to other network infrastructure nodes, and vertically to application/content providers or customers, but the value arises in the nodes, not their interconnection. This is not as odd as it might seem. All Coasian firms are networks, but they are subject to central and hierarchical control to minimize transaction costs (Coase 1937). In telecommunications, fixed investments for network deployment are generally more significant than recurring transaction costs. The mainstream view of the industry, therefore, emphasizes backward-looking cost recovery over the forward-looking catalytic potential of distributed activity on the interconnected network.

The one area of network theory that has made its way into the business and policy discussion around telecommunications infrastructure is network effects (Rohlfs 1974). "Network effects" refers to the positive externalities of networked activity, which, among other things, cause networks to enjoy increasing returns to scale. A bigger network gives users access to more users, and to more content or services that can be delivered through the network. As analyzed by Katz and Shapiro (1985), network effects have complex impacts in telecommunications-based markets. They allow new services, such as Google, Facebook, or Skype, to grow extremely rapidly, because their value proposition improves with more users. On the other hand, network effects mean that, even with absent anticompetitive behavior, network industries may tend toward concentration, as AT&T demonstrated in its early days by exploiting its larger network and strategically refusing to interconnect with others.

Recent developments in the telecommunications industry, such as the growth of the Internet, have only enhanced its network-centric characteristics (Shapiro and Varian

1998). Since the 1970s, the telecommunications sector has evolved from a collection of vertically integrated, often government-owned, monopoly telephone companies to a diverse mesh of interconnected wired, wireless, and data networks (Nuechterlein and Weiser 2005). Barriers between geographies, transmission modalities, legal structures, formats, services, and devices are collapsing dramatically. Where once AT&T and its brethren dominated as vertically integrated colossi, today the world's largest telecommunications company in subscribers is China Mobile (Xinhua Financial News 2008), and in capacity is, by some reckonings, Google.[3] Prices have plummeted as service offerings have exploded.

Today's telecommunications industry is, on some levels, radically interdependent. Even behemoths such as AT&T cannot always serve customers without handing off traffic to other carriers. A telephone call from an AT&T customer to a Comcast or Sprint customer is a collective effort of competitors, because both law and customer expectations dictate cooperation (Werbach 2008a). The rise of the Internet, a "network of networks" that significantly decentralizes intelligence and control, has accentuated this tendency (Werbach 1997; Werbach 2008b). A simple search query to Google, in a fraction of a second, can incorporate handoffs among multiple data network operators and swarms of distributed servers around the globe. As Benkler (2006) and Lessig (2001) elucidate in detail, the Internet is an open infrastructure platform, which allows for many different uses. Those uses are defined not by the network owner, but by network users. The network owner may offer specific services, but usage of the network is not limited to those services (Frischmann 2005).

The emergence of a diffuse, interconnected infosphere has so far failed to elevate network-based thinking in either the telecommunications boardroom or the academy. As we enter the broadband era, leading telecommunications carriers proclaim the need for "managed" networks (Yoo 2006). They lock out potential rivals, throttle peer-to-peer applications, lock mobile phones to particular networks, hatch plans to charge content and application providers for the privilege of reaching users, and develop standards to control rather than encourage usage (Wu 2003). It is no accident that the nation where this proprietary approach is most prominent, the United States, has gone from the dominant adopter of narrowband Internet access to a laggard in broadband penetration, near the bottom of Organization for Economic Cooperation and Development (OECD) and other rankings (OECD 2007).

---

[3] Google does not publicly disclose details about its network capacity. However, it operates a massive distributed network of hundreds of thousands of computers in data centers around the globe, which requires tremendous communications capacity. Both internal and external sources have anecdotally suggested that it now distributes more bandwidth than any telephone company.

The carriers are aided in their efforts by regulators and scholars, who either promote a return to centralized, proprietary control or advocate artificial barriers that ignore the essential fluidity of the networked information economy. On one side, "free market" thinkers ignore the voluminous evidence that network topologies are important in ways that simple rational-actor models do not capture, as explained in Crawford (2007) and Benkler (2006). On the other side, opponents of the incumbent carriers' vision of a managed network rally around "network neutrality" rules that would prohibit operators from blocking or degrading unaffiliated content and applications (Wu 2003). Neither camp is happy with the current situation. Incumbent telecommunications carriers fear their businesses will be hollowed out, and application providers fear that their growth and innovation will be constrained. As discussed later, there is some cause for optimism about the future.

Network Monists and Dualists: AT&T and Google

The strategies of two major players in the telecommunications and Internet marketplace—AT&T and Google—offer insights into two competing views of telecommunications networks. On the one hand, Monists, such as AT&T, see the physical infrastructure as the only "real" network, with applications, services, and content as subsidiary phenomena. In contrast, Dualists, such as Google, see additional layers of functionality on top of that infrastructure as the source of value for users, with the physical connections as merely a means to that end.

Although Google is not considered a telecom company, it resembles a traditional network operator such as AT&T in many ways.[4] Both invest billions of dollars annually in fiber-optic transmission links, and in geographically distributed data centers filled with computers that route and deliver services to the millions of users of their networks. Both generate billions of dollars of annual revenue from customers who value the services those networks provide. Both must interconnect their networks with others, because no single provider can control access to every user worldwide. Both think of themselves as their customers' trusted gateway to the richness of the Internet. Both are expanding aggressively into video, and both see wireless data services as an increasingly important growth area.

---

[4] Gilder (2006) and Carr (2008) discuss the development of "cloud computing" infrastructures by Google and others, which deliver information services through networked data centers.

Yet the two companies' business models are dramatically different. AT&T charges connection and usage fees for access to its network, by both customers and other operators. Google gives away its dominant service, search, for free, and also provides free access to application programming interfaces for third parties to "mash up" its services into their own offerings. AT&T charges well-defined prices that are carefully differentiated to maximize revenue based on its customers' willingness to pay. Google makes virtually all its money from advertisers participating in a continuous real-time auction for placement in its search results, with no payments until Google delivers a concrete result. AT&T defines specifications and purchases its software and hardware from a variety of providers, such as switch vendors, billing system providers, and mobile handset manufacturers. Google ties together commodity computers and open-source software with its own internally developed "cloud computing" software platform (Carr 2008; Gilder 2006). AT&T's new offerings emerge after multiyear development cycles and typically involve incremental fees. Google tweaks its search algorithms constantly, and constantly introduces new services with no business model other than driving usage of the core search/advertising platform.

AT&T and Google diverge in other ways as well. The company that today bears the name AT&T was formed through the consolidation of four of the seven regional "Baby Bells" and the long-distance operator that retained the AT&T name after the 1984 government-mandated divestiture. Google was founded in 1998 by two Stanford graduate students, and its acquisitions have been either small or, as with YouTube and DoubleClick, expansions into new markets. AT&T is a leading proponent of "tiered access," under which content and applications providers (including Google) would pay network operators for enhanced connections to AT&T's broadband customers (Werbach 2008a). Google is a leading advocate of "network neutrality" regulations to preclude such approaches, to the extent that they block or discriminate against unaffiliated providers. Many of these differences are rooted in history. AT&T built its infrastructure as a regulated utility, with competition prohibited and profits guaranteed under a rate-of-return system. Google could take the global network infrastructure as a given, allowing it to invest only in less-costly and more localized data centers, computers, and software.

These differences reflect a fundamental tension. There are two possible views of communications infrastructure, which I will call the Monist and the Dualist perspective. AT&T typifies the Monist viewpoint, whereas Google represents the Dualist approach. A successful vision for telecommunications in a network-centric world must take both views into account.

Monists and Dualists differ in critical ways. Monists emphasize the supply side, and control of physical networks of wires and switches. Dualists emphasize the demand side, facilitating applications such as telephone service, video distribution, or searching the Internet. Monists live in a world in which fixed costs are high, variable costs are negligible, and congestion is a negative externality to solve through pricing. Monists, therefore, seek managed hierarchical networks, metered pricing, value capture through proprietary advantage, and clear lines of service differentiation. Dualists draw more from network economics and complexity theory, stressing the positive externalities of network effects. They support radical openness and connectivity, and seek to drive the price of admission to zero, so as to more easily grow a community that can be monetized in other ways.

As shown in Figure 24-1, Monists and Dualists perceive the same world, but they understand the relationship of users and the network differently.[5] Monists see the infrastructure as the business, while Dualists see the infrastructure as a platform for experiences. Generally speaking, Monists include those who operate communications networks, and those who sell equipment to those operators. Dualists include most of the companies that deliver content and services through the Internet, such as Yahoo!, Amazon.com, Google, and Microsoft.[6] These two camps are largely on opposite sides of debates over network neutrality, wholesale access requirements for networks and wireless spectrum, unlicensed wireless access, and imposition of regulatory obligations on Internet-based services.

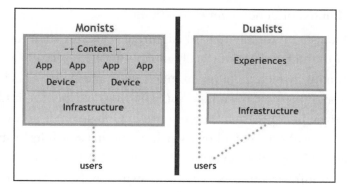

Figure 24-1 Monist and Dualist perspectives on the network

[5] The diagram is quite stylized for clarity. In the real world, the dividing lines are not always so clear. Many services "on top of" the network incorporate devices at the customer premises or within the network switching fabric, for example.

[6] Academics are split between the two camps. Anecdotally, the majority of economists seem to adhere to the Monist view, while the majority of legal scholars appear to favor the Dualist perspective. Engineers are divided, often based on whether their roots are in studying telecommunications or data networking.

The Monist Perspective

Monists see communications and information industries as integrated value chains, analogous to the traditional distribution chains in many industries. In their view, operators invest capital to deploy networks, and they are entitled to recover those costs from users of their networks. The benefits of telecommunications and information services accrue from these decisions to put capital at risk, and therefore strategy and public policy should make such investments as palatable as possible (Singer and Litan 2007). For a Monist, the goal is to maximize the value of the interconnected system of networks and what runs on top of them. Thoughtful Monists appreciate that this is not the same thing as centralizing all value in the network and crowding out the services on top. That may have been possible in the old days of the centralized, rigid telephone network, but even what we call the phone network no longer works that way, thanks to technological advances and newly possible competition.

Monists tend to be reductionists. They focus on the basic components of network connectivity, the networks themselves, because without them the ecosystem could not exist. A network without content or applications may be rigid and sterile, like the traditional phone network, but networked applications without a network are nothing. To a Monist, moreover, networks and what they carry are subject to the same basic economic laws, under which the apportionment of fixed and variable costs are critical. Physical infrastructure is dominated by high fixed costs and tremendous economies of scale, often leading to limited or nonexistent competition.

This leads Monists inexorably toward capturing a greater share of the ecosystem's value creation in the network, or vertically integrating higher-level functions with the network infrastructure, which amounts to much the same thing. This is in the natural interests of network operators, of course, but from their perspective it ultimately benefits everyone. Verizon benefits from the presence of Google on its network, the thinking goes, but Google *needs* Verizon, without which it couldn't reach its customers. Verizon doesn't just provide Google the benefit of connectivity; it frees Google from having to invest in the costly infrastructure of wires and switches itself. Thus, to a Monist, the Googles of the world should be responsible for their "share" of network costs, before considering any other economics of their business.

The Monist perspective is rooted in the history of telephony.[7] Unlike the telegraph, which was a point-to-point system between local offices and relay points, the telephone network is designed to connect all endpoints. The innovation of telephone carriers, led by

[7] This analysis draws heavily on the influential work of Huber (1987).

AT&T, was to construct a system that could affordably deliver calls between any individual or company in a city, a country, and eventually the world (Werbach 2008a). They did so through a hierarchical structure, using switching, regional lines, and high-capacity "long lines" spanning the country. This system was by nature centralized and hierarchical.

Because AT&T controlled its own switching hierarchy, and could decide whether to interconnect with other carriers, it recognized early on that network effects would determine the ultimate structure of the industry. Other networks could afford to build lines to a cluster of customers in a city or region, but not to duplicate AT&T's national footprint. They could, therefore, compete only by interconnecting with AT&T, which was initially under no legal obligation to do so. Under CEO Theodore Vail, AT&T skillfully used strategic denial of interconnection, standardization requirements, and acquisitions to achieve an unassailable position of dominance. The U.S. government, convinced by AT&T's argument that it was the only means of delivering "universal service" throughout the nation, ratified AT&T's monopoly position in the Kingsbury Commitment of 1913. It would remain largely unchallenged for decades.

Beginning in the 1960s and gaining speed in the intervening decades, the legally enforced AT&T monopoly crumbled (Nuechterlein and Weiser 2005). A combination of technological changes, new competitive entrants, and a shift in the government mindset undermined its hierarchical foundations. The introduction of computerized switching and digital communications links dramatically reduced the costs of the network. What Peter Huber (1987) famously labeled a geodesic network—a mesh of interconnected switches on multiple competing network platforms—became the efficient economic structure. Competitors such as MCI and Sprint entered the long-distance market, eventually with the blessing of the U.S. government, which forced a breakup of AT&T in the mid-1980s. The Federal Communications Commission, in its *Computer Inquiry* decisions, prevented AT&T and its descendents from interfering with the growth of computer-based information services (Werbach 2005).

In recent years, with the rise of digital transmission and the open internetworking environment of the Internet, the telecommunications sector has entered a new era of convergence. Any network operator can, in theory, offer virtually any service, from television programming to broadband Internet access. Thus, telephone companies deploying fiber-optic networks compete with cable television providers and direct broadcast satellite companies to offer multichannel video programming. Millions of customers have migrated their primary phone service from wireline to wireless, so much that mobile phone connections far outnumber fixed lines worldwide, and landlines in service in the United States have peaked after a century of growth. And services delivered entirely on top of network infrastructure, such as the peer-to-peer telephony service Skype, now compete directly with legacy network-based offerings (Werbach 2008a).

This diversity and fluidity of the converged communications environment poses serious challenges for communications policy (Huber 1997). Most acutely, it undermines the Monist pre-Copernican worldview, in which the network infrastructure is the immovable center of the universe, leading to a very different view of telecommunications networks.

The Dualist Perspective

At the other end of the spectrum are network Dualists, who see networks as a means to an end. Tim Wu, a leading network neutrality advocate, notes that information infrastructure is "most valuable as general purpose input into *other* activities" (Wu 2007).

The great benefit of the Dualist view is that it recognizes that services on top of physical networks, such as Skype's voice over Internet protocol software, Facebook's social networking platform, Google's search engine, and YouTube's video aggregation service, are themselves subject to network dynamics. Moreover, because the Internet and the World Wide Web provide an open, standards-based environment for such applications, they are increasingly coming together through "mashups" and other interactions (Benkler 2006). Google syndicates advertisements to independent Web sites, sharing a portion of its revenues, and Facebook encourages developers to create third-party applications for its tens of millions of users, to name two prominent examples. Customers think little about the broadband infrastructure that undergirds all these services; it is a doorway to the networks they experience, rather than the network itself.

The difficulty with the Dualist view is that it relentlessly squeezes value out of the network itself. The applications, services, and content delivered through the network grow in value, while the network itself is impoverished. This leads to what David Isenberg and David Weinberger (2002) have called "the paradox of the best network." Building on the work of financial analyst Roxanne Googin, they point out that the ideal from a Dualist perspective is one that offers network operators no hope of making money. Those offering services on top of the network depend on the network being built and enhanced, but that is difficult to expect when the network cannot capture the value of the entire system.

In response to the paradox of the best network, some network operators have tried to grow their way out of the box or offer their own networked applications and services.

So far, however, these offerings have done little to pry users away from their preferred unaffiliated services. Network operators also have tried to recapture some of the value that otherwise would accrue solely to the users of the network. Through pricing structures, restrictive services offerings, or discriminatory practices, they find ways to shift some of the economic gains from the network ecosystem into their own pockets.

Regulators and business leaders in telecommunications face the great challenge of squaring the past and the future. The paradox of the best network means that the right strategy for network operators today differs from the approach under which they undertook the massive investments needed to build their infrastructure. Internet-based service providers may not want to concern themselves with the settled expectations and property rights of their antagonists' investors. However, any comprehensive welfare-maximizing perspective must. Moreover, the Internet-based providers have no desire to see the network infrastructure collapse. It is essential to their businesses.

The Modular Future

The key strategic question for telecommunications today is to find a way out from the limitations of both the Monist and the Dualist worldviews. Networks have become increasingly complex, competitive, and densely interconnected. Yet, even as telecommunications has come increasingly to exhibit the distributed structures that researchers see in social, business, ecological, Web-based, and other networks, it has also gradually dissociated the processes of moving information from the content and uses of that information. Content and conduit increasingly inhabit separate spheres. Though often promoted for valid policy and business reasons, this rigid segmentation of applications and connectivity is ultimately counterproductive. Each depends on the other. And in a networked world marked by fluidity, diversity, openness, and decentralization, such immutable divisions are anachronistic.

A modular structure, emphasizing neither infrastructure nor applications, may offer a way out of this dilemma. End users would utilize services that combined content, processing, and transport, often from different providers, but as unified experiences. Google itself offers an example of how infrastructure and applications might come together. As a business, it is a search engine and an exchange for online advertising. Yet the physical instantiation of that virtual platform is a distributed network of hundreds of thousands of commodity computers, linked together into a massive distributed "cloud" computer (Gilder 2006).

Google is aggressively purchasing dark fiber and spending billions of dollars each quarter on physical data centers. It is even part of a consortium laying a new trans-Pacific undersea cable. It is doing so not to enable communications capabilities, although it offers a voice chat service and YouTube video sharing, among other services. Google is investing in capacity to power its cloud computing platform. The more devices and capability it can add to the network, the more data it can process and the more intelligence it can deliver. That "global brain" powers everything Google does, whether the outputs take the form of interactive data services, live communication, or media distribution. And Google is working to extend that platform beyond Internet-connected computers, seeing mobile phones, broadcast television, and even print magazines as potential endpoints.

At the same time as it grows, Google is opening up many elements of its platform. It provides interfaces for third-party developers to leverage its Google Earth mapping engine and other services. It syndicates its advertisements to thousands of other Web sites. And in its forays into spectrum policy, it is advocating "open access" rules under which wireless licensees would provide wholesale capacity without limitations on the devices and services that ride the network, in stark contrast to current business practices.

In short, Google is creating a modular platform, which can leverage outside resources and also deliver components of Google's internal capability for integration with other platforms. This approach is not unique. In fact, it lies at the heart of the "Web 2.0" trend that animates many of the established and up-and-coming companies in the Internet economy today. And as Google demonstrates, it is not a strategy that requires purely "virtual" operation, free from significant capital expenditure requirements. Yet there is nothing quite like it among infrastructure-based telecommunications providers.

Regulation can hasten the arrival of modular telecommunications. Europe and Asia have had some success in this effort. On the other hand, in the United States, the failure of early efforts toward government-mandated network "unbundling" hardened the conflict between incumbent network operators and other service providers.

Devices as Networks

Changes in end-user devices also are transforming telecommunications networks. The devices are gradually *becoming* the networks, at least in the minds of users. The rapid and continual improvement in computer processing power means that a standard consumer communications device, such as a mobile handset, is now a sophisticated multimedia computer. Intelligence is migrating from the network to the devices, which can perform a great deal of processing and service delivery on their own.

As a result of these trends, the interaction of devices and networks is a hot area for policy debate in telecommunications today. The Federal Communications Commission's 1968 *Carterfone* decision required AT&T to allow customers to attach standards-compliant devices of their choosing to the phone network (Werbach 2005). This opened the door not only for competition in telephone sales, but also for innovative new devices such as speakerphones, fax machines, and the digital modems used for Internet access. No phone company could ever keep up with the innovation and marketing prowess of the consumer electronics and computer industries, after they were unleashed to build devices that interfaced with the network. *Carterfone,* however, applied only to wireline devices, and only to the dominant incumbent carriers. It does not apply, for example, to wireless operators, who today select and specify the handsets that function on their networks.[8] A movement for "wireless Carterfone" rules has picked up steam recently, involving many of the same groups that back network neutrality rules.

The Internet took off as a platform for innovation because anyone could create and distribute new services, but mobile devices generally have built-in restrictions against customers loading their own applications or content (Wu 2007). With new transmission technologies and cheaper radios, wireless handsets will have the capability to hop among many different networks. They may even extend the network to other devices, by serving as relays. This "mesh network" approach, in which every endpoint is also potentially a transmitter, would make telecommunications networks more closely resemble the routers of the Internet or the peer-to-peer nodes of media-sharing applications (Werbach 2004). And such user-defined networks are not limited to mobile phone handsets. Vendors such as Intel plan to build wireless radios using next-generation technologies such as WiMAX into every computer and consumer electronics device they power.

The telecommunications providers of the future will incorporate infrastructure, applications, devices, and content interchangeably. Some early examples suggest the possibilities. Skype, free software that enables voice calling and other functionality through a peer-to-peer architecture, has more than 200 million customers worldwide. Fon, a start-up based in Spain, distributes Wi-Fi routers that make each user part of a communal voice and data network for other Fon subscribers. It is beginning to strike deals with broadband access providers, such as BT in the United Kingdom, to integrate with and support its virtual network. And Google is simultaneously pushing forward on a

---

[8] This practice is significantly more restrictive in the United States than in Europe.

range of communications-focused initiatives, including developing reference designs for mobile phones, operating a free Wi-Fi network in the city around its headquarters, and acquiring a company, Grand Central, which provides virtual phone numbers to link together a user's many communications endpoints.

Conclusion: A Network View of Networks

Both the Monists and the Dualists have a point. Yet they cannot both be correct. All that is clear is that, sooner or later, more decentralized and collaborative models will sweep telecommunications as they are sweeping so many other industries and disciplines. This story is likely to be unsettling for business readers. The fantastic growth of the Internet and other digital communications systems means that the dynamics of the telecommunications industry have deep implications across the global economy and society.

The telecom future, whenever it arrives, will look very different than the world of today. And the transition will be disruptive. It bears noting that the bulk of global telecommunications revenues, wireline and wireless, are still tied to voice telephone service. Yet from an engineering standpoint, voice is one of the least capacity-intensive applications on the network, requiring only a few kilobits per second. Data and, especially, video, will increasingly dominate network demand in the future. An industry geared to selling voice service by the minute will have to adapt. Those who succeed in the changing environment will be able to see network resources as pools of capacity that can be drawn on as needed to power evolving services, much as Google sees its computing infrastructure today. Only then will the network industry of telecommunications operate according to the principles of networks.

References

Albert, R., H. Jeong, and A.-L. Barabasi. 1999. Diameter of the World Wide Web. *Nature* 401, 130-131.

Benkler, Y. 2006. *The Wealth of Networks: How Social Production Transforms Markets and Freedom.* Yale University Press.

Carr, N. 2008. *The Big Switch: Our New Digital Destiny.* W. W. Norton.

Coase, R. H. 1937. The nature of the firm. *Economica* 4, 386-405.

Crawford, S. 2007. The Internet and the project of communications law. *UCLA Law Review* 55, 359-407.

Faloutsos, M., P. Faloutsos, and C. Faloutsos. 1999. On power-law relationships of the Internet topology. *SIGCOMM '99*, 251-262.

Frischmann, B. 2005. An economic theory of infrastructure and commons management. *Minnesota Law Review* 89, 917.

Gilder, G. 2006. The information factories. *Wired* 14, 178.

Huber, P. 1987. The geodesic network: 1987 report on competition in the telephone industry. U.S. Government Printing Office.

Huber, P. 1997. *Law and Disorder In Cyberspace*. Oxford University Press.

Isenberg, D., and D. Weinberger. 2002. The paradox of the best network. www.netparadox.com/.

Katz, M., and C. Shapiro. 1985. Network externalities, competition, and compatibility. *American Economic Review* 75, 424.

Lessig, L. 2001. *The Future of Ideas: The Fate of the Commons in a Connected World*. Random House.

Mitchell, D. 2006. Tail is wagging the Internet dog. *New York Times* (July 8).

Nuechterlein, J., and P. Weiser. 2005. *Digital Crossroads: American Telecommunications Policy in the Internet Age*. MIT Press.

OECD. 2007. Directorate for science, technology, and industry. Broadband statistics to December 2006, http://www.oecd.org/document/7/0,3343,en_2649_34225_38446855_1_1_1_1,00.html.

Pastor-Satorras, R., and A. Vespignani. 2004. *Evolution and Structure of the Internet: A Statistical Physics Approach*. Cambridge University Press.

Reuters. 2007. EU officials debate plan to split telecommunications companies (September 25).

Rohlfs, J. 1974. A theory of interdependent demand for a communications service. *Bell Journal of Economics and Management Science* 5, 16-37.

Shapiro, C., and H. Varian. 1998. *Information Rules: A Strategic Guide to the Network Economy*. Harvard Business School Press.

Singer, H., and R. Litan. 2007. Unintended consequences of net neutrality regulation. *Journal on Telecommunications and High Technology Law* 5, 533.

Spulber D., and C. Yoo. 2005. On the regulation of networks as complex systems: A graph theory approach. *Northwestern University Law Review* 99, 1687.

Werbach, K. 1997. Digital tornado: The Internet and telecommunications policy. Federal Communications Commission Office of Plans and Policy. Working paper 29.

Werbach, K. 2004. Supercommons: Toward a unified theory of wireless communication. *Texas Law Review* 82, 863.

Werbach, K. 2005. The federal computer commission. *North Carolina Law Review* 84, 1.

Werbach, K. 2008a. Only connect. *Berkeley Technology Law Review* 22, 1234.

Werbach, K. 2008b. The centripetal network: How the Internet pulls itself together, and the forces tearing it apart. Forthcoming.

Wu, T. 2003. Network neutrality, broadband discrimination. *Journal on Telecommunications and High-Tech Law* 2, 141.

Wu, T. 2006. Why have a telecommunications law? Anti-discrimination norms in communications. *Journal on Telecommunications and High-Tech Law* 5, 15.

Wu, T. 2007. Wireless Carterfone. *International Journal of Communication* 1, 389.

Xinhua Financial News. 2008. China seen issuing telecom restructuring plan after March NPC meeting—analysts (January 11).

Yoo, C. 2006. Network neutrality and the economics of congestion. *Georgetown Law Journal* 94, 1847.

25

Network-Based Strategies and Competencies for Political and Social Risk Management

Witold J. Henisz[1]

Abstract

From oil companies seeking rights to drill to consumer products firms attempting to forestall a consumer boycott, organizations often seek to influence political or social policy to achieve their own objectives. But to exert this influence, they need to understand the structure of political and social networks. In this chapter, Witold Henisz examines how information about the structure of political and social networks can be integrated into data acquisition and analysis, as well as strategy implementation. Although sophisticated companies have long relied on an informal understanding of networks of informants to gather information about social and political actors at home and abroad, the analysis of the information and design of an influence strategy has too often occurred without reference to that structure. As Henisz points out, a more rigorous approach to analysis described in this chapter is transforming political and social risk management from art to quasi-formal science. This chapter outlines the past, present, and future frontiers of political and social risk management with particular attention to using an understanding of the network structure of diverse actors in perceiving, analyzing, and influencing the political and social environment.

[1] Thanks to Stephen Kobrin, Bennet Zelner, and Paul Kleindorfer for their comments on previous drafts.

Organizations use political and social risk management to influence political or social policy outcomes that help or hinder them in realizing their own stated objectives, such as these:

- Oil or mining companies or the operators of infrastructure services (for example, electricity supply, telecommunications, water, or transport) to reduce the likelihood of expropriations or renegotiations of contract terms by governments of countries in which they operate

- Owners of intellectual property (for example, patents, copyrights, trademarks, or trade secrets) to maximize the revenue from their up-front fixed investments by maintaining the current state of protection or enforcement of intellectual property

- Holders of nonperforming loans in countries with nascent or weak bankruptcy laws to maximize the recovery of their exposure

- Organizations seeking to build political or social support, incurring short-term costs to generate medium- to long-term returns in the form of increased willingness of consumers to pay, members of the value chain to share rents, or policy-makers to desist from interventions

- Organizations seeking to defuse an activist campaign for a consumer boycott, overcome reluctance by suppliers to provide crucial inputs (for example, capital), or address increased media criticism or government intervention

In each of these cases, although technical, marketing, financial, and operational efficiency and capability are clearly important, a substantial driver of value creation and appropriation will be the actions and reactions of political and social actors that influence policy outcomes.

Despite the clear and widespread acceptance that political and social risks are of large and growing importance for multinational managers, the political and social risk-management capabilities are not that different in many corporations than they were four decades ago. At that time, Franklin Root surveyed large U.S. firms and concluded that "No executive offered any evidence of a systematic evaluation of political risks, involving their identification, their likely incidence, and their specific consequences for company operation" (Root 1968). Kobrin (1979) surveyed the literature and similarly concluded that "Rigorous and systematic assessment and evaluation of the political environment is exceptional. Most political analysis is superficial and subjective, not integrated formally into the decision-making process." A recent PriceWaterhouseCoopers-Eurasia report based on a 2005 survey echoes this conclusion, finding that 73% of firms surveyed were dissatisfied with the effectiveness of the political and social risk-management processes.

As the authors write:

> Risk managers, chief financial officers, and international division heads con-
> tacted for our survey said frequently that the complex web of information that
> would enable them to assess political risk was difficult to obtain and evaluate.
> Many expressed frustration that when they were able to glean information from
> local sources, the information was inevitably biased. Moreover, funding for spe-
> cific risk-management techniques (e.g., risk mapping) was often lacking within
> their organizations, because the benefits were not well understood. As a result,
> CEOs and boards of directors were not getting the timely, accurate information
> they needed to make good decisions about international exposures—or, con-
> versely, information was not effectively communicated and utilized to manage
> risk in the field (PWC Advisory and Eurasia Group 2006).

The scope and magnitude of the resulting financial losses can be acute. Merchant International Group reported that from 1995 to 1998, 84% of operations in emerging markets failed to reach their earnings targets, resulting in an 8% to 10% diminution of total corporate returns, or a loss of $24 billion in 1998 alone (Poole-Rob and Bailey 2003). A survey by PWC reported that a one standard deviation in a country's "opacity" was equivalent in its predicted financial impact to raising taxation rates by 33% to 46% or borrowing costs by 9% to 13% on the operations of an otherwise identical country with mean levels of opacity (Kurtzman, Yago, and Phumiwasana 2004).

To formulate an influence strategy to alter policy outcomes, one would need to know the identity, preferences, and power of various political and social actors, as well as the formal and informal processes of their interaction. To take a simple example, analyzing a committee vote in a legislative chamber would require information on committee members, their constituents, and fundraising sources. The preferences of each of these actors, their power (one vote for each committee member but a more complex function of votes, jobs, status, and dollars for constituents and fundraising sources), and the strength of each actor's preferences (for example, the extent to which they are willing to use their power on this issue) could be analyzed to assess the likely outcome of the committee vote. In countries with strong party systems, perhaps the analysis could be reduced to a consideration of the partisan affiliation of each committee member and the preferences and salience of the issue to each party. More complex issues would require consideration of a multistage policymaking process that might include committee votes, full chamber votes, presidential authorizations, regulatory enactments, legal rulings, and media campaigns by various interest groups to feed back into future policymaking or the enforcement of current policy.

Turning from the political to the social arena, the crucial actors shift to nongovernmental organizations, interest groups, media, and other opinion leaders. The policy outcome is an organization's reputation, which can be attacked or devalued by any of these actions with substantial financial consequences. Consumers may switch to competitors or demand lower prices to maintain their purchases of what they now perceive as an inferior good. Suppliers may restrict the availability of capital or other key resources or charge more for those inputs to offset their risk of becoming a target of the activists. Employees may seek to depart the company, demand higher wages for staying, or become less productive. Governments may also intervene to regulate or otherwise alter the operations that are the focus of the activist campaign. The focal organization seeks to protect its reputation and thus needs to understand how it is viewed by each of its stakeholders. The relative power of these stakeholders can be a function of an objective indicator such as their number of press mentions or a subjective judgment of their importance for the intangible "reputation."

In the remainder of this chapter, I outline the tools used to gather such information on the identity, preferences, and power of the relevant political and social actors, and then analyze that information to identify an influence strategy and implement that strategy. In each section, I note how over time a network methodology or perspective has enhanced a more traditional view of the political and social environment.

Sources of Information on Political and Social Risks

Corporate or regional managers often lack the information they need to make major strategic decisions affected by the political or social environment. Executives need to obtain knowledge about the political and social context of host countries from sources with more context-specific knowledge. In contrast to many external sources of uncertainty (for example, exchange rates, interest rates, and input prices), however, political and social risks cannot easily be priced and hedged via financial market instruments. The likelihood that a political or social actor will seek to alter the revenue stream of a corporation in a manner inimical to shareholders is typically neither a country- nor an industry-specific risk. Rather, the largest determinant of the risk of an adverse event is often the strategy of the investor. How do they enter? With whom do they ally? Whom do they hire and from whom do they source materials and credit? On what terms?

Where do they sell? What do they do with their returns? What are their future invest-ment or expansion plans? What sort of public relations, corporate social responsibility, and government affairs strategy do they pursue? Absent a sophisticated understanding of both the specific risks that the investor faces and the strategies that they pursue to mitigate these risks by insurers or traders, the market for cover or hedging instruments collapses.[2] In this manner, political and social risk management bears greater similarity to the management of uncertainty over technology, market demand forecasts, or com-petitor strategies than it does more exogenous financial risks. In short, it lies in the domain of management, not finance.

Information on such risks should be drawn from as wide an array of sources as pos-sible to avoid the insular focus of many homogenous deliberative bodies. These sources include the following:

- **Internal sources**—The obvious sources include the managers responsible for the geographic region or country together with relevant functional managers such as those responsible for government, public, and media affairs. A recent PriceWater-houseCoopers-Eurasia Group survey found that 70% of the largest multinational corporations rely most heavily on this source of information. This result echoes those of Kobrin (1979), who found that 74.6% of subsidiary managers and 68.9% of regional managers rely on these internal sources.

- **Value chain members**—These sources inside the firm should, however, be sup-plemented by consultation with actors across the focal organization's value chain. Any local partners (for example, joint venture partner, licensees, or franchise own-ers) should be given a central role in deliberations as the navigation of the local political and social environment may well be one of their distinct competitive advantages. Suppliers of labor, capital, goods, and services—particularly those that are local or have longer experience in the host country—may provide a richer or more independent analysis of the local context.

- **Consumers**—Analogous to Clay Christensen's pioneering work on technological uncertainty, managers of political and social risks should also speak to their con-sumers. Just as consumers are at the frontier of new technology and the demands that give rise to it, so too may they be at the frontier of new political demands, par-ticularly those with a strong social dimension. The impact of consumer demands

---

[2] A growing quantity of political and social risk coverage is available, but such coverage is typically limited to the value of the investment, not the revenue stream it is meant to generate; and costs frequently amount to 10% of the asset at risk, with coverage rarely available for more than 10 years. Given the 20- or 30-year exposure an investor is taking on and the gap between the cost of the investment and the rev-enue stream it is meant to generate in such a risky market, even investors who purchase such coverage are internalizing a substantial portion of residual risk management.

can be seen in campaigns against genetically modified organisms, sweatshops and child labor, and stem cell therapies. Activist groups target many individuals to generate policy changes. By listening carefully to the demands of sensitive classes of consumers, companies may be able to recognize and get out in front of these social challenges.

- **Activist groups**—In some cases, the activist groups themselves may be a powerful source of information. Yaziji (2004) argued that multinational corporations should transform their perspective of NGOs from that of gadflies to allies to avoid strategic surprises or to preempt attacks. For example, Royal Dutch Shell agreed to include Greenpeace in any substantive environmental discussions after the conflict between the two organizations over the disposal of the Brent Spar North Sea oil platform. Unilever also cooperated with the World Wildlife Fund to develop guidelines for sustainable fishing that led to the formation of the Marine Stewardship Council.

- **Outside experts**—Specialized lawyers or consultancies are another source of useful information. In fact, the aforementioned PWC-Eurasia Group report found that these are the most common sources of information after internal resources. Political risk consultancies range from well-positioned ex-government officials operating on retainer, to the stringers who write for the Economist Intelligence Unit, Stratfor, or Oxford Analytica, to global specialized political consultancies such as Political Risk Services or the Eurasia Group. Although suppliers, consumers, and activists may each have better information or better incentives to gather and filter information, they may lack the formal and specialized training in the art of politics that such specialists bring to the table. By focusing on the political incentives and constraints generally neglected by financial markets or other analysts, Eurasia Group was able to make predictions that contradicted the conventional wisdom. Two prominent examples were the early expression of concern that policy incoherence in Russia in 1998 could trigger a financial crisis and an early and sustained confidence in Brazilian President Luiz Inacio *Lula* da Silva's commitment to fiscal discipline in the run-up to his 2002 election (Bremmer 2006).

- **Independent third-party monitors**—The most distant set of actors from the focal organization—but still potentially valuable sources of information—are independent third-party monitors such as bankers, the media, or foreign governments. Although the information that they provide may not be sufficiently tailored to the needs of the focal organization, they do have substantial resources, in-country knowledge and expertise, and strong incentives to follow developments that may have a substantial macroeconomic, political, or social impact.

Aggregating Information: Developing a Network Perspective

Given the many sources of information about the political and social environment, companies face the challenge of aggregating these multiple perspectives into a coherent view. At one extreme, information can be sourced as needed or in response to a crisis-generated request, and then averaged or reduced to a point estimate with a distribution that treats each source of information equally. A more sophisticated, network-based approach would be to create an active scanning network that would report any relevant changes in the political and social environment in real time. The importance of reported changes could be assessed based on the structural position of the information source and the consistency of the information that they are providing with that of other sources.

For example, PWC-Eurasia notes that one of their survey respondents had established such a network to monitor political events that could disrupt their supply chain in any one of 120 countries. Companies such as Strategic Radar (see Chapter 16, "Extended Intelligence Networks: Minding the Periphery," by Day, Schoemaker, and Snyder) and the Probity Group develop such scanning networks for clients, monitoring shifts in the competitive, market, social, and government landscapes, as well as information from the media and other third parties. Attensity and Evolve24 offer similar scanning focused on the management of corporate reputation.

An extension of these outsourced scanning capabilities is the development of a network-risk scanning capability. Instead of merely listening for problems or negative reactions to corporate decisions and reacting to them, companies can engage stakeholders more deeply. They can listen before decisions are made, alter decisions based on that *ex ante* feedback, and agree on which decisions should be made in cooperation or partnership with a network of actors (Kytle and Ruggie 2005).

In monitoring and aggregating information, companies improve results by factoring in the consistency of information across the network and biases of individual sources. Potential biases from at least two structural dimensions of the network should be considered in the aggregation process:

1. *Geography*—PWC-Eurasia highlights that "long-term expatriates and local employees rarely provide an objective view of the political environment. These biases are largely unintentional but are inherent to their roles within the company." Given the trade-off between the greater quantity of information and the inherent bias in the provision of such information, disparities between the information provided by more proximate and distant sources should be evaluated with particular care.

2. *Alignment*—Actors may well perceive allied actors to have more closely aligned preferences than they actually do, whereas they may perceive opponents to be more extreme. Proximity of preferences thus plays an analogous role to geographic proximity in that it increases the quantity of information but also the need to filter that information and to pay special attention to disparities between reports from proximate and distant sources of information.

The structure of the network—geography and alignment—thus affects the quality of the information derived from it. A network approach can help enhance real-time information flow across the value chain and analyze the marginal value of new information based on its source within that network.

Developing a Strategy to Manage Political and Social Risks

Although many organizations traditionally have adopted formal structures or appointed C-level executives with responsibility for political and social risks (for example, Corporate Risk Officers or Corporate Responsibility Officers), the tools employed have evolved less quickly than organizational structures. Corporate Risk Officers are typically expertly trained in modeling financial and economic risks, but modeling political and social risks is more complex due to the need to incorporate individual and group beliefs, actions, and interactions that explicitly respond to stimuli other than price mechanisms (for example, perceptions of fairness, identity, or legitimacy). The lack of analytical tools to address these massively complex systems limits the ability to extend enterprise risk modeling frameworks to cover political and social risks. Similarly, although Corporate Responsibility Officers are well versed in compliance with a code of conduct or principles of behavior, the management of political and social risks requires assessing stakeholder preferences on a wide range of issues, the design of a set of practices and influence strategies to alter preferences, and the implementation and communication of those practices and strategies. Although a growing number of companies, particularly targets of negative stakeholder campaigns, are realizing the benefits of such a proactive and sophisticated stakeholder-relations strategy, it remains far from the norm even in many of the largest multinational corporations. The next step of linking those stakeholder relations to the value of an asset or the size of a net revenue stream associated with an asset represents a level of financial sophistication beyond the level of most corporate responsibility staffs (though Anglo-American Corporation is an important exception, as discussed later in the text).

Mechanisms for analysis range from the informal to the formal. At one extreme is the gut instinct of the decision maker who has spoken with the relevant sources or been briefed on their views, and draws upon her own experience in knowledge of similar cases to reach a decision based on what informally is known as the "tummy test." The likely accuracy of such judgments can clearly vary enormously according to the skill set, experience, and biases of the decision maker. One means of improving the accuracy of such judgments is to use specialized consultancies, which can draw upon a more diverse set of analogies and experiences from multiple firms and industries in the target country or a comparable one, before reaching a final recommendation.

A more sophisticated extension of the "tummy test" is the "war room," in which relevant staff come together for a one-off meeting or series of brainstorming sessions on how best to proceed. War room sessions may be scheduled regularly or triggered by a shock or an event that requires a strategic response. Such discussions are often guided by visual representations of the "battlefield" in which the positions and power of various players are captured graphically through the use of "influence maps." These diagrams graph the relationships of politically relevant actors, represented as bubbles that are proportional to the player's power. Linkages across actors or clusters of actors can be depicted by either location or dyadic ties. Although no formal analytic tools are deployed on the resulting visualization, influence maps do help guide "what if" discussions regarding various strategies that could be expected to improve the policy outcome.

For example, Figures 25-1 and 25-2 represents the threat of weakening international protection for intellectual property rights over pharmaceutical products in the past decade. The yellow, vertical bar represents the outcome of the influence game, with leftward moves representing weakening of intellectual property protection. This clear visual representation of the players, the ties between players, and the policy outcome helps guide a discussion to such questions as, "What if we target the emerging market producers of pharmaceutical products?" "What if we bring them into our value chain and thus shift their preferences on intellectual property?" and "What if they lobby their governments, who then similarly shift their preferences?" "What if we exploit the connection between the WTO and these governments?" The insights into strategy in this case are as good as the information brought into the room and the quality of the team analyzing it. Once again, specialized consultancies such as Hill & Knowlton's Commetric and Alan Kelly's Plays2run (Kelly 2006) can augment an internal capability, provide rich visuals, and consider substantially more complex "plays."

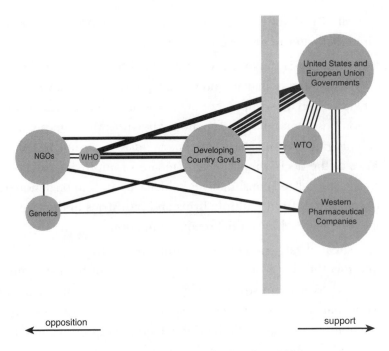

Figure 25-1   Intellectual property for pharmaceuticals, circa 1995

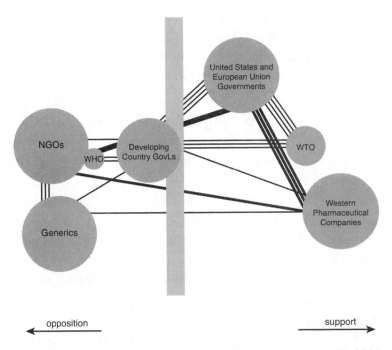

Figure 25-2   The threat to intellectual property for pharmaceuticals 1995–2005

Where the scope and range of uncertainty is high and the time horizon sufficiently long, depictions of the current battlefield, the movement of its players, and the plays they are making may not offer sufficient insight into key long-term strategies. Players may be too focused on today's battle and pay insufficient attention to sea changes over the horizon. Scenario planning exercises are a strategic tool that forces managers to consider the implications of combining known trends with a series of uncertainties to generate internally consistent narratives of future scenarios with vastly different strategic implications (Schoemaker 2002; also see Chapter 16 in this book). Like influence maps, such narratives are most useful for the questions that they trigger.

The most analytically rigorous process involves incorporating individual actors' preferences, power, and issue salience (for example, the extent to which they are willing to deploy their power on this issue) to develop a dynamic expected utility-based model. In such models (Bueno de Mesquita 1992), each actor makes a decision in each time period about whether to propose a policy, oppose a policy, or do nothing. The decision is made with the knowledge that proposals and opposition are costly and that the preferences, power, and salience of other actors on this issue are public information, though potentially measured with error or bias by some actors. Each actor therefore undertakes an exercise in expected utility maximization (for example, Will I be better off if I propose, oppose, or do nothing, given my expected utility from each choice?) and chooses accordingly. Each actor proceeds in a similar manner, generating a prediction of the likely policy outcome. The sensitivity of this outcome to various parameter estimates can then be calculated, giving guidance about the identity of the pivotal actor(s) in the policymaking process (for example, the actors for whom a change in preferences, power, or salience would have the largest impact on the predicted policy outcome), who can subsequently be made the focus of an influence strategy.

These models are widely used within the intelligence community, as well as by a growing number of multinational corporations. Engagements by Sentia Group (previously Decision Insights Inc.) spanned many issues: international security (the stability of the Soviet Union, Russia, Saudi Arabia, Iraq, Korea, Yugoslavia, and Northern Ireland); privatization and regulation (Poland, Czechoslovakia, and Italy); legislative reform of healthcare (United States), trade (United States), or investment liberalization (Sri Lanka); earmarking and other funding authorizations within the United States, EU, and China; regulatory rulings on rates of return in the United States and EU; and government approvals of mergers in the United States and EU.[3]

---

[3] See www.diiusa.com/experience.html.

A company at the frontier of current practice is Anglo-American Corporation, whose SEAT (Socio-Economic Assessment Toolbox) is a new standard against which many multinational corporations are measuring their political and social risk-management practices. This toolbox offers a comprehensive system for continuously improving and managing stakeholder relations based on frequent communications, formal data gathering and analysis, informal consultation, and tracking and quantification of activities, impact, monitoring, and stakeholder reactions. The process, which begins at the onset of any project and continues through its termination, involves a locally determined set of relevant stakeholders who are given voice and power, and incorporates transparent and credible monitoring and feedback loops. SEAT constitutes an actionable plan as opposed to a high-level checklist.[4]

Interdependent Strategy: A Network Perspective on Influence

Each of these analytical methods omits crucial elements of the network structure of policymaking and may, therefore, lead to a suboptimal influence strategy. However, modeling the interdependence among the reactions of each actor to each possible influence strategy will likely strain the capabilities of any informal process. It might be obvious that two actors will tend to move in tandem or that the efforts to sway one actor will have a negative impact on another, but capturing the full set of such interdependencies across political and social actors with different objective functions, world views, and locations will prove extremely difficult. The quasi-formal scenario planning exercise, by contrast, is a powerful means to model such interdependencies and the future states of the world that they may generate, as well as to focus attention on an organization's preparedness for that future. Unfortunately, these benefits come at the cost of sacrificing insight into the identification, design, and implementation of strategies that can alter the evolution of the future.

Relationships among different players in the network are more complex than can be recognized by examining expected utilities of individual actors. For example, environmental groups and American labor unions may both prefer restrictions on tuna fishing that require the deployment of modern nets. Environmental groups favor the legislation because it saves dolphins that might otherwise be caught in the old nets, whereas labor unions favor this policy because it raises costs for older fishing fleets, thus advantaging more modern American fleets against their Mexican competition. Absent a recognition

---

[4] For a more detailed overview of SEAT, see www.angloamerican.co.uk/aa/development/society/engagement/seat/.

that labor unions and environmentalists are typically *opponents* in the policymaking arena, an expected utility analysis might view them as close allies in this campaign. Although they are likely to cooperate on certain issues or elements of the campaign, incorporating their typically divergent positions into the analysis would more likely capture the inherent suspicion, tensions, or friction that would make such a coalition more difficult to maintain. In other words, not only must information on preferences be adjusted to reflect the current network structure of the policymaking environment, but we must bring a network perspective to analysis of how those preferences could evolve.

A network view can also help to understand how political and social risks, and actions to influence policy, affect the organization's internal value creation. How does a given change in the political and social environment affect the value of an asset and the net revenue stream generated by that asset? Absent the connection to observable consequences, the exercise stumbles in its efforts to provide guidance as to the allocation of scarce resources. The decision-making body ultimately must perceive not only the most efficient mechanism to influence policy outcomes, but also the value proposition in doing so. Here, building on well-established tools in enterprise risk management, specific policy outcomes need to be linked to assets within the firm (for example, capital equipment, reputation, intellectual property) and the impact of changes in the external environment need to be quantified in terms of potential costs or revenues. All too often, analysis stops at the point of increasing the threshold return for a project as opposed to actually modeling the implications of political and social risk for revenues and costs under various scenarios.

Network approaches to political and social risk-management strategies offer greater potential to incorporate information on relationships between various trends or uncertainties, stakeholder preferences or actions, and their combined impact on multiple asset values or net revenue streams. These advantages are increasingly important as international economic, political, and social interdependence expand.

Implementing Political and Social Risk-Management Strategies

Understanding the network also helps in strategic implementation. In contrast to typical discussions of implementation, however, the challenge in political and social risk management is heightened by the need to influence behavior and actions by nonemployees who often operate in response to a motive other than profit maximization.

Although influencing behavior among a diverse group of managers or workers is challenging, extending the focus to politicians, regulators, bureaucrats, activists, lobbyists, and other politically relevant groups spread across multiple organizations in multiple countries clearly magnifies the difficulty.

As compared to profit-maximizing organizations, political and social actors possess a far wider range of objectives, typically including reelection/reappointment or maintenance of status, social welfare maximization, and, in some instances, personal wealth or reputation maximization. They are often agents of or otherwise dependent on the favor of other political and social actors ranging from voters to interest groups to individual enterprises, each with its own blend of political, social, and economic objectives. How can one organization best influence such a heterogeneous playing field?

Only a few large entrenched organizations may possess enough leverage to influence such a complex playing field directly. For the vast majority, action requires assembling a coalition of actors and convincing them of a shared interest. The coalition may include other economic organizations, trade associations, consultants, lawyers, and lobbyists, as well as allied political and social actors. Relevant political or social actors include representatives of the home country embassy or government; host country politicians at the federal, subfederal, or local levels; political actors of powerful third countries; or multilateral organizations or nongovernmental actors from the home, host, or third countries. Ideally, the focal organization can coordinate both the message and the target of that message for all actors. Great skill is required in orchestrating such an outcome due to the need to understand the particular interests and capabilities of each member of the coalition, the direct and indirect ties that they have to the target, and the most effective means for the coalition members to present their case to the target.

One key trade-off in the implementation of influence is between a reliance on agents from the home country (for example, the government of the home country, international financial institutions including private and multilateral lenders, a chamber of commerce or other international trade association, management at headquarters, affiliated foreign firms, and international nongovernmental organizations) versus the host country (for example, local government officials, a local trade association, local financial institutions, the host country management team, affiliated local firms, and local nongovernmental organizations). On the one hand, foreign influence channels are relatively low-cost and expedient. In addition, particularly for large or otherwise more powerful home countries, they offer the focal organization a capability to use the leverage of linkage to other issues between the two countries. On the other hand, foreign influence can generate a perception of meddling, can stoke fears of nationalism, and may lack sufficient leverage to generate deep-seated structural reforms. There is also always the risk that the foreign actor will sacrifice the needs of the focal organization for another more salient issue. In contrast, local influence channels require greater up-front investment in political capital and even more careful ongoing management of the alignment of interests. In return for these higher fixed and ongoing costs, such coalitions have a greater likelihood of effecting deep-seated change that persists over the medium to long term.

A second key trade-off within the subset of local influence coalitions is between envelopment of and partnership with the focal organization's competitors or direct opponents. In some instances, it may be feasible to form alliances with members of the value chain in a country without going so far as to strike a deal with a local competitor. In other instances, where the battle is more over the size of the pie or where the local competitor has such power in the policymaking structure, sharing the spoils and investing in maintaining an alignment of interests over the medium to long term may be necessary.

Coalition Building: A Network View of Implementation

A network approach to implementation incorporates information on network structure and feedbacks more comprehensively and systematically to improve the efficacy of influence strategies. Just as the network position of information sources should influence the aggregation of that information, the network position of potential allies should influence the design and implementation of an influence strategy. Rather than focusing solely on the relationship between a potential ally and the target of an influence strategy, consider as well their structural position in the policymaking network, particularly as perceived by third-party actors. These actors will seek to interpret the behavior of your coalition allies and infer whether they are acting as proxies or as allies. Interventions by coalition partners that are dependent on the focal actor or otherwise always support the preferences of the focal actor will be discounted as compared to interventions by structurally independent actors (for example, those that are perceived to have come to their own conclusion on the issue). The design of an influence strategy should thus incorporate not only information on the power and preferences of each individual actor, but the structural position of that actor as perceived by others. This approach can help identify nontraditional or credible organizations to play a prominent role in implementation. For example, Nike used the Fair Labor Association to monitor and report on its efforts to improve accountability of suppliers in response to accusations of sweatshop labor. Were Nike to solely self-report this information, or have suppliers or a wholly funded "independent" entity do so, its credibility would have been substantially lower.

Second, a network approach aspires to go beyond partial analysis of individual interventions and consider seriously how various interventions will interact. Strategies designed to meet individual objectives (for example, the severing of a tie between two actors or the development of greater local support among undecided constituencies) may undermine each other when implemented together. Managers need to understand these reactions and interactions. The indirect effect of strong negative reactions from tied actors may overwhelm any beneficial direct effect of an influence strategy. Companies need to deploy coordinated and coherent strategies.

Conclusion: From Information Overload to Actionable Insight

Political and social risk management has typically been viewed as more art than science. As the previous discussion highlights, however, a network perspective and a set of analytic capabilities drawn from various social science disciplines offer the potential for increased rigor. These tools help in aggregating information, analyzing influence maps, developing comparative scenarios, and designing influence strategies to alter those scenario outcomes. Given the inherent complexity of the system of interactions among corporations, governments, nongovernmental organizations, and each of their respective stakeholders, it is unlikely that political and social risk monitoring will approach the level of sophistication of financial modeling of exchange rate or credit risk. We do, however, have the potential to move far beyond the "tummy test." Insights from the modeling of networks can help in making this shift.

The networks that provide information about the political and social environment—and influence this environment—evolve over time. Understanding these networks is vital to understanding this evolution. The accuracy of information sources is affected by the broader political and social structure in which they are embedded. Decision makers need to understand this network structure to identify and target pivotal actors. Managers also need to consider how these positions will change due to the interaction of these actors with others in the network. To understand policy making and how to influence it, decision makers need to move beyond viewing individual actors in isolation to understand the complete networks that influence political and social information and outcomes.

References

Bremmer, Ian. 2006. *The J Curve: A New Way to Understand Why Nations Rise and Fall.* New York: Simon & Schuster.

Bueno de Mesquita, Bruce. 1992. *Predicting Politics.* Columbus, OH: Ohio State University Press.

Kelly, Alan. 2006. *The Elements of Influence.* New York: Penguin Group.

Kobrin, Stephen. 1979. Political risk: A review and reconsideration. *Journal of International Business Studies* 10 (Spring), 67-80.

Kurtzman, Joel, Glenn Yago, and Triphon Phumiwasana. 2004. The global costs of opacity. *Sloan Management Review* 46 (1), 38-44.

Kytle, Beth, and John Gerard Ruggie. 2005. Corporate social responsibility as risk management: A model for multinationals. Harvard University's John F. Kennedy School of Government's Corporate Social Responsibility working paper 10.

Poole-Rob, Stuart, and Alan Bailey. 2003. *Risky Business: Corruption, Fraud, Terrorism and Other Threats to Global Business.* London: Kogan Page Ltd.

PWC Advisory and Eurasia Group. 2006. How managing political risk improves global business performance. http://www.pwc.com/extweb/pwcpublications.nsf/docid/6C7FE77BCC684D01852571620083BD9A

Root, Franklin R. 1968. Attitudes of American executives towards foreign governments and investment opportunities. *Economics and Business Bulletin* 20 (January), 14-23.

Schoemaker, Paul J. H. 2002. *Profiting from Uncertainty: Strategies for Succeeding No Matter What the Future Brings.* New York, NY: The Free Press.

Yaziji, Michael. 2004. Turning gadflies into allies. *Harvard Business Review* 82 (2), 110-115.

PART VII

A DOUBLE-EDGED SWORD: CONTAGION AND CONTAINMENT

Networks have a dark side. They speed the flow of communication and commerce but also can be conduits for diseases, terrorism, computer viruses, and other threats. The final section of the book explores the dark side of networks and strategies for addressing these challenges. In Chapter 26, **Boaz Ganor** takes up the challenge of terrorist networks and considers how antiterrorist agencies have had to build their own networks in response. In Chapter 27, **J. Shin Teh** and **Harvey Rubin** examine the role of global networks of air travel and connections in the spread of infectious diseases, and how these complex networks require a collaborative international solution. In Chapter 28, **Jere R. Behrman**, **Hans-Peter Kohler**, and **Susan Cotts Watkins** explore the power of informal social networks in preventing HIV infection in Kenya and Malawi, showing that the context and density of networks affect outcomes.

Chapter 26   Terrorism Networks: It Takes a Network to Beat a Network   453
Boaz Ganor

Chapter 27   Global Diseases: The Role of Networks in the Spread and Prevention of Infection   471
J. Shin Teh and Harvey Rubin

Chapter 28   Lessons from Empirical Network Analyses on Matters of Life and Death in East Africa   495
Jere R. Behrman, Hans-Peter Kohler, and Susan Cotts Watkins

26

Terrorism Networks:
It Takes a Network To Beat a Network[1]

Dr. Boaz Ganor

Abstract

As terrorist organizations such as Al-Qaeda have been transformed from hierarchical organizations to more fluid networks, countering terrorism requires an understanding of networks. These networks evolve rapidly in response to actions to thwart them, leading to an ongoing struggle of terrorist and antiterrorist networks. In this chapter, Boaz Ganor examines the evolving threat of terrorist networks and network-based responses. As he notes, "It takes a network to beat a network." He also examines direct and indirect implications for business organizations.

Until 2001, terrorist organizations such as Al-Qaeda had a clearly defined hierarchal structure, concrete leadership, clear decision-making processes, and a coherent chain of command (Mishal and Rosenthal 2005, 277). The leadership of Al-Qaeda, which was established in 1998 by a group of radical Muslims headed by Osama Bin-laden, was located at the head of a classic pyramid structure, with the activists executing the attacks at the bottom. The middle level of the pyramid consisted of various operative managers and functionalists, such as recruiters, trainers, weapons experts, intelligence officers, and activists in charge of the operational planning and preparations. The decision-making process was clearly defined. The heads of the organization determined the group's policy and its long- and short-term goals, and lower-level operatives carried out their commands.

---

[1] This paper was prepared for the Wharton-INSEAD Alliance and Impact Conference on Network-based Strategies and Competencies (November 8-9, 2007).

This hierarchical structure and the decision-making process that derived from it suited the operational method of a "direct layout" terror attack. A typical example of a direct layout terror attack is the famous September 11, 2001 (9/11), terrorist attacks in the United States. The 19 terrorists carrying out the attack were recruited by Al-Qaeda, trained at the organization's bases in Afghanistan, and provided military and operational supplies from the organization. They executed the terror attack under the initiative, command, and control of Al-Qaeda leadership.

Since 2001, the structure of Al-Qaeda has shifted, dangerously morphing itself from a hierarchical terror organization into a complex religious network, devoid of any clear organizational boundaries, which has penetrated many levels of Islamic society around the world. Responding to the invasion of Afghanistan and other attacks by the West, and utilizing the Internet and other emerging technologies, Al-Qaeda has transformed itself into a *network* with diffuse structure, indirect connections, and nontraditional modes of communication. Today's terrorist organizations are highly decentralized and dispersed, increasingly relying on network forms of organization to facilitate their actions, maintain their operational capabilities, and spread their message around the world. This structure has been described as "ideal" for the new wave of terrorism (Rodriguez 2005, 1).

Aided by new information-age technology and the Internet, Al-Qaeda has begun to rely more heavily on proxy organizations—nodes in the larger, complex global jihad terror network—to conduct its terrorist activities. Since the 9/11 terror attacks and subsequent wars in Afghanistan and Iraq, Al-Qaeda has managed to convince many Muslims around the world that Islam is persecuted by the "infidels"—Western regimes headed by the United States. Al-Qaeda invoked a divine religious decree obliging every Muslim to take part in the holy war, jihad, in defense of Islam. This global jihad complex network is a combination of isolated networks and localized, "homegrown" cells of terrorist activity, some of which have strong connections to Al-Qaeda's central leadership, and others of which are connected to the global jihad organization only through loose ties, inspiration, or ideology.

This emerging reorganization is a solution and survival mechanism for terrorist organizations that must operate under the radar and—under attack. Network forms of organization have allowed global jihad groups such as Al-Qaeda to maintain operational capacity and continue attacks despite damage to their hierarchal structure or central leadership in a given locale. These networks are more difficult to detect and, in their dispersed and resilient nature, all the more difficult to counter.

Terrorism and Social Network Analysis

In response to these less traditional—and increasingly deadly—terrorist threats after 9/11, national governments, academics, and even the mainstream media[2] expressed a surge of interest in social network theory, citing it as a valuable tool in understanding and combating modern terrorism (Ressler 2006, 3). Social network analysis (SNA) maintains that all social relationships, including organizations, can be understood as networks, defined as a set of actors (nodes) and ties (links) whose relationships have a patterned structure (Arquilla and Ronfeldt 2001a, 7). Classic social network analysis aims at mapping and measuring the ties and flows among different actors in a specific context, ultimately showing how a network can create opportunities or restrictions for its members (www.orgnet.com/sna.html; Arquilla and Ronfeldt 2001a, 8). The use of social network analysis in understanding terrorist organizations draws on methods similar to those previously used in charting criminal activity and secret societies.

After the September 11 attacks, several scholars applied social network analysis and organizational network analysis to terrorist organizations by visually mapping their networks and determining the strength of the links among members. Using public data available on the Internet and a software-based methodology, organizational networks consultant Vladis Krebs was able to map a portion of the network responsible for the September 11 attacks, providing a visual representation of the ties between the hijackers of the four airplanes (Krebs 2002). Using similar methods, Spanish sociologist Jose A. Rodriguez mapped the network responsible for the March 11 Madrid bombings—concluding that loose ties were a key feature of the network, which was linked to the larger and much more diffuse Al-Qaeda network (Rodriguez 2005, 4; Ressler 2006, 4).

Based on the biographies of 172 terrorist operatives, Marc Sageman's *Understanding Terror Networks* (2004) traces the social movement of the global Salafi Jihad, the violent Islamic movement led by Al-Qaeda, suggesting that this "new type of terrorism" is an emerging quality of social networks, established by alienated young men who follow the path of jihad (Sageman 2004, vii). His analysis produces four large terrorist clusters, one of which consists of Al-Qaeda central staff, and three others based in Arab states, Europe, and East Asia.

---

[2] Examples of Post-9/11 coverage of the terrorist networks theme: Garreau, Joel, "Disconnect the Dots; Maybe We Can't Cut Off the Terror's Head, but We Can Take Out Its Nodes," *The Washington Post*, September 17, 2001; Patrick Keefe, "Can Network Theory Thwart Terrorists?" *The New York Times*, March 12, 2006; Tom Siegfried, "Network Science Could Provide Patriotic Games," *Dallas Morning News*, September 9, 2002.

As these scholars noted, Al-Qaeda and terrorist organizations like it are indeed well suited for the application of social network analysis—they consist of networks of individuals spread across countries, continents, and social groups, and are all connected through a common ideology or goal. Social network analysis provides information on the characteristics of organizations—potentially revealing how a terrorist group or network accesses new ideas, recruits members, and plans attacks (Ressler 2006, 1). Such an approach identifies both the characteristics of the relationships between the main operatives involved in a terrorist attack, and the broader characteristics of the network that initiated or supported the attack—including the stability, flexibility, and cohesion of the group (Rodriguez 2005, 1).

Understanding these network forms of organization is critical in countering the terrorist threat. For example, although "leaders matter in networks," they are generally easier to replace and less critical as the leader's role in a hierarchy (Deibert and Stein 2002, 7). This is certainly the case when there are many leaders diffused throughout the network, who coordinate with each other but do not necessarily rely on central control and command (Arquilla and Ronfeldt 2001a, 15). In this way, networks tend to be more resilient in the face of targeted attacks; cutting off the head may no longer kill the beast. By keeping cells or nodes of a network distant from each other, damage to the network is minimized in the case of a member being captured (Krebs 2002, 5). As Sageman explains, the integrity of the network is not necessarily compromised even with the removal of its nodes (Sageman 2004, 140). It is thus essential for security agencies to know which members of a network have the most links to others—whether or not they serve as a "hub"—to determine whom to target and how to disable the larger network organization.

In addition, though denying a terrorist organization a secure environment or host state—destroying its physical base—would help weaken the organization, it would not necessarily prevent a globally dispersed network from committing attacks, as we have seen in the case of Al-Qaeda post-9/11 (Deibert and Stein 2002, 7). Flexibility and security are additional advantages to organizations adopting a network structure. As opposed to strong ties, loose connections enable cells to maintain operational cooperation while avoiding the layers of bureaucracy in a hierarchy, permitting last-minute changes and ensuring low visibility amid the surveillance efforts of security forces (Rodriguez 2005, 3).

Although interest in social network theory experienced a boost post-9/11, networks are not a new phenomenon in the world of terrorism; Bruce Hoffman notes that Palestinian terror organizations first started utilizing network structures as early as the 1970s as they maintained operational cooperation with the German RAF terror organization

(Hoffman 2006, 77). Earlier literature addressing the terrorist network theme (Demaris 1977; Kupperman and Trent 1979) cites evidence of alliances and an exchange of training and arms support between Palestinian groups and revolutionaries from Western Europe, Africa, South America, Asia, and North America, as well as between groups within South America and within Arab countries. Such literature argues that terrorist groups established global liaisons and networks, allowing them to secure financial and technological support through cooperation among national and international organizations (Stohl 1983).

At the time, some argued that extensive contacts between these organizations led to the creation of an international communist terror network, mastered by the Soviet Union (Stohl and Stohl 2002, 4). Similar to the current manifestation of terror networks, the nodes in the communist network were terror organizations that shared a mutual ideology, operated in different arenas and continents, and were all connected to the Soviet Union in one way or another—whether directly through financial support, weapons provisions, or the training of terrorist activists in soviet camps (Sterling 1981, 278).

Netwars

Years before the 9/11 attacks, John Arquilla and David Ronfeldt (1993) coined the term "netwar" to describe the increased tendency of criminal and terrorist groups to use network forms to engage in a new mode of conflict short of warfare. Netwar activists— consisting of dispersed organizations, small groups, and individuals— communicate and conduct their campaigns in an "inter-netted" manner, often without a central command (Arquilla and Rondfeldt 2001, 4). The concept, which they first introduced as early as 1993, relied on the notion that the information age favors network forms of organization, doctrine, and strategy.

Following the 9/11 attacks, the authors wrote an afterword for their 2001 book *Networks and Netwar: The Future of Terror, Crime and Militancy*, maintaining that the "[netwar] theory has struck home with a vengeance" (Arquilla and Rondfeldt 2001b, 363). They claimed the 9/11 attacks "confirmed the warnings" in their book about information-age terrorist groups such as Al-Qaeda increasingly turning toward these network forms of organization (Arquilla and Rondfeldt 2001b, 363). Determining whether the network is a single "hub" designed around Osama Bin-laden was essential, because his death or capture may not defeat the network if it has a more diffused structure. As they write, "The more a terrorist network takes the form of a multi-hub 'spider's web' design, with multiple centers and peripheries, the more redundant and resilient it will be—and the harder to defeat" (Arquilla and Rondfeldt 2001b, 364-365).

Network Structure

Arquilla and Rondfeldt recognized that the global jihad network is not one concrete network but a complex structure consisting of numerous networks operating simultaneously, characterized largely by horizontal coordination among semiautonomous groups (Arquilla and Rondfeldt 2001a, 15). The system includes a central network of organizations, groups, and cells dispersed all over the world with a tight or loose connection to Al-Qaeda. Yet the system also includes local networks in Muslim, Arab, and Western countries.

With Al-Qaeda serving as the epicenter, the complex global jihad network includes as its "nodes" other hierarchical terror proxy organizations, various offshoots and fragments of organizations, small networks of local activists that form terror cells, and other activists who all share a mutual ideology—they are motivated by radical religious fanaticism, faith in a divine mission, and the ultimate goal of establishing a worldwide Islamic republic ruled by Islamic Sharia law (see Figures 26-1 and 26-2). As these diagrams illustrate, the network includes a combination of relatively autonomous cells and more hierarchical structures. To achieve and maintain an effective, calculated, and coordinated terror campaign, rather than random activity based on the exploitation of local opportunities and weaknesses, international terrorist organizations must eventually sustain, alongside a network structure, some form of a unified and hierarchical control and supervision system (Matthew 2005, 625).

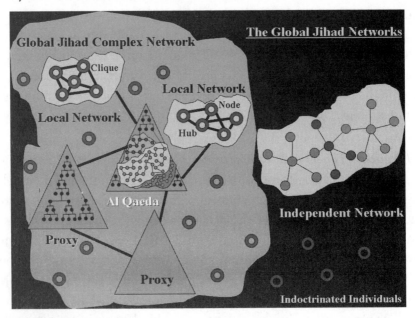

Figure 26-1   The global jihad networks

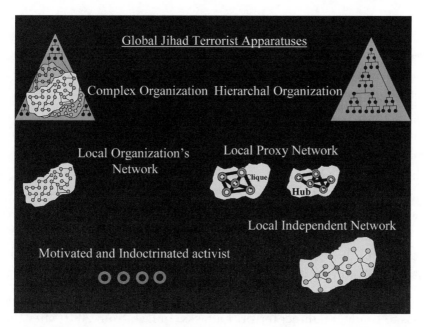

Figure 26-2   Global jihad terrorist apparatuses

In this complex central network, Al-Qaeda has continuously—and especially after September 2001—strengthened its status in the Muslim world in general and among radical Islamists in particular. It has used this status to facilitate interaction between various terrorist entities loosely unified by anti-Western positions. In this respect, Osama Bin-laden has succeeded in establishing Al-Qaeda as the *hub* of the global terror network (Matthew 2005, 621). The network is headed by leadership mainly composed of comradeship connections between "Afghanistan veterans," dominated by Egyptian terror activists (Sageman 2004, 152, 171).

The network established by Bin-laden, however, has taken on a life of its own. Cells in the network have, in fact, executed terrorist attacks without the involvement of Bin-laden—neither his leadership nor his funding—and will be capable of continuing to do so even if he gets caught or killed (Arquilla, Ronfeldt, and Zanini 1999, 63). This is a distinct characteristic—and advantage—of a network form of organization, in which, based on the nature of their connections, nodes can operate independently, without direct support from the central hub.

Cutting Off the Head

As noted previously, Al-Qaeda's own transformation from a hierarchical organization to a diffused network was driven in large part by external forces. Its shift in organizational structure was partly an outcome of the American military response to the 9/11 terrorist attacks. The occupation of Afghanistan, the destruction of the organization's administrative and operational infrastructure, and the demolition of training camps, recruitment offices, and facilities neutralized about 50% of the organization's activists. Many of these activists were arrested or killed during the conquest of Afghanistan by U.S.-led coalition forces. This damage effectively forced Al-Qaeda to change its structure and method of operation. Without autonomous territory in Afghanistan from which to operate, or freedom of movement for the organization's leaders and activists, the hierarchical structure of the organization and the control level of the organization's leadership over its activists were severely damaged.

As a result of these restraints, Al-Qaeda began to rely more on collegiate and proxy organizations to conduct indirect terrorist attacks. In fact, from 2001, after the occupation of Afghanistan, most global jihad terrorist attacks were carried out indirectly—by various jihad organizations, as opposed to actual Al-Qaeda operatives (Chandler and Gunaratna 2007, 24). Some of these organizations were affiliated with Al-Qaeda and others just shared the group's ideologies and narratives. Several of these organizations were members of the alliance established by Bin-laden in 1998, "The World Jihad Front against the Jews and the Crusaders," including the Egyptian Islamic Jihad, the Bangladeshi Islamic Jihad, and the Afghan Al Ansar Group.

Some of the terrorist attacks were carried out under the direction and initiation of the jihad organization itself, whereas others served as "proxies" of Al-Qaeda. For instance, the detonation of two explosive-laden automobiles in Istanbul in November 2003, was initiated by Al-Qaeda, which likely also aided in preparations. Yet despite Al-Qaeda involvement, the attack was eventually executed by a group identifying itself as "the Great Eastern Islamic Invaders' Front."

Al-Qaida's new modus operandi, which relies more on the activity of domestic jihad organizations in Muslim and Arab countries, has increased the severe threat that Al-Qaeda and its affiliated organizations pose for the stability of local regimes in the countries where they operate. This has, therefore, motivated these governments to operate more decisively against the organizations and has minimized the organizations' scope of local activity. In response, global jihad organizations headed by Al-Qaeda have once again been forced to change their modus operandi and even their organizational structure, a new means of overcoming the challenges posed by security forces.

Even beyond the nodes of the complex global jihad network, other groups located outside the network, such as Hamas, sometimes maintain tactical cooperation with Al-Qaeda. This cooperation generally stems from mutual local interests and not necessarily joint consent regarding the ultimate goals, long-term objectives, or even modus operandi of the organization (Stohl and Stohl 2007, 110).

The global jihad network is not, as said, a monolithic network composed of homogenous nodes; the nodes are heterogeneous, and they consist of many local networks, independent and semi-independent in nature. As social networks, these groupings create a shared space for identity-shaping emotions, world perspectives, and preferences. These networks are established, in many cases, by Muslim immigrants in the West who are exposed to incitement and radical Islamic indoctrination. They also include groups of like-minded young people who have decided to take a common step and join the path of jihad.

Sageman defines these groups as cliques—crowded little networks of nodes that are all connected to each other, based on local friendship or family ties, and on a mutual decision to join the global jihad movement. One example, among many, is the cell that planned the Bali nightclub terror attack in 2002. Four of its members were from the same family, and a fifth was their neighbor from childhood (Sageman 2004, 152-167). The members of these networks join the jihad movement through unique and ongoing processes—exposure to brainwashing, an extended process of radicalization, or, alternatively, due to a single traumatic event that motivates the individual to adopt the way of jihad. The networks often transcend national borders (Stohl and Stohl 2007, 107).

The structure of these networks is therefore dynamic, temporary, and flexible (106). Arquilla, Ronfeldt, and Zanini (2002, 91) determined that networks are generally divided into three types based on the characteristics of their activities and the extent of their ability to organize and preserve themselves:

1. *Chain or line network*—A network in which members are linked in a row and communication between one end and the other must pass through mediating nodes.

2. *Hub network*—A network in which communication between nodes must pass through a central hub. These networks usually create various star structures.

3. *General channel network or matrix network*—A network that lacks clear hierarchy. Each node is connected to the other and may have several leaders. The network's decision-making procedures are not centralized and allow for the growth of local and autonomous initiatives (Arquilla and Ronfeldt 1996, 7-8).

Mishal and Rosenthal take the typology of networks a step further by examining the structure and functioning of radical Islamic organizations. They propose the concept of "Dune organization," evaluating the process of vacillation between territorial presence and a mode of disappearance (Mishal and Rosenthal 2005, 275-293).

In practice, Al-Qaeda constructed a conceptual model that paved the way for many activists worldwide, allowing them to join the radical Islamic front by becoming one of the components of the global jihad network.

The Internet and Other Enabling Technologies

The Internet has served as a convenient platform and even a catalyst for the dynamic development of global jihad networks worldwide. Various aspects of the Internet, including Web sites, forums, blogs, chat rooms, file transfers, and e-mail messages, provide terror organizations and their leaders unprecedented channels for communication and activity. These channels serve, among other things, as a means for the following:

- *Distant incitement, propaganda, and indoctrination*—The Internet allows global jihad networks to reach distant target audiences. Messages of incitement conveyed on terrorist organizations' Web sites and supporter sites, using various forms of media—words, photography, musical messages, or video clips—are intended to influence potential activists. The Internet makes it possible to reach a large number of people without personal risk to the inciters, who could be located far away. It is difficult for security agencies to trace and stop the source of incitement.

- *Distant recruitment*—The Internet provides new, unprecedented channels to recruit activists, supporters, and financiers. Recruitment is an advanced stage in the radicalization process for potential activists, who—as they are exposed to messages of incitement—make the transition from passive to active actors by donating funds or deciding to join a terror organization, local terror network, or radical virtual community.

- *Distant institutionalization*—After potential activists go through a process of indoctrination and decide to transition from the passive to the active stage, some join local terrorist networks. These networks may be virtual in nature—Internet communities of like-minded people that essentially serve as support groups, unifying activists in solidarity despite the geographic distance between them. Alternatively, networks of activists in the real world, who are located in the same geographic vicinity, undergo the process of radicalization together via the Internet.

- ***Distant communication***—The Internet enables constant communication among nodes in the global jihad network, the leadership, and the sub-networks. The communication can be open or confidential—encoded messages determined in advance and transferred through specific Internet sites (Vidino 2006, 84). These messages may include administrative instructions or operational orders, all conveyed in a manner to make it difficult for the security establishment to trace and decode.

- ***Distant learning***—By using various Internet channels, global jihad organizations are able to train and teach their activists—from studying religion to providing operational training in areas such as surveillance, intelligence collection, withstanding interrogation pressures, the preparation of explosive devices, and counterfeiting documents. Such files and instructions have been nicknamed "cookbooks," popular among terror activists and their supporters, allowing jihad organizations to train their activists at a distance.

Terrorist Networks, Technology, and the "Homegrown" Phenomenon

The revolution in communication technology and the development of the Internet in the 1990s coincided with the rise of the global Islamic Jihad movement (Sageman 2004, 159). In fact, Al-Qaida's extensive use of the Internet is actually what allowed the organization to transform itself from a hierarchical terrorist organization into a worldwide network. By transcending the need for face-to-face interaction, Al-Qaeda has become a loose, decentralized network of terrorist activists empowered by a global communication network.

The propaganda spread through this communication network has captivated many young people, inspiring them to establish terrorist cells and networks among first- and second-generation Muslim immigrant communities all over the Western world. The Internet revolution has thus accelerated the development of *homegrown terrorism*. In many cases, these young people already feel alienated, unappreciated, and rejected by their host country. When they're exposed to messages of incitement associated with the global jihad movement, their feelings of alienation are only intensified, transforming into humiliation and the desire for revenge. Homegrown terrorism has made it possible for Al-Qaeda and other jihad organizations to compensate for the loss of Afghan territory, handle the limited freedom of movement of their leaders and activists, and overcome the severe limitations on their ability to maintain regular and operational communication.

Homegrown terrorism constitutes a dangerous threat to Western society because it is carried out by Western citizens in their own countries. These local activists have a clear advantage over external actors: They are embedded within these societies, know the societies' weak points better than others, can move about freely, know the local language, and operate alone or as part of small local networks that are often very difficult to infiltrate.

Groups of young Muslims in Western countries avidly absorbed the radical Islamic doctrines preached by Al-Qaeda leaders and their supporters through the Internet, via written and electronic media, and directly through religious preachers, friends, and family members. Some decided to establish local terror networks or to join a jihad organization as a result. In other cases, young people exposed to messages of incitement have decided to conduct a terror attack under their own personal initiative, without the guidance or support of any organization, and without membership in a local network.

Countering Terrorist Networks

In coping with domestic and international terrorism, the complex network structure of global jihad and the homegrown terrorism phenomenon place unique and critical challenges on security and intelligence services worldwide.

The first challenge to security establishments is the conceptual change needed to cope with the global jihad network system—shifting from conventional wisdom based on hierarchical models of classic terrorist organizations. According to Mishal and Rosenthal, "A hierarchical mode of thinking tends to ignore the potential and real influence of formal and informal ties among actors that cut across social categories and group boundaries. It also ignores other forms of informal everyday social relations that affect actors' identities, attitudes, and behavior" (Mishal and Rosenthal 2005, 178).

Security agencies must change their approach to terrorism, taking a network-based view of organizations as frameworks devoid of clear boundaries that maintain loose connections between their many components. Counterterrorist agencies also must comprehend the network structure and its connections in a specific context, which could change according to geographic, ethnic, or cultural contexts. They must differentiate between global and domestic networks and establish their counterterror strategies accordingly (Stohl and Stohl 2007, 107, 115).

The challenge here, for both scholars and government agencies, is that understanding and tracing the activities of terrorist networks, given their covert nature, is much more difficult than mapping other network organizations, or tracking hierarchical terrorist groups. In uncovering the network behind 9/11, Krebs realized he would essentially be mapping a "project team," similar to the groups he had mapped in countless business consulting assignments. He notes that "both overt and covert project teams have tasks to complete, information to share, funding to obtain and disburse, schedules to meet, and objectives to accomplish" (Krebs 2002, 2). However, data on terrorist groups, especially when access is limited to open sources, is often incomplete or inaccurate. The challenge is exacerbated by the fact that these networks are constantly changing, and boundaries between members and cells are "fuzzy"—often based on loose social ties that are not highly visible to intelligence agencies (Krebs 2002, 2).

Given the advantages network structure offers over hierarchies, the challenge of fighting these terror networks is formidable. Unlike hierarchical terror organizations, terror networks have greater durability; even substantial damage to the network, sustained through the neutralization (arrests, deaths, and so on) of a significant number of the network's nodes by security forces, will not necessarily lead to the collapse of the entire network. Contacts that have been exposed and neutralized can be substituted over time by other contacts, without significantly shocking the larger network structure. Significant network damage can occur if and when the nodes' commitment to the whole network is weakened or altogether disappears, or when network activities create alienation and antagonism among the community, which the network is supposed to represent (Stohl and Stohl 2002, 17).

On the other hand, terrorist organizations must take into consideration that although it is relatively easy to create networks, it is much harder to control them. It seems that the existence of terror networks has helped countries and organizations that support terrorism both promote their interests and carry out terror attacks rather easily, while simultaneously presenting domestic security forces with unusual challenges.

The traditionally hierarchical structure of government agencies may prove a challenge in fighting these emerging terrorist networks. As Arquilla and Ronfeldt (2001, 28) note: "Hierarchies have a difficult time fighting networks." This challenge forces all members of the counterterrorist community—security services, government ministries, first responders, decision makers, community lay leaders, and academic and private terrorist experts—to enhance not just their internal coordination and cooperation, or even just their regional and international ties, but also the informal connections between them.

Despite the fact that official counterterrorism institutions generally operate under strict secrecy and experience some form of interagency competition, it is essential that they acknowledge that the efficiency of counterterrorism efforts today are dependent on establishing national and international complex counterterrorism networks (see Figure 26-3). The preceding analysis of the complex global jihad network makes it clear that it "takes a network to beat a network." The traditional hierarchical systems of government agencies must transition along with terrorist organizations—not altogether abandoning hierarchical components, but drawing on similar network design principles to counter the threat, focusing on interagency, multijurisdictional, and transborder cooperation.

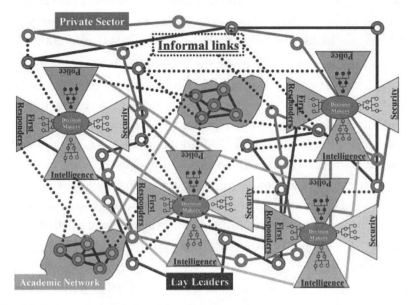

Figure 26-3 It takes a network to beat a network.

An Evolving Challenge

As illustrated by the transformation of Al-Qaeda from a hierarchical organization to a diffused network, terrorist organizations are constantly undergoing processes of transformation, gradually shifting their tactics, organizational structure, and sometimes even the political objectives that drive them. These changes, however, are not simply the result of a natural, evolutionary cycle. They are often a direct response to the challenges these organizations face from those trying to thwart them. This evolution of terrorist networks can create new and more difficult threats, so antiterrorist agencies need to evolve as well.

For example, terrorist bombings against the state of Israel in the 1960s and 1970s evolved into modern suicide attacks as a result of the give-and-take of terrorists and antiterrorist activities. Initially, Israeli security agencies responded to the reliance of terrorist groups on timer-activated explosive devices by educating the public to be aware of their immediate surroundings and report any suspicious objects in crowded places. The campaign was successful in thwarting this form of attack, allowing security forces to locate and deactivate bombs before they exploded. As an outcome, however, terrorist groups responded by using remote-detonated devices. This way, even upon discovery of a bomb, the group could still ensure an explosion—and casualties—before the bomb was neutralized. Security forces again responded, this time with the tightening of security at entrances to crowded places.

These remote-detonated devices, though more advanced technologically, were soon replaced by a new, more deadly modus operandi in the mid-1990s—the ultimate "smart bomb"—a wave of suicide terrorism, which allowed attackers to change their plan at any given time (Ganor 2001, 137). If a terrorist carrying an explosive device detects security guards at the entrance to its target, he or she can choose to instead execute the attack at a different destination, one that is not properly guarded, or simply carry out the suicide bombing against the guards at the entrance of the preselected destination—either way ensuring causalities.

Modern terrorism[3] is thus a dynamic, adaptive phenomenon, in which terrorists identify new challenges and threats and strive to find new solutions—means, technology, or a new modus operandi—to defeat security measures. This dynamic process is an outcome of ongoing, Sisyphean competition between security forces and terror organizations, with each one aspiring to precede and surprise its enemy.

---

[3] Modern terrorism is a form of political activity—a strategy of using violence against civilians to achieve political objectives (Ganor 2005, 17). The intent of a terrorist attack, however, is not only to kill or injure as many people as possible, but also to frighten the maximum number of people within the target population—whether an enemy country, rival ethnic group, different race, or community with certain socioeconomic characteristics. Terrorists seek to achieve their political goals indirectly, using psychological warfare as their weapon. The anxiety that terrorism creates in the target population translates into political pressure, intended to coerce decision makers into changing their policies based on the interests of the terrorists (Horgan 2005, 14).

Implications for Management and Business

The global jihad terrorism movement represents a special type of international, complex network that can reflect the complex networks of the international business world. Just as global jihad networks are a combination of hierarchal organizations, local and international networks, and individual actors, so too are international business networks a combination of international and local corporations, producers, financiers, industrialists, investors, and customers. The links between nodes in both these international networks differ in strength, direction, quantity, and importance.

Leaders of both networks need to balance control with flexibility. Leaders of the global jihad terrorism movement must develop and multiply their networks while simultaneously preserving their capacity to control and guide them into serving the organization's goals. International corporations face a similar challenge; they must extend their influence by creating and associating with other networks, but at the same time maintain control over a huge conglomerate and ensure that all actions taken by their subsidiaries ultimately serve their economic interests.

In this regard, it must be noted that sometimes, in the real world, these two global networks have mutual influence. First, the "products" of the global jihad complex network—terrorist attacks—have an immediate effect on international markets, the stock exchange, various industries (tourism, energy, transportation, and so on), and other aspects of an international business network. Second, some of the nodes in an international business network (banks, private companies, and so on) not only are influenced by the global jihad network but also are themselves influencing it through the contribution or transfer of funds to specific nodes of the jihad network. Company owners may be motivated to participate in such activities on the basis of ideology or out of economic considerations.

Aside from these connections, one of the most important lessons of global jihad networks on managing international business networks is the understanding that "it takes a network to beat a network." In the international economic arena, it may not be enough for a business to simply build a strong independent company or even its own complex international network to effectively promote its global economic interests. Sometimes that company, like the agencies involved in counterterrorism, must also work to narrow the influence and vitality of competing networks. Both counterterrorism agencies and international businesses need a strong network to be effective in general, but simultaneously need to reduce the influence of their competitors, be it other companies or global terrorist organizations. This task can be achieved only by creating new alliances, enhancing formal links, and developing informal ties between all parts of the complex network, always in a manner that strengthens the network in comparison to its competition.

References

Arquilla, John, and David Ronfeldt. 1993. Cyberwar is coming! *Comparative Strategy* 12 (2, April-June).

Arquilla, John, and David Ronfeldt. 1996. The advent of netwar. In *Networks and Netwars: The Future of Terror, Crime and Militancy.* Rand.

Arquilla, John, David Ronfeldt, and Michele Zanini. 1999. Networks, netwar and information age terrorism. In *Countering the New Terrorism.* Santa Monica: Rand.

Arquilla, John, and David Ronfeldt. 2001a. Networks, netwars, and the fight for the future. *First Monday* 6 (10, October). http://firstmonday.org/issues/issue6_10/ronfeldt/ index.html.

Arquilla, John and David Ronfeldt, eds. 2001b. *Networks and Netwar: The Future of Terror, Crime and Militancy*, RAND, http://www.rand.org/pubs/monograph_reports/ MR1382/index.html.

Arquilla, John, David Ronfeldt, and Michele Zanini. 2002. Networks, netwar, and information-age terrorism. In *Terrorism and Counter-Terrorism: Understanding the New Security Environment*, ed. Russell Howard and Reid Sawyer. McGraw-Hill.

Chandler, M., and R. Gunaratna. 2007. *Countering Terrorism.* Reaktion Books.

Deibert, Ronald J., and Janice Gross Stein. 2002. Hacking networks of terror. *Dialog-IO* (Spring).

Demaris, Oviad. (1977). Brothers in blood: The international terrorist network. *NFJ: Scribner's.* Epstein, E.C.

Kupperman, Robert and Darrell Trent. 1979. *Terrorism: Threat, Reality, Response.* Stanford Hoover Press .

Ganor, Boaz. 2001. Suicide attacks in Israel. In *Countering Suicide Terrorism.* The Interdisciplinary Center.

Ganor, Boaz. 2005. *The Counter Terrorism Puzzle.* Transaction Publishers.

Hoffman, Bruce. 2006. *Inside Terrorism.* New York: Columbia University Press.

Horgan, John. 2005. *The Psychology of Terrorism.* Routledge: Taylor & Francis Group.

Krebs, Valdis E. 2002. Uncloaking terrorist networks. *First Monday* 7 (4, April). http://firstmonday.org/issues/issue7_4/krebs/index.html.

Matthew, Richard. 2005. The limits of terrorism: A network perspective. *International Studies Review* 7.

Mishal, S., and M. Rosenthal. 2005. Al Qaeda as a Dune organization: Towards a typology of Islamic terrorist organizations. *Studies in Conflict and Terrorism.* Taylor & Francis.

Ressler, Steve. 2006. Social network analysis as an approach to combat terrorism: Past, present and future research. *Homeland Security Affairs* 2 (2, July).

Rodriguez, Jose A. 2005. The March 11th terrorist network: In its weakness lies its strength. XXV International Sunbelt Conference, Los Angeles.

Sageman, Marc. 2004. *Understanding Terror Networks.* University of Pennsylvania Press.

Sterling, Claire. 1981. *The Terror Network: The Secret War of International Terrorism.* Holt, Rinehart and Winston; New York: Readers Digest Press.

Stohl, Cynthia, and Michael Stohl. 2002. Networks, terrorism and terrorist networks. Paper adapted from the conference Communication in Action: The Communicative Constitution and its Implications for Theory and Practice, November.

Stohl, Cynthia, and Michael Stohl. 2007. Networks of terror: Theoretical assumptions and pragmatic consequences. *Communication Theory* 17.

Stohl, Michael. 1983. Review: The international network of terrorism. *Journal of Peace Research* 20 (1, April).

Vidino, Lorenzo. 2006. *Al Qaeda in Europe.* Prometheus Books.

27

Global Diseases: The Role of Networks in the Spread and Prevention of Infection

J. Shin Teh
Harvey Rubin

Abstract

Infectious diseases are complex, interdependent events that can be described as networks over enormous scales of time and distance from the molecular to the societal, from the local microenvironment to the global stage. In this chapter, Teh and Rubin argue that meeting this challenge effectively requires a solution that engages networks. This network-based perspective must inform not only the development and distribution of drugs and vaccines for infectious diseases, but also the development of strategies of primary prevention that use the knowledge of such networks to disrupt and limit disease spread. In this review, they analyze infectious diseases in the context of the networks underlying the evolution, establishment, and propagation of disease. They also review the network-based analyses for modeling disease spread and allowing a better understanding of the counter-interventions needed. Finally, they outline the future challenges in this area and propose a collaborative international solution based on a "global compact" that will allow effective diagnosis, prevention, and treatment of infectious diseases.

Introduction

Infectious diseases inflict global mortality and morbidity on a monumental scale. The Global Burden of Disease Study indicates that infectious diseases account for 22% of all deaths and 27% of disability adjusted life years (DALYs). They have a disproportionate impact on the developing world, where infectious diseases account for 52% of deaths and 50% of DALYs in sub-Saharan Africa compared to only 11% of deaths and 5% of DALYs in established market economies (Saker et al. 2004). The current realities are overwhelming. Each year, 300 million cases of malaria kill 2 million people. An estimated 3% of the world's population, or 170 million people, are chronically infected with hepatitis C virus. About 4 million people are newly infected each year, 80% of whom will progress to a chronic infection associated with cirrhosis in about 20% and liver cancer in about 5%. Roughly 2 billion people have been infected with hepatitis B (1 out of 3 people). Approximately 400 million people are chronically infected with the virus, and an estimated 1 million people will die each year from hepatitis B and its complications. One-third of the world is infected with *Mycobacterium tuberculosis* that causes tuberculosis, with 10 million new cases every year accounting for 2 million deaths. Approximately 50 million people worldwide are infected with HIV, which killed 3.9 million people in 2005, and the less-publicized spread of cholera causes close to 120,000 deaths per year. The physical suffering and loss of lives not only are devastating from a humanitarian perspective, but also place a tremendous economic burden on societies, as illustrated by Table 27-1. Nevertheless, the urgent need for action lines up with today's booming progress in research and technology development, which provide us with an unparalleled opportunity for effectively mitigating the costs and extent of infectious diseases. Indeed, novel methods and concepts are increasingly employed in finding new solutions.

TABLE 27-1 The Economic Costs Resulting from Infectious Diseases

Disease	Cost (USD)
Avian flu, Hong Kong 1997	$100 million in lost poultry production Air travel declined by 22%
Bovine Spongiform Encephalopathy (BSE), United Kingdom 1995	$9–$14 billion
Cholera, Peru 1991	$775 million dollars lost in ban on seafood exports
Plague, India 1994	$2 billion in losses to the Indian economy; half a million people displaced; aviation and tourism shut down

Disease	Cost (USD)
Hypothetical smallpox attack	$117 billion dollars/week
Potential H5N1 influenza in the USA	$600 billion dollars (Congressional Budget Office Report)

In addition, the deliberate spread of infectious diseases has emerged as one option for terrorists and is a major national security concern. However, nondeliberate spread remains the forefront threat, and overall constitutes a serious threat to security, more broadly defined. In 1992, the Institute of Medicine published the first comprehensive report on the subject, "Emerging Infections: Microbial Threats to Health in the United States" (Lederberg, Shope, and Oaks 1992). In its new version published in 2003, the global environment and microbial agents are brought into focus as threats to health. An unclassified report from the National Intelligence Council in 2000 examined "The Global Infectious Disease Threat and Its Implications for the United States" (National Intelligence Council 2000). Similarly, an unclassified 2003 CIA document analyzed "The Darker Bioweapons Future," in which the many benefits of modern molecular biology are weighed against the danger that "the effects of engineered biological agents could be worse than any disease known to man" (CIA 2003). This vexing problem was raised quite clearly in the 2006 "National Security Strategy": "Public health challenges like pandemics (HIV/AIDS, avian influenza)…recognize no borders. The risks to social order are so great that traditional public health approaches may be inadequate, *necessitating new strategies and responses…*" (italics added) (White House 2006). In this chapter, we consider the role of networks in the spread of diseases—accelerated by increased interaction and international travel—and the new strategies and responses that might be necessitated to meet this threat.

Network-Based Perspective of Infectious Diseases

Infectious diseases are established and spread through networks composed of pathogen reservoirs, vectors (for example, insects, animals), humans, as well as raw and processed biologic products. The complexities of vector-human and human-human networks have increased as human populations grew, human-related activities increased, and encroachment into forests expanded. Indeed, the substantial surge of international economic, social, cultural, political, and technological interchange, accompanied by the increased flow of goods, capital, and people across political and geographic boundaries, has helped to spread some of the deadliest infectious diseases known to humans (Daulaire 1999).

The pace of today's infectious diseases is faster and the stakes are much higher. Compare the spread of the bubonic plague in the fourteenth century and the Spanish flu pandemic six centuries later. The fourteenth-century transportation network consisted mostly of year-round shipping routes centered on key port cities around the world from the Pacific rim, South China Sea, and the Indian Ocean, right to the Mediterranean and Scandinavian seas. These ports served as areas for disease propagation, and this was clearly evident in the case of bubonic plague or "the black death," which spread in the span of roughly a year through the movement of infected sailors and black rodents harboring the pathogen *Yersinia pestis*. By comparison, the Spanish flu pandemic spread quickly and globally—propelled by rapid industrialization and modernization of transportation, not to mention WWI—killing somewhere between 50 and 100 million people (Knobler et al. 2005).

From a networks point of view, infectious diseases have geographical origins. In fact, many infectious diseases originate at areas of interface between humans and nature at specific endemic locations throughout the world. In these hot spots or niches, pathogens exist with high prevalence in certain members of the ecological system. Here, there is ample opportunity for the pathogens to survive and immunologically evolve, that is, undergo genetic mutations such as point mutation, gene deletion or insertion, and gene transduction, as well as gene segment and plasmid exchange. Insect or animal vectors as well as human populations around hot spots are endemically infected and reinfected. They evolve their immune system in tandem with the pathogens, and movement of this vector/human reservoir to other geographical areas unleashes these pathogens to immunologically "naïve" vulnerable populations and, hence, propagates the disease. The importance of geography is exemplified by the phenomena of antigenic drift (point mutations) versus shift (gene segment exchange, which leads to epidemics/pandemics) of the influenza A virus, whereby antigenic shifts preferentially occur in areas with significant avian hosts either naturally or from agriculture.

A review of emerging infectious diseases from 1940 to 2004 (Jones et al. 2008) found that emerging infections are most often (60%) related to zoonoses (infectious diseases that can be transmitted from wild or domestic animals to humans). The study also found that most emerging infections are bacterial or rickettsial (54.3%) related to the increased number of antibiotic resistance strains, and most emerging infections are correlated to socioeconomic, environmental, and ecological factors. The emerging infections arise in potential hot spots such as Central America, tropical Africa, and south Asia Drug-resistant strains of emerging bacterial infections arise in the more developed nations at higher latitudes, related to the widespread and often indiscriminate use of antibiotics.

This networks perspective of human and nature interplay is aptly formalized by the Institute of Medicine, which identified six major factors that contribute to the establishment and spread of infectious diseases (Lederberg, Shope, and S. E. Oaks 1992): (1) human demographics and behavior; (2) technology and industry; (3) economic development and land use; (4) international travel and commerce; (5) microbial adaptation and change; and (6) breakdown of public health measures.

Indeed, infectious diseases are excellent examples of complex network systems in motion, from the molecular level right up to the societal and global: Pathogens elaborate complex networks of genetic elements, the interplay of which determines metabolism, survival, and virulence; networks of environmental niches in turn naturally select animal and human reservoirs; and finally, networks of humans and populations predict risk of disease establishment and spread. Globalization further introduces higher levels of network complexities. Network-based analyses help us to understand how entities interact with one another and act collectively, and can identify strategies that can prevent deleterious outcomes, for example, expression of virulence factors, animal-human transmission, and epidemic/pandemic spread in human societies. In addition, analyses must boldly venture into uncharted areas of study to develop social, political, and business strategies that promote global multinational collaborations that *facilitate* disease surveillance, communications, knowledge sharing, research, and drug development, as well as specialist training. We live in a world of pandemic, epidemic, and endemic infectious diseases, which threaten personal, national, and international security—and demand global responses.

Applying Network Models to Infectious Diseases

Network-based strategies have brought new perspectives, methodologies, and analytical tools to diverse fields from basic microbiology, biochemistry, genomics, and systems biology, to epidemiology, diagnosis, and treatment. Network-based analyses apply graph, network, and complexity theories to the study of individuals, organizations, or other specific entities, and delve into their interdependent relationships. Graphically, entities or players are depicted as nodes, and their relationships are illustrated by lines that indicate various types of interdependencies or interactions, such as friendship, kinship, sexual relations, trade, values, ideas, conflict, web association, or airline links. Network-based analyses focus on structure/topology of the network, time-dependent changes in the network, and the composition and properties of the ties between constituent players and how they influence collective norms, behavior, or action.

Network-based approaches were avidly developed toward the end of the preceding century on the heels of greater appreciation of how individuals network with one another, with the discovery of small-world phenomenon (Travers and Stanley 1969; Watts and Strogatz 1998) (commonly known as six degrees of separation) and scale-free networks (Barabasi and Albert 1999). They aim to realistically model the manner in which entities collectively self-organize. It was soon discovered that these approaches can also be used to model other entities at various scales, such as genes, proteins, and cells.

We define networks in the broadest, nonmathematical sense as relationships between agents, individuals, or groups. These relationships can be mutually beneficial, stable, robust, and secure, or not, leading to a catastrophic state of affairs when security fails either by design or inadvertently, either anticipated or unanticipated.

There are different types of networks, varying in terms of topology, heterogeneity of contact formation, and degree distribution. For the classical random type of networks, there are three main classes (Bansal, Grenfell, and Meyers 2007):

1. The lattice network, in which all nodes have the same degree, and a given node is connected to other nodes that are physically close

2. The regular random network, in which all nodes have the same degree, but a given node is connected to other nodes in the network chosen at random

3. The Erdos-Renyi or Poisson random network, in which there is a preset total number of edges that are assigned to nodes at random, giving a Poisson degree distribution for the network that decreases exponentially (Bollobas 1985; Erdös and Rényi 1960)

The more heterogeneous network types include the exponential and the scale-free networks. The discovery of the scale-free nature of networks, so called because of a lack of a typical value (or range of values) for a network's "degreeness," provides closer approximations about how complex networks self-organize in reality; the observed degree distribution follows a power-law. This scale-free topology has been found to be characteristic of many natural and manmade network systems, such as protein interaction networks (Giot et al. 2003; Bork et al. 2004), the Internet (Albert, Jeong, and Barabasi 1999), and airway networks (Dorogovtsev and Mendes 2003). The model indicates that there is a higher probability of highly connected nodes in the network, as well as nodes with edges connecting the node's neighbors to each other, compared to networks constructed using the random model. In other words, a small fraction of nodes are very highly connected (for example, hubs). It also exhibits preferential attachment, wherein new nodes preferentially attach to nodes that are already highly connected.

Network-based studies have led to new technologies and strategies in human systems. For example, the study of pheromones and swarm intelligence in ants helped develop adaptive telephone switching to route phone calls toward uncongested routes, thereby improving traffic regulation in telecommunications (Bonabeau and Theraulaz 2000). In medicine, network-based perspectives have advanced understanding in various areas such as the promoter targets of transcription factors (Reddy, Delisi, and Shakhnovich 2007), protein complex formation (Zotenko et al. 2006), and anatomical and functional connectivity in the brain (Stam and Reijneveld 2007).

Modeling Disease Spread

Modeling disease spread is important for epidemiologists and public health officials to preemptively identify areas of rapid spread, obtain quantitative predictions, and devise appropriate containment strategies (which includes contact tracing, isolation, quarantine, and prophylactic vaccinations). It also informs the optimal distribution of drugs and vaccines for infectious diseases. It is an evolving field, increasingly incorporating newer network-based strategies in lieu of older, more simplistic methods. For example, for simplicity, traditional compartmental modeling in epidemiology, which is used to derive the number of secondary cases of disease resulting from a single initial case (R_0), assumes that population or subpopulation members are uniformly mixed, and everyone has an equal chance of becoming infected or infecting others. It is usual to categorize members of a population into three compartments: susceptible, infected, or recovered (thus giving the "SIR" model). This model is good for diseases that produce post-infection immunity, such as measles, mumps, and rubella. Other compartmental models include the SIS (susceptible-infectious-susceptible) model, the stochastic compartmental models (Bailey 1975), the pair or dyad models (Ferguson and Garnett 2000), and the branching process models (Farrington, Kanaan, and Gay 2003).

Despite previous successes, these epidemiological models have weaknesses stemming mainly from the fact that contact patterns in a population are neither random nor homogeneous. Furthermore, compartment modeling was recently shown to be unrealistic when used to model the spread of Severe Acute Respiratory Syndrome (SARS)

(Meyers et al. 2005). The early, abnormally high R_0 estimates that were based on transmission data from closed settings such as hospitals and crowded apartment buildings (where there are unusually high rates of contact between individuals [Lipsitch et al. 2003; Riley et al. 2003]) failed to be reproduced when subsequent worldwide epidemiologic data were analyzed. Indeed, although the range of 2.2 to 3.6 for R_0 would have predicted 30,000 to 10 million secondary cases in China alone in the first 120 days, there were only 782 actual cases. Accordingly, a study on the effects of SARS isolation strategies in Hong Kong, Singapore, and Toronto emphasized the importance of putting R_0 into context with the setting from which disease transmission data is obtained (Chowell et al. 2003). Indeed, R_0 is a function of both the transmissibility of the disease and the contact patterns of the population under analysis. Unrepresentatively high contact rates, such as those present in the hospitals and apartment buildings, yielded the high R_0, which were then erroneously applied when predicting outbreak numbers in the general community. This example highlights the inadequacies of models that do not factor in individual-level information, and instead rely on generalized factorials of population networking.

In truth, the spread of infectious diseases is highly heterogeneous, sometimes with only certain carriers efficiently spreading the disease (the "superspreaders") through their extensive contacts with other people (Lloyd-Smith et al. 2005), while most others spread the disease more locally. This more closely mirrors the exponential and scale-free, nonhomogenous network models of contacts between individuals in a specific population, with some members being well-connected (the "hubs") versus those who are integrated only locally, as exemplified by sexual contact networks (Liljeros et al. 2001). These attributes are somewhat at odds with the compartment models and, hence, call for the use of more realistic exponential (Bansal, Grenfell, and Meyers 2007; Amaral et al. 2000) and scale-free contact network models (Pastor-Satorras and Vespignani 2001) over random, compartment models (Lloyd and May 2001; Ancel Meyers et al. 2003). The benefits are numerous, with contact networks able to incorporate intelligent or realistic data-derived probabilities of interpersonal contact based on stratified social structures (for example, household, workplaces, and public foci such as schools and hospitals). Loci can be further subdivided to improve simulation accuracy, for instance, subcategorizing hospitals into normal wards, emergency rooms, and intensive care units, each with different infectious indices, or workplaces into bays, lunch rooms, and meeting/conference rooms. Also, there are several established methods for obtaining behavioral information for building realistic models (Bansal, Grenfell, and Meyers 2007), for example, contact tracing (Klovdahl et al. 1977), surveying individuals in populations

(Eubank et al. 2004), social characteristics information (Halloran et al. 2002), and census data (Lloyd and May 2001). In addition, certain statistical properties of networks are useful predictors of disease status in a population. For example, an increase in the standard deviation of the degree distribution actually lowers the epidemic threshold, which refers to the critical infection rate above which a disease may spread and persist (Anderson and May 1992).

However, certain shortcomings of these network models need to be addressed. For example, scale-free network construction was shown to be prone to sampling bias during data collection (Stumpf, Wiuf, and May 2005). Also, most networks employed are static. (For example, they assume that contact patterns remain the same over the course of the simulation.) They may, therefore, miss crucial networking and propagation dynamics in slow or chronic infectious diseases. Nevertheless, network-based approaches have heralded the advent of more sophisticated approaches to complex problems in infectious diseases, and will help generate innovative solutions with continued development.

Genetic and Metabolic Networks

In addition to studying the spread of disease across populations, network perspectives also have been applied to the study of infectious diseases at the molecular and cellular levels. Following decades of progress in genomic and proteomic research that has increased our understanding of how small networks of genes and proteins interact and function, molecular biology is increasingly focused on systems biology, which emphasizes a global understanding of cell physiology and metabolism. Cell metabolism ultimately determines phenotypic expression, including whether pathogens elaborate virulence factors that allow them to establish disease. This shift toward seeing biological systems as large networks needed new research tools and paradigms, particularly when it involves the integration of large amounts of heterogenous data at different scales, including bioinformatics, genomic, transcriptomic, proteomic, metabolomic, and phenomic data of immensely complex cellular networks (Bollobas 1985).

Analysis of cellular gene expression network patterns revealed the existence of a power-law or scale-free topology with few high-expression level genes and many low-expression level genes (Furusawa and Kaneko 2003). An experiment analyzing the gene expression pattern of *E. coli, S. cerevisiae, A. thaliana, D. melanogaster, M. musculus,* and *H. sapiens* under different growth conditions revealed that the absolute gene expression change for two different conditions is conserved among the species and proportional to the relative levels before the transition (Ueda et al. 2004), meaning that highly expressed genes change their expression levels more than low-expression genes, termed a "rich travel more" phenomenon. These high-expression level genes are important, as they may indicate areas of network vulnerability if attacked. Another study examined genome-wide disruption networks and revealed essential hub genes with high out-degrees, and these predominantly encode regulatory proteins. Genes with the highest in-degrees are mostly involved in carrying out metabolic reactions (Rung et al. 2002).

At the metabolic level, analysis of the metabolic networks of 43 organisms representative of the three kingdoms (archaea, bacteria, and eukaryotes) illustrated modularity (Ravasz et al. 2002; Ravasz and Barabasi 2003), as well as scale-free architecture (Jeong et al. 2000), and highlighted metabolite hubs that were heavily involved in various metabolic reactions and are, therefore, crucial in determining metabolic fluxes. A metabolic flux analysis of *Escherichia coli* further confirmed that only a few reactions operate high-flux values (Almaas et al. 2004). The implication of this is that these few hubs may be important in shifting the overall metabolic program of, for example, bacteria, toward expressing special phenotypes such as virulence, persistence, dormancy, and sporulation. Also, attacks on these hubs can lead to severe disruptions to the network as a whole and compromise robustness. These concepts are further corroborated by protein-protein interaction network analyses, which also revealed scale-free topology and thus the existence of only a few proteins participating in many protein complex interactions (Yook, Oltvai, and Barabasi 2004).

A good example of a network point vulnerability is the Rel enzyme widely found in prokaryotes. This enzyme is responsible for catalyzing the formation of hyperphosphorylated guanosine, an influential nucleotide that represents a highly connected metabolic node. This leads to many downstream cellular effects such as reduction of certain ribonucleic acids (RNA), induction of protein degradative pathways, stimulation of stationary phase genes, and modulation of genes that regulate DNA replication (Cashel et al. 1996; Chakraburtty et al. 1996; Xiao et al. 1991). In fact, researchers at present are focused on obtaining structural information of the Rel enzyme and generating inhibitory compounds against it. This is important in diseases such as tuberculosis, in which the causative *Mycobacterium tuberculosis* was also shown to elaborate a Rel-mediated mechanism of dormancy in infected murine lungs (Dahl et al. 2003). Also, newly developed genome-scale network computations were able to identify knocked-out biochemical species or metabolites following a particular gene deletion. The analyses also showed whether these metabolites were essential for a particular phenotype (for example, bacterial virulence) as determined from in vivo survivability data (Imielinski et al. 2005), thus further pinpointing potentially vulnerable nodes for attack.

Controlling Global Infectious Diseases

Although progress has been made at the basic science level in understanding the pathogenesis of many diseases, the overall situation in controlling infectious diseases has deteriorated for a number of interrelated reasons, including these:

- The increase in antibiotic-resistant bacterial infections
- The sparse pipeline of new molecular entities that lead to effective anti-infective agents
- The lack of participation of large pharmaceutical companies in anti-infective drug development and discovery
- Slow progress on developing antibacterial, antifungal, and especially antiparasitic agents (although antiviral research and development is progressing)
- The absence of harmonized regulatory processes, which hinders rapid development of anti-infective agents
- Woefully underdeveloped distribution of anti-infective agents to clinics and patients in many parts of the world
- Inadequate infrastructure for rapid and accurate diagnostic testing in the developing world
- Incomplete global infectious disease surveillance and reporting, and inadequate shared, interoperable, real-time databases
- An insufficient number of well-trained medical workers to ensure proper diagnosis, prescribing, and monitoring practices
- Lack of consideration of zoonotic and food-borne infections in the increased incidence of the spread of infectious diseases
- The increased incidence of national insurgencies and of failed states worsening the global communicable disease situation
- Different motivations of individual nations in generating policy for the use of first-, second-, and third-line anti-infective agents
- Globalization—economic globalization, demographic globalization (urbanization and refugee movement), technological global changes, and environmental/climate global changes that alter patterns of communicable diseases, frequently in unpredictable ways
- Lack of coordination of agencies that work for increased access to anti-infective agents with agencies that work to limit the emergence of resistance to anti-infective agents

- Increased number and availability of counterfeit drugs, contributing substantially to the spread and emergence of drug resistance of communicable diseases
- New threats from the emergence of new research in synthetic biology from the synthetic creation of new infectious agents, the reintroduction of infectious agents that no longer exist in nature, or the generation of infectious agents that exist in nature but are hard to isolate

A Network-Based Response—A Global Compact for Infectious Diseases

The daunting challenge of tracking, detecting, preventing, and treating infectious diseases is the arms race of the twenty-first century. The race is not between states; the race is between the global community and pathogens found in nature or pathogens nefariously disseminated. The challenge calls for new, network-inspired solutions that integrate basic science, technology, and social, political, legal, and economic realities (see Figure 27-1). The solution should optimize trade-offs in the interplay of international security, global health, the creation and open dissemination of new knowledge, and the maintenance and enhancement of the positive role of modern molecular biology on the economy of the developing world.

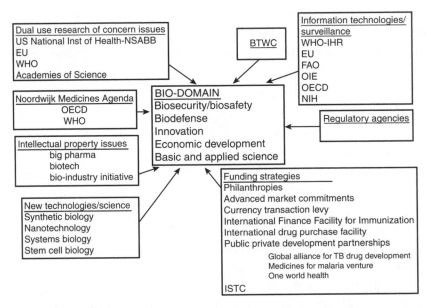

Figure 27-1   Response to infectious disease: a very complex organizational network

Beyond the undeniable moral significance of this state of affairs, our collective failure to give this problem the attention it deserves has implications for the economic well-being of both the developed and the developing world. International development scholars have described the role that infectious diseases play in the perpetuation of poverty in the developing world: destroying family structures and limiting economic and educational opportunities. However, infectious diseases are not merely an "over there" problem but a symmetric threat that imperils the economic security of all nations, given the global interconnectedness of populations. Although the social disintegration that accompanies an epidemic has filtered into the public consciousness, the resulting economic disruption is less well known. A few weeks after the identification of SARS, the disease had already cost nearly $30 billion, an amount sufficient to prevent 8 million deaths from infectious disease worldwide (Kickbusch 2003). A potential H5N1 pandemic carries an even higher cost, with economic losses approaching $600 billion in the United States alone, depending on the virulence and mortality rate of the pandemic strain (Lipsitch et al. 2006). Even without an epidemic, the spread of antibiotic-resistant strains of bacteria imposes a persistent cost in terms of both health and dollars. Medical and popular literature is replete with reports of life-threatening infections caused by bacteria that are increasingly resistant to existing antibiotics. The recent Infectious Diseases Society of America report observed, "In a growing and frightening number of cases, these bacteria are resistant to many approved drugs, and patients have to be treated with new, investigational compounds or older, toxic alternatives" (IDSA 2004).

A study of U.S. national security issues conducted by the Woodrow Wilson School of Public and International Affairs at Princeton University unequivocally states, "American national security in the 21st century…is likely to be threatened by pathogens as much as people. New diseases and antibiotic-resistant strains of old ones are on the rise" (Ikenberry and Slaughter 2006).

This challenge requires a solution that engages the entire network across which infectious diseases may spread. In this chapter, we introduce a new strategy based on the creation of a unique four-point International Compact for Infectious Diseases (the "Compact") characterized by a network-based view:

1. *Information and knowledge sharing*—Establish, maintain, and monitor a shared international data and knowledge base for infectious diseases, including but not limited to biosurveillance information, relevant pharmaceutical data, and suites of services and skills.

2. *Basic research centers*—Establish, maintain, and monitor a network of international basic science research centers that will support fundamental investigations into the pathophysiology of certain microbial threats to global health.

3. *Drug and vaccine development*—Expand capabilities for the production of vaccines and therapeutics expressly for emerging and reemerging infections.

4. *Laboratory and regulatory standards*—Establish, maintain, and monitor international standards for best laboratory and regulatory practices.

Through the implementation of these four core missions, the Compact will minimize the impact of infectious diseases on national and international health, social and economic development, and international security. As shown in Figure 27-2, these missions are interconnected; without a strong foundation of basic science, the drug and vaccine pipelines dry up. Similarly, in the absence of effective biosurveillance, it becomes difficult to project which strain of an emerging disease represents the most significant threat, which in turn hampers our ability to create countermeasures. Information technology and knowledge sharing will drive new science, which in turn can modify and inform regulatory initiatives. Standardized regulatory regimes enable new drugs and vaccines that will change global epidemiological patterns, and these patterns must be reintegrated into a central database, beginning the cycle again.

Addressing the problem as a whole creates powerful incentives for stakeholders to participate. For example, to access a central database containing information on current clinical trials, epidemiological data, and new compounds and targets, participants would pledge to implement best laboratory and regulatory practices. By bringing together government, the private sector, and academia, the Compact allows each group to institutionalize their relations with the others. Pharmaceutical companies and public-private development partnerships can find partners to help take promising leads through to development. With the inclusion of post marketing/post distribution clinical trial data in the database, philanthropic organizations and governments will be able to understand the effects their investments are having throughout the world. Academics will acquire additional funding streams for their research, as well as input from their colleagues all over the world. Finally, all parties will work together to harmonize regulatory processes across the board, reducing barriers to market entry for much-needed therapeutics and ensuring their wider distribution.

International Compact for Infectious Disease

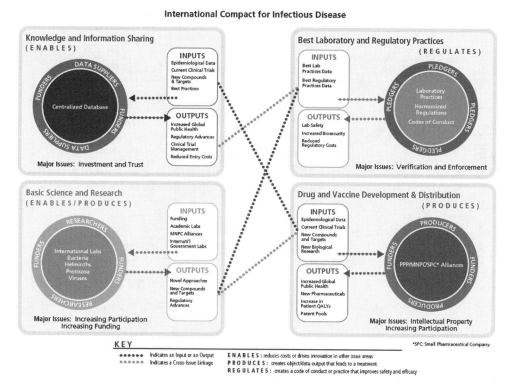

Figure 27-2   International Compact for Infectious Diseases

A large number of databases already address one or more of these issues, for example, the revised 2005 International Health Regulations (IHR). We propose developing an information technology architecture (see Figure 27-3) that will seamlessly integrate these databases and make them user-friendly, yet provide the necessary security and add new data as recommended by the wide user community. The challenges here are formidable, but hardly insurmountable. The greatest obstacle is the need for trust between signatory nations and a willingness to share data. There are technical challenges as well. Any attempt to create a common architecture for information systems would require common ontologies. New algorithms and models of disease spread need to be developed and validated. Lastly, the language of the Compact has to address the issue of member states that do not report, or significantly underreport, the incidence of communicable diseases.

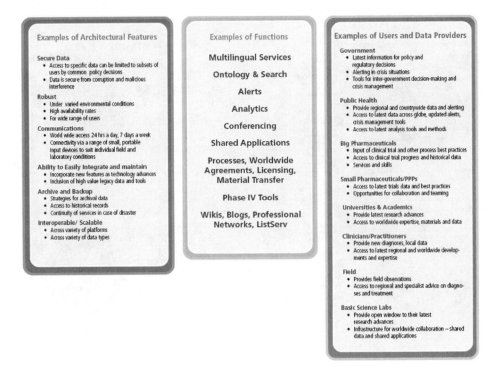

Figure 27-3   Information technology infrastructure

International biosurveillance and reporting, at the level of sophistication we envision, faces certain challenges (GAO 2005), including these:

- Integrating current initiatives into a national health IT strategy and federal architecture to reduce the risk of duplicative efforts
- Developing and adopting consistent interoperability standards
- Creating an open architecture that maximizes the use of off-the-shelf tools
- Creating enough flexibility to bring together disparate underlying IT languages and technologies to provide a common operating picture
- Generating the ability to accept multiple data formats used by agencies that provide the biosurveillance information
- Generating the ability to feed information back to the originating agencies providing biosurveillance information in a format each agency can accept
- Identifying data flows that will evolve during the developmental process
- Allowing the methods of analysis to evolve and adapt as new data become available or existing data sets are improved

- Knowing and evaluating the effectiveness of the current underlying algorithms, methods, and structures for biosurveillance data analysis

Organization and Governance

To accommodate the various interested parties and work within the limits of international law, the Compact will embrace a two-pronged approach, working with states in the form of a treaty and with other interested parties (NGOs, academic institutions, and the private sector) as a softer, pledge-based agreement.

These differences are structural rather than substantive, but both approaches have their limitations. Treaties must be ratified through domestic processes that vary widely from state to state and take an extended amount of time to enter into force. Furthermore, states jealously guard their sovereign prerogatives, and thus, enforcement regimes must be devised in a manner that maximizes both effectiveness and feasibility (Downs, Rocke, and Barsoom 1996). However, when in force, a treaty creates a body of "hard law" around an issue, providing a legal basis for international enforcement. A compact structure, in contrast, allows NGOs, the private sector, and academic institutions to submit a pledge of membership and voluntary compliance, making it quick to set up and allowing interested parties to coalesce around an issue (Rischard 2001, 2003).

By providing parallel frameworks for different parties, the overall project will, over time, achieve the benefits of each. Domestic groups that pledge their membership can apply pressure to their home states to speed ratification of the treaty framework. By bringing together both state and nonstate actors, the overall aims of the Compact will be debated from various viewpoints, thereby enhancing the legitimacy of the project and promoting a thorough understanding of its goals.

Conclusions: The Rising Challenge and Lessons from the Past

Can such an ambitious international initiative as this global compact succeed? Over the past 25 years, projects with international scope and impact demonstrate that efforts at resolving complex international issues are feasible from the perspectives of both implementation and end-stage achievements. We briefly discuss two of them.

In October of 1992, six NGOs met in New York City and founded the International Campaign to Ban Landmines (ICBL). By the end of 1997, a mere five years later, the Convention on the Prohibition of the Use, Stockpiling, Production and Transfer of Anti-Personnel Mines and on Their Destruction entered into force, and the ICBL was awarded the Nobel peace prize "as a model for similar processes in the future" (Sigal 2006). Of particular relevance for the struggle against infectious diseases is the way in which the ICBL—a coalition of nonstate actors—used normative rhetoric to compel government action on a previously neglected issue of little importance to the developed world. The essential issues surrounding infectious diseases possess similar normative force, which may indicate a similar potential for progress.

In the science and development domain, the Consultative Group on International Agricultural Research (CGIAR) achieved tremendous successes with a similarly broad approach to agricultural issues. Reacting to a projected crisis in the food supply, a series of high-level consultations were held in Bellagio, Italy, and elsewhere to devise a framework for addressing the situation. As a result of CGIAR's efforts, the world experienced a massive increase in cereal yield in the second half of the twentieth century, and the crisis was averted (CGIAR 2008). CGIAR is an important antecedent combining North/South representation with innovative research and has a truly lasting impact in some of the poorest regions in the world. The magnitude of the threat of infectious diseases also necessitates a major global, investigative effort. The example of the "Rice Institutes," funded by the Rockefeller Foundation for 15 years (Normile 1999) and sustained by the Consultative Group in International Agricultural Research, provides a framework for an interdisciplinary, collaborative, and synergistic network of Infectious Disease International Research Centers. These should have a permanent faculty and staff as well as visiting fellowships and studentships. The lasting positive impacts of international research centers are many, including fostering long-term relationships between scientists, establishing a culture of research responsibility, and serving as the nucleus for safe applications of interdisciplinary sciences globally.

The argument for taking such collective, network-based action to address infectious diseases is becoming more compelling. In particular, several highly probable trends may suggest we are losing the upper hand against infectious diseases:

- The emerging resistance to antiretroviral therapy for the human immunodeficiency virus (HIV)
- The emergence of multidrug resistance (MDR) and extremely drug-resistant (XDR) strains of *Mycobacterium tuberculosis*

- The emergence of hepatitis C, for which there are approximately four million carriers in the United States alone
- The next influenza pandemic, with a close watch on the continual evolution of the H5N1 strain
- The increasing rates of antimicrobial resistance displayed by, for instance, *Staphylococcus aureus*
- Naturally emerging new agents and food-borne illness, especially with the growing effects of global warming
- The ever-present threat of a biological terrorist attack

The key to any progress against infectious diseases is a structure that brings together diverse interests in a lasting fashion. Without such a structure, the commitment to reducing the impact of infectious diseases on our national, economic, and personal security will be subject to the political vagaries of the moment, leaving us unprepared for the next global health crisis.

Infectious diseases spread through networks, and a network perspective can help us understand their threats. At the same time, solutions to such network-based challenges cannot be developed by individual nodes in isolation. We need network-based approaches, such as the first *Global Compact for Infectious Diseases,* to address them. It takes a network-based approach to address the challenges created by networks.

References

Albert, R., H. Jeong, and A. L. Barabasi. 1999. The diameter of the World Wide Web. *Nature* 401, 130-131.

Almaas, E., B. Kovacs, T. Vicsek, Z. N. Oltvai, and A. L. Barabasi. 2004. Global organization of metabolic fluxes in the bacterium Escherichia coli. *Nature* 427, 839-843.

Amaral, L. A., A. Scala, M. Barthelemy, and H. E. Stanley. 2000. Classes of small-world networks. *Proceedings of the National Academy of Sciences USA* 97, 11149-11152.

Ancel Meyers, L., M. E. Newman, M. Martin, and S. Schrag. 2003. Applying network theory to epidemics: Control measures for Mycoplasma pneumoniae outbreaks. *Emerging Infectious Diseases* 9, 204-210.

Anderson, R. M., and R. M. May. 1992. *Infectious Diseases of Humans: Dynamics and Control.* New York: Oxford University Press.

Bailey, N. T. J. 1975. *The Mathematical Theory of Infectious Diseases and Its Applications.* New York: Hafner Press.

Bansal, S., B. T. Grenfell, and L. A. Meyers. 2007. When individual behaviour matters: Homogenous and network models in epidemiology. *Journal of the Royal Society Interface* 4, 879-891.

Barabasi, A. L., and R. Albert. 1999. Emergence of scaling in random networks. *Science* 286, 509-512.

Bollobas, B. 1985. *Random Graphs.* London: Academic Press.

Bonabeau, E., and G. Theraulaz. 2000. Swarm smarts. *Scientific American* 282, 72-79.

Bork, P., L. J. Jensen, C. Von Mering, A. K. Ramani, I. Lee, and E. M. Marcotte. 2004. Protein interaction networks from yeast to human. *Current Opinion in Structural Biology* 14, 292-299.

Cashel, M., D. R. Gentry, V. J. Hernandez, and D. Vinella. 1996. The stringent response. In *Escherichia coli and Salmonella: Cellular and Molecular Biology*, ed. F. C. Neidhardt, R. Curtis, J. L. Ingraham, E. C. C. Lin, K. B. Low, B. Magasanik, W. S. Reznikoff, M. Riley, M. Schaechter, and H. E. Umbarger. Washington, DC: ASM.

CGIAR. 2008. History of the CGIAR. www.cgiar.org/who/history/index.html.

Chakraburtty, R., J. White, E. Takano, and M. Bibb. 1996. Cloning, characterization and disruption of a (p)ppGpp synthetase gene (relA) of Streptomyces coelicolor A3(2). *Molecular Microbiology* 19, 357-368.

Chowell, G., P. W. Fenimore, M. A. Castillo-Garsow, and C. Castillo-Chavez. 2003. SARS outbreaks in Ontario, Hong Kong and Singapore: The role of diagnosis and isolation as a control mechanism. *Journal of Theoretical Biology* 224, 1-8.

Dahl, J. L., C. N. Kraus, H. I. Boshoff, B. Doan, K. Foley, D. Avarbock, G. Kaplan, V. Mizrahi, H. Rubin, and C. E. Barry III. 2003. The role of RelMtb-mediated adaptation to stationary phase in long-term persistence of Mycobacterium tuberculosis in mice. *Procedings of the National Academy of Sciences USA* 100, 10026-10031.

Daulaire, N. 1999. Globalization and health. International Roundtable on "Responses to Globalization: Rethinking Equity and Health."

Dorogovtsev, S. N., and J. F. F. Mendes. 2003. *Evolution of Networks: From Biological Nets to the Internet and WWW.* Oxford: Oxford University Press.

Downs, G. W., D. M. Rocke, and P. N. Barsoom. 1996. Is the good news about compliance good news about cooperation? *International Organization* 50, 379-406.

Erdös, P., and A. Rényi. 1960. On the evolution of random graphs. *Publication Mathematics Institute Hungarian Academy of Sciences.* 5, 17-61.

Eubank, S., H. Guclu, V. S. Kumar, M. V. Marathe, A. Srinivasan, Z. Toroczkai, and N. Wang. 2004. Modelling disease outbreaks in realistic urban social networks. *Nature* 429, 180-184.

Farrington, C. P., M. N. Kanaan, and N. J. Gay. 2003. Branching process models for surveillance of infectious diseases controlled by mass vaccination. *Biostatistics* 4, 279-295.

Ferguson, N. M., and G. P. Garnett. 2000. More realistic models of sexually transmitted disease transmission dynamics: Sexual partnership networks, pair models, and moment closure. *Sexually Transmitted Diseases* 27, 600-609.

Furusawa, C., and K. Kaneko. 2003. Zipf's law in gene expression. *Physical Review Letters* 90, 088102.

GAO. 2005. information Technology: Federal agencies face challenges in implementing initiatives to improve public health infrastructure. United States Government Accountability Office.

Giot, L., J. S. Bader, C. Brouwer, A. Chaudhuri, B. Kuang, Y. Li, Y. L. Hao, C. E. Ooi, B. Godwin, E. Vitols, G. Vijayadamodar, P. Pochart, H. Machineni, M. Welsh, Y. Kong, B. Zerhusen, R. Malcolm, Z. Varrone, A. Collis, M. Minto, S. Burgess, L. Mcdaniel, E. Stimpson, F. Spriggs, J. Williams, K. Neurath, N. Ioime, M. Agee, E. Voss, K. Furtak, R. Renzulli, N. Aanensen, S. Carrolla, E. Bickelhaupt, Y. Lazovatsky, A. Dasilva, J. Zhong, C. A. Stanyon, R. L. Finley, Jr., K. P. White, M. Braverman, T. Jarvie, S. Gold, M. Leach, J. Knight, R. A. Shimkets, M. P. Mckenna, J. Chant, and J. M. Rothberg. 2003. A protein interaction map of Drosophila melanogaster. *Science* 302, 1727-1736.

Halloran, M. E., I. M. Longini, Jr., A. Nizam, and Y. Yang. 2002. Containing bioterrorist smallpox. *Science* 298, 1428-1432.

IDSA. 2004. Bad bugs, no drugs: As antibiotic discovery stagnates…a public health crisis brews. http://www.idsociety.org/badbugsnodrugs.html.

Ikenberry, G. J., and A. Slaughter. 2006. Forging a world of liberty under law: U.S. national security in the 21st century. *The Princeton Project Papers.* Princeton University.

Imielinski, M., C. Belta, A. Halasz, and H. Rubin. 2005. Investigating metabolite essentiality through genome-scale analysis of Escherichia coli production capabilities. *Bioinformatics* 21, 2008-2016.

Jeong, H., B. Tombor, R. Albert, Z. N. Oltvai, and A. L. Barabasi. 2000. The large-scale organization of metabolic networks. *Nature* 407, 651-654.

Jones, K. E., N. G. Patel, M. A. Levy, A. Storeygard, D. Balk, J. L. Gittleman, and P. Daszak. 2008. Global trends in emerging infectious diseases. *Nature* 451, 990-993.

Kickbusch, I. 2003. A Wake-Up Call for Global Health. *International Herald Tribune*, April 29.

Klovdahl, A. S., Z. Dhofier, G. Oddy, J. O'Hara, S. Stoutjesdijk, and A. Whish. 1977. Social networks in an urban area: First Canberra study. *The Australian and New Zealand Journal of Sociology.* 13, 169-172.

Knobler, S. L., A. Mack, A. Mahmoud, and S. M. Lemon, ed. 2005. *The Threat Of Pandemic Influenza: Are We Ready? Workshop Summary.* National Academies Press.

Lederberg, J., R. E. Shope, and S. E. Oaks, Jr. 1992. *Microbial Threats to Health in the United States.* National Academies Press.

Liljeros, F., C. R. Edling, L. A. Amaral, H. E. Stanley, and Y. Aberg. 2001. The web of human sexual contacts. *Nature* 411, 907-908.

Lipsitch, M., T. Cohen, B. Cooper, J. M. Robins, S. Ma, L. James, G. Gopalakrishna, S. K. Chew, C. C. Tan, M. H. Samore, D. Fisman, and M. Murray. 2003. Transmission dynamics and control of severe acute respiratory syndrome. *Science* 300, 1966-1970.

Lipsitch, M., P. Mcinnes, C. Mills, W. Nordhaus, P. Palese, and H. Rubin. 2006. A potential influenza pandemic: Possible macroeconomic effects and policy issues. Report Presented to the Congressional Budget Office, July 27.

Lloyd, A. L., and R. M. May. 2001. Epidemiology. How viruses spread among computers and people. *Science* 292, 1316-1317.

Lloyd-Smith, J. O., S. J. Schreiber, P. E. Kopp, and W. M. Getz. 2005. Superspreading and the effect of individual variation on disease emergence. *Nature* 438, 355-359.

Meyers, L. A., B. Pourbohloul, M. E. Newman, D. M. Skowronski, and R. C. Brunham. 2005. Network theory and SARS: predicting outbreak diversity. *Journal of Theoretical Biology* 232, 71-81.

US National Intelligence Council. 2000. *The Global Infectious Disease Threat and its Implications for the United States (National Intelligence Estimate).* Washington: US National Intelligence Council. http://www.odci.gov/nic/pubs/index.htm

Normile, D. 1999. Rice biotechnology. Rockefeller to end network after 15 years of success. *Science* 286, 1468-1469.

Office of Transnational Issues, Central Intelligence Agency. 2003. "The Darker Bio-weapons Future." Unclassified. www.fas.org/irp/cia/product/bw1103.pdf

Pastor-Satorras, R. and A. Vespignani. 2001. Epidemic spreading in scale-free networks. *Physical Review Letters* 86, 3200-3203.

Ravasz, E., and A. L. Barabasi. 2003. Hierarchical organization in complex networks. *Physical review. E, Statistical, Nonlinear, and Soft Matter Physics* 67, 026112.

Ravasz, E., A. L. Somera, D. A. Mongru, Z. N. Oltvai, and A. L. Barabasi. 2002. Hierar-chical organization of modularity in metabolic networks. *Science* 297, 1551-1555.

Reddy, T. E., C. Delisi, and B. E. Shakhnovich. 2007. Binding site graphs: a new graph theoretical framework for prediction of transcription factor binding sites. *PLoS Computational Biology* 3, e90.

Riley, S., C. Fraser, C. A. Donnelly, A. C. Ghani, L. J. Abu-Raddad, A. J. Hedley, G. M. Leung, L. M. Ho, T. H. Lam, T. Q. Thach, P. Chau, K. P. Chan, S. V. Lo, P. Y. Leung, T. Tsang, W. Ho, K. H. Lee, E. M. Lau, N. M. Ferguson, and R. M. Anderson. 2003. Transmission dynamics of the etiological agent of SARS in Hong Kong: Impact of public health interventions. *Science* 300, 1961-1966.

Rischard, J. F. 2003. Global issues networks: Desperate times deserve innovative meas-ures. *The Washington Quarterly* 26, 17-33.

Rischard, J. F. 2001. High noon: We need new approaches to global problem-solving, fast. *Journal of International Economic Law* 4 (3), 507-525.

Rung, J., T. Schlitt, A. Brazma, K. Freivalds, and J. Vilo. 2002. Building and analysing genome-wide gene disruption networks. *Bioinformatics* 18 (Suppl. 2), S202-S210.

Saker, L., K. Lee, B. Cannito, A. Gilmore, and D. Campbell-Lendrum. 2004. Globaliza-tion and infectious diseases: A review of the linkages. *Special Topics in Social, Economic and Behavioural (SEB) Research.*

Sigal, L. V. 2006. *Negotiating Minefields: The Landmines Ban in American Politics.* Routledge.

Stam, C. J., and J. C. Reijneveld. 2007. Graph theoretical analysis of complex networks in the brain. *Nonlinear Biomedical Physics* 1, 3.

Stumpf, M. P., C. Wiuf, and R. M. May. 2005. Subnets of scale-free networks are not scale-free: Sampling properties of networks. *Proceedings of the National Academy of Sciences of the United States of America* 102, 4221-4224.

Travers, J., and M. Stanley. 1969. An experimental study of the small world problem. *Sociometry* 32, 425-443.

Ueda, H. R., S. Hayashi, S. Matsuyama, T. Yomo, S. Hashimoto, S. A. Kay, J. B. Hogenesch, and M. Iino. 2004. Universality and flexibility in gene expression from bacteria to human. *Proceedings of the National Academy of Sciences of the United States of America* 101, 3765-3769.

Watts, D. J., and S. H. Strogatz. 1998. Collective dynamics of "small-world" networks. *Nature* 393, 440-442.

White House. 2006. The national security strategy of the United States of America.

Xiao, H., M. Kalman, K. Ikehara, S. Zemel, G. Glaser, and M. Cashel. 1991. Residual guanosine 3',5'-bispyrophosphate synthetic activity of relA null mutants can be eliminated by spoT null mutations. *The Journal of Biological Chemistry* 266, 5980-5990.

Yook, S. H., Z. N. Oltvai, and A. L. Barabasi. 2004. Functional and topological characterization of protein interaction networks. *Proteomics* 4, 928-942.

Zotenko, E., K. S. Guimaraes, R. Jothi, and T. M. Przytycka. 2006. Decomposition of overlapping protein complexes: A graph theoretical method for analyzing static and dynamic protein associations. *Algorithms for Molecular Biology* 1, 7.

28

Lessons from Empirical Network Analyses on Matters of Life and Death in East Africa

Jere R. Behrman
Hans-Peter Kohler
Susan Cotts Watkins

Abstract

Information about life-and-death matters such as ways to attain good health or prevent disease is often diffused through informal social networks. Network-based strategies and competencies are probably even more important in poor societies with limited means of communication and less effective formal structures than in developed economies. In this chapter, the authors explore the nature of and impacts of informal social networks in reducing fertility and HIV infection in Kenya and Malawi, using longitudinal quantitative and qualitative data that they and their collaborators have been collecting and analyzing for over a decade. They find that social networks and informal interactions are relevant for many different health domains in developing countries. Their research shows that network effects may be nonlinear, that there may be multiple equilibria, and that networks may either reinforce the status quo or help diffuse new options and behaviors. They show that both the context (for example, the degree of market development) and the density of networks matter (possibly interactively), as well as the endogeneity of network partners. Their work demonstrates that multiple approaches, including both qualitative and quantitative analyses, can be informative in providing greater understanding of what networks do and how they function.

This paper builds on extensive collaboration among the authors on social networks and demographic behaviors in Kenya and Malawi. This research was supported in part by NIH RO1 HD37276-01 (Watkins PI, Behrman co-PI), the TransCoop Program of the German-American Academic Council (Kohler PI, Watkins co-PI), NIH P30-AI45008 (Watkins PI, Behrman co-PI), Social Science Core of the Penn Center for AIDS Research (Watkins PI, Behrman co-PI), NIH RO1 HD044228 (Kohler PI , Behrman and Watkins co-PIs), NIH RO1 HD/MH41713 (Watkins PI, Behrman and Kohler co-PIs), and NIH R01 HD053781 (Kohler PI , Behrman and Watkins co-PIs). The data used in this paper were collected with funding from, in addition to the above-mentioned NIH grants, USAID's Evaluation Project (Watkins and Naomi Rutenberg co-PIs) and The Rockefeller Foundation (for a larger project including Malawi with Watkins and Eliya Zulu co-PIs). Behrman is the William R. Kenan, Jr., Professor of Economics and Research Associate of the Population Studies Center at the University of Pennsylvania, Philadelphia. Kohler is a Professor of Sociology and Research Associate of the Population Studies Center at the University of Pennsylvania, Philadelphia. Watkins is a Professor of Sociology and Research Associate of the Population Studies Center at the University of Pennsylvania, Philadelphia, and a Visiting Research Scientist at the California Center for Population Research, University of California–Los Angeles.

Social change, such as the worldwide declines in fertility and responses to the spread of HIV, call for explanation. Some attempts have emphasized planned interventions to persuade individuals to change their behavior; others have pointed to the importance of structural and institutional changes in the context in which individuals make decisions. Although the social sciences have been largely committed to a model of social change that assumes individuals acting in isolation from one another, recent theoretical advances and innovative empirical work have recognized the importance of social interactions. This chapter explores this emerging field of inquiry in demography through empirical studies in Kenya and Malawi that demonstrate the significance of networks in facilitating changes that fundamentally affect life and death.

Theories of social interactions in demography rest on the interdisciplinary insight in the social sciences that individuals do not make decisions about demographic and other social behaviors in isolation, but rather with others. Although the basic insight about the relevance of social interactions is old, dating back at least to the nineteenth century with the work of the sociologist Georg Simmel (1922), research in the past decades has achieved substantial progress in specifying, measuring, modeling, and understanding the importance of network-based interactions on human behaviors on the micro level, and on societal, economic, and cultural dynamics on the macro level. In particular, recent research has documented how social interactions offer opportunities for individuals to exchange information, to evaluate information, to learn about the rigidity or flexibility of social norms, and to influence the attitudes and behaviors of one another.

A key insight of the recent work on social interactions has been a better understanding of micro-macro interactions, and, in particular, how interrelated individual behaviors can affect the dynamics of social change (see Chapter 27, "Global Diseases: The Role of Networks in the Spread (and Prevention) of Infection"). For example, social multiplier effects imply that the total societal change in response to an innovation or intervention is larger than it would have been in the absence of social interactions. Social interactions can also result in multiple social equilibria, situations in which a society may be "stuck" in an inefficient societal state; multiple-equilibria, however, can also result in rapid and irreversible societal changes, such as a rapid transition from a high to low fertility regimes. The interrelatedness of individuals' decisions through social interactions can also imply that the dynamics of social change depend on the intricacies of the web of social relations, including, for instance, the structure, extent, and heterogeneity of individuals' social networks. The availability of causal estimates of social interaction effects and new analytic or simulation-based modeling approaches also promise a quantum step toward establishing social science models of individual behavior that are cognizant of roles of social interactions and informed by detailed empirical findings of how these interactions shape individual decision processes and aggregate societal dynamics.

Several reviews have described origins of network theories and analyses (for example, Wellman 1988). Network studies were given an early applied focus by European anthropologists studying rapid social change associated with modernization in sub-Saharan Africa, who wrote of network connections of urban migrants with each other and with rural communities from which they came (Mitchell 1969) and by anthropologists studying class relationships in Britain (Bott 1971). An interest in social networks then developed among U.S. sociologists, who focused more on theories and methods of network analysis (Marsden 1990; Burt 1982; Valente 2005) than on substantive issues. Among the exceptions that later had dominant influences on the field, Fischer (1982) analyzed personal networks to investigate social and psychological consequences of urban life, and Granovetter (1973) emphasized the importance of "weak ties" that transmit unique and nonredundant information across otherwise largely disconnected segments of social networks, thereby facilitating the diffusion of new information; "strong ties" and dense networks, on the other hand, are more likely to enforce norms and conventions that represent "proper" behaviors. In a similar vein, Burt (1992) pointed to strategic informational advantages that may be enjoyed by individuals who bridge "structural holes," that is, those with ties into multiple networks that are largely separated from one another, and the "new science of social networks." Watts (1999) formalized the "small-world phenomenon"—the hypothesis that a short chain of social acquaintances connects most individuals—using a few random shortcuts in the midst of locally dense neighborhoods.

In demography, an important stimulus to incorporating social networks in analyses was a byproduct of interest in explaining fertility declines in historical Western Europe and the developing world. Although it was expected that fertility declines could be understood as individual responses to structural changes associated with modernization (for example, urbanization, the transformation of the labor force from agricultural to industrial, declines in infant and child mortality), associations between measures of these changes and fertility declines were typically modest (Coale and Watkins 1986; Cleland and Wilson 1987). This led to postulating the importance of interpersonal diffusion (Knodel and van de Walle 1979) and emphasis on social networks (Watkins 1991; Casterline 2001; Kohler 2001; Montgomery and Casterline 1996; Munshi and Myaux 2006). Applications in demography have also included perceptions of mortality change (Montgomery 2000), the onset of sexual behavior among teenagers (e.g., Rodgers and Rowe 1993), and international migration (Massey et al. 1994; Munshi 2003). The discipline of economics also contributed to analyses of social networks, with research on issues such as cascades.

Despite evidence that showed that developing country villagers talked to each other about family planning and family size, demographers paid little attention to social networks prior to the 1990s. In part, this was due to the absence of data on networks; that absence, however, was due to a dominant model of social behavior that privileged individual and family characteristics over social interactions. Only in the 1990s were new data collected in developing countries that permitted detailed descriptions of social networks and rigorous analyses of social network effects, for example, in Ghana (Casterline et al. 2000), Kenya (www.kenya.pop.upenn.edu), and Malawi (www.malawi.pop.upenn.edu).

Our work for well over a decade in investigating the roles of social interaction for important demographic behaviors has been based on data collected in Kenya and Malawi. In the text that follows, we summarize the key substantive findings of these studies of social interaction pertaining to life (fertility) and death (HIV/AIDS). We also highlight some specific lessons for the study of social networks in other contexts.

General Overview of Survey Data and Contexts

Our analyses are based on data from the Kenyan Diffusion and Ideational Change Project (KDICP) and the Malawi Diffusion and Ideational Change Project (MDICP). Both data sets consist of longitudinal household survey and qualitative data that we collected in rural areas during 1994–2000 for Kenya and 1997–2008 for Malawi.[1] The initial primary motive for collecting these data was to analyze roles of social networks in diffusion of innovations to increase use of "modern" family planning methods and to reduce fertility, but the focus shifted increasingly toward HIV/AIDS because of the rapid spread of the epidemic in the populations being studied. The basic sampling frame for the surveys was women of childbearing age (15–49) who had ever been married, and their husbands (if any).

Our quantitative data are unique because they also include detailed accounts about women's and men's interactions about family planning or the HIV/AIDS epidemic with social network partners (besides their spouses) that allow us to investigate the role and importance of these interactions.[2] In particular, the data include information on egocentric networks, that is, networks that contain the respondent and network partners with whom the respondent had chatted about family planning or HIV/AIDS. The term "chat" was used in survey questions to indicate informal conversations rather than lectures at clinics. The network data were collected by first asking the respondents how many people they had chatted with about these respective topics. They were then asked a series of questions about these network partners (covering a maximum of four network partners if more than four were identified). The questions asked of the respondent about her or his network partners included relationship (for example, co-wife, sister-in-law, sister); the degree of closeness (confidant, friend, acquaintance); network partners' age, sex, and wealth; and perceptions of the respondents about the views and behaviors of network partners on family planning or about the risk of becoming infected with HIV/AIDS. The survey areas are primarily characterized by subsistence agriculture, and though schooling was valued, few respondents had studied beyond the primary grade.

---

[1] Details of data collection and analyses of attrition and data quality are available at www.malawi.pop. upenn.edu and in a special issue of *Demographic Research* (Watkins et al. 2003).

[2] Other data sets on AIDS have information on respondents' sexual partners (information that we have for only some subsamples) but not on their social networks in which they discuss HIV/AIDS risks and ways of coping with such risks.

Social Networks and Life—The Diffusion of Family Planning

Social networks played a critical role in the decline of fertility in a rural area of Kenya, where between 1978 and 1998 changes in both family size ideals and contraceptive use led to a dramatic decline in fertility.[3] To illustrate this important role of social networks in the Kenyan fertility decline, we examine the results of three separate studies based on our data that focus on the following key aspects: the direct impact of family planning programs versus the total effect of programs and social interactions; the relationship between the density of networks and fertility decisions; and the role of networks in changing contraceptive use over time.

First, in Kohler, Behrman, and Watkins (2000), we analyzed the *direct* impact of increasing family planning program efforts versus the *total* effect for example, the direct effect modulated by social interactions) in both linear and nonlinear models. This analysis yielded three major results:

1. Estimates of direct program effects differ substantially in the nonlinear model from those in the linear model, and social multiplier effects are substantial (as much as 43% of total program effects), as illustrated in Figure 28-1a and b.[4] Thus, simple specifications that are linear or that do not include social multiplier effects may be quite misleading.

2. If the model is nonlinear (see Figure 28-1b and c), there may be a low-level Malthusian equilibrium in which contraceptive use remains relatively low despite ongoing program efforts, as well as an equilibrium in which contraceptive use is high.[5] If a population is at a low-contraceptive-use and high-fertility equilibrium,

---

[3] In the 1978 World Fertility Survey the total fertility rate in Kenya was 8.2 per woman and in Nyanza Province 8.1; 17% and 8%, respectively, of currently married women reported that they wanted no more children, and 8% and 9%, respectively, were using some method of family planning (Kenya, Republic of 1980). Subsequent Demographic and Health Surveys for Kenya and for Nyanza Province showed a steady decline in the total fertility rate and a steady increase in the proportion wanting no more children and practicing family planning. According to the 1998 Demographic and Health Survey, the total fertility rate for Kenya is 5.0 births per woman; for Nyanza the figure is 4.7.

[4] That is, if the social multiplier is 175%, the proportion of the total effect due to social interaction is 43% = 75 / 175.

[5] Related models of multiple equilibria and path dependency in the context of fertility decline are found in, for example, Becker, Murphy, and Tamura (1990), Galor and Weil (1996), and Kohler (1997, 2000b).

small program changes have relatively small effects, but large increases in program efforts—even if transitory—may cause a shift to a high-contraceptive-use and low-fertility equilibrium. Our empirical analysis, however, does not indicate the presence of multiple equilibria in our data. Thus, these estimates suggest that there is little likelihood that a sharp transitory increase in program activities in Nyanza would lead to a rapid shift to much higher sustained levels of contraceptive use. But such possibilities may exist in other contexts.

3. Intensified social interactions may either increase or decrease the total effect and social multiplier effect resulting from family planning program efforts. "More" social interaction can thus reinforce or retard the diffusion of an innovation. When a nonlinear (logistic) model is used, increasing social interactions reinforces the status quo, resulting in close to a stable equilibria (whether at low or high contraceptive use) in a multiple-equilibria situation. Our nonlinear empirical estimates for Nyanza District imply that when social interactions are intensified, they reduce the total effect associated with program interventions, but slightly increase the social multiplier effect. These findings are in contrast to the linear estimates that imply that more intense social interaction leads to a larger social multiplier effect and an increased total effect.

A second analysis (Kohler, Behrman, and Watkins 2001) considers the impact of the *density* of social networks on fertility decisions. This paper proposes that network structure modifies the impact of the content of the network interaction. We distinguish between dense networks, in which all the network partners know each other, and sparse networks, in which the network partners are mostly connected only through their ties to the respondent. We focus on two mechanisms by which social interaction influences behavior: *social learning* and *social influence*. Social learning is the exchange of information, whereas social influence reflects the impact of informal social networks on norms. We argue that when social learning dominates, network density should not matter. In situations of uncertainty, information is important. Because all members of a dense network are likely to possess the same information, we expect weak, possibly negative effects of density on the adoption decision when the content of the interaction is controlled. If social influence dominates, however, density is expected to be important. In particular, when the normative acceptability of contraceptive use is the issue, dense networks with a low proportion of contraceptive users should reduce the probability of using family planning; dense networks with a high proportion of users should increase that probability; and sparse networks should be relatively neutral.

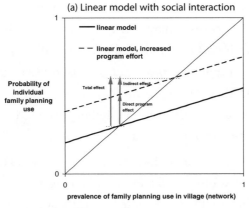

(a) Linear model with social interaction

(b) Nonlinear model with social interaction, single equilibrium

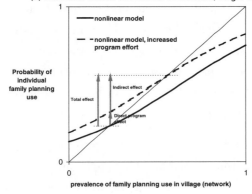

(c) Linear model with social interaction, multiple-equilibria

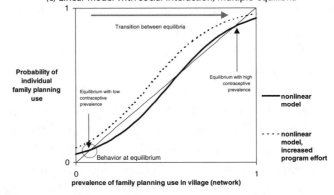

Figure 28-1   Linear and nonlinear model with social interaction (Kohler, Behrman, Watkins, 2000)

We estimate the probability of using modern contraception using KDIC data with a specification that includes the proportion of contraceptive users in the social network, the density of the network, and an interaction between these measures of content and structure. The results suggest that context determines whether social learning or social influence dominates. In Obisa, one of the regions of our study, the probability of a woman's contraceptive use is affected primarily by the measure of the content of the interaction; network structure has little relevance. In Obisa, social learning apparently is the mechanism through which social interaction affects contraceptive decisions. In Owich, Kawadghone, and Wakula South (OKW), the other regions, social influence appears to be the primary mechanism through which networks influence individual behavior. In OKW, the interaction between content and structure is critical: Dense networks discourage an individual from using contraception if the network includes few contraceptive users, but dense networks encourage use when contraceptive use in the network is relatively high. Thus, when social learning is the mechanism by which networks affect contraceptive decisions, a comparison across contexts confirms the simple account: *The higher the proportion of contraceptive users in a woman's network, the more likely she is to use family planning.* Where social influence dominates, however, the influence of networks is ambivalent: They may either facilitate or constrain the adoption of family planning.

These differential implications of social learning and social influence on the probability of using family planning are depicted in Figure 28-2. Given the same social network, the ever-use of contraception is higher in Obisa than in Owich, Kawadghone, and Wakula South. If we compare the lines for dense networks and sparse networks in Obisa, we see that a woman is more likely to have ever used modern contraception if she has a sparse network than if she has a dense network, given the same prevalence of family planning in a respondent's social network. Moreover, as the proportion of network partners using family planning increases, the lines diverge. Therefore, when the prevalence of users within the network is low, women with sparse networks are about as likely to use family planning as women with dense networks. When the prevalence of family planning in the network is high, however, women in sparse networks are more likely to use family planning than women in dense networks.

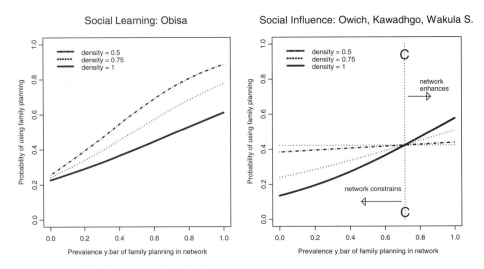

Figure 28-2   The effect of contraceptive prevalence in the network on the probability of adopting family planning for respondents with networks of different density (Kohler, Behrman, Watkins, 2001)

Market activities appear to make social learning more important. These two regions of Kenya are not distinguished by characteristics of the networks of the respondents who live there, but rather by the extent of market activities: In Obisa, more women are engaged in market activities than in OKW, and they buy and sell at a larger market. We find that social influence is important only where market activity is low. Where market activity is high, social learning dominates. Although the available data do not allow us to investigate in detail the interdependence of social interaction and market activities, the notion that higher market activities favor social learning is plausible. After all, the spread of information is an important aspect of markets, and market participants may focus more strongly on the information provided by their personal contacts than on the social acceptance regarding their family planning behavior. This finding also suggests predictions about the future of contraceptive use in South Nyanza. Even in areas where social interactions currently retard the diffusion of family planning, market development may help shift the dominance of conservative social influence to a dominance of social learning. Thus, interactions between network structures and market activities may be critical in fertility transitions.

A third study examined changes in social networks over time and the impact on contraceptive use in rural Kenya (Behrman, Kohler, and Watkins 2002). A limitation of the preceding analyses, as well as of much of the demographic literature on social interactions, is that the estimation methods used do not permit confident inferences regarding causal effects of social networks because unobserved factors that may directly affect attitudes and behavior may also directly affect choices of the units of social interaction. In particular, most existing literature on social interactions and demographic behaviors assumes, usually implicitly, that it is acceptable to treat networks as if they were formed randomly. There are at least two reasons to expect that this assumption of random network selection often is violated. *First,* empirical studies suggest a nonrandom selection of network partners (Watkins and Warriner 2003) because people discuss issues of family planning and AIDS with others who are perceived to be similar ("like me"), and some network partners are deliberately chosen because they are believed to have relevant information or competence. *Second,* theoretical consideration of learning under uncertainty suggests that social interactions about family planning are determined by costs and benefits of social learning. What has been interpreted as causal effects of social networks may simply be associations that are due to both contraceptive use and network partners' choices being determined, in part, by unobserved factors, such as preferences.

Using our longitudinal data to investigate the determinants of contraceptive use in high-fertility rural Kenya, we reached four major findings. *First* and foremost, social networks have significant and substantial effects, even with control for unobserved factors that may also determine the nature of the social networks. *Second,* estimates of the effects of social networks that are based on the implicit assumption that they are determined randomly, as in previous studies, may lead to a substantial misunderstanding of the impact of social networks. *Third,* the effects of social networks are not limited to women, even though in local stereotypes women are often characterized as gossiping much more than men. To the contrary, our estimates indicate that, if anything, men are likely to be more influenced by their network partners than are women. This finding may reflect cultural patterns of exogamy and patrilocality that result in men having known their network partners since childhood, whereas women alter their network partners after marriage. *Fourth,* the effects of social networks are generally nonlinear and asymmetric—and particularly large if at least one network partner is perceived to be using contraceptives. This combination of nonlinearity and asymmetry suggests that the exchange of information constitutes the primary aspect of social interactions about family planning—social learning, not social influence. In addition, the nonlinear and asymmetric pattern of network influences is consistent with stereotypic diffusion models (for example, Rogers 1995; Valente 1994). If there are just a few who initially adopt an innovation, they can have a relatively large influence because they interact with a relatively large number of individuals who have not yet adopted it; in such cases, they provide these individuals with at least one adopter, the influence of whom is relatively large.

Thus, adoption initially accelerates. As there are more innovators, however, the marginal influence of yet another adopter eventually starts to decline. Interaction processes therefore suggest that social networks are likely to have large effects on behavior as long as an innovation is not widely disseminated. As innovative behavior increases, the marginal effect of interactions is likely to be much smaller than in the early phase of the diffusion process.

Social Networks and Mortality and Death—The Diffusion of Worry About HIV/AIDS

Individuals facing the tsunami of the AIDS epidemic in eastern and southern Africa know well that HIV is primarily transmitted in their context by sexual intercourse and that reducing risky sexual interactions can help to protect them from infection and death. Whether correct or incorrect, the subjective perceptions of one's own HIV/AIDS risk and of one's sexual partner's risk have been shown to be important correlates of whether an individual adopts risk-reduction strategies (Cerwonka, Isbell, and Hansen 2000; Estrin 1999; UNAIDS 1999; Weinstein and Nicolich 1993). The processes through which these risk perceptions are formed, however, is only poorly understood (for example, Smith 2003).[6] In Kohler, Behrman, and Watkins (2007), we therefore investigate the determinants of subjective HIV/AIDS risk assessments, focusing in particular on the hypothesis that individuals assess their risk of infection through interactions with others in their social networks.

The MDICP survey measured perceived AIDS risk with a question frequently used in research on risk perceptions: "How worried are you that you might catch AIDS?" Responses to this question ranged from "not worried at all" to "worried a lot." Between 36% and 40% of women in Kenya responded in the 1996/1997 and 2000 surveys, respectively, that they perceived themselves to have a moderate or high risk of becoming infected with AIDS. For Malawi, 61% and 47% of women perceived a high risk of AIDS in 1998 and 2001, respectively; moreover, their responses are highly and positively correlated with a question about the subjective likelihood that the respondent will become infected with HIV/AIDS in the future. Respondents are generally also aware of several mechanisms by which HIV/AIDS is transmitted and several methods of protection. For instance, in 1996/1997, more than 90% of women in Kenya knew that AIDS can be

---

[6] For a general discussion of the need to better understand the formation of expectations, including risk perceptions, see Manski (2004).

transmitted by sex, and 48% knew about possible transmission by injections. Similarly high levels of knowledge prevail in Malawi.

Some of the survey responses suggest considerable talk about AIDS in social networks, as well as related issues such as extramarital partnerships and deaths that they suspect are due to AIDS. The networks are quite dense (most members know each other as well as the respondent) and highly gendered (men talk with men, women with women) (Watkins and Warriner 2003; Zulu and Chepngeno 2003). More than three-quarters of the women had talked with at least one person about AIDS, and more than two-fifths of the women had talked with at least one person who believes that he or she is at moderate or great risk of becoming infected with AIDS. In addition to talking with network partners about AIDS, husbands and wives discuss with each other their risks and how they can prevent infection.

On average, women report that they had talked with 3.9–4.8 network partners about AIDS, and men report slightly more interactions, ranging from close to 4 to about 7 network partners. In general, respondents report more interactions with network partners who perceive a high AIDS risk as compared with network partners who assess their risk as low. Neither the size of these networks nor having talked with at least one network partner about AIDS depends strongly on the respondent's risk perception (Kohler, Behrman, and Watkins 2007, Table3), whereas—as we expect based on the hypothesis that social interactions are important determinants of risk perceptions—network partners' assessments of HIV/AIDS risks are associated with the respondent's own risk perception.

Our major findings from analysis of these data are these: *First* and foremost, this analysis again shows that social networks have significant and substantial effects on individuals' AIDS risk perceptions, even when we control for unobserved factors that also may determine the nature of the social networks. Thus, to understand the dynamics and diffusion of behavioral change in response to AIDS, it is essential to incorporate the impact of social networks. *Second,* this effect of social networks extends to the area of spousal communication about AIDS risk, and interactions with network partners—independent of network partners' risk assessments—tend to increase the probability of husband-wife communication about the disease. *Third,* the effects of social networks that we have found contribute to a better understanding of diffusion. These effects are generally nonlinear and asymmetric. They are particularly large for having at least one network partner who is perceived to have a great deal of concern about AIDS. The inclusion of additional network partners with the same level of concern or with less concern generally has much smaller or insignificant effects. An exception to this asymmetry occurs in the network effects on spousal communication: Network partners, independent of their risk perceptions, have strong and significant effects. *Fourth,* social networks are associated with important social-multiplier effects that reinforce the effects of AIDS prevention programs. For women, for instance, about one-fifth of the influence of program efforts on respondents' HIV/AIDS risk perceptions is mediated through social networks.

These findings are of central importance for understanding the spread of HIV/AIDS because they document that social interactions constitute important determinants of how individuals and couples develop strategies for coping with the disease. In particular, this study shows that social networks exert systematic and strong influences on risk perceptions and the probability of spousal communication about HIV/AIDS risks in rural areas of two sub-Saharan African countries with high HIV prevalence, and that these influences are in addition to other factors such as program interventions that disseminate knowledge about the disease, provide access to condoms, and advocate changes in sexual behaviors within and outside marriage. Social networks are also likely to amplify program efforts aimed at increasing individuals' information about HIV/AIDS and their assessments of their own risks. Thus, social interactions are likely to have a substantial impact on the course of the epidemic and the magnitude of its consequences, and these should be taken into consideration in understanding and predicting behaviors in such high-prevalence contexts and in devising program interventions with respect to the HIV/AIDS epidemic.

Conclusion

The methods and results of studies of these social networks have several implications for studies of business networks. First, the insights may be directly relevant to social networks in healthcare, where understanding the contributions of social learning and social influence to changing perceptions and behavior are likely to be crucial in all societies. For example, what is the role of networks in the spread of knowledge about a new disease or treatment?

Second, the insights and approaches from these studies might offer a broader perspective on networks in business. Learning, for example, is vital in the adoption of any innovation, and this occurs through both the transfer of information and social influence. How many adopters of iPhone technology, for example, have extensive knowledge of its features or underlying technology? In this, and other cases, social influence is likely to play a significant role in adoption.

Our studies also demonstrate the importance of accounting for the endogeneity of network partners in analyzing network effects and show that networks are important even with control for endogeneity. These results show that network effects may be non-linear, that there may be multiple equilibria, and that networks may either reinforce the status quo or help diffuse new options and behaviors. This research also indicates that both the context (for example, the degree of market development) and the density of networks matter (possibly interactively). Finally, these studies have shown the power of using multiple approaches, including both qualitative and quantitative analyses, in providing in-depth understanding of what networks do and how they function.

References

Baum, C. F., M. E. Schaffer, and S. Stillman. 2003. Instrumental variables and GMM: Estimation and testing. Working paper no. 545, Boston College, Department of Economics. http://fmwww.bc.edu/ec-p/wp545.pdf.

Becker, G. S., K. M. Murphy, and R. Tamura. 1990. Human capital, fertility, and economic growth. *Journal of Political Economy* 98 (5, pt. 2), 12-37.

Behrman, J. R., H.-P. Kohler, and S. C. Watkins. 2002. Social networks and changes in contraceptive use over time: Evidence from a longitudinal study in rural Kenya. *Demography* 39 (4), 713-736.

Bott, E. 1971. *Family and Network: Roles, Norms and External Relationships in Ordinary Urban Families.* London: Tavistock Publications.

Burt, Ronald S. 1982. *Toward a Structural Theory of Action.* New York.

Burt, Ronald S. 1992. *Structural Holes: The Social Structure of Competition.* Cambridge, MA: Harvard University Press.

Casterline, John B. 2001. Diffusion processes and fertility transition: Introduction. In *Diffusion Processes and Fertility Transition*, ed. John B. Casterline, 1-38. Washington, DC: National Academy Press.

Casterline, J., M. Montgomery, S. Green, P. Hewett, D. Agyeman, W. Adih, and P. Aglobitse. 2000. Contraceptive use in Southern Ghana: The role of social networks. Paper presented at the Annual Meetings of the Population Association of America, March 22-25, Los Angeles.

Cerwonka, E. R., T. R. Isbell, and C. E. Hansen. 2000. Psychosocial factors as predictors of unsafe sexual practices among young adults. *AIDS Education and Prevention* 12 (2), 141-153.

Cleland, J., and C. Wilson. 1987. Demand theories of the fertility transition: An iconoclastic view. *Population Studies* 41 (1), 5-30.

Coale, A. J., and S. C. Watkins, eds. 1986. *The Decline of Fertility in Europe.* Princeton: Princeton University Press.

Estrin, D. 1999. In Ghana, young men's condom use is linked to lack of barriers, perceived susceptibility to HIV infection. *International Family Planning Perspectives* 25 (2), 106-107.

Fischer, Claude S. 1982. *To Dwell Among Friends: Personal Networks in Town and City.* Chicago, IL: University of Chicago Press.

Galor, O., and D. N. Weil. 1996. The gender gap, fertility and growth. *American Economic Review* 86 (3), 374-387.

Granovetter, M. S. 1973. The strength of weak ties. *American Journal of Sociology* 78 (6), 1360-1380.Kenya, Republic of. 1980. Kenya Fertility Survey 1977–1978. First Report, Vol. 1. Nairobi: World Fertility Survey and Kenya Central Bureau of Statistics and Ministry of Economic Development and Planning.

Knodel, J., and E. van de Walle. 1979. Lessons from the past: Policy implications of historical fertility studies. *Population and Development Review* 5 (2), 217-245.

Kohler, H.-P. 1997. Learning in social networks and contraceptive choice. *Demography* 34 (3), 369-383.

Kohler, H.-P. 2000a. Fertility decline as a coordination problem. *Journal of Development Economics* 63 (2), 231-263.

Kohler, H.-P. 2000b. Introduction to the special issue on lowest low fertility. *European Journal of Population* 17 (1), 1-2.

Kohler, H.-P. 2001. *Fertility and Social Interactions: An Economic Perspective.* Oxford: Oxford University Press.

Kohler, H.-P., J. R. Behrman, and S. C. Watkins. 2000. Empirical assessments of social networks, fertility and family planning programs: Nonlinearities and their implications. *Demographic Research* 3 (7), 79-126. www.demographic-research.org.

Kohler, H.-P., J. R. Behrman, and S. C. Watkins. 2001. The density of social networks and fertility decisions: Evidence from South Nyanza District, Kenya. *Demography* 38 (1), 43-58.

Kohler, H.-P., J. R. Behrman, and S. C. Watkins. 2007. Social networks and HIV/AIDS risk perceptions. *Demography* 44 (1), 1-33.

Manski, C. F. 1993. Identification of endogenous effects: The reflection problem. *Review of Economic Studies* 60 (3), 531-542.

Manski, C. F. 2000. Economic analysis of social interaction. *Journal of Economic Perspectives* 14 (3), 115-136.

Manski, C. F. 2004. Measuring expectations. *Econometrica* 72 (5), 1329-1376.

Marsden, P. V. 1990. Network data and measurement. *Annual Review of Sociology* 16, 435-463.

Massey, D. S., J. Arango, G. Hugo, A. Kouaouci, P. Adela, and J. E. Taylor. 1994. An evaluation of international migration theory: The North American case. *Population and Development Review* 20 (4), 699-751.

Mitchell, J. Clyde. 1969. The concept and use of social networks. In *Social Networks in Urban Situations*, ed. J. C. Mitchell, 1-50. Manchester, England: Manchester University Press.

Montgomery, M. R. 2000. Perceiving mortality decline. *Population and Development Review* 26 (4), 795-819.

Montgomery, M. R., and J. B. Casterline. 1993. The diffusion of fertility control in Taiwan: Evidence from pooled cross-section time-series models. *Population Studies* 47 (3), 457-479.

Montgomery, M. R., and J. B. Casterline. 1996. Social learning, social influence, and new models of fertility. *Population and Development Review* 22 (Supplement), 151-175.

Montgomery, M. R., and W. S. Chung. 1998. Social networks and the diffusion of fertility control in the Republic of Korea. In *The Dynamics of Values in Fertility Change*, ed. R. Leete, 179-209. Oxford: Oxford University Press.

Munshi, Kaivan. 2003. Networks in the modern economy: Mexican migrants in the US labor market. *Quarterly Journal of Economics* 118 (2), 549-599.

Munshi, Kaivan D., and Jacques Myaux. 1997. Social effects in the demographic transition: Evidence from Matlab, Bangladesh. Unpublished working paper, Boston University.

Munshi, Kaivan, and Jacques Myaux. 2006. Social norms and the fertility transition. *Journal of Development Economics.* 80:1, 1-38.

Rodgers, J., and D. Rowe. 1993. Social contagion and adolescent sexual behavior: A developmental EMOSA model. *Psychological Review* 100 (3), 479-510.

Rogers, E. M. 1995. *Diffusion of Innovations.* New York: Free Press.

Simmel, G. 1922. *Conflict and Web of Group Affiliations.* Trans. K. H. Wolff and R. Bendix, 1955. New York: Free Press.

Smith, K. P. 2003. Why are they worried? Concern about AIDS in rural Malawi. *Demographic Research,* Special Collection 1 (9), 279-317. www.demographic-research.org.

Tawfik, L., and Susan Cotts Watkins. 2007. Sex in Geneva, sex in Lilongwe, sex in Balaka. *Social Science & Medicine* 64 (5), 1090-1101.

UNAIDS. 1999. *Sexual Behavioral Change for HIV: Where Have Theories Taken Us?* Geneva: United Nations. www.unaids.org.

Valente, T. W. 1994. *Network Models of the Diffusion of Innovations.* Cresskill, NJ: Hampton Press.

Valente, Thomas W. 2005. Network models and methods for studying the diffusion of innovations. In *Recent Advances in Network Analysis,* ed. P. Carrington, S. Wasserman, and J. Scott.

Watkins, Susan Cotts. 1991. *From Provinces into Nations: Demographic Integration in Western Europe, 1870-1960.* Princeton, NJ: Princeton University Press.

Watkins, S. C., and I. Warriner. 2003. How do we know we need to control for selectivity? *Demographic Research,* Special Collection 1 (4), 109-142. www.demographic-research.org.

Watkins, Susan, Eliya M. Zulu, Hans-Peter Kohler, and Jere R. Behrman. 2003. Demographic research on HIV/AIDS in rural Malawi: An introduction. *Demographic Research,* Special Collection. www.demographic-research.org.

Watts, D. J. 1999. *Small Worlds: The Dynamics of Networks Between Order and Randomness.* Princeton: Princeton Studies in Complexity.

Weinstein, N. D., and M. Nicolich. 1993. Correct and incorrect interpretations of correlations between risk perceptions and risk behaviors. *Health Psychology* 12 (3), 235-245.

Wellman, Barry. 1988. Structural analysis: From method and metaphor to theory and substance. In *Social Structures: A Network Approach,* ed. Barry Wellman and S. D. Berkowitz, 19-60. Greenwich, CT: JAI Press.

Zulu, E. M., and G. Chepngeno. 2003. Spousal communication about the risk of contracting HIV/AIDS in rural Malawi. *Demographic Research,* Special Collection 1 (8), 247-277. www.demographic-research.org.

About the Authors

Franklin Allen

Chapter 21: Networks in Finance

Franklin Allen is the Nippon Life Professor of Finance and Professor of Economics at the Wharton School of the University of Pennsylvania. He has been on the faculty since 1980. He is currently Co-Director of the Wharton Financial Institutions Center. He was formerly Vice Dean and Director of Wharton Doctoral Programs and Executive Editor of the *Review of Financial Studies*, one of the leading academic finance journals. He is a past President of the American Finance Association, the Western Finance Association, the Society for Financial Studies, and the Financial Intermediation Research Society. He received his doctorate from Oxford University. Dr. Allen's main areas of interest are corporate finance, asset pricing, financial innovation, comparative financial systems, and financial crises. He is a co-author with Richard Brealey and Stewart Myers of the eighth and ninth editions of the textbook *Principles of Corporate Finance*.

Raphael Amit

Chapter 15: The Business Model as the Engine of Network-Based Strategies

Raphael ("Raffi") Amit is the Robert B. Goergen Professor of Entrepreneurship and a Professor of Management at the Wharton School of the University of Pennsylvania. Dr. Amit is the Academic Director of the Goergen Entrepreneurial Management Programs, which encompasses all of Wharton's entrepreneurial programs. He also co-founded and leads the Wharton Global Family Alliance (WGFA), a unique academic-family business partnership established to enhance the marketplace advantage and the social wealth creation contributions of global families through thought leadership, knowledge transfer, and the sharing of ideas and best practices among influential global families. Dr. Amit's research and teaching interests center on performance implications of family owned, controlled, or managed firms; entrepreneurship in independent and corporate settings; business models and business strategy; and venture capital and private equity investments. Dr. Amit holds BA and MA degrees in Economics and received his PhD in Managerial Economics and Decision Sciences from Northwestern University's J.L. Kellogg Graduate School of Management.

Ana Babus

Chapter 21: Networks in Finance

Ana Babus is currently affiliated with the University of Cambridge as a research fellow for Centre for Financial Analysis and Policy. She received her doctorate from Erasmus University Rotterdam in May 2008. Her research interests concern the economics of networks, games of network formation, microeconomics of banking, contagion and financial crisis, and risk-sharing in microfinance.

Steve Barnett

Chapter 18: Managing the Hyper-Networked "Instant Messaging" Generation in the Work Force

Steve Barnett, President of Bardo Consulting, is an anthropologist who has held academic and business positions. He has taught at Princeton, Brown, MIT, and the Wharton School of the University of Pennsylvania. He has been a senior executive at Nissan North America, Citibank, Ogilvy & Mather, as well as Managing Director/head of the New York office of GBN (Global Business Network). He has published widely on consumer culture, business strategy, and modernization. His PhD is from the University of Chicago.

Jere R. Behrman

Chapter 28: Lessons from Empirical Network Analyses on Matters of Life and Death in East Africa

Jere R. Behrman is the William R. Kenan, Jr. Professor and former Chair of Economics and Research Associate, and former Director of the Population Studies Center at the University of Pennsylvania. His research interests are in empirical micro economics, economic development, labor economics, human resources, economic demography, and household behaviors. He has published more than 300 professional articles and 32 books and monographs on these topics. He has worked as a research consultant with numerous national and international organizations, including the World Bank, the Asian Development Bank, and the Inter-American Development Bank. He received a PhD from the Massachusetts Institute of Technology in 1966 and has received various honors, including being selected a Fulbright 40th Anniversary Distinguished Fellow, a Fellow of the Econometric Society, a Guggenheim Foundation Faculty Fellow, and a Ford Foundation Faculty Fellow.

John Bell

Chapter 20: Relating Well: Building Capabilities for Sustaining Alliance Networks

Dr. John Bell is Head of Strategy & Partnerships at Philips Research, focusing on the strategy and partnerships of Philips Research. In addition, he is responsible for the Research Program Office and for strengthening account management. Before that he was VP Corporate Strategy & Alliances at Royal Philips. In this role, he was responsible for capturing the value potential in the alliances of Philips. In 2003, Dr. Bell became a Professor at Radboud University of Nijmegen, holding the Chair on Strategic Alliances. Here he established the Center for Strategy and Alliances (CSA), which is one of the few research centers on alliances around the globe. John has a PhD from Tilburg University.

Yvette Bordeaux

Chapter 7: Information Networks in the History of Life

Yvette Bordeaux, Director of Professional Masters Programs in Earth & Environmental Science in the School of Arts and Sciences, has been at the University of Pennsylvania since 1988. She received her PhD in Geology from the University of Pennsylvania in

2000 and has been Director for the Professional Masters Programs (Master of Environmental Studies and Master of Science in Applied Geosciences) there since 2007. Dr. Bordeaux teaches courses in Environmental Analysis, Paleontology, Environmental Chemistry, and Field Ecology. She studies marine organisms that live on the shells of other organisms, known as epibionts. Her work examines organisms more than 400 million years old as a way of determining water quality, ocean circulation patterns, and climate history of regions throughout the world.

Ryan Burg

Chapter 19: Missing the Forest for the Trees: Network-Based HR Strategies

Ryan Burg is a PhD candidate in Sociology and Business Ethics at the University of Pennsylvania. His sociology research explores the durability and value of social connections within and among organizations. His research in business ethics considers the intrinsic value of communities within organizations, asking how and when a corporation should be allowed to "die" despite the value of the connections it fosters for its stakeholders.

Eric K. Clemons

Chapter 18: Managing the Hyper-Networked "Instant Messaging" Generation in the Work Force

Eric Clemons is Professor of Operations and Information Management at The Wharton School of the University of Pennsylvania. For two decades, he directed the Wharton School's research program in information, strategy, and economics, and has long been at the forefront of the study of the intersection of information, economics, and corporate strategy. He has worked with clients and corporate sponsors to assess how emerging trends will affect corporate structure and strategy. Dr. Clemons has collaborated with Steve Barnett on a number of studies of consumer behavior, including the application of scenario planning to examine emerging long-term trends. His current research focuses on understanding the long-term interactions among information technology, individual behavior and economic choice, and corporate strategy. His education includes an SB in Physics from MIT and an MS and PhD in Operations Research from Cornell University.

Julia Clemons

Chapter 18: Managing the Hyper-Networked "Instant Messaging" Generation in the Work Force

Julia Clemons is an undergraduate at the University of Chicago with an interest in the social sciences, in particular individual behavior and the relationships between individual motivations and the functioning of groups and societies. Her previous research includes a study of online social networks and the behavior of gamers. As the only teenager on the research team, Ms. Clemons provided a constant sequence of reality checks, hypotheses, and alternative explanations for the other members of the research team. Ms. Clemons also arranged the participation of a substantial group of undergraduates as participants in the study and as readers of early drafts.

Colin Crook

Chapter 12: Complexity Theory: Making Sense of Network Effects

Colin Crook is a Fellow of the Royal Academy of Engineering (UK) and a Senior Fellow of the Wharton School of the University of Pennsylvania. He trained as an electrical engineer and subsequently worked in many key areas of advanced technology, in both engineering and managerial roles. He has been responsible for businesses in all parts of the world. Mr. Crook has served on many U.S. National Academy advisory committees and advised various U.S. government agencies. He has lectured widely and served on various company and nonprofit boards. During his career he has worked for the BBC, Canadian Marconi, Plessey, Eli Lilly, Motorola, Rank Organization, Zynar/Nestar, British Telecom, Data General, and Citicorp where he was Chief Technologist, reporting to the Chairman, John Reed. He is a co-author with Jerry Wind of *The Power of Impossible Thinking*.

George S. Day

Chapter 16: Extended Intelligence Networks: Minding and Mining the Periphery

George S. Day is the Geoffrey T. Boisi Professor, Professor of Marketing, and Co-Director of the Mack Center for Technological Innovation at the Wharton School of the University of Pennsylvania. Prior to joining the Wharton School, he was Executive Director of the Marketing Science Institute, an industry-supported research consortium. He has been a consultant to numerous corporations such as AT&T, Eastman Kodak, General Electric, IBM, Metropolitan Life, Marriott, Molson Companies, Unilever, E.I. DuPont de Nemours, W.L. Gore and Associates, Boeing, LG Corp., Best Buy, and Medtronic. He is Chairman elect of the American Marketing Association and a Director of TL Contact Inc. and the Biosciences Research and Education Foundation. His primary areas of activity are marketing, the management of emerging technologies, organic growth and innovation, and competitive strategies in global markets. His recent book *Peripheral Vision: Detecting the Weak Signals That Can Make or Break Your Company* (with Paul Schoemaker) published in 2006 is the foundation for this present paper. He was selected as the outstanding marketing educator for 1999 by the Academy of Marketing Science, and in 2003 he received the AMA/Irwin/McGraw-Hill Distinguished Marketing Educator Award.

Victor K. Fung

Chapter 17: Network Orchestration: Creating and Managing Global Supply Chains Without Owning Them

Dr. Victor Fung is the Group Chairman of the Li & Fung group of companies, which includes major subsidiaries in Trading, Distribution and Retailing, including publicly listed Li & Fung Limited, Integrated Distribution Services Group Limited, and Convenience Retail Asia. He also is Chairman of the Hong Kong University Council and the Greater Pearl River Delta Business Council. Dr. Fung holds a number of civic and professional appointments. He is Chairman of International Chamber of Commerce, a member of the Chinese People's Political Consultative Conference; and a member of the Commission on Strategic Development. Dr. Fung is Chairman, Asia Advisory Board of Prudential Financial, Inc (USA), an independent nonexecutive Director of Bank of China (Hong Kong) Limited and Orient Overseas (International) Limited in Hong Kong, Baosteel Group Corporation in the People's Republic of China, and CapitaLand Limited in Singapore. Born and raised in Hong Kong, Dr. Fung holds Bachelor and Master Degrees in Electrical Engineering from the Massachusetts Institute of Technology, and a Doctorate in Business Economics from Harvard University. He also taught as a professor at the Harvard Business School for four years before returning to Hong Kong in 1976.

William K. Fung

Chapter 17: Network Orchestration: Creating and Managing Global Supply Chains Without Owning Them

Dr. William Fung, SBS, OBE, JP, has been Group Managing Director of Li & Fung Limited since 1986. He joined the Group in 1972 and became a Director of the Group's export trading business in 1976. Dr. Fung graduated from Princeton University with a Bachelor of Science degree in Engineering. He holds an MBA degree from the Harvard Graduate School of Business and a Degree of Doctor of Business Administration, honoris causa, by the Hong Kong University of Science & Technology. Dr. Fung is a nonexecutive director of HSBC Holdings PLC and the Chairman of its Corporate Sustainability Committee. He is also an independent non-executive director of VTech Holdings Limited and Shui On Land Limited. Dr. Fung is co-author of the book *Competing in a Flat World* (Wharton School Publishing 2008). In 2008, Dr. Fung was awarded the SBS ("Silver Bauhinia Star") by the Government of the Hong Kong Special Administrative Region for his significant contribution to the development of Hong Kong and for his outstanding public service in the areas of trade promotion and economic development.

Boaz Ganor

Chapter 26: Terrorism Networks: It Takes a Network to Beat a Network

Boaz Ganor is the Deputy Dean of the Lauder School of Government and Diplomacy, the founder and Executive Director of the International Institute for Counter-Terrorism (ICT), and the head of the Homeland Security Studies Programs at the Interdisciplinary Center (IDC), Herzliya, Israel. At present Dr. Ganor is a Koret Distinguished Visiting Fellow at the Hoover Institution, Stanford University. Dr. Ganor received his doctorate from The Hebrew University, Jerusalem in 2002. Dr. Ganor is a member of the International Advisory Council of the International Centre for Political Violence and Terrorism Research at the Institute of Defense and Strategic Studies (IDSS), Nanyang Technological University, Singapore. Dr. Ganor is also a member of the Board of The International Centre for the Study of Radicalization and Political Violence (ICSR), London. Dr. Ganor has published numerous articles and edited several books on terrorism and counter-terrorism, including *The Counter-Terrorism Puzzle: A Guide for Decision Makers* (Transaction Publishers, 2005).

Robert Giegengack

Chapter 7: Information Networks in the History of Life

Robert Giegengack, Professor Emeritus of Earth & Environmental Science in the School of Arts and Sciences, has been on the faculty of the University of Pennsylvania since 1968. Dr. Giegengack is Faculty Director of the Master of Environmental Studies (MES) program, which currently enrolls approximately 150 students. He has also been Director of Penn's Summer Course in Geologic Field Methods, based at the facility of the Yellowstone-Bighorn Research Association (YBRA) in Red Lodge, MT. Giegengack teaches courses in Environmental Analysis, Paleoclimatology, Environmental Geology, and Field Geology. Dr. Giegengack studies geologic archives that enable paleoclimatologists to reconstruct the history of environmental change, primarily climate change, during the very long period of time (~4.5 billion years) that preceded acquisition, during the last ~200 years, of the instrumental meteorological record. That work provides a useful time perspective on environmental processes currently under way and an evolutionary perspective on the physical, biologic, and social configuration of the modern world. He has pursued field work on every continent except Australia. He received his PhD in Geology from Yale University in 1968.

Witold J. Henisz

Chapter 25: Network-Based Strategies and Competencies for Political and Social Risk Management

Witold J. Henisz is the UPS Visiting Associate Professor of Civil and Environmental Engineering at Stanford University. He is also an Associate Professor of Management at The Wharton School of the University of Pennsylvania. His research examines the impact of political hazards on international investment strategy. He analyzes the political and economic determinants of government attempts to redistribute investor returns to the broader polity and the determinants of the success of strategic responses by organizations to withstand such pressure. His research has been published in top-ranked journals in international business, management, international studies, and sociology. He is currently a principal in the political risk management consultancy PRIMA LLC and serves as an advisor to the World Economic Forum's Global Risks Project.

Dawn Iacobucci

Chapter 5: Social Networks: You've Lost Control

Dawn Iacobucci is the E. Bronson Ingram Professor of Marketing and Associate Dean of Faculty at the Owen Graduate School of Management, Vanderbilt University. Previously she was a Professor of Marketing at Kellogg (1987-2004), the University of Arizona (2001-2002), and Wharton (2004-2007). Her research focuses on the modeling of dyadic interactions and social networks. Her work has appeared in *Harvard Business Review*, *International Journal of Research in Marketing*, *Journal of Consumer Psychology*, the *Journal of Marketing*, the *Journal of Marketing Research*, *Journal of Service Research*, *Marketing Science*, *Psychometrika*, *Psychological Bulletin*, and *Social Networks*. She teaches Marketing Management, Marketing Research, Marketing Models, Services Marketing, and New Products to MBA and executive students and multivariate statistics in PhD seminars. She is recent editor of both the *Journal of Consumer Research* and *Journal of Consumer Psychology*.

Prashant Kale

Chapter 20: Relating Well: Building Capabilities for Sustaining Alliance Networks

Prashant Kale is a Professor of Strategic Management with the Jones School of Management, Rice University, and a visiting faculty for executive education at the Kellogg School of Management, Northwestern University, and at the Wharton School of the University of Pennsylvania. Before coming to Rice, he was a full-time faculty member at the Ross School of Business, University of Michigan. Dr. Kale does research in the areas of corporate strategy, strategic alliances, and mergers and acquisitions. His research has received awards from the Academy of Management and the Strategic Management Society, and his work has been published in leading international journals such as the *Strategic Management Journal*, *Harvard Business Review*, *MIT Sloan Management Review*, *California Management Journal*, and *Managerial and Decision Economics*. Dr. Kale has an undergraduate degree in mechanical engineering, an MBA from the Indian Institute of Management, Ahmedabad, and a Masters and PhD in Management from the Wharton School.

Alan M. Kantrow

Chapter 3: Knowledge as a Social Phenomenon: "Horse Holding" and Learning in Networks

Alan M. Kantrow is Professor of Management and Director of the Infrastructure Research Center at the Moscow School of Management Skolkovo. He also serves as Senior Advisor at Monitor Group, where, for nearly a decade and a half he was a senior partner and Chief Knowledge Officer. Before that, as a partner at McKinsey & Company, he was the editor of the *McKinsey Quarterly* and the Director of Communications, Europe and Asia-Pacific. And before that, for many years, he was senior editor of *Harvard Business Review*. He holds a PhD from Harvard University in the History of American Civilization.

Steven Kimbrough

Chapter 8: Artificial Intelligence: How Individual Agents Add Up to a Network

Steven Kimbrough is a Professor at The Wharton School of the University of Pennsylvania. His main research interests are in the fields of electronic commerce (and formal languages for business communication), knowledge and information management, and computational rationality. His active research areas include computational approaches to belief revision and nonmonotonic reasoning, formal languages for business communication, evolutionary computation (including genetic algorithms and genetic programming), and information discovery in unstructured and semi-structured databases (text). He was principal investigator for the U. S. Coast Guard's KSS (knowledge-based decision support systems) project, and co-principal investigator on the Logistics DSS project, which is part of DARPA's Advanced Logistics Program. He was most recently Principal Investigator in the NSF-funded project "Working Memory and Adaptive Choice Behavior."

Paul R. Kleindorfer

Chapter 1: The Network Imperative: Community or Contagion?

Chapter 23: Integration of Financial and Physical Networks in Global Logistics

Paul R. Kleindorfer is the Paul Dubrule Professor of Sustainable Development and Distinguished Research Professor at INSEAD, Fontainebleau, and the Anheuser Busch Professor of Management Science (Emeritus) at the Wharton School of the University of Pennsylvania. Dr. Kleindorfer graduated with distinction from the U. S. Naval Academy in 1961. He studied on a Fulbright Fellowship in Mathematics at the University of Tübingen, Germany (1964/65), followed by doctoral studies in the Graduate School of Industrial Administration at Carnegie Mellon University (PhD,1970). Before joining INSEAD in 2006, Dr. Kleindorfer held university appointments at Carnegie Mellon University (l968/9), Massachusetts Institute of Technology (1969/72), and The Wharton School (1973–2006). Dr. Kleindorfer's research has focused on risk management, ranging from major accident prevention to hedging and trading to mitigate supply and demand coordination risks. His current research is on sustainable operations for energy-intensive companies and carbon-leveraged investments arising from legislation and regulations to mitigate presumed consequences of industrial activity on the biosphere and climate.

Sonia Kleindorfer

Chapter 6: Biological Networks: Rainforests, Coral Reefs, and the Galapagos Islands

Sonia Kleindorfer is Senior Lecturer in Biodiversity and Conservation in the School of Biological Sciences at Flinders University in South Australia. She received her BA in Biological Basis of Behavior from the University of Pennsylvania (1988) and a PhD in Zoology (1995) from the University of Vienna. She undertook post-doctoral fellowships in animal behavior and reproductive endocrinology at the Konrad Lorenz Institute for Comparative Ethology and the University of Washington School of Medicine. She was site-director for the Animal Behavior Research Unit in Tanzania, environmental consultant with the Austrian Development Service in Ecuador, and research scientist with the Charles Darwin Research Station, Galapagos Islands. She began at the School of Biological Sciences in 2002 and is currently Head of Department. Her research addresses evolution in natural populations and the role of behavior for reproduction and survival.

Hans-Peter Kohler

Chapter 28: Lessons from Empirical Network Analyses on Matters of Life and Death in East Africa

Hans-Peter Kohler received a MA in demography (1994) and a PhD in economics (1997) from the University of California at Berkeley, and is currently a Professor of Sociology and a Research Associate at the Population Studies Center at the University of

Pennsylvania. His primary research focuses on fertility and health-related behaviors in developing and developed countries. A key characteristic of this research is the attempt to integrate demographic, economic, sociological, and biological approaches in empirical and theoretical models of demographic behavior. He is author of a recent book on fertility and social interaction, has co-edited a book on the biodemography of human reproduction and fertility, and has widely published on topics related to fertility, health, social and sexual networks, HIV/AIDS, biodemography and well-being in leading journals. Dr. Kohler has been awarded the Clifford C. Clogg Award for Early Career Achievement by the Population Association of America, has been a recent fellow at the Center for Advanced Studies at the Norwegian Academy of Science. He currently serves as the president of the Society of Biodemography and Social Biology.

Howard Kunreuther

Chapter 22: The Weakest Link: Managing Risk Through Interdependent Strategies

Howard Kunreuther is the Cecilia Yen Koo Professor of Decision Sciences and Public Policy at the Wharton School of the University of Pennsylvania, and Co-Director of the Wharton Risk Management and Decision Processes Center. He has a long-standing interest in ways that society can better manage low-probability/high-consequence events related to technological and natural hazards. His most recent work, *At War with the Weather: Managing Large-Scale Risks in a New Era of Catastrophes* (with Erwann Michel-Kerjan), provides a series of in-depth analyses of the efficiency and equity of current disaster insurance and mitigation programs in the U.S. It will be published by MIT Press in 2009. Dr. Kunreuther is a Fellow of the American Association for the Advancement of Science (AAAS); a member of the National Earthquake Hazards Reduction Program's Advisory Committee on Earthquake Hazards Reduction; and Distinguished Fellow of the Society for Risk Analysis, receiving the Society's Distinguished Achievement Award in 2001. He is co-chair of the World Economic Forum's Global Agenda Council on "Innovation and Leadership in Reducing Risks from Natural Disasters," and a member of the OECD's High Level Advisory Board on Financial Management of Large-Scale Catastrophes.

JoAnn Magdoff

Chapter 18: Managing the Hyper-Networked "Instant Messaging" Generation in the Work Force

JoAnn Magdoff has a PhD in Cultural Anthropology, augmenting her skills in observation, survey design, and data analysis. Currently, she is a psychotherapist in private practice: a Licensed Clinical Social Worker and a Marriage and Family Therapist. Contemporary Relational and Postmodernist therapeutic approaches inform her interpretation of the construction of the self, the assumptions underlying the team and the meanings invested in networks and the flattened hierarchies of the IM Generation. She welcomes the opportunity provided by working with a multidisciplinary team for the emergence of the analytically unexpected, particularly as it is reflected in use of symbols, construction of meaning, unforeseen values, and trends. A prior publication on the *Psychological and Social Usage of the Internet* provided a useful background for this project.

James G. Mitchell

Chapter 6: Biological Networks: Rainforests, Coral Reefs, and the Galapagos Islands

Jim Mitchell is Head of the School of Biological Sciences at Flinders University in South Australia. He received BA (1980) and MS (1982) degrees in Biology and Marine Sciences from the University of California, Santa Cruz, and a PhD (1988) in oceanography from the State University of New York, Stony Brook. He undertook post-doctoral fellowships in microbiology at the Autonomous University of Barcelona and the Center for Microbial Ecology at Michigan State University. Subsequently, he was Julian Huxley Instructor of Evolutionary Biology at Rice University. He began in the School of Biological Sciences in 1992 and since has founded the Lincoln Marine Science Centre in Port Lincoln, South Australia. He was an Associate Professor at the University of Tokyo in 2003 and 2004. His research interests center on how microscale biological processes influence and control global processes in the ocean.

Satish Nambisan

Chapter 9: Network-Centric Innovation: Four Strategies for Tapping the Global Brain

Satish Nambisan is an associate professor of technology management and strategy at the Lally School of Management, Rensselaer Polytechnic Institute in Troy, NY. A globally recognized researcher and thought-leader in the area of innovation and technology management, his recent research work has focused on customer co-innovation, network-centric innovation, and IT-enabled product development. His research has been published in premier management journals such as *Management Science*, *Academy of Management Review*, *Harvard Business Review*, and *MIT Sloan Management Review*. His new book *The Global Brain: Your Roadmap for Innovating Faster and Smarter in a Networked World* was published by the Wharton School Publishing in October 2007. Prior to joining the academia, Nambisan held executive positions at the consumer-product giant, Unilever Plc. in Mumbai, India.

Serguei Netessine

Chapter 13: Supply Webs: Managing, Organizing, and Capitalizing on Global Networks of Suppliers

Serguei Netessine is an associate professor in the Operations and Information Management (OPIM) department at the Wharton School of the University of Pennsylvania. Professor Netessine received BS/MS degrees in Computer Science and Electrical Engineering from Moscow Institute of Electronic Technology and, after working for several years for Motorola and Lucent Technologies, he also received MS/PhD degrees in Operations Management from the University of Rochester. His current research focuses on the strategic aspects of supply chain management, incentives, and contracting in supply chains. His current industry projects include adoption of performance-based logistics in defense industry, retail store execution strategies, and studies of supply chains in the automotive industry. His research has been published in the leading management journals, including *Management Science*, *Operations Research*, *Marketing Science*, and *Manufacturing & Service Operations Management*. Professor Netessine is also a recipient of the Early Career Achievement Award from Production and Operations Management Society. He holds Associate Editor and Senior Editor Positions at several leading academic journals, including *Management Science*, *Production and Operations Management*, *Operations Research*, and *Manufacturing & Service Operations Management*.

Russell E. Palmer

Chapter 4: Cross-Cultural in Networked Global Enterprises

Russell E. Palmer is the majority shareholder and Chairman and Chief Executive Officer of The Palmer Group, a corporate investment firm located in Philadelphia, Pennsylvania. Mr. Palmer served for ten years as Managing Partner and CEO of Touche Ross &

Co. (now Deloitte & Touche). He became CEO of Touche Ross at age 37, the youngest person ever to attain that position in a "Big Eight" firm. After 27 years in the accounting and consulting profession, Mr. Palmer became Dean of the Wharton School in 1983. He was instrumental in attracting more than 100 new faculty members to the School, building a new executive education program and complex and raising over $120 million for the School. In his current career he has acquired more than 30 companies, with the majority being in the educational field. Mr. Palmer has served on 12 New York Stock Exchange boards, including Honeywell International, Verizon Communications, The May Department Stores Company, and The Goodyear Tire & Rubber Company. He is a Trustee Emeritus of the University of Pennsylvania, a Trustee of the National Constitution Center, and a Member of the Smithsonian National Board. He serves on the board of Main Line Health and The Mann Center for the Performing Arts. Mr. Palmer graduated with a BA degree from Michigan State University and has received several honorary degrees. His articles and essays have appeared in *Business Week*, *The New York Times*, the *Journal of Accountancy*, and other publications. He is the author of the recently released book *Ultimate Leadership*.

CK Prahalad

Chapter 2: Creating Experience: Competitive Advantage in the Age of Networks

CK Prahalad, the Paul and Ruth McCracken Distinguished University Professor at the Ross School of Business, University of Michigan, specializes in corporate strategy. His books include *Multinational Mission: Balancing Local Demands and Global Vision* (1987), co-authored with Yves Doz; *Competing for the Future* (1994), co-authored with Gary Hamel and named the Best Selling Business Book of the Year in 1994; *The Future of Competition: Co-Creating Unique Value with Customers* (2004) (co-authored with Venkatram Ramaswamy), and translated into twelve languages. *The Fortune at the Bottom of the Pyramid: Eradicating Poverty Through Profit* (2004) was selected as one of the best books of the year 2004 by *The Economist, Fast Company*, and Amazon.com. He is also the author of numerous award-winning articles, including McKinsey Prizes from the *Harvard Business Review* for "The End of Corporate Imperialism," co-authored with Kenneth Lieberthal (1998); "The Core Competence of the Corporation," co-authored with Gary Hamel (1990); and "Strategic Intent," also co-authored with Gary Hamel (1989). He has been honored for his contributions with a Life Time Achievement Award by the Ross School of Business. He received several honorary doctorates for his work and was named number one in the Thinkers50 (the most influential thinkers in management alive today) poll conducted by Suntop media and the *Times of London*. He serves on the Board of Directors of NCR Corporation, Teradata Corporation, Hindustan Unilever Limited, and the World Resources Institute. He is a member of the Board of Trustees of The Indus Entrepreneurs (TiE), a global organization devoted to democratizing entrepreneurship.

Jan W. Rivkin

Chapter 11: Organizational Design: Balancing Search and Stability in Strategic Decision Making

Jan W. Rivkin is the Bruce V. Rauner Professor of Business Administration at Harvard Business School, where he leads the required first-year MBA course in business strategy. His research examines how managers make decisions whose ramifications cross functional and product boundaries. His scholarly papers use a mix of simulations, large-sample statistical techniques, field research, and case studies, and have appeared in journals such as *Management Science*, *Organization Science*, the *Strategic Management Journal*, the *Academy of Management Journal*, *Long Range Planning*, and *Research Policy*.

Harvey Rubin

Chapter 27: Global Diseases: The Role of Networks in the Spread and Prevention of Infection

Dr. Rubin is Professor of Medicine at the University of Pennsylvania with secondary appointments as Professor in the Department of Microbiology, the Department of Biochemistry and Biophysics, and as Professor of Computer and Information Sciences at the University of Pennsylvania School of Engineering and Applied Sciences. His research in infectious diseases has been funded by the NIH, NSF, DARPA, and the Global Alliance for TB Drug Discovery. In addition to his work on the basic biology of the disease, he has extended the investigations to mathematical modeling of complex biological systems. Dr. Rubin served on a number of national and international scientific review panels, including the NIH, NSF, NASA Intelligent Systems Program, DARPA, and The Medical Research Council, South Africa. He is a member of the United States National Science Advisory Board for Biosecurity (NSABB) and the Department of Defense/National Academy of Sciences Biological Cooperative Threat Reduction Program. Dr. Rubin is also the founder and Director of the Institute for Strategic Threat Analysis and Response (ISTAR) at the University of Pennsylvania.

James M. Salter II

Chapter 5: Social Networks: You've Lost Control

James Salter is a Principal of Customer Lifecycle, LLC, a customer loyalty consulting and research firm. Previously he was senior vice president of customer loyalty at Harris Interactive and Total Research Corporation and a senior executive with Gunneson Group International, a founding organization in Total Quality Management consulting and customer loyalty initiatives. His work focuses on the areas of customer loyalty measurement and management, strategic research platform development, and linking the voice of the customer to process improvements and financial outcomes. He has consulted across a wide range of industries, including financial services, information technology, diversified chemicals and manufacturing, as well as B2B and B2C on-line research applications. He is author of *Managing the Customer Satisfaction Process* and *Strategic Account Management*.

Mohanbir Sawhney

Chapter 9: Network-Centric Innovation: Four Strategies for Tapping the Global Brain

Mohan Sawhney is a globally recognized scholar, teacher, consultant, and speaker in strategic marketing, innovation, and new media. His research and teaching interests include marketing and media in the connected world, process-centric marketing, collaborative marketing, organic growth, and network-centric innovation. He has been widely recognized as a thought leader. *Business Week* named him as one of the 25 most influential people in e-Business. Crain's *Chicago Business* named him a member of "40 under 40," a select group of young business leaders in the Chicago area. He is a Fellow of the World Economic Forum. Professor Sawhney's recent books include *Collaborating to Innovate* (October 2008) and *The Global Brain: Your Roadmap for Innovating Smarter and Faster in the Networked World* (October 2007), which serves as a foundation for his research reported here. Professor Sawhney advises and speaks to Global 2000 firms and governments worldwide. He serves on the boards and advisory boards of several technology startup companies, including EXLService, Fieldglass, and Confluent Surgical. Professor Sawhney holds a PhD in marketing from the Wharton School of the University of Pennsylvania.

Paul J. H. Schoemaker

Chapter 16: Extended Intelligence Networks: Minding and Mining the Periphery

Paul J. H. Schoemaker, PhD, is the founder and Chairman of Decision Strategies International, Inc. (www.thinkdsi.com), a consulting and training firm specializing in strategic decision making, executive development, and multimedia software. He also serves as Research Director of the Mack Center for Technological Innovation at the Wharton School of the University of Pennsylvania, where he teaches strategy and decision making. For more than twelve years, he was a professor in the Graduate School of Business at the University of Chicago. He has a BS in physics and did his MBA as well as PhD at Wharton. He has written more 100 academic and applied papers, as well as several books including *Decision Traps and Winning Decisions* (with J. Edward Russo). With George Day, he edited *Wharton On Managing Emerging Technologies* (Wiley, 2000). His is the author of *Profiting from Uncertainty* (Free press, 2002) and with George Day wrote *Peripheral Vision* (Harvard Business School Press, 2006). Paul has published multiple *Harvard Business Review* articles, and his writings have been published in over ten languages and received several prizes. He has consulted with more than 100 organizations around the world (see www.paulschoemaker.com) and serves on the Board of the Decision Education Foundation in Palo Alto, CA.

Nicolaj Siggelkow

Chapter 11: Organizational Design: Balancing Search and Stability in Strategic Decision Making

Nicolaj Siggelkow is a tenured associate professor of management at the Wharton School of the University of Pennsylvania. He received a PhD in Business Economics from Harvard University. His current research focuses on the strategic and organizational implications of interactions among a firm's choices of activities and resources. His work has been published in the leading management journals, including *Academy of Management Journal*, *Administrative Science Quarterly*, *Journal of Industrial Economics*, *Management Science*, *Organization Science*, and *Strategic Organization*. In 2008, he received the *Administrative Science Quarterly* Scholarly Contribution Award. He is a member of the Editorial Review Boards of *Administrative Science Quarterly*, *Organization Science*, *Strategic Management Journal*, *Strategic Organization*, and *Academy of Management Perspectives*.

Harbir Singh

Chapter 20: Relating Well: Building Capabilities for Sustaining Alliance Networks

Harbir Singh is the William and Phyllis Mack Professor of Management, Co-Director of the Mack Center for Technological Innovation, and Vice-Dean of Global Initiatives at the Wharton School of the University of Pennsylvania. He has been past Chair of the Business Policy and Strategy Division of the Academy of Management and Chair of Wharton's Management Department. His main areas of research are on strategic alliance and network formation, alliance management, corporate acquisitions, management buy-outs, and corporate restructuring. He has worked with companies around the world and has published on these topics in journals such as the *Academy of Management Journal, Academy of Management Review, Strategic Management Journal*, and *Administrative Science Quarterly*. His research on the role of cultural distance in explaining the choice of entry mode by multinationals won the "JIBS Decade Award," presented by the *Journal of International Business Studies*. He has also received the Strategic Management Society's Award for Outstanding Research. He is on the Academic Advisory Board of the Indian School of Business, and has been a Visiting Professor at the London Business School and Bocconi University, Italy.

Scott A. Snyder

Chapter 16: Extended Intelligence Networks: Minding and Mining the Periphery

Dr. Snyder is the President and CEO of Decision Strategies International, a leading strategy firm focused on increasing the strategic aptitude of organizations through education, consulting, and tools. He is also a Senior Fellow in the Management Department at the Wharton School, and an adjunct faculty member in the School of Engineering and Applied Sciences at the University of Pennsylvania. He has more than 20 years of experience in business leadership, strategic planning, and technology management for both Fortune 500 companies and start-up ventures. Dr. Snyder has held executive positions with several Fortune 500 companies, including GE, Martin Marietta, and Lockheed Martin. He has worked with numerous Fortune 500 clients on business, legal, and technology strategy. He is co-author of the book *Inside the Minds: Small Business Growth Strategies: Goals for Successful CEOs* (Apatore Books, December 2007) and also contributed as a co-author to the recently released "Legal Transformation Study: Your 2020 Vision of the Future and Future of BioSciences 2020" from DSI. Dr. Snyder holds a patent for online decision aids and has been quoted as a thought leader in numerous publications including the *LA Times*, *The Wall Street Journal*, the *Philadelphia Inquirer*, and the *Philadelphia Business Journal*. He earned his BS, MS, and PhD in Systems Engineering from the University of Pennsylvania and has an executive degree from USC in Telecommunications Management.

Manuel E. Sosa

Chapter 10: Coordination Networks in Product Development

Manuel E. Sosa is associate professor of technology and operations management at INSEAD. He received his BS degree in mechanical engineering from Universidad Simón Bolívar (Caracas, Venezuela) and his S.M. and PhD degrees in mechanical engineering from Massachusetts Institute of Technology (MIT). Professor Sosa's research efforts are applied to improving product development systems. He is particularly interested in studying coordination and innovation networks in complex product and software development organizations. His research has been published in *Management Science*, *Journal of Mechanical Design*, *Research in Engineering Design*, and *Harvard Business Review*. Professor Sosa's teaching achievements include the development of a program with the Art Center College of Design (Pasadena, California) to integrate business and design disciplines for successful product development. His work experience includes systems engineering in the petrochemical industry, and development and deployment of computer-aided engineering software applications for the automobile and aerospace industries.

J. Shin Teh

Chapter 27: Global Diseases: The Role of Networks in the Spread and Prevention of Infection

Dr. Teh received a BA in Physiological Sciences in 1998 and his medical degree in 2001 from the University of Oxford, UK. He was a House Officer at Oxford's John Radcliffe Hospital and a House Surgeon at its sister site, the Horton Hospital. He is a member of the U.K. General Medical Council. He completed his postdoctoral research fellowship in infectious diseases at the School of Medicine of the University of Pennsylvania in 2005. He was subsequently a Research Specialist at Penn's Institute for Strategic Threat Analysis and Response (ISTAR) and has helped secure federal funding for numerous preparedness projects, curriculum development plans, and federal educational workshops. He was also a member of a committee that looked into ways of improving all-preparedness training in the four medical-related schools at Penn (medicine, nursing, dental, and veterinary). He currently serves as ISTAR's associate director.

Christophe Van den Bulte

Chapter 14: Leveraging Customer Networks

Christophe Van den Bulte is an Associate Professor of Marketing at the Wharton School of the University of Pennsylvania, which he joined in 1997. His research focuses on social networks, new product diffusion, and business-to-business marketing. He is an associate editor of the *Journal of Marketing Research* and also serves on the editorial boards of the *International Journal of Research in Marketing*, the *Journal of Business-to-Business Marketing*, the *Journal of Marketing*, and *Marketing Science*. Stefan Wuyts and he completed a short monograph on *Social Networks and Marketing*, published by the Marketing Science Institute in their Relevant Knowledge Series (2007).

Ilias D. Visvikis

Chapter 23: Integration of Financial and Physical Networks in Global Logistics

Dr. Ilias Visvikis holds a PhD in Finance from City University Cass Business School, London. He is elected as an Assistant Professor of Finance and is the Academic Director of the MBA in Shipping Program at ALBA Graduate Business School, Greece. He has lectured in several academic institutions and his research work, in the areas of finance and shipping, has been published in top international refereed journals and presented extensively in international conferences. Dr. Visvikis held posts in the Central Securities Depository of Greece, in the derivatives market of the Athens Exchange, and in shipping companies in various departments. He has provided consultancy services to private companies in the areas of finance and risk management.

Susan Cotts Watkins

Chapter 28: Lessons from Empirical Network Analyses on Matters of Life and Death in East Africa

Susan Cotts Watkins has been a professor of the Department of Sociology and an associate of the Population Studies Center, both at the University of Pennsylvania, since 1982. She studied social networks and demographic behavior in the past in Europe and the

United States; since 1995 she has focused on social networks and demographic behavior in Africa, where she has co-directed research projects with Jere R. Behrman, Hans-Peter Kohler, Agnes Chimbiri, and Eliya Zulu.

Kevin Werbach

Chapter 24: Telecommunications: Network Strategies for Network Industries?

Kevin Werbach is Assistant Professor of Legal Studies and Business Ethics at The Wharton School of the University of Pennsylvania. His research explores the legal and business dynamics of information and communications technologies. He is also the founder of Supernova Group, a technology analysis and consulting firm, and organizer of Supernova http://www.supernova2008.com, a leading executive technology conference. Formerly, Mr. Werbach was the Editor of *Release 1.0*, a monthly technology report published by Esther Dyson. He also served as Counsel for New Technology Policy at the Federal Communications Commission, where he helped develop the U.S. Government's Internet and e-commerce policies. He has testified before the U.S. Senate and Federal Communications Commission, and is the author of numerous academic and popular publications.

Yoram (Jerry) Wind

Chapter 1: The Network Imperative: Community or Contagion?

Chapter 17: Network Orchestration: Creating and Managing Global Supply Chains Without Owning Them

Yoram (Jerry) Wind is The Lauder Professor and Professor of Marketing at the Wharton School of the University of Pennsylvania. He joined the Wharton faculty in 1967, with a doctorate from Stanford University. He is founding director of The SEI Center for Advanced Studies in Management, the founding academic director of The Wharton Fellows Program, and was the founding editor of Wharton School Publishing. From 1995 to 1997 he led the development of the Wharton globalization strategy. Dr. Wind led the reinvention of the Wharton MBA curriculum (1991-93) and the creation of the Wharton Executive MBA Program (1974). Dr. Wind was founding director of the Joseph H. Lauder Institute (1983-1988) and the Wharton International Forum (1987). He has served in editorial positions for many top marketing journals. He has published more than 250 papers and articles and more than 20 books. Dr. Wind is a member of the advisory boards for various entrepreneurial ventures and a trustee of the Philadelphia Museum of Art. Dr. Wind's major marketing awards include The Buck Weaver Award

(2007), The Charles Coolidge Parlin Award (1985), AMA/Irwin Distinguished Educator Award (1993), the Paul D. Converse Award (1996), and the Elsevier Science Distinguished Scholar Award of the Society of Marketing Advances (2003). Dr. Wind is the former Chancellor of the International Academy of Management. He is co-founder of the Interdisciplinary Center, Herzliya (IDC) and chair of its academic council and university appointment and promotion committee. He received a PhD from Stanford University.

Stefan Wuyts

Chapter 14: Leveraging Customer Networks

Stefan Wuyts is an associate professor of marketing at Tilburg University, the Netherlands, where he has been teaching marketing strategy since 2005. His doctoral dissertation (Erasmus University Rotterdam, 2003) was a winner of the ISBM Doctoral Support Award Competition and a finalist for the Dutch Marketing Science Prize for innovative practice-oriented research. It was awarded by the Dutch Royal Society for Economics as the best dissertation defended at an Economics Faculty in the Netherlands in the years 2003 and 2004. His research interests include channel management, innovation and alliances, and social networks, with a focus on B2B markets. His work in these areas has appeared in the *Journal of Marketing*, the *Journal of Marketing Research*, the *International Journal of Research in Marketing*, and the *Journal of Organizational Behavior*, among others. In 2007, he wrote a monograph "Social Networks and Marketing" with Christophe Van den Bulte for the Relevant Knowledge Series of the Marketing Science Institute (MSI), and he was named a MSI Young Scholar. Wuyts serves as an Area Editor for the *International Journal of Research in Marketing* and as a reviewer for *Journal of Marketing*, *Journal of Marketing Research*, *Management Science*, *Journal of Operations Management*, and *Journal of International Business Studies*.

Valery Yakubovich

Chapter 19: Missing the Forest for the Trees: Network-Based HR Strategies

Valery Yakubovich is Associate Professor of Management at the Wharton School of the University of Pennsylvania and previously taught at the University of Chicago Graduate School of Business. He holds an MS in Mathematics from Moscow State University and a PhD in Sociology from Stanford University. His research explores the relationships between human capital, formal organizational arrangements and social networks in organizations and labor markets, and their implications for organizational and individual performance. His articles appeared in leading academic journals, such as *Organization Science* and *American Sociological Review*, edited volumes, and business publications. His current projects focus on technology-mediated management practices, the mutual reproduction of human capital and social networks in a classroom, and the interplay between formal structures and informal networks in Russian corporations.

Christoph Zott

Chapter 15: The Business Model as the Engine of Network-Based Strategies

Christoph (Chris) Zott is Associate Professor of Entrepreneurship at IESE and at INSEAD. His current research centers on business model innovation, the acquisition and mobilization of resources through innovators' social influencing actions, and the deployment of resources for organizational renewal and rejuvenation through dynamic capabilities. He has published on these topics in the *Administrative Science Quarterly*, the *Journal of Business Venturing*, *Organization Science*, and the *Strategic Management Journal*, among others. Moreover, he was an Associate Editor for *Management Science*, and he currently serves as a member of the Editorial Boards of the *Strategic Entrepreneurship Journal* and the *Journal of Business Venturing*. He also serves as a member of the Business Policy and Strategy Executive Committee of the Academy of Management. Chris teaches courses on entrepreneurship, innovation, and private equity at the MBA, EMBA, and Executive Education levels. He also consults for growth ventures and advises start-up companies, as well as larger firms interested in entrepreneurial leadership and innovation. Chris holds graduate degrees with distinction in Industrial Engineering from Universität Karlsruhe (Germany) and Institut National Polytechnique de Grenoble (France). He received his PhD in Commerce and Business Administration from the University of British Columbia (Canada).

Index

NUMBERS

3M, 148, 162
78 rpm shellac disks, 40
80-20 rule, 61-62

A

absorption capacity, 279
access
    distributed resources, need for, 32
    Internet, 420. *See also* Internet
    social networks, 324, 326
actionable insight, 448
activist groups, 438
actors, linkages across, 441
adaptation, 218
    capacity to adapt, 287
    processes, 91
Adner, Ron, 21
adopters, early, 254
advertising, 77
aerospace industry, supply webs, 231-234
Afghan Al Ansar Group, 460
Africa, 59, 457
agent-based models (ABMs), 133
    economic theories, 136
    Schelling's segregation model, 134-135
    sugarscape model, 135
agents, 6, 125-126
    cellular automata models, 127-132
    evolutionary models, 137
        ant colony optimization (ACO), 138
        particle swarm optimization (PSO), 139
    modeling, 220
aggregating information, political and social
    risks, 439-440
AIDS, 473
    social networks, 506-508
AIG (American International Group), 4, 388
air cargo logistics, 403, 405

Airbus, 166, 232
Al-Qaeda, 453, 458-466
Alcoa proper, 45
algorithms, 71
    genetic, 219
    methods, 126
alignment, 178, 440
Allen, Thomas, 40, 513
alliance capabilities, 354-355
    developing, 361-362
    relational capabilities, creating, 356-361
Alliance Managers Meetings, 359
Amazon.com, 305, 400-402, 423
    value-creation processes, 28
America Online (AOL), 148
American Chemistry Council (ACC), 395
American International Group (AIG), 4, 388
Amit, Raphael, 513
Amsterdam banks, 376
analysis
    empirical networks, 495-498, 509
        social networks, 72, 500-508
        survey data, 499
    social network analysis (SNA), terrorism and,
        455-457
    tools, 325, 441
Anglo-American Corporation, 441
animal husbandry, 106
ant colony optimization (ACO), 138
ants, 105, 114
AOL (America Online), 148
Apis mellifera, 114
Apple, 7
applications, 369-379, 420
    contagion, 370-373
    freezes in interbank markets, 374
    investment banking and, 376
    microfinance, 377-378
    social networks, 375-376
Archimedes screw, 113

architecture, 34, 418
Argentina, 59
armaments, 37
Arquilla, John, 457
arrays of networks, 267
Arthur Andersen, 387
articles, social networks, 72
artifacts (and artifice), 42-44
artificial barriers, 421
artificial intelligence (AI), 125-126
    agent-based models (ABMs), 133
        economic theories, 136
        Schelling's segregation model, 134-135
        sugarscape model, 135
    cellular automata models, 127-132
    evolutionary models, 137
        ant colony optimization (ACO), 138
        particle swarm optimization (PSO), 139
Asia, 457
Asia Pacific region, 59
assessment, risk, 393
assigning control, 246
Association of National Advertisers, 283
assumption of independence, social networks, 68
asymmetric links, 69
asymmetry of volatility, 412
AT&T, 417, 420
    as Monists, 421-426
Atlantic Ocean, 383
atomized approaches to human resources (HR),
    337-338
atoms to bits, 304
attacks, 456. *See also* terrorism
Audible, 305
Australia, 59
authenticity of social networks, 78
authority, 324
automobile designs, examples from, 170-171
automotive industry, supply web relationships,
    228-231
avian flu, 472
Aviva, value-creation processes, 28
awareness of social contagion, 250

B

Babus, Ana, 514
Baby Bells, 422
Bahama Banks, 112
balance of network orchestration, 312-313
Baltic Capesize Index (BCI), 408
Baltic Clean Tanker Index (BCTI), 408
Baltic Dirty Tanker Index (BDTI), 408

Baltic Handysize Index (BHSI), 408
Baltic Panamax Index (BPI), 408
Baltic Supramax Index (BSI), 408
Bangalore, 314
Bangladeshi Islamic Jihad, 460
banks. *See also* finance
    investment banking and networks, 376
    linkages between, 373
    microfinance, 377-378
Barings Bank, 387
Barnett, Steve, 318, 514
Basic Beliefs (IBM), 39
basic research centers, 484
battlefields, 441
Bear Stearns, 3
Bebo, 246
behavioral predictions, 76
Behrman, Jere R., 515
Beiersdorf, 361
Being Digital, 304
Belgian interbank markets, contagion, 373
Belgium, 386
beliefs, updating, 250
Bell, John, 515
bell-shaped curves, 249
benefits
    of reintegration, 195
    of unnecessary overlap, 199
Benkler, Yochai, 149
Berlin banks, 377
Berlin Wall, fall of, 402
Betamax technology, 7
Bhattacharya, Arindam, 7
Bhopal disaster, 394
bias in historical records, 41
BIG Idea Group, 155
Bin-laden, Osama, 453, 457. *See also* Al-Qaeda
biology, networks in, 85-89
    biological agents, 473
    biological communities, 105
biosurveillance, 486
black death, the, 474
black swans, 215
Blu-ray, 7
BMW, 166
Board of Management, 356
Boeing, 154, 234, 302
    supply webs, 232
Bordeaux, Yvette, 515
borderless manufacturing, 301
Boston Consulting Group, 7
boundaries, between firms, 264

Bovine Spongiform Encephalopathy (BSE), 472
Braille alphabet, 111
brands
  building, 246
  management, 77
Brazil, 59
breakdowns, 372
Brent Spar North Sea oil platform, 438
broadband customers, AT7T, 422
Brown, Frank, xliii
Brown, John Seely, 47, 302
Brussels, 59
bryozoans, 113-114
BT, 429
bubonic plague, 474
Build-a-Bear Workshop®, 25-26
building competencies, 299
Burberry, 246
Burg, Ryan, 516
Burt, Ronald, 281
Bush, George W., 308
business implications of terrorism, 468-469
Business Innovation Factory, 283
business models, xxi
  conclusions, 271-272
  networks, 266, 269
  product market strategies and, 269-270
  research, 262-263
  value drivers, 261
Business Round Table, 283
business-to-business (B2B), 400
business-to-consumer (B2C), 400
BzzAgent, 248

C

calcite (CaCO3) skeletal structures, 113
cancer, 472
capacities
  absorption, 279
  to adapt, 287
  planning, 405
capital, 336-337
caps, 410
capture
  of knowledge, 40
  network, 285
carbon-fiber composite materials, 232
cardiac pacemakers, 27
Caribbean Coral Reef Network, 87
Carnegie Mellon, 71
Carnegie, Andrew, 245
Carterfone, 429

cascading, 390-392
case studies, 71
cash settlements, 407
catastrophic loss protection, 387
cats, 96
cattle guards, 109
causation, 92
CBS Laboratories, 40
CDs, 304
cells, terrorism, 456
cellular automata models, 127-132
center (network) feature, 319
central locations of networks, 255
Cha, Chu Hui, xliv
chains, 461
  food, 90
  supply, 301. *See also* supply chains
  value, 263, 301, 437
Chairman of the Joint Chiefs, 328
change propagation, 172
channel networks, 461
charts, PERT, 167
Chase, 7
chemical plant investments, 388-389
Chief Marketing Officer, 358
Chile, 59
China, 42, 59, 300, 361, 402, 443
  industrialization, growth of, 402
Chinese toxic-milk scandal, 4
cholera, 472
Christensen, Clay, 437
Chrysler, 7, 148, 227. *See also* supply webs
CIA, 473
cirrhosis, 472
Cisco, 355
Clean Air Act Amendments (CAAA) of 1990, 391
clearing offers, 410
clearinghouses, 410
Clemons, Eric, 318, 516
Clemons, Julia, 318, 517
clusters, 172
  innovation, 281
CNN, 309
co-creating value, 27
coalition building, 447-448
Coase, Ronald, 149
Coasian firms, 419
coauthorship on papers, 281
collateral, social, 374
collection, data, 74-75
Colombia, 59
Colonial structures, communication in, 111-122
Columbia Pictures, 7

Comcast, 420

commander's intent, 328

commercial banks, 376

commercialization, 156

Commetric, 441

commons-based peer production model, 150

communication

  in Colonial structures, 111-122

  of design teams, 175-179

  instant messaging (IM), 328-329, 331

  senses and network, 108-111

  skills, 56

  social networks, 244-247

  telecommunications, 417-418

    modular future of, 427-430

    Monists and Dualists, 421-426

    networks, 418-421

  terrorism, 463

  trends in modern networks, 323-324

  word-of-mouth marketing, 247-256

competencies

  building, 299

  network orchestration, 307-309

  network-centric models, 158-160

  social risk management, 434-436

    aggregating information, 439-440

    implementing strategies, 445-448

    information sources, 436-438

    strategies, 440-445

  theory of the firm, 9-10

competition

  social contagion, 251

  supply webs, 228

competitive advantages, 25-27

  changing, 28-29

  competition paradigm shifts, 29-32

  diabetes network models, 32

  network impediments, 34

  sources of, 34-36

complementary network effects, 251

complex products as networks of components, 171-175

complexity theory, 91, 207-208

  accessing, 221-222

  implications for managers, 213-216

    organization, 219-220

    strategies, 216-219

  key concepts of, 208-213

  unanswered questions, 220

components, 302

  complex products as networks of, 171-175

computational methods, 126

computational paradigms, 139

Computer Inquiry, 425

concepts

  business models, 266, 269

  of complexity theory, 208-213

concepts in social networks, 72-75

conclusions

  business models, 271-272

  coordination networks, 180-181

Conference Board, 283

Conference Proposal, xliv

confidence in information, 325

configuration theory, 267

connectedness, networks and, 210

Connections, 71

connectivity, 76

consequences, social risk management, 434

constraints, 175

Consultative Group on International Agricultural Research (CGIAR), 488

contact

  patterns, 477

  tracing, 478

contagion, 249, 370-373

  occurrence of, 250-252

contamination, signal, 119-120

content of social networks, 72

contexts, overview of, 499

contextulization challenges, 150

contraceptive decisions, 503. *See also* family planning

contracts, options, 410

contractual-like interactions, 320

control

  assigning/regaining, 246

  in business, shift of, 80

  through empowerment, 311

Convention on the Prohibition of the Use, Stockpiling, Production and Transfer of Anti-Personnel Mines and on Their Destruction, 488

converged communications environments, 426

conversations about new products, 255-256

conversions, 158

Conway's Game of Life, 127

Coolskin alliance, 361

cooperators, triumph of, 130-133

coordinating mechanisms, 391

coordination networks, 165-166

  communication, 175-179

  complex products, 171-175

  development process, 166-171

  future of, 180-181

coral reefs, 85
    animals on, 112-113
    food webs, 89
core competencies, 29. *See also* competencies
    Theory of the firm, 9-10
Corporate Alliance Office, 358, 362
corporate board members, 375
corporate governance, 375
Corporate Responsibility Officers, 440
Corporate Risk Officers, 440
costs
    of idiosyncratic exchanges between firms, 264
    of infectious diseases, 472
    R & D, 45
    transactions, 149, 264
Cote, David M., 59, 61
Counter-Strike, 158
countering terrorism networks, 464-467
creation of knowledge, 40
Creative Bazaar model, 155
creativity, 180
    performance management, 344-345
credibility of network membership, 79
credit
    linkages between banks, 373
    risk, removal of, 410
critical infrastructures, 387
criticality of design dependencies, level of, 174
Crook, Colin, 517
Cross, Robert, 40
cross-cultural leadership, building, 62
Crosswalk.com, 270
crowds, understanding, 215
cultures
    cultural challenges, 150
    differences, 56-58
    diversity of, 58
    humor, bridging with, 61
    leadership across, 51-54
    respect of, 54
    social network research, 76
    strong organizational, building, 59-62
customers
    insights, 283
    loyalty, 79
    networks
        social networks, 244-247
        word-of-mouth marketing, 247-256
Customs-Trade Partnership Against Terrorism
  (C-TPAT), 386
cut, make, and trim (CMT), 300

cyanobacterial microbes, 86
Cyworld, 246
Czechoslovakia, 443

D

da SilvaLuiz Inacio Lula, 438
Daimler, 148
Daimler-Benz, 7
Daly, Dan, 328
"Darker Bioweapons Future, The", 473
Darwin, Charles, 137
    Darwin's Finches, 85, 89, 93-94
    Darwin's theory of speciation, 126
data collection, 74-75
databases, 34
Davenport, Tom, 40
Davis, Arthur Vining, 45
Day, George S., 517
death, social networks and, 506-508
Decision Insights Inc., 443
Decision Processes, 121
decision-making processes, 217
    investments, 375-376
    organizational design, 186-189
        models, 189-192
        Schwab (sequencing), 194-198
        searching effective strategies, 201-202
        Toyota (modularity), 198-200
declines in performance, 47
decomposition, 166
    products, 172
dedicated software, 71
defense industry, supply webs, 231-234
Defense Logistics Agency (DLA), 290
Dell Computer, 357, 402
Deloitte Consulting, 306
Deloitte Touche Tohmatsu, 50
Demographic Research, 499
deniability, 318
Department of Defense (DoD), 290
dependencies
    design, 174
    paths, 42-44
derivatives
    freight rate, 407-411
    impact on, 411-412
design
    business model research, 262-263
    change propagation, 172
    dependencies, 174
    development process, 166-171

interface matrix, 178
networks, 211, 310
novelty-centered business model, 269
organizational, 186-189
    models, 189-192
    Schwab (sequencing), 194-198
    searching effective strategies, 201-202
    Toyota (modularity), 198-200
team communication, 175-179
design structure matrix (DSM), 165-166
partitioning, 169
destabilizing spot market price volatility, 412
detritus feeders, 86
development
alliances, 361-362
theories, 72
training and, 342, 344
devices as networks, 428
Dewey, John, 140
DHL, 305, 400
diabetes network models, 32
diagrams, IDEF, 167
Dial, 156, 161
Dibiasio, Dolf, xxii
Didax, 269-270
Diesel Jeans, 246
differences
cultures, 56-58
recognizing cultural, 52
diffusion process, 252-253
Digitally Enabled Extended Enterprise in a Global Economy, 236
dimensions of network-centric innovation, 152
diploid females, 114
disabilities, 472
disability adjusted life years (DALYs), 472
discipline of social networks, 68-69
diseases, infectious, 471-473
controlling, 481-487
future of, 487-489
networks, 473-480
dispersion of labor, 302
distortion, historical records, 41
divergent attention, 278
diversity, 58, 426
DNA, 88
dogs, 96
donkeys, 96
Dreamliners, 154, 234
drivers
business model value, 267
contagion, 252-253
value, 261

drones, honeybees, 114
Drucker, Peter, 8, 11
drugs, development, 484
dry-bulk FFA contracts, 408-411
Dualists, 418, 421-430
Duke University, 156
Dune organizations, 462
DuPont, 162, 391
DVD standards, 7
dyads, 69

E

E. coli, 479
Earley, Christopher, 58
early adopters, 254
earmarking, 443
eBay, 4-9, 21, 305, 400
economics
design decisions, 6
theories, 136
Economist Intelligence Unit, 438
Ecuador, 59
Edison, Thomas, 245
effectiveness of traditional marketing, 245
effects, networks, 207, 370
efficiency in network structures, 90
egalitarianism, 320
eggs, insects, 115
El Verde Rainforest Network, 87
Eli Lilly, 355
emergence, 212-213
"Emerging Infections: Microbial Threats to Health in the United States," 473
empirical investigations, 76
empirical network analysis, 495-498, 509
social networks, 500-508
survey data, 499
empirical studies, 373
employee retention, 345-346
empowered users, understanding, 220
empowerment, control through, 311
enabling technologies, terrorism, 462-464
encrusting macroalgae, 86
endogenous discoveries, 135
engineering
biological agents, 473
chunks, 173
enterprises
global, 300
managing, 299
need for network orchestration, 314
risks, 11

environments
  with interactions, 192
  treaties, 386
equilibrium, punctuated, 212-213
Erdos-Renyi network, 476
Erez, Miriam, 58
Eskew, Mike, 305
Esourcing.airbus.com, 232
estimates, empirical network analysis, 500
Estonia, 386
Europe, 59, 376
European Union (EU), 400-402, 443
Evergreen IP, 156
evolution
  of air cargo and maritime logistics, 403-405
  algorithms, 137
  computation, 137
  computing, 137
  history, 92
  of a Life network, 128-130
  models, 137
    ant colony optimization (ACO), 138
    particle swarm optimization (PSO), 139
  of networks, 91-96
  of terrorism, 466
examples
  from automobile designs, 170-171
exchanges, 410
execution challenges, 151
existing
  databases, 34
  networks, extended intelligence networks,
    utilizing, 284-287
experience, creation of, 25-27
  Build-A-Bear Workshop®, 25-26
  changing, 28-29
  competition, 29-32
  diabetes network models, 32
  network impediments, 34
  sources of competitive advantage, 34-36
explosions, information, 279
exporting jobs, 32
extended intelligence networks, 277
  existing networks, utilizing, 284-287
  management, 292
  mining the periphery, 278-280
  optimization, 288-291
  research literature, 280-282
  types of, 283
extended internal labor market (EILM), 339
external interactions, 177
external labor market (ELM), 339

externalities, 6
extinction of species, 96

F

face-to-face interaction, 318
Facebook, 4, 7, 78, 246, 318, 419. *See also* social
  networks
fads
  driving, 220
  understanding, 215
failure of Prodigy, 263
Fair Labor Association, 447
family planning, 500-506
Fannie Mae, 3
Federal Communications Commission (FCC),
  425, 429
Federalists, 41
FedEx, 305, 400-403
feral goats, 96
fertility, World Fertility Survey, 500
fertilization, 116
filtering noise, 119
finance, applications to, 369-379
  contagion, 370-373
  freezes in interbank markets, 374
  investment banking and networks, 376
  microfinance, 377-378
  social networks, 375-376
financial flows, 304
financial risk management in shipping, 405-412
financial stability and contagion, 370
Financial Times, The, 207
firm, theory of the, 8-9
  firm-centric innovation, 148
  firm-centric view of value, 28
  networks, 11-12
  nodes, 11-12
  revolutions, 10-11
  strategies, 9-10
Five Forces model, 9
flagellum, 114
Flat World, 300. *See also* Friedman, Thomas
floors, 410
Floreana Island, 96
flowers, 115
flow of information, 285
fluidity, 426
food web stability, 89-90
Ford Motor Company, 166
  Model T, 31
  River Rouge plant, 31
  supply webs. *See also* supply webs, 228

Ford, Henry, 8, 301
forecasting outcomes, 218
formal analytic tools, 441
formalized communication channels, 280
formation of networks, 370, 372
Forward Freight Agreements (FFA) contracts, 407
four categories of explanation, 92
four flows, 302, 304-305
fractals, 211
fragility, 372
    (network) feature, 320
Franklin, Benjamin, 245
Freddie Mac, 4
free market thinkers, 421
freezes in interbank markets, 374
freight
    put options, 410
    rate derivatives, 407-411
French Connection UK, 248
French Revolution, 41
frequency of alleles, 91
Friedman, Thomas, xxii, 9, 299-300
Friendster, 78. *See also* social networks
function value, 92
funding authorizations, 443
Fung, Victor, 518
Fung, William, 518
future
    of coordination networks, 180-181
    implications of social networks, 327
    of instant messaging (IM), 328-331
    of research, security, 393-395
FutureMonitor, 283

G

Galapagos Islands, 85, 96
Game of Life (Conway), 127
games, 158, 218
    Prisoner's Dilemma, 130
Ganor, Boaz, 453, 519
Garvin, David, 40
Gattorna, John, 301
general linear modeling, 68
General Motors, 11, 28
    supply webs, 226. *See also* supply webs
    value creation, 27
generalized opinion leaders, 253
generics
    design structure matrix, 168
    infectious networks, 479-480

genetics
    algorithms, 219
    drift, 91
    pathways, 91
    variation, 92
geography, 439
Geography and Trade, 282
German banking systems, failure of, 373
Germany, 54
Gerstner, Louis, 39
Giegengack, Robert, 520
Gladwell, Malcolm, 249
Global Brain, The, 147
Global Burden of Disease Study, 472
Global Business Network, 283
global diseases, 471-473
    controlling, 481-487
    future of, 487-489
    networks, 473-480
global enterprises, 300
"Global Infectious Disease Threat and Its Implications for the United States, The," 473
global jihad networks, 458
Global Leadership and Organizational Behavior Effectiveness Research Program (GLOBE), 55, 58
global logistics, 399-401
    air cargo and maritime, 403-405
    financial risk management in shipping, 405-412
    infrastructure, impact on, 401-403
global supply-chain management, 385
globalization, 301
    networks, sustaining, 353
GM (General Motors), 328
Goldmark, Peter, 40
Googin, Roxanne, 426
Google, 4, 21, 400, 417, 419, 423
    as Dualists, 421-426
    value-creation processes, 28
Gore, Al, 308
Gould, Stephen Jay, 46
governance, 11, 375
Grameen banks, 377
Grand Central, 430
Granovetter, Mark, 281
Great Barrier Reef, 112
Greenpeace, 438
Grim, Patrick, 129
groups, activist, 438
growth of international trade, 405
Gunther, Robert, xxii

H

H. sapiens, 479
H5N1 influenza, 473, 483
Hagel, John, 302
Half-Life, 158
Hamas, 461
Hamburg banks, 376
hanging out, 323
Harvard University, 42
HCL Technologies, 302
HD-DVD, 7
Head of Strategy, 358
healthcare, 443
hearing, 109-110
Heathrow Airport, 383
hedging risk management, 405
Hemerling, Jim, 7
Henisz, Witold, 520
Henkel, 148
hepatitis B virus, 472
hepatitis C virus, 472
herbivores, 86
herding, ants, 106
hertz (Hz), 109
heterogeneous network types, 476
heuristic, 137
Heuristic Choice Theory, 140-141
hierarchical terror proxy organizations, 458
hierarchies, 320
high-technology manufacturing, 282
Hill & Knowlton, 441
hiring, 338
    Internet recruitment, 341-342
    passive recruitment, 338-341
history
    lessons learned from, 44
    of thought in social networks, 70-72
    records, 40-45
HIV, 472
    social networks, 506-508
Hoffman, Bruce, 456
holdings, 375. *See also* investments
holistic thinking, systems and, 212
Holland, 386
homegrown terrorism, 463
Honda supply webs, 230. *See also* supply webs
honeybees, 106, 114
Honeywell, 51, 59-62
Hong Kong, 67, 305, 478
horse holding, 38, 45-48

hubs
    global terror networks, 459
    networks, 461
Huber, Peter, 419, 425
human capital, 336
human networks, implications for, 119-122
human resources (HR), 336-347
    employee retention, 345-346
    performance management, 344-345
    recruitment, 338-342
    training, 342-344
humor, bridging cultures with, 61
Hurricane Katrina, 387
husbandry, animal, 106
Hyper-targeting, 79
hypothetical smallpox attacks, 473

I

Iacobucci, Dawn, 521
IBM, 39, 148
ICICI-Prudential, value-creation processes, 28
IDEF diagrams, 167
identifiable agents, 6
imitation, innovation versus, 92-93
impact
    of networks, 8
    of species invasions, 95-96
implementation of performance management, 344-345
implications
    for managers, complexity theory, 213-220
    of network orchestration, 307-309
in-country knowledge, 438
in-house training programs, 342
InBev, 356
incitement, 462
increasing (destabilizing) spot market price volatility, 412
independent third-party monitors, 438
India, 59, 377, 394, 402
indirect linkages on contagion, impact on, 372
individual genetic entities, 88
individualism in networks, 322
indoctrination, 462
Infectious Disease International Research Centers, 488
infectious diseases, 471-473
    controlling, 481-484, 487
    future of, 487-489
    networks, 473480

Infectious Diseases Society of America, 483
influence
  matrices, 192
  social, 501
information. *See also* networks
  access, 324
  communication in Colonial structures, 111-122
  explosions, 279
  flows, 285
  implications for humans, 119-122
  insects and, 105-107
  interpretation, 285
  overload, 448
  senses and communication, 108-111
  sharing, 483
  sources, 436-438
  transfer, 88
  understanding, 215
information and communications technology
  (ICT) architecture, 34
Information Systems Research, 236
infrared (IR) frequencies, 108
infrastructure, 419
  critical, 387
  logistics, 401-403
  social, 34
InnoCentive, 32
Innovation, 148-151
  clusters, 281
  Creative Bazaar model, 155, 157-158
  versus imitation, 92-93
  Jam Central model, 156
  models, 151-162
    organizational competencies, 158-160
  open, 283
  Orchestra models, 154
  research and practice, 161-162
  process of, 25-27
    changing, 28-29
    competition, 29-32
    diabetes network models, 32
    network impediments, 34
    sources of competitive advantage, 34-36
INSEAD Social Innovation Centre, xxi-xxii
INSEAD-Wharton Alliance, 13
insect colonies, 105
insights, 22
  actionable, 448
  customers, 283
  relaying, 286
instant messaging (IM), 317, 328-331
Institute of Medicine, 473, 475
institutionalization, 462

integration, 166, 399-401
  air cargo and maritime logistics, 403-405
  financial risk management in shipping, 405-412
  globalization, 401-403
  value through, 311
integrity, maintaining, 54
Intel, 429
  supply webs, 225
intellectual property for pharmaceuticals, 442
intelligence, sharing, 283
interactions, 177
  contractual-like, 320
  environments with, 192
  food webs, 90
  strategies, 237
interbank markets, freezes in, 374
interconnections, 75, 420
interdependencies, 6, 264
  social networks, 68-69
interdependent security (IDS), 383-385
  catastrophic loss protection, 387
  chemical plant investments, 388-389
  critical infrastructures, 387
  environmental treaties, 386
  global supply-chain management, 385
  nuclear reactor meltdowns, 386
  protection of shared network resources, 385
  research, 393-395
  tipping and cascading strategies, 390-392
interest, social contagion, 250
interfaces, 176-177
internal information sources, 437
internal labor market (ILM), 338
internal organizational rules, 391
International Campaign to Ban Landmines
  (ICBL), 488
International Compact for Infectious Diseases, 485
International Health Regulations (IHR), 485
international logistics operations, 403
International Network for Social Network
  Analysis, 71
International Standards Organization (ISO), 392
international trade, growth of, 405
international transactions, 11
Internet, 9, 476
  recruitment, 341-342
  social networks, 318-321
  telecommunications, 417
  terrorism networks, 462-464
introduction of species, 96
investments, 354
  decisions, 375-376
  investment banking and networks, 376

liberalization, 443
microfinance, 377-378
Iraq, 443
Isenberg, David, 426
ISO 14000 certification procedures, 395
Israel, 467
Italy, 443
iTunes, 304

J–K

Jam Central model, 156
Japan, 50
    automotive manufacturers, 230
jihad, 455, 458
JIT fulfillment strategies, 402
jobs, exporting, 32
Journal of Business Research, 133
Journal of Economic Geography, 281
JP Morgan, 7

Kale, Prashant, 521
Kantrow, Alan, 37, 522
keiretsu relationships, 230
Kelly, Alan, 441
Kenya, 495, 500
Kenyan Diffusion and Ideational Change Project
    (KDICP), 499
key concepts of complexity theory, 208-213
key decision points, creating relational
    capabilities, 356-362
key influentials, targeting, 252-253
key node (network) feature, 320
Kimbrough, Steve, 125, 522
Kingsbury Commitment of 1913, 425
Kleindorfer, Paul, 522
Kleindorfer, Sonia, 523
Kleisterlee, Gerald, 361
Klingon warships, 46
knowledge
    management, 247
    historical records, 40-45
    as social phenomenon, 40
    spillover, 282
    storage of, 38-39
Kohler, Hans-Peter, 523
Korea, 59, 300, 443
Krugman, Paul, 282
Kuhn, Thomas, 47
Kunreuther, Howard, 524

L

labor
    dispersion of, 302
    markets, 339
laboratory regulations, 484
Landes, David, 42
languages in historical records, 44
Latin American, 59
lattice networks, 476
Latvia, 386
leadership, 50
    across cultures, 51-54
    cross-cultural, building, 62
    cultures, 59-62
    global styles, 55, 58
leaf-cutter ants, 105
Lear supply webs, 227
learning
    distant (terrorism), 463
    research literature, 280-282
    social, 501
least squares, 68
Leonard, Dorothy, 40
lessons learned from history, 44
levels of criticality of design dependencies, 174
leveraging
    coordinating technology, 231-234
    customer networks, 244-247
    word-of-mouth marketing, 247-256
Levinthal, Dan, 21
Li & Fung, 300, 402
    value-creation processes, 28
limitations of analyses, 504
Lindegren, Len, xxii
line networks, 461
linear modeling, 68
LinkedIn, 318
links, 6
    across actors, 441
    affect on stability, 90
    contagion impact on indirect, 372
    interdependent security (IDS), 385
        catastrophic loss protection, 387
        chemical plant investments, 388-389
        critical infrastructures, 387
        environmental treaties, 386
        global supply-chain management, 385
        nuclear reactor meltdowns, 386
        protection of shared network resources, 385
        research, 393-395
        tipping and cascading strategies, 390-392
    social networks, 69

Linux, 149, 162
listservs, 71
literature, research, 280-282
Lithuania, 386
liver cancer, 472
living supply chains, 301
living systems, viewing businesses as, 214
Lloyd's, 403
lobbying, 441
local supply webs, 226. *See also* supply webs
location of networks, 255
Lockerbie, Scotland, 383
logistics, 399-401
　　air cargo and maritime, 403-405
　　financial risk management in shipping, 405-412
　　globalization, 401-403
London (LCH.Clearnet), 410
longitudinal studies, 71
　　theories, 74
low-cost manufacturing, 402
loyalty, 78
　　of social networks, 326-327
Luxembourg, 386

M

Mack Center for Technological Innovation, 283
macroalgae, 86
Magdoff, Joann, 318, 525
malaria, 472
Malawi, 495
Malawi Diffusion and Ideational Change Project (MDICP), 499
management, 50
　　across cultures, 51-54
　　brands, 77
　　business models, 271-272
　　cross-cultural, building, 62
　　cultures, 59-62
　　employee retention, 345-346
　　enterprises, 299
　　extended intelligence networks, 292
　　global styles, 55, 58
　　innovation, 180, 247
　　instant messaging (IM) generations, 329-331
　　knowledge, 247
　　networks, 310
　　performance, 344-345
　　risk, 395
　　　　catastrophic loss protection, 387
　　　　chemical plant investments, 388-389
　　　　critical infrastructures, 387
　　　　environmental treaties, 386
　　　　global supply-chain management, 385
　　　　hedging, 405
　　　　interdependent security (IDS), 385
　　　　nuclear reactor meltdowns, 386
　　　　protection of shared network resources, 385
　　　　research, 393-395
　　　　in shipping, 405-412
　　　　social, 434
　　　　tipping and cascading strategies, 390-392
　　Royal Phillips, 357
　　self-organization, 212-213
　　supply chain, 247
　　supply webs, 225-228, 237-238
　　　　leveraging coordinating technology, 231-234
　　　　networks, 235-237
　　　　relationships, 228-231
　　terrorism networks, 468-469
managers
　　complexity theory, 213-216
　　　　organization, 219-220
　　　　strategies, 216-219
　　organizations and, 192
manufacturing, modularization of, 305
Marine Rifle company, 328
Marine Stewardship Council, 438
maritime logistics, 403, 405
mark-to-marked, 410
marketing
　　products, 269-270
　　social networks, 77-79
　　traditional, effectiveness of, 245
　　word-of-mouth, 247-256
Marketing Science Institute, 245
markets, 4
　　derivatives, impact on, 411-412
　　dynamics, 412
　　freight rate derivatives, 407-411
　　interbank, freezes in, 374
　　labor, 339
　　spot, 407
mathematical representations, 126
matrices
　　influence, 192
　　networks, 461
　　organizations, 280
Matsushita, 7
McDonald's, 306
MCI, 425
meat space world, 318
Medtronic, 28
membership, social networks, 79
members of value chains, 437

messaging, targeted, 77
meta-heuristics, 137
metabolic infectious networks, 479-480
methods
    algorithmic, 126
    computational, 126
    procedural, 126
    social networks, 74-75. *See also* social networks
metrics, determining success, 160
Meyer, Chris, 47
microalgae, 86
microbes, 86
microfinance, 377-378
Microserfs, 327
Microsoft, 32, 423
Middle East, 59
minding the periphery, 278-280
mindset challenges, 150
mining the periphery, 277-280
MIT's Media Lab, 304
Mitchell, James, 525
mitigation of risk, 377
MOD Station model, 157-158
Model T Ford, 31
models
    agent-based models (ABMs), 133
        economic theories, 136
        Schelling's segregation model, 134-135
        sugarscape model, 135
    agents, 220
    business, xliii
        conclusions, 271-272
        networks, 266, 269
        product market strategies and, 269-270
        research, 262-263
        value drivers, 261
    cellular automata, 127-132
    commons-based peer production, 150
    evolutionary, 137
        ant colony optimization (ACO), 138
        particle swarm optimization (PSO), 139
    Five Forces, 9
    general linear, 68
    infectious diseases, 475-478
    network-centric innovation, 151-158
        Creative Bazaar, 155
        Jam Central, 156
        MOD Station, 157-158
        Orchestra, 154
    networks, impact of, 8
    organizational design, 189-192
        environments with interactions, 192
        Schwab (sequencing), 194-198

        searching effective strategies, 201-202
        Toyota (modularity), 198-200
    problems with, 237
    scanning, 282
    social networks, 74-75
modern networks
    paradox of, 321-322
    trends, 323
        access, 324-326
        communications technologies, 323-324
        loyalty, 326-327
modern terrorism, 467
modularity, 91, 172, 175
    future of telecommunications, 427-430
    of manufacturing, 305
    Toyota, 198-200
modules, 172
Monists, 418, 421-430
monopoly positions, 425
Moore, Tim, xliv
morbidity, 472
Morison, Elting, 37
mortality, 472
    social networks and, 506-508
motivations, 22
Multex, 269-270
multicelled organisms, 91
multicellular eukaryotes, 91
multilateral netting, 410
multilateral network broadcast technologies, 324
multiplayer games, 218
multiple selves, 318-322
Muslims, 453
    in Western countries, 464
mutation, 91
mutual fund managers, 375
mutual links, 69
Mycobacterium tuberculosis, 472, 480
MySpace, 7, 78, 246, 309, 318. *See also* social
    networks

N

N=1, R=G competitive environment, 35
Nambisan, Satish, 147, 525
narrowband Internet access, 420
national security issues, 483
natural selection, 91
Nature of the Firm, The, 149
nature of the innovation space, 152
near misses, 393
need for network orchestration, 306-307, 313-314
Negroponte, Nicholas, 304

NetBank, 269
Netessine, Serguei, 301, 526
Netflix, 7, 305
  value-creation processes, 28
NetLogo, 127, 134
netting, 410
netwars, 457
Network Dualists, 426
network-centric innovation, 148-151
  models, 151-158
    Creative Bazaar, 155
    Jam Central, 156
    MOD Station, 157-158
    Orchestra, 154
  organizational competencies, 158-160
  research and practice, 161-162
Network-Centric Thinking, 22
networks
  artificial intelligence (AI), 125-126
    agent-based models (ABMs), 133-136
    cellular automata models, 127-132
    evolutionary models, 137-139
  in biology, 85-89
  business models, 266, 269
  capture, 285
  central locations, 255
  challenge of, 21-22
  channels, 461
  and conceitedness, 210
  coordination, 165-166
    communication, 175-179
    complex products, 171-175
    development process, 166-171
    future of, 180-181
  design, 211, 310
  devices as, 428
  effects, 207-208, 370
    accessing, 221-222
    implications for managers, 213-220
    key concepts of, 208-213
    unanswered questions, 220
  empirical analysis, 495-498, 509
    social networks, 500-508
    survey data, 499
  evolution, 91-96
  extended intelligence, 277
    management, 292
    mining the periphery, 278-280
    optimization, 288-291
    research literature, 280-282
    types of, 283
    utilizing existing networks, 284-287

formation, 370-372
hub, 461
human resources (HR), 337-338, 346-347
  employee retention, 345-346
  performance management, 344-345
  recruitment, 338-342
  training, 342-344
information
  communication in Colonial structures,
    111-122
  implications for human networks, 119-122
  insects and, 105, 107
  senses and communication, 108-111
innovation, impediments to, 34
line, 461
logistics, 399-401
  air cargo and maritime, 403-405
  financial risk management in shipping,
    405-412
  globalization, 401-403
management, 310
matrix, 461
modern
  paradox of, 321-322
  trends, 323-327
neural, 126
orchestration, 299-300
  balance of, 312-313
  four flows, 302-305
  implications of, 307-309
  need for, 306-314
  roles of, 309-312
  unbundling supply chains, 301-302
overview of, 13-21
reach, 284
resilience, 287
rise of, 5-8
risk
  applications to finance, 369, 379
  contagion, 370-373
  freezes in interbank markets, 374
  investment banking and, 376
  microfinance, 377-378
  role of, 368-369
  social networks, 375-376
sharing, protection of, 385
social, 281, 309, 318-320
  discipline of, 68-69
  expansion of, 320-321
  future implications, 327-329, 331
  history of thought in, 70, 72
  marketing, 77-79

overview of, 244-247
research, 75-76
theories in, 72-75
speed, 286
spread of infectious diseases, 471-480
controlling, 481-484, 487
future of, 487-489
strategic theories, 265
structure, 89-90
supply chains, 235-237
supply webs, 226. *See also* supply webs
sustaining, 353-355
creating relational capabilities, 356-361
developing alliances, 361-362
telecommunications, 418-421
modular future of, 427-430
Monists and Dualists, 421-426
terrorism, 453-454
countering, 464-467
enabling technologies, 462-464
management and business implications,
468-469
social network analysis (SNA), 455-457
structure, 458-462
theory of the firm, 11-12
virtual, 321
word-of-mouth marketing, 247-256
Networks and Netwar: The Future of Terror,
Crime and Militancy, 457
neural networks, 126
New Delhi, 302
new ideas, 282
new interlinked enterprises, xxi
New York City, 313
New York Mercantile Exchange (NYMEX), 410
Nike, 306, 356, 361, 447
value-creation processes, 28
nodes, 6
pairs of, 69
random failure of, 90
terrorism, 456
theory of the firm, 11-12
noise, filtering, 119
Nokia, 357
non-Western markets, social network challenges
in, 247
nonconnected holdings, 375. *See also*
investments
normative pressure, 251
North America, 457
Northern Ireland, 443
Northern Rock, 368

not invented here view (NIH), 150
Noveck, Beth, 47
novelty-centered business model designs, 269
nuclear reactor meltdowns, 386
Nyanza Province, 500

O

Obama, Barack, 4
occurrence of social contagion, 250-252
offers, clearing, 410
offshoring, 9, 402
olfactory information, 110
omnivores, 86
OnStar, 28. *See also* General Motors
ontogeny, 92
open innovation, 283
Open Source movement, 150
operations
control of logistics, 405
readiness, 159
risks, 407
optimization of extended intelligence networks,
288-291
options, 410
Opuntia cacti, 96
Orchestra models, 154
orchestration, networks, 299-300
balance of, 312-313
four flows, 302-305
implications of, 307-309
need for, 306-314
roles of, 309-312
supply chains, 301-302
ordinary least squares, 68
organization
complexity theory, 219-220
network-centric innovation, 158-160
supply webs, 225-228, 237-238
leveraging coordinating technology,
231-234
network management, 235-237
relationship management, 228-231
Organization for Economic Cooperation and
Development (OECD), 420
Organization Man, The, 327
organizational design, 186-187, 189
models, 189-192
Schwab (sequencing), 194, 196, 198
searching effective strategies, 201-202
Toyota (modularity), 198-200
Orkut, 318

Oslo-based International Maritime Exchange (IMAREX), 410
outbreaks, 478
outcomes, forecasting, 218
outsourcing, 9, 402
overlaps (network) feature, 320
over-the-counter (OTC), 407
Owich, Kawadghone, and Wakula South (OKW), 503
Oxford Analytica, 438

P

P&G (Procter & Gamble), 4, 38, 148, 156, 361
    word-of-mouth marketing, 248
Pace, Peter, 328
pacemakers, 27
pairs of nodes, 69
Pakistan, 300
Palmer, Russell E., 526
Palmer Group, 51
Pan Am flight 103, 383
pandemics, 473, 483
panopticon self, 322
paradox of modern networks, 321-322
Parry, Charles W., 45
partial conversions, 158
particle swarm optimization (PSO), 138-139
partitioning DSMs, 169
passive recruitment, 338-341
paths, 6
    dependence, 42-44
    of energy, 88. *See also* networks
patterns, 47, 108
    contact, 477
Pearl Harbor, 286
peer-to-peer applications, 420
people, understanding, 215
perception of risk, 394
performance
    declines in, 47
    employee retention, 345-346
    management, 344-345
periphery
    mining the, 277-280
    network feature, 319
    scanning, 290
perspectives on value creation, 263-266
PERT charts, 167
pharmaceuticals, 441-442
phenomenon, knowledge as social, 40
pheromones, 110, 477
Philadelphia, 41

Philippines, 54
Philips, alliances, 356-362
Philornis downsi (fly), 96
photosynthesis, 112-113
phylogeny, 92
physical flows, 304
physical infrastructure, 419
physical markets, impact of derivatives on, 411-412
pistils, 115
plague, 472, 474
planning
    capacity, 405
    family, 500-506
plausible deniability, 318
Plays2run, 441
plug and play, 76
points, seeding, 252-253
Poisson random network, 476
Poland, 443
Political Risk Services, 438
political risks
    aggregating information, 439-440
    information sources, 436-438
    strategies, 440-441, 444-448
Porter, Michael, 9, 281, 301
portfolio of innovation, 160
power
    in business, shift of, 80
    of self-interest, 53
practice, network-centric models, 161-162
Prahalad, CK, 307, 527
predators, 86
predictions, behavioral, 76
prephotosynthetic chemautotrophs, 111
Presby, Tom, 56, 58
pressure, normative, 251
price
    discovery, 406, 412
    discrepancies, 412
Priceline.com, 259, 269
PriceWaterhouseCoopers-Eurasia, 434, 437
principles, universal, 52, 54
Principles of Economics, 282
priori, 79
Prisoner's Dilemma, 125, 129-132
privatization, 443
procedures, 126, 139
Proceedings of the National Academy of Sciences of the United States, 133
processes, 302
    development, 166-171
    dimension, 159

innovation, 25-27
  changing, 28-29
  competition, 29-32
  diabetes network models, 32
  network impediments, 34
  sources of competitive advantage, 34-36
Procter & Gamble (P&G), 4, 38, 148, 156, 361
  word-of-mouth marketing, 248
Prodigy, 263
Product Development Group (PDG) LLC, 155
products, 302
  conversations about, 255-256
  decomposition, 172
  development, 165-166
    communication, 175-179
    complex products, 171-175
    future of, 180-181
    process of, 166-171
  freight rate derivatives, 407-411
  marketing, 269-270
  product-centric view of value, 28
  updates, 254
professional networks, 281
professional societies, 281
profits, trends, 400
prokaryotes, 91
propaganda, 462
propositions, 79
proprietary knowledge, 281
protection
  against catastrophic loss, 387
  of shared network resources, 385
proximity of preferences, 440
Prusak, Larry, 40
Ptolemaic astronomy, 47
public sector, roles of, 391-392
punctuated equilibrium, 212-213
pupation, 115
purposeful networking, 260
put options, 410
Putnam, Hilary, 140

Q–R

queens, honeybees, 114, 118

R & D (research and development), 44, 159
  management, 40
radical Muslims, 453
radio-frequency identification (RFID) tags, 232
rainforests, 85
  food webs, 89

random failures of nodes, 90
rankism, 326
rats, 96
RCA, 44
reach, networks, 284
readiness, 159-160
real-time, 289
  tracking, 405
recombination, 91
recommendations for instant messaging (IM)
  generations, 329-331
reconfiguration strategies, 402
recording industry, 40
records
  historical, 40-45
  uneven, 40-41
recruitment, 338
  Internet, 341-342
  passive recruitment, 338-341
  terrorism, 462
Red Bull, 246
reductionists, 424
redundancy, 91
regaining control, 246
regular random networks, 476
regulations, 443
  International Health Regulations (IHR), 485
  laboratories, 484
  networks, sustaining, 353
regulators, 421
reintegration, benefits of, 195
relational capabilities
  creating, 356-361
  developing, 361-362
relationships, 53
  keiretsu, 230
  social networks, 244-247
  supply webs, 228-229, 231
  word-of-mouth marketing, 247-256
removal of credit risk, 410
Rendell, Paul, 128
representation, 76
reproduction, ants, 106
research
  business models, 262-263
  literature, 280-282
  network-centric innovation, 161-162
  organizational design, 186-189
    models, 189-192
    Schwab (sequencing), 194-198
    searching effective strategies, 201-202
    Toyota (modularity), 198-200

security, 393-395
   social networks, 75-76
   supply chains, 235-237
research and development. *See* R & D
resilience of networks, 287
resource-based view (RBV), 264
resources
   allocation, 6
   networks, protection of shared, 385
respect of cultures, 54
responses to infectious diseases, 482
Responsible Care initiative, 395
retention of employees, 345-346
revenue-tone-kilometers (RTKs), 404
revolutions, theory of the firm, 10-11
RFID (radio frequency identification), 232,
   290, 405
ribonucleic acids (RNA), 480
risk
   assessment, 393
   credit, removal of, 410
   interdependent security (IDS), 385
      catastrophic loss protection, 387
      chemical plant investments, 388-389
      critical infrastructures, 387
      environmental treaties, 386
      global supply-chain management, 385
      nuclear reactor meltdowns, 386
      protection of shared network resources, 385
      research, 393-395
      tipping and cascading strategies, 390-392
   management, 395
      hedging, 405
      in shipping, 405-412
   networks
      applications to finance, 369, 379
      contagion, 370-373
      freezes in interbank markets, 374
      investment banking and, 376
      microfinance, 377-378
      role of, 368-369
      social networks, 375-376
   operational, 407
   perception, 394
   social, 434. *See also* social risk management
Risk Management Plan (RMP), 391
Rivkin, Jan, 528
Robertson, Tom, xxi
robustness in network structures, 90
Rockefeller Foundation, 488
Rodriguez, Jose A., 455
Rohan, Katherine, xxii

roles
   of network orchestration, 309, 312
   of networks
      applications to finance, 369, 379
      contagion, 370-373
      freezes in interbank markets, 374
      investment banking and, 376
      microfinance, 377-378
      shaping systemic risk, 368-369
      social networks, 375-376
   of the public sector, 391-392
   specialization of, 119
Ronfeldt, David, 457
Root, Franklin, 434
RosettaNet, 236
routers, Wi-Fi, 429
Royal Dutch Shell, 438
royal jelly, 116
Royal Philips, 355
   alliances, developing, 361-362
   relational capabilities, creating, 356-361
Rubin, Harvey, 528
rule-based expert systems, 126
rules (80-20), 61-62
Russia, 443

S

S. cerevisiae, 479
Sageman, Marc, 455
Saharan Africa DALYs, 472
Salafi Jihad, 455
Salomon bond trading desks, 328
Salter, James, 529
sampling, 76
Santa Cruz Island, 96
Sara Lee, 356, 361
Saudi Arabia, 443
Sawhney, Mohanbir, 147, 529
scale-free topology, 476
scanning, 280-282
   models, 282
   periphery, 290
Schelling, Thomas, 134-135
Schering, 356
Schoemaker, Paul, 530
scholars, 421
Schwab (sequencing organizational structures),
   194-198
Science Center at Harvard University, 42
Scott, James, C., 335
searching for effective strategies, 201-202
SEAT (Socio-Economic Assessment Toolbox), 444

security, interdependent (IDS), 383-385
  catastrophic loss protection, 387
  chemical plant investments, 388-389
  critical infrastructures, 387
  environmental treaties, 386
  global supply-chain management, 385
  nuclear reactor meltdowns, 386
  protection of shared network resources, 385
  research, 393-395
  tipping and cascading strategies, 390-393
seeding points, 252-253
Seeing Like a State, 335
segmentation, 79
segregation models, Schelling's, 134-135
self-contained units, 280
Self-Help Groups (SHGs), 377
self-interest, power of, 53
self-organization, 212-213
Senseo, 361
senses and network communication, 108-111
Sentia Group, 443
September 11, 2001, 387, 454, 456-457
sequencing organizational structures, 194-198
Sert, Jose Luis, 42
Severe Acute Respiratory Syndrome (SARS), 478
sexual selection, 91
SGV Group, 54
shadow of society, 140
Shanghai, 314
Shannon's Law of Information Theory, 286
shaping forces, 214
shared network resources, protection of, 385
sharing
  information, 281, 483
  intelligence, 283
Sharp Beaked Ground Finch (*G. difficilis*), 94
shipping, financial risk management in, 405-412
shocks, 372
short-term lending, 368
Siggelkow, Nicolaj, 530
sight, 108
signal contamination, 119-120
significance (network) feature, 320
simulations, 218, 237, 289
Singapore, 410, 478
Singh, Harbir, 531
Sirkin, Hal, 7
skills, communication, 56
Skype, 356, 400, 419, 426
slack, creating, 284
smallpox, 473
smart bombs, 467

smell, 110
Smith's invisible hand, 126
Smith, Adam, 8, 10, 402
Snyder, Scott, 531
social capital, 336-337
social collateral, 374
social contagion, occurrence of, 250-252
social influence, 501
social infrastructure, 34
social learning, 501
social network analysis (SNA), terrorism and, 455-457
social networks, 281, 309, 318-320
  access, 324-326
  discipline of, 68-69
  empirical network analysis, 500-508
  expansion of, 320-321
  future implications, 327
        instant messaging (IM), 328-331
  history of thought in, 70-72
  and investment decisions, 375-376
  loyalty, 326-327
  marketing, 77-79
  overview of, 244-247
  research, 75-76
  theories in, 72-75
  trends, 323-327
Social Networks, 70-71
Social Networks and Marketing, 245
social phenomenon, knowledge as, 40
social risk management, 434-436
  aggregating information, 439-440
  information sources, 436-438
  strategies, 440-448
social structures, 11
software, 71
Sony, 7, 357
Sosa, Manuel, 532
Sound Surveillance System (SOSUS), 109
sources of competitive advantage, 34-36
South America, 457
South Nyanza, 504
Southwest Airlines, 402
Soviet Union, 443, 457
Spanish flu, 474
specialization of roles, 119
species invasions, 95-96
speed, 286
  of network development, 21
spermatatheca, 117
spillover, knowledge, 282
spot markets, 407

spot price volatility, 412
spread of infectious diseases, 471-473
    controlling, 481-484, 487
    future of, 487-489
    networks, 473-474, 476-478, 480
Sprint, 420, 425
Sri Lanka, 443
stability, 370
stability (network) feature, 320
stamens, 115
standards
    comprehensive text, 71
    contracts, 410
    laboratories, 484
Staples, 161
Star Trek, 46
Starbucks, value-creation processes, 28
stereotypes, cultural, 5- 58
storage of knowledge, 38-39
Strategic Radar, 439
strategies, 299
    alliance, 357
    complexity theory, 216-219
    interactions, 237
    JIT fulfillment, 402
    network-centric innovation, 148-151
        Creative Bazaar models, 155
        Jam Central models, 156
        MOD Station models, 157-158
        models, 151-158
        Orchestra models, 154
        organizational competencies, 158-160
        research and practice, 161-162
    networks
        orchestration, 307-309
        sustaining, 355
        theory, 265
    organizational design, 186-189
        models, 189-192
        Schwab (sequencing), 194-198
        searching effective strategies, 201-202
        Toyota (modularity), 198-200
    product marketing, 269-270
    radar, creating, 289-290
    reconfiguration, 402
    recruitment
        Internet, 341-342
        passive, 338-341
    social risk management, 434-445
        aggregating information, 439-440
        implementing, 445-448
        information sources, 436-438

theory of the firm, 9-10
    tipping and cascading, 390-392
    value creation, 263-266
Stratfor, 438
structure
    of air cargo and maritime logistics, 403-405
    of networks, 89-90
    of terrorism networks, 458-462
studies, empirical, 373
styles
    global leadership, 55, 58
    facts, 136
success metrics, 160
sugarscape model, 135
suicide terrorism, 467
Sunbelt Social Networks Conference, 71
Sung Dynasty, 42
supply chains, 299
    global supply-chain management, 385
    management, 247
    multiple actors in global, 404
    unbundling, 301-302, 402
supply webs, 225-228, 237-238
    leveraging coordinating technology, 231-234
    network management, 235-237
    relationship management, 228-231
survey data, overview of, 499
survival value, 92
susceptible, infected, or recovered (SIR model), 477
sustaining networks, 353-355
    alliances, developing, 361-362
    relational capabilities, 356-361
swarm intelligence meta-heuristics, 137
symbiotic microalgae, 86
synchronized commerce, 305
systems
    architecture, 418
    breakdowns, 372
    decomposition, 166
    and holistic thinking, 212
    integration, 166
    risk, 368-369

T

tags, RFID, 232
Taiwan, 59
tamper-proof containers, 405
Tapscott, Don, 7
targeting
    key influentials, 252-253
    messaging, 77

teams
  design, communication, 175-179
  interaction matrices, 178
technology
  embeddedness of social networks, 76
  interfaces, 176
  networks, sustaining, 353
  speculation, 21
  using, 215
Teh, J. Shin, 532
telecommunications, 417-421
  modular future of, 427-430
  Monists and Dualists, 421-426
termites, 114
terrorism networks, 387, 453-454
  countering, 464-467
  enabling technologies, 462-464
  management and business implications, 468-469
  social network analysis (SNA), 455-457
  structure, 458-462
testing, theories, 73
that versus why, 38-39
theories
  complexity, 207-208
    accessing, 221-222
    implications for managers, 213-220
    key concepts of, 208-213
    unanswered questions, 220
  configuration, 267
  development, 72
  economic, 136
  Heuristic Choice Theory, 140-141
  in social networks, 72-75
  longitudinal studies, 74
  Shannon's Law of Information Theory, 286
  strategic network, 265
  testing, 73
theory of the firm, 8-9
  networks, 11-12
  nodes, 11-12
  revolutions, 10-11
  strategies, 9-10
Third-Party Logistics (3PL) providers, 404
threat to intellectual property for
  pharmaceuticals, 442
Time Warner, 148
Tinbergen, Niko, 92
tipping, 390-392
Tipping Point, The, 249
Tohmatsu Awoki & Co, 50

Tomita, Iwao, 50
tools
  analysis, 441
  visualization, 291
Tora! Tora! Tora!, 286
Toronto, 478
Toshiba, 7, 225
total conversions, 158
touch, 111
Touche Ross International, 50
Toyota, 4, 234, 301, 328, 402
  modularity, 198-200
  supply chains, 230
tracing, contact, 479
tracking, 405
trade, 443
  growth of, 405
traditional marketing, effectiveness of, 245
traffic modeling, 418
training, 342-344
transactions, 11
  business model research, 262-263
  costs, 149, 264
  FFA, 410
transformation from atoms to bits, 304
transmission
  of knowledge, 40
  of sound, 110. See also senses
transmit forces, 175
treaties, environmental, 386
Tremor, 248
trends
  modern networks, 323
    access, 324-326
    communications technologies, 323-324
    loyalty, 326-327
  profits, 400
triumph of cooperators, 130-133
Tropical Disease Initiative (TDI), 156
tsunami (December 2006), 289
tuberculosis, 472
Twain, Mark, 44
Twitter, 4, 318
types
  of agents, 133
  of design dependencies, 174
  of extended intelligence networks, 283
types of interdependency, 6

U

U.S. Department of Homeland Security (DHS), 386
U.S. Environmental Protection Agency (EPA), 391
U.S. national security issues, 483
ubiquitous access to information, 325
UCINET, 71
UCLA, 71
Ultimate Leadership, 51
ultraviolet (UV) frequencies, 108
unbundling
  global supply chains, 402
  supply chains, 301-302
Understanding Terror Networks, 455
uneven records, 40-41
unicellular photosynthesizing organisms, 111
Unilever, 162, 361
Union Carbide, 394
United Kingdom, 429
United States, 443
universal principles, 52, 54
University of California at Berkeley, 156
University of California at Irvine, 71
University of California at San Francisco, 156
University of Pennsylvania, 51
unmatched interfaces, 177
unnecessary overlap, benefits of, 199
unobserved motivations, 22
updates
  beliefs, 250
  products, 254
UPS (United Parcel Service), 305, 403

V

vaccine development, 484
Vail, Theodore, 425
value
  chains, 263, 301s, 437
  creation, 25-27, 259, 263-266
    changing, 28-29
    competition paradigm shifts, 29-32
    diabetes network models, 32
    network impediments, 34
    sources of competitive advantage, 34-36
  drivers, 261
  through integration, 311
  propositions, 79
Value Chain, 402
Valve Corporation, 158

Van den Bulte, Christophe, 533
Van Wassenhove, Luk, xxii
Vans, 246
venture capital (VC) firms, 375
Verizon, 424
video games, 158
video sharing sites, 246
views, network-based, 267
virtual networks, 321
visualization tools, 291
Visvikis, Ilias, 533
Vocalpoint, 248
volatility, 412

W

waggle dance, 117
Wal-Mart, 78, 236, 306
Wash SyCip, 54
Watkins, Susan Cotts, 533
Watson, Thomas, Sr., 39
we know everything (WKE) view, 150
weak signals for relevance, 278
weak-ties argument, 338
Wealth of Nations, The, 10, 401
Weber, Steve, 47
webs, supply, 225-228, 237-238
  leveraging coordinating technology, 231-234
  network management, 235-237
  relationship management, 228-231
Weinberger, David, 426
Weiss, Leigh, 40
Werbach, Kevin, 417, 534
West, Al, xx
Western Europe, 402, 457
Wharton Risk Management and Decision Processes Center, 393
Wharton School, 51
Wharton SEI Center for Advanced Studies in Management, xxii
Wharton-INSEAD Alliance, xxii
Wi-Fi routers, 429
Wikinomics, 7
Wikipedia, 21, 308
Williams, Anthony D., 7
WiMAX, 429
Wind, Yoram (Jerry), 534
wireless *Carterfones*, 429
Woodrow Wilson School of Public and International Affairs at Princeton University, 483
word-of-mouth marketing, 247-256
work flows, 305

workers, honeybees, 114
Working Families for Wal-Mart, 78
World Fertility Survey, 500
"World Jihad Front against the Jews and the Crusaders, The," 460
World Trade Organization (WTO), 400, 402
World War II, 37
World Wide Web (WWW), 419. *See also* Internet
World Wildlife Fund (WWF), 438
Worldspan Central Reservation System, 260
Wu, Tim, 426
Wuyts, Stefan, 535
www.opacityindex.com, 11

X–Z

X-teams, 327

Yahoo!, 361, 423
Yakubovich, Valery, 535
yellow fever epidemic, 41
Yersinia pestis, 474
YouTube, 4, 246, 309, 318
Yugoslavia, 443

Zara, 402
Zooxanthellae, 113
Zott, Christoph, 536